The Mentally Retarded and Society

Proceedings of the conference,
"The Mentally Retarded and Society: A Social Science Perspective,"
held in Niles, Michigan, April 18–20, 1974.
The Conference was supported by the National Institute of Child Health and
Human Development of the United States Public Health Service

THE MENTALLY RETARDED AND SOCIETY:

A Social Science Perspective

Edited by

Michael J. Begab, Ph.D.
Head, Mental Retardation Research Centers Program
National Institute of Child Health and
  Human Development

and

Stephen A. Richardson, Ph.D.
Professor, Departments of Pediatrics and
  Community Health
Albert Einstein College of Medicine
Rose F. Kennedy Center for Research in
  Mental Retardation and Human Development

University Park Press
Baltimore · London · Tokyo

UNIVERSITY PARK PRESS
International Publishers in Science and Medicine
Chamber of Commerce Building
Baltimore, Maryland 21202

Copyright © 1975 by University Park Press

Typeset by The Composing Room of Michigan, Inc.
Printed in the United States of America by Universal Lithographers, Inc.

Library of Congress Cataloging in Publication Data

Main entry under title:

The Mentally retarded and society:

Proceedings of a conference held in Niles,
Mich., Apr. 18-20, 1974, sponsored by the National
Institute of Child Health and Human Development
and the Rose Kennedy Center at Albert Einstein
College of Medicine.
Includes index.
1. Mentally handicapped - - United States - -
Congresses. I. Begab, Michael Jay, 1918 -
II. Richardson, Stephen A. III. United States.
National Institute of Child Health and Human
Development. IV. Rose F. Kennedy Center for
Research in Mental Retardation and Human
Development. [DNLM: 1. Mental retardation
- - Congresses. 2. Sociology - - Congresses. WM300
M5543 1974]
HV3006.A3M45   362.3'0973   75-33173
ISBN 0-8391-0751-X

Contents

Historical and Contemporary Issues in Mental Retardation

Attitudes and Values

Social Competence and Socialization

Conference Contributors

Conference Chairmen

Michael J. Begab, Ph.D.
Mental Retardation Program
National Institute of Child Health
  and Human Development
Bethesda, Maryland

Stephen A. Richardson, Ph.D.
Department of Pediatrics
Albert Einstein College of Medicine
Bronx, New York

Conference Secretary

Ruth Markham, M.S.
Mental Retardation Program
National Institute of Child Health
  and Human Development
Bethesda, Maryland

Conference Participants

Margaret Adams, M.S.
Department of Mental Health
Walter E. Fernald State School
Waverly, Massachusetts

Richard D. Ashmore, Ph.D.
Department of Psychology
Rutgers University
New Brunswick, New Jersey

Arnold Birenbaum, Ph.D.
Department of Pediatrics
Albert Einstein College of Medicine
Bronx, New York

Elizabeth M. Boggs, Ph.D.
National Advisory Council on
  Services and Facilities for the
  Developmentally Disabled
HEW South Building
Washington, D.C.

Philip L. Browning
Research and Training Center in
  Mental Retardation
University of Oregon
Eugene, Oregon

Esther R. Brummer
Research and Training Center in
  Mental Retardation
University of Oregon
Eugene, Oregon

Aaron V. Cicourel, Ph.D.
Department of Sociology
University of California, San Diego
LaJolla, California

Herbert J. Cohen, M.D.
Department of Pediatrics
Albert Einstein College of Medicine
Bronx, New York

Robert B. Edgerton, Ph.D.
Department of Psychiatry
University of California, Los Angeles
Los Angeles, California

Amitai Etzioni, Ph.D.
Center for Policy Research, Inc.
New York, New York

Bernard Farber, Ph.D.
Department of Sociology
University of Texas
Austin, Texas

Howard Garber, Ph.D.
Waisman Center on Mental Retardation
  and Human Development
University of Wisconsin
Madison, Wisconsin

Erving Goffman, Ph.D.
Department of Anthropology
University of Philadelphia
Philadelphia, Pennsylvania

Jay Gottlieb, Ph.D.
Research Institute for Educational Problems
Cambridge, Massachusetts

Herbert Grossman, M.D.
Illinois State Pediatric Institute
Chicago, Illinois

Andrew S. Halpern
Research and Training Center in
  Mental Retardation
University of Oregon
Eugene, Oregon

Robert E. Kleck, Ph.D.
Department of Sociology
Dartmouth College
Hanover, New Hampshire

Richard A. Kurtz, Ph.D.
Department of Sociology and Anthropology
University of Notre Dame
Notre Dame, Indiana

Albert Kushlick, M.B., B.Ch., D.P.H.,
  F.F.C.M., M.R.C. Psych., M.R.C.P.
Health Care Evaluation Research Team
Highcroft, Romsey Road
Winchester, SO22 5DH, England

Marvin Lazerson
Faculty of Education
University of British Columbia
Vancouver, British Columbia

Phyllis Levenstein, Ed.D.
Verbal Interaction Project
Mother Child Home Program
Freeport, New York

Jane R. Mercer, Ph.D.
Department of Sociology
University of California, Riverside
Riverside, California

Lloyd E. Ohlin, Ph.D.
Harvard Law School
Cambridge, Massachusetts

Earl S. Schaefer, Ph.D.
Department of Maternal & Child Health
University of North Carolina
Chapel Hill, North Carolina

Zena Stein, M.A., M.B., B.Ch.
Division of Epidemiology
Columbia University
New York, New York

Conference Rapporteurs

John Borkowski, Ph.D.
Department of Psychology
University of Notre Dame
Notre Dame, Indiana

Peter Forsythe
Edna McConnel Clark Foundation
New York, New York

Mervyn Susser, M.D., B.Ch.
Division of Epidemiology
Columbia University
New York, New York

George Tarjan, M.D.
Mental Retardation Program
The Neuropsychiatric Institute
Los Angeles, California

Thomas Whiteman, Ph.D.
Center for the Study of Man
University of Notre Dame
Notre Dame, Indiana

Conference Host

William T. Liu, Ph.D.
Center for the Study of Man
University of Notre Dame
Notre Dame, Indiana

Foreword and Acknowledgments

The topics and organization of the conference reflect the experience of the editors. At the National Institute of Child Health and Human Development, Dr. Begab has been in close touch with the social science component of the research programs at the mental retardation research centers. These centers have provided opportunities for social scientists in different parts of the United States to come in touch with some of the major issues related to mental retardation and, through research, to develop knowledge needed for social policy, for prevention, and for planning and evaluating services that can ameliorate the consequences of mental retardation. The opportunities have come about through contact with the biological scientists and the clinical programs at the research centers and with the professionals and consumers in the community whose primary concern is mental retardation. Dr. Begab also has been closely connected with many of the national and international conferences where information is exchanged and discussed.

Dr. Richardson is a Professor in the Departments of Pediatrics and Community Health at Albert Einstein College of Medicine, Yeshiva University. He is also a Senior Investigator at the Rose F. Kennedy Center for Research in Mental Retardation and Human Development, one of the regional centers. The Center was described in one of the earlier conferences in this series which dealt with methodological approaches to the study of man. At the Kennedy Center he directs a Social Ecology Research Unit where the emphasis is on biosocial, epidemiological, and social science research. Studies at the Unit have included the long-term consequences of severe malnutrition in infancy to determine whether intellectual and functional impairment is found at school age; a long-term follow up of young people with mental retardation between the ages of ten and twenty-two to determine what happens in the transition from childhood to adulthood; the nature of the communication problems that develop between parents and professionals at a multidisciplinary diagnostic and evaluation clinic for children with developmental disabilities; a register of cases of severe mental retardation to assist in the community planning and evaluation of services; and a study of the consequences for mentally retarded adults who move from a large, traditional, isolated mental retardation institution to a small residential care unit in the community.

The Unit was founded in the hopes of building research and concepts between two groups of investigators who traditionally have little communication or engage in collaborative research. One group is the medical and biological scientists who have focused on issues such as metabolic and karyosomal factors, physiological insult, and brain pathology as the causes of severe mental retardation. The second group is made up of behavioral scientists who have been largely concerned with social environment and cultural disadvantages as causal agents. In examining the consequences of mental subnormality the medical and biological scientists have focused on a variety of forms of pathology, how these may be identified, and therapeutic intervention with the goal of alleviating the disorders or preventing further deterioration. The behavioral science group, in examining the consequences of mental retardation, have concerned themselves with the nature and measurement of intellectual functioning, learning deficits, the intellectual and social development of retarded children, home and institutional environments, and behavior modification.

The separation of the research of these two groups in many university settings has largely prevented the development of a biosocial approach to the study of mental retardation. There have been few efforts to determine the relative and interacting contributions of genetic, biological, and social environmental factors in the etiology or functional development and socialization of children who are mentally subnormal.

In planning the conference a series of background papers were prepared by Ashmore, Begab, Farber, Kleck, Kurtz, Lazerson, Richardson, Schaefer, Stein, and Susser. They were read by participants before attending the conference. At the conference the other participants presented papers, which were discussed. The present book has included the background papers in the general organization of the content but does not include discussion of these papers because this did not occur at the meeting.

The conference was jointly sponsored by the National Institute of Child Health and Human Development and the Rose Kennedy Center at Albert Einstein College of Medicine. The host sponsor was the Center for the Study of Man in Contemporary Society, directed by Dr. William Liu at the University of Notre Dame. Dr. Liu arranged for the conference to be held at the Associates Lodge, Niles, Michigan, and he and his staff arranged for the technical facilities needed for the conference. The facilities of the Lodge were made available by Mrs. Ernestine Carmichael. The participants are deeply grateful to her for her hospitality and generosity. Ruth Markham, secretary to Dr. Begab, was conference secretary and attended to the myriad of details connected with the conference with competence and charm.

Stephen A. Richardson
Michael J. Begab

Preface

Mental retardation as a social problem varies from culture to culture and is differentially distributed within a given culture, although its concentration among the most disadvantaged segments of the population seems universal. Considering the greater vulnerability of impoverished families to disease, trauma, and disorders of pregnancy, and to social environmental factors affecting intellectual development and the quality of life, this is not surprising. Assortative mating, whether viewed genetically or behaviorally, also contributes to this phenomenon.

The symptom of mental retardation, whatever its etiology or severity, manifests itself in some form of behavioral impairment. Such impairment is in turn socially defined. Thus society perceives as retarded those individuals who fail to measure up to its norms, expectations, and demands because of presumed intellectual inadequacies. Since norms vary as a function of age, locality, and subgroup values, we might well expect that similarly limited people, if mildly retarded, will not always be similarly perceived and that the same individual will slip in and out of the category as he moves through different phases of the life span.

This conceptualization of the problem suggests that focus on the retarded person alone and efforts to improve his adaptation to the environment through education, training, and rehabilitation services are not enough. Increasingly, in our efforts to understand and find solutions to retardation, we are compelled to look to the economic forces that shape social organization, to the values and mores that regulate conduct and influence attitudes, and to the social opportunities that affect behavior and development. From this broader perspective, the individual *and* society are seen as inseparably linked and mutually interacting forces.

Never before in our history has the role of social forces and conditions assumed such prominence in guiding the fortunes of the mentally retarded as today. Given impetus by the civil rights movement, organized citizen groups, professional societies, and human rights-minded lawyers have embarked on aggressive campaigns of public education and class action suits to secure for the retarded the basic rights presumably guaranteed by our Constitution. In the process, old concepts such as community integration of the retarded and normalization have been rejuvenated.

Although these principles are widely accepted by the professional community as a general philosophy, many barriers remain to their full implementation in practice. Some believe that institutions have a legitimate role in the spectrum of services for selected retarded persons and that the concept of normalization must be drastically modified to accommodate the more severely handicapped. Other barriers to implementation are deeply rooted in public attitudes, legal constraints, and inadequate service delivery systems and resources. Lack of precise knowledge, however, may be the greatest stumbling block. Much of the research data available on significant issues involving special education, the impact of classification, the relationship of IQ to impaired behavior, the affect of alternative patterns of care on development, and social competence are inconclusive.

The social sciences are in part responsible for our limited understanding of the societal elements impinging on the mental retardation problem. The knowledge gap is more one of omission than commission. Few social scientists in academic settings have as yet applied their investigative talents to health and social service issues, and in particular, to mental retardation. To some, research bearing on practical matters is scientifically uninteresting and atheoretical. Perhaps this is a symptom of our continuing preoccupation with "pure theory," deductive reasoning and the experimental approach.

There is need in the social sciences for applied research with imaginative interplay between inductive and deductive conceptualization, taking as a starting point central issues and problems related to mental retardation.

The objectives of the Conference held in Michigan implicitly deny the validity of this view. Although we clearly advocate the importance of theory and conceptualization, we should recognize the distinct likelihood that theory building may follow from, rather than necessarily precede, a proper consideration of practical issues. A technological approach to social science research, invoking testable hypotheses, may well prove fruitful in advancing theory.

For the last several decades, researchers into the social aspects of mental retardation have attempted to integrate the goals of practical utility and theoretical relevance. Epidemiological studies, for example, have identified associations between social-demographic variables and developmental outcomes, thus pointing the way to more precise exploration of the etiology and pathogenesis of mental retardation. Studies on the factors affecting the quality of care in residential facilities and other living arrangements contribute to our understanding of social organization and family theory. Differing models for intervention with vulnerable children are beginning to sharpen our concepts of critical periods in child development. The current impact of social change and concern with human rights—still to be explored scientifically—adds another dimension to the potential linkage of practical issues and theory refinement.

This Conference, in its emphasis on theories relevant to mental retardation and the current state of knowledge, and its application to emerging issues and program trends, is another step in this direction. Hopefully, in this careful assessment of the knowns and unknowns regarding the mentally retarded and society, we may determine what can be done today and what must await the findings of future research.

In this manner, we can be more confident that neglects of the past will not be compounded by mistakes of the future.

Michael J. Begab

Introduction

This book addresses some of the major issues of social concern and policy posed by mental retardation in our society. In many of its chapters, it offers a conceptual and theoretical framework for a fuller understanding of the current and potential status and role of mentally retarded persons in society and of the values, attitudes, and processes underlying social change and program development. The book is designed to synthesize and review existing knowledge about mental retardation on a range of topics, to identify limitations or gaps in research and theory, and to point to new directions for future research. The information and perspectives contained in this volume, however, are not oriented to the social scientist alone, but have significant implications for professional practitioners of many disciplines, for social policy formation, and ultimately for the mentally retarded person and his family.

The structure of the conference for which the papers in this book were prepared included a series of background articles, largely conceptual, historical, and state-of-the-art in nature, and the presentation of ongoing research. They included consideration of issues, trends, and the factors and processes in social change affecting the relationship between the mentally retarded and society. Some reports of current research were added to the book to complement the more general reviews. The summary discussions inserted at the end of specific sections, although focusing on papers presented at the conference, nevertheless reflect the influence of the background articles on the group's deliberations.

HISTORICAL AND CONTEMPORARY ISSUES IN MENTAL RETARDATION

The first section represents an analytic and conceptual approach to historical and contemporary issues in mental retardation. In the Begab chapter, the changing status of the retarded in society is examined as a function of the interplay between changing concepts about the capacities and limitations of the retarded, developments in the behavioral sciences and community values, attitudes, and expectations. The author, in a review of the research literature, notes the continuing weaknesses in the quality and organization of existing services, but cautions against the full acceptance of drastic change in social institutions based on sociopolitical processes rather than scientifically tested concepts. He argues that the application of such currently fashionable concepts as normalization, deinstitutionalization, mainstreaming, and declassification is not appropriate to all of the retarded and, indeed, may prove a disservice to many. The social concerns addressed in this paper are reflected in many portions of the book.

Lazerson brings to this volume the perspective of a social and educational historian. His view of American social and educational history and its impact on social change adds a new dimension to earlier treatises on the relationship between mental subnormality and the educational system. He examines two major developments. The first considers the emergence of the asylum movement for various types of social deviants and the assumptions behind their founding and eventual acceptance as custodial facilities. The second development focuses on the public school system itself and the evolvement of educational differentiation, testing, and special classes. Lazerson's analysis of the origin of the special class system and its relationship to administrative, vocational, classificatory, and pedagogical problems of education in general, offers an excellent framework for looking at the special versus regular education controversy in mental retardation.

Stein and Susser approach contemporary issues from an epidemiological and public health vantage point. They note the need for more precise classification schemes and the importance of case registers in improving the efficiency of care systems and providing a base for rational policy and planning. As in other chapters, these authors discuss the conflict between traditional values (e.g., confidentiality of records), ethics (e.g., immunization directed toward "herd immunity:" antenatal diagnoses and therapeutic abortion), and the responsibilities of public health agencies for preventive programs. In discussing means for the prevention of specific diseases associated with mental retardation, it is clear that even conditions of biological origin for which there are remedial biomedical technologies also require systematic attention to social aspects of the problem.

ATTITUDES AND VALUES

The second section examines in greater depth some of the attitudes and values discussed in earlier papers. Richardson suggests that the role of stigma in mental retardation may have been overgeneralized and overstated, and he challenges the presumed largely negative consequences of administrative classification. Although the concept of stigma is unquestionably significant and a legitimate target for continued research, Richardson stresses the need for systematic attention to other common reactions to mental retardation—for example, anxiety, fear, and withdrawal—and describes many of the cues by which the mentally subnormal are identified. These cues, transmitted in interpersonal transactions, directly influence social relationships and the nature of the labeling process and its consequences.

Gottlieb, in a review of the research literature, dissects some of the personal and social components underlying attitudes and values toward the retarded. His analysis indicates equivocal findings in attitude studies, based in part on weaknesses in methodology and research design, variations in instrumentation, and different conceptualizations of attitude components. Notable are his conclusions that general education teachers are not favorably disposed toward retarded children and that length of teaching experience alone does not promote positive attitude change. He concludes, therefore, that means must be found to change teacher attitudes if current efforts at integrating the retarded into regular classes are to succeed. He argues for more research on the relationship between expressed attitudes and overt behavior, how the retarded internalize the behavior of others, what aspects of their behavior are responded to by others, and the impact of proximity to the retarded on attitude formation or change.

The chapter by Edgerton reports on his followup of adults discharged from a state hospital for the retarded about fifteen years ago. The participant observer method in this study stands as a relatively unique approach in mental retardation. Edgerton stresses the importance of processes rather than social structures in mental retardation research, and the insights derived from his anthropological orientation contribute to understanding the complexity of these individuals' lives and the multiplicity of sociocultural factors impinging upon adult adjustment.

Mercer is concerned with the limitations of intelligence testing of minority group children, their possible misclassification as retarded, and the stigmatizing effects of special class placement. She suggests the need for more comprehensive assessment procedures and proposes the use of pluralistic norms as an important dimension in estimating a child's learning potential. The quantification and measurement of such norms offers another tool for more precise diagnoses and classification. Applied together with measures of adaptive behavior, social role performance in nonacademic settings, and health status, more appropriate decisions about educational placement are possible.

The chapter by Ashmore concludes this section of the book. Whereas previous papers focus mainly on identification and measurement of attitudes and values and assessment of their consequences, Ashmore is concerned with the factors and processes of attitude formation and with their change. To create more favorable attitudes toward the retarded, he suggests careful identification and specific programming for the target group; the initiation of forced compliance and self-confrontation procedures rather than mass media campaigns to affect attitude change; more emphasis on the strengths and heterogeneity of retarded persons in mass media educational programs; and the development of educational curricula designed to make children more aware of and comfortable with "differences" in others.

SOCIAL COMPETENCE AND SOCIALIZATION

The chapters on social competence and socialization in the third section are clearly an integral part of any discussion of mental retardation and the status and roles of these individuals in society. In fact, although low intelligence has obvious implications for behavior, it is only when maladaptive behavior is manifest that the problem is viewed with concern by families, communities, and the larger society. Thus, an understanding of the dynamics of the socialization process and the interaction of forces that contribute to the development or impedance of social competence is crucial.

Kleck provides the introductory chapter in this section. He emphasizes the need for greater attention to therapeutic intervention methods for embracing social competence in the retarded and the need for de-emphasizing the more traditional concerns with intelligence quotients, literacy, and scholastic achievement. He argues for an interactional model and the identification of factors that may limit the occurrence of effective social interaction patterns by the mentally handicapped. Changes in the stigmatizing attitudes of those who interact with the retarded—a concept expressed by many of the authors—are seen as one vital factor in promoting social competence among the mentally subnormal. Significantly, Kleck ends his chapter by suggesting that the scientific knowledge essential to wise social policy remains to be developed.

Schaefer, in an exhaustive review of the research literature on socialization and family interaction, focuses on the social stresses in the family environment as the primary influential force impeding the process of socialization. The roles of heredity and neurological impairment are acknowledged but are given relatively less attention than family relationships in accounting for asocial or antisocial behavior and deficits in intellectual performance. The author proposes a model for parent-child interaction that focuses on the contribution of that interaction to socialization and mediated learning of the child. In our provision of substitute parental care to protect children from abuse or neglect, Schaefer cautions that we supplement, not supplant, family care. Such programs must be child-centered, not based primarily on cost-effective considerations, and should maintain parental attachment and involvement in child care.

The complexities of social competence to which the chapters in this section are directed are further reflected by Cicourel. He contends that our understanding of the mentally retarded is guided by a narrow view of oral communication and non-oral representations of information processing. We are further hampered by the ambiguity in our notions of normal social competence and our limited understanding of how language is acquired and its role in the development of social competence. Cicourel proposes that a more realistic model of communicative competence in the mentally retarded can be approximated by studies of the blind or deaf in whom key modalities for communication are lacking. The emphasis on language acquisition and cognitive processes as central to adult forms of behavior suggests that, in family interaction processes, the achievement of social competence in the retarded child is influenced by the development of communication skills, which are not necessarily oral or written representations of language.

FORMS OF FAMILY ADAPTATION AND INTERVENTION

The second half of the book deals more directly with programs of social intervention and newly emergent patterns of community-based services generated in part by dissatisfaction with traditional forms of care and concern with human rights. The diverse nature of current programmatic efforts in mental retardation, and the ferment and controversy surrounding these efforts, does not permit an exhaustive consideration of alternative concepts and theories, or delivery systems. The chapters in this part of the volume, however, are exemplars of approaches for preventing or ameliorating mental retardation among individuals formerly given little consideration by community-based social institutions.

It seems apparent that the present emphasis on deinstitutionalization will place increasing demands on families to maintain their retarded children at home, with consequent stress on their resources and stability. In the first chapter of this section of the book, Farber points out that families of the retarded derive their roles and values from events similar to those experienced by other families and that their special plight stems from the necessity of coping with various kinds of offensive situations associated with their offspring's retardation. Families differ greatly in how much they are able or willing to change their mode of existence to integrate the retarded child into the family's normal life style. Farber approaches this problem in the context of adaptational processes—the creation of means for dealing with functional problems. In his presentation of assumptions about the adaptational process, he offers a meaningful conceptual framework for the sociological analysis of family crisis, not only with respect to mental retardation but to other stressful conditions as well.

Clearly, many retarded children able to profit from a family-type living experience cannot be cared for in their own homes. Theoretically at least, foster family care, designed originally to care for children deprived of parental protection and nurture, should have similar application to the retarded. As Adams notes, however, foster home care for intellectually handicapped children can be an invaluable social resource only if certain conditions are met. She points to the importance of systematically selecting foster parents with specific qualifications and aptitudes; the need for substantial and consistent professional support and guidance; a network of supplementary supportive services; efforts to rehabilitate the child's natural family; and fiscal policies and in-service training procedures designed to lend higher status and paraprofessional perspectives to the role of the foster parent.

The Garber chapter reports on a now well-known intervention project in Milwaukee with children at high risk for the development of mental retardation. Significantly, despite the apparent success of this program in raising intellectual performance and its implications for the role of environmental stimulation and the critical period of development concept, Garber indicates that many theoretical issues remain to be resolved. Among these, he highlights the threshold effect of genetic factors on mental performance; the methodological weaknesses of IQ tests and their repeated application in longitudinal studies; the potential disparities between the preschool and school curriculum; the inadequacies of the ghetto school; and the continuing oppressive effects of an unmodified seriously disadvantaged home. Garber also suggests that the presumed irreversible effects of a deprived early environment need to be questioned and that much learning takes place between the early years and adulthood. Early intervention, he maintains, in the absence of continuing, positive reinforcement, may be insufficient to prevent social environmental based mental retardation.

Levenstein, in contrast to the child-focused intervention studies dominant in our society, reports on a program directed toward helping mothers stimulate the cognitive development and language acquisition of their children through verbal interaction. She points out that college-educated, middle-class mothers carry on such "intervention" spontaneously as part of a "hidden curriculum," but that similar situations do not prevail in the lower-class home. Building on the notion that the child's intrinsically motivated play represents opportunities for cognitive development, Levenstein has introduced the guided and demonstrated use of toys and books to achieve this goal. The IQ gains in children exposed to this form of intervention are noteworthy, but the long-range effects remain to be documented. Conceptually, this approach to improving the interactional process between mothers and their children is partially responsive to Garber's expressed concern that the benefits of early enrichment outside the home can be quickly lost in a nonstimulating atmosphere inside the home.

The role of the family in the causation of certain forms of retardation, the stresses posed to family stability, and the contributions of this fundamental social institution to ameliorating the impact of intellectual handicap and promoting social competence provide one important facet of conceptual unity to this book.

EMERGENT PATTERNS OF SERVICE FOR YOUNG PEOPLE AND ADULTS

The section on emergent patterns of services describes several innovative approaches to implementing community-based programs of residential care and rehabilitation services. The Kushlick chapter speaks to the necessity of epidemiological surveys if community programs are to be properly planned and responsive to needs. Ascertainment of prevalence by degree of mental handicap is clearly insufficient. Data also must be obtained on types of disability and inappropriate behaviors, associated clinical conditions, family support structures, and availability of specialized services. Given this kind of information on mentally handicapped persons in the community, program development can proceed in an orderly, rather than crisis-oriented, manner. Kushlick's outline of the stages to be followed in an action and research program is one to which most professionals in mental retardation would subscribe, but which few have implemented.

The study reported by Birenbaum on residential care in an American city contrasts in some meaningful ways with the more carefully planned approach of the Wessex Regional Hospital Board mentioned above. Because of the preliminary nature of this program, definitive conclusions on the benefits of such care for deinstitutionalized retarded adults cannot yet be formed, although some gains in social behavior and independent functioning are evident. The value of Birenbaum's chapter at this point lies in its prospective nature and the opportunity afforded the author and his readers to examine the process and problems of transition from the large institution to the community while it is occurring. This examination cautions against massive and rapid resettlement. Birenbaum indicates we must define more precisely the social skills needed to live in different residential settings and the appropriateness of socially learned skills in state schools for community living. The achievement of these goals would permit better prediction of success in community placement and enable institutional personnel to relate more effectively preplacement training to community-living requirements.

The vocational status of the retarded and programs of training directed toward an enhancement of their adjustment have focused largely on the development of work skills and proper work habits. Halpern reminds us that an appropriate theory of work adjustment demands a dual correspondence of the individual and his work environment, manifested in satisfactory work performance and individual satisfaction. Our failure to attend to the work interests of retarded people, and to develop instruments for such assessment, may well account for observed inadequacies in vocational training. Halpern reviews the presumed relationship between social and prevocational skills and voccational adjustment adaptation of training technologies to severely handicapped persons formerly considered totally incapable of productive work. Like many of the other authors in this book, Halpern approaches his special topic in a broader environmental context. Vocational adjustment, in this sense, depends not only on work skills, but on motor, affective, and cognitive development, and communication and interpersonal skills as well.

Advocacy for the mentally retarded is another recent social development resulting from concern with the protection of human rights and ensuring the mentally retarded person's access to services. Thus it represents a new addition to delivery systems with potentially profound impact on professional decision-making processes and authority, the implementation of legislative decrees, and the range and structure of community programs. Experience with advocacy programs is too limited at this time to yield any meaningful data, but the analysis by Kurtz of some of the significant issues involved offers direction to needed research and contributes to the spirit of inquiry that characterizes this book. As with other emerging concepts in mental retardation, the functional utility of advocacy programs awaits empirical testing. A number of important issues are identified: the potential conflict between advocates and parents, professionals, and administrators regarding the retarded person's needs; conflict between the rights of the retarded and rights of others; the likely appointment of middle-class advocates for lower-class retarded persons; possible undesirable latent consequences of the advocacy role, such as the prolongation of dependency patterns; and public resistance to the advocate-sponsored principle of full human rights for the mentally retarded. The role of the advocate in social change is an important sociological phenomenon in need of scientific investigation.

SOCIAL CHANGE: PROBLEMS AND STRATEGIES

Changes in the status of the mentally retarded in society ultimately depend on the application of theory and knowledge to practice. The gap is considerable between our philosophical ideals of utilizing all human resources to their fullest potential and the establishment of a comprehensive network of services to meet the needs of all retarded persons. Social change, especially when new social institutions threaten old ones, is not likely to be accomplished without problems. Barriers to change must be identified and strategies to overcome them, devised.

The final section of this book addresses this objective. Cohen describes the practical problems encountered in developing a network of services for the mentally retarded in an urban community. Undoubedly, the obstacles noted are common to many local communities: greater complexity of fiscal procedures and controls; bureaucratic resistance to change; consumer participation in decision-making processes; professional and lay attitudes; overlapping jurisdiction; and the pervasive issue of community priorities. The problems are common, but the strategies employed for their resolution may well vary as a function of leadership style, staff resources, legislative mandates, and unique local conditions. The personal case study deals with issues and problems that also have been encountered by other professionals in the development of community services for the mentally retarded.

On casual observation, it may seem to the reader that Ohlin's paper, concerned with new approaches to delinquent youth, has little relevance to the sociological aspects of mental retardation. The relevance is clear, however, both theoretically and practically. Delinquency and mental retardation are both forms of social deviance involving socially undesirable patterns of behavior. The negative reactions that these behaviors evoke in others are similar, if not identical, as are the consequences of stigma for self-concept formation and adjustment. As Ohlin notes, the shift from large, isolated institutions to local, community-based programs has characterized efforts in mental retardation, mental illness, and delinquency, with striking parallels in the kinds of alternative models developed and obstacles to change encountered. Ohlin's analysis of the deinstitutionalization process for youthful offenders in Massachusetts, and the barriers encountered and strategies for overcoming these barriers, is particularly timely and relevant to professionals in mental retardation.

The contribution by Boggs to this volume stems from her unique and extensive experience with social organizations of various kinds, bureaucratic structures at all levels of government, and paraprofessional and consumer groups. She approaches from a very different perspective some of the fundamental issues examined by other authors in this book. She notes that classification in categorical aid programs, for example, determines eligibility for service and may be greatly complicated by vague definitions and criteria in legislation, denying "due process" protections for the individual. Applying the case study method, Boggs clearly documents many of the processes and factors involved in the formulation of legislative acts and rules and regulations in varied programs such as immigration, housing, vocational rehabilitation, and institutional care. In her analysis of organizational dilemmas in mental retardation, the impact of concepts such as normalization is carried beyond its affects on the individual and family to the structure of governmental agencies responsible for the delivery of services. Her comments on the legal, legislative, and bureaucratic process highlights the role of social science principles in public policy-making affecting the retarded.

Discussion summaries appear at the end of specific sections. These summaries reflect the vigorous debate and differing viewpoints generated by the papers presented at the Conference itself. These differences, as well as variations in concepts, strategies, and philosophical orientation of the author-participants, fairly represent our current state of knowledge about the mentally retarded and society.

The need for more research in the social sciences, and the direction such research might take, we hope are apparent in these pages.

Michael J. Begab
Stephen A. Richardson

HISTORICAL AND CONTEMPORARY ISSUES IN MENTAL RETARDATION

The Mentally Retarded
And Society:
Trends and Issues

Michael J. Begab

New concepts and program developments in the field of mental retardation and the research issues arising therefrom are inextricably tied to the changing values and conditions in our society. Today's actions emerge from yesteryear's attitudes, concerns, and discoveries and portend tomorrow's events. There is, however, a serious cultural lag in applying new knowledge to societal goals. Even in periods of rapid social change, the structure and organization of our social institutions, deeply entrenched biases and beliefs, and economic and political considerations serve to slow down the process. Sometimes these represent barriers to progress, but in other instances they may act as a stabilizing force, compelling a thoughtful examination of the consequences of change and providing an opportunity to test new ideas and programs for their functional or dysfunctional properties in mainstreaming a viable collective society.

Unfortunately, the rational approach these comments imply does not characterize the modern complex society. We are not, and have not been, especially successful in looking ahead in the formulation of solutions to major social problems. Alcoholism, drug addiction, mental illness, mental retardation, soaring divorce rates, illegitimacy, delinquency and crime, and poverty continue to plague us. Several reasons for this predicament, other than our state of knowledge and technology, could be advanced. The first of these is a failure in conceptualization. We do not yet appreciate the interrelated and interdependent nature of social, economic, and technological events. It is not too difficult to link, in an oversimplistic way at least, legislative action on farm subsidies to food supply, prices, and malnutrition among the poor; the civil rights movement of the 1950's to class action suits on behalf of the retarded today; changing attitudes toward sexual permissiveness to social concerns for marriage and sterilization among socially incompetent retarded persons. Our failure to conceptualize the linkage between such social movements and events and their possible outcomes partly accounts for our predictive ineptitudes.

3

The second reason is, in part, implicit in the first. Multiple factors, interacting in endless combinations, greatly complicate analysis and prediction. A single event often has diverse consequences and each of these creates its own "ripple effects." Thus, the energy crisis not only affects major segments of the economy and employment, but may also, if severe enough, markedly influence extended kinship relationships, neighboring behavior, and patterns of family interaction. Conceivably, if marital partners must stay home more and go to bed earlier to conserve electrical energy, efforts at population control would be dissipated. These relationships are not part of an isolated system. Many factors, unrelated to the energy crisis, more directly affect interpersonal relationships. The consequences of different inputs to the system are sometimes reinforcing, other times counteracting. The patterns which emerge are not readily discernible and, therefore, difficult to predict.

A third reason for deficiencies in foresightful planning is the preoccupation with the past and overconcerns with the present. We still have to identify the harbingers of social change in our environment, to measure these forces qualitatively as well as quantitatively, to understand the processes involved, how they interact and how to intervene to achieve desired outcomes. Our society, and most others for that matter, is crisis oriented and reaction motivated. Legislation is enacted and resources mobilized in response to *expressed,* not *anticipated,* needs. We incarcerate offenders, hospitalize the mentally ill and retarded, and ostracize the amoral. Seldom do we address ourselves to the conditions in the family and society which foster these problems. And when we do plan ahead, as in comprehensive health programs, community mental health centers, and national health insurance, for example, we look primarily to treat and rehabilitate the sick and disabled, rather than to maintain good health among the well. These admittedly worthy activities are, nevertheless, reactions to demonstrated need. In the past year, seven states have passed laws establishing health screening, diagnosis, and preventive measures in mental retardation and other birth defects. Other examples could also be cited, such as mass immunization, well-child and prenatal care clinics, early intervention programs, nutritional supplementation, the campaign against smoking. Such forward-looking activities are, however, the exception to the rule.

HISTORICAL HIGHLIGHTS IN MENTAL RETARDATION

The fortunes and misfortunes of the mentally retarded in our society have varied over the years with changes in behavior technology, social and economic conditions, shifting values, new knowledge, and the predominant social ethos of the American way of life. For the major part of our history, we have been guided by the credo that the individual is in essence master of his destiny. Ambition, hard work, the rational and efficient use of time, morality, and independence were the gateways to success and the door of opportunity was open to all who possessed these virtues. Values of rugged individualism and self-reliance served as cornerstones for public school teaching and social policy. Failures in this presumed "open-ended" system were attributed to personal weaknesses and deficiencies. (Levine and Levine, 1970) With this perspective, solutions had to be person centered and oriented toward the remediation of individual deficits for better adaptation to the social milieu.

The mentally retarded, by definition, have "weaknesses and deficiencies." According to the American Association on Mental Deficiency (Grossman, 1973), "Mental retardation refers to significantly subaverage general intellectual functioning existing concurrently with deficits in adaptive behavior, and manifested during the developmental period." Whether these weaknesses are indigenous to the individual is a matter for continuing debate and research, if not for the severely handicapped person, at least for the mildly retarded, disadvantaged, who are without demonstrable central nervous system pathology.

The potentially depressing effect of social environmental factors on intelligence and behavior was not considered in early approaches to the problem. Early pioneers such as Itard, Seguin, Howe, and others focused their efforts on the educational remediation of deficiencies, but unfortunately, only seriously pathological and clinical forms of retardation were identifiable at that time and existing technologies were clearly unequal to the task. The optimism generated by these pioneers in the rehabilitation potential of these individuals through teaching and training programs in institutional settings did not long prevail. The limited capabilities of this group fall significantly outside the margins of variability and diversity communities were willing to tolerate, and the institutions were transformed into custodial care facilities. Correspondingly, attitudes shifted from habilitation to humanitarianism. Regarded as dysfunctional elements to community stability and disruptive to family life, the mentally retarded came to be thought of with an "out of sight, out of mind" philosophy. The location of these facilities in isolated, rural settings transformed this philosophy into reality for the general public, if not for the parents and relatives of the retarded. Nevertheless, a milestone had been passed: the acceptance of public responsibility and support for the retarded.

The concept of the retarded as severly damaged persons underwent dramatic change with the invention of intelligence tests and research relating to genetics early in the 20th century. For the first time an instrument was available to measure the intelligence of a large proportion of the country's population. Persons whose behavior previously went unnoticed or was attributed to various forms of character defect were thrust into the public limelight. The application of these tests to army troops in World War I revealed an alarming number of young men performing at a mentally subnormal level. Overnight, historically speaking, mental retardation became recognized as a social problem of the highest magnitude.

The public image of the retarded as damaged, very dependent, casualties of the reproductive process and, therefore, deserving of humane care could not survive these new revelations. Practically all of the studies conducted during this period concentrated their attention on impoverished, socially troublesome families. Applying Mendelian concepts of heredity and IQ tests, they uniformly concluded that mental retardation was transmitted through heredity (Goddard, 1912; 1914; Brock, 1934). Despite many hundreds of studies bearing on this issue, the role of genetics in intelligence remains unresolved.

The most alarming information from these studies was the extremely poor social behavior of the families involved. Antisocial, immoral, criminal, and other undesirable traits characterized these families. The fact that these traits were often coupled with high birth rates, convinced many people that civilization was in jeopardy unless effective measures of control could be devised. The public image of the retarded was mirrored in the words of Dr. Walter E. Fernald, an authority in the field, in a speech made in 1912.

> The social and economic burdens of uncomplicated feeblemindedness are only too well known. . . . The great majority ultimately become public charges in some form. . . . Feebleminded women are almost invariably immoral and if at large usually become carriers of venereal disease or give birth to children who are as defective as themselves. . . . Every feebleminded person, especially the high grade imbecile, is a potential criminal needing only the proper environment and opportunity for the full development and expression of his criminal tendencies. (Davies, 1959).

These views generated the eugenics movement of the early 1900's which were further buttressed by sociological theories current at the time. Most prominent was the concept of Social Darwinism advanced by Herbert Spencer (1877). According to this theory, society was subject to the same principles of natural selection as plants and animals and only the fittest would survive.

For many, solutions to the societal threat posed by these retarded persons could not be entrusted to natural processes of selection and more drastic remedies were put forth. Some proposed that all defectives be put to death. Others advocated restrictive marriage laws. Some of the more far-sighted recommended a general improvement of the environment. Control through life segregation and sterilization, however, received the most popular support. Thus, by 1915, 12 states had passed compulsory sterilization laws and most others soon after embarked on a program of indefinite detention for those persons considered to be social risks and a menace to society.

Community perspectives of the severely retarded as objects of pity and of the mildly retarded as sources of threat dominated public thought for nearly a century, even though the proportion institutionalized of all levels of retardation never approached 10% of the retarded population. Attitudes were tempered in part by the passage of compulsory education acts very early in the 20th century and the problems this posed for the less able learners. This movement led to a system of teaching children *en masse* in large classes with stringent standards for scholastic promotion. The slow learners, many of whom were members of minority groups, foreign language-speaking immigrants, and children of migrant families, could not compete in this system. In 1929, in the San Francisco elementary school program, one-third of the children were behind in grade level; at the junior high school level with even more demanding curriculum requirements, 46% of the students were considered retarded. This situation was fairly typical for the large city.

Homogenous grouping according to ability was the proposed solution to this problem. This concept became the foundation of special education and has been largely unchallenged until recent years. In the intervening years, educators have introduced many variations: special schools, special classes within the regular school, ungraded classes, track systems, resource rooms, tutoring, integration with "normal" students in non-academic subjects. The underlying premise has always been, however, that unequal competition breeds failure, frustration, low self-esteem, and disruptive behavior. Children, it was felt, needed to be protected from these consequences if they were to assume productive adult roles in society.

Significantly, opposition to ungraded classes came from two different sources. On the one hand, despite more than 20 euphemisms to choose from, some clearly not pejorative in connotation, parents often resented the classification of their children as subnormal and withheld consent for placement. School executives, for quite opposite reasons, objected to the expense of educating children of low mental ability. In some school systems, per pupil costs for atypical classes ranged 2 to 3 times as high as for normal children. Such expenditures were justified by proponents of special education, however, as less costly economically and socially than caring for the potential future criminal or dependent individual.

Special classes were also thought to contribute to teacher efficiency. The regular class teacher, it was argued, needed to devote a disproportionate amount of her teaching activities to the retarded child, to the neglect of other children from whom self-support and responsible behavior was expected. To leaders in the professional community, use of regular teachers was a foolish and extravagant waste of personal resources and unfair to the normal child and his parents.

Many of these issues are as relevant today as they were 50 years ago.

CONCEPTS IN CHANGE

Some of the public's concern about the retarded dissipated with the growth of institutional facilities and the practice of segregation and control through sterilization. While there is no compelling evidence that these policies effectively reduced the incidence of mental retardation or "protected society," the disappearance of many graduates of special education from public visibility and the highly selective placement practices of the public institutions, pushed mental retardation temporarily into the background of social consciousness.

The great depression of the 1930's and World War II diverted attention still further from mental retardation to more pressing national concerns. But once again, the spotlight was focused on the large number of males in the population considered unfit by the Selective Service System for military service. Fully one-third were considered ineligible, and the large majority of these, by virtue of intellectual handicap (President's Task Force on Manpower Conservation, 1964). The rejected males, however, 14 times more prevalent in the South than Northwestern states, did not demonstrate the negative behavioral traits revealed by the early pedigree studies noted earlier. The vast majority of these young men (approximately 94%) had made a reasonable adjustment to civilian life. They were economically self-sufficient, socially responsible, and law abiding (Ginzberg and Bray,

1953). Furthermore, the mentally retarded were productive workers in the labor force and contributed meaningfully to the war effort.

The aftermath of the war brought to social awareness millions of dislocated and disabled veterans. A grateful nation, confronted with problems of serious dependency and shattered lives, embarked upon a massive program of rehabilitation, urged employers to hire the handicapped and retrained veterans for new careers. Perhaps the most significant outcome of these efforts was the new insights gained regarding the remarkable restorative capacities of the human organism and resilience of the human personality.

In this climate of reawakened humanitarianism and a more enlightened view of human capabilities, the potentialities of the retarded came in for re-examination. The American Association on Mental Deficiency, established in 1876, and long a champion and spokesman for the retarded, found more receptive listeners and provided professional leadership and direction to expanded programs of care, training, and treatment. They were more than ably abetted in these efforts by the establishment of the National Association for Retarded Children in 1950. Motivated to secure for their children the rights and opportunities available to other children and essential to their development and fulfillment, members of this Association lobbied aggressively to secure services. The profound impact of the parent group movement on Federal and State legislation, on the demonstration of innovative services, the quality of programs, and expansion of educational and rehabilitation opportunities, stands forth as an important social phenomenon in the field of human services. Many other parent groups representing different forms of handicap were developing similar models. Frequently these groups, often sharing common interests, compete with each other for limited supportive resources.

With the interest and the pressure of parent groups and the personal involvement of the late President Kennedy, the federal government in the early 1960's moved actively to redress the long-standing neglect of the retarded. In a landmark and unprecedented message to Congress on mental illness and mental retardation, President Kennedy committed the resources of the nation to the prevention and treatment of this major social problem. The enactment of PL 88-164 and 88-156 (implementing some of the recommendations of the President's Panel Report), authorized the construction of research centers in mental retardation, university-affiliated facilities for training and service demonstration, and community mental health centers. Provision was also made for training teachers in special education and for planning grants to states. The latter, while offering only limited funds, compelled interdepartmental and interdisciplinary cooperation, thus bringing to bear a range of resources and programs previously only marginally committed to serving the retarded.

From this modest beginning only 10 years ago, Federal and State expenditures for programs for the handicapped have escalated sharply (Table 1). In 1970, over $4.7 billion were spent on a variety of programs (Conley, 1973). Clearly the foundation has been laid for a continuing assault on the problem of mental retardation and the amelioration of its consequences for the individual, his family, and society. This goal has been achieved only through broadly based community support, national leadership, and extensive educational efforts to make visible the magnitude and nature of the problem.

Table 1. Expenditures on selected programs serving the retarded[a]

Program	1968	1970
	$	$
Residential care	1,284,400,000	1,619,500,000
Special education	1,057,900,000	1,463,600,000
Regular academic education	648,000,000	748,600,000
Clinical program	26,000,000	54,400,000
Employment programs	75,000,000	124,800,000
Construction	46,500,000	41,500,000
Training of personnel	183,000,000	235,000,000
Research	50,000,000	62,000,000
Income maintenance	263,500,000	364,600,000
Agency operating expenses	7,100,000	11,800,000
Total	3,641,400,000	4,725,800,000

[a]Reprinted from Conley, R. W. The Economics of Mental Retardation. The Johns Hopkins University Press, 1973.

EMERGING ISSUES AND DEVELOPMENTS

The variable visibility of mental retardation to the lay and professional community has probably been a mixed blessing, depending in large measure on the nature of the image created. Professionals in the field, mainly in institutional settings in years past, were mindful of this factor. They recognized that the severely handicapped child from the average or disadvantaged family was a threat to family stability and the mildly retarded acting-out adolescent or adult a threat to community values. The latter group is generally admitted to public institutions between the ages of 15 and 19 years, with histories of aggressive, delinquent, unmanageable, or sexually promiscuous behavior. They are community rejects whose behavior and life styles violate the standards of the cultural, dominant majority. Rhodes (1972) describes these relationships by a threat-recoil hypothesis. According to this view, communities exist in a constant state of uneasiness arising from the coexistence of individuals with diverse needs and behavior patterns. From time to time, an individual or group's behavior exceeds the community's tolerance and upsets its equilibrium. Widespread delinquency, drug abuse, or social militancy increases stress to the point that a recoil reaction is generated and corrective measures demanded. Even an individual's behavior, if looked upon as representative of a certain group, can evoke this response. To the extent that agencies or social institutions act effectively to reduce the threat, the community calms down and equilibrium is restored.

Many examples, some old, some current, support this hypothesis. The eugenics movement, the segregation and control approach, the denial of civil rights for persons adjudicated as retarded, the establishment of maximum security facilities for defective delinquents are historical cases in point. Less than 15 years ago, several states appointed Governor's Commissions on Defective Delinquents because a retarded person had allegedly sexually molested a child, committed rape or some other "heinous" offense. Today, in many communities, citizens join forces to block the establishment of a residential center for disturbed children or a sheltered workshop for retarded adults or any other invasion by "undesirable" elements.

Early practitioners, guarded as to the changes in behavior institutional regimes could effect, learned to approach the task of community placement very selectively. This caution resulted from repeated failures in community adjustment where individuals persisted in the same behavior patterns communities were unwilling to tolerate. The strategy was to present a low-key profile, to reduce visibility and facilitate assimilation. At the time (1940's and 1950's) wage-home placements as domestics and child care aides or as hospital and nursing home assistants were popular for female adults. Males were frequently placed on farms or in unskilled industrial work. Most of these placements required that the employer assume some degree of personal interest and supervisory responsibility. In many instances, domestics became a part of the family's activities, participating in their social and recreational pursuits and visits to extended family members. Invariably, they lived in and their success was largely determined by how well their "foster parent-employers" fulfilled the "benefactor" role so aptly described by Edgerton (1967). Industrial workers, in the absence of supportive family ties, were generally placed in "half-way houses" managed by a married couple who carried similar parental functions. In these group settings (ranging from four to ten persons as a rule), peer relationships served as the primary outlet for leisure time needs. Efforts to integrate the retarded into community recreation programs were not especially fruitful. For some, physical appearance and interests and for others, socially dependent behavior, often a consequence of regimented institutional experiences, tended to stigmatize them and disqualify them from full social acceptance (Goffman, 1963). For the most part, although the evidence is more anecdotal than truly scientific, the avoidance response of the normal adults with whom they came into contact stemmed from interpersonal encounters rather than knowledge of their institutional backgrounds. While sometimes able to conceal their histories of commitment and *official* label of mental retardation, they could not mask, in direct encounter, their intellectual and social limitations.

DEINSTITUTIONALIZATION AND RESEARCH ISSUES

The careful evaluation of potential "benefactors" and the equally careful selection of candidates for placement whose credentials were "gold plated" stand in marked contrast to current, massive efforts to depopulate public institutions. While heroic efforts are being launched to find suitable foster parents and to develop alternative patterns of care and service such as group homes, day centers, activity centers, etc., there are little scientific data available to ensure constructive outcomes. Questions regarding the kind of retarded child most likely to profit from foster family care and the essential character-istics of foster parents await answers from research. Some of the background and personality factors to be explored are suggested in a study by Fanshel (1961). He notes that foster fathers who have not suffered deprivation in their own childhoods are more successful with aggressive foster children. Some foster families too, are especially effective with a range of handicapped children sharing the essential element of dependency. Successful foster parents have been effective with their own children and many come from large, closely knit families. Perhaps, as Fanshel conjectures, such families provide added social supports and contribute to an understanding that *all* family members are to be valued.

These observations were not derived from studies of retarded children in foster care, although some of the concepts may be applicable and certainly deserve testing. That foster home placements for retarded children have not widely applied these concepts seems clear from a study by Maas and Engler (1959). Their findings indicate that in general retarded children are among the least successfully placed, being shifted frequently from home to home. In a critical review of research by Windle (1962), management and discipline problems, inordinate demands for supervision or medical care, and lack of environmental supports were frequent causes of failure in family care for the moderately retarded. Interpersonal difficulties were primary factors for failure in vocational and home leave placements for the mildly retarded. In these instances, professional supervision could not compensate for family deficiencies which precipitated admission in the first place.

Clinical insights can provide some meaningful starting points for the development of foster family care programs as an alternative to institutions. These must be validated, however, if children are to be protected from the harmful effects of constantly changing homes. Professional attitudes may be another barrier to widespread implementation. As Begab (1963) has noted, foster family placements as treatment resources are used sparingly for retarded children with organic damage, except as a stopgap measure pending admission to an institution. Social workers, reflecting upon the helplessness and despair natural parents feel toward their retarded children, may well underestimate the number of foster parents willing to accept such children, but this defeatist attitude is not entirely unfounded. Foster parents, like natural parents, must derive gratification from their parenting tasks to maintain their motivations and endure the extraordinary burden of care that severely handicapped children pose. Few children are totally unresponsive to affection and attention, but such children are poor candidates for foster family care.

For the young, mildly retarded child from a disadvantaged home, this form of care is clearly the preferred choice of treatment and with few exceptions has been an integral part of social agency practice for more than a decade. The commitment of whole families of functionally submarginal and mentally subnormal individuals to state institutions, so common even 20 years ago, is an increasingly rare event. From our knowledge of developmental processes in children, family living is clearly better designed to maximize potentials than institutional environments. However, there is little research data on the outcomes of this shift in placement policies.

There are some indications that seriously deprived parents of limited intelligence can be helped through intensive intervention programs to provide more stimulating, growth-promoting environments (Heber et al., 1972). For these parents, retention of the child in the home or return at a later period in time when pathological conditions have been corrected can avoid institutionalization altogether. Our technology for modifying the behavior of these multiproblem families, however, is still very limited and economically and politically difficult to apply on the broad scale required.

The number of young children from adverse homes currently admitted to institutions because of neglect, dependency, or abuse is small. They will play a minor role in deinstitutionalization activities. As an alternative to institutional placement, however, it poses a number of issues other than those involving selection criteria for foster parents and their charges already noted. Foster care is traditionally time limited. It provides substitute parental care for parents who are ill, neglectful, abusive, economically destitute, or otherwise unable to discharge their responsibilities. A major goal of foster care programs is to restore the natural home to more adequate performance levels and to return the child to his family. In cases of serious family pathology, it is used as a transitory placement pending termination of parental rights and adoption plans. As a rule, the time span does not exceed a few years, but when it stretches beyond adolescence (or begins during that period) it terminates with the achievement of independent status.

This general pattern of foster family care may not suffice for the retarded. More time will be required to restore family adequacy, a significant proportion will be unamenable to change, and a greater percentage of the children, as compared to those with normal intelligence, will fail to reach fully independent status. The situation is more obvious for the less able retarded child who needs prolcnged, even lifetime supervision, care, and guidance. It seems most unlikely that foster parents could or would assume such excessive burdens on an indefinite basis even with comprehensive supportive services.

Small group homes (7 to 12 persons) are probably a better alternative for this latter group. It combines some of the advantages of family life and peer interaction in the socialization process (Begab, 1963). Some of the problems relevant to prolonged care, however, apply here, too. Independent operators, often married couples seeking additional sources of income, offer little assurance of long range stability. The disruptive impact to the retarded, the agency, and the community of precipitate closings can be very devastating. This problem can be largely forestalled by the establishment of agency-operated homes, where the "foster-parents" are employees of the agency (Gula, 1964).

In this form of care, as in many other types of community-based services for the retarded, there is little experience upon which to build quality programs. There are, indeed, numerous isolated examples of effective half-way houses, hostels, and group homes, but, with few exceptions, environmental and program ingredients have not been sufficiently specified and evaluated to permit replication in diverse communities and subcultures (Kushlick, 1968; Tizard et al., 1972). Research into these areas demands the highest national priority if community-based services are to be any better than the institutional conditions they are intended to replace.

The urgency felt by state administrators to depopulate the institutions by one-third before the end of this decade has been generated in large measure by recent class action suits before the courts and the Federal government's expressed goals. The movement from institution to community orientation and the normalization concept which underlies it are not new to the mental retardation field. Exposés of the deplorable conditions in many of our large public institutions have occurred many times in the past, but repercussions have been local, not national, and corrective measures, when invoked, have been handled at the administrative level. The right to treatment litigation decisions in Alabama, New York, and other states, with the aid of television and the mass media have now given the problem national visibility and aroused the conscience of the public and the Congress.

The public response for immediate action has placed great stress on community resources. On the basis of anecdotal evidence at least (time and inclination have not permitted careful assessments as yet), the consequences have been of questionable value. Partly this results from a lack of knowledge of what to do, how to do it, and for whom. We might also anticipate, based on the threat-recoil hypothesis discussed earlier, that with increased visibility and citizen awareness, communities will feel a sense of uneasiness and erect barriers to the integration of the retarded in their midst. While this should not deter us from this ultimate goal, it points to the need for selective placement and strategies for positively influencing public attitudes. A gradual, low-key approach will demonstrate to communities that the retarded are not a substantial threat to their cultural norms and values. The retarded child who is subjected to stigmatizing and rejecting experiences by an ill-prepared citizenry and peers stands to gain little by his placement from the institution into the community.

The problem is especially acute for the mildly retarded. A small fraction of this segment of the retarded population resides in state facilities for the retarded and mental hospitals. Some are inmates of prisons or juvenile correction facilities. Many seem able to adjust to community expectations, albeit marginally in many instances, and are identified as deviant only during their school years when intellectual prowess is at a premium. In adult life, many assume the roles of wage earners, marital partners, and parents, although definitive knowledge of their performance in these roles is quite limited. Nevertheless, whatever negative reactions they provoke are seen in the context of proverty and corresponding social ailments rather than mental retardation per se. Essentially, they lose their official labels as retarded persons.

The mildly retarded who are committed to state institutions have a far higher frequency of behavioral disorders than those who remain in the community. These individuals are seldom placed primarily because of low intelligence. They are removed from their homes and communities because of emotional disorders, serious behavior problems, delinquency, and the lack of family supports. Such behaviors are intolerable to the community, especially when retardation and its presumed (although not scientifically demonstrated) causal role in delinquent behavior is evident. These individuals who violate the law, like their counterparts in penal facilities, most frequently commit crimes against property: burglary, breaking and entering. In a survey of penal facilities, mentally retarded inmates surprisingly were reported to be more involved in homicide than the non-retarded offenders. Equally surprising, in light of the general public's indignation when a retarded man is indicted or convicted of a sexual crime, was their comparatively infrequent (5%) incarceration for rape and other sexual offenses (Brown and Courtless, 1971).

In the same study of 90,000 cases of reported IQ scores in state prisons, nearly 10% had IQ's under 70. Data are not available, however, on the nature and frequency of delinquent acts committed by residents in mental retardation institutions. Major crimes such as homicide and rape, even when the offender is definitely retarded (IQ under 55), generally are handled through the correctional system. Comparatively less serious offenses, against property, for example, may be channeled either through the corrections or mental health systems. The courts do not apply uniform criteria in their disposition of such cases. Often decisions are based on the judge's views of the community's need for protection, the potential of the retarded person to profit from education and rehabilitation programs, and the availability of such programs in the respective facilities. Sentencing under the criminal code has time limitation advantages for the retarded offender, but the rate of recidivism reported for this group suggests a reinforcement of their delinquent and criminal behavior. On the other hand, these facilities have very few programs of special education or vocational training geared to the retarded offender and even fewer psychiatric services. Conversely, while placement in an institution is generally for an indefinite period of time, programs are undeniably more available and particularly oriented toward this population.

As in the mental retardation field, there is a beginning movement in some state programs to treat delinquent youth in the community and to avoid the allegedly harmful effects of labeling and learned criminal behavior. These programs are of recent origin and their effectiveness remains to be evaluated. It seems likely that certain retarded youth offenders could be treated in similar fashion, thus negating the need for separation and readjustment to community life and the stigmatizing impact of being housed with more seriously handicapped individuals. But here too, there is a need to discriminate between the mildly disturbed, acting-out youth and markedly deviant behavior. For the latter, temporary segregation from the source of his conflicts while behavior is being brought under better control can be highly advantageous. In these instances, the institution may serve as a refuge. The abolition of institutional care for this group, as some have advocated, would deprive them of a potentially important treatment resource and relegate them to the largely discredited jails and hospitals for the criminally insane.

Placement programs for mildly retarded persons with preadmission histories of antisocial behavior have been marked by varying degrees of failure, (Windle, 1962). As indicated in Table 2, patient actions, largely in the realm of interpersonal difficulties, are primarily responsible. Inadequate work performance is another common reason for failure, but here too, authority conflicts, poor work habits, anxiety, and low self-esteem rather than lack of work skills appear operative. By contrast, the moderately retarded are more likely to fail because of lack of family and environmental supports, poor health, or intolerable behavior.

It could be argued that the institutional subculture and program deficiencies contribute to failure and that readjustment problems are minimized when treatment is provided in the community setting to which the individual is expected to return. There is some merit to this view, but the potential reactions of the community to the threatening behavior of disturbed, antisocial youth urges caution and appropriate safeguards if this

Table 2. Percentage of failures for various reasons, by type of leave[a]

Reason for failure	Vocational leave (N = 27)	Home leave (N = 49)	Family care (N = 71)
	%	%	%
Patient's actions	92	83	44
Antisocial behavior: crimes, sexual misbehavior, pregnancy, minor antisocial actions	(14)	(63)	(4)
Intolerable behavior: unhygienic, untidy, temper, hyperactive, destructive, sleeping problems	(0)	(0)	(21)
Inadequate interpersonal relations: jealousy, disrespectful, quarrels, dominates	(26)	(2)	(7)
Inadequate work performance: cannot take orders, anxiety, poor self-evaluation	(30)	(2)	(3)
Voluntary return and escape	(18)	(6)	(3)
Mental illness: commitment to mental hospital, psychotic, depressed	(4)	(10)	(6)
Health: medical problems, seizures, or too much care required	4	2	21
Environmental lack of support: parental disinterest, home closed, parental interference, community objection	4	15	35

[a]Reprinted from Windle, C., Prognosis of Mental Subnormals. Monograph Supplement to American Journal of Mental Deficiency, March, 1962, 66, p. 23.

approach is to succeed. Experimental programs and careful evaluation should precede any large-scale community-based effort of this nature.

Over the past decade, institutions, with the help of Federal funds from the Hospital Improvement Program, have accelerated efforts to prepare the mildly retarded better for integration into the community. The declining percentage of this group in the institutional population suggests some remediation of earlier deficiencies. The establishment of preplacement units in the institution serves as a motivator to residents and source of status and often involves day-work activities in the community. Half-way houses have also been used to effect transition from institution to community life. In this model, substitute parents offer psychological support, and contact with the natural parents, where adverse conditions prevail, is consciously discouraged. A vital component in this rehabilitation process is to protect the individual from the source of family deprivation that contributed to his behavior. The dismal record of these persons released to home leave status indicates the wisdom of this view (Windle, 1962, p. 24).

Residential care has been effectively used for disadvantaged adolescents in an experimental program in Israel to modify cognitive functioning and enhance social adaptation (Feuerstein and Karasilowsky, 1972). The adolescents in this study, mainly immigrants from very deprived Moroccan families, ranged from 60 to 80 IQ and first to third grade in scholastic achievement. Many were school dropouts or special education students with histories of maladaptive behavior, not unlike the mildly retarded in our own society.

This project challenged the critical age hypothesis. The Hebbian theory which underlies much of the current emphasis on early intervention postulates that the deprivation of perceptual stimuli during critical periods of development may result in deficits in the neurophysiological substratum of the organism to the point that later recovery is not possible. Utilizing a highly ingenious method of assessing the cognitive modifiability of these low functioning adolescents (Learning Potential Assessment Device, LPAD) and a structured program of instrumental enrichment, Feuerstein has been able to document marked improvement in cognitive performance in an overwhelming majority of his subjects. Exercises to promote cognitive capability, viewed by this investigator as an essential tool for adaptation, were supplemented by a planned intervention program of induced socially accepted regression.

The adolescent, it was assumed, needs to emancipate himself from adult supervision and identify with his peer group. His failure in school and rejection by his age mates increase his need to establish independence from hostile adult figures and society. This provokes conflict with socially accepted norms. This type of behavior is reinforced by the uncontrolled quality of the adolescent culture and no significant redevelopment is possible while these factors prevail. Furthermore, to learn at his existing low level of functioning, the adolescent must enter into a child-teacher relationship characteristic of younger children. This requires the individual to reconcile his quasi-adult strivings with "first grade" behavior. In Feuerstein's words,

> Our program seeks to induce socially accepted regression. This in turn is used as a technique to unify and make compatible the various levels of functioning and role playing. Ultimately, this allows the youngsters to use learning as a way of becoming significantly modified. Such a strategy becomes possible only within a residential setting where the total environment is structured so as to allow the individual to indulge in such a regressive process (Feuerstein and Krasilowsky, 1972, p. 579).

The success of this program suggests that institutional care is not inherently evil and that educational strategies combined with structured peer activities may have certain advantages for disadvantaged adolescents.

Another experiment in Israel uses entire villages and communities in rural areas as foster placements for deprived adolescents in the Youth Aliyah Program. Individuals are placed in work-home situations similar to the farm-home placements in this country. Unlike our placements, however, the employer is not asked to assume supervisory functions and responsibilities for the adolescent's non-work-related personal behavior or to become a parent surrogate. While the family may well develop close personal relationships with the adolescent placed in their home, the primary source of social and psychological support as well as moral constraints comes through structured peer experiences in the Youth Aliyah program.

It should be noted that a major problem in the community adjustment of the retarded on work-home placement is the lack of peer contact and social and recreational outlets. For many retarded youth who enjoy social dances, movies, sports, and other planned uses of leisure time while in the institution, the change to independent status in the community is not sufficiently compensating. This model, in its de-emphasis of the parental role, is consistent with the adolescent's need for independence. With the formation of peer groups under skilled leadership, it could probably be adapted to our own culture. The stress on deinstitutionalization and the limited success of placement efforts merit experimentation with a variety of innovative programs.

THE FUTURE ROLE OF THE INSTITUTIONS

The concept of institution-community relations and the free flow of retarded persons between these settings according to their needs and the needs of their families at specific times in the life process have been the hallmark of professional philosophy for decades. Similarly, the idea that the retarded should have life experiences and be treated as much like normal persons as possible, the principle of normalization, is not new. Admittedly, the implementation of this philosophy in practice has varied widely. Differences in the availability of community resources, public attitudes, funding capabilities, legal barriers, and the level of knowledge enjoyed by practitioners contribute to this variation.

The current agitation to depopulate our public facilities, given great impetus by recent court decisions and the inhumane conditions disclosed at court hearings, rests heavily on the normalization principle. For many, this old concept dressed in new terminology has assumed ideological and doctrinaire proportions and the status of a philosophical absolute. Often ignored in the application of this principle is the significant qualifying phrase "as nearly normal *as possible.*" Despite our growing awareness that even the most severely disabled have greater capacities than we have been willing to credit them with in the past, the marked heterogeneity of the retarded population clearly indicates that what is possible for some is not so for others. While IQ is not the only determinant, and accompanying physical and emotional disorders must also be considered, it is obvious that, in general, the higher one goes on the intellectual spectrum, the better the possibility of normalization and integrating the individual into the mainstream of community services. Nevertheless, much doubt has been cast on the future role of public institutions, and indeed, if they should have any role at all.

Opponents of the view to abolish institutions totally point to the experience in many states of moving individuals into group homes, day care centers, nursing homes, private and proprietary facilities, and even foster family homes, with consequent poorer care and far less supportive services than the large institutions provide. In some states, increased placement in the community is accompanied by markedly reduced admissions and, thus, rapid overloading of the service delivery system. The diversion of state and federal funds from the institution to the community tends to deteriorate further the quality of care in these facilities and exacerbate the very conditions in urgent need of remediation.

The criticism of community resources, less visible because of the difficulty of monitoring and lack of systematic evaluation, is not a valid argument for institutional care any more than dissatisfaction with institutions argues for community services. Inadequate services, wherever they may be located, are indefensible.

The TV horror story that filled millions of living rooms with the indignities of back ward life in Willowbrook and Rosewood have generated an overreaction to the institution as a form of care. Certainly, such conditions cannot continue to exist unchanged, and some may well be beyond redemption. In the process, however, all institutions have been tainted and community-based services have taken on a saintly glow. Both notions distort the facts. Within a given institution, excellent programs in work training, occupational and physical therapy, education, and recreation for the mildly and moderately retarded stand in marked contrast to starkly barren, unstimulating conditions for the severe and profound. Even among large institutions, as with community services, some come closer to meeting standards than others. Variations in leadership, patterns of organization, caretaker-resident staff ratios, training and orientation of child care staff and how their time is spent, professional resources, etc., all influence the program.

The polarity of opinion concerning the future role of institutions cannot be resolved by ideologies, court actions, or philosophical discourse on human rights. Congregate forms of care have certain characteristics which commend them, others which condemn them. The issue confronting society is to specify these characteristics and their impact on child development and to adjust programs and structures accordingly. In this effort, it must always be kept in mind that the heterogeneity of the retarded population and the diversity of their needs militates against any single pattern or program.

Historically, institutions have served a variety of highly useful purposes. Much of the knowledge about retardation and personnel expertise have come from these environments. Concentrated, specialized experience on a given problem has always been the gateway to in-depth knowledge and quality service. This approach has marked every area of human endeavor. In the field of mental retardation, institutions have served as a focal point for research into clinical conditions and behavioral capacities and have provided the leadership and staff training for many community programs.

Some children with little comprehension of personal danger, uncontrolled aggressive behavior, and management problems are exceedingly difficult to supervise in the home and community. Others have a need for therapeutic and restorative services requiring skilled staff and equipment. Still others need constant medical attention. These are logistically difficult to provide in scattered facilities serving individual or small groups of children, especially in rural areas or small towns where the prevalence of retarded children is too low to justify special resources. They can assure lifelong care for those who need it and whose families may want it. For the antisocial retarded person discussed earlier, the institution may offer protection not only for society, but for the individual himself, providing a haven from continuing conflict and retaliation. And theoretically at least, total daily living experiences can be structured toward specific goals.

The disadvantages of institutional care, as currently practiced, are well known. Children are exposed to numerous caretakers presenting different parental models and thereby inhibiting identification and the socialization process. Child care and nursing staff spend a good deal of their time in administrative and housekeeping duties rather than in interpersonal relations with the child. Language, communication, and other developmental processes are thereby adversely affected.

The routine and regimentation thought essential to group living are additional drawbacks. These approaches allow little opportunity for decision making and self-determination and tend to foster prolonged dependency. Institutionalization may stigmatize the mildly retarded individual and lower his self-esteem, but it may also lead to a sense of self-aggrandizement as the individual compares himself favorably with his more handicapped peers (Edgerton, 1962). In tandem, dependency and low self-esteem, where they occur, greatly complicate successful return to the community. Some have also noted declining intellectual performance.

This brief and incomplete listing of the merits and demerits of institutional care is derived from both observation and research. For the most part, it describes *what* takes place, rather than *why* it does. More analytically oriented research is needed before points for intervention can be identified and directions for modification determined. Without such information, social planning will continue to be crisis driven. Proposals for change will come from public scandal and pressure by citizens for immediate remedies. Strategic planning is impossible under these circumstances. The systematic evaluation of new services after huge investments are made in their development is not only wasteful, but new programs are difficult to abandon once started.

Investigators interested in the impact of institutional programs on the mentally retarded have used many different outcome criteria. Some have looked at changes in IQ or behavior problems, others at global estimates of social adjustment in the institution following some form of treatment, still others at post-release adjustment. Selection biases, methodological deficiencies, and faulty matching procedures make interpretation of results somewhat speculative, but nonetheless of value.

The emotional immaturity and impulsive behavior of mildly retarded disturbed adolescents seem to deter successful community adjustment. These same reasons precipitate their admission. When they elope or are released by parental insistence, they tend to fail (Tarjan et al., 1960). It is possible that older elopers are imprisoned or discharged because the institution has little more to offer them. However, the greater success of older residents on planned placements suggests a positive relationship between age and community success (Whitney, 1948; Shafter, 1954; Hartzler, 1951). By the same token, individuals admitted between the ages of 14 and 18 years are the most likely to be released 6 to 8 years later (Kramer et al., 1957). As noted earlier, they are also the brightest and, thus, regarded by staff as having the most potential (Krishef, 1959).

Substantial evidence exists that children reared in stimulating environments tend to have higher IQ's than comparable children from deprived environments. This observation has particular relevance here, because institutional settings, universally condemned on this basis, have in some studies been shown to increase IQ scores. The effectiveness of environment in altering IQ does seem related to age and critical periods of development (Gray, 1958), although change of lesser magnitude may be possible at various ages. The data are, in fact, inconclusive, due in large measure to failures in properly controlling for age, diagnosis, length of institutionalization, and family-related factors. Whereas Crissey

(1937) and Kephart and Strauss (1940) reported losses in Binet IQ for the mildly retarded, Skeels and Dye (1939) and Clarke et al. (1958) reported gains. In both of the latter studies, individuals were removed from adverse, nonstimulating environments, an orphanage and deprived home conditions, respectively. For the young children and adolescents in these studies, the institution was comparatively stimulating. Even more surprising are the findings by Chambers and Zabarenko (1956) that patients with postnatal brain damage gained more in mental age through increased attention than those with familial or other conditions. These conflicting findings suggest that differences between institutional environments may be as great as those between categories of retardation. Undoubtedly, the same qualification applies to families and community-based programs. Failure to specify the nature of these environments in measurable terms raises much doubt about the validity of studies on institution versus home-reared children.

The institutionalization of the mentally retarded is based on the premise that limited intellectual ability precludes their being able to care for themselves in society. This presumption is seldom reflected in practice, however. Families of the less able choose this course of action because of marital problems, real or anticipated adverse effects on other children, despair about the future, high medical and care expenses, sense of stigma, and lack of attention. Frequently, these retarded persons have associated physical defects and serious emotional disorders. The mildly retarded, by contrast, are prone to delinquent or other unacceptable behaviors. For all of the retarded, intelligence is undoubtedly a contributing factor to institutional placement, but social, familial, and secondary deficiencies are crucial determinants. The mildly retarded, especially, are better characterized as victims of their environment than of their low mental abilities.

This suggests that the emphasis on IQ as a criterion for placement from the institution to vocational placement may be misguided, except of course at the extremes of the intellectual spectrum. The vast majority of studies on adjustment after release report no significant relation between IQ level and community success (Windle, 1962), with an actual trend toward an inverse relationship. The paradox is more apparent than real, for the brighter the individual (at the upper ranges of the definition of mental retardation), the more serious must be his personality and behavior problems to warrant his placement in the institution.

Critics of institutionalization argue that the longer an individual remains in care, the more difficult his later adjustment to community life (Sarason, 1957), his debilitation through hospitalization (Spitz, 1945), and stigmatization (Goffman, 1957). Conversely, the length of stay is also an index as to how much opportunity has been available for the individual's training or rehabilitation (Krishef, 1957).

The generalizations regarding the deteriorating effects of long term care are not supported by research. Most studies show either a positive relationship between length of stay and adjustment or no relation at all. This is consistent with findings cited earlier about age at release. Certainly, this should not be construed as an argument for long term care of the mildly retarded. Nevertheless, it does imply that with greater maturity and control of behavior through training, the potentials for adjustment may be enhanced.

This brief and highly circumscribed review of the research literature on the effects of institutionalization in no way denies the extremely adverse conditions to which some retarded individuals are exposed. For the most part, the "warehousing" conditions described at court hearings and via the mass media apply to the severely and profoundly retarded for whom caretaker personnel are woefully inadequate. Furthermore, it implies a value-oriented priority system within the institutional environment that allocates a greater share of limited resources to those deemed more able to profit therefrom. For the moderately and mildly retarded, however, generalizations regarding the deleterious effects of institutions are at best equivocal, at worst contradicted. Too often, institutions are charged with causing personality disorders that emerge from the child's life experiences before he got there. And as noted earlier, experiences between institutions differ greatly, thus invalidating many of the generalizations made about them.

Only recently have some efforts been addressed to specifying these differences. In an intensive investigation by King and his associates (1971) of hostels, institutions, and foster care homes, differences in patterns of child management were explored. Hospital wards were clearly oriented toward child management practices while hostels demonstrated child-oriented practices. The size of the institution or living unit, contrary to widespread belief, did not account for differences in child management practices. Nor did staff ratios account for variations in child care practices. The principal determinant of differences in patterns of child care was the organizational structure. In the child-oriented units, caretakers had greater responsibility for decisions affecting all aspects of the units' functioning. The responsibilities of senior staff were shared with junior colleagues and more time was spent in child care than on administrative and domestic work, as was true for the institutional settings. There was less staff mobility within the facility and more involvement of the children in their activities. The social organization of the institution and staff training largely accounted for differences in staff behavior. Children in the child-oriented facilities were more advanced in self-care skills and speech and had fewer symptoms of disturbed behavior.

It seems quite possible that once the significant characteristics of institutional regimes can be identified, social organization reform can be initiated. More research in this area is urgently needed.

CHANGING ROLE OF THE FAMILY IN MENTAL RETARDATION

The trend toward deinstitutionalization, the expansion of community resources, and the recent court decisions upholding the right of every child, however severely handicapped, to public education can be expected to have significant impact on the role of families toward their retarded children. They may also be expected increasingly to play roles as consumer-citizens in the planning and implementation of services.

The impact of retardation on family life has received much attention in the literature (Begab, 1966; Adams, 1971; Schreiber, 1970). Some parents are able to cope successfully with the problem, maintain family stability and integrity, and provide growth-promoting experiences for their handicapped child. The trauma of having a retarded child presents for many others a seriously disruptive force to the family's life style. The physical and emotional stress of 24-hour care, the anxiety and guilt in giving birth to an "imperfect" child, the sense of hopelessness about the future, the neglect of normal children and their consequent disturbance, the exacerbation of marital frictions, all of these reactions make difficult the retarded child's retention in the home.

The establishment of community resources can markedly relieve the burden of constant care and surveillance some retarded children require. It could also enable parents to devote more time to their normal children and thus reduce potential parent-child conflicts. For many parents of the more severely handicapped, however, the threat to their self-esteem, the lifelong child care roles, and the unwillingness to change drastically their aspirations and manner of living make such relief not sufficiently compensating. These parents may still find care outside the home necessary and, because of its greater stability, prefer the institution. Whatever disposition is sought, the expansion of services will provide parents more options to choose from and, thereby, greater responsibility in the decision-making process. To extend these options to embrace the diverse needs of the retarded, collective action to resolve conflicts between primary groups (the family) and bureaucratic organizations will need to be expanded.

There are many examples of consumer participation in the mental retardation field. At the Federal and State level, the National Association for Retarded Children has lobbied aggressively and successfully for legislation to expand services, training, and research. They participate in standard setting, advisory councils, institutional committees, health and welfare planning councils, and a wide range of other linkage activities.

Despite this type of involvement, citizen and parent groups claim insufficient input into decision-making processes and a sense of alienation by the "bureaucracy." To combat this problem, some states, New York for example, have created offices for Community Involvement and Citizen Affairs or similarly titled enterprises. The basic charge to such offices is to explore means for effective linkages and cooperation between legitimate representative groups and the providers of service.

Although citizen-consumer involvement is a well established public policy, relatively little is known regarding its impact on programs. The processes and dynamics of these organizations, their internal organization and efficiency, membership composition, and the "linkage" barriers that may impede goal achievement need clarification.

In the field of mental retardation and related disabilities, a large number of organizations have been formed in recent years. Some of these groups, perhaps seeking to avoid the stigma associated with the term mental retardation, have resorted to other terms such as learning disabilities, developmental disabilities, autism, cerebral palsy, etc. There are indeed some real differences in the clientele represented, but in all of these conditions, intellectual limitations are a common, although not universal, corollary and the needs and services required overlap. The proliferation of organizations has often resulted in fragmentation of effort and competition for resources, but the consequences for programs are unknown. It is an empirical question whether the independent activities of each group have achieved a greater or lesser yield than might have been accomplished through cooperative effort. The categorical approach to funding at the Federal level, now being attacked in preference for general revenue sharing, nevertheless has many supporters. These individuals point to the rapid growth of mental health and mental retardation services, among others, that have prospered through national visibility, public education, and intensive consumer lobbying. By contrast, legislation to serve *all* children or groups of handicapped children has lagged, perhaps because the task appears economically over-whelming or self-interest groups feel their special clientele will be relegated to a lower priority status.

Additional issues arise from the heterogeneity of the mentally retarded, even within organizations devoted exclusively to this client group. Parents of the severely retarded, for example, are concerned primarily with lifetime support services or substitute care, whereas parents of the more able stress educational and vocational training opportunities. The mildly retarded from disadvantaged families often have no spokesmen at all. These parents are seldom part of organized groups and program development on their behalf has relied for the most part on the initiative of professional groups such as the American Association on Mental Deficiency.

The relationships between consumer and professional groups and the factors which influence them are not thoroughly understood. The demand by parents in the late 1950's to mandate special education classes for the "trainable" child (IQ 35 to 50) is a case in point. This movement was strongly resisted by many educators who felt that such children could not profit from academic instruction and that teachers were not suffi-ciently trained for this purpose. With the enactment of permissive or mandatory legisla-tion in most states, the professionals ostensibly lost this battle. However, the still inadequate status of educational resources for trainable children suggests that professional resistance may act as barriers to change when citizen pressures challenge professional judgment.

The more recent "right to education" decision in Pennsylvania and the District of Columbia, placing responsibility on the departments of education for the severely and professionally handicapped, raises the same spectre of possible passive resistance. Here too, change was stimulated by parent group action with a consequent shift in superordi-nate-subnordinate relationships. Thus far, court directives have not been fully imple-mented. Undoubtedly, community failure to provide the necessary supportive resources is a contributing force, but honest differences in professional opinion about the appropriate role of the schools for these children and the proposed shifts in agency responsibility are also operative. Better understanding of the relationships between citizen-action and professional groups could facilitate goal achievement.

The conceptualization of family organizational linkage systems offers a convenient framework for analysis in this area. Sussman (1969) has identified several underlying assumptions. Linkage is a process whereby patterns of interrelationship are formed between the groups, organizations, and institutions of society or by individuals represent-ing such units. It also denotes a condition: a relationship between a parents' group and other professional societies on an advisory council, for example.

As noted above, reversals of subordinate-superordinate relationships may occur as group needs, functions, and situations change. In linkages, the family may succeed to the latter role, wielding influence over the policy and activities of the bureaucracy. Legislation recently passed in California requiring parental consent before a retarded child could be placed in special classes illustrates this point. In effect, the consumer is in the position of dictating to the school system the kind of educational environment a specific child should have, thus sharply curtailing (should many parents oppose placement recommendations) the responsibilities and functions of guidance personnel.

Another assumption is that most groups, in order to survive and maintain their territory, attempt to develop the competence of their members. At the organizational level, the techniques applied are well known. For the primary group, the family, socialization of members is the key to competence. Sussman's final assumption is that intergroup relationships exist within some system of exchange, reciprocity, and bargaining. Reciprocities are maintained when the payoff for preserving the relationship is greater than that of the alternative of discontinuing it. These conditions may not prevail where there is no cooperation and change is enforced through legal edict. The class action suits brought against state institutions, however warranted they may be, have polarized the professional community and, indeed, the primary groups directed affected. In the process, new linkages have been formed, parent groups and legal societies, and old ones disrupted. The impact of these changes compels further study.

The role of parents toward their retarded children *within* the family structure is also likely to undergo change as a function of the current re-emphasis on community care. The movement to depopulate institutions can be effective only if admissions are also reduced. There are beginning indications that this is taking place in some states, although for the decade between 1960 and 1970 for the U.S. as a whole, the number of residents per 100,000 population in public institutions for the retarded increased from 91.9 to 94.2 (Mental Retardation Source Book of DHEW, 1972). With supportive services increasingly available or, at least, on the drawing boards, more parents will be enabled to keep their children at home for most of their childhood years. Some will find substitute parental care a reflection on their own parental adequacies and will choose to care for their child despite considerable personal and family sacrifice.

Whatever the social or personal dynamics involved, supplementary parental care services such as day care, homemaker services, respite care, preschool education, etc. may not be sufficient to optimize the child's development and family stability.

Furthermore, in many rural or sparsely populated sections of the country, the number of retarded persons in a given geographical area is too small to justify special resources and the less capable may be difficult to integrate into generic programs. These are not insurmountable obstacles, however, and experimentation with regional residential facilities allowing the child to return home on weekends is one compromise solution to serving the child while maintaining family integrity.

Faced with these prospects and the limitation of trained personnel to man widely dispersed programs, parents will need to assume more active roles as teachers and therapists for their retarded children. Success in teaching would probably help dissipate the sense of frustration and despair these parents commonly feel, but failure might well have further depressing effects. The importance of this parental function has only recently been recognized and given credence by the development of behavior modification technology. Significantly, this approach has been effectively applied both with lower class, deprived families of the mildly retarded and with middle class families with more severely handicapped and emotionally disturbed children.

Parents of children with normal or retarded intelligence have been largely involved in the modification of single, specific behaviors such as enuresis (Baker, 1969), fire setting (Holland, 1969), stealing, fighting, or truancy (Tharp and Wetzel, 1969), speech (Risley and Wolf, 1967), or incontinence (Graziano, 1971). More recent reports have addressed multiple behavior problems (Gardner et al., 1968) or behaviors and skill deficiencies (Pascal, 1973).

The nature and extent of parental involvement have varied widely. Sometimes this took the form of advice on what the clinic and school were doing, with instructions to carry out the same approach in the home. By contrast, other parents have been engaged in highly structured educational programs on the theory and techniques of behavior modification, including assessment and data recording and the development of their own programs (Walder et al, 1969). Clearly, only highly educated parents could benefit from such instruction. Gradually, parent responsibility has shifted from a focus on discrete behavior of the child to the parent-child interaction system and maintenance of new desirable behaviors (Berkowitz and Graziano, 1972).

The training of parents for teaching and therapeutic functions has been conducted largely in group sessions often with follow-up home visits, under the skilled professional leadership of psychologists, generally in or near university or clinic settings. The procedure is time consuming and costly and such resources are not accessible to the vast majority of parents who need them. One solution to this dilemma is to provide parents with instructional materials they could use to shape the behavior of their children without benefit of professional training and reinforcement. The issue in this proposed remedy is whether media materials, by themselves, can achieve this goal.

Except for a very recently published study by Baker, Heifitz, and Brightman, 1973), few research projects have attempted to evaluate scientifically the effectiveness of instructional materials, although several "how to do it" books have been on the market for a few years (Patterson and Gullion, 1968; Vallet, 1969; Becker, 1971). Families in this study were randomly assigned to five experimental conditions: four groups of parents, ranging in training exposure from a manuals-only condition (MO) without professional assistance, to manuals and group training and home visits (MGV), plus a control group. The data in this study clearly indicate that parents in the MO condition were able to effect positive change in their children's behavior. The total gain in *programmed skills alone* for children in this group was equal to the gain in *all* self-help skills for control children. This difference extended as well to unprogrammed skills offering support for the generalizing effects of the manuals. More significant than the absolute improvements shown by the MO children were the comparative gains over the other experimental groups. Contrary to expectations, the most effective condition was MO. The practical significance of this finding for incorporating parents in the manpower teaching pool is self-evident. The differences in cost benefit between the two extreme conditions (MO and MGV), namely, $38 per family versus $211 per family is equally compelling (Baker et al., 1973, p. 154).

The integration of the retarded into the mainstream of society demands that social institutions adapt to the needs of the retarded and that the retarded be helped to adapt more adequately to social institutions. Currently, normalization is more a philosophy of human rights than a prescription for treatment. Until the retarded are taught the skills necessary for at least minimal participation in family and community life and for the proper exercise of their "rights," the repeated presentation of rights at professional and public forums will be of little use. The utilization of parents as teachers has promise in this regard and may prove critical to the implementation of community-based service programs.

THE IMPACT OF LABELING

Throughout this chapter, references have been made, some more explicit than others, to the impact of labeling on the retarded child and his family and the organization of services. The seriousness of this problem stimulated the establishment of a special Project on the Classification of Exceptional Children funded by the Department of Health, Education, and Welfare. The findings of this project are to be published under the title of *The Futures of Children.*

The ramifications of the labeling process and its consequences are far too complex for a detailed review in this paper. Yet, because it relates to institutionalization, the adjustment of the retarded in society, program planning, access to opportunity, and the organization of service delivery systems, some attention to unresolved questions arising from this national concern is in order.

As a first step, it is important to distinguish between classification and labeling. While the former is not possible without the latter, each has distinctive purposes and uses. Classification systems are impersonal. They are designed primarily to furnish statistical data about groups of cases. Without such data, we would have no basis for measuring incidence, prevalence, characteristics, and related information or the success of programmatic efforts aimed at prevention or amelioration. Classification systems increase precision in communication, highlight research needs, and offer direction to administrative and program planning.

Any effort to categorize the totality of any individual by multiaxial indices is clearly not possible and is subject to many imperfections. Paradoxically, the more we learn about mental retardation, the more difficult classification becomes. At the upper levels of retardation, where discrepancies between adaptive behavior and measured intelligence are frequent, the determination of who should be classified is often confounded by sociopolitical processes.

Much agitation has been expressed in recent years about IQ testing as a basis for classifying and programming for individuals. The limitations of intelligence tests are not always appreciated: errors in measurement (often approximating as much as 10 IQ points for an individual), errors in test construction, and errors in test administration. Such errors, if used as a single source of information, can improperly label a child and markedly influence his life course.

Of greater concern is the presumed cultural bias of intelligence tests. In the past, "culture-free" and "culture-fair" tests have been devised to combat this bias. The first deleted items which seemed to reflect a culture context, the second to draw upon elements presumably existing in any human culture. Both of these approaches have yielded even lower scores for disadvantaged children than they obtained on traditional tests. One view of the value of tests, a still unresolved controversy, has been succinctly stated by Anastasi (1968).

> To criticize tests because they reveal cultural influences is to miss the essential nature of tests. Every psychological test measures a sample of behavior. Insofar as culture affects behavior, its influence will and should be reflected in the test. . . . The same cultural differentials that impair an individual's test performance are likely to handicap him in school work, job performance, or any other activity we are trying to predict. . . . To conceal the affects of cultural disadvantages by rejecting tests or by trying to devise tests that are insensitive to such affects can only retard progress toward a genuine solution of social problems.

Even more difficult problems of measurement apply to the assessment of social competence. Behavior that is maladaptive to the society at large may be highly adaptive to a delinquent subculture, for example. These caveats urge caution in the application of test results, but do not deny their fundamental utility. Supplemented by clinical judgment, life history data, and biomedical information, meaningful programming for individuals is possible.

Labeling, in contrast to classification, is highly personal. The process takes place largely through interpersonal encounter. Individuals perceive themselves as others see them and the normal child is apt to react to his perception of the retarded child's competence, rather than his label. Thus, it may be argued that the poor self-image of the retarded is not the consequence of an "official" label as evidenced by special class placement or institutionalization. Long before the label is applied, the child has been exposed to attitudes and reactions that make him feel inferior. Children with limited intelligence start off in school the same way, but academic failure and disruptive behavior in the early years of schooling by some generate teacher rejection and peer ridicule. These encounters probably result in self-labeling. Subsequent placement in a special class only confirms the image the child has already formed of himself, but this adverse effect has to be weighed against the unlikely potential for developing higher self-esteem in the setting which precipitated the negative self-labeling process in the first place. The issue of self versus external labeling has direct bearing on strategies to protect the individual against stigmatizing influences. Despite a voluminous literature on the subject, much of it oriented to the harmful effects of the official labeling process, the evidence is very inconclusive. Studies are confounded with variables other than labeling, there are weaknesses in methodology and research design, sampling biases are common, and instruments are of questionable validity or vary from one project to another. The phenomenon of labeling is not sufficiently understood to abandon specialized services and facilities for the mildly retarded because of its presumed effects.

For the child who visibly deviates from the norm in a socially undesirable direction, stigma may be inevitable. Only as societal values are changed and all forms of difference not only tolerated, but accepted, can this component of human behavior be eliminated. It has been argued that the integration of handicapped children with normal children at a young age would provide useful imitative models for the handicapped child and an appreciation and tolerance of individual differences in the other children. Conversely, sustained interaction may also reinforce the sense of difference. These are testable issues. Answers to these speculations require longitudinal research. For the present, they must remain a long range goal.

Labels are essentially shorthand terms to facilitate communication about individuals or categories of individuals. Every label, especially when it has been assigned perjorative meanings by the public, conjures up an image and stereotype of the person labeled which conceal his differences and individuality. Thus, blindness is immediately associated with disability, delinquency with "badness," and retardation with dependency and, often, stigmata. In mental retardation, the problem is especially acute, for there is greater herterogeneity among those sharing this label than perhaps in any other category of exceptionality. Clearly, labels are not a substitute for a diagnostic profile. Used only as a signal that a child may be "different" and in need of special help and as a stimulus to in-depth evaluation, mislabeling can be minimized and harmful effects at least partially avoided. Labels can be changed and their use better controlled, but generalization and communication is impossible without them.

Historically, as we have noted earlier, the label of mental retardation has been applied with differential effects on the well-being of this group. Seguin used it (or its euphemism) to identify those in need of special education and treatment techniques. The eugenicists used it to segregate and control. President Kennedy applied the label as a clarion call to national action and expanded services. Labels, in short, are not inherently evil, although they can be, and admittedly are, sometimes abused.

Increased knowledge and more enlightened attitudes account in large measure for the constructive uses to which labeling has been put in the past two decades. This does not deny the inaccurate classification of large numbers of minority group children, but here the problem lies in our failure to apply our diagnostic skills, and consequent *mislabeling*. The individual who has low measured intelligence and clearly impaired behavior is by definition mentally retarded. Whether he requires services from a specialized agency or can be served by a generic agency in a special way, unless his peculiar problems are well understood, his needs will be poorly met.

Much of our progress to date in mental retardation stems from its national visibility. Television spot announcements proclaim that the retarded child can be helped. International societies advocate their basic rights as human beings. Professional organizations explore their problems and needs and how to satisfy them. Special interest groups lobby for legislation and resources.

It is unlikely that these activities and outcomes can be maintained without the rallying point labels represent. The task before us is to appreciate the informative limitations of labels, apply them more discriminately, and ensure that the service provided is not inferior in quality.

Opponents of special education contend that children in these classes are stigmatized, that teachers have low expectancies of them, and that the learning opportunities offered them are inadequate. The same accusations are made against the ghetto school. The relative merit of special versus regular class attendance for the retarded child with respect to achievement and personal/social adjustment is still an open question. Yet, these children may indeed need special help in the management of their behavior and realization of their potentials. Whether the regular classroom teacher, who is the initial source for referral of these children to special classes, is better equipped to handle these problems than the specially trained teacher is a moot point. In either situation, teacher competencies and expectations can be changed.

Similar arguments apply to institutionalization. It is not true, as some contend, that classification as retarded can lead to commitment. The overwhelming majority of the *designated* mildly retarded population resides in the community. The very small minority, as noted earlier, is confined because of intolerable family or community behavior, not low intelligence. Classification in these instances directs the individual to the resource presumably best equipped to instruct and treat him. Should these facilities prove inadequate, they too are subject to change.

At the service organizational level, it is undoubtedly true that the proliferation of agencies to serve special categories of children has resulted in some duplication of effort, competition for scarce resources, a lack of service for those children who do not fit neatly into any given classification, and difficulties in coordination. Here too, these problems are potentially remediable. Alternatively, the organization of services for *all* children, without regard to their exceptionality, could result in poorer quality of services and a priority system that once more relegates the retarded to their former state of chronic neglect. Experimentation with different models for the delivery and organization of services is needed to resolve these issues.

Current developments and trends in the mental retardation field have in some instances polarized the professional community and created new alliances or antagonisms between special interest groups. Issues have arisen which owe their origin to sociopolitical processes and the concern with civil and human rights. Court decisions and the accelerated demand for community alternatives to institutional care have created a sense of crisis and urgency for reform. Unquestionably, there are many weaknesses in the quality and organization of services at every governmental level of operation and in the private sector as well. But our present state of knowledge, particularly in the sociological aspects of the problem to which this paper is primarily directed, is not sufficiently precise to warrant massive change and the wholesale abandonment of established social institutions.

It is imperative that new approaches to meeting the needs of the retarded be guided by science, not emotion or metaphysics. Research and demonstration can, it is hoped, point the nation in the right direction.

REFERENCES

Adams, M. 1971. Mental Retardation and Its Social Dimensions. Columbia University Press. New York/London.

Anastasi, A. 1968. Psychological Testing. 3rd Ed. Macmillan. New York.

Baker, B. L. 1969. Symptom treatment and symptom substitution in enuresis. J. Abnorm. Soc. Psychol. 74: 42–49.

Baker, B. L., L. J. Heifitz, and A. J. Brightman. 1973. Parents As Teachers. Behavioral Education Projects, Inc., Read House, Harvard University. Cambridge, Mass.

Becker, W. 1971. Parents Are Teachers. Research Press. Champaign, Ill.

Begab, M. J. 1963. The Mentally Retarded Child: A Guide to Services of Social Agencies. DHEW, Children's Bureau Publication 404, U.S. Government Printing Office. Washington, D.C.

Begab, M. J. 1966. The mentally retarded and the family. In I. Phillips (ed.), Prevention and Treatment of Mental Retardation. Basic Books, Inc. New York/London.

Berkowitz, B. P. and A. M. Graziano. 1972. Training parents as behavior therapists: A review. Behav. Res. Ther. 10: 297–317.

Brock, L. G. 1934. Report of the departmental committee on sterilization. Sessional Papers (Great Britain) 15: 1–137.

Brown, B. S. and T. F. Courtless. 1971. The Mentally Retarded Offender. DHEW Pub. No. (HSM) 72-039./U.S. Government Printing Office. Washington, D.C. pp. 25–26.

Chambers, G. A. and R. N. Zabarenko. 1956. Effects of glutamic acid and social stimulation in mental deficiency. J. Abnorm. Soc. Psychol. 53: 315–320.

Clarke, A. D. B., A. M. Clarke, and S. Reiman. 1958. Cognitive and social changes in the feebleminded—three further studies. Br. J. Psychol. 49: 144–157.

Conley, R. W. 1973. The Economics of Mental Retardation. The Johns Hopkins University Press. Baltimore/London. p. 143.

Crissey, O. L. 1937. The mental development of children of the same IQ in differing institutional environments. Child Develop. 8: 217–220.

Davies, S. P. 1959. The Mentall Retarded in Society. Columbia University Press. New York. p. 47.

Edgerton, R. B. 1962. From mortification to aggrandizement: Changing self-concept in the careers of the mentally retarded. Psychiatry 25: 263–272.

Edgerton, R. B. 1967. The Cloak of Competence. University of California Press. Berkeley.

Fanshel, D. 1961. Specializations within the foster parent role: A research report. Child Welfare 40(4)II: 19–23.

Feuerstein, R. and D. Karasilowsky. 1972. Interventional strategies for the significant modification of cognitive functioning in the disadvantaged adolescent. J. Am. Acad. Child Psychiat. 11 (3): 572–582.

Gardner, J. E., D. T. Pearson, A. N. Bercovici, and D. E. Bricker. 1965. Measurement, evaluation, and modification of selected social interactions between a schizophrenic child, his parents, and his therapist. J. Consult. Clin. Psychol. 32: 537–542.

Ginzberg, E. and D. W. Bray. 1953. The Uneducated. Columbia University Press. New York. pp. 41–43.

Goddard, H. H. 1912. The Kallikak Family: A Study in the Heredity of Feeblemindedness. Macmillan. New York.

Goddard, H. H. 1914. Feeblemindedness: Its Causes and Consequences. Macmillan. New York.

Goffman, E. 1957. Characteristics of total institutions. In Symposium on Preventive and Social Psychiatry. Walter Reed Army Institute of Research. Washington, D.C. pp. 43–84.

Goffman, E. 1963. Stigma: Notes on the Management of Spoiled Identity. Prentice-Hall. Englewood Cliffs, N. J.

Gray, P. H. 1958. Theory and evidence of imprinting in human infants. J. Psychol. 46: 155–166.

Graziano, A. M. 1971. Behavior Therapy With Children. Aldine-Atherton. New York.

Grossman, H. 1973. Manual on Terminology and Classification in Mental Retardation. American Association for Mental Deficiency. Washington, D.C.

Gula, M. 1964. Agency Operated Group Homes. DHEW, Children's Bureau Pub No. 416. U.S. Government Printing Office. Washington, D.C.

Hartzler, E. 1951. A follow-up study of girls discharged from the Laurelton State Village. Am. J. Ment. Defic. 55: 612–618.

Heber, R., H. Garber, S. Harrington, and C. Hoffman. 1972. Rehabilitation of Families at Risk for Mental Retardation. Progress Report, SRS, DHEW. U.S. Government Printing Office. Washington, D.C.

Holland, C. J. 1969. Elimination by the parents of fire-setting behavior in a seven-year-old boy. Behav. Res. Ther. 7: 135–137.

Kephart, N. C. and A. A. Strauss. 1940. A clinical factor influencing variations in IQ. Am. J. Orthopsychiat. 10: 343–350.

King, R. D., N. V. Raynes, and J. Tizard. 1971. Patterns of Residential Care: Sociological Studies in Institutions for Handicapped Children. Routledge and Kegan Paul. London.

Kramer, M., P. H. Person, G. Tarjan, R. Morgan, and S. W. Wright. 1957. A method for determination of probabilities of stay, release, and death for patients admitted to a hospital for the mentally deficient: The experience of Pacific State Hospital during the period 1948–1952. Am. J. Ment. Defic. 62: 481–495.

Krishef, C. H. 1957. An analysis of some factors in the institutional experience of mentally retarded discharges from the Owatonna State School that influence their successful or unsuccessful community adjustment. School of Social Work, University of Minnesota, Minneapolis. (Unpublished manuscript)

Krishef, C. H. 1959. The influence of rural-urban environment upon the adjustment of discharges from the Owatonna State School. Am. J. Ment. Defic. 63: 860–865.

Kushlick, A. 1968. The Wessex Plan for evaluating the effectiveness of residential care for the severely subnormal. Proceedings, 1st International Congress for the Scientific Study on Mental Deficiency. Surrey: Michael Jackson, Montpelier.

Levine, M. and A. Levine. 1970. A Social History of Helping Services: Clinic, Court, School, and Community. Appleton-Century-Crofts. New York.

Maas, H. and R. Engler. 1959. Children in Need of Parents. Columbia University Press. New York.

Mental Retardation Source Book of DHEW. 1972. Office of Mental Retardation Coordination. U.S. Government Printing Office. Washington, D.C.

Pascal, C. E. 1973. Application of behavior modification by parents for treatment of a brain-damaged child. In B. A. Ashem and E. G. Poser (eds.), Adaptive Learning: Behavior Modification with Children. Pergamon Press. New York.

Patterson, G. R. and M. E. Gullion. 1968. Living With Children: New Methods for Parents and Teachers. Research Press. Champaign, Ill.

President's Task Force on Manpower Conservation, The. 1964. One Third Of A Nation. U.S. Government Printing Office. Washington, D.C. January.

Rhodes, W. C. 1972. Behavioral Threat and Community Response. Behavioral Publications. New York.

Risley, T. and M. M. Wolf. 1967. Establishing functional speech in echolalic children. Behav. Res. Ther. 5: 73–88.

Sarason, S. B. 1957. Individual psychotherapy with mentally defective individuals. *In* C. L. Stacey and M. F. DeMartino (eds.), Counseling and Psychotherapy with the Mentally Retarded. Free Press. Glencoe, Ill. pp. 22–24.

Schreiber, M. 1970. Social Work and Mental Retardation. John Day Company. New York.

Shafter, A. J. 1954. The vocational placement of institutionalized defectives in the United States. Am. J. Ment. Defic. 59: 279–307.

Skeels, H. M. and H. B. Dye. 1939. A study of the effects of differential stimulation on mentally retarded children. Proc. Am. Ass. Ment. Defic. 44: 114–136.

Spencer, H. 1877. Principles of Sociology. Appleton. New York.

Spitz, R. A. 1945. Hospitalism: An inquire into the genesis of psychiatric conditions in early childhood. Psychoanal. Stud. Child. I: 53–74.

Sussman, M. B. 1969. Cross national family studies: Some conceptual issues in family-organizational linkages. Presented at the 64th Meeting of American Sociological Association, San Francisco, California.

Tarjan, G., H. F. Dingman, R. K. Eyman, and S. J. Brown. 1960. Effectiveness of hospital release programs. Am. J. Ment. Defic. 64: 609–617.

Tharp, R. G. and R. J. Wetzel. 1969. Behavior Modification in the Natural Environment. Academic Press. New York.

Tizard, B., O. Cooperman, A. Joseph, and J. Tizard. 1972. Environmental effects on language development: A study of young children in long-stay residential nurseries. Child Develop. 43: 337–358.

Vallet, R. E. 1969. Modifying Children's Behavior. Flaron. Palo Alto, Cal.

Walder, L., S. Cohen, D. Breiter, P. G. Daston, I. S. Hirsch, and J. M. Leibowitz. 1969. Teaching behavioral principles to parents of disturbed children. *In* B. G. Guerney (ed.), Psychotherapeutic Agents: New Roles for Non-professionals, Parents, and Teachers. Holt, Rhinehart, and Winston. New York.

Whitney, E. A. 1948. A statistical study of children admitted and discharged from Elwyn. Am. J. Ment. Defic. 53: 182–186.

Windle, C. 1962. Prognosis of mental subnormals. Am. J. Ment. Defic. 66: 23–25.

Educational Institutions And Mental Subnormality: Notes on Writing a History [1]

Marvin Lazerson

The historiography of most social service professions tends to be a litany of progress. Inspirational in content and intent, it is a history of humanitarians seeking to overcome ignorance and adversity. Failures are usually caused by the opponents of reform; less often, the reforms themselves are deemed insufficient. Less concerned with the past than with the politics of the present, it is a history designed to enhance the prestige of contemporary professionals. This conventional wisdom about the past assumes what is problematic, the inevitability of progress, and by so doing, it makes historical alternatives difficult to comprehend. History becomes the unfolding of a predetermined plan, the victory of good over evil, truth over falsehood. Opponents of reform are delegitimized; they are viewed as obstacles to progress. When reforms fail or do not live up to expectations, the blame is external. But failure is also redemptive. It allows for a rededication of energy and faith in the powers of new reforms. The assumptions of the reformers, however, remain unexamined.

Until recently this has been the case in the writing of American educational history. Historians seldom questioned the importance of a rapidly expanding, highly professionalized educational system. They presented the common school as essential to a democratic society, necessary to melt America's heterogeneous masses and to provide equality of opportunity. The changes that accompanied this expanding educational system, compulsory attendance, differentiation of the curriculum, professionalized administration, certification of the teaching staff, to name just a few, were invariably seen as progressive steps toward the triumph of democracy (Bailyn, 1961).

[1] The author wishes to thank the University of British Columbia Committee on Research for its research support, and Neil Sutherland, David Tyack, and Harold Troper for their criticisms.

Since the mid-1960's, this conventional wisdom has come under sharp challenge. At their most extreme, revisionist historians accuse the schools of being racist, bureaucratic, class biased, and antidemocratic in their origins and continuing practices. Others, less radical, point to the failures of reforms, the misplaced assumptions, and the unintended consequences of previous decisions. In both the radical and the moderate version, however, the past ceases to be a series of triumphs, and instead becomes a challenge to educational decision-makers to re-examine the ongoing assumptions that continue to mold their institutions (Lazerson, 1973).

Like the educational system more generally, the educational treatment of mental subnormality has had its conventional historical wisdom (Kanner, 1964; Dunn, 1961). This wisdom has tended to emphasize the inevitable and progressive nature of reform, the importance of humane and path-breaking individuals, and an unwavering faith that further improvements will come with greater scientific knowledge and professional expertise. Two developments particularly stand out in this history: the emergence of segregated residential institutions for feebleminded and idiots during the nineteenth century and the establishment of special classes for the mentally deficient in the public schools during the first decades of the twentieth century. The first, the creation of residential facilities, sought to distinguish mental retardation from mental illness, made the feebleminded an object of concern as opposed to neglect, and claimed for them a humanness they had previously been denied. At first naive and overconfident in their claims, the conventional wisdom tells us, the institution builders soon became more realistic about the limitations of their reform, and adapted asylums to the realities of feeblemindedness and insufficient funding.

The residential institutions of the nineteenth century are thus generally seen as the first major step in the proper care of the mentally subnormal. They also laid the foundation for the second major development: the establishment of special education classes for mental defectives within the public school system. This development drew upon the scientific and clinical findings of Binet and Simon in Europe and of Goddard, Terman, and the World War I psychological testers in the United States. These findings led to the belief that mental deficiency was widespread in the population at large. The special education movement also drew upon more general trends to diversify and individualize the educational system. Although seriously limited by lack of public support, and sometimes harmed by overzealous classifiers, by confusion over the relationships between educability and trainability, and by concern for what happens after the mentally deficient leave school, the institutionalization of special education is seen in the conventional history as the breakthrough upon which contemporary progress is based.

The story is thus an unfinished morality play. Out of small beginnings, service to the mentally subnormal has steadily improved. Better today than yesterday, largely because we can now diagnose mental retardation and provide special services by trained professionals, reforms today will make tomorrow even better. This approach to history was well summarized by Harold M. Williams and J. E. Wallace Wallin who concluded after reviewing progress in the treatment of mental retardation that "one does not always have the opportunity to observe democracy in action in as neat a package as this. . . . To those who do not understand how a democracy operates, or whose faith in it sometimes wavers, this story is a truly inspiring lesson" (Williams and Wallin, 1961).

The thrust of this kind of history is thus to inspire. But in so doing, it produces a sense of inevitability about the past and undermines our ability to postulate alternatives. By phrasing reforms in terms of neglect versus responsibility, the same terms used by the reformers themselves, historians of mental subnormality make it easy to praise or condemn but difficult to sort out why events occurred. Aside from the overoptimism of the nineteenth century institutional founders, little attention has been paid to the social context within which residential institutions became custodial. Nor can we understand why special education in the public schools has not fulfilled its promise, and gives little evidence of being able to do so. To understand these issues requires a rethinking of the conventional wisdom. This chapter attempts to begin that rethinking, by focusing on the social and institutional contexts within which residential institutions were established and special education begun.

ASYLUMS, DEVIANCY, AND DEPENDENCY

The most striking feature of nineteenth century America's response to deviancy and dependency was the movement to construct specialized segregated residential institutions. Asylums for the criminal and delinquent, for the insane and feebleminded, and for the poor and the orphaned became the pre-eminent response to all forms of social disorder. While Americans had always been concerned about these issues, during the colonial period they did not define crime, poverty, or illness as critical social problems. Where deviancy existed, adjustments had to be made, and punishments imposed, but the assumption was that family and communal responsibility would suffice. Religious values, the punishment of sin and the charity of Christians, a sense of a hierarchical, well ordered society with the family at its center, and a belief in the efficacy of communal responses were deemed sufficient. Both aid and punishment were direct; rarely were they mediated through special institutions. In the case of the dependent, the insane, the infirm, the aged and homeless, society used the family and the local community as the agencies of care. Only where dependency threatened family and community, as in the case of the uncontrollably insane, or where infirmity was too severe, or where individuals were strangers to the community, did institutions come into play. Although some cities built special institutions, until the eighteenth century, almshouses, insane asylums, and hospitals were places of last resort, homes for the homeless, to be used when all else failed (Rothman, 1971; Grob, 1973).

During the nineteenth century, these assumptions and practices were dramatically altered. Institutions, asylums, grew in number and importance. They became the preferred treatment for those who stepped outside the social code and the bounds of normality. Almshouses were erected for the poor, insane asylums for the mentally ill, penitentiaries for the criminal, orphan asylums and reformatories for dependent and deviant juveniles, and schools for the feebleminded. Why? What led to this extraordinary reversal of traditional practices? What were these institutions supposed to accomplish? What happened once they were erected? These questions can be asked separately for each of the institutional categories mentioned above, and the answers will be determined by the differences between care of criminals, the insane, the poor, or the feebleminded. Yet the questions also suggest the commonalities of the asylum movement. For those interested in the treatment of mental subnormality, it is these commonalities that provide the social context for understanding the establishment and subsequent development of residential institutions for the mentally retarded.

The movement to establish asylums revealed the fears early and mid-nineteenth century Americans had about social disorder. The appearance of large numbers of people in American cities, many of them transient and immigrant, undermined the sense of social cohesion upon which traditional approaches to welfare depended. Family, church, and local community no longer seemed adequate to care for individuals in need or protect the community from the rapid increase in dependency and deviancy. It was as if the centrifugal forces of the new republic threatened to fragment the social order Americans so highly prized. Whether these fears were well founded is difficult to determine, particularly since notions of dependency and deviancy depend so heavily upon definitions and the systemization of policy. But America was clearly changing, and many Americans expressed fear for the young republic, assumed that dependency and deviancy were rising, and agreed that measures had to be taken to stem the tide. Asylums were one of those measures (Rothman, 1971; Grob, 1973).

In its initial phases, the asylum movement showed an extraordinary faith in the curative effects of a well ordered environment. Social fragmentation and declining moral values could be countered by placing dependents and deviants in segregated model institutions. Run on strict and regularized routine and free from the pressures of an urbanizing world, these institutions would counter the social chaos that undermined individual stability and health, while simultaneously serving as an example to the public at large. The dependent and deviant could thus be educated to participate in society; society, in turn, would profit from the model offered by the institutions.

These assumptions can be seen in the movement to institutionalize the mentally ill, a trend especially important in the treatment of mental subnormality, since insanity and feeblemindedness were often lumped together. During the colonial period, little interest was shown in the biological and social origins of insanity. The mentally ill suffered, like those with other diseases, from God's will, and they required attention because of their dependency. Reports of cures for insanity from Europe helped modify this view, especially those emphasizing the importance of humane care in special residential institutions, a procedure that came to be known as "moral treatment." By the late eighteenth century, those concerned with improving the treatment of insanity were urging that more attention be paid to the physical and emotional comfort of the afflicted. At the same time, the belief that insanity was a physical disorder of the brain often produced by other bodily ailments (stomach disorder, malnutrition, menstruation, or blows on the head) heightened interest in insanity as a medical and physiological problem (Dain, 1964; Deutsch, 1949).

Interest in improving the therapeutic environment and in the biological basis of insanity was important in laying a basis for special institutions for the mentally ill. But in both cases, this interest was filtered through a set of social assumptions that were even more influential. Especially propagated by lay reformers and psychiatrists, insanity was viewed as a product of America's social, economic, and political environment. Everywhere they looked, the reformers "found chaos and disorder, a lack of fixity and stability. The community's inherited traditions and procedures were dissolving, leaving incredible stresses and strains. The anatomical implications of this condition were clear: the brain received innumerable abuses, was weakened, and inevitably succumbed to disease" (Rothman, 1971).

These assumptions led doctors and reformers to devote themselves to social rather than biological analyses. A highly fluid social order, for example, encouraged excessive ambition, causing individuals to overreach themselves, ultimately placing too much pressure on their mental powers. Even where economic and social success were achieved, the stress undermined mental stability. The poor, too, were affected: temptations to vice, poor health, and the daily struggle for existence brought insanity. Adopting a nostalgic view of an orderly society in the past, the leading advocates of improved treatment for the mentally ill contended that an unstable world was creating an unstable people.

By locating the etiology of insanity in a social context, reformers laid the basis for an environmental approach to therapy, either by reconstructing American society directly or by creating model environments. The latter expectation underlay the rapid and sudden growth of insane asylums in early and mid-nineteenth century America. Before 1810, most mentally ill lived with family and friends, or languished in local jails and poorhouses. By 1860, 28 of the 33 states had public institutions for the insane, most established between 1830 and the 1850's. More important, institutionalization was assumed to be the most proper method of treatment.

The early asylum builders revealed an enormous optimism about their work, especially contrasting the benefits of institutionalization with the neglect and barbarism of earlier periods. Yet it seems likely the contrast was overdrawn. The pre-institutional treatment of the mentally ill and feebleminded is exceedingly difficult to determine. Where care of deviancy and dependency was accepted as a familial and communal responsibility, extensive discussion and analysis did not occur. Most of our assumptions about early care are thus based on nineteenth century reformers' claims of neglect and their examples of inhumane treatment. Since these were usually designed to marshall political and financial support for institutionalization, they should be treated with care.

Like the stress on the social origins of disease, the optimism of the asylum movement was environmental. An institution that provided the stability of fixed routines and that curbed impulses and passions without resorting to undue force or punishment could cure the mentally ill. This belief in a reordered and stable environment led the reformers and the medical superintendents who ran the asylums to emphasize physical construction and the internal details of management and administration. "Precision, certainty, regularity, order—these became the bywords of asylum management, the main response in the battle against insanity" (Rothman, 1971). By promptly removing the mentally ill from the social environment that had caused their illness, by placing the asylum in a tranquil, natural, and rural setting, and by imposing order in a humane fashion, the asylum builders would effect their cures (Grob, 1973).

To mid-twentieth century observers, the optimism of the early asylum builders seems naive at best, even vicious in light of the subsequent development of their institutions. Over time the expectations for therapy and re-entry into the community were not fulfilled. Within a few decades insane asylums had become places of custody complete with an ideology that justified custodial care. Why? Why should institutions that began with the promise of cure have become custodial non-therapeutic environments?

In part, of course, the early expectations had been excessively grandiose. A society diagnosed as ill was hardly going to be cured by a few institutions for the deviant. Neither crime, nor insanity, nor poverty, nor feeblemindedness disappeared in nineteenth century America, and that fact alone would have forced a re-evaluation of the asylum's role. In part, too, the limited financial support given asylums by public authorities undermined the possibilities of cure. Overcrowded, understaffed institutions made a mockery of the classification systems necessary to a well ordered environment. Work therapy fell into disuse, while mechanical restraints and harsh punishments increased. As important, was the discrepancy that emerged between those who actually came to the asylum and those reformers had expected to come. The initial patients of insane asylums had been middle and upper class, often only mildly deviant, with whose life styles psychiatrists were empathetic and who provided the income to keep institutions small and intimate.

Public financing and the optimistic projections of the founders quickly led to a demand that the worst cases, those chronically ill for years, the violent, the most costly to maintain by families and local communities, be institutionalized. As public asylums became homes for the severely ill and for the poor and foreign born whose lives were seen as deviant almost by definition, a cycle of withdrawal among the middle and upper classes and among the mildly ill set in, as did an increased acceptance of the limits of curability. "A vicious circle developed. The poor and foreign born did not receive the same care as the well-to-do; since they recovered less easily, doubt about their ability to recover ensued, and fewer efforts were made to treat them therapeutically, which again reduced their rate of recovery and engendered further pessimism" (Dain, 1964).

Under the impact of these developments, the expectation that asylums would be curative gave way to an ideology of custodial care. The tenuous balance between warmth and regularity, guidance and coercion was replaced by the authoritarian dictates of control. Discussions of institutional treatment soon emphasized the difficulties and unlikelihood of cure and fixed on the importance of protecting the community from deviants (Rothman, 1971; Grob, 1973).

The change from therapeutic to custodial was not simply a product of external pressures. Nor did it occur solely in overcrowded, underfinanced state institutions for the indigent. Private hospitals that remained asylums for the middle and upper classes underwent a similar process. In part, the reformers' ideology opened the way for such an emphasis. By confusing moral treatment with administrative and mechanical operations, the reformers implied that the existence of segregated, residential institutions was sufficient for amelioration and therapy. Once constructed, institutions were assumed to be curative; if they were not, the problem undoubtedly lay with the disease and the patients. Moreover, in order to justify their institutions, in order to sell them to policy makers and the public, the reformers had to emphasize the social threat deviancy brought to the community. Asylums were not simply to improve the lot of individuals but to protect communities from the social menace within. As that menace came increasingly to be defined as the poor, foreign born, and black, those who ran the asylums quickly accepted the identification of deviancy and dependency with social treat and came to believe that institutions for the poor had inevitably to be custodial. By the last decades of the century, the patients took the blame for the institutions' failures (Dain, 1964).

The choices confronting the asylum builders were not easy, and the complexity of their task should not be minimized. Forced to manage overcrowded and underfinanced institutions, they were convinced that institutionalization of deviants and dependents was preferable to neglect and barbaric treatment by the community at large. However, by phrasing their arguments so starkly, the institutionalists soon became incapable of resisting pressures for a predominantly custodial role, and indeed came to advocate such a role in order to justify the continuing expansion of their asylums. In the end, they made an asset out of what they once perceived to be adversity.

The movement to establish segregated residential facilities for idiots and the feebleminded began soon after the founding of asylums for the mentally ill. The first institution for the feebleminded was established in 1848. Nine more were founded before 1866 and another ten between 1876 and 1893. The development of these institutions paralleled what occurred in the treatment of the insane. Indeed, for much of the nineteenth century the categories insanity and feeblemindedness were linked in professional and lay minds; both categories were defined by notions of irresponsibility, i.e., the inability to tell right from wrong. Early journals of insanity carried articles on idiocy, while the feebleminded and insane were often grouped together in legislative statutes and were routinely placed in the same institutions even after the drive for separate asylums for the feebleminded was well underway. Reformers overlapped the two causes; Dorothea Dix and Samuel Grindley Howe were only the most prominent in this regard, and they were joined by psychiatrists who treated both groups (Deutsch, 1949; Kanner, 1964).

Not surprisingly, then, many of the assumptions in the founding of asylums for the feebleminded were remarkably similar to those applied to the institutionalization of the mentally ill. While feeblemindedness was a physiological condition that could be brought about by physical problems, bad health, or blows on the head, its primary cause was a social environment that failed to provide order and stability. Reiterating a theme prominent in almost all mid-nineteenth century discussions of deviancy and dependency, the director of the Pennsylvania Training School for Idiotic and Feeble-Minded Children declared that cities were increasing the amount of feeblemindedness in the population: "extreme poverty, business excitement, and intemperance [found in the cities], naturally tend to the exhaustion of vitality, and the consequent production of an increased proportion of idiocy" (Royfe, 1972).

As was the case with insanity, the cause dictated the cure. Since feeblemindedness originated in the malfunctioning of society, special therapeutic environments that would classify the feebleminded and bring order and precision to their lives were necessary. Strict attention was thus paid to physical construction and layout, scheduling, labor, and exercise. Therapeutic environments would withdraw individuals from their community, convert them into useful and productive citizens, and return them to society trained to "habits of industry, cleanliness and self respect." The expectations were clearly formulated in the first annual report of the Pennsylvania Training School:

> The experience now abundantly furnished by [institutions in Europe, Massachusetts, and New York] fully justifies the assertion, that in nearly all the less-marked cases of idiocy, the mind may be so far improved as to be pronounced sane, that the individual may be trained to such skill as to enable him to support himself, and that his conduct in society will be in all respects as proper as that of the mass of his fellow-men. For the worst class of idiots, grovellers on the earth, of undeveloped speech and unclean habits, so successful a result, though frequently attained, cannot in general be assured; but, at the very least, they may be taught decency of habits, ability to converse, and property of conduct in their social intercourse. Taking all the classes of idiots together, it is believed that by far the larger proportion can be trained to become useful and self-supporting members of the community (Royfe, 1972).

The first institutions were thus seen as educational and therapeutic environments, committed to returning individuals to their communities. Although doubts existed that all could be made normal, the expectation was to make the deviant as much like the non-deviant as possible. In this sense, the early institutions were, in Samuel Grindley Howe's words, "a link in the chain of common schools—the last indeed, but a necessary link in order to embrace all the children of the State." Believing that change was possible, these institutions allowed for frequent public inspection, built vacations and returns home into their schedules, rejected involuntary retention, and placed great emphasis on the improvement of their patients in the institutions' annual reports. And, during their early stages, it appears that a substantial proportion who entered institutions for the feebleminded soon left (Wolfensberger, 1969; Tyor, 1972; Deutsch, 1949; Kanner, 1964).

The expectation that the feebleminded could be educated and trained for self-sufficiency soon gave way to custodial practices and a custodial ideology. One aspect of this trend was the growing concern for where those released might go. An 1872 survey in Pennsylvania, for example, claimed that of the 3500 feebleminded in the state, only 700 came from homes that could support them, a little less than that from homes that could half support them, and the remainder from families too poor to provide any support (Tyor, 1972). The assumption was that it might be better for the feebleminded to remain institutionalized to spare them from the outside world, an assumption Wolfensberger calls "protecting the deviant from the non-deviant" (Wolfensberger, 1969).

This concern, however, rested uncomfortably with the continuing hopes for the early release of those institutionalized. The founders of asylums for the feebleminded had expected to cater to the mildly retarded, but soon found themselves flooded with the most serious cases, individuals communities wanted the least contact with. As it became clear that moral treatment would not effect cures among the seriously retarded, and as overcrowding threatened to alter the nature of the treatment, those who ran the asylums protested that their therapeutic programs were being strangled by custodial pressures (Royfe, 1972).

Custodial care thus initially met with some opposition and a great deal of ambivalence. The Pennsylvania Training School reported in 1869 that it was "compelled" to receive a few of the worst cases of idiocy because there were no suitable alternatives. Such cases "are hardly admissible applicants," the School's director wrote, and "their number shall not so increase . . . as to conflict seriously with the proper classification of our household, or the interests of our school children" (Royfe, 1972).

To cope with the demands of increased numbers and long term care, institution superintendents called for an enlargement and diversification of their facilities, allowing for greater classification of residents. But they also changed the focus of their activities. Nowhere was this more evident than in the approach to work. Originally work was to be educational and moral; it would help people become self-sufficient in the outside world and was uplifting in teaching traditional moral values. With the emergence of a custodial ideology, work came to be justified more for its aid in producing institutional self-sufficiency than individual self-sufficiency. Especially through agricultural productivity, long term residents could pay for their maintenance (Tyor, 1972; Wolfensberger, 1969).

By 1885 the men who ran institutions for the feebleminded had been converted to a belief in custodial care for the benefit of both the feebleminded and society, with the trend flowing toward protecting the latter from the former. Educational goals were not abandoned, but they were in a drastic decline. As institutional leaders searched for the reasons why the feebleminded should remain in custody, they turned to the hereditarian passage of subnormality, its incurability, and the limitations of educational training. As occurred with insane asylums, moreover, much of the increase in numbers of committed came from the poor and foreign born. When tied to studies that showed that feeblemindedness and criminality were correlated, the essential basis for a custodial ideology was forged. The feebleminded were a potential menace to society, "moral imbeciles," and had to be permanently segregated so that they would neither contaminate others nor reproduce. For more than 30 years, those most responsible for the care of the feebleminded articulated a common message. Wolfensberger summarized it as follows: "between about 1890 and 1918, I found not a single speaker or writer in opposition to the prevailing views of the retardate as a sinister menace" (Wolfensberger, 1969; Tyor, 1972; Royfe, 1972; Kanner, 1964; Deutsch, 1949).

The patterns of development found in the institutionalization of the feebleminded paralleled those found in the treatment of other forms of deviancy and dependency. Without understanding this commonality, the educational treatment of mental subnormality in American society cannot be understood. The findings here suggest that idiocy and feeblemindedness were responded to primarily as social problems, and that the ideas of leading reformers, Seguin and Howe are excellent examples, were applied largely because they fit an emerging set of propositions about the therapeutic effects of institutionalization. And the transformation of institutions for the feebleminded from residential schools to custodial asylums was acquiesced in and, indeed, by 1885, fully supported by the professionals who ran the institutions. The professionals did not create the "menace of the feebleminded," but they supported its propagation, sought to benefit from it, and prior to the 1920's, opposed alternative provisions to residential segregation such as day educational facilities and family care (Wolfensberger, 1969).

SCHOOLING AND MENTAL DEFICIENCY

The last decades of the nineteenth century saw discussion of the care and education of the mentally subnormal turn from asylums to the public schools. This reorientation was not a rejection of institutionalization nor even an explicit criticism of the custodial nature of the asylums. Rather, the drive for special education assumed the necessity for custodial care, but argued that there were large numbers of mentally subnormal who should not be institutionalized. It demanded public school facilities for the handicapped, and a means of identifying, classifying, and training them. Like the earlier asylum movement, however, special education depended upon broader institutional changes, in this case the transformation of the American educational system that occurred between 1880 and 1930.

At the end of the nineteenth century the public school system seemed well on its way to completion. Its basic structure had been established: tax-supported, tuition-free, age-graded. Most states were moving toward compulsory attendance. In the larger cities, enrollment figures even before compulsory legislation showed that almost all children between ages 7 and 14 years were in school. Although still only a small percentage of the eligible age group, high schools had shown sharp enrollment gains in the 1890's, growth that would continue. Yet if public education was here to stay, it was also being subjected to its severest criticism since the early phases of the common school movement. Faced with massive numbers whom they were expected to teach at limited economic cost, educators had to respond to accusations that schools were economically inefficient, partisan and non-professional, and teaching an irrelevant curriculum by archaic means. Their responses dramatically altered the nature of public education.

For our purposes, four developments are worth particular attention: the school's responsibility for social problems, the emergence of a corporate-industrial bureaucratic model, vocationalism and the definition of equality of educational opportunity that grew with it, and the rise of intelligence testing to prominence after World War I. The first of these, the expansion of the school's concern with social problems, was not new. Earlier reform efforts had called for an expanded governmental and public role in traditionally private and individual concerns. But turn-of-the-century social reform greatly enlarged the sphere of public responsibility, and called for more active intervention by publicly funded professionals and experts. As the major public institution for the young, schools were increasingly called upon to train for civic, social, and economic roles. Health problems were to be met by school nurses, doctors, baths, and playgrounds. Fears for the melting pot were transformed into citizenship education and Americanization programs. Inadequate homes required earlier school entrance, and various forms of what was later called compensatory education developed. Whereas the school had once been expected to share its social responsibilities, it was now seen as the primary defender of the social order, a prophylactic against social ills. By the 1920's, it was assumed that any social problem could be effectively treated by making it an educational problem (Cremin, 1962; Lazerson, 1971).

The adoption of a corporate-industrial model of organization also profoundly affected American education. The criticism schoolmen most anxiously sought to counter was the attack based on their inefficiency. Efficiency has always been a moral value for Americans, but through most of the nineteenth century it was defined in terms of individuals and technology; that is, one either worked hard or used a machine to produce more. The rise of large scale corporate enterprise, with its emphasis on centralized decision making, hierarchy, specialization of function, assembly lines, and cost accounting, created a new model of efficiency that was managerial and organizational, a model quickly adopted by twentieth century educators. As mass urban school systems confronted charges of inefficiency, they moved to adopt industrial organizational techniques. Hundreds of school surveys were undertaken with the intention of bringing efficiency, cost and pupil accounting, and greater productivity to the educational system. School boards were centralized, superintendents and specialized administrative staff appointed, and university level programs in educational administration begun. Departments of budgeting, research, and testing were organized. In some cases, the industrial model was made explicit: school boards were the analogues of boards of directors, superintendents and administrative staff the managers, teachers the workers, the curriculum the technology, and the students the raw material to be processed (Spring, 1972; Cohen and Lazerson, 1972; Callahan, 1962).

Closely tied to the emphasis on efficiency was a new definition of equality of educational opportunity. Originally it was assumed that schools provided equality of opportunity by being open to all at no expense and by providing a curriculum that would increase the student's knowledge, literacy, and understanding of the world. In practice, of course, many were excluded from participating, but the assumption remained that once in school, all had pretty much the same opportunity to rise. It was soon clear, however, that a mass system did not treat all equally. The most striking evidence came from the score of dropout and "retardation" studies conducted in the first decades of the twentieth century. Numerous school surveys (the most well known were by E. L. Thorndike of Columbia Teachers College in 1907, Leonard Ayres of the Russell Sage Foundation in 1909, and the U.S. Immigration Commission published in 1912) revealed that large numbers of students were leaving school without completing their elementary course work and that many more repeated grades one or more times. Such retardation—students more than a year older than their peers at the same grade level—and elimination were held to be inefficient, costing millions of dollars annually for students to repeat grades and failing to increase the likelihood that repeaters would stay in school longer. In addition, early school leaving undermined the presumed economic benefits of going to school: dropouts, surveys showed, tended to drift into "dead-end jobs," unskilled occupations with little likelihood of advancement. Although a number of reasons were given for dropping out: economic need, health, parental hostility to schooling, the most common reasons advanced were the dullness and economic irrelevancy of the curriculum. The answer to most educational reformers was an economic revitalization of the curriculum: vocational education and a redefinition of equality of educational opportunity (Lazerson, 1971).

Vocationalism was tied to a number of assumptions about American life and schooling. It assumed that social mobility in an urban-industrial society was circumscribed, that individuals could no longer expect to go from rags to riches. Vocationalism also assumed that a society that valued institutional efficiency, and in which work was fragmented and specialized, demanded schools that fit individuals for the vocational roles they would play. In order to appeal to youth who had traditionally failed at school, coursework had to be directly relevant to future economic and social status. Equality of educational opportunity thus became tied to providing a differentiated course structure that allowed students to choose the area of study most suited to their interests and abilities (Lazerson and Grubb, 1974).

Vocationalism raised as many questions as it answered. None was more important, however, than how the fit between individual needs and abilities and school courses should take place. Who was to decide, how were the decisions to be made? What determined a curriculum best suited to the individual's abilities? From their inception, these questions formed a major part of vocational education programs. Assuming that most of the "manually motivated" and the weak school achievers would come from among the lower socioeconomic classes, educators were faced with finding a democratic means of placement; father's occupation or nationality were not adequate bases for categorization no matter how highly correlated to school success they might be. Upon these issues of choice and classification, so crucial to vocationalism, intelligence testing in America's schools grew.

The rise of intelligence and educational tests from insignificance before 1910 to a major subindustry of the educational system by 1930 deserves special attention. Before 1900, measures of intelligence in the U.S. centered on physical, motor, and sensory development with some attention paid to memorization and tests of vocabulary. These had attracted little attention, however, beyond raising the possibility that teaching and teachers might be standardized and evaluated. With the appearance between 1906 and 1911 of the Binet-Simon scale for measuring intelligence, mental testing took on greater prominence, particularly through the efforts of Henry C. Goddard (Goodenough, 1949; Weinland, 1970).

Director of the Vineland, New Jersey Training School for the Feebleminded, Goddard was the first American to use tests of intelligence on a large scale. Like Binet, Goddard assumed that mental defectives needed special training, and he began using the former's scale in 1910. Quickly finding that its classifications neatly accorded with the Training School's expectations, Goddard concluded that "experience with these tests has continually reassured us as to their amazing accuracy; their usefulness as a means of understanding the mental development of children is beyond question." Turning to the testing of public school children, he found that at least 2% of the school population was mentally defective, unable to achieve in the traditional classroom, and ignored by the schools. But Goddard also claimed that his findings provided scientific evidence for the belief that mental deficiency was both hereditary and a cause of social deviancy. Using his findings to attack what he considered the educational system's archaic attachment to equality, Goddard urged the use of mental testing to classify individuals by their inherent trainability and called for the isolation and sterilization of the worst cases of mental deficiency (Binet and Simon, 1916; Haller, 1963; Kanner, 1964).

Goddard's missionary zeal attracted considerable attention, especially among those concerned with social deviancy and the feebleminded, but it was Lewis Terman and the use of psychological tests of intelligence during World War I that made mental testing a major influence in American education. Terman's *The Measurement of Intelligence,* published in 1916, became the Bible of mental testing, his test results the standard by which to determine a child's potential. Introducing the concept of IQ, giving step-by-step administrative and scoring instructions, and emphasizing the representativeness of his sample, Terman stated that all levels of intelligence could be measured. Of the 1916 revision of the Binet scale, Florence Goodenough, herself an influential tester, wrote, "Once and for all, intelligence testing had been put on a firm basis. Terman's spectacular findings were duplicated by dozens of other experimenters who tried out the new instrument." Within a decade, the Stanford-Binet dominated mental testing in the U.S. and Europe; IQ became synonymous with intelligence (Goodenough, 1949; Terman, 1916).

Terman's work received enormous impetus from the application of group tests to large numbers of army recruits during World War I. Although the specific findings became highly controversial after the war, the overall thrust of the Alpha and Beta tests reinforced the belief that all levels of intelligence could be measured and classified in immediately practical ways. The tests confirmed most of the stereotypes about the relationships between social class, race, nationality, and intelligence. And, they showed that testing could be done on a massive scale at low cost (Yoakum and Yerkes, 1920; Yerkes, 1921; Weinland, 1970).

By the early 1920's, then, a substantial body of support had emerged to press intelligence testing on the American public. Although Stanford-Binet was dominant, nonverbal tests for the young and non-English speaking, educational achievement tests in particular areas, tests of motor and perceptual abilities, and tests for vocational guidance were being popularized. Nowhere, however, was the testing movement more significant than in the schools. "The educational significance of the results to be obtained from careful measurements of the intelligence of children can hardly be overestimated," wrote Ellwood P. Cubberley, one of the nation's leading educators, in his introduction to Terman's *Measurement of Intelligence.* "Questions relating to the choice of studies, vocational guidance, schoolroom procedure, the grading of pupils, promotional schemes, the study of the retardation of children in schools, juvenile delinquency, and the proper handling of subnormals on the one hand and gifted children on the other,—all alike acquire new meaning and significance when viewed in the light of the measurement of intelligence. . . ." Between World War I and 1930 the testing movement was in its heyday, "the age of innocence," Goodenough wrote, "when an IQ was an IQ and few ventured to doubt its omnipotence" (Terman, 1916; Goodenough, 1949).

The question, of course, is why. Why was testing's growth so dramatic? In part, testing was a response to the establishment of a mass educational system, a development that significantly heightened demands for efficiency and categorization. Measurement could be used to standardize the curriculum and evaluate teachers and students. And, it could do this while simultaneously opening the way for a greater recognition of individual differences, allowing schools to take into account, in Terman's words, "the inequalities of children in original endowment." The tests thus could account for the system's failures: those who were age-grade retarded or dropped out did so because programs had not been created to conform to their inherent limits of intelligence. This was the basis upon which a new definition of equality of educational opportunity was being forged.

But the early intelligence tests also seemed to provide scientific evidence on the causes of social deviancy and on the relationships between heredity and intelligence. While here little new was added to previous assumptions, traditional stereotypes were given an authority they had rarely possessed in the past. Goddard, Terman, and others argued that mental deficiency was a primary cause of criminality, since moral judgment, the ability to see right from wrong and to exercise self-restraint, was a product of intelligence. This reasoning had significance for public policy when the tests found that 2 to 3% of the total school age population possessed an intelligence so low that "they cannot be taught to meet new conditions effectively or to think, reason, and judge as normal persons do." These people threatened society: "there is no investigator who denies the fearful role played by mental deficiency in the production of vice, crime, and delinquency," and, the findings showed, such deficiency was most likely to be found among the lower social classes and selected racial and nationality groups. "Not all criminals are feeble-minded," Terman concluded, "but all feeble-minded are at least potential criminals. That every feeble-minded woman is a potential prostitute would hardly be disputed by any one" (Terman, 1916; Haller, 1963; Marks, 1973).

Finally, important in testing's growth in the schools were the claims that IQ was a constant and that it caused or predicted (the distinction was often blurred) school achievement. Since the latter was assumed to lead to adult economic and social success, intelligence tests were predictive of the future. The schools now had their institutional capstone: an instrument that scientifically classified students for their future social roles. The time will soon come, Terman told his readers, when "we shall know fairly definitely the vocational significance of any degree of mental inferiority or superiority. Researches of this kind will ultimately determine the minimum 'intelligence quotient' necessary for success in leading occupations." Moreover, the findings could be gotten swiftly and accurately. "One who knows how to apply the tests correctly and who is experienced in the psychological interpretations of responses can in forty minutes arrive at a more accurate judgment as to a subject's intelligence than would be possible without the tests after months or even years of close observations." More cogently, Terman wrote,

"There is nothing else about a child as important as the IQ" (Terman, 1916; Terman, 1920).

The early testers thus established a number of key relationships: IQ was inherited and immutable. IQ and intelligence were synonymous and predicted school achievement. Socioeconomic status was a product of intelligence. Intelligence determined social and occupational behavior. As these relationships were articulated, however, they became the object of intense debates during the 1920's and 1930's. While most of the arguments concentrated on the mechanics of testing, substantive issues were raised: what was the nature of intelligence? Did IQ measure more than school-based learning? Was intelligence a product of environment or heredity? To what extent did intelligence determine socioeconomic status? Could IQ tests predict future occupational and social success? Increasingly, many of the basic assumptions upon which the tests were grounded came under challenge and, in some of their most extreme forms, revised (Weinland, 1970).

What effect these challenges had upon the actual use of tests in the schools is difficult to determine. Undoubtedly they moderated the expectations of testing's powers and presumably raised major questions about the nature of intelligence. But it also appears that the challenges and the questions they raised were passed over in the rush for efficient evaluatory and sorting devices. To a great extent, tests were adopted as a means of sorting individuals into the differentiated curriculum in preparation for their future social roles. As long as they classified, their use grew. What should have been "a continuous inquiry," the noted historian Richard Hofstadter has written, "had a way . . . of being exalted into a faith—not so much by those who were actually doing research as by those who were hungry to find its practical applications and eager to invoke the authority of science on behalf of their various crusades." Accepting increasing responsibility for America's social problems, adopting a corporate industrial model of organization, and agreeing that a differentiated curriculum oriented toward future vocational roles was the essential ingredient of equality of educational opportunity, educators bought intelligence tests as basic to the way they ran their schools (Hofstadter, 1962; National Society for the Study of Education, 1922, 1925, 1936).

The changes in the organization and assumptions of public education that occurred in the first three decades of the twentieth century underlay the emergence of special education. The creation of a mass educational system highlighted the problems of group and individual differences and raised in a cogent way the phenomenon of "failure," i.e., those who did not achieve despite the availability of opportunity. The triumph of public education, near universal attendance, had thrown "a new burden on the public schools," Ellwood Cubberley declared in the introduction to J. E. Wallace Wallin, *The Education of Handicapped Children.* Children from inferior stock and environments, truants and incorrigibles, and those suffering from physical and mental defects were now the school's responsibility. But a mass educational system also presented schoolmen with their greatest opportunity. A captive audience of nearly all children ages 7 to 14 years made the public school, in Arnold Gesell's words, "potentially the most powerful of all social agencies in the vast field of human engineering." The obligations of social responsibility and the possibilities of social engineering strengthened the case for special education of the handicapped (Wallin, 1924; Gesell, 1921).

So, too, did the new emphasis on curriculum differentiation and vocational training. The need to classify and provide distinctive curriculum by learning capability and for expected vocational roles (the two were usually tied together) meant that claims for special education accorded with prevailing trends in the educational system as a whole. Cubberley made the point explicitly when he suggested that the problem of special education was essentially the problem of the school more generally: "diagnosis, proper classification, curriculum adjustment, restatement of educational objectives, revision of teaching methods, differentiated instruction, and proper training and habit formation" (Wallin, 1924). Similarly, vocationalism was most consistently applied to those deemed inadequate in the traditional school setting. In their focus on vocational preparation, then, special educators could thus draw upon a newly accepted role for schooling more generally.

Most important of all, however, the popularization of intelligence testing provided the basis for special education for the mentally deficient. This was not surprising. Binet and Goddard's original use of intelligence tests was directed at separating the feebleminded from the normal, and much of the debate after 1910 was over the extent to which tests could be applied to standard populations. But the popularization of the tests for all further reinforced the movement for special education in three ways. First, widespread testing showed that large numbers of the population were subnormal: between 2 and 3% severely deficient and 14 to 16% borderline. These numbers were too large for residential institutions to accommodate. Second, the tests combined an emphasis on the inherent limits of learning ability and the possibilities of categorizing with the argument that most individuals were trainable, i.e., they could learn habits of survival and some vocational skills, and could thus be converted into productive citizens, a theme that had been prominent in the founding of the first residential institutions for the feebleminded. Third, the tests reinforced the ties between mental deficiency, low socioeconomic status, and deviancy. Although the assumption that feeblemindedness inevitably led to crime was weakened by studies in the 1920's and thereafter, the belief remained strong that without proper controls criminality was exceedingly likely (Wallin, 1924).

Special education was thus part of a broader transformation of the American school. While it had its own particular components, its development often reflected these larger trends. One example of this involved the benefits thought to come from segregating the mentally deficient from regular classrooms. Here the arguments closely resembled those being made for ability grouping more generally. The benefits were two-fold. Segregation would free normal pupils from the restrictions imposed by the deficient. Declaring that an educational system's highest obligation was to its normal and brightest pupils, Wallin wrote, "By removing the 'clinkers' and the 'drags' the regular grades will be thrown open to the normal progress pupils, thereby enabling these pupils to advance more rapidly, and materially reducing the extent of pedagogical retardation." Having them out of the classroom, teachers would be relieved of worry, discouragement, and nervous tension. At the same time, the "mentally underprivileged" could receive aid and encouragement as opposed to scorn and ridicule, could be taught by specially trained and sympathetic teachers, and be relieved of a "maladjusted curriculum" (Wallin, 1924).

In its initial phases, the special education movement had great expectations both in its ability to categorize and to train for economic usefulness and social decorum. Ideally school systems would undertake mental surveys of all their pupils. When that was unfeasible, other ways of finding the mentally deficient would suffice: children 3 or more years behind their normal grade level or those children teachers thought particularly slow at their work. Whatever the initiatory process, however, the expectation was that placement would depend on the Stanford-Binet or some revision of it. Through the use of such tests, a consistent public policy with regard to the mentally defective could be established, curriculum standardized, and the retarded brought to their fullest potential (Wallin, 1924; White House Conference on Child Health and Protection, 1931).

While special education thus began optimistically, although more guarded and conservative than the earlier asylum movement, it never achieved full public acceptance. An initial outburst of enthusiasm during the 1910's and the early 1920's soon waned. Although some cities at the end of the 1920's had substantial numbers of pupils in special classes (in 1929, Cleveland had 6.29% of its elementary school population in special education classes, Philadelphia 3.52%, Rochester 3.21%, and Detroit 2.10%) most school systems provided for less than 2%, the absolute minimum for special educators, while statewide figures went from 1.49% (Minnesota) to 0.31% (Wisconsin). Where classes did exist, they were usually in the least desirable buildings and rooms. Equipment and materials were scarce, few of the teachers specially trained, and the curriculum a watered down version of what the regular classes did. Parental hostility to classes for mental defectives was high, forcing school systems to resort to such euphemisms as ungraded, opportunity, Binet, and adjustment classes. Finally, the distinctions between mental deficiency, behaviorally disruptive and truant children, and the physically handicapped were frequently ignored, with the special classes dumping grounds for those the system could not accommodate or tolerate (Wallin, 1924; White House Conference, 1931).

The failure of special education to gain widespread commitment in practice, despite its acceptance in theory, did not lead to a re-examination of basic premises. Questions about the effects of labeling or why special classes were so readily seen as custodial were rarely raised. Instead, special educators reintensified their pleas for support of policies already articulated by the 1920's. They called for sharper distinctions between mental defectives and other problem children, and between various grades of mental deficiency. Better facilities, trained teachers, a curriculum more suited to the educability of the mentally subnormal and tied to their limited vocational expectations were demanded. Hostility by parents had to be overcome, especially by showing the child's behavioral improvements when placed in special classes (Anderson, 1922).

There was much to be said for these demands. School systems were neglecting the mentally subnormal, and such children were undoubtedly rejected by their peers and teachers. Nor should the problems confronting special educators be minimized. With little community interest and support, special educators were isolated and alienated from their colleagues. The tendency of school systems to lump all "problem" children together seriously hindered their work. Confusion over etiology and terminology and uncertainty over what was possible made consistent procedures difficult. And despite expressions of concern for individualized learning, school systems rarely went beyond conventional mass instruction at any level.

Yet there was more to the problem than insufficient support and the need for consistent procedures. Even after special education began a substantial growth after mid-century, basic inadequacies remained apparent. Seemingly liberal ideas had a way of becoming illiberal in practice. The common assumption was that the ideas had been perverted, often by inadequate application. But the original assumptions themselves remained unquestioned. Although concern was always expressed over mislabeling, the expected benefits of categorization always outweighed the disadvantages. Underplayed was Binet's warning that "It will never be to one's credit to have attended a special school. We should at least spare from this mark those who do not deserve it." Parental opposition was seen as an obstacle to overcome. Debates over the efficacy of segregated learning environments abounded, but little effort was made to rethink the phenomeonon of segregation. Nor was much effort made to examine the assumptions of an educational program built on the notion of failure, and what role this negative characteristic played in equating special education with second class citizenship. Despite some modification, the stress on IQ as an irremedial constant remained intact, effectively undercutting the significance of cultural and psychological variables. This induced what Burton Blatt has called "a predeterministic mental set" that tended to be fatalistic, and it confused diagnosis and treatment with classification. Moreover, it assumed that a lack of competence in traditional school work, almost definitional on the basis of IQ score, was equivalent to a lack of competence in other areas of social activity. But as long as special educators attributed their problems to external sources, the unwillingness of the public to support them and the limited vision of public school administrators, valid as those complaints were, there was little likelihood that the education of the mentally subnormal would substantially change (Mercer, 1973; Blatt, 1961; Kirk and McCarthy, 1966).

CONCLUSION

What has been offered here is an approach to writing a history of the educational system and mental subnormality. It argues that one way of understanding that history is to look at the social and institutional contexts within which change occurred. And, it argues, those contexts are not simply background material, the social setting often presented in the literature, but integral to the ways in which institutions treated the mentally subnormal.

It should be kept in mind, however, that the arguments presented here are incomplete. Fuller development and modification require more intensive explorations into the relationship between the treatment of mental subnormality and social change. We need to know more about how the mentally subnormal were treated within and outside institutions, what changes they underwent, and the limitations imposed by physiological and emotional disorders. More is necessary on the transmission and uses of medical knowledge, especially the social assumptions under which such knowledge is used. And we need a fuller understanding of the alternatives actually available at any particular time. This essay is thus just a start for historians of mental subnormality, but it is a necessary one.

REFERENCES

Anderson, M. L. 1922. Education of Defectives in the Public Schools. World Book Co. Yonkers-on-the-Hudson.

Bailyn, B. 1961. Education in the Formation of American Society. Vintage. New York.

Binet, A. and T. Simon. 1916. The Development of Intelligence in Children. Translated by Elizabeth S. Kite. Vineland Training School. Vineland, New Jersey.

Blatt, B. 1961. Some persistently recurring assumptions concerning the mentally subnormal. In J. H. Rothstein (ed.), Mental Retardation. Holt, Rinehart and Winston. New York. pp. 113–125.

Callahan, R. 1962. Education and the Cult of Efficiency. University of Chicago Press. Chicago.

Cohen, D. K. and M. Lazerson. 1972. Education and the corporate order. Socialist Revolution 2: 47–72.

Cremin, L. A. 1962. The Transformation of the School. Alfred A. Knopf. New York.

Dain, N. 1964. Concepts of Insanity in the United States, 1789–1865. Rutgers University Press. New Brunswick.

Deutsch, A. 1949. The Mentally Ill in America: A History of Their Care and Treatment from Colonial Times. 2nd Ed. Columbia University Press. New York.

Dunn, L. 1961. A historical review of the treatment of the retarded. In J. H. Rothstein (ed.), Mental Retardation. Holt, Rinehart and Winston. New York. pp. 13–17.

Gesell, A. 1921. Exceptional Children and Public School Policy. Yale University Press. New Haven.

Goodenough, F. L. 1949. Mental Testing: Its History, Principles, and Applications. Rinehart and Co. New York.

Grob, G. N. 1973. Mental Institutions in America: Social Policy to 1875. Free Press. Riverside, New Jersey.

Haller, M. 1963. Eugenics: Hereditarian Attitudes in American Thought. Rutgers University Press. New Brunswick.

Hofstadter, Richard. 1962. Anti-Intellectualism in America. Alfred A. Knopf. New York.

Kanner, L. 1964. A History of the Care and Study of the Mentally Retarded. Charles C Thomas. Springfield, Illinois.

Kirk, S. and J. McCarthy. 1966. The Illinois test of psycholinguistic abilities—An approach to differential diagnosis. In T. E. Jordan (ed.), Perspectives in Mental Retardation. Southern Illinois Press. Carbondale. pp. 273–290.

Lazerson, M. 1971. Origins of the Urban School: Public Education in Massachusetts, 1870–1915. Harvard University Press. Cambridge.

Lazerson, M. 1973. Revisionism and American educational history. Harvard Ed. Rev. 43: 269–283.

Lazerson, M. and W. N. Grubb. 1974. American Education and Vocationalism: Documents in the History of Vocational Education, 1870–1970. Teachers College Press. New York.

Marks, R. 1973. Testers, Trackers and Trustees: The Ideology of the Intelligence Testing Movement in America, 1900–1954. Ph.D. dissertation. University of Illinois.

Mercer, J. R. 1973. Labeling the Mentally Retarded: Clinical and Social System Perspectives on Mental Retardation. University of California Press. Berkeley.

National Society for the Study of Education. 1922. Twenty-first Annual Yearbook. National Society for the Study of Education. Chicago.

National Society for the Study of Education. 1925. Twenty-fourth Annual Yearbook. National Society for the Study of Education. Chicago.

National Society for the Study of Education. 1936. Thirty-fifth Annual Yearbook. National Society for the Study of Education. Chicago.

Rothman, D. J. 1971. The Discovery of the Asylum: Social Order and Disorder in the New Republic. Little, Brown and Co. Boston.

Royfe, E. H. 1972. A Systems Analysis of an Historic Mental Retardation Institution: A Case Study of Elwyn Institute, 1852–1970. Ed.D. dissertation. Temple University.

Spring, J. 1972. Education and the Rise of the Corporate State. Beacon Press. Boston.

Terman, L. 1916. The Measurement of Intelligence. Houghton Mifflin Co. Boston.

Terman, L. 1920. The use of intelligence tests in the grading of school children. J. Ed. Res. 1: 30.

Tyor, P. L. 1972. Segregation or Surgery: The Mentally Retarded in America. Ph.D. dissertation. Northwestern University.

Wallin, J. E. W. 1924. The Education of Handicapped Children. Houghton Mifflin Co. Boston.

Weinland, T. P. 1970. A History of the IQ in America, 1890–1941. Ph.D. dissertation. Columbia University.

White House Conference on Child Health and Protection. 1931. Special Education. The Century Co. New York.

Williams, H. M. and J. E. W. Wallin. 1961. Education of the severely retarded child. In J. H. Rothstein (ed.), Mental Retardation. Holt, Rinehart and Winston. New York. pp. 334–338.

Wolfensberger, W. 1969. The origin and nature of our institutional models. In R. B. Kugel and W. Wolfensberger (eds.), Changing Patterns in Residential Services for the Mentally Retarded. President's Committee on Mental Retardation. Washington, D.C. pp. 59–171.

Yerkes, R. M. (ed.). 1921. Psychological Examining in the U.S. Army. Vol. 15. Memoirs of the National Academy of Sciences. Washington.

Yoakum, C. S. and R. M. Yerkes. 1920. Army Mental Tests. H. Holt and Co. New York.

Public Health
And Mental Retardation:
New Power
And New Problems

Zena Stein and Mervyn Susser

In recent decades, there has been a focusing of scientific interest on the field of mental retardation. This focus has brought us to the brink of a new era, in which scientific developments can find their full expression in public health practice. Excepting some rare spirits, scientists up to this latest period had shown slight interest in mental retardation. In the 1950's, under the brilliant illuminations of molecular biology, the true number of human chromosomes and then the chromosomal anomaly of Down's syndrome were discovered, and the field began to burgeon. Human genetics lost the stigma acquired from the abominations of Nazi Germany, and there were rapid advances at the molecular as well as the cellular level. In an opening address to the First Scientific Congress on Mental Deficiency in London in 1958, Lionel Penrose, himself a pioneer, remarked that mental retardation had at last begun to excite scientists as they sensed the opportunities for generalization. Epidemiologists began to go beyond descriptive statistics to search for causes of disordered development. Psychologists studied the genesis and treatment of learning disabilities. Social scientists began to examine the structure and the effects of residential institutions. The scientific harvest has opened up possibilities for a new phase of prevention. Such developments will be attended by issues of human rights and ethics, economics, public health practice, and technical manpower. Our discussion will be concerned with several of these issues.

MEASURES OF MENTAL RETARDATION IN THE POPULATION

We shall start by clarifying the epidemiological issues of incidence and prevalence, and of case definition and classification. We shall then draw these themes together with respect to planning and evaluation of services, and to surveillance and prevention.

53

Incidence and Prevalence: Definitions, Limitations

Incidence measures the frequency with which disorders arise anew in a population during a defined period of time. The search for causes is best pursued by studies of incidence. Most incidence rates in mental retardation must take their data from cases clinically identified on entry to some form of care. Such rates are an approximation in at least two ways. First, entry to service rarely coincides with the onset of disorder and yet ordinarily must be used to indicate the time of onset. In theory, this limitation can be overcome by modifying the definition to suit the circumstances, for example, the incidence of entry to clinics or to hospitals. In practice, the limitation is a serious one for studies of causation; in such studies the aim of the measure is to bring the point of recognition of disorder as near as possible to the point of impact of the causal factor in order to uncover the connection between them. A second approximation of incidence derived from service agency data is that all who suffer the disorder may not be represented. Some may not seek care and others may die before they come into care. Incidence rates usually reflect disorders in which a need for service has been recognized and met; only when a disorder is severe and when services are adequate will the measured rates reflect the "true" incidence in the population.

Prevalence describes a disorder existing in a population at one particular time. This measure ignores the time of onset of a disorder, and with chronic disorders greatly limits inference about the connection between cause and effect. Although an obvious requirement in establishing cause is to show that it is antecedent to effect, the information about both is collected at the same time. On the other hand, for the purposes of determining community need[1] in chronic disorders, prevalence is more satisfactory than incidence precisely because it represents the load of disorder existing at the time of need. Prevalence estimates also have some technical advantages over incidence estimates, in that investigators can set up case definitions, and then go out and discover existing cases without having to depend on what emerges at the service level from the social process of referral. Thus, incidence gives the best view of the circumstances in which disorders arise in a population over a period of time, but depends heavily on service usage; prevalence gives the better view of needs at a particular time, and need be less dependent on service usage.

Prevalence is a function of incidence and duration, $P = I \times D$. Prevalence is therefore affected by a change in either one of these terms. In acute disorders of short duration, prevalence has been of little interest. The main service need is for flexible response to epidemic periods of peak incidence. In long-lasting disorders, the reverse is true. The main service need flows from the accumulation of cases which is governed by the duration of time over which newly arising disorders remain active, of which prevalence is the measure. To simplify discussion at this point, we shall treat mental retardation as lifelong; that is, duration equals survival. This assumption is appropriate to severe mental retardation, but as we shall see later, not necessarily to mild mental retardation.

---

[1] The measurement of "need" and its relation to values about health is material enough for another essay.

Figure 1 illustrates changes in the incidence and prevalence of Down's syndrome, produced by the dynamics of incidence and survival. There is not much doubt that during this century the incidence at birth of Down's syndrome has declined somewhat. There is no doubt that the expectation of life, or duration, has increased markedly. Children with Down's syndrome have been protected by antibiotics and immunization from the respiratory and other infections to which they are especially vulnerable. Affected by many potentially lethal congenital anomalies, they have also profited from advances in cardiac and pediatric surgery.

Uses of Incidence

Incidence measures rely heavily on clinical identification. In severe mental retardation, this is largely a matter of identifying congenital disorders. In societies with well developed medical services, several conditions associated with severe mental retardation can be identified at birth or soon after. The clinical diagnosis of other forms of mental retardation, particularly mild retardation, most often must be deferred until later in childhood. In Table 1 we have listed the incidence of a number of conditions which can

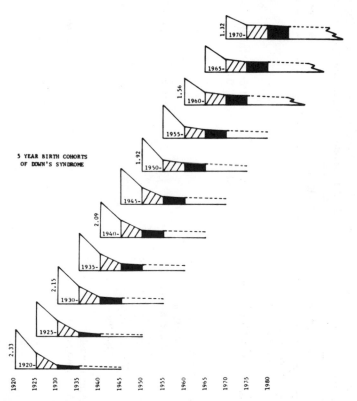

Figure 1. Incidence, survival, and prevalence of Down's syndrome.

Table 1. % mental retardation in child survivors with selected conditions present at birth, and % these conditions among various populations of A.) Incidence at birth; B.) Prevalence in childhood; C.) % mentally retarded; D.) % among institution residents

Condition	Rate	Source	Comment
Cerebral Palsy			
A. Incidence at birth	?		Usually diagnosed some time after birth. Probably declining. Prevalence in 11,645 school age children born in Isle of Wight, England, 1/5/50 to 8/31/60 at 5 to 15 years, 2.9:1000. Additional 12% borderline, (IQ 71–85).
B. % mentally retarded	36% severe } 54% 18% mild	Rutter, Graham, and Yule (1970)	
C. Residents in institutions with condition Point prevalence	20% (?)	Moser and Wolf (1971)	Walter E. Fernald State School, Mass., USA "Mentally retarded, etiology unknown, with significant neurological signs."
% consecutive admissions	3.0%	McIntire and Adams (1963)	Mental Retardation Project at the Nebraska Psychiatric Institute, ⩾ 6 years of age.
Anencephaly			
A. Incidence at birth	1.1:1000	Czeizel and Révész (1970)	Total live and stillbirths, Budapest, 1963–1967.
	3.95:1000	Elwood (1970)	Total live and stillbirths, Belfast, 1950–1966.
	0.73:1000	Janerich (1973)	Total live and stillbirths, New York State, 1945–1971.
B. % mentally retarded	—		No survivors.

Spina bifida (without anencephaly)

A. Incidence at birth	1.63:1000	Czeizel and Révész (1970)	Total live and stillbirths, Budapest, 1963–1967
	1.55:1000	Spain (1973)	Total live and stillbirths, London, 1965–1969 (18% of total cases were stillborn).
	0.51:1000	Kurent and Severe (1973)	Collaborative Perinatal Study, USA, births 1955–1966.
	0.96:1000	Janerich (1973)	Total live and stillbirths, New York State, 1945–1971.
B. % mentally retarded	54%	Spain (1973)	London, England.
C. Residents in institutions with condition	?		No satisfactory report located.

Hydrocephaly

A. Incidence at birth	0.76:1000	Czeizel and Révész (1970)	Total live and stillbirths, Budapest, 1963–1970.
B. % mentally retarded	35% mild	Hemmer (1971)	Following treatment with ventricular-uricular shunts, in 140 cases.
C. Residents in institutions with condition			
Point prevalence:	1.7%	Moser and Wolf (1971)	Walter E. Fernald State School, Mass., USA
% consecutive admissions	6.8%	McIntire and Adams (1963)	Mental Retardation Project at the Nebraska Psychiatric Institute, $\leq$ 6 years of age.

continued

Table 1. *continued*

Condition	Rate	Source	Comment
Phenylketonuria			
A. Incidence at birth	1.37:1000	Allen, Flemin, and Spinito (1967)	Michigan: 104,785 births.
B. % mentally retarded	84% if untreated	Smith and Wolfe (1974)	Treated index cases and untreated sibs (28 pairs), London.
C. Residents in institutions with condition			
Point prevalence	0.7% 0.48%	Yannet (1966) Allen, Lowrey, and Wilson (1960)	Southbury, Connecticut Michigan.
% consecutive admissions	1.6%	Rostafinski (1964)	New admissions children ≤ 10 years, Virginia, USA.
Down's Syndrome			
A. Incidence at birth	1.45:1000 0.89:1000 2.4:1000	Collman and Stoller (1962) Stark and Mantel (1966) Harlap (1973)	Victoria, Australia hospitals, agencies. Michigan, USA, hospitals, agencies. West Jerusalem: consecutive births; clinical and cytogenetic confirmation.
B. % mentally retarded	100% (2% mild, 98% severe)	Carter and Gold (1972)	
C. Residents in institutions with condition			
Point prevalence	8.5% 17.0%	Yannet (1966) Moser and Wolf (1974)	Southbury, Connecticut. 21% of severely retarded, Walter E. Fernald State School, Mass., USA.
% consecutive admissions	12.6%	McIntire and Adams (1963)	Mental Retardation Project at the Nebraska Psychiatric Institute, ≤ 6 years of age.
	7.4%	Rostafinski (1964)	New admissions, children ≤ 10 years, USA.

Tay-Sachs			
A. Incidence at birth	0.15:1000	Holmes et al. (1972)	In Ashkenazi Jews.
	0.0015:1000		In others.
B. % mentally retarded	100%	Holmes et al. (1972)	
C. Residents in institutions with condition	–		Early death.
Point prevalence	0.1%	Yannet (1966)	Southbury, Connecticut.
% consecutive admissions	0.35%	Rostafinski (1964)	New admissions, children ≤ 10 years, Virginia, USA.

be diagnosed early in life. Down's syndrome, hydrocephalus, spina bifida, cerebral palsy, and certain metabolic disorders are recognizable at birth, and some countries and states require a record of the anomaly on the birth certificate. Such records make community surveillance possible. If the returns are examined promptly, they provide an early warning of change. Clusters of cases in time or place can be speedily investigated. Although the degree of mental retardation in the individual case will often be unclear at first, diagnosis can be sufficiently precise to serve for surveillance.

The community benefits from a reporting system if it is put to use for epidemiologic surveillance, and for planning and evaluating services. The affected child and family benefit if the system is put to use to mobilize services and to avoid the ill consequences of delay. Thus, in some communities the initial report of a case institutes a continuous relationship with a professional helper who brings to bear and coordinates an array of services. In most of the United States however, only cases with the particular biochemical defect of phenylketonuria (PKU) receive such services. Case finding and the early institution of treatment, primarily an advantage to individual child and family, but also an advantage to the community in relieving the burden of cases by reducing duration, have properly been recognized as a function of public health. Effectiveness is limited by techniques and skills: retarded children without physical or biochemical abnormalities often cannot be recognized early in life. Among those who can be recognized, levels of future function often canot be reliably predicted.

Uses of Prevalence

In communities where the likelihood of using the services is high, the prevalence of conditions diagnosable at young ages can be, as with incidence, estimated from service usage. Estimates are much more sound for severe than for mild mental retardation, as will appear, and this discussion of uses will attend to severe mental retardation. In Western Europe and Canada, and in much of the United States, estimates from services of the prevalence of severe mental retardation yield reliable rates that differ little from those of community surveys. Table 2 gives examples based on services in Britain, Canada, Sweden, The Netherlands, and the United States. (See the Table for references.) The age-specific rates in the teens are surprisingly constant in the range 3.5 to 4 per 1000. The prevalence rates based on communities without reference to service usage, also shown in the Table, are in the same range. The most substantial study is of a Dutch population of 400,000 men systematically examined at military induction in their nineteenth year; the prevalence of severe mental retardation among them was 3.8 per 1000. In a few of the prevalence studies based on the population at large, for instance, in Amsterdam, Sweden, and Maryland, higher rates have been found. We tend to seek the reasons for these inconsistent results in the methods used.

We conclude that in developed countries services yield good estimates of true prevalence for severe mental retardation (although not for mild mental retardation). This should hardly come as a surprise, since compulsory education ensures visibility of the severely retarded at school age. What is surprising is not the adequacy of the prevalence

Table 2. Age-specific prevalence studies of severe mental retardation

Authors	Year of study	Location	Age group years	Rates/1000 M	Rates/1000 F	Agency or population: method: criteria
Lewis (1929) (Table 14)	1925–27	England	7–14	4.39 7.11	3.13 5.12	3 urban areas, Agencies: key informants, 3 rural areas, schools. Denominator is based on school attenders; more rural than urban children were not in school
Goodman and Tizard (1962)	1960	Middlesex, England	10–14	3.61		Agencies: records of all mentally sub-normal children under 16.
Kushlick and Susser (1968)	1961	Salford, England	15–19	3.62		Agencies: active cases supervised by mental health service of local authority.
Taylor (1962)	1962	Oregon	12–14	3.3		Agencies: statewide survey of mentally retarded known to all social, medical, educational, and custodial agencies, services, and facilities.
Akesson (1967)	1964	Western Sweden	10–20	5.5		Agencies: institutions, mental hospitals, and clinics, parish records and information from doctors, teachers, clergy, and nurses in each district.
Kushlick (1964)	1964	Wessex, England	15–19	3.2		Agencies: records of local health authorities, hospitals, private homes.
Rutter, Tizard, and Whitmore (1970)	1964	Isle of Wight, England	5–15	3.4		Prevalence in 11,685 school age children born in Isle of Wight, England, 1/5/50 to 8/31/60.

continued

Table 2. continued

Authors	Year of study	Location	Age group years	Rates/1000 M	F	Agency or population: method: criteria
Wald (1965)	1964–65	Poland	7–13	3.4		Agencies: official population records, school records.
Imre (1973)	1966	Maryland, U.S.A.	10–14 15–19	4.6 13.9	4.8 13.8	Household interviews, screening and clinical examination of all families in one county (15,000 or 17,000 individuals in Maryland, USA contacted).
			10–14 15–19	1.8 16.3	5.7 22.6	Adjusted for race (Conley, 1973).
Wing (1971)	1967	London, England	10–14	3.81	3.51	Agencies: population registers, contacts.
Sorel (1970)	1968–69	Amsterdam	10 13	7.25 7.34		Agencies.
Drillien (1966)	1962–64	Edinburgh	8–14	5.0		Agency records, from hospitals, schools, health agencies.
Birch et al. (1970)	1970	Aberdeen, Scotland	8–10	3.7		Records of births in 1952–1954, followed by health visitors and researchers.
McDonald (1973)	1973	Quebec, Canada	10	3.8		Agencies: records of hospitals, institutions, schools, and homes for retarded, social and welfare agencies, and M.R. associations.
Stein et al. (1975)	1973	Netherlands	19	3.8		Military induction records.

measure, but the constancy of the apparently true rate across communities, countries, and continents that vary in population structure, social structure, economic level, and geography. Ineligibility for education in the ordinary school ordinarily means eligibility for special services reserved for the severely retarded, and legal proof of eligibility, based on individual examination, is recorded.

Knowledge of prevalence rates makes possible the planning of services for affected individuals and their families on a community basis. Kushlick (1964) and Wing (1971) have each furnished us with estimates of the expected disabilities associated with severe mental retardation together with estimates of the expected numbers of severely retarded individuals. An approximation of their findings is shown in Table 3. Official reports have sometimes defended deficient services for the mentally retarded on the grounds that it is difficult to provide for a need the size of which is unknown. This defense is no longer available. In our view, to repeat prevalence studies with the sole object of counting cases has limited value at this time. Sufficient change may have occurred within about a decade, however, to make fresh counts again worthwhile.

Yet no estimated prevalence rate drawn from another population can do for a community-based mental retardation service what a register can do. A register gives an unduplicated record of every identified person with mental retardation, including his current location within a system of services. While a prevalence study is a sortie at one particular time, constant updating is the essence of a register. The newborn and the newly identified are added; deaths, recoveries, emigrants, and immigrants are noted. An efficient register rests on the linked records of a network of services. As indicated in the discussion of incidence above, there is interaction and exchange in the benefits to be drawn from a register by communities and individuals. For the community a register can yield essential feedback for the preventive and planning functions of public health. It provides continuing counts of incidence and prevalence, and a population base for evaluating treatment programs and for epidemiological research. For affected individuals, a register can promptly signal the need for services, ensure continuity in their care, and promote the comprehensive planning and integration of necessary services. The dangers that attend the maintenance of registers we shall discuss below.

Definition of a Case

Measures of incidence and prevalence must be based on cases, and a case to be counted must be distinguished from a non-case. The difficult problems relate to mild mental retardation, and thus this discussion is relevant more to mild than severe retardation. As with many health disorders, lines of demarcation are blurred. Like sickness, recognized mental retardation is a social attribute (Susser, 1968). Failure to perform social roles at a particular stage of life identifies mentally retarded individuals. Social roles vary over the life course, with time, and among societies, and we may anticipate that the variation in the demands of social roles will be manifest in variation in the frequency of failures in role performance, and of those identified as mentally retarded.

Although mental retardation is ultimately a social attribute, it comprises at least three components: organic, functional, and social. The organic component we term impair-

Table 3. Incapacities with severe mental retardation: % distribution in children 5–14 years (based on Kushlick (1970) and Wing (1971) and rounded)

Cannot walk	15
Can walk	85
Severely incontinent	10
Behavior disorder	10
Incontinent and behavior disorder	10
None of the above	55
Total severely mentally retarded	100

ment; the functional component we term disability; the social component we term handicap. There is by no means a one-to-one relationship among these three criteria. Hence epidemiological understanding of the condition will be quite different depending on which among these three components is counted. For each component, age distribution, treatment, and service needs will differ. It follows that for many epidemiological purposes an undifferentiated concept of mental retardation is futile. Compare, for instance, cerebral palsy with Down's syndrome, both impairments that can often be recognized at birth. In cerebral palsy, the association of impairment with disability and handicap is much less constant than in Down's syndrome (Table 1), and unfolds only with aging over time. Other children with functional disability, apparent in retarded speech and verbal comprehension and in poor performance on psychological tests, cannot be diagnosed as impaired. Even with severe mental retardation, the presence of an organic impairment must sometimes rest on assumption. At autopsy of cases of severe mental retardation with impairments undiagnosed in life, no organic, biochemical, or structural impairments can be found in about 30% (Crome, 1972).

In mild mental retardation the absence of recognized impairment is almost the rule. In the cultural-familial syndrome, by far the most common syndrome of mental retardation, there is by definition no detectable organic impairment. By definition also, functional disability measured in terms of an IQ below a given threshold must be present, but the accompanying degree of social handicap varies by age and by social setting.

The social role of mental handicap, on the other hand, is sometimes conferred on individuals without either brain impairment or functional disability. Both in the United States and in England, individuals with IQ's well within the normal level have been placed in institutions for the retarded and thereby acquired the social role of mental retardation. The common attributes of such cases are a combination of behavior disorders and lack of social support. The consequence for population measures of the fickle choices among multiple criteria for defining cases is inconstant and changeable rates. Prevalence rates of mild mental retardation display this character, as Table 4 shows.

The case is the unit of enumeration in statements of incidence and prevalence, and usefulness of the statements is influenced by the criterion used. In incidence studies, the order of usefulness for each criterion descends from organic, through functional, to social. The object of the incidence study is to identify the case at the earliest possible stage. The greater the component of organic impairment, the earlier a case can be

Table 4. Age-specific prevalence studies of mild mental retardation

Authors	Year of study	Location	Age group	Rates/1000 M	Rates/1000 F	Comment
Lewis (1929) Table 14	1925–1927	England	7–14	18.21 34.92	16.08 32.10	3 urban areas, Agencies: key informants, 3 rural areas, schools. Denominator is based on school attenders.
Kushlick and Susser (1968)	1961	Salford, England	15–19	8.65		Agencies: active cases supervised by mental health service of local authority.
Taylor (1962)	1962	Oregon	12–14	30.3		Agencies: Statewide survey of mentally retarded known to all social, medical, educational, and custodial agencies, services, and facilities.
Kushlick (1964)	1964	Wessex, England	15–19	2.97		Agencies: Records of local health authorities hospitals, private hostels.
Rutter, Tizard, and Whitmore (1970)	1964–6	Isle of Wight, England	9–11	25.3		Random sample of 159 children given WISC; total sample 2334.
Imre (1973)	1966	Maryland, USA	10–14 15–19	81.7 85.9	80.2 83.0	Household interview of all families; a county in Maryland, USA
Birch et al. (1970)	1970	Aberdeen, Scotland	8–10	23.7		Records of births in 1952–54, followed by health visitors and researchers.
Stein et al. (1975)	1975	Netherlands	10	66		Diagnosis of 'Moron' at assessment for military service.

identified. Psychological dysfunction may be detectable from early childhood, but social handicap is unlikely to emerge until later. In Down's syndrome impairment is apparent at birth, psychological dysfunction in the nursery, and handicap emerges with social demands for adaptation through the life cycle.

In prevalence studies the order of usefulness of these criteria is reversed. The frequency of the social components of handicap (which encompasses the other two components) is more easily established than is the frequency of impairment or disability. Those who are identified as mentally retarded through their backwardness in school or their failure in occupational roles can often be identified from records or interviews. The data from which to determine levels of functional disability in terms of psychometric tests are less likely to be available. To determine levels of impairment in terms of neurological investigation in a population, data are still less likely to be available, and to obtain them requires an elaborate undertaking.

Classification: Level and Diagnosis

The unitary concept of cognitive dysfunction conjured up by the word "mental retardation," it can now be seen, refers in reality to a concept that is unitary only with respect to social handicap. Aside from social handicap, it is difficult to make a single useful statement about mental retardation that remains true across grade of defect, diagnostic category, and age. Preliminary to any analytic epidemiology, a first distinction needs to be drawn between severe and mild retardation (a useful cutoff point is an IQ of about 50).

We have noted that severe mental retardation can be diagnosed at an early age. The dysfunction and handicap are rooted in persisting organic or chemical impairments of the developing brain. The impairments have many known and unknown causes most of which arise prenatally or even before conception, and are distributed fairly evenly across the social classes. It follows that the origin and prevention of much severe retardation must be sought in factors that are antecedent to conception or to birth and that affect all classes.

Mild mental retardation comprises at least three-quarters of the recognized mentally retarded population[2]; it can be diagnosed with confidence only in later childhood (sometimes not until pubescence), and in not more than one-quarter are dysfunction and handicap rooted in organic impairment (of heterogeneous cause). The remaining three-quarters of those described as mildly retarded comprise mainly the cultural-familial

---

[2] In surveys which depend on direct screening and testing of all the target population, this proportion depends on the ceiling for IQ above which cases are not admitted to the diagnosis of mild mental retardation. It depends also on the extent to which criteria other than intellectual performance are taken into consideration in the case count. Examples of surveys illustrating these differences are noted in Table 4. In surveys depending on service records, obviously many other considerations enter into case identification.

In the national population of 19-year-old Dutch men which we studied, the proportion of mild to severe mentally retarded is about 16:1. In this series, the diagnosis is made in terms of anticipated roles to be required of inductees, and there is no intention of providing services. The IQ ceiling for

syndrome noted above; they have functional disabilities without detectable organic impairment, and they have a socal handicap that is, for some, temporary and age bound. This syndrome is heavily over-represented in the social classes at the bottom of the social scale, where precarious incomes, inadequate diet, and large or dysmorphic families are also concentrated (c.f. Susser, 1968). the origin and prevention of much mild mental retardation must be sought in postnatal factors and those that interfere in the acquisition of functional abilities and social roles (Stein et al., 1975).

To our way of thinking, these distinctions need to be drawn early and kept clear. Yet to define grades of defect by applying these "pass/fail" classification systems may influence the careers of individual children adversely, just as creating the dichotomy between normality and mental retardation may do. To create special services for a class of handicapped persons tends to segregate them and often stigmatizes them as inferior, and the true integration of mentally retarded children within a general education and health system is to that extent hindered. Such considerations, as they affect individuals, have fostered the impression that classification as such is an evil to be avoided, even as it affects populations. Thus, one is obliged to argue a case that should be self-evident for the usefulness, indeed the necessity, of classification in the epidemiology of mental retardation. The distinctiveness of clinical syndromes must be recognized in order to make meaningful studies of etiology, to mount effective programs of prevention, and to provide appropriate treatment and care. Without classification, there is no epidemiology and no science.

Uses and Misuses of Records

We have earlier noted the advantages of record systems designed for the purposes of creating and evaluating population-based services. Westin (1967) and others (U.S. DHEW, 1973) have emphasized the dangers inherent in such identification of individuals in a linked record system. Individuals could be harmed and stigmatized through the misuse of records.

Here too the case of the severely retarded population needs to be considered separately from that of the mildly retarded population. The impairments of severe mental retardation are often physically manifest, and the handicaps always socially manifest. Administrative identification through formal registration can hardly add to this visibility, except perhaps in a legal sense.

The case of the mildly retarded stands in sharp contrast. Many people with mild mental retardation escape early identification, for they seldom appear impaired, and their "coming out" is deferred. In some social groups, social visibility is only partial, perhaps

---

mild mental retardation corresponds to about 75. Many subjects who were given the diagnosis had not attended special classes or schools, but few had left school with an achievement beyond elementary school level. Their performance was poor on both IQ and educational achievement tests.

The Dutch population is homogeneous in ethnic terms but not social. There was a six-fold difference in prevalence of mild mental retardation as between sons of manual and non-manual workers. The prevalence of severe mental retardation is much more constant across the classes.

confined to the classroom alone. The usual purpose of administrative identification is to transfer a backward child in a local public school to another class or school that provides for the special needs of slow learners. Whether such transfers achieve their purpose is an important question often asked but not yet clearly answered. Does the slow learner do better in special schools? Do the other interests involved in the transaction (fellow pupils in the original school, teachers, the community educational system) have advantage from the identification and segregation of the mildly retarded child? Does administrative identification of young persons as mentally retarded harm their chances of employment and their social status by stigmatizing them? Does failure to identify such individuals ignore their special needs and allow society to evade responsibility for discovering and providing for those needs?

If there is a benefit from special education and if administrative identification is shown to be harmful to the individual child, then the benefit might be achieved without the unintended harm. Rational policy therefore requires the study of two questions. First, is administrative identification as such likely to be deleterious for the individual child? Second, what are the effects of special classes and schools for backward children for all concerned?

Whatever the effects of administrative identification of affected individuals may turn out to be, both the conduct of such enquiries and the continuous process of creating rational policy require the identification of the affected populations. As we noted above, registers aid greatly in the task of describing needs and evaluating the effects of intervention. Although the purposes and effects of identifying individuals and of identifying populations can and should be kept analytically distinct, in either instance the procedures used and the safeguards needed are much the same. With a feedback system that involves epidemiological surveillance, registration and computerized records, problems of confidentiality take on new dimensions.

To make technology work for and not against citizens and under their control will require special effort. There seems little hope of preventing breaches of confidentiality through unauthorized access to records. There is much better hope of preventing the misuse of confidential information through laws and licensing. Constraints on record usage need not entirely stifle research (Lasker, 1973). For instance, epidemiological surveillance of populations can be carried out, within an acceptable margin of error for unduplicated counts, without the naming of individuals. There is thus every reason to recommend, at the least, the maintenance of anonymous registers for developing policy and maintaining programs for the mildly retarded. On balance, we would incline to go beyond this, and support the maintenance of nominal registers in circumstances where a serious public commitment to the provision of services exists. These registers help to improve the efficiency of care and its evaluation for the individual case.

Prevention

The scientific momentum of the recent historic phase in mental retardation has brought us to the verge of preventive public health programs. There are now some specific possibilities for prevention (Stein, 1975). The realization of each possibility calls for new public health policies that will have many consequences of social concern. We consider five conditions: three conditions, Tay-Sachs disease, a Down's syndrome, and phenylketonuria, are associated with severe mental retardation; a fourth condition, the cultural-familial syndrome, is associated with mild mental retardation; a fifth condition, congenital rubella, may be associated with either severe or mild mental retardation.

In Tay-Sachs disease, which results in death in early childhood, the condition is transmitted by recessive Mendelian inheritance, and the following steps are involved in a preventive program:

Parents must have their blood tested, to see if both are carriers. A pair of carriers can eschew marriage, or the bearing of their own children. Or they may marry and risk pregnancy, monitor each pregnancy by amniocentesis, and elect an induced abortion if the fetus proves to be affected.

In Down's syndrome (mongolism) a preventive program would focus on older women, since older mothers have a greatly increased chance of bearing an affected child. During pregnancy, older women may be monitored by amniocentesis. If the diagnosis of Down's syndrome is made from the presence of an extra 21 chromosome in cells cultured from the amniotic fluid, then, as with Tay-Sachs disease, parents may elect an induced abortion. Thus the prevention of Down's syndrome has been made technically feasible by prenatal diagnosis and elective abortion.

A general question is germane to other conditions like these where the possibility of prevention exists. Should prevention be an option reserved for those who have the good fortune to be informed of it, and who, once informed, are in a situation where the means are available to take the necessary action? Or should a preventive program depend not on individual but on public initiative (Stein, Susser, and Guterman, 1973)? If so, at what stage of technical development should public health agencies undertake the responsibility for setting up programs based on communities rather than on individuals who sporadically come into conjunction with the needed information and the means to act? At present, facilities are available for aminocentesis in a limited number of centers across the United States, mainly to private patients. One of the largest centers is in New York City, and probably more than 75% of high risk pregnant women wover 40 years of age do not at this time have access to these facilities.

In Down's syndrome, the community case for prevention may be more cogent than in Tay-Sachs, because in Down's syndrome, the life expectancy for the condition is much longer, prevalence is rising, and it comprises a sizeable proportion of the severely retarded population. On the other hand, the yield from amniocentesis will be much smaller. The risk of 1 in 4 among couples both of whom carry the Tay-Sachs gene must be compared with 1 in 50 in Down's syndrome even among women over 40 years, and perhaps 1 in 1000 at the youngest ages.

Phenylketonuria (PKU) provides a paradigm for rare metabolic disorders, of which it is the most common. About 1 in 15,000 births are affected, and thus carriers of the recessive trait are about 1 in 50. In PKU, the disorder can be identified among the newborn by simple blood- and urine-screening tests. Dietary treatment of those with the disorder, carried out over 6 or 7 years, can avert the associated mental retardation.

Once screening for PKU is accepted as worthwhile, the question arises as to why screening of the newborn for metabolic defects should be confined solely to this particular defect? The common sense answer is that the balance of benefits and costs with an incidence of about 1 in 15,000 makes it a rational undertaking, but that the lesser yield of still rarer conditions does not. Not all communities make the same assumption. Quebec, for instance, maintains a province-wide program of screening allied with treatment for a wide range of metabolic disorders (Clow et al., 1973). New York State recently extended its screening program of the newborn to cover five metabolic disorders in addition to PKU.

Each of the three causes of severe mental retardation discussed illustrates different strategies for preventive programs. Parents may be screened for abnormal traits. The fetuses at special risk, or all fetuses, may be tested in time for a specific pregnancy to be terminated. The infant may be screened at birth and treated preventively. If all these strategies were adopted, and if at each stage the testing were to include all currently known disorders, the prevalence of severe mental retardation at an early age might be reduced by about 30%.

Cultural-Familial Syndrome

With regard to mild mental retardation, the main hope for prevention is to alleviate the cultural-familial syndrome by modifying the learning environments of children. Strong evidence of environmental effects in individuals comes from studies that have produced IQ changes in children by planned intervention on an experimental model. In at least two instances the intervention achieved dramatic results. One (Garber, "Intervention in Infancy: A Developmental Approach") is reported in this volume.

These studies suggest that if an appropriate intervention starts early enough, continues long enough, and is executed intensively enough, the incidence of the most widespread form of mild mental retardation could be radically reduced.

Intra-uterine infection, exemplified by rubella, but known to occur also with cytomegalovirus (CMV) and toxoplasmosis, is undoubtedly responsible for some cases of mental retardation. Rubella is the best documented example (Chess, Korn, and Fernandez, 1971). Unlike CMV and toxoplasmosis, the main impact occurs in epidemics. Even if epidemic years are averaged out, rubella could be said to have caused mental retardation of recognizable degree in a considerable number of children over the past decade in the United States. Immunization is the first resort for a preventive program against infection. With rubella, CMV, and toxoplasmosis, the approach is eminently feasible, but not without a special ethical problem. Excepting effects on the fetus early in gestation, rubella, like CMV and toxoplasmosis, is virtually harmless. The present program of immunization against rubella, in the United States, is aimed at the total population of school children, with the object of protecting the offspring of the girls among them who may later fall pregnant. The program seeks not so much to provide individual protection as to produce a level of "herd immunity" that will reduce the chances of epidemics occurring. Although no immunization programs are free of costs and complications, they are usually designed for the good of the individual being immunized; he suffers for his own sake. In the case of rubella we have an analogue of a gift relationship, but with the donor probably seldom aware of his gift. Boys and girls are immunized primarily to protect the next generation. Immunization to attain levels of herd immunity sufficient to protect communities is not a new principle in public health. To do so in order to protect generations not yet born may be. Indeed, in Britain, immunization programs for rubella are at present aimed at adolescent girls only. Other preventive approaches against intra-uterine viral infections have been suggested, for instance, monitoring women during pregnancy in order to detect signs of infection.

CONCLUSION

These preventive methods can together bring about remarkable changes in mental retardation. Cases that are in no way preventable are becoming less frequent as we push back the borders of ignorance. The significance of preventive approaches for societies will vary according to values, technical capacity, resources, and the influence of unequal wealth on access to services and culture. These factors will now in turn influence the epidemiology of mental retardation. It is easy to prophesy that the higher the value placed on mental competence, and the more capable, privileged, and aware are particular families, subcultures, and societies, the more will individuals and groups reduce their chances of bearing and rearing children with mental retardation. In these circumstances, societies that value equality of opportunity may not long accept that preventive services are available to parents who are informed and can pay, and to no others. Public health agencies may thereby be provoked to resume their traditional responsibilities for the active pursuit of prevention in communities. With new power, new problems and new responsibilities arise. Decisions will have to be made that will require the creation of new rules and a review of traditional values.

REFERENCES

Akesson, H. O. 1967. Severe mental deficiency in a population in Western Sweden. Acta. Genet. 17: 243.

Allen, R. J., L. Flemin, and R. Spinto. 1967. Variations in Hyperphenylalaninemia in Amino-Acid Metabolism and Genetic Variation. McGraw Hill. New York.

Allen, R. J., G. L. Lowrey, and J. L. Wilson. 1960. The search for phenylketonuria in Michigan. J. of Mich. State Med. Soc. 59: 1809.

Birch, H., S. Richardson, D. Baird, G. Horobin, and R. Illsley. 1970. Mental Subnormality in the Community. Williams & Wilkins. Baltimore.

Carter, C. O. 1958. A life table for mongols with the causes of death. J. Ment. Def. Res. 2: 64.

Chess, S., S. J. Korn, and P. B. Fernandez. 1971. Psychiatric Disorders of Children with Congenital Rubella. Brunner/Mazel. New York.

Clow, C. L., F. C. Fraser, C. Laberge, and C. R. Scriver. 1973. On the application of knowledge to the patient with genetic disease. Prog. Med. Gen. 9: 159.

Collman, R. D. and A. Stoller. 1962. A survey of mongoloid births in Victoria, Australia, 1942–1957. Am. J. Public Health, 52: 813.

Conley, R. W. 1973. The Economics of Mental Retardation. John Hopkins University Press. Baltimore and London.

Crome, L. 1972. Non-specific developmental abnormalities and unclassified mental retardation. In J. B. Cavanagh (ed.), The Brain in Unclassified Mental Retardation. The Williams & Wilkins Co. Baltimore. pp. 283–289.

Czeizel, A. and C. Révész. 1970. Major malformations of the central nervous system in Hungary. Br. J. Prev. Soc. Med. 24: 205.

Davie, R., N. Butler, and H. Goldstein. 1972. From Birth to Seven. Humanities Press. New York.

Drillien, C. M., S. Jameson, and E. M. Wilkinson. 1966. Studies in mental handicap Part I: Prevalence and distribution by clinical type and severity of defect. Arch. Dis. Child. 41: 528.

Ellwood, J. H. 1970. Anencephalus in Belfast. Br. J. Prev. Soc. Med. 24: 78.

Goodman, N. and J. Tizard. 1962. Prevalence of imbecility and idiocy among children. Br. Med. J. 1: 216.

Grossman, H. J. 1973. Manual on Technology and Classification of Mental Retardation. American Association of Mental Deficiency. Washington, D.C.

Hansen, H. 1970. Epidemiological considerations on maternal hyperphenylananinemia. Am. J. Ment. Def. 75: 22.

Harlap, S. 1973. Down's syndrome in West Jerusalem. Am. J. Epidemiol. 97: 225.

Hemmer, R. 1971. The development of hydrocephalic infants treated with ventricular auricular shunts. Dev. Med. Child Neur. Suppl. 25, Vol. 13, No. 6.

Holmes, L. B., A. L. Moser, S. Halldersson, C. Mack, S. S. Pent, and B. Matzolwich. 1972. Mental Retardation. Macmillan Co. Toronto. p. 62.

Imre, P. D. 1973. In P. W. Conley (ed.), The Economics of Mental Retardation. Johns Hopkins University Press. Baltimore.

Kushlick, A. and M. Susser. 1968. Cited in M. Susser, Community Psychiatry. Chapts. 11, 12. Random House, Inc. New York.

Kushlick, A. 1964. The prevalence of recognized mental subnormality of I.Q. under 50 among children in the south of England. Proc. of the Int. Congress on the Scientific Study of Mental Retardation. 2: 550.

Lassker, G. 1973. EEG records for indicating the termination of diet in treatment of Phenylketonuria. Paediatr. Paedol. 8: 187–194.

Lewis, E. O. 1929. Report of the Mental Deficiency Committee, Part IV, His Majesty's Stationery Office, London.

McDonald, A. H. 1973. Severely retarded children in Quebec: prevalence, causes and care. Am. J. Ment. Def. 78: 2.

McIntire, M. S. and H. Q. Adams. 1963. Congenital anomalies associated with mental retardation. Nebraska S.M.J.

Milunsky, A. 1973. The Prenatal Diagnosis of Hereditary Disorders. Springfield, Illinois.

Moser, H. and P. Wolf. 1971. The nosology of mental retardation: Including the report of a survey of 1378 mentally retarded individuals at the Walter E. Fernald State School. Birth Defects: Original Article Series. Vol. 7, No. 1.

Penrose, L. S. 1949. The incidence of mongolism in the general population. J. Ment. Sci. 95: 685.

Postafinski, M. J. 1964. The incidence of preventable forms of brain damage. Virginia Med. Monthly 91: 22.

Rutter, M., P. Graham, and W. Yule. 1970. A Neuropsychiatric Study in Childhood. J. B. Lippincott Co. Philadelphia.

Rutter, M., J. Tizard, and K. Whitmore. 1970. Education, Health and Behaviour. Longman. London.

Schneck, L., C. Valenti, D. Amsterdam, J. Friedland, M. Adachi, and B. W. Volk. 1970. Prenatal diagnosis of Tay-Sachs disease. Lancet 1: 582.

Smith, I. 1974. (letter) Duration of treatment of phenylketonuria. Lancet I: 1229.

Sorel, F. M. 1972. Onderzoek Geestelijk Gehandicapten Amsterdam, Tilburg, Institute for Social Research.

Spain, B. 1973. Treatment patterns and outcomes for spina bifida within Greater London. Dev. Med. Child. Neurol. 15: 115, Suppl. No. 29.

Stark, R. S. and N. Mantel. 1966. Effects of maternal age and birth order on the risk of mongolism and leukemia. J. Natl. Cancer Inst. 37: 687.

Stein, Z. A. 1975. Strategies for the prevention of mental retardation. Bull. N.Y. Acad. Med. 51: 130.

Stein, Z. A., M. W. Susser, and A. V. Guterman. 1973. Screening programme for prevention of Down's syndrome. Lancet 1: 305.

Stein, Z. A., M. Susser, G. Saenger, and F. Marolla. 1975. Famine and Human Development: The Dutch Hunger Winter of 1944/45. Oxford University Press, New York.

Susser, M. W. 1968. Community Psychiatry. Random House. New York.

Susser, M. W. and W. Watson. 1971. Sociology in Medicine. Oxford University Press. London, New York.

Taylor, J. L. 1962. Mental retardation prevalence in Oregon. Oregon State Board of Health.

Tredgold, A. F. 1914. Mental Deficiency. Wood. New York.

U.S. DHEW. 1973. Records, Computers and the Rights of Citizens.

Wald, I. 1968. Epidemiology of low-grade mental deficiency in Poland: organization of the study and method of sampling. Epidemiological Review 12: 245.

Wing, L. 1971. Severely retarded children in a London area: prevalence and provision for services. Psychological Medicine 1: 405.

Yannet, H. 1966. The prevention of mental retardation through control of infectious diseases. U.S. DHEW 1692. p. 28.

ATTITUDES
AND VALUES

Reaction to
Mental Subnormality

Stephen A. Richardson

A prerequisite for examining reactions to mental subnormality is some description of what is encompassed by mental subnormality, mental retardation, mental deficiency, terms which have been used interchangeably. It is clearly not a single etiological entity or a homogeneous syndrome of dysfunction. A characteristic common to all types of mental retardation is intellectual impairment and inability to reach some minimal level of expectation for functioning as a member of society. These expectations vary depending on age and also to some extent on the society in which a person is placed. There may be additional functional impairments: motor, emotional, sensory, and perceptual, and the probability of their occurrence is greater with severe than with mild intellectual impairment. Abnormalities of appearance occur in some clinical subtypes including Down's syndrome, microcephalies, and those with some endocrine disorder. Clearly, in considering reaction to a person, the reaction is to the appearance, manner, and overall functioning of the person and not just the level of intellect. Once a person has been defined as mentally retarded for administrative purposes, people's reactions may be influenced by this classification if they are aware that it has been made. The influence can occur whether the classification was made correctly or incorrectly. The definitions and criteria used in diagnosing mental retardation have varied so much at different times and places and are so generally lacking in explicitness of definition and reliability of measurement that errors in diagnosis have not been uncommon.

In comparing studies of reactions to retardation, a major difficulty is determining to which particular subtype of mental subnormality the results apply, and what reasonable generalizations may be drawn. As will be discussed later, investigators often do not have the information to identify their subjects in an overall epidemiological framework and, reading the studies, one is reminded of the blind men describing the same elephant but differing in their descriptions depending on the part of the elephant they had felt. The range of reports is broadened by the inclusion of those who have been misclassified as mentally retarded. Perhaps the only overall picture of mental subnormality now available is that derived from epidemiological studies.

While mental subnormality, mental handicap, and similar terms are used for administrative purposes, these terms may not be used by or even relevant for many persons in their casual or more intimate social encounters. The process of perceiving a person is influenced by the situation in which the perception takes place and the purpose for which it is being used. For these reasons it is useful to consider the identification of mental retardation in the context of diagnosis and administrative placement for inclusion in special programs, facilities, or services provided for different subtypes of mental subnormality. The form of designation of mental subnormality will be related to the consequences that stem from being administratively classified as mentally subnormal. We shall then consider identification of mental subnormality or some equivalent category used by persons in social contact with others but where the perceiver's judgments are primarily used to guide their own conduct in the interpersonal relation. Throughout, it is necessary to consider the age of the person being judged and the nature, clarity, and multiplicity of cues provided by the person being judged.

HOW IDENTIFICATION OF MENTAL SUBNORMALITY FOR PURPOSES OF ADMINISTRATIVE CLASSIFICATION INFLUENCES REACTIONS   TO THOSE CLASSIFIED

Preschool

For a very small proportion of all cases of mental retardation, positive identification can be made around the 16th week of fetal growth using amniocentesis. Determination of chromosome and enzyme abnormalities can be made from the amniotic fluid, e.g., Down's syndrome. The use of amniocentesis and the termination of pregnancy if the findings are positive, depend on decisions of the pregnant woman and her husband. It is likely that only people who very much want a child will consider amniocentesis, because they have the alternative of terminating the pregnancy without amniocentesis. If their values are strongly against abortion, they may refuse amniocentesis. These values, however, will have to be weighed against their attitudes toward having a child who may be severely mentally handicapped.

The procedure of amniocentesis is used in the hope that the results will be negative and no decision will be necessary about termination of pregnancy. Some medical centers will provide amniocentesis only on the condition that the woman consents in advance to termination of pregnancy in the event of a positive finding. At present far more is known about the medical procedures of amniocentesis and the termination of pregnancy than is known about the psychological reactions and values related to them. The pregnancy woman's values toward Down's syndrome will be influenced by her prior experience and what she learns about the lives of persons with Down's syndrome from the staff at the facility which provides amniocentesis. We also need to know more about a woman's psychological reactions after she has undergone a termination of pregnancy. It is likely that the reactions will include grief and guilt because, as has been noted, amniocentesis will be undergone only by a woman who wants a child.

When amniocentesis is not used, the conditions with the same chromosome and enzyme abnormalities can be identified clinically and by test at birth. A few other medical conditions evident at birth also are highly indicative of retardation. These include microcephaly and hydrocephaly with myelomeningocele. Confident prognosis of mental retardation can be made, however, only on a very small proportion of those who at some time in their lives will be so classified.

We need to know more about how parents are told, following the birth of their child, that the child will be mentally retarded, how parents react, and in what ways parents can best be helped to deal with the news.

In the perinatal and infant stages of development, biological factors can provide statistical indicators of heightened risk of mental retardation when used for a large population. These factors, however, do not provide reliable prediction for individual cases. They include a maternal history of repeated spontaneous abortions, and some complications of pregnancy, low birth weight, and clinical signs of central nervous system damage. Delays in reaching developmental landmarks such as sitting, walking, and speaking are considered at a later age. These kinds of indicators have been used in high risk registers to determine which infants should be followed with especial care because of their greater likelihood of handicap. It should be emphasized that a sizable number of children who may be considered "at risk" develop normally. To the extent they are aware of the risk, parents whose infants have indicators of heightened risk of mental retardation may suffer a considerable period of anxiety and concern until the child reaches the age at which a definitive diagnosis can be made. Among those in health care who identify the indicators of risk and know something about the probabilities of mental retardation there is considerable uncertainty of what to tell the parents and what their role should be in relation to the parents.

So far we have described situations in which the physician is the first to see evidence of mental subnormality and in some cases to make an accurate prediction before or at birth. Perhaps a more common pattern is one in which the initial suspicion and concern that the infant or preschool child is not developing normally arises in the parent, or in a friend, relative, or neighbor who has had experience with other children. Alternatively, staff members of day care centers and kindergartens may be the first to suspect mental retardation for a child in their care. The arousal of concern that something is wrong with the development of the child will occur at different ages depending on the amount of evidence the infant or child provides.

Depending on the kind and severity of the mental subnormality, the identification process may be sudden and definite, or slow and insidious. Where the identification is early, the retardation is likely to be severe. For the parents, the adaptation to the knowledge that their child will be severely retarded can involve a profound shock. Most parents, prior to the birth of their child, have developed some picture of the life course their child will follow. A period of acute grief and mourning for the death of these initial hopes appears to be a necessary early stage in adaptation to the child's handicap. This stage is often accompanied by deep depression and a withdrawal from other people (Strasser and Sievert, 1963; Richardson, 1969). A person undergoing this experience can be helped by the comfort and emotional support of a spouse, relative, friend, or a professional. Unfortunately those who are in the best position to comfort and support have difficulty in playing the role because they also have suffered the same emotional shock. Being a professional does not provide immunity from being strongly emotionally affected.

The more ambitious and aspiring the original hopes and expectations parents have for their child, the greater will be the discrepancy between these hopes and realistic expectations for the future of a mentally subnormal child.

A difficulty for parents is their lack of knowledge or misconceptions about the life course of people with differing degrees of severity of mental subnormality, a lack shared with many professionals. Parents and advisers will react in terms of what limited knowledge or experience they possess. For example, in the film made by the Kennedy Foundation, "Who Should Survive" (1971), the parents withheld permission to operate on their child shortly after birth. Without the operation, the child died. Refusal was based on knowledge that their child had Down's syndrome. The mother was influenced in her decision because she was a nurse and the only children with Down's syndrome she had seen were in a large ward of severely retarded children in a residential institution.

If recognition of mental retardation occurs shortly after birth, if facilities are available for institutionalization, and if this course is advocated by professionals, the parents may take this option. However, institutionalization shortly after birth is often not possible and the infant is cared for at home at least for some years. This gives parents time to get to know their child. While these parents may well need supporting services with the extra burden of care the handicap imposes, they can generally care for the child. Later, in the light of the experience gained with the child at home, they are in a better position to decide whether or not to place the child in residential care, and are better able to evaluate whether or not a particular residence is suitable for their child.

The social and intellectual expectations for the preschool child are less demanding than during school age and the discrepancy in functioning between mentally retarded children and other children is often less marked than at later ages.

School Age

Epidemiological cross-sectional studies show that most severely and moderately retarded children are administratively classified before or shortly after the age of school entry. The remaining mildly retarded children generally become administratively classified around 7 to 8 years of age which is about as early as IQ tests can predict performance over the school years (Mercer, 1973, Birch, et al., 1970). In school, large groups of children of the same age are generally together in classes where they can easily be compared with peers. Furthermore, teachers have training and experience in evaluating behavior, especially those behaviors which interfere with the teaching task. While parents may have evidence that their child seems somewhat backward in development, it is the teacher who often initially identifies mild and moderate retardation. Cues leading to identification vary. A child who is slow in learning and perhaps impeding the teacher's tasks may be seen as disruptive to the class and someone to get rid of. The child may be withdrawn and unresponsive but not a disturbance. Where special educational facilities are available in the school system, the teacher may feel that the child would be better off in these facilities. In general, the more the school system and educational methods emphasize classes which equalize the abilities of the pupils, the more difficult it becomes for the teacher to deal effectively with a child who is a poor learner or lacks social competence.

Generally, the classroom teacher initially identifies slow learners, but it is usually a school psychologist who is primarily responsible for the administrative classification as mentally retarded. While the teachers predict that the child is likely to continue to fail in school work on the basis of classroom performance, the psychologists use intelligence tests. The combined teacher and psychologist evaluations weigh heavily in the decision of whether or not to place the child in special educational facilities. In some school systems a physician is involved in the administrative classification of mental retardation, and he will use a number of medical indicators including a history, evidence of seizures, central nervous system damage, sensory or perceptual impairment.

The three general criteria used in arriving at a clinical decision as to whether a child is mentally retarded are social competence, school performance, and IQ test results. School systems vary greatly in the criteria and procedures used in making an administrative decision that a child is mentally retarded. An influential factor is the extent and nature of special educational facilities available within and outside the school system for children with different degrees and types of mental handicap. Where special educational facilities are inadequate or non-existent, the determination of mental retardation may be used in deciding that a child should be placed with children younger than himself. It has also been used as a reason for removing the child from the educational system.

Once a child is administratively classified as mentally retarded in a school system, it is unlikely that the child will be declassified during the remainder of his schooling. This is partly because the pace is slower in special classes and it becomes increasingly difficult to catch up with the work covered in regular classes. Also, in the cases of errors of classification it may be difficult for the system to admit to having made a mistake. To avoid misclassification some school systems use the benefit of the doubt principle. The child is given the opportunity to stay in a regular class until it is clear that he is unable to cope and is steadily failing in school work. When a shift is made to special education, the child will first be given a trial in a class for educable children even if those responsible believe that the child may be better suited to a class for trainable children.

The parents' reaction to the school's administrative classification of their child as mentally subnormal may be initially negative, although the reaction will be related to many factors: the parents' conception of mental subnormality, how much their knowledge of the child's functioning agrees or disagrees with the view of the educational authority, the kinds of special services available and their reputation locally, the parents' aspirations for their child, and the extent to which the parents have been involved in making the decision.

During the school years, some of the more severely retarded children who had been cared for at home may be moved into residential facilities because the parents may no longer be able to cope with the problems involved in home care. There may be many reasons why the parents are unable to cope. For example, the increased size and weight of the child may make the care of the young person beyond the capacity of the parents' physical strength. The onset of a chronic illness or handicap for the parent may make him or her unable to cope with the daily task of care. The family may break up because of death, divorce, or separation. The parents' decision to seek residential care may be torturous when the only options they have are to go on caring for their child at home with no outside help, or to send their child to a distant residential institution where visiting is difficult and where the quality of care is poor. These alternatives unfortunately have been all that were available to many in the past. Recently, as illustrated in the papers by H. Cohen and A. Kushlick in this volume, more flexible patterns of service have been instigated which include residential care close to the parents' home so that parents can visit and the child can go home for weekends and holidays, short term residential stays when parents need a respite in caring for the child, and various supporting services for the family in the home. Again, the parents' reactions will be heavily influenced by the nature, range and quality of services available.

Post-school Career

After the years of compulsory schooling, the criteria for the administrative classification of mental subnormality do not change very much for the more severely subnormal, but there is considerable change in criteria for evaluating mild mental subnormality. This is suggested by the difference in age-specific prevalence rates for different subtypes. The prevalence of severe retardation remains fairly constant before and after the school years, while the prevalence of mild mental subnormality drops by approximately 50% between the later school years and the middle and late twenties (Susser, 1968; Gruenberg, 1964). Very little is known about what happens to the 50% of the mildly subnormal young people who disappear from administrative note. It is reasonable to expect that most of them attempt to make the steps in socialization expected after leaving school: to find and keep a job, to develop financial independence, to organize their own lives and make their own decisions, to marry and have children, to function as a parent, to develop and maintain some network of family and friendship ties, and to have some spare time interests. There is some evidence that some succeed in taking some or all these steps (Saenger, 1957; Kennedy, 1966; Henshel, 1972). For those unable to succeed, various facilities designed especially for the mentally retarded may be considered, if available. Such facilities include a daytime occupational center, a sheltered workshop, hostel living arrangements with some supervision, or a more total institutional residential facility. An adult may also come to the attention of those who administer special services through the courts as the result of displays of inappropriate, immature, or antisocial behavior. Many kinds of people may be involved in the identification of and services for those who cannot meet the minimal level of intellectual and social expectations appropriate to a given age and role. Parents may seek help, either in the form of service or direct financial aid, if their young adult child continually fails in attempts to get a job and is home all the time, apparently unemployable and with nothing to do. Employers indirectly influence the administrative classification through either refusing to hire a person based solely on previous record, or, after hiring, through dismissing a person as too slow, or incompetent to hold the job. The police and the judicial system apprehend and judge persons who exhibit deviant behavior. In criminal cases in which there is evidence that the person was not responsible for his actions because of intellectual impairment or social incompetence, the case may be referred to those responsible for mental retardation or psychiatric services even though the person had achieved some of the adult socialization steps, such as finding employment. An additional reason for a person coming to administrative attention may be an indirect result of the young person not being accepted by anyone as a spouse. The help and support a spouse can provide may enable a limited young adult to function without special services, whereas without this help, the young adult may fail to manage (Edgerton, 1967). In those communities with well developed social and welfare services, these may provide support sufficient to bridge the gap for the mentally retarded between the two extremes of independence and total dependence.

Older Adulthood

Most adult residential facilities for the mentall retarded take in a sizable number of adults around and after the age of 35 years (Innes, 1973). It is around this time that parents who have been able to maintain their retarded adult children at home become infirm or die, and alternative living arrangements become essential. It is a time dreaded by most parents if the residential facilities for the retarded are of poor quality or far removed from those who have been significant in the life of the retarded adult. It is this older group of parents which have been emphasizing so strongly the need for small group homes or hostels where, after their death, their retarded adult children can continue to live in a familiar environment and maintain long established social relations.

ADMINISTRATIVE CLASSIFICATION
OF MENTAL SUBNORMALITY WHEN FAMILY SUPPORTS FAIL OR DO NOT EXIST

The foregoing description of the administrative classification of individuals is in line with a customary assumption of society that individuals, especially children, form part of a family and that there are adults in the primary or extended family who will take continued responsibility for the children until adulthood. This not only includes care and socialization, but the protection of the rights of the child and functioning as advocates for the child if the agencies of society make mistakes. It is where family supports are weak, fail, or have not existed that many of the errors of classification and placement of the retarded occur.

A second set of conditions in which administrative classification breaks down is where special services of any kind are inadequate, undifferentiated adequately to meet individual needs, or badly overcrowded and understaffed. When these two sets of conditions occur conjointly, severe social injustices may occur to individuals classified under these circumstances. For those who try to operate these services, the fit between individual need and what is available to meet the need is at best a crude approximation. Placement in such traditional institutions as orphanages, reform schools, prisons, mental subnormality and psychiatric institutions may be dictated more by what exists and what is available than by what is most suitable. Under these conditions, administrative classification is sometimes used to provide a label to allow entry into a service facility where there is space, rather than a classification which best fits the individual. There are certain rational bases for mislabeling individuals. A person with administrative authority confronted with a person who has lost all family sources of help and for whom there is an immediate urgent need for some placement may choose a classification which provides the only form of service available and, given this restricted set of options, may be acting in the belief that it is in the best interest of the person who needs help.

Historically some relatively competent persons were retained in mental retardation institutions because they were of value to the institution either through providing skilled unpaid labor, or because they were presented to impress visitors to the institution with the effectiveness of the training and rehabilitation purported to take place at the institution (Binet and Simon, 1914). It is hoped that such practices no longer occur.

OTHER CONSIDERATIONS
OF ADMINISTRATIVE CLASSIFICATION AND ITS CONSEQUENCES

A characteristic of administrative classification of retardation is the separation of the classifier from responsibility for the consequences that stem from that classification. The school psychologist who classifies a child as retarded is not generally involved in organizing or reviewing the quality of the programs in the special classes or schools. The physician who diagnoses a child as severely subnormal and recommends placement in a residential institution usually has no responsibility for the standards of care or the program of the institution and may never have visited the institution or feel a responsibility for evaluating the quality of the institution before recommending placement. Is this separation of responsibility in the best interests of those served by professionals? Exemption of the professional from responsibility for the consequences of his decision reduces the likelihood that collective concern and pressure to improve services will come from professionals.

The values of those engaged in administrative classification of mental retardation and those who operate the services where the retarded person is placed are influenced by the frame of reference developed during their professional training. Specialized training and the ensuing selective attention to different aspects of a person have strongly influenced how the retarded have been regarded, e.g., medical training leads to a physiological, etiological, and pathological conceptual framework. The earlier heavily emphasized genetic view led to concerns about segregation and sterilization, custodial care with emphasis on bodily needs, and an ignoring of social, emotional, and educational needs.

Residential care was also heavily influenced by physicians in administrative positions transferring the hospital model of organization and care to residential institutions for the mentally subnormal, a model which was developed for the care of acute illness when bodily needs are given primary attention, with little or no regard for the social supports and ties that might be provided by the family, neighbors, and friends. At best a benevolent paternalism existed between staff and residents. The belief that mental retardation is predetermined by genetic factors led to a fatalistic view that little could be achieved through social habilitation or rehabilitation. It is interesting that in this country the concept of support of rehabilitation for the physically handicapped is seen as a financial investment that will result in a major return and has been accepted by government. The application of the same concept to mental retardation has gained slower acceptance and is less readily considered by government in setting priorities. And yet some degree of benefit from training and socialization will occur with almost all retarded people. Toilet training and self-feeding for the severely retarded lead to major savings in care over a lifetime, in addition to increasing self-dignity for the retarded person. For the mild mentally subnormal, careful training and socialization in the school years can make the difference between employment and self-support as an adult and the need for continued costly special services and care throughout life.

The training of the teacher and that of the school psychologist provide different perspectives and sets of professional values. The teacher's task is primarily to communicate effectively the school curriculum to the child with predominant emphasis on learning and cognitive ability. The school psychologist is heavily influenced by intelligence test results which were originally devised to predict school performance but which are often used to predict life performance, a highly questionable assumption except at extremes of the test in the mental subnormality range. Both teacher and psychologist are involved in determining whether a child should stay in regular classes or be placed in alternative educational programs. They, like the physicians, get to know the child in a specific setting and often do not consider the child in the context of his home environment and the influence his home has on the child.

THE IDENTIFICATION OF MENTAL RETARDATION
OUTSIDE OF THE ADMINISTRATIVE CLASSIFICATION PROCESS

The administrative classification process of mental retardation has been discussed first because the consequences of classification, both positive and negative, can be profound and long lasting for the person classified. A different recognition process occurs in the daily round of social intercourse. In every social interaction the perceiver's behavior is influenced by the characteristics of the person perceived. Further, individuals differ in the cues of behavior they pay attention and react to in others. What, then, is the evidence that is used in social interaction in forming judgments that a person is retarded, slow, stupid, or whatever categories the perceiver uses in assessing others? The general classes of evidence are cues of behavior, appearance, and movement.

Behavior

A person shows unusual slowness in grasping ideas or concepts.

A person's speech shows a limited vocabulary, simple and sometimes incorrect sentence structure, little use of ideas, concepts, and abstractions, and sometimes slow tempo. The topics and interests expressed are limited.

The behavior and interests appear immature and more appropriate to a person of a younger age.

The behavior exhibited appears inappropriate to the social context in which it occurs, or is behavior not generally exhibited in public.

Forms of non-verbal behavior such as eye contact, facial expression, use of personal space, and gesture do not conform with norms and expectations.

More generally, a person seems broadly lacking in social competence and interpersonal skills.

Appearance

There appears to be a widespread belief that mental retardation can be identified by physical cues. These beliefs stem in part from phrenology and the work of Lombroso that led to the belief that there are physical stigmata of degeneracy. Later studies by Galton and Tredgold and Burke indicated far more uncertainty in the relation between physical stigmata and mental retardation (Clarke and Clarke, 1965). Clarke and Clarke concluded, "But apart from physical signs associated with specific diseases, no useful correlation has been found between physical abnormalities and mental growth or development" (p. 168). Nevertheless, it is not unusual to hear the comment that someone does or does not "look like a retarded person." The physical cues that may be used include characteristics associated with Down's syndrome, body proportions which are asymmetrical or abnormal, unusual facial features, and unusual degrees of ugliness. In addition to the physical features, unusual, inappropriate, or bizarre clothing may be considered as evidence of mental subnormality.

Movement

Cues which may be used as supporting evidence of mental subnormality include unusual gait, clumsiness, lack of control of bodily movements and facial expression, drooling and lack of mouth, eye, and tongue control. In general, any physical handicap which is visible, with or without a person moving, may be used as evidence. A review of epidemiological studies of more severe retardation (IQ less than 50) concludes that about half of this population have associated handicaps (Abramowicz et al., 1975). For the population with cerebral palsy, for example, about half will have an IQ of less than 75 (Rutter et al., 1970, p. 138). This places this population at increased risk of retardation but does not permit confident prediction of intelligence for individual cases from appearances and movement.

Common to the perception of behavior, appearance, and movement cues is that the person perceived does not meet the minimal or normative expectations of the perceiver. There is evidence that very early in life people develop a schema or set of norms they expect others to exhibit in their behavior, appearance, movement, and manner. This schema allows for some variation around the expected norms. If, however, the variation is too great, a violation of expectation occurs. This violation evokes responses in the perceiver which have important consequences for the socialization and interpersonal relations of the person who commits the violation. The responses in the perceiver include fear and anxiety (Kagan, 1968), a lessened preference for the violator (Richardson et al., 1972a), formal, inhibited, overcontrolled behavior, avoidance of intimacy, and an absence of spontaneity and emotional arousal (Kleck et al., 1966). The violation often leads to a focus on the characteristic which caused the violation with relative neglect of the violator's other personal attributes (Davis, 1961). From the initial violation of expectation, more general consequences may follow. For the violator there will be a reduction in the quality and quantity of experiences needed to learn and develop social skills as the result of being left out of social events and avoided in interpersonal contacts. There is a tendency to shelter and protect the violator to such a degree that he or she is often not given the opportunity to learn from the experience of mistakes (Richardson, 1972b). The focus on what is wrong with the violator of expectations deflects attention from helping him to develop skills that are esteemed in the society and which would result in successes and increased prestige for the violator.

The studies which report these consequences of inappropriate behavior and appearance have focused primarily on the initial phases of interpersonal relationships. There is some evidence that the characteristic which initially causes the violation of expectation becomes of decreasing importance as other attributes of the violator become known (Davis, 1961). The extent to which violations of expectation occur will vary with the prior experience of the perceiver and with the particular form of the violation. Among those without prior experience there is considerable variation in the extent to which their behavior is influenced by the violation (Kleck et al., 1966).

In addition to cues of appearance, movement, and behavior, a person may be told that someone is retarded or see that person in or connected with a special service for the retarded, e.g., a child is seen waiting on the corner to take a special bus which transports children to a special school for educable children. A person may also be influenced in their behavior toward someone if they are told that he or she is "slow," "stupid," "dumb," etc. We need to know more about what the term mental retardation and equivalent terms conjure up for a person given this information, and how it influences that person's behavior toward the person who has been so classified. How is it related to that person's prior direct experience with mental retardation and how does it relate to secondhand experience gained from individuals, literature, and the mass media? To what extent does reaction include any understanding of the wide range of subtypes included in the general term?

The amount of personal experience people have with those who are administratively defined as retarded will be influenced by the nature of the services provided. Where services emphasize segregation of the mentally retarded, in special schools, by exclusion from schools with the child homebound, or by placement in large total institutions in isolated locations away from population centers, interpersonal contact between those who are and are not retarded will be reduced. Where services are maintained within the local community with encouragement of participation by retarded persons in community activities and organizations, contacts between those who are and are not retarded will be greater. More generally, the more the society is stratified and segregated by income, color, ability, and handicap, the narrower becomes the body of interpersonal experience a person gains. Where the personal characteristics of the individuals in a community are more heterogeneous and when over time there is a high level of interpersonal relations, then it may be expected that violation of expectations will occur less often with resultant reduction in fear and anxiety.

So far the negative consequences of violation of expectation have been emphasized. They may be more common when the violating attributes of the person are strikingly apparent and/or multiple. For the majority of persons who are mentally subnormal, violations of expectation will be few and not strikingly apparent. When differences are noted by the perceiver, they may provide him with cues which enable him to adapt in ways which are beneficial to the interpersonal relationship. The perceiver may adapt his language, expression of thought, tempo of speech, and level of expectation and thereby enable the retarded person to function in a way that is comfortable and congenial and prevent him from feeling inadequate or incompetent. The perceiver may also be able to identify the functional assets of the retarded person and encourage their use. How often this occurs, the ways in which it occurs, and with whom are questions that need further research. It has been pointed out that these attempts are sometimes clumsy or patronizing (Edgerton, 1967). This does not mean they have to continue to be so.

The minimal level of expectation for another's appearance, manner, and behavior is influenced by the social history of the perceiver and the particular setting in which the interpersonal relation occurs. For example, there is evidence (Birch et al., 1970; Douglas, 1956) that the average IQ is related to social class. In Aberdeen, for example, children in families where the head of the household had a non-manual occupation had an average IQ 15 points higher than children in families where the head of the household was a non-skilled manual laborer. Between these extremes there is a step progression downward in IQ from upper to lower social class families. In upper social class settings, a child with a low IQ will probably be more noticeable because of higher levels of expectation. The extent to which low intelligence will be a source of serious concern may also vary depending on the social ambitions and aspirations of the parents. When these are high and central in their thinking, a child who is even marginally mentally subnormal is likely not to meet their minimal level of expectations for intellectual performance. The schools also reflect different intellectual expectations for their pupils. A school whose aim is to prepare the maximum number for admission to socially prestigious, private schools and colleges will be less accepting of a retarded child than one that has a broader concern for the overall development of a child's personal characteristics and abilities. The value placed on intellect in the overall scale of human values will also influence reaction to mental subnormality (Lippman, 1972). It has been suggested, for example, that in Israel, kibbutzim members who are emotionally disturbed are given support and understanding and helped within the kibbutz, whereas the reaction to mental retardation is less tolerant, and the retarded person may well be placed for care outside of the kibbutz (Chigier, Personal Communication).

It is difficult to give a general picture of the identification and reaction to mental subnormality, given the wide differences in values. These vary from place to place at any one time and even more across time. Statements of objectives and policies by those responsible for retardation services are difficult to find. Kushlick (1965), in a paper on residential services points out:

> It has been noted by many students of organizations that the top management of organizations which process people (schools, social agencies, hospitals, etc.) seldom, if ever, declare in documents their specific objectives, or the specific tasks which are necessary to ensure that these objectives are to be achieved. If stated at all, the objectives are very *general,* and it appears to be assumed by top management that the specific objectives are not only obvious, and therefore agreed by everyone concerned in the organization, but that the necessary tasks are being carried out as effectively as is possible by all concerned.

One of the few clear and direct statements of principles to guide the care of those who are mentally subnormal and in residential care has been written by Karl Grunewald (1969), Head of the Division for Mental Retardation, National Board of Health and Welfare, Sweden. He states that every attempt should be made to achieve the following aims:

> retardates should live in as normal a way as possible, with their own room, and in a small group; they should live in a bisexual world; retardates should experience a normal daily rhythm; they should work in an environment different from that in which they live; they should eat in a small group, as in a family, with food and drink standing on the tables; they should be able to choose between different ways of spending their free time; their leisure pursuits should be individually designed, and differentiated according to the time of year; the environment should be adjusted to the age of the retardate; retarded young people should be given the opportunity to try out adult activities and forms of life, and be able to detach themselves from their parents.

Further, Grunewald outlines the following requirements for any institution in which those who are mentally retarded live:

> that it be organized on the principle of the small group; that the physical standard of the institution reduces collective facilities to a minimum, i.e. in respect to toilets, basins and showers, bedrooms, etc.; that the institution be situated within a community; that the institution should not be larger than would permit the assimilation of those living there into the community; that the social contacts of the institution be freely developed in both directions; that the institution should consistently work in cooperation with parents, relatives and the retarded person themselves.

A statement made 60 years ago by Fernald reflects some of the changes in reactions to mental retardation since that time:

> . . . The feebleminded are a parasitic, predatory class, never capable of self-support or of managing their own affairs. The great majority ultimately become public charges in some form. They cause unutterable sorrow at home and are a menace and danger to

the community. Feebleminded women are almost invariably immoral. . . . Every feebleminded person, especially the high grade imbecile, is a potential criminal, needing only the proper environment and opportunity for the development of expression of his criminal tendencies (Quoted in Clarke and Clarke, 1965, p. 16).

It is difficult, in reading recent behavioral studies of mental retardation, to know where, in time, values, and kinds and quality of services, to set the results.

In examining studies which have focused on mild and moderate retardation, it is useful to consider the potential population of those who might be administratively defined as retarded including both those who are and are not classified and then for each of these subsets to consider the beneficial and harmful consequences of each status. This approach is summarized in Table 1.

Predominant attention has been paid to those who are classified as retarded and to the harmful consequences (cell 4).

Two recent books by Edgerton (1967) and the Braginskys (1971) have selected for study people who had been or were, at the time of the study, in residential facilities. For Edgerton, a major theme was the "stigma in the lives of the mentally retarded," the subtitle of the book. Edgerton was influenced in his conceptualization by Goffman's book, *Stigma,* (1963). In the concluding chapter, Edgerton writes that ". . . stigma . . . galvanizes the most basic feelings of these retarded persons into a single-minded effort to 'pass' and to 'deny'," and ". . . To find oneself regarded as a mental retardate is to be burdened by a shattering stigma." Since the purpose of the study "was to examine some of the ways in which mentally retarded persons manage their lives and perceive them-selves when left to their own devices in a large city, the choice of a population was decidedly limited. Most such persons are either formally institutionalized or have their lives managed for them by their own relatives, by foster families or by other parental surrogates" (p. 9). Subjects were selected for the study on the following criteria: 1) they were near the upper limits of the mildly retarded range, in terms of both their measured IQ and their estimated social competence; 2) they must have been free of the supervision or guardianship of parents, relatives, or friends; 3) they had been residents of a mental retardation institution. They "represented the upper stratum of the hospitals' mildly retarded patients in regard to their IQ, their demonstrated social competence, and their demonstrated emotional stability" (p. 10). Fifty-five men and 55 women were studied whose mean age was 34.6 years. What is striking is that their average stay in the institution had been 20.6 years, an average of well over half their lives, so that many must

Table 1. Potential candidates for administrative classification as mentally retarded

Consequences of administrative classification	Not classified	Classified
Beneficial	1	2
Harmful	3	4

have been in institutions since childhood. Nothing is said about the reasons why they were initially institutionalized, but with the changes in values and ways of identifying and classifying mental retardation, it is likely that, were they 20 years younger, most would not have been institutionalized. The 20 years of institutional life had two major effects. One was the limitation on socialization and social experience resulting from the confinement. The other was their recognition of how they had been misjudged and mistreated by being placed among people who were clearly far more intellectually impaired then they were. These particular circumstances may have been a major contributing factor to their feelings of stigma.

The Braginskys studied children in residential institutions for the mentally retarded and examined their effectiveness in interpersonal manipulation and their styles of adaptation to the institution. They also examined the values of the staff. They summarize their findings as follows:

> The portrait of the retardate that has emerged in this book is that of an adept, rational, sensitive, resourceful and intelligent human being . . . we found that they had not only acquired a manipulative interpersonal orientation, but that they were able to carry out successfully subtle manipulative strategies. They were capable of protecting the self-interests by using complex tactics of impression management, such as ingratiating themselves with the staff and controlling their IQ test scores in order to appear either bright or dull (p. 174).

The title of the book, *Hansels and Gretels,* was chosen on the assumption that today these children from the folktale would be diagnosed as mentally retarded. "Their lack of formal education, their rejecting parents and their general impoverishment would ensure poor performance on intelligence tests" (p. 159). The authors are influenced by Farber's view that, "The so-called culturally disadvantaged are included in the surplus population but the surplus population is by no means restricted to them" (Quoted from p. 163 of Braginsky). The Braginskys summarize their position as follows:

> In short, society's response to the surplus poor is to stigmatize them (with a helpful hand from the professionals) by invoking putative defects in order to explain why their behavior is different from that of the mainstream. The first step in this process is to misconstrue the meaning of lower-class behavior and to create a negative myth about the basic "nature" of the poor. After they have been defined as deviant, criteria which offer evidence of their deficiencies are constructed, which, in turn, allow for their exclusion from meaningful participation in society.
>
> This procedure is, in fact, identical to the steps taken to transform a child into a mental retardate.

The Braginskys develop the view that the milder forms of mental retardation are largely a myth and a way that society has developed for handling surplus children.

Again, it is important to consider the nature of the population which provides the bases for the findings. The study was done at two training schools. "First they were large, having a resident population of well over 1000" (p. 41). It is not clear if this number is for each school or is the combined number, so it may be approximately 1200 or 2400. "The subjects met the following criteria: a) educable; b) probably cultural familial retardates—that is they did not have any obvious organic impairment accounting for the low IQ scores; c) judged by the training school staff to be capable of a relatively high degree of self-management. These criteria were met by approximately 40% of the residents" (p. 42). Forty percent gives 480 or 960 children. From this group, 177 subjects were selected. For some of the experimental studies, smaller samples were used. No information is given on how the 177 subjects or smaller samples were selected. The total of 177 subjects represents 37% or 18½% of the population who met the criteria for the study and 15% or 7½% of the total population of the training schools. The average age of the subjects was 20 years and the average residence in the school 10 years or half their lives. The Braginskys' findings strongly suggest that their subjects were not mentally retarded, taking into account the criterion of social competence, a central criterion after leaving school. The findings and methods of selection suggest their subjects may be among the most intellectually competent at the institution. From this highly atypical population within the institutions studied widespread generalizations are made about mental retardation. Seen in this context, the conclusions of the Braginskys appear unfounded.

Examination of the Edgerton and Braginsky studies suggests that in both cases a highly select subpopulation of institutional residents formed the basis for the findings. The administrative classification was made for subjects in these studies 10 to 20 years ago and consisted of young people whose family supports had failed or were missing and where misclassification was used to fit them into an inadequate undifferentiated set of social services. The studies make major contributions in highlighting the negative consequences of some administrative classification 10 to 20 years ago and there is reason to believe that where poor services still exist the same thing is happening today. The studies have also helped show that there are people in institutions who could function in the society with considerable degrees of independence and the results have contributed to the major thrust now being made in the direction of moving institutionalized people back into the community and trying to undo injustices that have been done.

However, the studies are misinterpreted if the results are generalized to condemn all forms of administrative classification of mental subnormality as having largely negative consequences, or to regard the persons studied as generally representative of mild or moderate mental subnormality. The consequences for persons classified as mentally subnormal in the present or future may be very different than for those of the past and may no longer be as detrimental.

The concern for the negative consequences of classification has been growing in recent years, and studies of children not institutionalized but placed in special classes have been conducted to examine the stigmatization that may arise out of special school placement (MacMillan et al., 1974). The overdependence on IQ as a major criterion in making administrative decisions on classification has been attacked in a number of court cases. The term "labeling" has increasingly been used in place of "administrative classification." Labeling has picked up many negative connotations to the point that it has become almost synonymous with stigmatizing. Mercer, in her recent book on *Labeling the Mentally Retarded* (1973), has studied those who are called mentally retarded by the different private and public agencies in a community covering many facets of community life. She also studied the steps in the labeling process in the public schools. It is implied, but not shown, that being labeled as mentally retarded will have deleterious consequences for the child, but the possibility of benefits of special classes is not examined. This is obviously a difficult issue to study. First, it is clearly necessary to go beyond cell 4 of Table 1 and study the other cells of the two-way table. Again, implicit in the recent focus on cell 4 has been the assumption that the consequences of classification are always harmful.

Because of the almost total absence of studies of children in cells 1, 2, and 3, comments of teachers and parents have to be depended on. In a follow-up of young adults who had attended special schools for the retarded in a city in Scotland, we interviewed a number of parents who recalled that they were initially upset by the news that their child was being moved to a special school. However, many also reported that after the child had attended the special school for a while, his behavior improved, there was reduction in anxiety, a gain of self-confidence, and a feeling of greater security and happiness in the special school. Often, for the first time, the child began to learn. Many parents came to feel that the shift had benefited the child and they came to support the action of special placement (cell 2).

For the children with borderline mental subnormality who remain in regular classes, the absence of being labeled as mentally retarded does not mean that they have no problems. Yet, the social system approach to mental retardation sounds at times like the third of the three baseball umpires discussing how they called balls and strikes. The first umpire said, "I calls it as it is." The second said, "I calls it as I sees it," while the third umpire said, "It ain't nothing until I calls it." Children, unlike pitches, can have real problems and difficulties in regular classes without being "called" or administratively classified as mentally retarded. Further, if the intellectual impairment is sufficiently severe, identification of the child may occur whether or not the child is labeled as mentally retarded. The absence of classification also prevents the child from receiving whatever services are received by those classified. The overall consequences of classification cannot be considered without knowing the quality and nature of these services and balancing their possible advantages to the child with the disadvantages that obtain if the child is classified. For the child who is having real problems with school work, remaining in regular classes is likely to mean that he will have difficulty in achieving any form of legitimate success or status at school, and it can be devastating for a child's self-confidence to be continually failing to live up to others' expectations. Without a classification which exempts them from normal expectations, their poor performance may be interpreted as the result of inattention, laziness, or poor study habits. They can easily become the scapegoat of teachers and peers and develop resentment against authority figures. They may also seek to achieve some status among peers through delinquent and deviant behavior. Where classes are large and teachers are not highly skilled, the teacher may give up trying with the child who is then tolerated but not taught. Such children, if they are classified as retarded and placed in special classes or special schools, can receive more care and understanding, and a pace and type of education that will better enable them to develop their functional capacities and prepare them for living after the school years. A careful study of the advantages and disadvantages may lead to findings which suggest how the harmful consequences of classification may be reduced.

An unintended but beneficial consequence of classifying children as mentally retarded has been the impetus to the development of parent organizations which have been and continue to be a powerful social and political influence in drawing attention to the problems of retarded children and obtaining better services and better public understanding of mental retardation.

A major purpose of schooling is to prepare children for adult life. Evaluation of the consequences of placing a child in a special program should then include a follow-up of children in adulthood. A number of these studies has been carried out (Charles, 1953; Ferguson and Kerr, 1955, 1958; Kennedy, 1948, 1966; Ramer, 1946; Saenger, 1957; Tobias et al., 1969). These studies have shown that of the young people who were the products of special education were able to live in the community away from their parents' home, many found employment and some married, raised families, and were able to function in the adult society. Others required various degrees of social and economic assistance and some experienced real problems in achieving satisfactory living conditions. The results have contributed to the development of a more balanced view of both the possibilities and the limitations of persons with various degrees of mental retardation. They have focused attention on serious and neglected problems and have challenged earlier dogmatic and limited conceptualizations of mental retardation, dealing with both the causes and consequences of mental retardation and the effects of educational and vocational training.

There are, however, a number of methodological and substantive limitations which make it difficult to generalize about the studies or apply them to some of the contemporary issues in the field of mental subnormality:

1. The studies are largely retrospective, with limited information on the subjects when they were of school age.

2. The criterion for inclusion in the studies has predominantly been placement in special educational facilities for the mentally handicapped, and sometimes the availability of the IQ score.

3. Often the study population includes a heavy representation of individuals from minority groups or recent immigrants.

4. The nature of the selection process for special educational placement is not known.

5. Few of the studies have any comparison group obtained from the same school or residential area, so it is not possible to interpret the extent to which their functioning in later life and place in society are consequences of intellectual impairment. Kennedy did use a comparison population. In these studies, subjects were selected who had been classified in the 1938 census as "morons" and who had IQ's of 45 to 75. Comparisons were chosen from classmates in the first grade and matched on a number of variables. Unfortunately, no IQ scores were available for the comparisons.

6. Because total populations of mentally subnormal young persons have not been followed-up, it has not been possible to examine the subsequent life histories of young persons with different subtypes of mental subnormalities living in the same community.

There are a number of questions and issues which have been largely ignored in all follow-up studies. No study encompasses all degrees and subtypes of mental subnormality from the most severe to borderline. Further, children who are borderline or mildly retarded but were allowed to remain in regular schools have been ignored. It is not known how they function in later life compared to the children who have equivalent IQ's, but were placed in special classes for mentally subnormal children.

The studies have not examined the socialization processes of young people with different levels of mental subnormality as they progress from childhood through adolescence to adulthood. Rather, the emphasis has been on cross-sectional analysis of adults, examining such questions as proportion employed or unemployed, type of job, and marital status. Missing from the studies is a dynamic approach emphasizing process and dealing with the nature of the social environment at different age levels and stages of their development, their experiences with their families, and the various institutions that impinge on and influence their lives.

In summary, then, there has been major attention in recent years given to the negative consequences of administrative classification of children as mentally retarded, with widespread search for evidence to illustrate the nature and manifestations of stigma. The studies have not sufficiently considered the kinds and quality of the services which follow classification. A more balanced view is now needed to focus on the possible benefits of administrative classification, and on both the harmful and beneficial consequences of withholding the administrative classification of retardation when a child is referred for consideration.

Previous work has provided important advances in knowledge. But the role of stigma in mental retardation may have been overgeneralized and overstated because of studies of persons who were misclassified as mentally retarded 1 or 2 decades in the past. There is need in future research for an examination of the interpersonal transactions between those who are and are not mentally subnormal: the perceptual cues used in identification, how these vary, the meaning of terms such as mental retardation and how these influence the social relationship, and how the behavior of a person changes when he recognizes that he is encountering someone who is intellectually impaired.

REFERENCES

Abramowicz, H. and S. A. Richardson. 1975. Epidemiology of severe mental subnormality: Review of community studies. Am. J. Ment. Defic. (In press)

Binet and Simon. 1914. Mentally Defective Children. Longmans, Green and Co. New York.

Birch, H. G., S. A. Richardson, D. Baird, G. Horobin, and R. Illsley. 1970. Mental Subnormality in the Community: A Clinical and Epidemiologic Study. The Williams & Wilkins Co. Baltimore.

Braginsky, D. D. and B. M. Braginsky. 1971. Hansels and Gretels — Studies of Children in Institutions for the Mentally Retarded. Holt, Rinehart and Winston, Inc. New York.

Charles, D. C. 1953. Ability and accomplishment of persons earlier judged mentally deficient. Genet. Psychol. Monog. 47: 3—71.

Clarke, A. M. and A. D. B. Clarke. 1965. Mental Deficiency — The Changing Outlook. Methuen & Co. Ltd. London.

Davis, F. 1961. Deviance disavowal and normalization. Social Problems 9(2): 120—132.

Douglas, J. W. B. 1956. Mental ability and school achievement of premature children at 8 years of age. Br. Med. J. 1: 1210—1214.

Edgerton, R. B. 1967. The Cloak of Competence — Stigma in the Lives of the Mentally Retarded. University of California Press. Berkeley.

Ferguson, T. and A. W. Kerr. 1955. After-histories of girls educated in special schools for mentally handicapped children. Glas. Med. J. 36: 50—56.

Ferguson, T. and A. W. Kerr. 1958. After histories of boys educated in special schools for mentally handicapped children. Scot. Med. J. 3: 31—38.

Goffman, I. 1963. Stigma—Notes on the Management of Spoiled Identity. Prentice-Hall Inc. Englewood Cliffs, N.J.

Gruenberg, E. M. 1964. Epidemiology. In H. A. Stevens and R. Heber (eds.), Mental Retardation. University of Chicago Press. Chicago.

Grunewald, K. 1969. The Mentally Retarded in Sweden. Publication of the Division for Mental Retardation, National Board of Health and Welfare.

Henshel, A. 1972. The Forgotten Ones. University of Texas Press. Austin and London.

Innes, G. 1973. Multi-disciplinary study of mental subnormality in northeast Scotland. Third World Congress, I.A.S.S.M.D., the Hague.

Kagan, J. 1968. The many faces of response. Psychology Today 1: 22—27, 60.

Kennedy, R. J. 1948. The Social Adjustment of Morons in a Connecticut City. Mansfield-Southbury Training Schools. Hartford.

Kennedy, R. J. 1966. A Connecticut Community Revisited: A Study of the Social Adjustment of a Group of Mentally Deficient Adults in 1948 and 1960. Connecticut State Department of Health, Office of Mental Retardation. Hartford.

Kleck, R., H. Ono, and A. H. Hastorf. 1966. The effects of physical deviance upon face-to-face interaction. Human Relations 19(4): 425—436.

Kushlick, A. 1965. Community services for the mentally subnormal: A plan for experimental evaluation. Proc. R. Soc. Med. 58: 5, 374—380.

Lippman, L. 1972. Attitudes Toward the Handicapped. Charles C Thomas. Springfield, Illinois.

MacMillan, D. A., R. L. Jones, and G. F. Aloia. 1974. The mentally retarded label: A theoretical analysis and review of research. Am. J. Ment. Defic. 79: 241—261.

Mercer, J. R. 1973. Labeling the Mentally Retarded. University of California Press. Berkeley.

Ramer, T. 1946. The prognosis of mentally retarded children. Acta. Psychiat. Neurol. 41(Suppl.): 1—142.

Richardson, S. A. 1972a. People with cerebral palsy talk for themselves. Develop. Med. Child Neurol. 14: 524—535.

Richardson, S. A. and M. J. Friedman. 1972b. Social factors related to children's accuracy in learning peer group values toward handicaps. Human Relations 26: 77—87.

Richardson, S. A. 1969. The effect of physical disability on the socialization of a child. *In* D. A. Goslin (ed.), Handbook of Socialization Theory and Research. Rand McNally & Co. Chicago.

Rutter, M., P. Graham, and W. Yule. 1970. A Neuropsychiatric Study in Childhood. Spastics International Medical Publications in Association with William Heinemann Medical Books Ltd. London.

Saenger, G. 1957. The Adjustment of Severely Retarded Adults in the Community. A report to the New York State Interdepartmental Health Resources Board. Albany, New York.

Strasser, H. and G. Sievert. 1963. Some psycho-social aspects of ectromelia: A preliminary report of a research study. *In* C. A. Swinyard (ed.), Proceedings of a Conference on Human Limb Development and Mal-development with Special Reference to Experimental Teratogenesis and Medical Management of Limb Deficiencies. Association for the Aid of Crippled Children. New York.

Susser, M. 1968. Community Psychiatry. Random House. New York.

Tobias, J., A. Alpert, and A. Birenbaum. 1969. A Survey of the Employment Status of Mentally Retarded Adults in New York City. Report to the Office of Manpower Research, Manpower Administration, U.S. Department of Labor.

Who Should Survive. 1971. Joseph P. Kennedy, Jr. Foundation, International Symposium on Human Rights, Retardation and Research: Choices on our Conscience. Charles Guggenheim, Producer. Washington, D.C.

Public, Peer, and Professional Attitudes toward Mentally Retarded Persons[1]

Jay Gottlieb

Of what value is it to retarded people to study the attitudes of others toward them? One answer to this question is that a knowledge of attitudes is of importance in providing clues as to why certain programs exist, how professional services are delivered, what legislation becomes enacted, and generally, how the retarded person's life style is affected. The underlying assumption is that when attitudes toward retarded people are favorable, more enlightened treatment of them will ensue; when attitudes are not favorable, the retarded will continue to suffer, as they have in the past, and remain in a more unenviable position in society than may be necessary. The intent here is to review the literature of public, peer, and professional attitudes toward the retarded, and some of its limitations, as an indicator of actions having impact on the lives of mentally retarded people.

In very recent years, there has been an increasingly accelerating movement to provide normalizing experiences for mentally retarded people, both in the community and in school. Plans for deinstitutionalization are being developed across the country. Many of these plans call for the establishment of community-based facilities to house, care for, and, in some cases, employ mentally retarded adults. Similarly, plans are being developed to deinstitutionalize mentally retarded children by sending them to community day schools in towns where their parents reside. Undoubtedly, the extent to which the community-based programs will be successful will be determined, in large part, by the acceptance of the community residents. We have only to look at similar programs to deinstitutionalize mentally ill individuals, who are the victims of similar public stereotypes as are the mentally retarded (Guskin, 1963) to realize the importance of community acceptance (*New York Times,* April 28, 1974). It is doubtful that a community-based program can succeed without community acceptance.

[1] The author wishes to thank Dr. Louise Corman for her critical reading of the manuscript and her many helpful editorial suggestions.

99

Public schools, too, are providing normalizing experiences for their retarded populations. Motivated by court suits, legislative mandates, the failure of research to demonstrate the superiority of special classes, and the purported negative effects of labeling, many school systems are abolishing their segregated, special classes and reintegrating their mentally retarded populations into the regular grades. Here also it is not unrealistic to expect that the attitudes maintained by the regular class teachers and peers will influence the newly integrated child's adjustment to his educational placement.

Given the importance of knowing attitudes toward the mentally retarded, a logical question at this time is, what do we know about these attitudes? Unfortunately, a simple answer to this question is not forthcoming. Research data regarding attitudes toward the mentally retarded are, for the most part, confusing and contradictory. To illustrate, relative to non-retarded children, peer attitudes toward mentally retarded children have been found to be rejecting (Johnson, 1950; Johnson and Kirk, 1950; Heber, 1956), nonaccepting (Miller, 1956), tolerating (Lapp, 1957), similar (Renz and Simensen, 1969), and significantly more accepting by same-sex peers (Bruininks, Rynders, and Gross, 1974). Retarded children are said to be stigmatized and described in negative terms by their non-retarded peers (Dunn, 1968; Christoplos and Renz, 1969), yet data indicate that non-retarded children do not employ denigrating terms when describing them (Clark, 1964; Renz and Simensen, 1969). Contact with retarded people has been found to be related to positive attitudes (Jaffe, 1966; Gottwald, 1970), negative attitudes (Goodman, Gottlieb, and Harrsion, 1972; Gottlieb and Budoff, 1973), and not related (Strauch, 1970). Further, knowledge of retarded individuals has been hypothesized to be associated with more favorable attitudes (Christoplos and Renz, 1969), yet special education teachers who have greater knowledge of mental retardation than general education teachers do not express more favorable attitudes (Semmel, 1959; Greene and Retish, 1973). Finally, we have often heard how attitudes toward the retarded in Europe, particularly in Scandinavia, are more favorable than in the United States (Lippman, 1972). Yet, the few studies that compared attitudes cross-culturally have failed to substantiate these differences (Jordan, 1969; Gottlieb, 1972).

Before the question regarding what we know about attitudes toward the retarded is answerable, we must first establish who the retarded are who are the objects of the attitude statements.

THE OBJECT REFERENT IN ATTITUDE STUDIES

One of the most critical limitations in the study of attitudes toward retarded people is the failure of most research to specify precisely the characteristics of individuals whom the respondent believes to be mentally retarded. If the referent of attitude studies is not constant, but varies from study to study, it becomes exceedingly difficult to synthesize the information and develop a meaningful statement regarding attitudes toward mentally retarded people. Although the referent, mentally retarded person, may differ in any number of ways that could logically affect attitude scores, two of the most compelling are: 1) the severity of retardation and chronological age of the mentally retarded referent, and 2) the manner in which the concept of mental retardation is presented to the subject.

Severity of Mental Retardation and Chronological Age

As we are aware, the range of intellectual capabilities of individuals who are labeled as mentally retarded varies enormously. Some are labeled mentally retarded because they have difficulty in coping with some of the situational demands placed on them during a particular time in their lives, e.g., the demand to read and write at a given level of proficiency. When the demands are removed the individual no longer functions as a mentally retarded person. Other individuals are afflicted with mental retardation that is so severe that it prevents them from functioning on even the simplest tasks during their entire life span.

Severity of mental retardation may also be confounded with chronological age in many studies. We are all aware that mental retardation is defined partly in terms of its developmental origins. Just as infants may be retarded, so can toddlers, preadolescents, adolescents, and adults be retarded. Although the demands placed on individuals differ by chronological age levels, failure to cope with the demands, whatever they may be, may result in the individual being labeled mentally retarded. It is probable that children identified at birth as mentally retarded or who are labeled prior to entry into school are more likely to be organically and/or genetically impaired, and more severely retarded, than are children who are not identified until the third or fourth grade (Mercer, 1973). Also, if most school-identified retarded children disappear into society as adults (Goldstein, 1964), it is likely that those individuals who remain identified as mentally retarded during their adult years are apt to be more severely retarded than those who managed to adapt to society and disappear from the roles of the mentally retarded. Therefore, if attitudes are related to severity of retardation and the latter is at times related to chronological age, attitudes toward retarded people may be dependent on the chronological age of the mentally retarded referent. Thus, when interpreting data from studies of public, peer, or professional attitudes toward the mentally retarded, it is essential that the referent of the attitude be clearly identified.

The Concept of Mental Retardation

The object referent in attitude studies may differ not only in the particular characteristics the subject attributes to the mentally retarded person about whom he is expressing his attitude, but also in the manner that the investigator presents the concept to the subject. Some researchers required their subjects to evaluate the concept mental retardation in its most abstract form, i.e., the label "mentally retarded person," without the benefit of any additional information (Jaffe, 1966; Strauch, 1970; Gottlieb, Cohen, and Goldstein, 1974; Holliger and Jones, 1970), while others asked their subjects to indicate the way they felt about a particular mentally retarded person (Johnson, 1950; Bruininks, Rynders, and Gross, 1974; Goodman, Gottlieb, and Harrison, 1972; Gottlieb and Budoff,

1973). Various intermediate amounts of information regarding the concept "mental retardate" have also been provided to the subjects. For example, Meyers, Sitkei, and Watts (1966) provided a label, "slow learner" or "retarded," accompanied by a statement indicating that retarded persons will never be able to read better than about a fourth grade level and will always be like a 9-year-old child. A few investigators supplied a sketch of a mentally retarded person and asked their subjects to rate the person indicated by the sketch (Jaffe, 1966; Smith and Greenberg, 1974; Gottlieb and Miller, 1974). Other experimenters presented mentally retarded persons through the use of video tapes (Guskin, 1963a; Gottlieb, 1974) or live encounter situations (Gottlieb and Davis, 1973; Strichart and Gottlieb, 1975).

The question arises as to whether these alternative methods of presenting the concept of mental retardation are likely to elicit similar attitudes. Most probably they are not. Jaffe (1966), for example, found that the label mentally retarded was evaluated more unfavorably and with greater variability than the sketch of a retarded person. If an abstract label and a sketch of a retarded person are evaluated differently, it is likely that a label and/or sketch may be evaluated differently from a video-taped presentation of a mentally retarded person. This may be so because the subject is able to witness a greater variety of behavior from the video-taped display than from the sketch of a person. Similarly, it is also likely that a video-taped presentation may elicit different expressed attitudes from a live behavioral encounter with a retarded person. One important difference between the two situations is that in the latter, the subject may be more likely to believe the consequences of his actions are real and could affect him (Kiesler, Collins, and Miller, 1969).

To summarize, the study of attitudes toward retarded people is interpretable only in relation to a precise statement regarding the referent of the investigation. Studies of public attitudes toward the mentally retarded will now be reviewed. First, the potential biasing effects of the attitude referent will be examined in relation to studies of public attitudes. Then, subject characteristics associated with particular attitudes will be presented. Finally, the literature on attitude change will be indicated.

PUBLIC ATTITUDES TOWARD THE MENTALLY RETARDED

Influence of the Attitude Referent

One of the ironies in the field of mental retardation is that although it is well known among professional workers that the overwhelming proportion of retardation is attributable to cultural and/or environmental differences and not to observable organic and/or genetic anomalies, the predominant view of mental retardation among the public at large is that of a mongoloid or physically damaged person. This view persists despite numerous attempts in the last decade to inform the public about mental retardation, attempts that often included television campaigns involving a retarded person having organic deficits (Begab, 1968). Evidence for the public view regarding mental retardation comes from several sources, the most detailed of which is Gottwald's (1970) study. As part of his inquiry, Gottwald asked respondents to indicate what the phrase "mentally retarded" meant to them. Those subjects who responded with a causal explanation most often attributed mental retardation to birth injury, defects, or brain damage, the forms that are in a numerical minority of all cases diagnosed as mental retardation but that are associated with the more severe cases. Gottwald's additional finding that only 1.1% of his sample (N = 1515) attempted to distinguish among different levels of retardation may indicate that not only does the public tend to view mental retardation as being associated with moderate or severe instances, they may not be aware that the majority of cases represents only mild forms. It may also be possible that the public may not be aware that such a condition as mild mental retardation even exists. Therefore, to the extent that the popular conception of a mentally retarded person is represented by a mongoloid or brain-damaged individual, studies that fail to consider the level of retardation in their study of attitudes are most probably obtaining a picture of attitudes that is generalizable to only the restricted range of moderate and severe cases.

Begab (1968), too, observed that retarded people were viewed as sick and physically handicapped. Begab further found that attempts to modify the attitudes of social work students through educational exposure, except for those in special field instruction placements, were largely unsuccessful. Since extreme attitudes have been found to be more resistant to change than neutral ones (Tannenbaum, 1956), Begab's data attest not only to the fact that the mentally retarded are viewed as being sick and physically damaged people, they also indicate that these attitudes are intensely held by many people.

The failure of some investigators to differentiate among levels of mental retardation in attitude studies may be one of the reasons for a recurring pattern of data indicating essentially negative attitudes. For example, Greenbaum and Wang (1965) reported that the public view (N = 330) of mental retardation was consistently more negative than for mental illness. This is in contrast to other data which indicated that attitudes toward mental retardation and mental illness were quite similar (Harasymiw, 1971) and that the two conditions are often confused by the public (Guskin, 1963a; Hollinger and Jones, 1970; Lattimer, 1970; Winthrop and Taylor, 1957). However, the negative attitudes expressed by Greenbaum and Wang's subjects are more easily understandable if they were referring to moderate and severe instances of retardation, as opposed to more mild forms. The fact that the authors obtained attitude scores by averaging responses to four concepts regarding mental retardation (mentally retarded, moron, imbecile, idiot), each of which was rated on a 21-item semantic differential, does not broaden the range of applicability of the findings as the authors indicated, if the subjects were not aware of the differences in the degrees of mental retardation implied by the concepts they were rating. Conceivably, all four concepts were viewed as representing moderate to severe cases of retardation.

When Winthrop and Taylor (1957) asked 133 subjects (24 of whom had a retarded child) to agree or disagree with nine popular misconceptions regarding "feeblemindedness," they found that many misconceptions which were prevalent 3 decades prior to their research were still common. Included among the misconceptions were the beliefs that feeblemindedness is a mental disease and that sterilization was the best solution to the problem. However, given the debates regarding pseudofeeblemindedness that permeated the professional literature of that period (Bialer, 1970), it is not unrealistic to expect that there was gross distortion and confusion regarding the term "feeblemindedness" among the public at large. It is quite possible that the incidence of misconceptions would have been greatly reduced had the authors defined "feebleminded."

The label "slow learner" has also been used to assess public attitudes. Hollinger and Jones (1970) administered two eight-item social distance scales each to 114 men and women ranging in age from 18 to 87 years. The two social distance scales were identical except that one referred to mentally retarded people and the other to slow learners. The investigators did not define the labels for their subjects, but asked them to provide their own definitions of the terms. Of 16 comparisons between the concepts mentally retarded people and slow learners (each of the social distance items was analyzed separately by sex of subject), 15 comparisons indicated that attitudes toward slow learners were significantly more favorable than toward mentally retarded people. Interestingly, two of the eight social distance items pertained to mentally retarded and slow learning *children,* with similar results being obtained, i.e., slow learning children were rated significantly more favorably than mentally retarded children. When the investigators asked the subjects to define slow learner and mentally retarded, 63% saw no similarities between the two concepts, but most could not explain how they were different. Those subjects who did explain the nature of the difference indicated that, for the most part, mental retardation was associated with physical disability and mental illness, while slow learners were characterized by a general "slowness" that did not necessarily involve intellectual ability. Again we notice that the popular conception of the label "mentally retarded" involves physical disability, most often associated with the more severe degrees of retardation. Slow learners, on the other hand, were not often viewed as being mentally retarded. The latter finding is of particular interest since the community where the investigation was conducted had special classes for *slow learners* for 23 years prior to the community interview, whereas most other states refer to identical children as educable mentally retarded. Thus, the importance of a label as an influence on community attitudes is clearly illustrated: the labels "slow learner" and "mentally retarded" elicit different attitudes.

The fact that the public might differentiate slow learners from mentally retarded people was not considered by Meyers, Sitkei, and Watts (1966), who conducted a household interview of 188 randomly selected individuals and 24 adults who had children enrolled in special classes for the mentally retarded. The investigators compared attitudes toward mildly and severely retarded children and supplied a brief description of both degrees of mental retardation. Mildly retarded people were described as "people who are slow learners . . . who are retarded . . . who will not be able to read better than the fourth grade level . . . like a 9-year-old." Within this definitional framework, equating slow learners with mentally retarded people, the majority of the random and special samples (188 and 24, respectively) felt that public schools should provide education. However, the majority of the random sample also felt that public schools should *not* have programs for the more severely retarded (who were defined as "extremely retarded . . . never be able to dress or even feed themselves . . . will always need someone to look after their needs and to care for them"). The sample of special class parents was equally divided on the question of public school provisions for the more severely retarded. The Meyers et al. investigation indicates that when mental retardation is equated with slow learners by the investigators, public attitudes are favorable, at least with respect to the provision of public school services. Attitudes toward the more severely retarded were less favorable in this respect.

Guskin (1963b) also demonstrated the importance of brief descriptions of handicapping conditions on expressed attitudes. He employed two different brief descriptions of eight handicapping conditions (e.g., "educationally inadequate" was defined either as "a child who has been left back in school two or three times" or "a child who reads and writes very poorly for his age") and found that the degrees of relationship between the two sets of definitions were sufficiently different so that they could not be combined for statistical treatment in a single analysis, but had to be treated separately.

Finally, the importance of the label was also well demonstrated by Belinkoff's (1960) attempt to enroll 5- to 7-year-old children with IQ scores between 50 and 75 in an experimental education program. When the project was renamed from "Mental Retardation Project" to "Special Education Project," significantly more parents came to discuss the possibility of their children's enrollment. Belinkoff indicated how the parents were more willing to accept the fact that their children were "slow" than "retarded."

To summarize, the label that accompanies community attitude surveys has a profound effect on the attitudes that will be elicited. In the absence of any descriptive information regarding the attitude object, the public is likely to imagine a physically damaged individual and respond negatively. It is doubtful whether the public views the milder forms of mental retardation as being a serious handicap at all. This finding is not restricted to this country alone. In Germany, Von Bracken (1967) asked a varied sample of 120 adults which of seven handicapping conditions was the most severe. Included in the list of seven were severely and mildly retarded children. Von Bracken reported that severe retardation was mentioned 83 times but that mild mental retardation was not mentioned even once.

In spite of the relatively wide array of labels employed in community attitude studies, several patterns emerge. Attitudes toward the mildly retarded are more favorable than toward the severely retarded. Mental retardation is often confused with mental illness. Last, there is a general ignorance among the public regarding the retarded themselves (Winthrop and Taylor, 1957) as well as to the services available for the mentally retarded (Lattimer, 1970).

Factors Associated with Public Attitudes toward the Mentally Retarded

Many studies of public attitudes toward the retarded have attempted to relate attitudes to subjects' (i.e., raters') characteristics. The characteristics most often examined in their studies are the subject's sex, age, level of education, socioeconomic status (SES) level, and degree of contact with retarded people.

Harasymiw (1971) reviewed literature on differences in attitudes of males and females toward the disabled in general. He concluded that the majority of evidence collected in this country indicates that females tend to express more favorable attitudes than males. Greenbaum and Wang (1965), who examined attitudes toward the mentally retarded specifically, also reported that females expressed significantly more positive attitudes than males. Gottwald (1970) found that, as might be expected, women were more aware than men of the causes of mental retardation, especially as they related to birth injury and prenatal factors. Men and women in his study did not differ significantly in their responses to the social worth of a retarded person (e.g., what proportion of the mentally retarded would make good friends, neighbors, citizens, etc.). In other categories, such as the proportion of retarded persons who could be expected to learn to add and subtract, use public transportation, drive, and have a regular job, women tended to be significantly more "conservative" than men.

Gottlieb and Corman (1975) administered many of Gottwald's questions to 430 adults, of whom 57% were female. These investigators found that well educated females expressed significantly more favorable attitudes than males with similar education on a factor representing "positive stereotype toward the mentally retarded." Male and female subjects did not differ on two factors that emerged from this investigation, "segregation in the classroom" and "perceived physical and intellectual handicap."

Studies which have examined the relationship between attitudes and subject's age have generally found that younger subjects express more positive attitudes than older ones toward the mentally retarded (Gottwald, 1970; Gottlieb and Corman, 1975; Hollinger and Jones, 1970). Greenbaum and Wang (1965), on the other hand, reported no statistically significant relationship between age and attitude favorability (although there was a tendency for *older* subjects to express more favorable attitudes).

The data relating amount of education and attitudes are not so consistent as those on sex and age. Gottwald (1970) reported that, in general, level of education was correlated with positive attitudes, as well as with factual knowledge of the mentally retarded. Greenbaum and Wang (1965), on the other hand, reported that individuals who did not complete high school posited more favorable attitudes than those with more education. With a well educated sample, Gottlieb and Corman (1975) failed to detect significant differences due to educational level on two of the four attitudinal factors they identified. On the "perceived physical and intellectual handicap" factor, however, subjects who were high school graduates expressed a less negative stereotype than either college graduates or individuals who did not complete high school. Results of studies which have examined the relationship between education and work-related attitudes toward the retarded have also been inconsistent. Both Phelps (1965) and Cohen (1963) studied attitudes of employers toward the retarded. Phelps found a significant positive relationship, i.e., the more highly educated employers expressed more favorable attitudes. Cohen, on the other hand, observed a significantly negative relationship, with the more highly educated employers positing less favorable attitudes.

Gottwald (1970) examined the relationship between SES and attitudes and reported no significant differences among subjects of various income levels regarding their view of the "social worth" of a retarded person. On other assigned characteristics of the retarded, however, upper income groups tended to be more sophisticated and realistic about the mentally retarded. Greenbaum and Wang (1965) observed that low SES subjects expressed significantly more favorable attitudes than either middle or upper class subjects. No significant differences in attitudes emerged between the latter two SES levels.

The relationship between attitudes and contact with retarded people has an inherent appeal to investigators who implicitly hope that more favorable attitudes will result when individuals have an opportunity to interact with retarded people. The data on this point are not conclusive. Gottlieb and Corman (1975) found that those subjects who had not known a retarded person were most apt to favor segregation of the retarded in the community. No difference emerged on any of the three remaining factors as they related to the contact variable. Hollinger and Jones (1970) failed to find reliable relationships between exposure to slow learners and attitudes toward them. Indirect evidence for the negative effects of contact on attitudes is available in Phelps (1965), who studied attitudes of personnel managers toward the employment of the mentally retarded. He found that the longer the subject was in personnel work, the less likely he was to hire a retarded person. Thus, research does not consistently indicate that contact with retarded people is associated with more favorable attitudes. Additional data on this subject are available in studies on attitude change toward the retarded, which have generally hypothesized that physical contact will produce favorable attitude change.

Studies of Attitude Change

Studies of attitude change toward the mentally retarded usually predict that exposure to retarded people will change attitudes, hopefully rendering them more favorable. Unlike data on attitudes collected at one particular time, investigations that focus on change must provide an intervening treatment and therefore require greater subject commitment. For this reason, these investigations have typically employed high school and college students, a more captive population than the public at large, but also a more restrictive one in terms of generalizability.

Cleland and Chambers (1959) conducted a tour through an institution in an effort to modify the attitudes of high school and college students. The investigators found that the tour was effective in improving students' attitudes toward the institution. However, after the tour students were more likely to favor institutionalization of retarded patients. The investigators' attempt to relate attitude change to SES level was unsuccessful for the most part because the range of SES levels was too restricted. There was a significant tendency, however, for the lower SES group to express a greater acceptance of repeated future visits to the institution. This finding is consistent with data presented previously which indicate that low SES individuals are more apt to express favorable attitudes toward the retarded.

The use of an institutional tour to modify attitudes was examined in a subsequent study by Cleland and Cochran (1961), who employed a contrast group of high school students who were given written factual information relating to the institution but did not receive a tour. No significant differences appeared between the groups who received the tour and the contrast group.

Kimbrell and Luckey (1964) administered a ten-item attitudinal scale to 96 of 281 subjects before they took a 90-minute guided tour of an institution for the mentally retarded and again immediately following the tour. Significant pre-post-test differences emerged on five of the ten items, three of which revealed that attitudes toward the patients became more negative after the tour. Two items reflecting attitudes toward the institution changed in a positive direction.

Sellin and Mulchahay (1965) also found that an institutional tour elicited both positive and negative components of attitude change. Like Kimbrell and Luckey, these investigators found that attitudes toward the institution became more positive as a function of the tour but that attitudes toward the patients themselves did not. Sellin and Mulchahay observed that attitudes toward the mentally retarded patients were unrealistic both before and after the tour: prior to the tour the subjects underestimated the patients' ability while after the tour they overestimated the patients' ability.

Perhaps the most detailed investigation regarding attitude change was conducted by Begab (1968), who studied the impact of differences of curricula and experiences on social work students' attitudes and knowledge about mental retardation. Most pertinent to the present discussion was Begab's finding that exposure per se resulted in attitude change which was predominantly, although not entirely, in the positive direction. Other factors in addition to mere exposure were important determinants of attitude change, such as the esteem in which the students held their field instructor. Similar findings were also reported by Vurdelja-Maglajlic and Jordan (1974), who observed that enjoyment of contact rather than extent of contact was most significantly related to attitudes. One can speculate that enjoyment of the contact might also be related to favorable attitude change toward mentally retarded people.

To summarize, the brief literature on attitude change indicates that exposure per se does not necessarily produce favorable attitude change toward mentally retarded people. The problem is far more complex. For example, very little information is available regarding the tour itself. Only the temporal sequence of the high and low shock value patients was systematically varied (Cleland and Chambers, 1959; Cleland and Cochran, 1961). On what other dimensions that might have affected attitude scores did the institutions differ? Similarly, how did the subjects differ? Future studies will have to consider various subject characteristics that may serve to impede or facilitate attitude change. One such variable could be the subject's initial attitude, both in terms of its intensity and direction. Intense attitudes are more resistant to change than neutral attitudes (Tannenbaum, 1956). Also, subjects whose initial attitudes toward the retarded are negative may use the institutional tour experience as a vehicle to justify their initial attitude rather than to change it (Zajonc, 1968).

To the extent that any general statements regarding the effects of institutional tours on attitude change are possible, it appears that attitudes toward the patient become more negative while attitudes toward the institution become more positive. This combination of attitudes toward the patients and the institution is easily interpretable if one considers that the more likely people are to believe that retarded people have a limited prognosis and should be segregated, the greater will be their belief that institutions are necessary to achieve these ends.

PEER ATTITUDES TOWARD THE MENTALLY RETARDED

The nature of the attitude referent has been less of a problem in studies of peer attitudes than it has been in investigations regarding public attitudes. The majority of research on peer attitudes toward the mentally retarded has focused on attitudes toward mildly retarded children within a school context. A major difference between studies of public and peer attitudes is the fact that there has been a strong reliance on sociometric instruments in studies of peer attitudes, thus eliminating the problem of the specificity of the attitude referent. Peer attitude studies have traditionally employed sociometric and attitude scales. Occasionally, other data-gathering instruments have been used, such as adjective check lists (Willey and McCandless, 1968), overt behavioral interactions (Gottlieb and Davis, 1973; Strichart and Gottlieb, 1975), and open-ended descriptions (Clark, 1964). Most of what we know concerning the attitudes of peers toward mentally retarded children, however, has been obtained from sociometric investigations and studies using more traditional scales.

Sociometric Studies of Peer Attitudes

Sociometric inquiry represents a subcategory of attitude measurement (Lindsey and Byrne, 1968), insofar as it reflects a person's feelings toward another individual. In the general literature on attitudes, sociometric responses constitute the *conative* component of an attitude (McGuire, 1968) when they represent how a person behaves or would behave toward the attitude object, *under circumstances where the person believes that his choices may have consequences for himself.* When the subject does not believe that the consequences of his actions are real and could affect him, sociometric responses are "scarcely more overt than those required by the usual self-report inventories" (Scott, 1968, p. 217). In the latter situation, sociometric assessment may be interpreted as a measure of the *affective* component of an attitude, dealing with the subject's feelings of liking and disliking the attitude object. The majority of sociometric research regarding the social status of retarded children may be viewed as measuring the affective component of an attitude, since there are seldom any implied consequences directed toward the subject for his choices. Most sociometric studies are conducted primarily to obtain a ranking of the social position of the retarded child, usually in relation to non-retarded children, in various types of class and/or school organizations. Other studies have been concerned with the relationship between social status of retarded children and social class of the rater, as well as with techniques to improve social status.

Social Status and Class Placement Investigations that relate sociometric scores of non-retarded and retarded children do so to determine the type of educational models, *vis-à-vis* classroom arrangements, that will result in the highest possible acceptance of retarded children. Educational models may vary from total segregation of retarded children to a situation in which the educable mentally retarded (EMR) is fully integrated into regular classes. Many intermediate arrangements are also possible, such as when EMR children are assigned to a segregated special class but spend part of their school day in regular classes.

The most often cited sociometric investigation was conducted by Johnson (1950), who studied the social status of EMR children who were totally integrated into regular classes. Of 698 children in 25 classes, Johnson identified 39 as mentally retarded on the basis of a Binet IQ score under 70. Individual sociometric data were then obtained from all children. The results indicated that non-retarded children were accepted approximately twice as often as the retarded, while retarded children were rejected approximately four times as often as non-retarded children. More than twice as many retarded children as non-retarded children were isolated. When Johnson asked the subjects to indicate the reasons for their sociometric choices, he found that antisocial behavior, and not academic incompetence, was the reason most often given for the rejection of retarded children. Johnson concluded that although the retarded children were physically integrated into the regular grades, they were socially and psychologically isolated.

Johnson and Kirk (1950) replicated the previous study in a less traditional school system that placed greater premium on social adjustment and less emphasis on academic achievement. The authors again found that the retarded were rejected significantly more often, with antisocial behaviors most often cited as the reason for the rejection.

Miller (1956) investigated the possibility that the results of the preceding studies could have been an artifact of the method which allowed only for accepting or rejecting responses. He asked his subjects to respond on a five-point continuum to questions about other children. Miller concluded that retarded children were nonaccepted, but not socially rejected. He did find, however, that they were accepted less often than mentally typical and mentally superior children.

Heber (1956) also employed a five-point rating system to obtain an index of the social position of high, average, and low IQ children. He observed that the decremental effect of low IQ on social status scores was more than 2½ times as great as the incremental effect of high IQ. Children of low IQ are at a greater disadvantage in terms of their social status than children of high IQ are at an advantage.

The preceding studies clearly indicate that retarded children in the regular grades in schools without special classes enjoy a less favorable social position than children of superior ability. It could be anticipated that regular class retarded children in schools having special classes would occupy a more favorable social position since the least acceptable children would likely be enrolled in the special class. Baldwin (1958) studied the social position of 31 IQ-defined EMR children who remained in the regular grades in schools containing a special class for retarded children. Non-retarded classmates attributed significantly fewer desirable and significantly more undesirable qualities to the retarded children than to the non-retarded ones. As was the case in Johnson's (1950) investigation, retarded children were found to be rejected because they were seen as engaging in antisocial behavior. Baldwin did not compare the social status of those

IQ-defined EMR children in regular classes with those in special classes, so no direct comparisons between the two groups are possible.

One of the first studies to compare attitudes toward retarded children in different class placements was conducted by Thurstone (1959). As part of the Thurstone report, Jordan compared the social position of EMR children in segregated classes with IQ-defined EMR children in regular classes who had never been identified for special class placement. The data indicated that special class EMR children were selected as friends more often and rejected less often than retarded children in the regular grades. As the author acknowledged, however, special class EMR children were rated by their special class peers while regular class EMR children were rated by their non-retarded classmates. The difference in the two reference groups used by the raters when making their choices makes the findings difficult to interpret. The regular class EMR children were judged by children who were better academic performers and who might tend to reject other children who performed very poorly (Gronlund, 1959). Since differences in academic performance tend to be less pronounced in the special class, different criteria may have been employed in selecting friends. More direct comparisons of the social status of segregated and integrated EMR children could have been made if only non-retarded children rated both groups of EMR children. Such an approach was used by Gottlieb and his colleagues in a series of investigations (Goodman, Gottlieb, and Harrison, 1972; Gottlieb and Budoff, 1973; Gottlieb and Davis, 1973), as well as by Iano, Ayers, Heller, McGettigan, and Walker (1974).

Goodman et al. began with the commonly held "contact hypothesis," shared by other special educators (e.g., Christoplos and Renz, 1969), i.e., because retarded children in the regular grades are better known to their non-retarded peers, attitudes toward integrated retarded children would be more favorable than toward segregated EMR children. The data, however, did not support the contact hypothesis. No differences in the acceptance of integrated and segregated retarded children were observed. In fact, male raters judged the integrated retarded children as significantly less acceptable than the segregated children. Gottlieb and Budoff (1973) replicated that study in a small rural town and obtained similar results. The integrated children tended to be rejected more often than the segregated ones. Finally, Gottlieb and Davis (1973) studied the social position of the same children that Goodman et al. observed, but in an overt play situation. A regular class child had to select a partner for a beanbag toss game from a pair consisting of a regular class child and an EMR child. Of 28 possible choices, 27 regular class children were selected as partners, regardless of whether the EMR child was in the special class or had been integrated. Again, the integrated children were not more socially acceptable than the segregated ones. In all three studies, the retarded children were always accepted significantly less often than non-retarded children.

Iano et al. (1974) compared the sociometric status of non-retarded children, children who were referred to a resource room program but were never diagnosed as mentally retarded, and special class EMR children who had resource room services available to them. Employing Johnson's (1950) sociometric questionnaire, these investigators found that non-retarded children were most accepted by their peers, followed in order by the non-retarded children referred to the resource room, and the EMR children who were referred for the resource room services. Similarly, the non-retarded children were rejected least often, followed by the non-retarded resource room-referred children and the EMR children. The rejection rates for the latter two groups did not significantly differ from each other. The investigators concluded that the EMR children who had the benefit of resource room help were not more highly accepted than EMR children in previous studies who had not received such services.

We have noted that regular class retarded children are socially accepted significantly less often than non-retarded children both when they are in schools with no special classes and when they are in schools with special classes. It was also observed that non-retarded children do not tend to be more accepting of integrated retarded children than of segregated ones. The last type of educational placement for which social acceptance data are relevant includes children who are formally assigned to a special class but spend part of their school day in the regular grades, either in academic or non-academic classes.

Lapp (1957) employed Johnson's (1950) sociometric questionnaire and found that rejection scores of EMR children who were partially integrated did not differ from a chance basis, but that their social acceptance scores were significantly higher than would be expected by chance. The author concluded that EMR children who were partially integrated were not overtly rejected by their peers but were tolerated by them. Rucker, Howe, and Snider (1969) also studied the social status of partially integrated children, but with different conclusions than Lapp's. These authors observed that partially integraded EMR children were rejected more often than non-retarded children both in academic and nonacademic classes.

A summary of the sociometric literature indicates convincingly that regardless of the particular educational model employed, EMR children are not so well accepted as are non-retarded children. However, the previous sociometric investigations were solely concerned with the status of retarded children in different models but did not consider the possibility that rejecting responses might interact with the characteristics of the person who did the rejecting. Conceivably, not all children reject retarded pupils equally. Although there has been very little research on rater characteristics that are associated with accepting and nonaccepting choices, the variable that has been studied most often is SES level.

Social Status and SES Level While the majority of sociometric research was conducted to examine how social acceptance differs with various administrative and/or educational arrangements within the school, several studies have investigated the relationship between social class of the respondents and their sociometric ratings of mentally retarded children. Bruininks, Rynders, and Gross (1974) recently reported that low SES urban raters were significantly more accepting of same-sex retarded children than non-retarded children. Contradictory results were obtained with their middle class samples, i.e., they rated same-sex non-retarded children more favorably than retarded children.

The studies by Goodman, Gottlieb, and Harrison (1972) and Gottlieb and Budoff (1973), previously described, both employed identical procedures to assess the social status of EMR children in an affluent middle class and poor rural area respectively. Although no direct statistical comparisons were made between the data in the two studies, an examination of the percentage of rejection scores from both samples indicated that EMR children were rejected more often by the middle class sample than by the poor rural sample of subjects.

Monroe and Howe (1971) indicated that the social class of the retarded child was an important factor in his acceptance, with higher SES EMR children accepted more often than lower SES EMR children. Fuchigami and Sheperd (1968), on the other hand, reported that in-school friendship patterns between retarded and non-retarded adolescents did not appear to be related to the income level of the retarded child's family, but that low income EMR adolescents tended to have more non-retarded friends outside of school than was the case for higher income EMR adolescents. The data of this last study, however, were collected by interviews with the adolescent retarded individuals, and no validating data were gathered from the non-retarded "friends."

The influence of the socioeconomic variable was controlled by Meyerowitz (1967), who compared the neighborhood peer relationships of 7-year-old EMR children in special and regular classes with a contrast group of non-retarded children matched for SES levels. Meyerowitz observed that there were no differences in the neighborhood acceptance of segregated and integrated EMR children, that the retarded children, regardless of placement, were isolates, and that both EMR groups were derogated equally, but considerably less than were non-retarded children. The basic pattern that emerges from this study is that special or regular class placement does not affect the neighborhood interaction patterns of retarded children; they tend to be ignored regardless of their placement.

Improving Social Status   The sociometric literature demonstrated that EMR children are not accepted as well as non-retarded children. The only point of contention is whether retarded children are sociometrically rejected or nonaccepted. Regardless of whether the data are to be interpreted as representing rejection or nonacceptance, the fact remains that retarded children are assigned to an inferior social position by their non-retarded peers, and methods to improve this situation must be identified.

Very few studies have appeared in the literature pertaining to the improvement of the social status of mentally retarded children. Chennault (1967) attempted to improve the social acceptance of special class EMR children through interaction, in organized group activities, with the most popular children in their classes. Low status junior high school age EMR children participated in a dramatic skit with high status retarded children for two 15-minute periods weekly over a 5-week period. Sociometric testing after the skit was performed revealed that the isolates who participated in the experimental skit improved their social position scores significantly more than the EMR children who did not participate.

McDaniel (1970) employed a similar approach to improve the social status of EMR adolescents by having them participate with each other in square dancing and basketball over a 6-week period. Sixteen EMR adolescents of comparable chronological age (CA) and IQ, who participated only in regular classroom activities, constituted the control group. At the end of every week, experimental and control subjects were asked to indicate with whom they would like to sit and play, and with whom they would not like to sit and play. Analysis of the data indicated that the experimental group obtained higher social acceptance scores as well as higher social rejection scores. For some retarded children, contact between themselves and other retarded children resulted in greater incidences of rejection.

It has been demonstrated that it is possible to improve the social status of EMR children by having them interact with other retarded children. How durable are these changes? Does the formerly rejected child revert to his original social position when the opportunities for social interaction are removed?

Rucker and Vincenzo (1970) extended Chennault's investigation by having the two least accepted special class pupils interact in carnival preparation activities with the most popular members of their special class. The authors predicted that low accepted special class children who participated in the planning would improve their social acceptance scores significantly more than a control group but that the gains would not persist 1 month after the completion of the treatment. Both predictions were supported. Immediate sociometric improvements did result but they were not permanent, disappearing on the post-post-test.

Lilly (1971) incorporated various refinements in the nature of experimenter and peer interactions that might be a contributing factor to improved social status and relate to the permanence of improved social acceptance *in regular grades*. Lilly had two low sociometric status, low achieving children participate with two other children in making a film to be shown to the class. Depending on the treatment conditions, the other children were either high or low status, and the experimenter either participated fully or minimally. The investigator observed that all treatments were equally effective in improving social acceptance change with 1 week following the completion of the treatment, but that the gains were lost on the post-post-test 6 to 7 weeks following the initial post-test. Lilly did not analyze his data to reveal whether there were differential changes in the sociometric scores assigned to the rejected children by the children with whom they interacted, as opposed to the remaining nonparticipating classroom members.

Attitudinal Studies of Attitudes toward the Mentally Retarded

The second major approach to the study of attitudes toward mentally retarded children has been through the administration of a variety of questionnaires. Unlike sociometric inquiries, which require subjects to indicate whether they like or dislike a particular mentally retarded child, attitudinal studies typically require the subject to indicate his feelings about mentally retarded children in general. The specificity with which the attitude referent is defined varies with the particular methodology employed by the investigator. Some investigators have required the subjects to rate the abstract concept of "mentally retarded" (e.g., Gottlieb, Cohen, and Goldstein, 1974). Others have asked the subjects to interact with a retarded person and then to rate mentally retarded people on attitudinal questionnaires (Strichart and Gottlieb, 1975).

Attitudinal studies are more varied than sociometric studies with respect to the dependent measures employed. Although several varieties of sociometric questionnaires have been employed in studies of the mentally retarded, attitudinal questionnaires are far more heterogeneous in their response formats. Questionnaires have appeared in Likert, semantic differential lists, true-false formats, as well as adjective check lists and open-ended descriptive formats. Since investigators often employ different instruments and define the attitude referent in different ways, it is almost impossible to compare results across attitudinal studies.

The literature in this section will be reviewed under three headings. First, general attitude studies will be reviewed with particular attention given to the treatment and the dependent measures. Then, studies will be presented that attempt to relate subject (i.e., rater) characteristics to their attitudes toward mentally retarded peers. Finally, the very brief literature on attitude-behavior consistency will be indicated.

Studies of Attitudes of Normal Children toward Mentally Retarded Peers   Clark (1964) tested the prediction that retarded children are described in terms of their own stimulus value rather than their intellectual abilities or special class placement by asking 214 fourth and fifth grade elementary school children to tell about one EMR child (from among 13) whom they knew best. Subjects attended classes in the same wing of the school as the special class pupils. The investigator categorized peers' responses into four categories: identification, description, evaluation, and association. Several interesting findings emerged. First, EMR children were described in terms of their individual stimulus properties. One EMR child was known best by 41% of the 212 subjects whereas 11 of the remaining 12 EMR children were known best by less than 10% of their non-retarded peers. Further, 27% of the responses were classified as evaluations, with significantly more favorable than unfavorable attributes ascribed to EMR children. Only 2.25% of the responses were unfavorable evaluations. Also, EMR children were described more often in terms of their appearance and athletic ability than in terms of their intellectual and/or academic ability. Finally, EMR children were accepted twice as often as they were rejected. The data do not indicate a persistent rejection of retarded children. Clark did not include a contrast sample, however, and no comparative statements vis-à-vis the relative rejection of retarded and non-retarded children are possible.

Renz and Simensen (1969) used Clark's method and included a non-retarded contrast group. The investigators reported that retarded children were perceived similarly to non-retarded children by their non-retarded peers. They also reported that the retarded children were not rejected with greater frequency than non-retarded children. These data are in contrast to previous sociometric investigations that did find retarded children to be less well accepted than non-EMR children.

The results from the Clark and Renz and Simensen attitudinal studies indicate that retarded children are not rejected to a greater degree than non-retarded children, and appear to contradict the findings of sociometric investigations. On closer inspection, however, the results from the two types of studies are easily reconcilable. Sociometric investigations have typically employed group means to obtain social status rankings of retarded and non-retarded children. That is, the social status of all EMR children and some proportion of all non-EMR children within the class is determined and analyses are computed on the two distributions of scores. With any variance in these distributions, and there invariably is, some EMR children are likely to be accepted to a greater extent than some non-retarded children. The two attitudinal studies just reviewed, on the other hand, required subjects to tell about *one* EMR child whom they knew best. It is quite possible that the subjects chose the children whom they *liked* best as well as knew best. Furthermore, since the attitudinal studies provided data on one EMR child per subject, whereas the sociometric investigations provided data for all EMR children per subject, the two sets of data are not directly comparable. A more direct comparison between attitudinal and sociometric studies would require non-EMR subjects to tell about several EMR children whom they knew.

Willey and McCandless (1968) administered a 46-item adjective check list to fifth graders, EMR and orthopedically handicapped children. The non-retarded fifth grade subjects ascribed 25 adjectives on a non-random basis as describing the mentally retarded, 24 of which were negative. Other fifth grade children and orthopedically handicapped children were rated more favorably than the EMR pupils. Thus, the familiar pattern of negative evaluations of mentally retarded children surfaced again. While the negative evaluation of retarded children is easily observed, we know little about the reasons for these evaluations. What behaviors do the EMR pupils engage in that cause them to be rejected? Are they rejected because of the negative social stereotype that is associated with the label "mentally retarded" or is rejection the result of inappropriate or incompetent performance? Put another way, which is more influential in the rejection process, the label "mentally retarded" or the behaviors exhibited by the children who are labeled?

Gottlieb (1974) studied the relative influence of the label "mentally retarded" and the variable of academic competence on attitudes of non-EMR children toward EMR pupils and found that children who were academically incompetent were judged less favorably than academically competent children, regardless of whether the children judged were labeled mentally retarded or normal (i.e., fifth grade pupil). The label itself did not affect attitudes to a significant degree, as measured by a rating scale and a modification of the Cunningham Social Distance Scale.

The influence of academic incompetence on the rejection of EMR children was also studied among Norwegian school children (Gottlieb, 1971). The investigator studied the situational context of attitudes toward EMR pupils, both in class and at play. Gottlieb contended that since EMR pupils are labeled as a result of their academic deficiencies rather than their athletic ineptness, attitudes of normal children toward them would be more favorable during play than during classroom activities. The prediction was supported: EMR children at play were evaluated more favorably than EMR children in class. Further, female EMR children were evaluated more favorably than male EMR's, a finding consonant with Clark's (1964) results.

The Relationship between Rater Characteristics and Attitudes toward Mentally Retarded Children   While it is important to know the attitudes of normal peers toward their mentally retarded age-mates, it is equally important, if not more important, to identify characteristics of raters that are associated with favorable attitudes. Unless the characteristics are identified, attempts to improve attitudes are likely to be largely unsuccessful.

One of the first studies to investigate the relationship between rater characteristics and attitudes toward mentally retarded children was conducted in Norway by Gottlieb

(1969). The investigator studied the influence of the rater's psychological adjustment and chronological age on attitudes towards EMR's as measured by a semantic differential. In this study, adjustment was defined as the discrepancy between the rater's ideal self-concept and actual self-concept, with a higher discrepancy indicating less favorable adjustment. The findings revealed that well adjusted individuals posited more favorable attitudes than less well adjusted subjects toward EMR children. Attitudes did not significantly differ among subjects between the ages of 8 and 16 years.

Gottlieb, Cohen, and Goldstein (1974) partially replicated Gottlieb's (1969) investigation but failed to find that well adjusted individuals expressed more favorable attitudes toward the mentally retarded, although the data were in the predicted direction ($p < 0.10$). These authors did find, however, that non-EMR children who had opportunities to observe or interact with EMR pupils expressed more negative attitudes than children not having opportunities to interact, a finding similar to those reported elsewhere (Goodman et al., 1972; Gottlieb and Budoff, 1973). However, Strauch (1970) observed that there were no differences in the expressed attitudes of subjects, measured by a semantic differential, as a function of whether they reported that they had previous contact with mentally retarded people. Jaffe (1966), too, found no differences in attitudes measured by the semantic differential as a function of reported contact but did find that subjects who indicated that they had contact with retarded people assigned significantly more favorable traits to them.

Studies of Attitude-Behavior Consistency   The studies cited were concerned with verbally expressed indices of an attitude. The implicit assumption in much of this research is that verbally expressed attitudes represent an index of overt behavior toward retarded people. That is, it is thought that people who express negative attitudes will behave differently toward the retarded than people who express positive attitudes. In the general literature of attitude-behavior consistency, various explanations are offered as to why attitudes should reflect overt behaviors and why they should not (Kiesler, Collins, and Miller, 1969). Among the reasons advanced for the lack of expected congruence between a verbally expressed attitude and overt behavior is the lack of similarity between the two measures of an attitude. To illustrate, a verbal attitude represented by a score on a semantic differential bears little resemblance to a behavior that requires an individual to befriend a retarded person, possibly at some psychological or status cost to himself. There are instances when it is expedient *not* to behave as one says he will (Thurstone, 1946). Without belaboring the many arguments concerning the degree of attitude-behavior consistency that is to be expected, it is sufficient for our purposes to indicate that there has been a paucity of research in this area that is relevant to mentally retarded people. Very few studies have examined the relationship between verbal attitudes and overt behavior toward the retarded.

Gottlieb and Budoff (1973) examined the relationship between non-EMR children's sociometric choices toward mentally retarded children and their classroom behavior toward these same EMR children over a period of approximately 4 weeks. These investigators found a significant relationship between social rejection and verbally aggressive behavior, as well as a significant relationship between social acceptance and a lack of verbally aggressive behavior. EMR children who engaged in verbally agressive behavior were usually rejected. Those who did not were usually socially accepted. Similar findings were reported by Bryan (1973) with learning-disabled children.

Strichart and Gottlieb (1975) studied the relationship between two overt measures of an attitude: the extent to which a retarded child's behavior will be imitated by others, and others' choice of the EMR as a play companion. The investigators sought to determine whether non-EMR children would imitate and choose as play companions highly competent EMR children (as predetermined by E on a rigged task) more often than non-competent EMR children. The data indicated that highly competent EMR children were imitated more often and that there was a significant correlation between imitation and choice behavior. In another study, however, Gottlieb (1972) was unable to find significant consistency between verbally expressed attitudes toward EMR children and overt behavior, both among American and Norwegian non-EMR children.

PROFESSIONALS' ATTITUDES TOWARD THE MENTALLY RETARDED

Professionals are the primary dispensers of a variety of information and services to the mentally retarded and their families. Physicians fill a primary need of physically and/or genetically impaired individuals with whom they typically become involved soon after the patient's birth. Social workers may serve to maintain the family integrity after the child is diagnosed as mentally retarded, regardless of the particular age at which the labeling occurs. While physicians are apt to deal with seriously retarded individuals, it is not clear whether families with a severely retarded member have a more critical need for social workers than families with a mildly retarded member. Grossman (1973) reported that the existence of a retarded sibling was more closely associated with the adjustment of non-retarded college age siblings than was the severity of the sibling's retardation.

The chief providers of services to retarded children in school are, of course, teachers. Since teachers service the greatest numbers of retarded children and are the professionals who most accessible to researchers, it is not surprising that the majority of research regarding professionals' attitudes has been conducted with teachers. Only scattered reports are available regarding the attitudes of physicians and even fewer are available regarding social workers' attitudes. The author was unable to locate any studies of psychologists' attitudes toward the mentally retarded, although Bialer and Sternlicht (1969) investigated the issues in mental retardation that psychologists considered important. Teachers are the only group of professionals for whom a "body" of literature regarding attitudes toward the mentally retarded exists.

Teacher Attitudes toward Mentally Retarded Children

The attitudes or expectancies of teachers toward particular children have been theorized to have a significant effect on the children's academic performance (Rosenthal and Jacobsen, 1968). Although the extent to which teacher expectancies affect retarded children's performance is open to considerable debate (see MacMillan, Jones, and Aloia,

1974, for a review of this issue), it is safe to assume that teachers' attitudes may be transmitted to the child and that these, in turn, will, at the very least, influence his social status among his peer group (Lapp, 1975).

What kinds of attitudes toward the mentally retarded do teachers possess? Efron and Efron (1967) identified six dimensions of attitudes toward EMR pupils through factor analytic techniques: 1) segregation via institutionalization, 2) cultural deprivation, 3) non-condemnatory etiology, 4) personal exclusion, 5) authoritarianism, and 6) hopelessness. The investigators reported that special class teachers expressed more favorable attitudes than regular grade teachers on four of the six factors, including the desire to have intimate contact with retarded children (personal exclusion factor). The investigators also reported that respondents in the field of mental retardation (special education teachers and students) possessed significantly more factual knowledge about mental retardation than individuals who were not in the field. The latter finding was also reported by Semmel (1959). Semmel, on the other hand, did not find special education teachers to have more favorable attitudes than general education teachers. Semmel's findings are similar to those of Greene and Retish (1973) who administered the Minnesota Teacher Attitude Inventory (MTAI) to special and regular education student teachers and also observed no differences in attitude scores. In a subsequent study, Alper and Retish (1972) administered the MTAI to special education, elementary education and secondary education student teachers prior to and following their student teaching experience. Special education students failed to register more favorable attitudes after their experiences with mentally retarded children. No significant changes in attitudes were found for either the special education and secondary education student teachers. Elementary education student teachers posited significantly more negative attitudes on completion of student teaching.

Shotel, Iano, and McGettigan (1972) studied the attitudes of teachers toward learning-disabled, emotionally disturbed, and educable mentally retarded children in schools with supportive resource room programs or self-contained special classes. Several interesting findings appeared from this study. First, pretesting at the beginning revealed that in the control schools with at least two self-contained classes, only 7.3% of regular class teachers ($N = 55$) favored regular class placement for retarded children, even though the placement would be supported by a resource room program. While 37.3 ($N = 59$) of the teachers in the experimental schools initially favored regular class placement for mentally retarded children, following 1 year's experience with an integration program, this percentage dropped to 13.6%. In contrast, no significant reduction occurred in the percentage of teachers who felt that emotionally disturbed, or learning-disabled children should attend regular classes. After 1 year of resource room programming, almost three times as many teachers favors regular class placement for emotionally disturbed children than for mentally retarded children. Combs and Harper (1967) noted that children labeled mentally deficient were the recipients of less favorable attitudes than children in other categories of exceptionality, e.g., psychopathy, schizophrenia, cerebral palsey. Since these investigators did not precisely specify the attitude referent, however, it is difficult to know how respondents defined "mentally deficient." These investigators did not detect differences in attitudes toward mentally retarded children due to length of teaching experience. Experienced and inexperienced teachers expressed equally unfavorable attitudes toward mentally deficient children.

The Shotel et al. (1972) and Combs and Harper (1967) results appear contradictory to those reported by Jones and Gottfried (1962), who found that a higher proportion of regular class teachers expressed preference for teaching mildly retarded children than emotionally disturbed children. Given the likelihood that the teachers sampled by Jones and Gottfried may not have had either retarded or disturbed children in their classes, their responses may be based on limited knowledge of mentally retarded children. This fact may account for the difference in results in this study and the Shotel et al. study, in which the teachers presumably had had contact with retarded children.

With regard to the need to define precisely the attitude referent, Jones and Gottfried asked teachers' preferences for several categories of exceptional children and noted that not a single regular class teacher expressed a preference to teach severely retarded children. Warren and Turner (1966) also reported that professionals and students in various professional disciplines least preferred to work with moderately to severely retarded children.

It will be recalled that the creation of special class education for the mentally retarded in this country originally grew from regular class teachers' desires to rid themselves of troublesome children (Esten, 1900). An 80-year history of educational exclusion is very rapidly coming to a close. Regular class teachers suddenly find themselves in the position of being forced to accept mentally retarded children into their classrooms. Studies have shown that regular education teachers do not possess especially positive attitudes toward children labeled mentally retarded (Combs and Harper, 1967), that length of experience in teaching in the regular grades either does not promote positive changes in attitudes (Alper and Retish, 1972) or else results in more unfavorable attitudes (Shotel, Iano, and McGettigan, 1972). Given these findings, serious attempts will have to be made, very quickly, to develop training programs designed to improve regular class teachers' attitudes toward mentally retarded children. While the impact of teacher expectancies on children's performance still awaits final resolution, we cannot afford to wait for the research to resolve the question. Too many children are being reintegrated so very quickly that we do not have the leisure to decide whether teachers' attitudes can and do influence children's performance. Attempts to promote positive attitudes among regular class teachers will in no way harm the children and very possibly could help them. Begab's (1970) study with social work students offers some leads as to the most effective way to change student teachers' attitudes, i.e., provide them with field work experiences, not classroom lectures. EMR pupils will have to be presented to the teachers in a positive light, at least initially, so that negative attitudes do not develop and interfere with the training process.

SOME FUTURE RESEARCH NEEDS

It was pointed out in the introductory section that knowledge of expressed attitudes toward mentally retarded persons might provide us with some indication of how people act toward them. However, the literature review revealed that very few studies have directly investigated whether expressed attitudes are in fact manifest in actual behavior. While there are numerous difficulties in relating expressed attitudes to indices of overt behavior, at the very least, future investigations should place greater emphasis on the study of behavior toward mentally retarded people.

A parallel concern is to ascertain the manner in which the retarded persons internalize the behavior of others. To the extent that the interpretation and internalization of increasingly subtle affective cues is limited by cognitive development, a logical set of questions that should be raised regards the retarded person's ability to recognize and react to these cues. While it is apparent that retarded people recognize that the label "mentally retarded" is not complimentary (e.g., Edgerton, 1967; Gozali, 1972), what is not nearly so apparent is how they come to perceive the negative feeling connoted by the label. Another set of basic questions that must be addressed concerns the kinds of behavior that retarded people engage in that are responsible for attitudes toward them. These questions are especially critical within the public school, a situational context that imposes proximity between EMR and non-EMR pupils. What do the EMR children do that results in their sociometric rejection? We are told that retarded children are rejected because they manifest antisocial, aggressive behavior (Johnson, 1950; Baldwin, 1958). Yet other data indicate that retarded children do not engage in significantly more negative behavior than non-retarded children (Gampel, Gottlieb, and Harrison, 1974; Gottlieb, Gampel, and Budoff, in press). We are further informed that academic proficiency is a cause of differential attitudinal expressions (Gottlieb, 1974). Yet other studies indicate that academic competence is not the cause of EMR children's rejection (Johnson, 1950). Extensive research is needed to resolve these ambiguities.

The relationship between proximity to the mentally retarded and attitudes toward them is not at all clear. The majority of evidence indicates that proximity is associated with increased rejection of mentally retarded individuals. The extent and nature of the contact, however, require explication. Information regarding the extent of contact has been obtained in several ways, most often by asking the subject. This information is of limited value, however, since there is almost no way to corroborate the subject's statement. For example, when a subject indicates that he knew a retarded person, how can we be sure that the person he knew was actually retarded?

The problem is especially critical in studies of physical proximity and its relationship to attitudes toward EMR pupils. While it is typically assumed that the retarded child's participation in the regular class will foster greater contact with non-retarded pupils than would have been possible in a special class, the extent of extra contact generated by regular class placement has not been established. All too often this writer has seen regular class EMR pupils totally ignored by their classmates. The EMR's physical life space within the classroom appeared to be far more limited than that of his non-EMR classmates. Can physical proximity under such circumstances be considered a valid indicator of contact?

Finally, what are the dimensions of an attitude toward the mentally retarded? The majority of research has focused on unifactorial measures of attitude favorability. Very few studies have attacked the measurement problem in a more complex form. A notable exception has been the work of Jordan (1971) and Efron and Efron (1967). One of the more pressing needs at the present time is to develop reliable, multifactorial instruments to measure attitudes. Perhaps, with the ability to measure the many facets of an attitude, we will be in a better position to predict more varied aspects of overt behavior.

REFERENCES

Alper, S. and P. M. Retish. 1972. A comparative study of the effects of student teaching in the attitudes of students in special education, elementary education, and secondary education. Training School Bulletin 69: 70–77.

Baldwin, W. D. 1958. The social position of the educable mentally retarded in the regular grades in the public schools. Exceptional Children 25: 106–108.

Begab, M. J. 1968. The effect of differences in curricula and experiences on social work student attitudes and knowledge about mental retardation. U.S. Department of Health, Education and Welfare, Public Health Service, National Institutes of Health, Bethesda, Maryland.

Begab, M. J. 1970. Impact of education on social work students' knowledge and attitudes about mental retardation. Am. J. Ment. Defic. 74: 801–808.

Belinkoff, C. 1960. Community attitudes toward mentally retarded. Am. J. Ment. Defic. 65: 221–226.

Bialer, I. 1970. Relationship of mental retardation to emotional disturbance and physical disability. In H. C. Haywood (ed.), Social-cultural aspects of mental retardation, pp. 608–660, Appelton Century Crofts, New York.

Bialer, I. and M. Sternlicht. 1969. Psychological issues in mental retardation: Report of a survey. Ment. Retard. 6: 35–37.

Bruininks, R. H., J. E. Rynders, and J. C. Gross. 1974. Social acceptance of mildly retarded pupils in resource rooms and regular classes. Am. J. Ment. Defic. 78: 377–383.

Bryan, T. H. 1973. Peer interactions and sociometric choices. Unpublished manuscript.

Chennault, M. 1967. Improving the social acceptance of unpopular educable mentally retarded pupils in special classes. Am. J. Ment. Defic. 72: 455–458.

Christoplos, F. and P. Renz. 1969. A critical examination of special education programs. J. Spec. Ed. 3: 371–380.

Clark, E. T. 1964. Children's perceptions of educable mentally retarded children. Am. J. Ment. Defic. 68: 602–611.

Cleland, C. C. and I. L. Chambers. 1959. The effect of institutional tours on attitudes of high school seniors. Am. J. Ment. Defic. 64: 124–130.

Cleland, C. and I. Cochran. 1961. The effects of institutional tours in attitudes of high school seniors. Am. J. Ment. Defic. 65: 473–481.

Cohen, J. 1963. Employer attitudes toward hiring mentally retarded individuals. Am. J. Ment. Defic. 67: 705–712.

Combs, R. H. and J. L. Harper. 1967. Effects of labels on attitudes of educators toward handicapped children. Exceptional Children 33: 399–403.

Dunn, L. M. 1968. Special education for the mildly retarded—Is much of it justifiable? Exceptional Children 34: 5–22.

Edgerton, R. B. 1967. Cloak of Competence. University of California Press, Berkeley.

Efron, R. E. and H. Y. Efron. 1967. Measurement of attitudes toward the retarded and an application with educators. Am. J. Ment. Defic. 72: 100–107.

Esten, R. A. 1900. Backward children in the public schools. J. Psychoaesthenics 5: 10–16.

Fuchigami, R. Y. and G. Sheperd. 1968. Factors affecting the integration of educable mentally retarded students. Mental Retardation 6: 18–22.

Gampel, D. H., J. Gottlieb, and R. H. Harrison. 1974. A comparison of the classroom behaviors of special class EMR, integrated EMR, low IQ, and nonretarded children. Am. J. Ment. Defic. 79: 16—21.

Goldstein, J. 1964. Social and occupational adjustment. *In* H. A. Stevens and R. Heber (eds.), Mental Retardation. University of Chicago Press, Chicago.

Goodman, H., J. Gottlieb, and R. H. Harrison. Social acceptance of EMRs integrated into a nongraded elementary school. Am. J. Ment. Defic. 76: 412—417.

Gottlieb, J. 1969. Attitudes toward retarded children: Effects of evaluator's psychological adjustment and age. Scand. J. Ed. Res. 13: 170—182.

Gottlieb, J. 1971. Attitudes of Norweigian children toward the retarded in relation to sex and situational context. Am. J. Ment. Defic. 75: 635—639.

Gottlieb, J. 1972. Attitudes of Norwegian and American children toward mildly retarded children in special classes. Unpublished doctoral dissertation. Yeshiva University.

Gottlieb, J. 1974. Attitudes toward retarded children: Effects of labeling and academic performance. Am. J. Ment. Defic. 79: 268—273.

Gottlieb, J. and M. Budoff. 1973. Social acceptability of retarded children in nongraded schools differing in architecture. Am. J. Ment. Defic. 78: 15—19.

Gottlieb, J., L. Cohen, and L. Goldstein. 1974. Social contact and personal adjustment as variables relating to attitudes toward EMR children. Training School Bulletin 71: 9—16.

Gottlieb, J. and L. Corman. 1975. Public attitudes toward mentally retarded children. Am. J. Ment. Defic. 80: In press.

Gottlieb, J. and J. E. Davis. 1973. Social acceptance of EMRs during overt behavioral interaction. Am. J. Ment. Defic. 78: 141—143.

Gottlieb, J., D. H. Gampel, and M. Budoff. Classroom behavior of retarded children before and after reintegration into regular classes. J. Spec. Ed. In press.

Gottlieb, J. and M. Miller. 1974. Effects of labeling on behavioral expectations. Unpublished manuscript.

Gottwald, H. 1970. Public awareness about mental retardation. Research Monograph, Council for Exceptional Children.

Gozali, J. 1972. Perception of the EMR special class by former students. Ment. Retard. 10: 34—35.

Greenbaum, J. J. and D. D. Wang. 1965. A semantic-differential study of the concepts of mental retardation. J. Gen. Psychol. 73: 257—272.

Greene, M. A. and P. M. Retish. 1973. A comparative study of attitudes among students in special education and regular education. Training School Bulletin 70: 10—14.

Gronlund, N. E. 1959. Sociometry in the classroom. Harper, New York.

Grossman, F. K. 1973. Brothers and sisters of retarded children. Syracuse University Press, Syracuse.

Guskin, S. 1963a. Social psychologies of mental deficiency. *In* N. R. Ellis (ed.), Handbook of Mental Deficiency. pp. 325—352. McGraw-Hill Book Company, New York.

Guskin, S. L. 1963b. Dimensions of judged similarity among deviant types. Am. J. Ment. Defic. 68: 218—224.

Harasymiw, S. J. 1971. Relationship of certain demographic and psychological variables toward the disabled. Research Development and Evaluation Bulletin, Series 1: Attitudes toward the disabled. Boston University, Boston.

Heber, R. F. 1956. The relation of intelligence and physical maturity to social status of children. J. Ed. Psychol. 47: 158—162.

Hollinger, C. S. and R. L. Jones. 1970. Community attitudes toward slow learners and mental retardates: What's in a name? Ment. Retard. 8: 19—23.

Iano, R. P., D. Ayers, H. B. Heller, J. F. McGettingan, and V. S. Walker. 1974. Sociometric status of retarded children in an integrative program. Exceptional Children 40: 267—271.

Jaffe, J. 1966. Attitudes of adolescents toward the mentally retarded. Am. J. Ment. Defic. 70: 907–912.

Johnson, G. O. 1950. Social position of mentally handicapped children in regular grades. Am. J. Ment. Defic. 55: 60–89.

Johnson, G. O. and S. A. Kirk. 1950. Are mentally handicapped children segregated in the regular grades? Exceptional Children 17: 65–68, 87–88.

Jones, R. L. and N. Gottfried. 1962. Preferences and configurations of interests in special class teaching. Exceptional Children 28: 371–377.

Jordan, J. E. 1969. Attitudes toward education and physically disabled persons in eleven nations. Latin American Studies Center, Michigan State University, East Lansing, Michigan.

Jordan, J. E. 1971. Construction of a Guttman facet designed cross-cultural attitude-behavior scale toward mental retardation. Am. J. Ment. Defic. 76: 201–219.

Kiesler, C. A., B. E. Collins, and N. Miller. 1969. Attitude change: A critical analysis of theoretical approaches. John Wiley & Sons, Inc., New York.

Kimbrell, D. L. and R. E. Luckey. 1964. Attitude change resulting from open-house guided tours in a state school for mental retardates. Am. J. Ment. Defic. 69: 21–22.

Lapp, E. R. 1957. A study of the social adjustment of slow-learning children who were assigned part-time to regular classes. Am. J. Ment. Defic. 62: 254–262.

Lattimer, R. 1970. Current attitudes toward mental retardation. Ment. Retard. 8: 30–32.

Lilly, M. S. 1971. Improving social acceptance of low sociometric status, low achieving students. Exceptional Children 37: 341–348.

Lindsey, G. and D. Byrne. 1968. Measurement of social choice and interpersonal attractiveness. In G. Lindzey and E. Aronson (eds.), The Handbook of Social Psychology, Vol. 2, pp. 452–524. Addison-Wesley, Reading.

Lippman, L. 1972. Attitudes toward the handicapped. Charles C Thomas, Springfield, Ill.

MacMillan, D. L., R. L. Jones, and G. F. Aloia. 1974. The "mentally retarded" label: A theoretical analysis and review of research. Am. J. Ment. Defic. 79: 241–261.

McDaniel, C. O., Jr. 1970. Participation in extracurricular activities, social acceptance, and social rejection among educable mentally retarded students. Ed. Training Ment. Retard. 5: 4–14.

McGuire, W. J. 1968. The nature of attitudes and attitude change. In G. Lindzey and E. Aronson (eds.), The Handbook of Social Psychology, Vol. 3, pp. 136–314. Addison-Wesley, Reading.

Mercer, J. R. 1973. Labeling the mentally retarded. University of California Press, Berkley.

Meyerowitz, J. H. 1967. Self-derogations in young retardates and special class placement. Ment. Retard. 5: 23–26.

Meyers, C. E., E. G. Sitkei, and C. H. Watts. 1966. Attitudes toward special education and the handicapped in two community groups. Am. J. Ment. Defic. 71: 78–84.

Miller, R. V. 1956. Social status of mentally superior, mentally typical and mentally retarded children. Exceptional Children 23: 114–119.

Monroe, J. D. and C. E. Howe. Effects of integration and social class on the acceptance of retarded adolescents. Ed. Training Ment. Retard. 6: 20–24.

New York Times, April 28, 1974.

Phelps, W. R. 1965. Attitudes related to the employment of mentally retarded. Am. J. Ment. Defic. 69: 575–585.

Renz, P. and R. J. Simensen. 1969. The social perception of normals toward their EMR grade-mates. Am. J. Ment. Defic. 74: 405–408.

Rosenthal, R. and L. Jacobson. 1968. Pygmalian in the classroom: Teacher expectation and pupils' intellectual development. Holt, Rinehart and Winston, New York.

Rucker, C. N., C. E. Howe, and B. Snider. 1969. The participation of retarded children in junior high academic and nonacademic regular classes. Exceptional Children 35: 617–623.

Rucker, C. N. and F. M. Vincenzo. 1970. Maintaining social acceptance gains made by mentally retarded children. Exceptional Children 36: 679–680.

Scott, W. A. 1968. Attitude measurement. In G. Lindzey and E. Aronson (eds.), The Handbook of Social Psychology, Vol. 2, pp. 204–273. Addison-Wesley, Reading.

Sellin, D. and R. Mulchahay. 1965. The relationship of an institutional tour upon opinions about mental retardation. Am. J. Ment. Defic. 70: 408–412.

Semmel, M. L. 1959. Teacher attitudes and information pertaining to mental deficiency. Am. J. Ment. Defic. 63: 566–567.

Shotel, J. R., R. P. Iano, and J. F. McGettigan. 1972. Teacher attitudes associated with the integration of handicapped children. Exceptional Children 38: 677–683.

Smith, I. L. and S. Greenberg. 1974. Test of assumptions underlying the six hour retardate. Unpublished manuscript, Yeshiva University.

Strauch, J. D. 1970. Social contact as a variable in the expressed attitudes of normal adolescents toward EMR pupils. Exceptional Children 36: 485–494.

Strichart, S. S. and J. Gottlieb. 1975. Imitation of retarded children by their non-retarded peers. Am. J. Ment. Defic. 79: 506–513.

Tannenbaum, P. H. 1956. Initial attitude toward source and concept as factors in attitude change through communication. Pub. Opinion Quart. 20: 413–425.

Thurstone, L. L. 1946. Comment. Am. J. Sociol. 52: 39–40.

Thurstone, T. G. 1959. An evaluation of educating mentally handicapped children in special classes and in regular grades. (U.S. Office of Education Cooperative Research Program, Project No. OE SAE-6452), University of North Carolina, Chapel Hill.

Von Bracken, H. 1967. Attitudes concerning mentally retarded children. Paper presented at meeting of the First Congress of the International Association for the Scientific Study of Mental Deficiency, Montpelier, France.

Vurdelja-Maglajlic, D. and J. E. Jordan. 1974. Attitude-Behaviors toward retardation of mothers of retarded and non-retarded in four nations. Training School Bulletin 71: 17–29.

Warren, S. A. and D. R. Turner. 1966. Attitudes of professionals and students toward exceptional children. Training School Bulletin 62: 136–144.

Willey, N. R. and B. R. McCandless. 1968. Social stereotypes for normal, educable mentally retarded, and orthopedically handicapped children. Unpublished manuscript.

Winthrop, H. and H. Taylor. 1957. An inquiry concerning the prevalence of popular misconceptions relating to mental deficiency. Am. J. Ment. Defic. 62: 344–348.

Zajonc, R. B. 1965. Cognitive theories in social psychology. In G. Lindzey and E. Aronson (eds.), The Handbook of Social Psychology, Vol. 1, pp. 320–411. Addison-Wesley, Reading.

Issues Relating to The Quality of Life among Mentally Retarded Persons[1]

Robert B. Edgerton

For the past two years, my associates and I have been attempting to assess what we have called "the quality of life" of mentally retarded persons in residential facilities throughout Southern California. Using more or less traditional ethnographic techniques of field work, we have accumulated thousands of hours of firsthand observation and participation in the everyday lives of several hundreds of persons who at one time in their lives were labeled mildly or moderately retarded. In the discussion that follows, I shall first describe how we have carried out this field work, then I shall point to a number of issues that bear upon either the practicalities of providing residential care for the mentally retarded or the conceptual problems that relate to the presence in the world of such retarded people.

RESEARCH BACKGROUND AND PROCEDURES

In Southern California, as in any other large urbanized area in the United States, there are presumed to be hundreds of thousands of persons who could be labeled mentally retarded if they were to come to the attention of some part of the mental retardation system as represented by our medical facilities, our schools, or our legal apparatus. Although our research has inadvertently come upon many such people, and we have chosen to study some of them, our emphasis has been placed elsewhere. We have taken as our population of interest those persons who have been labeled as mental retardates and who have, at one time or another, taken up residence in some sort of publicly supported residential facility. Our population, then, is those people for whom the "principle of normalization" was most directly intended. A decade ago, such people would have spent a sizable part of

[1] The research on which this paper was based was supported in part by PHS Grant #HD04612 NICHD, the Mental Retardation Research Center, UCLA, and #HD-05540-02, Patterns of Care and the Development of the Retarded.

their lives in a large institution for the mentally retarded. Some still do, even today, but more and more of these moderately and mildly retarded young adults have been offered residential care in what has come to be known as "the community," that is, in small "family"- or "hostel"-like facilities scattered throughout the less expensive parts of Southern California. A few have undertaken supervised or independent living in apartments or houses. Some live their lives secluded in these various places, rarely emerging for any purpose. Others go to workshops, ride buses, play miniature golf. A few achieve competitive employment, get married, and are never seen again by the agencies that once provided them with aid.

To date, our fieldwork has involved over 500 retarded adults in more than 50 separate residential settings (exclusive of independent living arrangements). These individuals range in estimated abilities from moderate to borderline retardation, but most fall into the mild range and although many have a record of emotional disturbance, few have overt physical handicaps. The residential settings range from a large state institution, through smaller "board-and-care" and smaller yet "family-care" establishments, through various kinds of small experimental or "normalized" facilities, to independent or semi-independent living. We have not examined foster care settings. Prolonged and intensive observation and participation have been carried out in all of the above mentioned kinds of settings, with some 100 retarded persons, including 32 persons who had been the subjects of a follow-up study begun in 1960 (Edgerton, 1967). Parents, caretakers, social workers, and agency personnel have also been interviewed, and many of their interactions with retarded persons have been observed.

Our ethnographic procedures require familiarity with as many aspects of a retarded person's life as possible. Our methodological philosophy derives primarily from "naturalism," rather than behavioral science, or experimentalism. Naturalism calls for an investigator to attempt to comprehend and interpret the phenomena under study as faithfully as possible; the goal is to be true to the phenomena themselves. We believe that such a true rendering can best be approximated, although never fully accomplished, by following three principles: 1) that phenomena be seen in their relevant context, 2) that these phenomena be seen not only through the observer's eyes, but those of the subjects as well, and, 3) that reactive procedures be avoided at the same time that the investigator regards himself as a part of the phenomenon under investigation (Edgerton and Langness, 1974).

No existing methodology for the study of human behavior adequately satisfies those three principles. Ours is no exception, for our practice of naturalism is only partial. Nevertheless, our procedures differ markedly from those commonly employed in the study of mentally retarded people (interviews, tests, formal observation, or secondhand accounts), and do, we believe, provide a more complete and accurate interpretation of their lives than is possible by these other methods. Needless to say, the force of this assertion comes not from the fervor with which the method is advocated, but from the materials the method generates. I shall illustrate some of these materials here, but since an elaborate examination of these materials will not be possible, I shall also describe our procedures a bit more fully so that our claims to a naturalistic understanding can be better evaluated.

Our contact with a retarded person begins with a full discussion of our purposes and that person's rights, as is now generally required by HEW in order to safeguard human rights. Our procedures will antedate the HEW mandate and university "human use" committees, however. We rely on rapport, and rapport requires that our "subjects" have a clear understanding of what our research is all about. It also requires a clear statement of what we cannot do: provide better jobs, remove an unpopular caretaker, offer compensation for past injustices, etc. What we say is that we wish to try to understand their lives in the hope that through such understanding we may be able to help others like them to find a more meaningful existence. Usually they both understand and approve. Rapport depends upon reciprocity also, so we do offer help with some aspects of everyday life and we do sometimes give advice or information, but most of all, we offer concern, companionship, and a little fun.

To do so and to carry out such ethnographic naturalism, we must have prolonged contact with people. We must become, if only relatively so, a "natural" part of their lives. When we succeed, and sometimes we do not, we eventually gain access to more than the public domain of their lives. With Goffman, we assume that retarded people, and those normal people who manage one or another aspect of their lives, say and do many things in order to present a favorable face to others. Our ethnographic procedures are attuned to the Janus-faced quality of self-presentation, and by virtue of our prolonged and somewhat unpredictable presence in their world, we hope to be able to see more than the obvious. We drop by, we take retarded persons away from their residences, and we stay in their residences overnight or for a week or more. We attend important events in the lives of the people (and their caretakers), going to weddings, family gatherings, or weekend outings, and we introduce them to new recreational experiences. We videotape many of these encounters so that we and the participants themselves can discuss and interpret the behavior that took place (we also erase these videotapes if the people find anything in them that is objectionable). Our procedures do not "break down" all deception (efforts to deceive are, after all, part of the reality we hope to study), nor do they reduce the complexities of human life to a clear and simple truth. However, they do lessen the likelihood that an obvious deception will go unnoticed and that the contradictory complexity of a human life, even a retarded life, will be seen as simple and straightforward. The method is not intended to provide simple answers; it is intended to provide the empirical grounds for rejecting simple answers in favor of fuller and more accurate understanding. I shall return to this issue at the conclusion of this paper. First, we should examine the kinds of understandings, and puzzles, that we have come to in our study of retarded persons.

"ALTERNATIVE CARE": THE RESIDENTIAL WORLD OF THE RETARDED

Mildly retarded persons in Southern California live in a variety of settings. Large institutions continue to offer programs and facilities, but there are now various community-based alternatives. Some retarded persons reside in apartments by themselves or with roommates where they live under conditions that vary from close supervision by a social worker to virtual independence. Others live in so-called "experimental" or "normalized" settings such as apartment complexes that simulate a normal environment and ordinary hostel-like residences that adhere to the spirit of normalization. In one such place, for example, residents live two to a room with almost no supervision. Alcohol is permitted for those over 21 and discreet sexual relations are accepted. Residents are expected not only to work as normals, they are encouraged to travel into the outside community as normal persons would. The goal here is to provide an environment that will lead each resident toward an independent living arrangement.

But by far the largest number of alternative care facilities is of two kinds: "family care" homes with six or fewer residents, and "board and care" facilities which may house 30, 40, or even more persons. Family care homes are state licensed and supervised. While the milieux there places provide vary greatly, some of these places make an effort to provide more nearly normal experiences, and a few succeed well enough that their residents go on to live more independently. Board and care facilities are typically not licensed and even though their residents receive ATD (aid to the totally disabled)[2] as mentally retarded persons, these places are not effectively supervised. They are, quite simply, private enterprises. For example, residents receive about $280 per month from ATD and around $250 of this goes directly to the caretaker. Some board and care facilities are "open" settings which provide more nearly normalized experiences than large institutions typically do. Most, however, are closed, ghetto-like places, whose residents are walled off from any access to community life. Such places frequently lack most medical, psychological, and recreational services and their amenities are few indeed. Perhaps more significant still, the residents of such facilities are given to understand, in no uncertain terms, that they can hope for nothing different in the future. Since the residents in these closed settings appear to possess the same array of backgrounds, skills, and capabilities as residents in many of the more normalized settings, some explanation is called for.

Before attempting this explanation, a word about sampling is necessary. Since no complete roster of board and care facilities is maintained by any given agency, we collected as many rosters as possible from several agencies. From these lists we picked some facilities at random along a 100-mile radius inland from the coast. We also asked agency personnel to identify what they regarded as "good" and "bad" facilities. Our final sample of some 30 facilities was approximately one-third random, and two-thirds nominated, evenly divided into "good" and "bad" places. A few caretakers refused to cooperate with us. We assume that the majority of those who refused were operating facilities that would not be considered "normalized." Thus the conclusions presented here are drawn from a range of facilities which may be slightly biased toward, not away from, normalization. None of this is to suggest, of course, that conditions in these facilities are necessarily reflective of conditions in other parts of the country.

---

[2] Although there have been recent changes in this nomenclature, I retain it here to reflect the conditions that prevailed during the period of research under discussion.

The closed quality of most of these board and care facilities seems to derive from several sources, including the backgrounds of the caretakers, their experience in management, and their conceptions of mental retardation, its remediability and its dangers. But the primary source seems to be their profit motive. Caretakers, almost all of whom are women without any professional or post-high school training, are quite openly in business to make a profit. A caretaker receives not only a direct payment per resident from ATD, but several additional payments as well (for medical needs, special therapy, etc.). Since much of the residents' allocation of private money and their earnings from workshop also go to the caretakers for one reason or another, sizable sums of money can be involved, averaging $250 per bed per month. Actual operating costs cannot be obtained, but it is clear that a sizable profit is quite possible. Our best estimates (confirmed by experienced social workers and agency personnel) would be that a 30-bed facility would easily show a $25,000 annual profit. Indeed, some caretakers readily admit that they do make money and none has denied that a profit is essential. In more marginal facilities the question of profit may be even more relevant, since, as caretakers regularly tell our research staff (usually quite plainly), they cannot afford to lose a resident unless they are guaranteed a replacement. Empty beds, especially in a marginally profitable facility, could mean financial ruin. Since there is no guarantee of a replacement, the wise caretaker holds on to her residents.

Related to this profit motive and the need to keep one's beds full, is the near universal practice of withholding information about a resident's right to decide for himself or herself whether he or she wants to live in that facility. Even some social workers are remiss in telling their ATD clients about their rights. Almost all caretakers not only fail to tell their residents about such a right, most actually assure these residents that the caretakers have complete control *in loco parentis*. Some caretakers threaten to return an offending resident to "the hospital" (the large institution from which many have come and about which most know). It is interesting in this regard, that caretakers often demand to be called "mom." So pervasive is this deficit in knowledge among residents, that even when we have informed a resident of his rights (as we have sometimes felt obligated to do), the resident has refused to believe us, even when written confirmation has been supplied. One lingering consequence of institutionalization seems to be the belief among retarded persons that one is never again a free agent, instead, one is always "under the state." What is more, the state's agents are thought to be omnipresent: parents, caretakers, even researchers. An illustration of how far this feeling can go is provided by two young adult women of borderline intelligence who, when we first took them on an outing and asked where they wanted to go, directed us to a social agency and then asked to be photographed in front of the building. Asked why, the wistful but respectful response was, "that's where they keep our records."

The quality of life in the alternative care facilities we have studied is highly variable, with evidence here and there of exciting progress toward the goal of normalization. For most mentally retarded people in this system, however, the little institutions where they now reside appear to be no better than the large ones from which they came, and some are manifestly worse. This conclusion is based not only on our judgments about Klaber's

(1970) five criteria of inadequacy, but also on the subjective evaluations of the residents themselves.

There are many reasons why successful normalization will not be easy for these and other mentally retarded persons. But one current barrier to such an achievement parellels an older one. As in earlier years when the best and most reliable workers in large institutions were sometimes denied discharge because their skills were valuable to the staff, today, some apparently capable residents of board and care facilities are being denied access to more nearly normal lives because of the economic needs of their caretakers. Needless to add, caretakers who do not want to lose a profitable resident cannot only take direct measures to thwart normalization opportunities, they can and do create a covert culture in which dependency and incompetence are rewarded.[3]

PROCESSES OF DEPENDENCY

As should be apparent, while these caretakers are neither evil nor cruel in any literal sense, neither are they citizen advocates. There is perhaps a lesson here, if a somewhat metaphorical one, about the inimical relationship between monetary payment and advocacy (Wolfensberger, n.d.). Instead of relying upon advocates (who are few in number and consist primarily of parents and agency personnel), this population of retarded persons seems to be caught up in elaborate and tenacious dependency relationships. As was mentioned earlier, some of these dependencies are fostered by caretakers who receive and bank residents' money, inspect residents' clothing as if these normal appearing adults were small children, and who herd groups of residents about quite as if they were prisoners or the victims of a tour guide's officiousness. Many, like the lower class children Bruner (1971) writes about, are never allowed to solve problems for themselves, being continually interrupted in any such task by the caretaker or aide who not only completes the task, but usually adds a remark that the task was "too hard" or "don't try that, you'll just mess it up."

It is not merely the more profit-oriented caretakers who foster such dependencies. Our experiences with independently-living retarded persons showed again and again that these people did not look upon us as potential advocates of their rights, but as resources for the maintenance or augmentation of their everyday dependencies: for small loans, transportation, advice about bureaucratic matters, help in medical or dental appointments, shopping, handling money, reading, and the like. Not only does one become a resource for these people, one becomes part of a conspiracy to prevent the retarded person from being perceived as such by helping to cover up his incompetencies when in public.

So regular and visible are these demands that we have consciously attempted to avoid them, only to find ourselves, inexorably it seems, slipping back into the role the retarded person has structured. Indeed, efforts to break out of this role into a more normal-

---

[3] For another view see Bjaanes and Butler (1974).

appearing one very often causes consternation or brings the interaction to a complete stop. Such so-called dependency behavior may be a product of an institutional history, but it may also reflect real incapacity. For this reason, help or a cover-up may well be adaptive for the retarded person. Even if it is not, it so quickly becomes reciprocal or symbiotic (since normal persons are parties to the system too) that any change is difficult to achieve.

Consider the story of John, a man of 21 years, who was labeled mentally retarded at the age of 4 years. Since the age of 15 years he had lived in family care homes until about a year ago when he moved to a highly normalized board and care facility. After about a year in this place, he was tested and found to have a full scale WAIS of 102. He was not only suddenly normal, he was just as suddenly offered a job as a custodian at this same residential facility. There are many intriguing aspects about John's literal "normalization," and some of these will be discussed shortly, but one of the most revealing is his struggle to break out of his past dependency relationships, and to achieve, overnight as it were, responsible independence. The challenge was at first too great and he ran away. After his return he has made progress, but his efforts provide an evocative record of how basic such dependencies can be. As John said only a week before this was written: "I want freedom, but I want it regulated. It was much easier to be retarded."

More typical is Mel, a 35-year-old with a withered arm whose IQ is about 55. Mel has gone from a large institution, through board and care, to an independent living arrangement, and finally, to marriage. Mel presents himself in a reasonably normal manner and he has held a job for several years. His malapropisms, while numerous, do not quite give him away. At times his competence is impressive, as for example, during the time when he was "studying" for a driver's license in order to operate the motorcycle he had just bought. Since Mel can barely read, his chances of passing a written test did not seem promising, so we were puzzled when he did not seem to want help in applying for a special non-literate test or in tutoring to improve his reading skills. We were surprised and impressed to learn that Mel got the license entirely on his own by making the discovery that there were only five versions of the exam. Although he scored only a few correct answers on his first exam, the examiner routinely marked the errors on the answer sheet. Mel concluded that he would try again, surreptitiously matching his first answer sheet to each new exam, until he hit the same form and scored 100% correct. This he finally did. Since he can drive the machine quite skillfully and has had no mishaps in it in a year of driving, perhaps there is no injustice in what he accomplished. Despite such skills, Mel is incorrigibly dependent and makes the most of his opportunities for assistance. Often he seems not even to notice when assistance is given. For example, when we once took him to a restaurant for dinner, he spilled food on his jacket soiling it visibly. We ignored it, so did Mel. But as Mel left the restaurant, a perfect stranger at a nearby table stopped him and cleaned his jacket with a napkin. Mel said "thank you," but seemed neither embarrassed nor surprised by the action. He seemed to expect it.

An instructive example is provided by a further follow-up study of the people originally discussed in *The Cloak of Competence* (Edgerton, 1967). I reported that many of these people relied on "benefactors" for help with various aspects of everyday life, including the problems of passing as normal. When we looked these people up 12 to 14 years later, we found that as a group their reliance upon benefactors had lessened somewhat. Nevertheless, it was remarkable how many of these people not only asked us, new-found potential benefactors, to aid them with the same dependencies seen 12 years earlier, but also that their tactics in initiating and maintaining such relationships were unchanged. Since their lives had changed in so many other ways, this degree of constancy in their dependency upon normals is impressive. It is more impressive still because many of these people had for years managed their own lives without much help from benefactors, only to seize upon a benefactor's assistance once one came into being. One is tempted to assume that reliance upon a benefactor is easier than independence; it may also be more efficient.

STIGMA AND LABELING

If we rely upon our fundamental theories from social psychology or from symbolic interactionist sociology, there can be no doubt that what we think about ourselves, what we are, in effect, is a product of what other people think about us. In Mead's classic terms, *I* cannot become *me* without others, who react, judge, approve, and sometimes reject. We all know, intuitively, from our training, or from our experiences as social scientists, that "labeling" *can* set into motion a self-fulfilling prophecy, and that expectancies *can* have a "Rosenthal" effect.

My earlier work with mentally retarded persons here and in other societies has only confirmed these convictions. I found that "mental retardation" was not only a strongly stigmatizing label, but in our society perhaps the most stigmatizing label of all (Edgerton, 1967). But I also reported that this same label when applied to institutionalized persons could motivate them to seek release, and, if the label were not felt to be stigmatizing, that the probability of release, and success after release, would both be reduced (Edgerton and Sabagh, 1962). I still believe that these views, however qualitative their support, are correct. However, our current research has provided refinement in the form of additional possibilities, and I would like to mention several of these here.

First, it would appear that there is a widespread tendency on the part of normal persons to construe the everyday problems of retarded persons as "problems of retarded persons," not as "everyday problems." We have assembled a large collection of examples of this phenomenon, many of which are truly remarkable. I offer only one sample here. Sarah, a mildly retarded woman of 45 years with a long history of retardation and emotional upset, was placed in an apartment with three roommates—all under 20 years of age. Sarah was the mother of a college-educated daughter of the same age, a daughter with whom she had recurrent problems, involving among other things, dependence of mother upon daughter. In her new quarters this woman had problems. She was unhappy and so were her young roommates who complained that Sarah depended upon them to clean, produce meals, and pay bills. Sarah complained that she felt unwanted by the younger girls (and their inevitable boyfriends): an "old" lady who was out of place, useful only as a maid or a contributor to monthly expenses. How was this "problem" assessed? It was felt by Sarah's social worker that the problem was not one of an impossible situation for *any* 45-year-old woman, but a problem of mental retardation: Sarah lacked the adaptive skills to cope with independent living.

Another pattern involves the often apparent requirement that someone who has been labeled mentally retarded must be "super"-normal before ordinary normalcy will be granted. Again, we have assembled many instances. A particularly sad one involves a parallel with slavery. As far as we have been able to determine, mentally retarded residents of small community facilities are expected, indeed required, to be happy. A slave who did not smile affronted his master. A retarded person who is not conspicuously happy is said to be unstable, unready for greater normalization. So profound is this otherwise absurd expectation that one young woman said, in response to our question of what led her to believe that she was retarded, that she was sometimes sad. Alas, she is not alone in believing that perpetual joviality is a mark of normalcy.

Another point involves the extent to which the label, mental retardation, is character defining in the sense of penetrating into all domains of a person's life. It can be, there is no doubt, but it may not always be so. We have several cases of young and older adults who appear to think of themselves as retarded when they are around their caretakers or parents, but who think of themselves as more or less normal when they are in another setting. Some of the people in *The Cloak of Competence* sample appear to have developed this situationally specific definition of self. Another phenomenon involves displays of retarded behavior in the company of protective social workers, and more nearly competent behavior out of their presence. Here the issue is one's ability to continue to qualify for personal and financial support, and the conclusion is that retarded persons sometimes choose to appear even less competent than they are in order to maintain their source of income.

We have also found that persons whose capacity to cope with the demands of independent living were once markedly reduced by their sense of stigma from the label of mental retardation are no longer so strongly afflicted. Of the 32 members of *The Cloak of Competence* follow-up cohort studied in 1972 to 1974, almost all felt the stigma strongly in 1960 to 1961. In 1972 to 1974, a dozen of these people still feel it, but the remainder do so to a lesser degree, for reasons I shall shortly discuss. Efforts to deny stigma no longer obsess many of these people. They now have other problems and their adaptive skills have changed too. As one woman who was highly stigmatized in 1960 put it: "that's something past and over with."

Finally, there are some retarded people who seem to draw strength from their label. Like the righteously indignant everywhere, they mobilize their resources to attack the injustice that has been done to them. It is the stigma and its unjust application that gives their lives a focus, that gives them a purpose and that seems to keep them going. Such people are not common among the retarded persons we have encountered, but we have known two or three who fit this description. Their existence, however uncommon, adds complexity to the phenomenon of labeling and its consequences.

THE SOCIOCULTURAL CONTEXTS OF INCOMPETENCE

The recognition of incompetence, or mental retardation in our terms, is a cultural phenomenon, as everyone knows (Edgerton, 1970). But cultural differences in what is reckoned as stupidity are notoriously deceptive as signs of "mental retardation." For example, many Australian Aboriginals traditionally lacked words for numbers larger than four, relying on their fingers to designate higher numbers. In the broken "pidgin" English used intertribally, they used wonderfully imprecise phrases such as "little mob" (any number up to 10), "little-bit-big-feller mob" (between 10 and 20), "big mob" (more than 20) and "properly-big-feller-mob" (100 or more). But they had no words, pidgin or their own, for 7, or 21, or 73 (Waipuldanya, 1962).

Such people would be horribly incompetent in our culture, but in theirs they were fully competent. Since Aboriginal children learn our mathematics and number terms readily enough when they attend Western schools, presumably everyone would agree that their failure to use number terms in their traditional culture does not indicate mental retardation. But some cultural differences are not as easy to understand, especially those in our own society. Consider the following description of children (Gazaway, 1969):

> None has played with finger paints, puzzles, or blocks. Their 'toys' consist of broken bottles, sharp metal, discarded tin cans. Ask them about Goldilocks, and they will look at you in bewilderment—they have never heard a fairy tale. I made a beanbag from an old rag and asked some of the older boys to catch it. They had difficulty. With an old string ball and a heavy stick, I tried to involve them in batting practice. I was unsuccessful. Not only do games fail to interest them, they are almost completely unable to participate in most activities. They could not be taught to whistle, sing, or even hum a simple tune. I wrote: 1111 2222 3--- -4- -55- on a sheet of paper and asked a number of eight-year-olds who had never been to school to fill in the missing numbers. They could not. Nor were they able to draw a circle, a square, raise their right arms, raise their left arms, extend their fingers, or spell their names.

Are these children retarded? We cannot say. They are the impoverished, isolated, thoroughly deprived inhabitants of a remote part of Eastern Kentucky. We cannot say that when they go to school they, like the Aboriginals, prove to be intellectually competent. Some do, but others do not. Few attend school regularly, fewer still graduate, and almost none shows an interest in academic learning. The world is full of children such as these and we are not quite sure what to say about them (Scribner and Cole, 1973; Cole and Scribner, 1974). Is the problem simply one of cultural difference, or have these differences produced lasting deficits as well?

Cultural differences also play an obvious role among the retarded persons we have studied. Their lives often reflect the kinds of experiences that have afflicted the children of Appalachia or an urban slum. But these matters are well known and it is another, more simple, cultural difference that I wish to emphasize here. The retarded persons we have focused upon are seldom from "middle class" families; those that are did not themselves attend college, nor have they established a comfortable pattern of middle class living. Those who are most responsible for charting the course of their present-day welfare, social workers and other agency professionals, are typically both college graduates and practitioners of a middle class style of life. When these personnel set goals for more normalized community living and when they evaluate progress toward these goals, they often reveal a marked "middle class" cultural bias. For example, it is commonplace to expect retarded persons who are given the opportunity to live more independently to have quite extensive homemaking skills. The following list of such skills is taken from a more comprehensive guide for independent living currently in use:

Meal preparation skills:

a. Can follow directions of simple recipes
b. Knows how to measure ingredients
c. "Cooks" an adequate complete meal (may use canned and frozen food for this purpose)
d. Mixes and cooks simple food, e.g., frying eggs, making pancakes, hamburgers, etc.
e. Prepares simple foods requiring no mixing or cooking, e.g., making sandwiches, preparing cold cereal, etc.
f. Knows how to: control top burners, preheat oven, and clean stove safely
g. Knows how to store food.

Aside from the fact that many middle class bachelors would fail to meet these criteria, it happens that so would many perfectly normal working class men and women in our society, particularly those from ethnic minority groups. Even if the retarded persons in our study might possess these skills, they rarely employ them. Instead, they eat hot dogs, or open cans, or heat frozen "TV" dinners. Sometimes, they eat at inexpensive hamburger stands or the like. But since they know that they are expected to behave like a graduate of a home economics class, they become adept at lying about their homemaking and culinary skills. Such performances are sometimes quite convincing and earn praise which is surely deserved even if its source is misunderstood. Thus, even if a mentally retarded person eats a can of beans for breakfast, he knows that he should say that he prepares a weekly menu and husbands his money so that he can have a balanced diet even at the end of a month.

As a good many experienced social workers realize, there are many culturally acceptable styles of life in our society that diverge drastically from the middle class model. The mentally retarded persons in our study usually establish one of these styles of life and find it satisfying. However, there is still a strong tendency among persons who guide the welfare of retarded people to behave as if there were but one culture, and that normalization should therefore be judged by middle class standards of speech, dress, hygiene, nutrition, and even recreation.

There are many other ways in which the sociocultural system influences the ways in which we interpret incompetence. In this regard, the lives of the men and women from

The Cloak of Competence cohort may be instructive. Although 16 of the persons studied in 1960 to 1961 could not be located, those who were found provide us with an interesting longitudinal lesson. Of these 32 people, some 14 were living very much the same way in 1972 to 1974 as they were in 1960 to 1961, while the others had changed their lives more or less substantially. If each of these 32 individuals is looked at, first in 1960 to 1961, then some 12 years later, we have a sort of "individual-as-his-own-control" perspective upon things. This perspective leads to some complex and difficult problems which are not appropriate here, since the similarities and differences we see in these lives require a more sophisticated analysis than can here be attempted. But some of these life changes are consistent and appear to be linked to basic social and economic conditions.

To illustrate, in 1960 to 1961, only 3 of these 32 persons were receiving social welfare payments. In 1972 to 1974, 14 were recipients of such aid. Does this change reflect a general reduction in the competence or independence of this cohort? We think not. Our subjective evaluation of competence and independence indicate that the cohort as a whole has increased its capacity in both regards. The increased utilization of social welfare suggests, we believe, not a reduction in competence, but a reduction in employment opportunities, and an increase in access to social welfare eligibility. In 1960 to 1961, the nation's economy was robust, hope was commonplace, and there was both an expectation, and a semblance of reality to the suggestion, that the mentally retarded could be, and some would be, employed. In 1972 to 1974, the economy had turned down, as we are all keenly aware, but the availability of social welfare payments for the mentally retarded, at least in Southern California, had greatly increased. In 1972 to 1974, being out of work was hardly exceptional, and while the retarded were often unemployed, so were a great many normal, previously employed people. Thus, changes in economic opportunity and access to social welfare assistance can radically alter the way we construe the adaptive success of retarded persons.

At the same time, a more fundamental change was taking place. These people were getting older. In 1960 to 1961, the mean age of the cohort was 35. Twelve to 14 years not only increased the *mean* age, it brought some members of the cohort well into their 50's, and some even into their 60's. Overall, and particularly for these older persons, a remarkable shift in status has taken place. These people now tend to live near normal people of similar age, often in trailer camps. They, and their normal neighbors, tend to have multiple physical complaints, and to be unemployable. As a result, the retarded people are seen, and see themselves, as no different from anyone else. When one is younger, physical illness and unemployability stand out. But when one is growing old, such problems are perfectly natural. So we see that changes in socioeconomic patterns and in aging bring about changes in how incompetence is evaluated, both by us as observers, and by the incompetent persons themselves. We as observers rate the cohort as being more competent in 1972 to 1974 than it was in 1960 to 1961, and more independent as well. Cohort members generally share this view. This may be due, as Cobb (1972) has suggested, to greater familiarity with community living, but it would also seem to reflect changes in the nature of this community itself.

It should be obvious that the incompetence of retarded individuals, like normals, varies from time to time and place to place. How we evaluate a person's competence therefore depends in part upon our knowledge of change and circumstance.

CONCLUSION

All of the investigations discussed here are continuing. Circumstances will change and so, hopefully, will our understandings of what we see. I say this not to offer a disclaimer; what I have reported seems to me to be accurate. Nor is it meant as a promissory note about how much more we will one day learn, although we do hope to learn more. I make this point (by now laboriously) in order to underscore the importance of looking at the reality of mental retardation as a process, not a static structure. In one sense, this is a truism, as all reality undergoes change. I mean more than this. I mean that what mental retardation "is" and what we can understand of it is changable depending, among other things, upon the setting in which the retarded person behaves, the sociocultural system that informs those settings, and the maturation and aging of the person himself. All social science is a search for stable, regular features that we call structures, and more changable ones that we call processes. In my opinion, studies of mental retardation have emphasized structures to the neglect of processes, and our knowledge has suffered accordingly.

The lives of the mentally retarded are changable, but they are also complex. Most of us, myself included, are sometimes guilty of writing (and perhaps believing) that the mentally retarded and their lives are simpler than they really are. Granted, writers about any aspect of human reality could be similarly accused, but the charge here may not be entirely gratuitous since the retarded are by definition "simple" and our accounts of them cannot often be praised for their efforts to discover complexity.

In this regard, a few general observations may be in order. First, it is an anthropological cliché that what, after 1 year of field work, seems perfectly simple, seems altogether different after 2 or 3 years of research. In time, one can not only learn something more, one can learn things that are altogether different. Try as they may, anthropologists have learned that they rarely achieve a complete understanding of any cultural event and when it comes to understanding the people who participate in the event, completeness is even less attainable. Clifford Geertz (1973) has put it well:

> Cultural analysis is intrinsically incomplete. And, worse than that, the more deeply it goes, the less complete it is. It is a strange science whose most telling assertions are its most tremulously based, in which to get somewhere with the matter at hand is to intensify the suspicion, both your own and that of others, that you are not getting it right.

But then science itself, at least according to some, is not the reduction of complexity to simplicity, but the process of understanding complexity in its own right.

I say all of this because I have come to realize that there is far more to mentally retarded persons than I had previously realized. My own writing about mentally retarded persons does not seem to me wrong, it is simply unfinished. Not only have I not got to the bottom of things, I cannot even guess where the bottom is. So I end with a cautionary note, for myself, if no one else: mentally retarded persons, even though they may have lesser skills and capacities than the rest of us, are nevertheless complex persons who live immensely complicated lives, like the rest of us.

ACKNOWLEDGMENT

I am grateful to my colleagues on this research project for their excellent field work and for their help in preparing this paper: Karen Joseph, Gordon Creed, Don Sutherland, Judy Myers, David Goode, and especially the group's coordinator, Sylvia Bercovici. The hard work is theirs and in many respects so is this paper. Their individual interests and accomplishments will be reflected in forthcoming papers and monographs.

REFERENCES

Bjaanes, A. T. and E. W. Butler. 1974. Environmental Variation in Community Care Facilities for Mentally Retarded Persons. Am. J. Ment. Defic. 78: 429–439.

Bruner, J. S. 1971. The Relevance of Education. W. W. Norton, New York.

Cole, M. and S. Scribner. 1974. Culture and Thought. A Psychological Introduction. John Wiley & Sons, New York.

Edgerton, R. B. 1967. The Cloak of Competence. University of California Press, Berkeley and Los Angeles.

Edgerton, R. B. 1970. Mental Retardation in Non-Western Societies: Toward a Cross-Cultural Perspective on Incompetence. In H. C. Haywood (ed.), Social-Cultural Aspects of Mental Retardation, pp. 523–559. Appleton-Century-Crofts, New York.

Edgerton, R. B. and L. L. Langness. 1974. Methods and Styles in the Study of Culture. Chandler & Sharp Publishers, Inc., San Francisco.

Edgerton, R. B. and G. Sabagh. 1962. From Mortification to Aggrandizement: Changing Self-Concepts in the Careers of the Mentally Retarded. Psychiatry. 25: 263–272.

Gazaway, R. 1969. The Longest Mile. Doubleday & Co., Garden City, New York.

Gertz, C. 1973. The Interpretation of Cultures. Basic Books, New York.

Klaber, M. M. 1970. Retardates in Residence—A Study of Institutions. University of Hartford, West Hartford, Connecticut.

Scribner, S. and M. Cole. 1973. Cognitive Consequences of Formal and Informal Education. Science 182: 553–559.

Wolfensberger, W. n.d. Citizen Advocacy for the Handicapped, Impaired, and Disadvantaged: An Overview. Washington, D.C.: DHEW Publication No. (OS) 72-42, President's Committee on Mental Retardation.

Sociocultural Factors
In Educational Labeling[1]

Jane R. Mercer

This paper is a report on the current status of a project designed to develop a multi-cultural, pluralistic method of educational assessment which will evaluate the child as a multi-dimensional person being socialized within a particular sociocultural setting. The need for such a system was demonstrated in earlier research studies which established that 1) disproportionate numbers of children from lower socioeconomic levels and from minority group backgrounds are being labeled as mentally retarded by the public schools and placed in classes for the mentally retarded, 2) minority students labeled as mentally retarded have significantly higher IQ scores and fewer identified physical anomalies than their Anglo-American counterparts, and 3) the public schools rely almost entirely upon individually administered tests of "intelligence" as a diagnostic tool and do not systematically take the sociocultural background of the student into account when interpreting the meaning of his or her score on the test or in making decisions about educational programs (Mercer, 1973).

An earlier paper argued that present psychological assessment practices in the public schools violate five rights of children: their right to be evaluated within a culturally appropriate normative framework, their right to be assessed as a multi-dimensional human being, their right to be fully educated, their right to be free of stigmatizing labels, and their right to ethnic identity and respect (Mercer, 1974).

The present paper will deal specifically with the issue of evaluating students within a culturally appropriate normative framework which takes his or her sociocultural background into account when interpreting the meaning of a test score. Before presenting

[1] Public Health Service Grant MH 20646-02, from the National Institute of Mental Health, Department of Health, Education and Welfare. The opinions and conclusions stated in this paper by the author are not to be construed as officially reflecting the policy of the Department of Health, Education, and Welfare.

We wish to thank James Frane of the Health Services Computer Center at the University of California at Los Angeles, for his kind assistance in doing the analysis of differences between the slopes and intercepts of the equations for the three ethnic groups for us using a program recently developed by him and his staff.

141

findings from our study, there are five premises which form the basis for our approach which must first be clarified and made explicit.

First, tests measure only what a person has learned. Biological intellectual capacity (the genotype) cannot be measured directly. An individual's genetic potential is always expressed through behavior acquired in a social and cultural setting, his phenotype. Thus, all tests are basically measures of achievement and all test scores are influenced by a wide variety of environmental factors as well as the person's innate capacity for learning.

Because all learning takes place in a sociocultural setting, no test is "culture free." However, some types of tests may be more "culture fair" than others because the materials covered in the test are present in more than one cultural tradition and persons from different cultural traditions have equal opportunities to acquire those particular skills or master those particular concepts.

Third, the distinction between tests of "intelligence" or "aptitude" and tests of "academic achievement" is erroneous. Jencks makes a succinct statement on this point.

> In practice, however, all tests measure both aptitude and achievement. . . . If two students have had the same opportunity to acquire verbal skills, and if one has picked them up while the other has not, the test does indeed measure 'aptitude.' But if one child has been raised speaking Spanish and another English, the test measures the Spanish-speaking child's mastery of a foreign language. If the Spanish-speaking child does worse than the English-speaking, this shows lower achievement in this area, but it need not imply less aptitude. . . . When everyone is equally well prepared, achievement tests become aptitude tests. When people are unequally prepared, aptitude tests become achievement tests (Jencks, 1972, p. 56).

Thus, whether a test can be interpreted as a test of "achievement" or a test of "aptitude" or "intelligence" depends upon the extent to which the persons whose performances are being compared have had an equal opportunity to learn the material in the test. The differentiation between "achievement" and "intelligence" or "aptitude" tests does not rest upon the test form or content, per se.

Our approach to pluralistic norms is based upon the fundamental premise that all tests are achievement tests which can be interpreted as measures of "aptitude" only when an individual's performance is being compared with others who 1) have had similar opportunities to learn the skills and information covered in the test and 2) have been similarly motivated and rewarded for learning those skills. Additional factors may also influence performance on a test so that an individual's score cannot be interpreted as a measure of "aptitude." Among these other factors are the person's familiarity with test procedures and test taking, the person's emotional state and anxiety level, and the state of the person's sensory equipment, i.e., vision, hearing, and so forth. In our System of Multi-cultural, Pluralistic Assessment (SOMPA), we are incorporating measures which will attempt to evaluate some of these other factors.

From this perspective, the technical problem in assessing "aptitude" is one of *identifying as precisely as possible the appropriate normative framework within which to interpret each individual's performance so that he is being compared only with others who have had similar opportunities to learn the materials in the test.*

Fourth, the norms for the standardized, norm-referenced tests currently used by the public schools are *not* universally applicable to all children attending the public schools as the basis for estimating the child's *aptitude*. Standard norms do provide information on the child's current level of *achievement* relative to other students of his age but they may or may not provide valid information on his learning potential. Such inferences can be made only when the student is being compared with persons of the same age from the same sociocultural background.

Evidence from our earlier studies (as well as the present study) indicates that identifying the appropriate normative framework for interpreting a particular test score as a measure of "aptitude" will require more than simply categorizing students by ethnic or racial group. Using a five-question index, we classified 595 Mexican-American children into five categories according to the extent to which their family background corresponded to the modal cultural configuration of the dominant Anglo-American society. The group of children from homes most like the Anglo-American mode had a mean IQ score on the Wechsler Intelligence Scale for Children (Wechsler, 1949) of 104.4. The least Anglicized group had a mean score of 84.5. A similar analysis of 339 Black children produced almost identical results. The children from homes most like the Anglo-American mode had a mean IQ of 99.5 while those from the least Anglicized homes had a mean score of 82.7 (Mercer, 1973, p. 245). Clearly, both of these Black and Mexican-American populations are culturally heterogeneous and cannot be treated as single populations. Thus, pluralistic norms must go beyond simple ethnic/racial classification systems and be based on more precise identification of relevant sociocultural factors.

Some recent work by educational historians provides valuable insights into the historical factors producing systematic racial, ethnic, and socioeconomic differences on standardized tests of academic tests (Karier et al., 1973; Katz, 1971). A complete review of their work goes beyond the scope of this paper, but a brief summary helps to place the relationship between public education and the testing movement into proper perspective.

Katz (1971) describes four alternative models of educational organization which competed for ascendency during the early nineteenth century: democratic localism, corporate voluntarism, paternalistic voluntarism, and incipient bureaucracy. Democratic localism developed in rural areas and was based on the principle that complete operation and control of the community school resides in the families whose children attend the school. There was close parental control and supervision of teachers, the curriculum, and the values taught in the community school. Because of local control, each school reflected the values and culture of its neighborhood. As a result, these schools had a highly decentralized, pluralistic educational configuration. Secondary education was handled through the educational model which Katz defines as corporate voluntarism. Single academies were operated as corporations with self-perpetuating boards of trustees and were financed privately through tuition and endowments. In the early years, some states viewed academies as public institutions because they served a "nonexclusive clientele" and states promoted their establishment through land grants (Katz, 1971, p. 23). During the first half of the nineteenth century, a large number of academies offering a wide variety of curricula were established by various private groups and denominations.

Coexisting with democratic localism and corporate voluntarism in education was the markedly different model of paternalistic voluntarism which developed in urban centers. Paternalistic voluntarism is exemplified by the New York Free School Society, established by leading citizens in 1805, for the purpose of socializing the unchurched poor, "to counteract the disadvantages resulting from the situation of their parents." Administered by an unpaid, self-perpetuating board, this system of education "provided the vehicle for the efforts of one class to civilize another and thereby ensure that society would remain tolerable, orderly, and safe" (Katz, 1971, p. 9). Strict discipline, humiliating punishments, keen competition among students, and educational drill characterized the system which assumed "exclusive" control of children without permitting their parents any participation in the management of the school, development of the curricula, or selection of teachers. To be eligible for "free" school, parents had to be certified as paupers. Those who administered the "free" schools, "did not deisgn the system for their own children nor for the children of their friends. Rather, they attempted to ensure social order through the socialization of the poor in cheap, mass schooling factories" (Katz, 1971, p. 11).

The fourth organizational mode which incorporated the basic social philosophy of the paternalistic "free schools," and eventually became the dominant one, was called incipient bureaucracy (Katz, 1971, p. 28). The central issue in the controversy among these four models was the extent to which American education should be standardized in structure, content, and program. Horace Mann and Henry Barnard, promoters of the bureaucratic form, attacked democratic localism because its decentralized administration was inefficient. They argued that the heterogeneity of urban neighborhoods would result in intense political battles among local parents for control of the moral and political ideas taught in the schools and the urban poor were incompetent to provide the proper education for their children. Standardization rather than pluralism won the day. The new definition of "public school" as a school established, controlled, and supported by the public without charge for tuition, resulted in the demise of the academy and democratic localism to be replaced by a bureaucratic form standardized to be the culture bearer for the Anglo-American cultural tradition.

According to Katz, incipient bureaucracy, which reproduced in the schools the organizational forms of the developing industrial order, has the following structural characteristics: compulsory attendance with emphasis on the importance of time, elimination of the local elementary school district by consolidation into the larger high school district, centralization of administrative control, classification of scholars into grades, and emphasis on teacher training and professionalism, and standardization of the curriculum. Although the schools were officially religiously and politically neutral, the values taught were those of Benjamin Franklin and the Puritan ethic, "a fear of poverty, a desire for wealth, a respect for work, a need for thrift, and a keen sense of duty to be a productive, useful citizen of the community" (Karier, 1973, p. 10). Fear that the illiterate immigrant might destroy American institutions led to public school programs intended to acculturate and "Americanize" immigrant children. "Religious values taught in the common school were Protestant; social values, White Anglo-Saxon; and economic values, Puritan" (Karier, 1973, p. 12). "Cultural homogenization" stemmed from a "gut fear of the cultural divisiveness inherent in the increasing religious and ethnic diversity of American life" (Katz, 1971, p. 39). Education functioned to blur cultural distinctions through a monocultural, educational "melting pot" in which all children were to be Anglicized.

Typically, all instruction was in English and the curricular content focused on Anglo-American institutions, history, literature, and values. Thus, almost from its inception, American public education has taught the cultural tradition of only one of many cultural streams brought by migrants to this continent. From these historical beginnings, we have the public schools as they exist today: Anglocentric, monocultural, class-biased, standardized, and centralized bureaucracies administered by professional educators.

The history of the testing movement has been intimately associated with public education. Binet's original "intelligence" test was designed to identify those children who would not succeed academically and should be placed in special schools for the mentally subnormal (Binet and Simon, 1905). After the idea of "intelligence" testing was adopted in the United States, the primary criterion for testing the validity of measures of "intelligence" has continued to be their ability to predict which children would be successful in a single social institution, the public schools. Thus, "intelligence" came to be equated with success in a social institution that was monocultural and class biased in its operation. Not surprisingly, children's relative performance on tests reflects quite accurately the extent to which their sociocultural backgrounds match the cultural and social class biases of the school. Correlations between test scores and school success are high because correlations between any test and a criterion which are both biased in the same direction will, inevitably, be high (Williams, 1974).

Although multi-cultural programs and bilingual education have recently appeared in some public schools, the programs in most schools remain monocultural, class biased, and Anglocentric. Standard tests of academic achievement and so-called "intelligence" tests continue to be constructed to predict success in monocultural public schools and are very school system specific in their predictive powers. Persons from lower class backgrounds and/or non-Anglo backgrounds have more difficulty with the tests just as they have, historically, had more difficulty coping with an American educational system originally designed by the dominant Anglo majority to "socialize" the children of "foreign" cultures.

We can only speculate how the types of tests and the criteria for "validity" would have differed if democratic localism had prevailed as the dominant educational pattern. If the United States had multi-cultural public schools perpetuating many different cultural traditions, in addition to the Anglo-American tradition, multiple criteria for validity and many different tests geared to a variety of cultural heritages would probably have been developed.

This brings us to the fifth premise on which pluralistic assessment is based, the role of public education as an intervener and labeler. Numerous studies have documented the fact that a primary function of educational institutions as they now function is allocating persons to adult roles and statuses in American society (Parsons, 1959; Cicourel and Kitsuse, 1963; Turner, 1960). Indeed, Jencks takes the position that "schools serve primarily as selection and certification agencies, whose job is to measure and label people, and only secondarily as socialization agencies, whose job is to change people" (Jencks, 1972, p. 135).

Using inappropriate normative frameworks for making inferences about the intellectual potential of students is one aspect of the process by which schools recreate in microcosm the unequal status relationships of the larger society and help perpetuate social inequalities. If schools are to shift from labeling children to educating children, it is essential that methods be devised for identifying a student's aptitude, i.e., learning potential, as well as his level of current functioning, i.e., his achievement. We are proposing that both achievement and aptitude can be estimated with the same standardized instrument by using different sets of norms.

RESEARCH DESIGN

Sample

During the 1972 to 1973 school year, the mothers of 2100 children (700 Black, 700 Chicano/Latino, 700 Anglo-American), 5 through 11 years of age, were interviewed. Using the data from the ethnic survey conducted annually by the state Department of Education (California State Department of Education, 1972), each subsample was independently selected to represent the public school population of California for that ethnic/racial group. We were able to locate 1924 of the children and test them with the 1974 revision of the Wechsler Intelligence Scale for Children (WISC-R). The tested subsamples consisted of 616 Black, 620 Chicano/Latino, and 699 Anglo-American children.

The sampling frame for each ethnic subsample consisted of 50 clusters of 14 children, 1 male and 1 female at each age level, 5 through 11 years of age. The multi-stage procedure first selected 50 school districts on a probability basis determined by the number of students of a particular ethnic group enrolled in that district. Rural districts with a total enrollment of less than 200 children of a particular ethnic group were combined with other districts to form "contrived" districts. Districts with large enrollments were selected more than once for some samples. For example, the Los Angeles Unified School District, which enrolls over 600,000 students appeared in the Black sample 19 times, the Chicano/Latino sample 10 times, and the Anglo-American sample 5 times. Schools were selected within districts on a probability basis according to the number of students of a particular ethnic group enrolled in the school. Individual children were randomly selected from the attendance records of each school to fill the cluster of 14 children from that school. The ethnic identity of a child was based on his social identity and his surname. The Spanish surnamed children have been designated as Chicano/Latino because that subsample consists of Spanish surnamed children not only from a Mexican heritage but from other Latino cultures, i.e., Cuba, Puerto Rico, Central America, and South America.

Data Collection Procedures

Mothers were interviewed in their homes by women of the same ethnic group as the mother. Altogether, 27 Anglo-American, 42 Black, and 38 Chicano/Latino women served as interviewers following an average of 10 hours of training which included two supervised interviews. Chicano/Latino interviewers were required to speak, read, and write Spanish. The Spanish version of the interview was used when preferred by the respondent, 31.8% of the Chicano/Latino cases. Most interviewers were recruited through recommendations made by administrators in the various school districts and lived within the attendance area of the districts in which they were interviewing. However, most interviewers did not live in the attendance area of the individual school from which children were chosen for the sample and did not know the respondent prior to the interview. Mothers were paid for the interview and signed consent forms permitting their children to be tested. The percentages of mothers of children initially selected for the sample who agreed to participate was 87.4% for Anglo-American mothers, 84.1% for Chicano/Latino mothers, and 73.3% for Black mothers. Mothers who declined to participate were replaced by randomly selected alternatives from the same school.

The WISC-R (Wechsler, 1974) was administered to the children during school hours. A total of 71 certified school psychologists and second-year graduate student interns did the testing. Twelve percent of the tests were administered by the school psychologists employed by the school districts in the study. The revised version of the scale, the WISC-R, was normed on a population of 2200 children, 100 boys and 100 girls at each age level. A quota sampling procedure was used. Whites and non-whites were included in the sample in the same proportion found in the 1970 Census for the age range tested. Non-whites included Blacks, American Indians, and Orientals.

The Measure of Sociocultural Modality

During the interview, each mother was asked a series of 40 questions relating to the sociocultural characteristics of the family. These questions were factor analyzed and nine factors were identified. Each factor was given a name which describes the items appearing in the factor. In the following descriptions of the content of the nine factors, factor loadings for each item are presented in parentheses.

The factor analysis program used for these computations does principle factoring with iteration. The initial estimates of the commonalities are the squared multiple correlations. An iterative procedure is used to improve these estimates. The factor matrix is rotated using VARIMAX computational routines with a maximum of 25 iterations (test criterion = 0.001). Given these parameters, factors are generated which are as orthogonal as possible.

Factor 1: Family Structure Family structure is based on three variables: the sex of the head of household (0.93), the marital status of the mother or mother substitute (0.78), and whether the child is living with both biological parents or with only one biological parent (0.92). This factor accounted for 32.5% of the total variance. (Scoring Range 0—3.)

Factor 2: Anglization Anglization consisted of five questions: highest grade completed by the head of household (0.49), highest grade completed by the mother or mother substitute (0.53), whether the head of household was reared in the United States outside the South versus reared in a foreign country or reared in the South (0.81), whether the mother was reared in the United States outside the South versus reared in a foreign country or reared in the South (0.86), and an interviewer rating of the level of English language usage of the respondent (0.68). This factor accounted for 23.3% of the total variance. (Scoring Range 0—10.)

Chicano/Latino respondents were asked a series of questions relating to how frequently they spoke Spanish at home, with relatives, in the neighborhood, and in the community. This scale was significantly correlated with an interviewer rating of the English language usage of the respondent. We concluded that the interviewer ratings were relatively valid indicators of language usage. Therefore, we decided to include the interviewer ratings rather than the language scale in the sociocultural modality measure because the interviewer ratings would provide information for Black and Anglo-American respondents as well as Chicano/Latino respondents.

Factor 3: Occupation of Head Occupation of head consisted of a single variable. The respondent described the occupation of the person who provided the primary financial support for the family and that occupation was coded into nine occupational levels corresponding to the gradations on the Duncan Socioeconomic Index (Reiss, 1961). These levels can be generally described as unemployed, laborers, operatives, craftsman, clerical workers, salespersons, self-employed proprietors, salaried managers and officials, and professionals. This factor accounted for 9.0% of the total variance. (Scoring Range 0—9.)

Factor 4: Family Size Family size consisted of two items: the number of full brothers and sisters of the sample child (0.78) and the total number of persons living in the household at the time of the interview (0.81). This factor accounted for 8.0% of the total variance. (Scoring Range 0—16.)

Factor 5: Parent-Child Relationship Parent-child relationship consisted of two items: the biological relationship between the child and the head of the household (0.61) and the biological relationship between the child and the mother or mother substitute. This factor accounted for 7.4% of the total variance. (Scoring Range 0—2.)

Factor 6: Sense of Efficacy Sense of efficacy included three Likert-type questions dealing with the respondent's locus of control and sense of powerlessness. Persons with low scores on the efficacy measure believe that a person's success or failure is predetermined at birth (0.54), that a person has to live for today and let tomorrow take care of itself (0.60), and that planning makes people unhappy since plans hardly ever work out (0.69). This factor accounted for 6.5% of the total variance. (Scoring Range 0—3.)

Factor 7: Source of Income Source of income includes two questions: Whether or not the head of household provides most of the family income (0.79), and an ordinal ranking of sources of financial support for the family (0.82). This factor accounted for 5.5% of the total variance. (Scoring Range 0—3.)

Factor 8: Urbanization Urbanization consists of the size town in which the head of household was reared (0.72) and the size town in which the mother was reared (0.75). Responses were categorized farm, small town, small city, and large city. This factor accounted for 4.3% of the variance. (Scoring Range 0—6.)

Factor 9: Community Participation Community participation contained four questions which asked the respondent to report how often she participated in meetings and events at the child's school (0.54), how often she participated in meetings at church or with religious groups (0.41), how often she met with groups working for the welfare of the community but not related to church (0.41), and how often she participated in social affairs with other persons not related to church (0.28). This factor accounted for 3.5% of the total variance. (Scoring Range 0–6.)

Measures of Socialization

Role Boundaries During the interview with the mother, the interviewer asked the mother a series of questions intended to measure the child's adaptive behavior, the Adaptive Behavior Inventory for Children (ABIC). These questions asked about the child's social role performance in the family, neighborhood, and school. Each question had three categories of response: a latent category which indicated that the child had never performed a particular role, an emergent category which indicated that the child performed a role occasionally and/or under supervision, and a mastered category which indicated that the child regularly performed a particular social role without supervision or adult assistance. Some respondents, however, reported that the child did not have an opportunity to perform certain roles or had not been allowed to perform certain roles. Thus, a child's role performance could be bounded by environmental factors, such as living in a rural area which did not provide opportunities for some types of activities. Role performance could also be bounded by cultural restrictions on the types of activities permitted a child of his or her age and sex. For example, many Mexican-American mothers reported that they did not permit their daughters to participate in any activities which would keep them away from home overnight. Such behavior is not culturally permissible for unmarried Mexican-American girls from traditional families.

We totaled the number of "no opportunity" and "not allowed" responses given by each mother and designated the score as a measure of Role Boundaries. Scores ranged from 0 to over 30. The average score was 11.25 with a standard deviation of 9.75.

Anonymity was a second measure derived from responses to the Adaptive Behavior Inventory. It consists of the total number of "Don't Know" responses given by the mother or mother substitute. We theorized that caretakers who know relatively little about the activities of the child are providing a socialization setting in which the child is relatively anonymous, an unknown. The mean number of "Don't Know" responses was low, 2.35, and skewed. The standard deviation was 3.00. Scores ranged from 0–10.

FINDINGS

Ethnic Differences in Sociocultural Modalities and Socialization

Table 1 presents the mean scores for each ethnic group on each sociocultural and socialization factor and tests the statistical significance of differences across the three ethnic groups using one-way analysis of variance. The significance of difference between

Table 1. Mean sociocultural modality and socialization scores for 1924 Black, Chicano/Latino, and Anglo-American children 5 through 11 years of age

	Black N = 616		Chicano/ Latino N = 620		Anglo-American N = 688		One way ANOVA (F-Ratio)	Scheffé test[a]		
								Black versus Chicano/ Latino (F)	Black versus Anglo-American (F)	Anglo-American versus Chicano/ Latino (F)
	(Mean)	(SD)	(Mean)	(SD)	(Mean)	(SD)				
Sociocultural modalities										
Family structure	1.75	1.35	2.39	1.09	2.45	1.01	65.36**	102.25***	122.50**	NS
Anglization	6.10	1.97	4.24	3.02	8.05	1.78	460.42***	172.95***	190.10***	725.80**
Occupation head	2.95	2.25	2.75	2.08	5.26	2.52	258.02***	NS	266.80**	315.00***
Size of family	7.78	3.80	9.17	4.10	6.80	2.80	76.37***	38.64**	19.20**	112.32***
Parent-child relationship	1.75	0.57	1.85	0.43	1.80	0.49	7.19***	6.25**	NS	NS
Sense of efficacy	2.21	0.98	2.00	1.13	2.69	0.59	97.69***	8.11**	44.78**	92.27**
Source of income	2.11	1.31	2.51	1.03	2.81	0.63	79.63**	23.95**	77.29**	14.24***
Urbanization	3.87	1.80	3.65	1.73	3.88	1.71	3.50*	NS	NS	NS
Community participation	4.25	1.94	2.72	2.01	4.19	1.78	141.22**	99.44**	NS	96.90**
Socialization factors										
Role boundaries	7.18	7.48	11.89	10.37	14.53	9.57	110.73***	40.19***	102.97**	13.33**
Anonymity	2.25	2.96	2.94	3.45	1.88	2.40	23.81**	8.46**	NS	21.07**

[a]Since all F-ratios for the one-way analysis of variance comparing Black, Chicano/Latino, and Anglo-American means were significant beyond the 0.05 level, the Scheffé test was used to determine the significance of difference between pairs of means. * indicates an F-ratio significant beyond the 0.05 level; ** indicates an F-ratio significant beyond the 0.01 level; NS indicates the differences are not statistically significant.

pairs of ethnic groups was tested using the Scheffé test of significance of difference of means.

The average scores of the three ethnic groups differ significantly beyond the 0.01 level on every sociocultural modality factor except Urbanization. Anglo-American and Chicano/Latino children are significantly more likely to come from families with intact structures. Anglo-American children are more likely than Black children to come from well educated families in which the parents were reared outside the South, while Chicano/Latino children are most likely to come from families in which the parents have relatively little formal education, are foreign born, and do not speak English. Anglo-American children are more likely to come from white collar homes while Black and Chicano/Latino children are more likely to come from blue collar homes. Anglo-American parents have the greatest sense of efficacy. They feel that they can influence their own destiny while Chicano/Latino mothers feel most powerless. Anglo-American families are more likely to be supported by the earnings of a family member while Black families are least likely to be self-supporting. On the other hand, Black families are most likely to participate in community affairs and Chicano/Latino families are least likely to participate. Anglo-American mothers are most likely to report Role Boundaries for their children and Black parents are least likely to report such boundaries. Finally, Chicano/Latino mothers are less likely to have a comprehensive knowledge of their child's activities than Black or Anglo-American mothers, especially those activities which take place in a school context. We conclude that the Anglo-American, Chicano/Latino, and Black children in our three subsamples come from significantly different sociocultural backgrounds and cannot be treated as if they were a single population with a common lifestyle and a similar cultural heritage.

Table 2 reports the Pearson correlation of each sociocultural and socialization factor with the Full Scale WISC-R IQ of the children in the three subsamples. The only factor which is not significantly correlated with Full Scale IQ for at least one of the ethnic groups is Parent-Child Relationship. On those factors most highly correlated with scores on the WISC-R (Occupation of Head, Anglization, Sense of Efficacy, and Source of Income), as shown in Table 2, we saw in Table 1 that Anglo-American children are clearly in the most advantaged positions. We cannot draw any conclusions about the relative learning potential of the children in our sample on the basis of the standard norms. Their scores on the standard norms can be interpreted as a measure of their relative *achievement* in relation to the culture of the public school but they provide no basis for making any inferences about their relative *aptitude*, i.e., intelligence or learning potential.

The average score of the children in each of the subsamples on the Full Scale WISC-R was 87.6 for Black children, 91.5 for Chicano/Latino children, and 103.0 for Anglo-American children. The differences in these mean scores is statistically significant (p < 0.001), indicating that the children in the three subsamples *cannot* be treated as a single population. The Scheffé test was statistically significant for all comparisons, p < 0.01 for Black versus Anglo-American comparisons, p < 0.01 for Chicano/Latino versus Anglo-American comparisons, and p < 0.01 for Chicano/Latino versus Black comparisons.

Table 2. Linear correlations of sociocultural and socialization factors with full scale WISC-R IQ for 616 Black, 620 Chicano/Latino, and 688 Anglo-American children 5 through 11 years of age

	Black	Chicano/Latino	Anglo-American
Sociocultural modalities			
Family structure	0.09^a	−0.04	0.15^b
Anglization	0.26^b	0.33^a	0.24^b
Occupation of head	0.20^b	0.17^b	0.31^b
Size of family	-0.21^b	-0.21^b	-0.12^b
Parent-child relationship	0.04	0.04	0.05
Sense of efficacy	0.18^b	0.29^b	0.13^b
Source of income	0.24^b	0.05	0.25^b
Urbanization	0.05	0.10^a	0.08
Community participation	0.11^a	0.21^b	0.12^a
Socialization factors			
Role boundaries	0.15^b	−0.03	0.07
Anonymity	0.01	-0.12^a	0.02

^{a}Significant beyond the 0.05 level.
^{b}Significant beyond the 0.01 level.

We calculated three stepwise multiple correlation coefficients (R), one for each ethnic group, using the nine sociocultural factors and the two socialization factors as independent variables and Full Scale WISC-R IQ as the dependent variable. Table 3 presents the results of those calculations. The eleven variables accounted for approximately 17% of the variance in Full Scale WISC-R IQ for the Chicano/Latino group, 15% of the variance for the Black group, and 16% of the variance for the Anglo-American group. However, the first five variables in the stepwise solution were able to account for most of the explained variance for each group: 16% for the Chicano/Latino sample, 14% for the Black sample, and 15% for the Anglo-American sample. For this reason, we decided to use the regression equation derived from the first five variables for estimating pluralistic norms.

Table 4 presents the multiple regression equations for each ethnic group. We found that the intercepts and slopes for the multiple regression equations for the three ethnic groups were significantly different ($p < 0.001$). This finding is further evidence of the sociocultural differences between the three populations and the inappropriateness of combining them in a single stardardization sample for norming so-called tests of "intelligence" or "aptitude." Because the relationships between the various sociocultural characteristics and IQ are significantly different for each group, we have calculated pluralistic norms using a different equation for each group. However, actual differences between predicted IQ scores based on a single equation when all ethnic groups were combined and predicted IQ scores based on separate equations for each ethnic group are not, substantively, very large. Differences range from two to six points.

Family size and Anglization appear in the equations for each ethnic group. Source of Income appears in the Black and in the Anglo-American equations, but does not appear in

Table 3. Stepwise multiple correlations using full scale WISC-R IQ as the dependent variable for Black, Chicano/Latino, and Anglo-American children, and sociocultural and socialization factors as independent variables

Black	(R)	(% Var.)	Chicano/Latino	(R)	(% Var.)	Anglo-American	(R)	(% Var.)
Anglization	0.26	6.7	Anglization	0.33	10.9	Occupation	0.31	9.5
Source of income	0.33	10.6	Sense of efficacy	0.37	13.7	Source of income	0.35	12.0
Size of family	0.36	12.7	Size of family	0.39	15.0	Anglization	0.36	13.3
Sense of efficacy	0.37	13.7	Role boundaries	0.40	15.6	Size of family	0.37	14.0
Role boundaries	0.38	14.4	Occupation	0.40	16.2	Family structure	0.38	14.5
Urbanization	0.38	14.6	Community participation	0.41	16.7	Parent-child relationship	0.39	14.9
Community participation	0.38	14.8	Parent-child relationship	0.41	17.2	Sense of efficacy	0.39	15.1
Family structure	0.39	14.8	Family structure	0.42	17.3	Anonymity	0.39	15.4
Occupation	0.39	14.9	Source of income	0.42	17.4	Urbanization	0.39	15.6
Parent-child relationship	0.39	15.0	Urbanization	0.42	17.4	Community participation	0.39	15.6
Anonymity	0.39	15.0	Anonymity	0.42	17.4	Role boundaries	0.39	15.6

Table 4. Multiple regression equations for predicting full scale WISC-R IQ from sociocultural and socialization factors for Black, Chicano/Latino, and Anglo-American children 5 through 11 years of age

---

Black equation
 Anglization (1.01) − Family size (0.47) + Source of income (1.92) +
 Sense of efficacy (1.30) + Role boundaries (0.15) + 77.00 = predicted
 full scale WISC-R IQ for Black children
  Standard error of estimate = 12.2
Chicano/Latino equation
 Anglization (0.93) + Sense of efficacy (2.1) − Family size (0.39) −
 Role boundaries (0.10) + Occupation of head (0.51) + 86.75 = predicted
 full scale WISC-R IQ for Chicano/Latino children
  Standard error of estimate = 12.3
Anglo-American equation
 Anglization (0.87) − Family size (0.51) + Occupation of head (1.14) +
 Source of income (2.78) + Family structure (1.17) + 82.79 = predicted
 full scale WISC-R IQ for Anglo-American children
  Standard error of estimate = 13.0

---

the Chicano/Latino equation. Sense of Efficacy and Role Boundaries appear in both the Black and the Chicano/Latino equation but not the Anglo-American equation. Family Structure appears only in the Anglo-American equation. These findings should not be interpreted to mean that variables not appearing in the equations are necessarily unimportant. Many variables not in the equations have significant linear correlations with WISC-R IQ's. Many of those variables not in the equations are significantly correlated with other sociocultural characteristics which are in the equations and, consequently, make only a small *unique* contribution to the explained variance. Because of co-variance with other sociocultural characteristics, they do not appear among the first five variables in the stepwise solution.

The estimated Full Scale IQ score is the estimated mean score for persons having a particular combination of sociocultural characteristics. We would expect 66% of the scores for persons from that sociocultural background to fall within one standard error from that mean and 95% of the scores to fall within two standard errors from that mean. Using the unique configuration of each person's sociocultural background and ethnic group, we can estimate the mean Full Scale IQ score for a normative population consisting of persons from similar backgrounds. We can then determine where the individual falls in the distribution of scores for the culturally appropriate normative population by converting the IQ into a standard score based on the pluralistic norms. Of course, standard scores can be readily converted into percentile scores and the child's relative position in the distribution of scores for persons of similar sociocultural background can be reported either as a standard score or a percentile. This procedure should provide a more accurate basis for making inferences about a child's estimated learning potential.

Three examples will suffice to illustrate how pluralistic norms might be useful in interpreting a child's performance on the WISC-R. Juan is a 7-year-old Chicano/Latino boy who scored 113 on the standard norms for the WISC-R. Thus, his school functioning level (SFL), i.e., his achievement in terms of the dominant culture of the school, is well above average but not outstanding. He is performing at approximately the 80th percentile in relation to the standard norms. We would predict that he will probably succeed in the regular program of the school without supplementary help, will be an adequate student, and will probably perform well in college. However, when we interpret Juan's performance relative to the pluralistic norms, we get a slightly different picture of his potential. His sociocultural modality scores are as follows: Anglization, 7; Family Size, 5; Occupation of Head of Household score, 1; Role Boundaries, 23; and Sense of Efficacy score, 1. Translating these scores into a more meaningful description, we find that Juan comes from a family of four. He lives with his mother and two other children. His mother is head of the household. The family's income comes from welfare and child support. Juan's mother, who spent most of her childhood in Los Angeles and did not finish high school, does not work outside the home. The family lives in a four-room rented house and has moved three times in the last 5 years. Juan's mother feels powerless, unable to control her future. The family speaks Spanish some of the time in their home and when they are out with friends in the community. Although Juan's mother speaks English fluently, her Spanish accent is noticeable.

The average IQ score for children of Juan's sociocultural modality is 91.6. His score of 113 is 22.4 points higher than the mean for his normative group, about 1.8 standard errors, approximately the 96th percentile. Interpreted against the pluralistic norm, Juan's estimated learning potential (ELP) is probably in the upper 5% of the population. An educational plan geared to his estimated learning potential, not just his school functioning level (SFL), might further enrich Juan's educational opportunities and eventual achievements.

Peter is a 7-year-old Anglo-American boy who scored 107 on the standard norms (approximately the 68th percentile). We would predict that his academic performance will be above average. However, we see a slightly different picture using pluralistic norms. His sociocultural background received close to the maximum score on most factors: Anglization, 10; Family Size, 5; Occupation of Head, 7; Source of Income, 3; and Family Structure, 3. Peter comes from a relatively advantaged background. Translated into a verbal description, Peter lives with his mother and father and one other sibling. His father provides the family's income and is a nonacademic employee of the University of California. Peter's father has 4 years of education beyond high school and his mother has 1 year of college. They expect that Peter will graduate from college. Both parents spent their childhoods in Colorado. The father was reared in Denver, and Peter's mother was reared in a small town. The family has moved three times in the past 5 years and now lives in a six-room home which they are buying. Peter's mother feels that the family determines its own success or failure and can make plans for the future that will work out.

The average score for children from similar sociocultural backgrounds is 108.8. Therefore, Peter's score of 107 is average for a child of his sociocultural modality and places him at about the 44th percentile for his normative group. His school functioning level (SFL) is above average compared to the total population but his Estimated Learning Potential (ELP) is average when his sociocultural advantage is taken into account.

Fred illustrates a case at the lower end of the continuum. He is a 7-year-old Black boy with a standard WISC-R score of 69, about the 2nd percentile on the standard norms. This score is low enough to make him eligible for classes for the mentally retarded in most public schools and indicates that he will probably have serious difficulty with the regular school program at his school level of functioning (SFL). His sociocultural modality scores are: Anglization, 1; Family Size, 3; Role Boundaries, 3; Efficacy, 3; and Source of Income, 0. Translating these scores into a verbal description, we find a family of six living in a four-room, rented dwelling. The family consists of five children: two full siblings to Fred, and two step-siblings. Fred's mother is divorced from her spouse, does not work outside the home and the family is on welfare. Fred's mother was born in rural Jamaica and speaks in an English dialect which is difficult to understand. She never finished high school herself but expects that Fred will finish college and has a high sense of efficacy and control over the future.

The average score for a child of Fred's sociocultural modality is 80.9. His score of 69 is about 12 points or 1.0 standard error below the mean for his sociocultural group and would place him in the 33rd percentile for his normative group. Although his estimated learning potential (ELP) is low, he does not appear to be mentally retarded. His very low school level of functioning (SFL) appears to reflect an impoverished family background and socialization by a mother who has relatively little familiarity with the dominant Anglo-American society. He needs an enriched education program which will acquaint him with the roles and skills needed in urban America. His educational program should probably be planned with this in mind, providing other aspects of the assessment confirm the diagnosis.

CONCLUSION

It is important to emphasize in conclusion that estimates of learning potential based on pluralistic norms are only *one* aspect of a comprehensive assessment procedure. Although knowledge of the estimated potential of Juan, Peter, and Fred provides a method for taking their cultural background into account when assessing the meaning of their scores on the WISC-R, this information alone is not sufficient for planning an educational program. We do not anticipate that pluralistic norms will be used in isolation from other measures.

We are currently developing a system of multi-cultural assessment which will also include measures of adaptive behavior and social role performance in nonacademic settings, careful screening for physical disabilities which might interfere with learning, and a thorough review of the child's health history. However, there is not space within the present discussion to describe the entire battery of measures. Pluralistic norms are one part of this larger system of assessment which looks at many aspects of the child's socialization milieu before reaching conclusions about an appropriate educational program. Such a system does not take away any of the information provided by present procedures, but adds a broader framework for interpreting the meaning of a child's performance.

REFERENCES

Binet, A. and T. Simon. 1905. Sur la necessité d'establir un diagnostic scientifique des états inferieurs de l'intelligence. Ann. Psychol. 11: 1–28.

California State Department of Education. 1972. Racial and ethnic survey, Sacramento.

Cicourel, A. and J. Kitsuse. 1963. The Educational Decision-makers. Bobbs-Merrill Company, New York.

Jencks, C., et al. 1972. Inequality: A Reassessment of the Effect of Family and Schooling in America. Basic Books, Inc., New York.

Karier, C. J., C. Violas, and J. Spring. 1973. Roots of Crisis: American Education in the Twentieth Century. Rand McNally, Chicago.

Katz, M. B. 1971. Class, Bureaucracy, and Schools. Praeger Publishers, New York.

Mercer, J. R. 1972. IQ: The lethal label. Psychology Today. Vol. 6, No. 4.

Mercer, J. R. 1973. Labeling the Mentally Retarded. University of California Press, Berkeley, California.

Mercer, J. R. 1974. A policy statement on assessment procedures and the rights of children. Harvard Ed. Rev. Vol. 44, No. 1.

Parsons, T. 1959. The school class as a social system; some of its functions in American society. Harvard Ed. Rev., 29: 297–315.

Reiss, A. J. 1961. Occupations and Social Status. The Free Press, New York.

Turner, R. 1960. Sponsored and contest mobility and the school system. Am. Soc. Rev. 25: 855–867.

Wechsler, D. 1949. WISC manual, Wechsler intelligence scale for children. The Psychological Corporation, New York.

Wechsler, D. 1974. WISC-R manual, Wechsler intelligence scale for children–revised. The Psychological Corporation, New York.

Williams, R. 1974. Scientific Racism and IQ. Psychology Today, No. 32.

Background Considerations In Developing Strategies For Changing Attitudes And Behavior toward The Mentally Retarded

Richard D. Ashmore

In the above title the most important words are the first two: "Background Considerations." I have very little direct experience with individuals labeled mentally retarded and only slightly more knowledge about research concerned with attitudes and perceptions about such individuals. I have had, on the other hand, a long interest in the topics of attitudes and attitude change, particularly as applied to intergroup relations. I will attempt in this paper to summarize first one of the more promising approaches to conceptualizing attitudes and then some of the factors influencing the success or failure of programs designed to change attitudes. Although much of the discussion will focus on research involving racial or ethnic attitudes, it is hoped that at least some of the general ideas might also be applicable to the development of more positive attitudes toward the mentally retarded.

The body of the paper is divided into four sections. In the first two I will present some basic ideas on the formation, maintenance, and change of attitudes. Section one is a discussion of Rokeach's (1973) schema for conceptualizing the arrangement of attitudes in relation to other internal behavioral predispositions (e.g., self-concept, values) and of how this schema relates to some major theories of attitude change. In the second section I will outline three cognitive-affective syndromes which are prominent in the development and maintenance of prejudice. Section three involves discussion of three general attitude change strategies and an evaluative review of these strategies as they have been operationalized in the area of race relations. The final section of this paper covers two new directions in psychological research and theory regarding intergroup relations.

TOWARD A SCHEMA
FOR CONCEPTUALIZING ATTITUDES AND ATTITUDE CHANGE

"Attitude" has been a central, if not *the* central, construct during the relatively brief history of social psychology. Although many definitions of this term exist, most social psychologists would probably agree to greater or lesser extent with the general definition put forth by Thurstone: "The intensity of positive or negative affect for or against a psychological object" (1946, p.39). Attitudes, then, are internal to a person (affect) and range along a continuum of positive to negative (i.e., for or against, pro or con). And most social psychologists would agree that they study attitudes as a shortcut to understanding behavior, i.e., attitudes and attitude change are assumed to be correlated with behavior and behavior change.[1]

With regard to mental retardation, who or what is the "psychological object" of the attitude? And with whose attitudes are we to be concerned? These two questions are covered more comprehensively by Gottlieb (in this volume). Gottlieb distinguishes three groups whose attitudes toward mental retardation are of interest: the general public, professionals who deal with the mentally retarded (e.g., doctors, teachers, social workers), and peers (e.g., "normal" children in the same school or classroom with other children somehow identified as mentally retarded). In this paper I will be concerned primarily with the attitudes of the public and secondarily with those of professionals and peers.

A wide range of intellectual-social impairments are subsumed under the rubric "mental retardation" but to date there has been little systematic research on the lay public's attitudes toward and perceptions of mental retardation. Such work would seem an important first step in developing attitude change programs based on the models discussed below. Although systematic research is lacking and the extant research is somewhat inconsistent, Gottlieb was able to make three generalizations about public attitudes regarding mental retardation. First, most people view the mental retardate as moderately or severely retarded and as having physical abnormalities (e.g., mongolism). Second, attitudes toward "mental retardation" and toward severely retarded individuals are generally negative while attitudes toward individuals labeled "slow learners" (i.e., the mildly mentally retarded) are more positive. Finally, the public is generally ignorant regarding mental retardation and societal programs for the retarded.

Until now the vast majority of social psychological research on intergroup relations has focused on intergroup attitudes and associated beliefs and perceptions, and most discussions of changing intergroup relations have involved theories of attitude change. Rokeach (1973) has recently proposed a broader schema for conceptualizing belief and behavior change. He posits a cognitive system composed of ten hierarchically arranged, interdependent subsystems of beliefs. As can be seen in Figure 1, "cognitions about self"

---

[1] This assumption, of course, is open to empirical test. A number of instances of attitude-behavior inconsistency have been noted (see Wicker, 1969, for a review), but the classic studies on this are open to alternative explanations (see Collins, 1970, pp. 82–87). Furthermore, social psychologists do not argue that attitudes are the only determinants of behavior; they recognize that personality factors and situational constraints are also important.

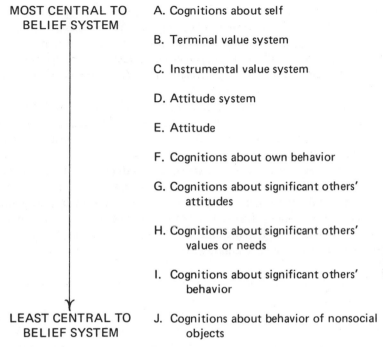

MOST CENTRAL TO
BELIEF SYSTEM

A. Cognitions about self

B. Terminal value system

C. Instrumental value system

D. Attitude system

E. Attitude

F. Cognitions about own behavior

G. Cognitions about significant others'
attitudes

H. Cognitions about significant others'
values or needs

I. Cognitions about significant others'
behavior

LEAST CENTRAL TO
BELIEF SYSTEM

J. Cognitions about behavior of nonsocial
objects

Figure 1. Hierarchical organization of elements in the belief system. Adapted from Rokeach (1973), pp. 220–221.

(taken together they comprise "self-concept") are the most central part of the belief system, followed in order by terminal values (desired end-states such as "a world at peace"), instrumental values (desired modes of behavior such as "honesty"), attitude systems (organized sets of attitudes as in a political ideology), individual attitudes (e.g., attitude toward abortion), and so on.

According to Rokeach the hierarchical arrangement of the belief system implies two things: 1) higher order elements serve to organize lower order elements (e.g., an attitude system such as conservatism brings together and gives order to individual attitudes regarding authority, religion, sexuality, rate of social change, and so on), and 2) higher order elements are generally more stable and resistant to change, but if they can be changed there is pressure to change lower order elements to which they are functionally related (e.g., if one's attachment to conservatism can be reduced this exerts pressure to modify one's beliefs regarding authority, religion, etc.) Rokeach extends his schema to belief and behavior *change* by assuming that individuals are motivated to reduce cognitive inconsistency. In this he is generalizing the ideas of other cognitive-consistency theorists (for the most comprehensive review see Abelson, Aronson, McGuire, Newcomb, Rosenberg, and Tannenbaum, 1968). Dissonance theory (Festinger, 1957) has been most often applied to situations in which an individual behaves inconsistently with respect to an attitude or belief, e.g., "I smoke cigarettes" yet "I believe that cigarette smoking causes lung cancer." According to dissonance theory, holding these two cognitions is psychologically uncomfortable, and the individual is motivated to reduce dissonance in some way, e.g., by changing the behavior (stopping smoking) or by denying that smoking causes cancer. Rokeach's conceptualization subsumes dissonance theory by treating it as an instance of perceived inconsistency between "attitude" and "cognitions about own behavior" (elements E and F in Figure 1).

Balance theory (Heider, 1958) is another cognitive consistency theory which is representable in terms of the Rokeach schema. According to balance theory, an individual is motivated to maintain balance between his own attitudes and those he perceives to be held by others. For example, my belief that smoking is OK would not be in balance with my belief that my best friend feels that smoking is a stupid and disgusting habit. Such imbalance is, as with dissonance, assumed to be motivating, with the result that I should feel it necessary to take some step to reduce the inconsistency, such as stopping smoking or finding a new "best friend." Rokeach sees balance theory as concerned with inconsistency between elements D or E and element G in Figure 1. In sum, the Rokeach schema is congruent with, and actually is a simple generalization of, existing cognitive consistency theories.

Rokeach goes beyond existing theories in one important respect. Although it is not explicit in Figure 1, Rokeach assumes that perceived inconsistency within the belief system leads to change only when that inconsistency causes the individual to be dissatisfied with himself, i.e., only when self-concept is somehow violated. According to Rokeach dissatisfaction with self-concept takes two forms: perceived incompetence or perceived immorality. That is, self-dissatisfaction can arise either from the perception that one lacks ability, intelligence, etc. ("I am incompetent") or from the perception that one has hurt himself or someone else ("I am immoral"). Rokeach draws on a considerable amount of social psychological research and theory (and could bring in more) to support his claim that self-dissatisfaction is an important part of belief change. (Whether it is a *necessary* condition for change is as yet undemonstrated.)

Although it is quite new and as yet not subjected to critical conceptual and empirical analysis by independent workers, the Rokeach schema draws our attention to several important factors in understanding attitudes and social behavior. First, attempts to change attitudes (and related behaviors) must take into consideration how these attitudes are related to higher order values and self-conceptions. For example, if the attitude change advocated by a particular message were incompatible with an individual's values or self-concept, resistance is to be expected. This caution seems obvious, but with only a few scattered exceptions, techniques to change social attitudes have ignored the values and self-conceptions of the target group. Second, belief change can be set in motion by perceived inconsistency *anywhere* in the belief system. To date, two types of intervention strategies have predominated: 1) clinical psychologists and psychiatrists have sought to change *personality* through highlighting or bringing into awareness contradictions involving self-conceptions (element A of Figure 1), 2) social psychologists (particularly consistency theorists) have concentrated on *attitude* change using inconsistencies involving attitudes (elements D and E). There are numerous, as yet untapped, belief system inconsistencies that might be employed to alter attitudes and behavior. Third, the central role of self concept in attitude formation and change is highlighted in Rokeach's schema. Although I can imagine successful attitude change procedures which do not involve a significant amount of self-dissatisfaction, for example, classical and instrumental conditioning of attitudes (e.g., Staats and Staats, 1958), I think that it is wise to consider self-concept when planning attitude change strategies.

COGNITIVE-AFFECTIVE SYNDROMES
AND NEGATIVE INTERGROUP RELATIONS

Although Rokeach's approach to attitudes has much to offer, his schema unfortunately tends to underplay the importance of the affective component of attitudes and how affect combines with beliefs in shaping behavior toward the attitude object. (Although it is not explicit in his presentation, Rokeach would probably include feelings at either the level of self-concept or values.) That is, attitudes as positive-negative behavioral predispositions are accompanied by specific feelings and beliefs and a negative attitude may be supported by a variety of different feelings and beliefs. Let me use the case of black-white relations in the U.S. as an example of the importance of considering the beliefs and feelings that accompany negative intergroup attitudes.

Van den Berghe (1967) has identified two major types of negative intergroup interdependence, dominance and competition, each of which produces a consistent set of negative intergroup attitudes, beliefs, and feelings. During slavery a clear dominant-subordinate relationship existed between whites and blacks and the white image of blacks as childlike (in the sense of being an incomplete or inferior form of adult) predominated. The Civil War and attendant legislation formally ended slavery and led to a brief period of open black-white competition; but competition was abridged through Jim Crow laws, Ku Klux Klan intimidations, etc. Thus, from about 1890 on, there was black-white competition in theory but not in fact. It is not surprising, then, that the paternalistic anti-black stereotypes (e.g., lazy, dumb, undependable) persisted well into the 20th century.

The Civil Rights Movement of the late 1950's and more importantly the black militancy of the middle and late 1960's have produced a new image of blacks in the minds of many white Americans. Blacks are seen, not as dumb and undependable, but as hostile, violent, pushing, unforgiving.[2] Accompanying this image are feelings of fear and anger rather than the contempt which characterized the paternalistic image.

In both the paternalistic and the competitive stages whites held negative attitudes toward blacks. There is a large difference, however, in the beliefs and feelings accom-

---

[2] Certain elements of the paternalistic stereotype do persist. In particular, most whites continue to see blacks as less motivated or more lazy than whites (see Ashmore and McConahay, 1975, Chapter 7, for one explanation of the persistance of this stereotype).

panying and supporting the negative attitude. In putting together an attitude change program, one would probably be wise to consider the possible varying cognitive and affective components of negative attitudes.

Although highly tentative at this time, it seems possible to identify three general cognitive-affective syndromes associated with negative intergroup attitudes. The first two, beliefs of inferiority accompanied by feelings of contempt, and threatening images accompanied by feelings of anger or fear, have already been discussed above. A third possibility is beliefs of strangeness or "non-normalcy" (or lack of a clear set of beliefs at all) coupled with feelings of being uneasy or uncomfortable. Reactions to stuttering appear to be a prime example of this syndrome. Rosenberg and Curtis (1954) found a large amount of avoidance behaviors (e.g., loss of eye contact) by non-stutterers in the presence of stutterers. Zajonc (1968) has hypothesized that unfamiliar stimuli arouse negative affect and attitudes. He further posits that simple exposure to initially unfamiliar and negatively evaluated stimuli will increase positive evaluation. Although some research has failed to support this idea, there is evidence that people prefer reasonably familiar objects and that exposure to negatively valued and unfamiliar stimuli *in a positive context* can reduce this negative evaluation (Perlman and Oskamp, 1971).

It is plausible that all three syndromes are implicated in negative attitudes toward mental retardation. Mental retardation is seen by many people as a form of mental illness, and Rosenhan (1973), in his study of reactions by hospital personnel to pseudo-patients who were "normal" but had been labeled "mentally ill" found that the "patients" evoked contempt, fear, and uneasiness in their attendants. D'Alton (1970) has argued that negative conceptions of retardation may result from the ethic of industrial society that everyone must carry his own weight, and from the high value placed on "having a good IQ." Also, there is some indication that "normals" see the seemingly unpredictable behavior of the mentally ill and the mentally retarded as threatening and potentially dangerous, i.e., fear arousing. And finally, there is the strong possibility that mental retardation is a strange topic and mentally retarded people "different." (As noted above, most people are relatively ignorant regarding mental retardation and the images of a mental retardate usually involve physical and behavioral abnormality.) Both the topic and individual people make us feel uneasy and uncomfortable. Why is this so? First, we do not have much experience with the problem since obviously retarded persons comprise only about 1% of the general population. Those individuals classified as unable to "make it" in society are separated from us. Those who are officially labeled as mentally retarded but who can function among us may not be identified by us as mentally retarded. Only family and friends would have both the official label and the retardate's behavior to shape their beliefs about and attitudes toward retardation. Second, like all forms of non-normalcy and conflict, retardation is a "touchy" topic. Touchy topics are avoided by schools (cf. Ashmore and McConahay, 1975, Chapters 7 and 8) and the mass media, particularly television (e.g., Colle, 1967). And when retardates *are* portrayed in the media, the image of extreme abnormality is stressed rather than the "fact" that most retardates do not exhibit such physical or behavioral symptoms. Thus, Americans can learn about mental retardation neither through firsthand experience nor through two of the major channels of socialization: schools and television. (In the final section of this paper this point will be discussed in more depth.)

PROCEDURES FOR ALTERING INTERGROUP ATTITUDES AND BEHAVIOR

Although there is a host of published attitude-change studies, the procedures used to bring about change can be reduced to three general paradigms: 1) a person "learns" that his attitude is inconsistent with that of a significant other, 2) a person is led to behave in a manner not consistent with his own attitude, 3) a person is confronted with some inconsistency that exists within his belief system (Ashmore, 1970; McGuire, 1969; Rokeach, 1973). The first category I will call the "Communication Paradigm" since it was most fully developed by Hovland and his co-workers in the Yale Communication Research Program. The second paradigm has been labeled "forced compliance" and (counter-attitudinal) "role playing" by attitude change theorists and "enforced contact" by those more directly interested in changing intergroup attitudes. I will used the "forced compliance" label because it is the most general. The final paradigm I will refer to as "self-confrontation" although others have used the title "self-insight" (see Ashmore, 1970, pp. 301–304) and Rokeach (1973) might prefer "education through self-information" (see his pp. 233–234).

The Communication Paradigm and Attitude Change

Research using the communication paradigm has been largely of the laboratory-experimental variety and has focused on questions such as: What distinguishes an effective communicator from an ineffective one? How should the arguments in a persuasive communication be organized? What personality variables in members of the audience increase persuasibility? (For reviews of the literature regarding such questions, see Cohen, 1964, and McGuire, 1969). Unfortunately, very little of this work has concentrated on intergroup attitudes and little attention has been paid by workers within the paradigm to the problem of arranging attitude change communications outside of the laboratory.

There have, however, been numerous attempts to change intergroup attitudes using persuasive communications, but these have been done by individuals more concerned with changing the specific attitudes in question than with understanding communication and persuasion. Thus, studies aimed at changing intergroup attitudes through persuasive communications have a non-theoretical flavor. Also, such studies have generally employed multifaceted experimental treatments. The resultant confounding of independent variables makes it hard to specify what reduces prejudice and what does not. Nevertheless it is possible to make at least a preliminary evaluation of the efficacy of the communication paradigm in altering intergroup attitudes.

Communication paradigm approaches to intergroup attitudes can be grouped into two categories on the basis of how the persuasive message is conveyed. In the first group are studies of the effectiveness of mass media pro-tolerance campaigns while the second group includes evaluation studies of educational programs to reduce prejudice.

Mass Media Campaigns to Reduce Prejudice   These attempts have involved newspaper comic strips, magazine advertisements, and radio and TV programs. They have been remarkably unsuccessful in *changing* attitudes (Hovland, 1959; Ashmore, 1970). One major reason for this lack of success is that such campaigns often do not get to those whom they are designed to change. For example, a study of a series of radio programs aimed at increasing ethnic tolerance showed that the listening audience for each program was predominantly of the ethnic group which was being discussed and not those most likely to be prejudiced against that group (Lazarsfeld, 1944).

This finding is consistent with others on the mass media indicating that persuasive communications tend to get through to those who already agree with the position expressed. As Freedman and Sears (1965) have argued, however, such *de facto* selectivity in exposure does not necessarily mean that individuals are psychologically motivated to seek out supportive information and avoid potentially non-supportive information. In fact, they present considerable evidence against the idea of motivated selective exposure (especially the avoidance of non-supportive information). Most important for the present purposes, they suggest the conditions under which people will attend to potentially non-supportive information. The strongest predictor of such exposure is *"perceived utility of the information."* Thus, mass media campaigns regarding mental retardation (or any topic) should seek to maximize the perception by the potential audience that the information could be useful or relevant to their lives. Also, Freedman and Sears report that *positive information* is preferred, especially during the initial stages of forming an opinion or when commitment to the opinion is low. Although most Americans probably have somewhat negative attitudes regarding mental retardation, their commitment to this attitude and their knowledge about the topic are probably not great. Thus, it would seem advisable to construct information campaigns that stressed the strengths, abilities, potentialities, etc. of the mentally retarded. In addition to these two considerations, Freedman and Sears point out that upper class and better educated individuals more often attend to the mass media in general and thus have higher rates of exposure to both consonant and dissonant persuasive campaigns. Campaigns designed to alter attitudes regarding mental retardation either should be directed toward such individuals or special efforts should be made to increase the appeal of the "message-plus-media" for those lower in educational background. Mass media campaigns can also be enhanced by identifying "opinion leaders" within the target population and enlisting their help in planning and carrying out the campaign. These leaders not only help fashion a campaign best suited for the target group but there is also considerable evidence that the word-of-mouth support of such leaders is important in gaining acceptance for new ideas (McGuire, 1969, pp. 231–235).

Failure to reach the intended audience is just one problem with mass media campaigns. Such programs are further hindered by conscious and unconscious evasion tactics by those who are exposed to them. Cooper and Jahoda (1947) describe such tactics in detail. Here I will note only two, "changing the frame of reference" and "message is too difficult," which seem to have particular relevance to the topic of mental retardation attitudes. In changing the frame of reference, the receiver's preconceptions and prejudice cause him to misperceive or selectively perceive the incoming information. This may dilute the impact of the campaign, or in some cases, produce a boomerang by inadvertently "reinforcing" the preconceptions. Television "commercials" designed to increase sympathy for the mentally retarded may be self-defeating if they portray individuals whose behaviors or facial expressions either fit cultural stereotypes of "idiocy" (*they* are all the same and different from *me*) or make the viewing audience "uncomfortable." The second mechanism is quite simple: often mass media programs fail because they aren't comprehended by the audience. This lack of comprehension is sometimes due to educational limitations of the audience and sometimes to the unclarity of the message.

The above difficulties of mass media persuasive campaigns should not lead to the conclusion that all such programs be abandoned. Pro-tolerance campaigns provide support for those already low in prejudice and they can help "justify" attitude and behavior change by someone whose negative intergroup attitude has been challenged in some way (e.g., a contact experience). Thus, although mass media campaigns should not be counted on as the major component of a total attitude change strategy, they can play an important supportive role if designed carefully.

That mass media attitude change programs are relatively unsuccessful also does not mean that the media have no impact on social attitudes. In fact quite the opposite is true. The mass media not only reflect cultural stereotypes about groups but they tend to teach and reinforce these stereotypes. The role of TV dramatic series is particularly noteworthy. A survey conducted by the Survey Research Center revealed that one reason listed by a majority of Americans for watching TV is that it is educational. When asked to list programs high in educational value respondents often cited "The FBI," "Bonanza," "Marcus Welby." If, in fact, Americans are learning about crime, Western history, medical problems, etc. from such TV programs, it seems important that these programs present material which will increase intergroup understanding rather than perpetuate negative stereotypes. As a consequence, any comprehenisve program to alter attitudes toward mental retardation must involve some attention to influencing the image of mental retardates in media "entertainment."

Educational Programs to Alter Ethnic Attitudes Such programs (e.g., an academic course, a symposium, a movie or lecture plus discussion) have been numerous and the reported success-failure ratio is about 2:1 (Ashmore, 1970, p. 311). Most such programs have been confounded and little systematic research has been done to identify the crucial aspects of a successful program. Two obvious, but often overlooked, factors in the success (or failure) of such programs are the attitude of the instructor and his or her relationship to the students: attitude change is maximized when the instructor believes in or at least understands and accepts the position being advocated and has a positive affective relationship with the students.

There is considerable evidence that "drug education" programs often fail because these points are not considered (Nowlis, 1970). That is, teachers' over generalized and rigid anti-drug attitudes influence the way they present "factual information" and reduce their credibility. And disliked teachers who espouse such attitudes can serve as negative role models: "If he doesn't like ___, maybe I better try it." Any educational attitude change program, then, must involve careful selection and training of those teachers who will mediate the program. This may be very difficult to achieve with regard to mental retardation since the available data indicate that regular classroom teachers generally have a negative attitude on the topic (e.g., Combs and Harper, 1967) and special education teachers often are not much more positive (e.g., Semmel, 1959). Thus educational programs for children must be preceded by teacher-training curricula which will positively influence the people who are to teach these programs.

Forced Compliance Paradigm and Attitude Change

Two types of forced compliance (i.e., inducing behavior contrary to a negative attitude) have been used to reduce intergroup prejudice: role playing and enforced contact. In role playing the target person is asked to write an essay, make a speech, or enact a dramatic role which espouses an egalitarian or non-prejudiced position. Although this could involve the presence of an outgroup person (especially in the case of dramatic enactment) it generally has not. Enforced contact research, on the other hand, has involved bringing the target person into direct, personal contact with outgroup members under conditions thought to be conducive to attitude change.

Role Playing Culbertson (1957) had anti-black whites participate in a psychodrama in which they advocated integration of educational facilities. This role-playing experience resulted in a significant decrease in anti-black attitudes. And Gray and Ashmore (1974) have recently presented evidence that simply writing an essay in favor of creating jobs for minorities can reduce outgroup prejudice. These and other studies suggest that role playing can be used to alter ethnic prejudice. Two conditions which seem to strengthen the effectiveness of role playing are: 1) perceived choice: the more choice the individual feels he or she has to engage or not engage in the counter-attitudinal role playing, the greater the attitude change, and 2) perceived consequences: the more important the role playing (e.g., "the role-played essay will be used as part of a report to policy makers") is perceived to be, the greater the attitude change (Collins and Hoyt, 1972).

Enforced Contact A large number of studies have assessed the impact of intergroup contact on prejudice. Reviews of this research (especially Amir, 1969; Ashmore, 1970; Cook, 1970) indicate that contact is not always conducive to reducing prejudice and conflict. In fact contact can often heighten conflict and reinforce prejudices. On the other hand, these same reviews suggest that several factors are known to increase the probability that contact will have an ameliorative effect. These ingredients are as follows: 1) cooperative interdependence (shared means and goals): majority and minority group members should not only work toward shared goals but also should share task responsibility for achieving these goals, 2) equality of status: minority group members should not all occupy low status positions, 3) norms favoring equality: institutional, authority, and peer group norms surrounding the contact situation should favor contact and tolerance in general, 4) success: the contact situation should be as rewarding as possible or if the contact group is unsuccessful the failure should not be linked to performance deficits by minority group participants, 5) acquaintance potential: the situations should allow the participants to exchange personal information and develop friendships (Cook, 1970), 6) stereotype destruction: at least some significant proportion of minority group members in the contact situation must not conform to cultural stereotypes.

Although there is some disagreement about how or why these factors do work, there is evidence and theoretical rationale (see Ashmore, 1970; Cook, 1970) for believing that the above listing is in the rough order of priority, i.e., cooperative interdependence is the most important ingredient, then equality of status, and so on. This would seem to have implications for structuring interaction between the non-severely retarded individuals (yet identified as mentally retarded) and others (e.g., community volunteers, peers, institutional staff). To achieve or approximate cooperative interdependence and equality of status, mentally retarded individuals will have to be given positions or duties of maximal possible responsibility and not simply be the recipients of help.[3] To achieve normative support, institutional arrangements and authority figure role models must favor such sharing of responsibility and discourage subgroup formation along "normal" versus "mentally retarded" lines. To maximize the possibility of successful cooperative experiences the responsibilities shared with mentally retarded individuals must not exceed their capabilities and past experiences. *And,* non-retarded individuals in the contact situation must have the interpersonal skills to be productive group members, i.e., a community volunteer who, even though highly motivated to help, becomes nervous and uncomfortable in egalitarian-cooperative contact with mentally retarded individuals will lessen the possibility of successful contact.

A number of studies have been conducted to see if contact reduces prejudice against the mentally retarded (see Gottlieb, in this volume, for a review). Unfortunately, few of these studies have considered the above "requirements" for successful contact and consequently it is not surprising that positive results are the exception and not the rule. For example, a number of investigators (e.g., Cleland and Chambers, 1959) have shown that simply visiting an institution for the mentally retarded does not produce a more positive attitude toward the retarded. On the other hand, where the contact experience has involved greater cooperative activity with roughly equal status and authority support, positive change in attitudes toward the retarded have been noted (e.g., Lilly, 1971). Furthermore, Begab (1968) has shown that the most positive attitude change by social work graduate students takes place when contact (through field placements) occurs under conditions approximating those described above as optimal for prejudice reduction.

Self-Confrontation Techniques and Attitude Change

The earliest form of self-confrontation as an attitude change induction was self-insight training. Katz, Sarnoff, and McClintock (1956) reasoned that if prejudice is (for some

---

[3] Rosenhan's (1973) work in mental hospitals suggests a potential side benefit of such sharing of responsibility: increases in treating patients as responsible individuals may counter the tendencies toward depersonalization which pervade such institutions.

people at least) rooted in personality needs and results from displacement and projection, then prejudice can be reduced by giving people insight into their use of "irrational" defense mechanisms. Three studies have provided support for the effectiveness of their self-insight training (involving primarily information on the dynamics of scapegoating and projection along with a case history example), but the psychodynamic theory underlying the technique has not been well supported (see Ashmore, 1970, pp. 301–304). The self-insight technique seems to work best when coupled with a message urging respondents to be consistent in their attitudes and behavior. This suggests that self-insight may work because it helps respondents adopt ethnic attitudes more consistent with higher order elements of their belief system (i.e., values and self-concept).

Rokeach (1973, Chapters 10, 11, 12) has done several experiments testing this latter notion more directly. Basically, his self-confrontation technique for reducing anti-black prejudice of whites involves three steps. First, subjects fill out his Value Test, which involves rank ordering 18 terminal and 18 instrumental values in terms of personal importance. Second, they are made aware of their tendency to place a higher value on their own freedom than on freedom and achievement possibilities for others (particularly members of underpriviledged groups), i.e., they rank "freedom" higher than "equality." Third, Rokeach further points out how this difference in value rankings makes the condition of the underpriviledged more difficult. In general, the results indicate that such self-confrontation not only leads to changes in value rankings but also to reductions in ethnic prejudice and discrimination *and* that such change persists over a relatively long period of time (in some cases up to 21 months after the treatment).

At this time it is not known how attitudes and behaviors toward the mentally retarded relate to values. If negative attitudes toward mental retardation also correlate with a high ranking of "freedom" relative to "equality" then Rokeach's procedure might easily be adapted. Or it might be that such attitudes are linked to such values as "capable" or "helpful" and that slightly different forms of self-confrontation must be developed. In either case the general procedure of self-confrontation seems worthy of further investigation.

A second type of self-confrontation might be helpful in improving the condition of the mentally retarded. If, as was hypothesized above, non-retarded individuals tend to feel uncomfortable in the presence of retardates they may engage in behaviors (e.g., simplifying their speech, avoiding eye contact) which hinder the development and maintanance of social interaction skills by the retardate. *And* they may do this unconsciously. Thus, it may be useful to videotape interactions between retardates and non-retarded individuals (e.g., parents, institutional personnel) and then present these tapes to the non-retarded individuals together with an interpretation of how their behavior influences that of the retarded individual in the interaction.

BEYOND STRATEGIES TO CHANGE THOSE WHO ARE PREJUDICED

Up to this point I have been concerned primarily with strategies for changing the attitudes and behaviors of individuals who have clearly negative orientations toward some socially defined group. This coverage reflects the state of intergroup relations research: it focuses on individuals who are prejudiced and how they can be changed. In this section I want to propose two new directions for thinking about negative intergroup relations: 1) what early learning experiences set the stage for prejudice development?, and 2) how do the attitudes and behaviors of the ostensibly "non-prejudiced" contribute to negative intergroup relations? First, I will discuss the early socialization of basic orientations toward people and societal institutions. Second, I will review a series of studies on the antecedents and consequences of "tokenism" by "non-racist" whites in black-white relations. In each case I will try to suggest its relevance for attitudes regarding mental retardation.

Socialization of Basic Social Orientations

Although individuals change their conceptions of both self and others at all points in the life cycle, there is considerable evidence that during childhood we learn basic orientations that serve to shape how we react to later learning experiences. In the area of political socialization, Americans, particularly white middle class Americans, learn prior to adolescence 1) to have a vague positive attachment to the American political and economic system, 2) to see voting as the best (only?) way to effect change in this system, 3) to have an aversion to open political conflict, and 4) to respond negatively to those who challenge the existing political and economic status quo (see Ashmore and McConahay, 1974, Chapter 8). Although these same children go on to develop partisan preferences (e.g., Republican or Democratic party allegiance) and related attitudes, these early basic orientations toward politics serve as continuing inputs to adult political behavior. And, the schools help in building these early orientations, especially by avoiding touchy issues (which almost by definition involve conflict) and by teaching about formal political systems and not about informal politics (e.g., lobbying, vote trading).

It is quite possible that early socialization in our schools also predisposes us to a vague positive feeling toward "normalcy." The avoidance of touchy issues (mental and physical deviations as well as politics and race) together with the segregation of those who are "different" (special schools or classes within schools for the blind, deaf, mentally retarded, etc.) means that American children are sheltered not only from conflict but from "differences" as well. Even though schools also socialize sympathy for the physically and intellectually handicapped, this sympathy is not accompanied by learning experiences which allow children 1) to be comfortable in situations involving those who are "different" or 2) to implement the general principle of sympathy in specific situations. This latter point is particularly important. For example, American schools also teach children about the Bill of Rights, but only at the level of general principles. Adult Americans are certainly not overly generous in extending freedom of speech to *specific* individuals who have *specific* political or social proclivities which differ from the majority.

A useful area for future research, therefore, would be to develop educational curricula which constructively expose children to the wide variety of human capabilities and existence and to head off the orientation that "differences" are anxiety arousing and bad.

Such a program might be guided by the work of Zellman and Sears (1971), who have presented preliminary evidence for the efficacy of a school curriculum to increase tolerance for political conflict.

Look at the Good Guys, Too

As noted above, most race relations research has been concerned with the prejudiced individual, the person who endorses stereotyped beliefs and engages in discriminatory behavior. A recent series of studies by Dutton (see Dutton, 1974, for a review) suggests that certain behaviors of "non-prejudiced" whites may lessen the likelihood of significant reductions in intergroup conflict.

In his first two studies, Dutton demonstrated that middle class whites with little contact with blacks actually discriminate against whites on a relatively trivial issue, e.g., seating a black man wearing a turtleneck sweater contrary to a restaurant's "coat-and-tie-only" policy. Next he showed that such "reverse discrimination" may result from a wish to look non-racist. Experimental subjects who scored low on an anti-black prejudice measure and who ranked equality high either were or were not led (through false autonomic feedback) to believe they might have racist tendencies. Those in the "high threat of being prejudiced" condition gave significantly more money to a black than a white panhandler while no such difference occurred in the "no threat" condition.

Dutton's final study suggests that the reverse discrimination shown in the previous studies may reduce the chances of more socially significant behaviors to improve black-white relations. The same type of subjects (i.e., "non-prejudiced") as in the previous study were used and all were exposed to the high threat procedure. After leaving the laboratory each subject was panhandled by either a black or white confederate or was not panhandled. As in the previous study, the black panhandler received more "contributions" than his white counterpart. More importantly, however, those subjects who gave money to the black panhandler volunteered less time for an "inter-racial brotherhood campaign" than subjects in the other two conditions when contacted the next day. Although Dutton's research is far from unequivocal, it does suggest that non-prejudiced individuals may engage in "token" acts of intergroup altruism and that such tokenism may reduce their commitment to more significant acts to ameliorate intergroup relations. A logical question is: Does such tokenism exist with respect to mental retardation?

SUMMARY AND CONCLUSIONS

The foregoing analysis suggests four background considerations which should guide programs to create more positive attitudes toward the mentally retarded. First, the target group for a particular program must be carefully identified, and the program specifically geared for this group. It is quite important in this identification process to ascertain how negative attitudes are integrated in the individual's total belief system and what affective-cognitive syndromes are implicated. Second, attitude change procedures involving forced compliance and self-confrontation seem to offer more promise than mass media campaigns. Forced compliance programs, however, must be built around the principles found to enhance prejudice reduction and not be implemented on the assumption that simple contact or exposure produces more positive attitudes. Third, mass media campaigns can be an important adjunct in a comprehensive program to improve attitudes toward the mentally retarded, particularly if they stress the strengths of and diversity among retarded individuals and if they are supported by opinion leaders. Fourth, educational curricula designed to make children more aware of and comfortable with "differences" and "non-normalcy" promise to be a significant factor in increasing acceptance of not only the mentally retarded but also others whose physical or social attributes differ from those of the majority.

ACKNOWLEDGMENTS

The preparation of this paper was facilitated by a grant from the Rutgers University Research Council. The quality of the final manuscript was greatly enhanced through the suggestions of the following individuals: Ronald Abeles, Robert Apsler, Margaret Bacon, Michael Begab, David Gray, Stephen Richardson, and Milton Rokeach.

REFERENCES

Abelson, R. P., E. Aronson, W. J. McGuire, T. M. Newcomb, M. J. Rosenberg, and P. H. Tannenbaum. 1968. Theories of Cognitive Consistency: A Sourcebook. Rand McNally. Chicago.

Amir, Y. 1969. Contact hypothesis in ethnic relations. Psychol. Bull. 71: 319–342.

Ashmore, R. D. 1970. Prejudice: Causes and cures. In B. E. Collins (ed.), Social Psychology: Social Influence, Attitude Change, Group Processes, and Prejudice. Addison-Wesley. Reading, Massachusetts. pp. 243–339.

Ashmore, R. D. and J. B. McConahay. 1975. Psychology and America's Urban Dilemmas. McGraw-Hill. New York.

Begab, M. J. 1968. The effect of differences in curricula and experiences on social work student attitudes and knowledge about mental retardation. Doctoral Dissertation. The Catholic University of America. Washington, D. C.

Cleland, C. C. and I. L. Chambers. 1959. The effect of institutional tours on attitudes of high school seniors. Am. J. Ment. Defic. 64: 124–130.

Cohen, A. R. 1964. Attitude change and social influence. Basic Books. New York.

Colle, R. D. 1967. Color on TV. The Reporter. Nov. 30: 23–25.

Collins, B.E. 1970. Social Psychology: Social Influence, Attitude Change, Group Processes, and Prejudice. Addision-Wesley. Reading, Massachusetts.

Collins, B. E. and M. F. Hoyt. 1972. Personal responsibility for consequences: An integration and extension of the "forced compliance" literature. J. Exper. Socl. Psychol. 8: 558–593.

Combs, R. H. and J. L. Harper. 1967. Effects of labels on attitudes of educators toward handicapped children. Exceptional Children 33: 399–403.

Cook, S. W. 1970. Motives in a conceptual analysis of attitude-related behavior. In W. S. Arnold and D. Levine (eds.), Nebraska Symposium on Motivation, 1969. University of Nebraska Press. Lincoln, Nebraska. pp. 179–231.

Cooper, E. and M. Jahoda. 1947. The evasion of propaganda: How prejudiced people respond to anti-prejudice propaganda. J. Psychol. 23: 15—25.

Culbertson, F. M. 1957. Modification of an emotionally held attitude through role playing. J. Abnorm. Socl. Psychol. 54: 230—234.

D'Alton, S. O. 1970. Concepts of retardation in industrial society. Aust. J. Ment. Retard. 1: 38—39.

Dutton, D. G. 1974. Tokenism, reverse discrimination, and egalitarianism in interracial behavior. To appear in R. D. Ashmore (ed.), Journal of Social Issues.

Festinger, L. 1957. A Theory of Cognitive Dissonance. Row Peterson. Evanston, Illinois.

Freedman, J. L. and D. O. Sears. 1965. Selective exposure. In L. Berkowitz (ed.), Advances in Experimental Social Psychology. 2. Academic Press. New York. pp. 58—97.

Gray, D. B. and R. D. Ashmore. 1974. Comparing the effects of informational, role-playing, and value-discrepancy treatments on racial attitude. Unpublished manuscript.

Heider, F. 1958. The Psychology of Interpersonal Relations. Wiley. New York.

Hovland, C. I. 1959. Reconciling conflicting results derived from experimental and survey studies of attitude change. Am. Psychol. 14: 8—17.

Hovland, C., I. Janis, and H. H. Kelley. 1953. Communication and Persuasion. Yale University Press. New Haven, Connecticut.

Katz, D., I. Sarnoff, and C. McClintock. 1956. Ego-defense and attitude change. Hum. Rel. 9: 27—45.

Lazarsfeld, P. F. (ed.). 1944. Radio and the printed page. Duell, Sloan, Pearce. New York.

Lilly, M. S. 1971. Improving social acceptance of low sociometric status, low achieving students. Exceptional Children 37: 341—348.

McGuire, W. J. 1969. The nature of attitudes and attitude change. In G. Lindzey and E. Aronson (eds.), The Handbook of Social Psychology (2nd Ed.), 3. Addison-Wesley, Reading, Massachusetts. pp. 141—160.

Nowlis, H. H. 1970. Student drug use. In F. F. Korten, S. W. Cook, and J. I Lacey (eds.), Psychology and the Problems of Society. American Psychological Assn., Washington, D.C. pp. 408—419.

Perlman, D. and S. Oskamp. 1971. The effects of picture content and frequency exposure on evaluations of Negroes and whites. J. Exper. Socl. Psychol. 7: 503—514.

Rokeach, M. 1973. The Nature of Human Values. The Free Press. New York.

Rosenhan, D. L. 1973. On being sane in insane places. Science 179: 250—258.

Rosenberg, S. and J. Curtiss. 1954. The effect of stuttering on the behavior of the listener. J. Abnorm. Socl. Psychol. 49: 355—361.

Semmel, M. L. 1959. Teacher attitudes and information pertaining to mental deficiency. Am. J. Ment. Defic. 63: 566—567.

Staats, A. W. and C. K. Staats. 1958. Attitudes established by classical conditioning. J. Abnorm. Socl. Psychol. 57: 37—40.

Thurstone, L. L. 1946. Comment. Am. J. Sociol. 52: 39—40.

Van den Berghe, P. 1967. Race and racism. John Wiley & Sons, Inc. New York.

Wicker, A. W. 1969. Attitudes versus action. The relationship of verbal and overt behavioral responses to attitude objects. J. Socl. Issues 25: 41—78.

Zajonc, R. B. 1968. Attitudinal effects of mere exposure. J. Personality Socl. Psychol. Monograph Supplement. 9 (2, Part 2): 1—27.

Zellman, G. L. and D. O. Sears. 1971. Childhood origins of tolerance for dissent. J. Socl. Issues 27: 109—136.

Discussion:
Attitudes and Values

The discussion of Gottlieb's paper focused the debate on special schooling, with emphasis shifted from the effects as measured in cognitive terms to the effects as measured in sociometric terms.

It was noted that the observations of the author had been made on children who had never been segregated in this way. On the other hand, a study in Aberdeen, Scotland, showed a tendency for children to make sociometric choices of children who were close to themselves in IQ. Practically no choices were made across the median and, in general, children with an IQ 3 to 5 points higher than the subject were chosen.

It was evident from the paper that the assumption that true integration followed from placing children within the same classroom was wishful thinking. The contrary view was put, however, that special classes allowed a collusion of irresponsibility towards the individual child. It was argued that with integration, a teacher has to pay attention to the problem of the individual child. Operant conditioners examine the actual situation of the failing child. They seek out specific elements in the situation: whether the child has appropriate material, what he does in the learning situation, and what the teacher does in the situation. The author maintained that his own studies did not support that view as a general effect of integration. For example, one school he observed touted the degree of individualization achieved. Yet he watched a child who for almost an hour engaged in no learning activity whatsoever, without any perusal of the situation by the teacher. It is never wise to assume that a program's philosophy reflects what actually occurs in practice.

Remedies other than simple integration to improve social contact after desegregation stressed the need to set up special conditions which could promote better attitudes among the children and teachers. By the sole measure of placing children together in the same classroom, one will at best set up the mentally retarded role as a paradigm of how not to behave. A final position has it that special versus regular schooling was a false issue, just as the debates on special testing presented a false issue. The real issue was whether or not children were being properly taught. If they were not being properly taught, then their location in one or another classroom with one or other set of children was not going to make any difference. Most children do get overlooked in classrooms, and so the fight should center on how children are taught. Debates solely in terms of target groups were doomed to fail.

The discussion on Edgerton's paper centered on the themes of dependency, roles, and labeling, all of which to some extent are interrelated. Dependency was seen as the core problem to resolve for the mentally retarded individual returning to the world at large. Yet much ambivalence centered around the question of dependency for the retarded individual himself, the social workers assigned to care for them, the homes set up with caretakers to provide places for them in the community, and even the participant observer-researcher. For the individual, dependency was in many respects adaptive for the mentally retarded person who exploited dependency to acquire as much help and care as he could. On the other hand, by doing so, he thwarted his own advance to full independence.

The discussion searched for those elements of the social role of the mentally retarded that were central to its deviation from the assumptions of competency. No stereotype seemed to fit, and Edgerton noted that the phenomenon of role playing could be documented on some of his films. The same individual might display normal behavior in some situations and mentally retarded behavior in others. Naturally, this passing from one role to another was a facility enjoyed mainly by the mildly retarded without physical stigmata. Those with stigmata, like Down's syndrome, could not function in this way so easily. A key test of role-playing ability, of which the mentally retarded themselves were fully aware, was a capacity to use numbers, for example, to identify such matters as money, duration of time, and so on. An ex-patient who wanted to play the role of mental retardation, would often fail deliberately when tested in his use of numbers.

Edgerton thought that a good deal of positive reinforcement was needed to counter dependency. Punishment only caused a retreat into dependency. The social workers assigned to the care of mentally retarded persons returned to the community were often unaware of the source and the nature of the role problems with which they were dealing. Thus, for fear that mentally retarded individuals could not cope on their own and manage their own budgets, social workers tended to collude with the managers or owners of proprietary homes to which the mentally retarded persons were assigned. These homes were private enterprise activities and unlicensed and the usual incentive for setting them up was a financial one. The mentally retarded individual was provided for under the act for "assistance for the totally disabled" (ATD). Eighty percent of these funds usually went directly to the caretaker. Legally the money should go to the disabled individual unless he was shown to be incompetent; in practice it usually went to the caretaker.

The return to the community of the mentally retarded individual could be seen as a process of moving in and out of variously labeled roles. On the removal from the institution, a process of normalization and "delabeling" was encouraged. At the same time, however, there was entry into the social welfare track, with "relabeling" in terms of welfare dependency. It might well be that retarded individuals were worse off in the new welfare track, where there was no legal aftercare responsibility exercised for them.

However many of Edgerton's sample of mentally retarded individuals returned to the community were exploited by their caretakers, and however much they themselves exploited the potential of their dependent roles, everyone found it encouraging that many of them were nonetheless in a materially better situation than that in which Edgerton had found them in his first observational study a decade before when they were in the process of re-entering the community. Many had acquired a number of coping skills and a reasonable adaptation to the community at large.

Two main themes emerged in the discussion of Mercer's paper. One was the validity of the modified and standardized assessment of the cognitive performance of children in the light of their cultural background. The other was centered around the efficacy of special classes and special schools.

The question was raised as to why ethnic differences should be seen in a different light from social class differences. The picture on Riverside for ethnic groups did not seem to differ, in any fundamental respect, from the picture for social classes in, say, Lancashire or Aberdeen. Thus it was pointed out that the IQ does have significance as to mental performance and that re-interpretation of the score by allowing for cultural backgrounds might divert from the appropriate action rather than facilitating it. Was not the issue to find means of preventing or alleviating the poor mental performance of deprived groups, and of testing the various approaches to them to find out what might help? The author's view was that the use of this standardized IQ resulted in the blame for the poor mental performance being placed on the child who comes from a deprived background rather than on the school which failed to remedy these deficiencies. The introduction of allowances for cultural background could be seen as a means to more precise diagnosis of the child in terms of his situation.

A similar theme, whether the central issues would be evaded or confronted by following this approach, involved the discussion of special classes and special schooling. One view was that the abolition of special classes for culturally deprived children could lead to their being treated with greater attention to their individuality if "bi-cultural" programs were introduced. Under these conditions it should be possible to recognize the hangups specific to schools.

A number of questions was raised about the proposed school program, however. Might not the bi-cultural school simply lead to a new form of segregation within the schools? Might not the unusual and difficult behavior of children functioning at a retarded level be avoided and simply brushed out of sight if it were not specifically recognized? The special problems of retarded children, for instance the necessity for precision in the detection of minimal brain damage, might be overlooked. Finally, the abolition of special classes for mildly retarded persons granted implicit recognition to the social deprecation and stigmatization of mental retardation and might have the untoward effect of increasing the stigmatization of those organically damaged children who continue to be assigned to special classes.

The discussion then turned to the question of the function of special schools and the effects of special schooling. One view was that the special school was invented simply to remove troublesome children from the regular class milieu. Another view was that its function is to protect them from the adverse effects on personality and behavior of unequal academic competition. Retention in the regular classroom and continued exposure to teacher and peer rejection and conflict could further aggravate behavior disorders and heighten self-deprecation. The effect of special schooling has been little explored and little understood and while admittedly falling below early expectations for the program, it might still have advantages over regular class placement and could be strengthened. The author's view was that the effect of special schooling was equivocal and that the best approach was to keep a child in the mainstream classes as long as possible. She observed that Spanish-speaking children had been educated in the schools of California for 100 years, but special attention to their problems of language had been given only in the past 5 years. Hence she saw it as vital that the educational system be made to pay attention to the problems of ethnic groups who were at a social disadvantage because of language and culture.

Current efforts by some school systems to integrate the retarded into nonacademic activities with their normal classmates and to provide tutorial services, remedial or special classes for academic pursuits, were considered by most participants to be the most effective approach. In this way, stigmatization could be reduced and the retarded individual's self-confidence protected from the erosion of repeated failure.

SOCIAL COMPETENCE
AND SOCIALIZATION

Issues in Social Effectiveness: The Case of The Mentally Retarded[1]

Robert E. Kleck

Special educators have long recognized that the ability of a handicapped person to succeed in society depends, in large measure, on his skill to get along with his fellow man. Yet we have done little to develop his social living skills, a complex area of paramount importance [Dunn, 1968, p. 19].

Dunn's acknowledgment of the importance of social skills to the successful integration of the mentally handicapped into society is not a new phenomenon. Over 20 years ago Tregold (1952) argued that social competence is the "most logical and scientific concept of mental deficiency" [p. 5] and, hence, the only criterion we should employ in the identification of such individuals. Edgerton (1967) has observed that it is frequently the social incompetence of the mentally subnormal which causes them to come to our attention in the first place.

What needs to be explained in the light of numerous and sometimes eloquent calls for a concern for the social inadequacies of the mentally handicapped is the relative absence of what Gunzburg (1968) calls "social education" [p. 2]. Instead, what we find is that three-quarters of the way through the twentieth century, IQ quotients, literacy, and scholastic achievement still serve as principal indexes of human development. In the U.S. alone, millions of individuals fare rather poorly against these criteria and, as a consequence, are stigmatized and in various ways and to various degrees excluded from meaningful participation in their own society. Further, because of the tenacity of intellectual achievement criteria, they are exposed to intervention programs which in many cases serve to exacerbate the deficits in social functioning which they experience and which might be ameliorated were these deficits to become the primary foci of therapeutic efforts.

---

[1] The final version of this chapter was prepared while the author was a Visiting Research Scientist with the Boy's Town Center for the Study of Youth Development, Stanford University, Stanford, California.

It is informative to examine the possible reasons which lie behind the continued tenacity of IQ to serve as the "major yardstick of development and the principal criterion of the effectiveness of early education programs" [Anderson and Messick, 1974, p. 284]. One of its major holds on scientist and educator alike is that it is easily and relatively reliably measured. If one seeks a parallel set of measures of social skills, one encounters "both a paucity of valid and reliable measures and a confusing abundance of inadequate and idiosyncratic tests, indexes, and schedules" [Anderson and Messick, 1974, p. 284–85]. Undeniably, one of the factors blocking the development of these other measures and thus contributing to the reliance on existing measures of IQ has been the lack of consensus among social scientists regarding the components of socially competent behavior. If we are to learn anything from the history of mental testing, it is that such agreement must be achieved before the assessment of social competence and concern for its facilitation become part of our current educational practices.

A second major reason for the continued reliance on intelligence measures rests with the presumption that social performance covaries with intelligence so directly that any measure of the latter would tend to be highly redundant with the former. A corollary typically linked to this argument states that we should not expect to see any improvement in social functioning independent of changes in general intelligence. If one is interested in improving social competence, therefore, such changes will have to be mediated by intervention programs aimed at improving general intellectual skills.

It would be difficult to deny that level of social functioning and intelligence, as measured by a standard test battery, are related. The general intellectual resources of the individual may well place some upper limit on the social competence of an individual. What we do know, however, is that within limited ranges of intellectual functioning one sees broad differences in the level of social skill achieved, and further, that such differences are critical to the nature of the social outcomes experienced by mentally handicapped individuals. It should be kept in mind that it is not being argued that intellectual competence and social competence are distinct entities and that we can focus on the latter and ignore the former. Edgerton (1967) is quite correct in his assertion that "the two competencies—intellectual and social—cannot be separated" [p. 216] in the reality of the everyday lives of the mentally handicapped, where the ability to deal with spatial, temporal, and numerical concepts is essential to effective social behavior. What is being argued is that we need to expand our conception of human abilities, particularly those in the social domain, and employ this expanded conception in the identification and treatment of the mentally subnormal.

It is a central thesis of this paper that to the extent that we can come to understand socially competent behavior and the conditions promoting or inhibiting its occurrence and to the extent that we can develop appropriate programs of intervention and prevention, we will make it possible for increasing numbers of mentally handicapped individuals to live relatively independent lives in non-institutional settings. What is equally important is that such a concern may result in a reduction in the current emphasis on intelligence and scholastic achievement as central markers in child development and thus also serve to increase the quality of the lives of mentally subnormal persons not only as adults but while they are being socialized into their society. Such outcomes would clearly be consistent with Nirje's (1969) principle of normalization, by which he means "making available to the mentally retarded patterns and conditions of everyday life which are as close as possible to the norms and patterns of the mainstream of society" [p. 181].

PREVIOUS ATTEMPTS TO DEFINE SOCIAL COMPETENCE

The concept of social competence or interpersonal skill has proved an elusive notion to say the least. When all else has failed, the preferred strategy for elucidating the concept appears to be to convene a group of interested and talented professionals and to allow them to wrestle with the issue for an average of 2½ days (e.g., Gladwin, 1967). Participants in one of the more recent of these conferences (Anderson and Messick, 1974) were able to identify 29 distinct facets of social competency in young children.

Several general approaches to identifying the dimensions of interpersonal skill are represented in the literature. Perhaps the most popular has been referred to as the "bag of virtues" strategy, in which one seeks to specify all those characteristics of socially skillful, well functioning persons. Into such a bag might go the elements identified by Foote and Cottrell (1955), i.e., health, intelligence, empathy, autonomy, judgment, and creativity; or those of Smith (1965), i.e., self-conficence, commitment, energy, responsibility, autonomy, flexibility, and hopeful realism.

The difficulties with such an approach are not far to seek. Clearly, not everyone will agree on 1) which traits or characteristics should go into such a set or 2) the relative importance of the various items. Further, the characteristics chosen are frequently at such a high level of abstraction that getting from the characteristic to an operational definition permitting measurement is difficult or impossible. Finally, the approach typically neglects the temporal or developmental aspect of competence. Emotional expressiveness may be important at early stages of development, for example, in that it facilitates correct labeling of one's feelings but may be disruptive at an adult stage when it will serve to interfere with more complex social interactions.

A second general approach to the task of identifying social competence might be labeled the "normative" tack. Here, a set of what are hoped to be critical social skills are identified and the age levels at which such skills are typically mastered are empirically determined. The widely used Vineland Social Maturity Scale (Doll, 1953), for example, establishes the age norms for no fewer than 117 distinct "social" skills. Again, there is a number of rather obvious limits to this strategy and the way in which it has been employed. There is an understandable tendency to select as social skills those behaviors which can be easily and reliably measured, but one is thus left with a very delimited conception of social functioning. Further, such an approach by definition indexes quality of social functioning against the status quo and provides little or no insight into potential levels of functioning and achievement in this domain. A specific problem with the Vineland Scale when employed to assess social competency level in the mentally subnormal is that the comparison group is always the normal population. Thus, we cannot assess whether the mentally handicapped individual is socially retarded or advanced in comparison to other mentally handicapped individuals (Gunzburg, 1968).

Yet a third approach to defining the elements or components of social competence is one which is guided by theoretical conceptions of the nature of social interaction or the nature of the developing organism or both. Desirable as such an approach might appear to be to social scientists, it has had few practitioners. An interesting exception to the atheoretical trend is the effort of Weinstein (1966; 1969). This theory of interpersonal tactics and competence draws heavily upon Goffman's (1959) earlier functional analysis of social interaction. Weinstein's (and, indirectly, Goffman's) notions of social competence and its development are worth reviewing for a number of reasons: 1) they derive from a reasonably well articulated conception of social interaction, 2) they have received less attention to this point than they deserve, and 3) they provide a reasonable context within which to introduce a number of issues regarding social incompetence in mentally subnormal individuals.

Weinstein (1969) begins by defining social competence as "the ability to manipulate others' responses" [p. 755]. At this level his definition differs little from those offered by Argyris (1965) or Foote and Cottrell (1955). It goes beyond many other conceptions, however, by emphasizing social interaction as the legitimate starting point in the analysis of competence rather than seeking a set of individual characteristics which identify the socially effective person. While the latter approach is prone toward the presumption of competence as a stable trait of individuals, Weinstein leaves the issue of trans-situational generality where it belongs, i.e., as an empirical question. Weinstein's model will be reviewed with specific concern for identifying those factors which may limit the occurrence of effective social interaction patterns on the part of the mentally handicapped. It is important to note at the outset that the approach is more helpful in delineating the aspects of the social context and the interpersonal skills which result in effective social functioning than it is at explicating the processes by which such contexts are created or such skills are acquired.

WEINSTEIN'S MODEL

For Weinstein, the establishment and maintenance of face-to-face interaction requires substantial agreement as to who everyone is and what is going on in a particular encounter. The "situational identities" necessary to encounters include all the attributes imputed to an individual and may derive in part from the nature of the context in which the interaction takes place, the past history of the interactions between the individuals involved, the nature of the specific behaviors engaged in, etc. Agreement in regard to situational identities is critical to the creation of what Goffman (1959) had earlier labeled the "working consensus" of an interaction. For both Goffman and Weinstein, this constitutes an "agreement as to whose claims concerning what issues will be temporarily honored" [Goffman, 1959, p. 9–10]. Consensus is achieved through a process of "identity bargaining," in which persons both call attention to aspects of self which might serve to establish a preferred identity and also attempt to withhold or disguise information which may contribute to an undesirable identity or one which will undermine the claims they wish to make on one another. Identity bargaining also involves the complementary process of assigning identity to others or "altercasting" (Weinstein and Deutschberger, 1963). Establishing the attributes of oneself and others in a social encounter is critical to the pursuit of interpersonal goals in that "the claims one person makes on another and the lines of action used to present those claims are legitimized on the basis of normative expectations regarding the behavior of particular kinds of people" [Weinstein, 1969, p. 757].

It follows from the above that at central issue in interpersonal competence is the ability to maintain and establish certain kinds of perceptions of oneself and of others. From Weinstein's point of view, three things are essential to this ability. First, the individual must be able to take the role of the other in the sense of being able to assess accurately the other person's definition of a given social situation. He notes that this is what we usually mean by the concept of empathy. Second, the person must possess a reasonably extensive repertoire of interpersonal tactics permitting him to control and influence others. And finally, the person must be capable of employing these tactics appropriately.

While this is but a bare outline of Weinstein's model, it is sufficient to focus attention on a number of factors which may be critical to effective social functioning on the part of the mentally handicapped. In what follows, attention is directed primarily to those factors which serve to disrupt encounters between the mentally subnormal and normal individuals or which act to deprive the mentally handicapped of the experience necessary to the learning of effective interpersonal tactics.

STIGMATIZED IDENTITIES AND SOCIAL EFFECTIVENESS

The process of establishing a situational identity obviously depends heavily on the initial information that an individual displays to and acquires from his interactants. As Goffman (1959) notes, "the individual's initial projection commits him to what he is proposing to be and requires him to drop all pretenses of being other things" [p. 10]. To the extent that a person is not able to project an initial impression or self-definition which is consistent with the goals he hopes to achieve in the interaction, the likelihood of successful outcomes is seriously reduced.

One of the primary difficulties faced by the mentally handicapped individual regarding the initial impression he presents to others is the stigmatizing nature of mental subnormality. Goffman (1963) has discussed the dynamics of encounters between stigmatized and non-stigmatized individuals, and Edgerton (1967) focuses on the implications of the specific stigma of mental retardation for the quality of the lives of those individuals. I do not wish to repeat their discussions in detail here but, rather, want to focus on the social psychological research evidence which has accumulated suggesting that the stigmatized individual may get involved in interactions or experience interaction outcomes which preclude socially effective functioning. It should be noted, though obvious, that to the extent that the stigma condition leads to active avoidance of interaction on either the part of the stigmatized or non-stigmatized individual, the issue of socially competent functioning is irrelevant. What is at issue in the case of interaction avoidance, however, is the way in which such limitation of interaction experience may seriously degrade the ability of the handicapped individual to develop the social skills and behavioral repertoire essential to social effectiveness. We will return to the issue of social deprivation, its implications for competence, and potential remedial strategies, near the end of this paper.

For the moment, our focus is on the nature of the behavioral exchange which takes place when stigmatized individuals interact with the non-stigmatized. In a series of studies extending over the last several years, this author has examined several dimensions of the behavior elicited from physically normal individuals by physically stigmatized persons. In these experiments, a convincing physical disability was simulated through the use of a specially constructed wheelchair, which allowed the same person to play the role of a physically normal person or an amputee. A central finding of the research is that the behavior emitted by a physically normal person differs in important ways as a function of whether he is interacting with a physically normal other or a physically stigmatized other. Kleck, Ono, and Hastorf (1966) found, for example, that when interacting with a stigmatized person, individuals tended to be more emotionally aroused, terminated an encounter more quickly, and expressed attitudes that were less representative of their actual beliefs than did individuals interacting with a non-stigmatized individual. This analysis was subsequently extended to the nonverbal dimensions of interactive behavior (Kleck, 1968; Kleck et al., 1968; and Kleck, 1969), and important differences in gestural activity, duration of eye contact, and the use of personal space by normals were detected as a function of the presence or absence of a stigmatized individual.

The nature of the differences which were observed in these studies obviously has essentially negative implications for the social functioning of the stigmatized individual. It could be argued, however, that with experience the stigmatized person learns to counter-act the behavioral biases of the normal and learns to manage successfully the strained interactions in which he finds himself (e.g., Davis, 1961). A number of laboratory studies have been done in which the behavior of the stigmatized individual rather than the behavior of the non-stigmatized person has been the focus of attention. Freedman and Doob (1968) have attempted to study the social interactive effects of deviancy per se without regard to the particular characteristics which define the deviancy or stigma. To achieve this, they produced feelings of "differentness" in young adults and compared their behavior to that of individuals who had been made to feel similar to others. The central manipulation was one in which all persons completed a complex personality inventory and were subsequently told either that they were quite similar to others in the group or that they were quite dissimilar to those others based on the inventory profiles. No explicit negative or positive evaluation was given to the feedback of being similar or different. The major findings of this research can be summarized quite directly. First, when social pressure is exerted on the individuals, those who feel deviant are more likely to conform than those who have not been induced to feel deviant, and the tendency toward greater compliance by the deviant is strongest when the person exerting the social pressure is perceived as non-deviant. Secondly, persons with feelings of deviancy, but for whom their deviancy is not public knowledge, tend to avoid social contact with others. Finally, persons in whom feelings of deviancy have been created prefer to associate with other individuals who have been identified as deviant rather than as non-deviants.

One must clearly be hesitant to generalize these results beyond the particular methods employed by Freedman and Doob. What the relationships are between these manipulated feelings of deviancy and those presumed to occur in persons who are stigmatized by some particular failing of mind, body, or character is an empirical question which as yet has no answer. They do seem to fit well with some of Goffman's (1963) speculations regarding the effect of stigma conditions on behavior, particularly as these apply to the issue of managing information about one's person. We will want to return to this issue shortly because of its importance to the question of training mentally handicapped individuals in the social skills they need in order to "pass" in society.

Finally, a study by Comer and Piliavin (1972) should be mentioned, in which the responses of physically stigmatized individuals to normals were examined, employing a paradigm parallel to that of Kleck (1968). The results can perhaps best be described as a "mirror image" to those earlier obtained by the author. That is, the behavior of actual amputees was more disrupted and less spontaneous when they were interacting with physically normal confederates than when they were interacting with confederates simulating an amputation. Thus, rather than counteracting or overcoming the behavioral biases of the normals, the responses of the stigmatized individuals would appear to jeopardize further the possibility for successful and satisfying encounters between stigmatized and non-stigmatized individuals.

The research reported above, with the exception of the Freedman and Doob studies, has dealt with individuals who could do little to manage or control the information necessary to establish their situational identity as stigmatized persons. In the case of the mentally handicapped, however, it is possible to conceal this information from others, at least during the initial stages of an interaction, and thus maintain for themselves a greater range of situational identities and hence a greater possibility for effective social functioning. Goldschmidt (1967) in the foreword to Edgerton's book *The Cloak of Competence* goes so far as to propose that the first element in any program of rehabilitation with mentally handicapped individuals is to train them in those minimal social skills which will "help them to weave their garment of concealment" [p. ix]. On the basis of what happens in social encounters when such information is disclosed, this would appear to be reasonable advice. It neglects, however, Goffman's (1963) speculations regarding the behavioral implications that follow from the need to manage discrediting information when in encounters with non-discredited other. Since any information disclosed about the self through what is said or what is done may lead by necessity or accident to the revelation of the discrediting characteristic, this eventuality can be defended against by avoiding intimate social interaction generally. The less time spent with another and the less personally involving the interaction is, the less likely it is that the stigma will be exposed.

This line of reasoning has been supported in the research of Freedman and Doob (1968) reported earlier and in a study of epileptics who had their disability under drug control (Kleck, 1968). In this latter study interviews with 18 individuals who were passing as "normals" in most of their social interactions revealed that the fear of having their disability discovered by others was a primary block to intimate social contact. Social relationships of a significant sort, e.g., engagements, were frequently terminated in preference to revealing the stigmatizing information.

The dilemma is therefore an acute one. So long as the mentally handicapped individual's situational identity is actually or potentially constrained within certain limits by stigmatizing information, any social skills he may have tend to be rendered ineffective for achieving outcomes which he desires. When he is taught those skills necessary to "pass," the demands of managing information regarding self may motivate him to avoid social interactions in general, or at least those in which the risk of exposure is high. One possible solution to this dilemma is to direct intervention efforts toward the normal and attempt to change those attitudes and response patterns which serve to undermine the development and performance of socially effective behaviors on the part of the mentally handicapped. Social effectiveness, to reflect back to Weinstein's model, is after all an interactive process. It depends not only upon the effects an individual intends and is capable of having but also upon the "identities" we permit these individuals to assume.

A slightly different way to phrase this issue is in terms of the expectations which normals bring with them into interactions with the mentally subnormal. It has been demonstrated by Rosenthal and Jacobson (1968) and confirmed by extensive subsequent research (Rosenthal, 1973) that expectations we hold concerning the intellectual capabilities of children can operate as self-fulfilling prophecies. In the original study, the authors gave each of 18 elementary school teachers the names of children in the classroom who might be expected to show dramatic intellectual growth. These predictions were supposedly derived from careful testing, though in actual fact the children were chosen randomly. All children were retested after one, two, and four semesters and their IQ change scores compared to those of a matched control group from the same classes. A significant expectancy effect was demonstrated for the "special" children in that they made larger IQ gains over the course of the study than did the children for whom no expectancy of IQ increases had been created.

It is primarily for ethical reasons that this study by Rosenthal and Jacobson, as well as those which have followed, has chosen to examine the effects of positive teacher expectancies on subsequent intellectual development. There is every reason to expect, however, that negative expectations can also function as self-fulfilling prophecies. Prior to Rosenthal's research, many authorities in mental retardation had suggested that when we first label a person as mentally retarded, we set in motion a biasing process which may affect in a negative manner most, if not all, of the social interactions and socialization experiences that the individual will have. The important point growing out of this is not that we should avoid the formulation of expectations regarding others but, rather, that we should encourage expectations of a positive sort which are consistent with the potential of the individual. In the case of the social competence of mentally handicapped persons, we have encouraged or endorsed expectations which are less positive than justified and in the process have helped preclude the development of even minimal levels of social effectiveness in such individuals.

While expectancy effects have been demonstrated frequently, such research is just beginning to focus on the mechanisms by which the outcomes are mediated. Subtle aspects of face-to-face interaction are undoubtedly involved (e.g., Rosenthal and Jacobson, 1968, pp. 178–181), and much more research on this issue is needed.

PHYSICAL APPEARANCE AND SOCIAL EFFECTIVENESS

In discussing the case of "May," a previously institutionalized mentally handicapped woman, Edgerton (1967) observes that "she is now so unattractive that she is greatly handicapped in most interpersonal relations" [p. 39]. Physical appearance cues constitute information which we bring to our encounters which others may well employ to establish our situational identities. As discussed previously, if these appearance cues include discrediting information such as a physical deformity, the social interactive implications may be quite negative. Consistent with the case of "May" above, recent research suggests that general physical attractiveness, and not just remarkable appearance characteristics, greatly influence both the way in which we are perceived and the manner in which we are treated.

Dion, Berscheid, and Walster (1972) demonstrated that a physical attractiveness stereotype exists, at least among young adults, in that attractive persons are perceived to be more warm, responsive, sensitive, kind, interesting, strong, poised, modest, sociable, and outgoing than are persons of lesser physical attractiveness. When the stereotype is phrased in terms of expectations regarding the future of attractive and unattractive persons, the former are anticipated to lead more fulfilling lives both professionally and socially.

In evaluating the ways in which or the extent to which an individual's social interactions may be affected by that individual's general level of physical attractiveness, it is important to establish the age at which an attractiveness stereotype develops and the precise implications it has for the nature of the social exchanges which occur. If, because we are less attractive than average, we experience consistent biases in our social outcomes, attractiveness stereotypes may function as self-fulfilling prophecies *vis-à-vis* social competence much as Rosenthal's induced IQ expectations serve as self-fulfilling prophecies *vis-à-vis* intellectual competence.

While there are few data available on children, a study by Dion and Berscheid (1974) does provide evidence that the "popularity" of preschoolers with their peers is directly and strongly related to physical attractiveness. They also found that the child's social behaviors were perceived and interpreted in a manner suggesting a positive bias toward physically attractive peers. Data consistent with these were collected in a summer camp setting by Kleck, Richardson, and Ronald (1974). An important finding of this latter study is that physical appearance cues continue to be related to social acceptance even after significant periods of interaction. A study by Kleck and Rubenstein (1975) offers yet further confirmation of a difference in social acceptance as a function of attractiveness but also demonstrates that we respond differently on a number of behavioral dimensions to attractive and unattractive others. For young adults, an attractive person was more frequently 1) engaged in direct eye contact, 2) smiled at, 3) sought out for social interaction, and 4) recalled accurately than was an unattractive individual.

What the data collected to date do not tell us is whether superficial physical cues continue to be more potent elicitors of social responses than behavioral information or whether positive/negative physical cues tend to co-occur with positive/negative behavioral cues. Clearly, if the unattractive child experiences negative social outcomes early on, the pattern is set for the development of a negative self-image and for the acquisition of a socially ineffective behavioral repertoire.

The data from Kleck and Rubenstein (1975) are suggestive in this regard but were collected with young adults in a situation in which individuals were encountering each other for the first time. A study by Dion (1972) is more informative in that it deals with children and their primary agents of socialization. Behavior descriptions of 7-year-old boys and girls were supposedly taken from the journal logs of elementary teachers. These descriptions involved either a mild or severe social transgression and were presented along with the child's name, age, and photograph. Young adult females were asked to read the descriptions and to give their impressions of how the child behaved on a typical day. Although there were no differences as a function of the mild transgression, when the transgression was severe, the women were more likely to attribute chronic antisocial dispositions to physically unattractive boys and girls than to attractive children.

Much more research is needed on this issue before we know the extent to which and the conditions under which low levels of physical attractiveness are related to negative social outcomes. We already have enough data, however (e.g., Berscheid and Walster, 1974), to suggest that the individual who enters an encounter under conditions in which he or she is perceived to be physically unattractive will be at a distinct disadvantage in the social exchange which follows. The implications for those concerned with social effectiveness in the mentally subnormal are obvious. Social education should include training in a self-presentation which involves a reasonably normal and acceptable physical appearance. Whether this is accomplished through the kind of behavior modification and token economy system employed by Lent (1968) or in a more casual home training procedure is probably irrelevant. What is important is that we not continue to underestimate the importance of this factor for effective social functioning.

NONVERBAL BEHAVIOR AND SOCIAL EFFECTIVENESS

The last decade has witnessed a resurgence of interest in the nonverbal dimensions of social interaction (e.g., Knapp, 1972; Mehrabian, 1971; Weitz, 1974). This renewed concern stems in part from the growing awareness that much of the communication which takes place between persons is mediated by nonverbal or body movement cues.

Birdwhistell, for example, has estimated that in a two-person conversation verbal components carry only 35% of the social meaning with the remainder being carried by nonverbal elements (Knapp, 1972). In addition, nonverbal behaviors appear to be of critical importance to the maintenance and regulation of social encounters (e.g., Condon, 1968; Kendon, 1967; 1970).

It has been demonstrated with nonhuman species that the inability to generate normal patterns of nonverbal or expressive behavior can seriously disrupt mother-child relationships and social relations generally (Rosenblum, 1969). Scott (1969) has argued that the inability of blind persons to employ typical gestural behavior or to respond to the nonverbal behavior of others may seriously disrupt encounters between the blind and the sighted. It is, according to Scott, one of the factors contributing to the development of social relations in which the blind individual becomes socially dependent.

Lack of vision is not the only condition contributing to the development of inappropriate gestural and nonverbal behavior. It is clinically commonplace that the mentally subnormal tend to be characterized by aberrant, stereotyped, or clumsy gestural and motor patterns (Tizard, 1965). Such patterns undoubtedly constitute a major block to effective social functioning and, as in the case of the blind, serve to move their social relationships toward one characterized by dependency. Research on the modifiability of gestural behavior and of the more subtle aspects of the nonverbal repertoire such as patterns of gaze behavior is minimal. Some attempts have been made to teach Foreign Service personnel the culturally variable aspects of nonverbal behavior (e.g., appropriate interpersonal distancing in American versus Near Eastern countries), but no systematic research has been conducted with the mentally subnormal in this regard.

Just as the ability to generate an appropriate and highly synchronized nonverbal repertoire is essential to effective social functioning, so is the reciprocal ability to interpret accurately and respond to the nonverbal behavior of others. While we know something of the correlates of sensitivity to the expressive behavior of others (e.g., Tagiuri, 1969), we know relatively little regarding how such skills might be trained. Argyle (1969) argues, however, that "while the . . . evidence is small, it seems that it is possible to train people to discriminate and interpret [nonverbal] cues" [p. 416]. Whether the procedures which have shown some success with normals can be extended to the mentally subnormal or whether special procedures will have to be developed is an important question for future research.

SOCIAL DEPRIVATION AND INTERPERSONAL EFFECTIVENESS

In what has gone before we have focused primarily on those factors which preclude meaningful and productive face-to-face encounters with others. These factors, however, have been primarily ones which obtain within the context of the interactions themselves or which the mentally handicapped individual brings to those encounters. Obviously, many other variables are critical in limiting the nature of the social experience and social outcomes which are available to such individuals. Socioeconomic conditions of birth, early decisions to place the person in an institutional setting, placement in special education classes, etc. all may be associated with greatly restricted social experience. Since it is primarily within the context of such experiences that interpersonal skills are incidentally learned, these factors serve directly to exacerbate the social inadequacy of the mentally retarded.

The research on experiential deficits and the development and maintenance of adaptive behavior has been recently reviewed by Haywood and Tapp (1966), as well as others, and there is no point in reproducing their review here. While most of the data derive from nonhuman species, these authors argue that the work with humans does "indicate that 'unstimulating' rearing conditions are accompanied by limited . . . social functioning" [p. 144].

Just as most of the research relating the effects of social deprivation to subsequent social inadequacy has been conducted with nonhuman species, much of the recent work on social rehabilitation has focused on dogs, cats, and nonhuman primates. Some of the most interesting of this work is being conducted by Harlow and his associates with isolate-reared rhesus monkeys. When members of this species are separated from their peers for 6 months, their behavioral repertoire becomes dominated by self-directed activities, stereotypic rocking, and an absence of age-appropriate social and exploratory behavior (e.g., Harlow, Dodsworth, and Harlow, 1965; Harlow and Harlow, 1962).

There have been two theoretical propositions advanced to account for the disruptive effects of isolation and social deprivation on social functioning. According to the critical period notion, an individual deprived of appropriate social stimulation during a particular period of development will be incapable of subsequent social maturation when returned to non-isolated conditions. The second theoretical notion derives primarily from work with dogs and suggests that when an individual shifts from the unstimulating environment associated with isolation to a more normal social one, he experiences a trauma of overstimulation which debilitates behavior.

Early attempts to rehabilitate isolate-reared monkeys by gradual introduction of environments of increasing complexity met with little success (e.g., Clark, 1968) and repeated exposure to socially competent age mates served primarily to exaggerate the disturbed behavior (Suomi and Harlow, 1972). Such results would appear to argue against the trauma hypothesis and in favor of the critical period notion. The most recent research, however, suggests that neither explanation is adequate. Suomi and Harlow (1972) hit upon the ingenious strategy of using immature females as "therapists" for their isolate-reared males. Immature females were selected for this role because they "predictably initiate social contact with an isolate without displaying social aggression and . . . exhibit simple social responses which gradually . . . become more sophisticated" [p. 133]. After only 26 weeks of interaction with these therapists, the isolate-reared males revealed recovery of most of the behavioral deficits. While Suomi and Harlow are justifiably cautious in making cross-species generalizations, these results do have potential implications for intervention strategies with socially deprived or retarded humans. They suggest both that rather striking deficits can be overcome and that the nature of the interactive experience provided is more critical than is its intensity or frequency.

Having said this much, we have gone little beyond what is already obvious. The problem remains, however, that the research which would allow us to specify the details of appropriate intervention strategies or the selection of "social therapists" who could be as effective as Suomi and Harlow's immature females has not yet been accomplished. Smith (1968) states the case appropriately in the following:

> What are the precursors of competent selfhood? By what processes and subject to what essential conditions does the baby human animal get set on a trajectory that creates the grounds for its favorable development? Recent research on infancy and early childhood identifies some of the possibilities. . . . But it still does not provide the answers we need. Wise social policy must still hedge its bets while entertaining alternative views of what is strategic in the course of development [p. 290].

REFERENCES

Anderson, S. and S. Messick. 1974. Social competency in young children. Dev. Psychol. 10: 282–293.

Argyle, M. 1969. Social Interaction. Atherton Press. New York. 504 p.

Argyris, C. 1965. Organization and Innovation. R. D. Irwin. Homewood, Illinois. 274 p.

Berscheid, E. and E. Walster. 1974. Physical attractiveness. In L. Berkowitz (ed.), Advances in Experimental Social Psychology, Vol. 7, pp. 157–215. Academic Press, New York.

Clark, D. L. 1968. Immediate and delayed effects of early, intermediate, and late social isolation in the rhesus monkey. Unpublished doctoral dissertation, University of Wisconsin.

Comer, R. J. and J. A. Piliavin. 1972. The effects of physical deviance upon face-to-face interaction. J. Pers. Soc. Psychol. 23: 33–39.

Condon, W. S. 1968. Linguistic-kinesic research and dance therapy. American Dance Therapy Association Proceedings: Third Annual Conference. Pp. 21–44.

Davis, F. 1961. Deviance disavowal; The management of strained interaction by the visibly handicapped. Soc. Prob. 9: 120–132.

Dion, K. K. 1972. Physical attractiveness and evaluations of children's transgressions. J. Pers. Soc. Psychol. 24: 207–213.

Dion, K. K. and E. Berscheid. 1974. Physical attractiveness and peer perception among children. Sociometry 37: 1–12.

Dion, K. K., E. Berscheid, and E. Walster. 1972. What is beautiful is good. J. Pers. Soc. Psychol. 24: 285–290.

Doll, E. A. 1953. The Measurement of Social Competence; A Manual for the Vineland Social Maturity Scale. Educational Publishers. Minneapolis. 664 p.

Dunn, L. M. 1968. Special education for the mildly retarded—Is much of it justifiable. Except. Children 35: 5–22.

Edgerton, R. B. 1967. The Cloak of Competence. University of California Press. Los Angeles. 233 p.

Foote, N. N. and L. S. Cottrell, Jr. 1955. Identity and Interpersonal Competence; A New Direction in Family Research. University of Chicago Press. Chicago. 305p.

Freedman, J. L. and A. N. Doob. 1968. Deviancy; Notes on the Psychology of Being Different. Academic Press. New York. 158 p.

Gladwin, R. 1967. Social competence and clinical practice. Psychiatry 30: 30–43.

Goffman, E. 1959. The Presentation of Self in Everyday Life. Doubleday and Company. New York. 225 p.

Goffman, E. 1963. Stigma; Notes on the Management of Spoiled Identity. Prentice-Hall. Englewood Cliffs, New Jersey. 147 p.

Goldschmidt, W. 1967. Forward to R. B. Edgerton's The Cloak of Competence, pp. v–xi. University of California Press. Los Angeles, California.

Gunzburg, H. C. 1968. Social Competence and Mental Handicap; An Introduction to Social Education. Bailliere, Tindall and Cassell. London. 384 p.

Harlow, H. F., R. O. Dodsworth and M. K. Harlow. 1965. Total social isolation in monkeys. Proc. Natl. Acad. Sci. 54: 90–97.

Harlow, H. F. and M. K. Harlow. 1962. The effect of rearing conditions on behavior. Bull. Menn. Clinic. 26: 213–224.

Haywood, H. C. and J. T. Tapp. 1966. Experience and the development of adaptive behavior. In N. R. Ellis (ed.), International Review ofResearch in Mental Retardation, pp. 109–146. Academic Press. New York.

Kendon, A. 1967. Some functions of gaze direction in social interaction. Acta Psychol. 26: 22–63.

Kendon, A. 1970. Movement coordination in social interaction. Acta Psychol. 32: 100–125.

Kleck, R. 1968. Physical stigma and nonverbal cues emitted in face-to-face interaction. Hum. Rel. 21: 19–28.

Kleck, R. 1969. Physical stigma and task-oriented interactions. Hum. Rel. 22: 53–60.

Kleck, R., P. L. Buck, W. L. Goller, R. S. London, J. R. Pfeiffer, and D. P. Vukcevic. 1968. The effect of stigmatizing conditions on the use of personal space. Psychol. Rep. 23: 111–118.

Kleck, R., H. Ono, and A. H. Hastorf. 1966. The effects of physical deviance upon face-to-face interaction. Hum. Rel. 19: 425–436.

Kleck, R. E., S. A. Richardson, and L. Ronald. 1974. Physical appearance cues and interpersonal attraction in children. Child Devel. 45: 305–310.

Kleck, R. E. and C. Rubenstein. 1975. Physical attractiveness, perceived attitudinal similarity, and interpersonal attraction in an opposite-sex encounter. J. Pers. Soc. Psychol. (In press)

Knapp, M. L. 1972. Nonverbal Communication in Human Interaction. Holt, Rinehart and Winston. New York. 213 p.

Lent, J. R. 1968. Mimosa cottage; Experiment in hope. Psychol. Today 2: 51–58.

Mehrabian, A. 1971. Silent Messages. Wadsworth. Belmont, California. 152 p.

Nirje, B. 1969. The normalization principle and its human management implications. In R. B. Kugel and W. Wolfensberger (eds), Changing Patterns in Services for the Mentally Retarded, pp. 179–195. President's Committee on Mental Retardation. Washington, D.C.

Rosenblum, L. 1969. Mother-infant interactions and the development of interindividual attachment in nonhuman primates. Presented at the Conference on the Nonverbal Dimensions of Social Interaction, June, Glen Cove, New York.

Rosenthal, R. 1973. On the social psychology of the self-fulfilling prophecy; Further evidence for pygmalion effects and their mediating mechanism. Psychol. Today 7: 56–63.

Rosenthal, R. and L. Jacobson. 1968. Pygmalion in the Classroom; Teacher Expectation and Pupils Intellectual Development. Holt, Rinehart and Winston. New York. 240 p.

Scott, R. A. 1969. The Making of Blind Men. Russell Sage Foundation. New York. 145 p.

Smith, M. B. 1965. Socialization for competence. Soc. Scien. Res. Coun. Items. 19: 17–22.

Smith, M. B. 1968. Competence and Socialization. *In* J. A. Clausen (ed.), Socialization and Society, pp. 270–320. Little, Brown and Company. Boston.

Suomi, S. J. and H. F. Harlow. 1972. Social rehabilitation of isolate-reared monkeys. Dev. Psychol. 6: 487–496.

Tagiuri, R. 1969. Person perception. *In* G. Lindzey and E. Aronson (eds.), Handbook of Social Psychology, Vol. 3, pp. 395–449. Addison-Wesley. Reading, Massachusetts.

Tizard, J. 1965. Individual differences in the mentally deficient. *In* A. M. Clarke and A. D. B. Blarke (eds.), Mental Deficiency; The Changing Outlook, pp. 1–6–187. Free Press. New York.

Tregold, A. F. 1952. A Textbook on Mental Deficiency. Williams & Wilkins. Baltimore. 327 p.

Weinstein, E. A. 1966. Toward a theory of interpersonal tactics. *In* C. Backman and P. Secord (eds.), Problems in Social Psychology, pp. 394–398. McGraw-Hill, New York.

Weinstein, E. A. 1969. The development of interpersonal competence. *In* D. A. Goslin (ed.), Handbook of Socialization Theory and Practice, pp. 753–775. Rand McNally. Chicago.

Weinstein, E. A. and P. Deutschberger. 1963. Some dimensions of altercasting. Sociometry 4: 454–466.

Weitz, S. 1974. Nonverbal Communication. Oxford University Press. New York. 351 p.

Factors That Impede
The Process of Socialization

Earl S. Schaefer

This analysis of factors that impede socialization will focus upon major dimensions of child adaptation that have been identified in clinical and personality research. A model for major dimensions of child adaptation that includes both social adjustment and social competence will be proposed. Emphasis will be placed on environmental and social determinants of the socialization of those dimensions and on family variables that have an early, continuing, and cumulative impact on child development instead of on specific traumatic events and specific child-rearing practices that have been related to socialization of systems of behavior (Child, 1954; Zigler and Child, 1969). Major dimensions of parent behavior, the network of family relationships, processes of socialization, and family variables that influence the major dimensions of adaptation will be discussed. In addition, evidence that social stresses and supports influence the family's ability to socialize the child will be interpreted as supporting family-centered intervention programs designed to strengthen and support family care of the child. Finally, suggestions will be made concerning the implications of the analysis for the professions and institutions that relate to families and children.

Among neo-Freudian theorists, as well as personality researchers, there is a shift in emphasis in analyses of socialization from a focus upon specific biological systems of oral, anal, and sexual behavior to a focus upon global social behaviors such as trust, intimacy, industry, and generativity (Erikson, 1959). Congruent with this changing emphasis in research on socialization is the dictionary definition of the term. *Socialize* is: "1. to make social; adjust to make fit for cooperative group living. 2. to adapt or make conform to the common needs of a social group" (*Webster's New World Dictionary, College Edition*, 1968). Thus, that socialization emphasizes social adjustment and social competence is supported by theory, research, and the dictionary definition.

In developing a model for major dimensions of child behavior that includes both social adjustment and competence, a number of clinical and statistical studies of major dimensions of child behavior will be integrated into a two-dimensional circumplex model of social adjustment. Evidence from comprehensive studies of child behavior in the classroom that a dimension of task-oriented behavior can be isolated will be presented. Since intelligence is also a major dimension of adaptation that contributes to prediction of social achievement, a hierarchical model for adaptation with two major dimensions of social competence, intelligence and task-oriented behavior, and with two major dimensions of social adjustment, extraversion versus introversion and love versus hostility, will be proposed.

Research on the ecology of child development, particularly the interaction of the child with his social environment, is needed to analyze the factors impeding socialization. In this area, both theory and research are contributing to the development of a psychology of relationships to complement the current emphasis on a psychology of personality. For example, Burgess' (1926) discussion of the family as a "unity of interacting personalities" and Handel's (1965) review of the "psychological study of whole families" have emphasized the need to study family relationships. The fruitfulness of research on the entire network of family relationships among mother, father, child, and sibling will be illustrated by a review of processes of socialization and of evidence of family influence upon the major dimensions of child adaptation.

The need for a more detailed analysis of factors that influence family relationships has been shown both by naturalistic studies of the social stresses and supports that influence family care of children and by family-centered early intervention programs. Researchers and clinicians are no longer content with the finding that parent behaviors influence child behavior, but are searching for modifiable factors that may foster both positive parent behavior and child development. Thus, research is becoming more comprehensive by studying the child and the family as they are influenced by social, cultural, and community variables.

Implications of research on the factors that impede socialization for development of more effective services for children are noted. Intervention research suggests the need to move from intervention programs to a re-evaluation of traditional professional roles in child health, child care, and education, for research and demonstration programs will have limited impact on children unless they can influence the development of more effective professions and institutions. In such a re-evaluation, this analysis suggests the need for a shift from child-centered to more family-centered training and practice in the professions that relate to children and families.

IDENTIFICATION OF MAJOR DIMENSIONS OF SOCIAL ADJUSTMENT AND COMPETENCE

Despite the controversies about interpretation and etiology, the identification of a major dimension of intelligence has contributed in countless ways to both behavioral research and clinical practice. In the area of personality research, converging findings from many different researchers on normal and clinical populations and from different types of data suggest that much of the variance in social adjustment and competence can be included in a limited number of major dimensions. These dimensions, while often similar in their behavioral content, have been given very different labels by different investigators. However, several reviews of personality research have recognized similarity in the different concepts and have isolated similar major dimensions (Anthony, 1970; Schaefer, 1971; Quay, 1972). Work on the identification of major dimensions of adjustment and competence will be reviewed to contribute to future research on socialization and to description of behavior in clinical practice.

Ackerson's (1942) analysis of 125 behavioral problems from over 3000 case histories resulted in the development of two clusters of personality and conduct problems. The personality problems score correlated with depression, an unhappy appearance, mental conflict, sensitivity, worrisomeness, nervousness, and feelings of inferiority, while the conduct problems score correlated with cruelty, destructiveness, truancy, stealing, lying, swearing, and disobedience. A similar study of child guidance clinic records by Hewitt and Jenkins (1946) also isolated clusters of traits which were interpreted as the overinhibited child, which appears similar to Ackerson's child with personality problems; the unsocialized aggressive child, which is similar to Ackerson's child with conduct problems; and the socialized delinquent with less evidence of hostility. Jenkins, Nur Edlin, and Shapiro (1966) later reported subgroups within the major group of inhibited children of shy-seclusive and overanxious neurotic and subgroups within the aggressive group of hyperactive, undomesticated, and socialized delinquents. Achenbach (1966) also analyzed child psychiatric case records and factor analyzed the intercorrelations of symptoms separately for boys and girls. The major bipolar factor of internalization versus externalization, anxious, fearful, withdrawn behavior versus aggressive, delinquent behavior, appears to be related to Ackerson's (1942) and Hewitt and Jenkins' (1946) clusters. Anthony (1970), in an integration of statistical approaches to classification of childhood behavior disorders, also suggests that Collins, Maxwell, and Cameron's (1962) anxiety and rebelliousness factors can be interpreted as defining inhibition and aggression. Despite the unrepresentative samples and the difficulties of analyzing psychiatric records, the degree of consensus on major patterns of child adjustment as derived from child clinical case records is high.

Ratings by school teachers also have revealed two major dimensions of child adjustment which are similar to those found in analyses of psychiatric records. From teachers' ratings of behavior problems, Peterson (1961) isolated two major dimensions of personality problems and conduct problems which were similar to Ackerson's clusters. Peterson (1960) had earlier identified major dimensions of extraversion-introversion and adjustment-maladjustment in the first two factors of several factor analyses of child behavior ratings. Perhaps Peterson's (1960, 1961) analyses might be integrated by interpreting conduct problems as combinations of extraversion and maladjustment and personality problems as combinations of introversion and maladjustment. Schaefer (1961) developed two-dimensional circumplex organizations of school behavior ratings and labeled the major dimensions introversion-extraversion and love-hostility. Becker and Krug (1964) also utilized Guttman's (1954) circumplex model to organize a set of bipolar behavior ratings within major dimensions of extraversion versus introversion and emotional stability versus emotional instability. Similarly, Baumrind and Black (1967) organized Q-sort data into a circumplex model that they related to Schaefer's (1961) and Becker and Krug's (1964) models. Thus, convergence on a two-dimensional circumplex model for child behavior can be seen in the syntheses of different investigators utilizing a number of different sets of empirical data.

Both Anthony's (1970) and Quay's (1972) integration of clinical studies of psycho-pathology have agreed upon two major patterns: 1) personality problems, overinhibition, anxiety, internalization, and withdrawal, and 2) conduct problems, rebelliousness, anti-social aggressiveness, and externalization. Quay (1972) cites 15 representative empirical studies that define the two dimensions of conduct problems or aggression and personality problems or withdrawal. Both Anthony (1970) and Quay (1972) attempted to integrate studies of psychopathology with less attention to variations in behavior in more represen-tative populations. Yet many of the dimensions isolated from psychiatric patients are similar to those found in more representative samples. Therefore, a two-dimensional circumplex model is used to integrate studies of both clinical and more representative populations in Table 1. Both two-dimensional and circumplex organizations of behavior are included, with the columns that represent different angular locations in a circumplex organization including concepts proposed by different investigators. Only the labels used for different dimensions or different sectors of the circumplex orderings are included, but a more comprehensive mapping could be developed by also plotting the more specific behaviors included in the different analyses.

The bipolar dimension of extraversion (360/0°) versus introversion (180°) show the clearest consensus in the labels assigned by different investigators. Externalization, which is clearly more related to conduct problems, was included with extraversion only because of its statistical independence of "severe and diffuse pathology" in Achenbach's (1966) study of symptoms of child psychiatric cases. Studies of more comprehensive samples of behavior and of more representative samples of children show a different factor structure. The neighboring sector of the circumplex organization includes the extraverted adjusted behavior (45) of social participation, friendliness, loving, stable, and interest-participation and the polar opposite sector of introverted maladjusted behaviors (225) of personality problems, overinhibition, withdrawal, anxiety, distrusting, unstable, neurotic, and apathy-withdrawal. Despite the great diversity of concepts and the varying emphasis upon pathological symptoms, the behaviors included in the concepts are very similar.

The bipolar sectors of adjustment versus maladjustment (90° to 270°), which are completely independent of the sector of extraversion versus introversion (360/0° to 180°), again show a great diversity in labels: ego strength, adjustment, love, good socialization, emotional stability, and responsible versus neurosis, ego weakness, mal-adjustment, hostility, poor socialization, emotional instability, irresponsible, and severe and diffuse pathology. However, the model suggests that these labels are defining the same sector of a circumplex model. Examination of the behaviors included in the labels by different investigators suggests that they are synonyms for the same behaviors. The bipolar sectors at 135° and 315° that are neighbors of adjustment versus maladjustment and extraversion versus introversion have more similar labels: intellectual control, con-formity, submissiveness, and cooperation-compliance versus conduct problems, unsocialized aggression, impulsivity, aggressiveness, rebelliousness, assertive, non-conformity, anti-social, and anger-defiance. This sector of hostile aggression would not conflict with an interpretation of the sector of maladjustment at 270° as highly related to less open expression of hostility. Becker and Krug's (1964) label of distrusting in the introverted maladjusted sector suggests that distrust may be a more introverted type of hostility. Schaefer's (1971) identification of a dimension of hostility also found both introverted and extroverted types of hostility, but with the factor of hostility statistically independent of the factor of extraversion-introversion.

Because the concept of hostility refers to more specific behaviors, the concept of love versus hostility will be used here to refer to the dimension that might also be labeled adjustment versus maladjustment. In contrast, maladjustment might refer also to personality problems and to conduct problems. Despite the problem of labeling the dimensions, this analysis suggests that concepts derived from studies of symptoms of clinical populations and those derived from behaviors of more representative populations can be integrated in a single circumplex model with major dimensions of love versus hostility and extraversion versus introversion.

The emphasis upon social behavior in labeling major dimensions of adjustment is supported by a number of theorists, including Horney's (1945) dispositions of moving away from others or moving against others, Rosenzweig's (1945) description of intropunitive and extropunitive responses to frustration, Fromm's (1947) description of destructiveness and withdrawal in social relationships, and Zigler and Phillips (1960) analysis of behavioral tendencies to turn against the self and to turn against others. Since clinical research focuses upon psychopathology rather than adjusted behavior, these concepts emphasize less adaptive responses.

The possibility that emotion concepts, trait concepts, and diagnostic concepts might be integrated into a unified conceptual scheme was supported by Schaefer and Plutchik (1966). Experienced clinicians rated the extent to which specific diagnostic concepts implied a set of emotions and a set of personality traits. Statistical analyses of these judgments showed that emotion and trait concepts were integrated in a unified circumplex organization in which the basic emotions of fear and anger were at the negative poles of the two major dimensions. The diagnostic concepts, as well as the traits and emotions, were integrated by circumplex organizations that correspond closely to the circumplex organization of social adjustment as seen in Table 1.

Identification of a Dimension of Task-Orientation versus Distractibility

Despite the fact that task-oriented behavior is involved in a high proportion of referrals to child guidance clinics, particularly referrals by the school system (Wender, 1971), that dimension has not been clearly identified in the research on social adjustment reviewed above. However, emphasis on task-oriented behavior is emerging from research on minimal brain dysfunction, which Wender (1971) states is the most common disorder seen by child psychiatrists. Child behaviors which Wender related to minimal brain dysfunction include: short attention span, poor concentration, learning difficulties shown

Table 1. A circumplex organization of social adjustment concepts

	360°/0°	45°	90°	135°	180°	225°	270°	315°
Ackerson (1942)						Personality problems		Conduct problems
Hewitt and Jenkins (1946)						Over-inhibition		Unsocialized aggression
Eysenck (1953)	Extraversion				Introversion		Neurosis	
Kassenbaum, Couch, and Slater (1959)	Extraversion	Social participation	Ego-strength	Intellectual control	Introversion	Withdrawal	Ego-weakness	Impulsivity
Peterson (1960)	Extraversion		Adjustment		Introversion		Mal-adjustment	
Peterson (1961)						Personality problems		Conduct problems
Schaefer (1961)	Extraversion	Friendliness	Love	Conformity	Introversion	Withdrawal	Hostility	Aggressive-ness

Collins, Maxwell, and Cameron (1962)								
Digman (1963)	Extraversion		Good Socialization		Introversion	Anxiety	Poor socialization	Rebelliousness
Becker and Krug (1964)	Extraversion	Loving	Emotional stability	Submissive	Introversion	Distrusting	Emotional instability	Assertive
Baumrind and Black (1967)	Active	Stable	Responsible	Conformity	Passive	Unstable	Irresponsible	Non-conformity
Achenbach (1966)	Externalization				Internalization		Severe and diffuse pathology	
Rutter (1967)						Neurotic		Antisocial
Kohn and Rosman (1972)		Interest-participation		Cooperation-compliance		Apathy-withdrawal		Anger-defiance
Quay (1972)						Withdrawal		Aggression

by poor school performance despite adequate intelligence, poor impulse control including low frustration tolerance and low perseverance, emotional lability, and antisocial behavior. Although several of these concepts have also been included in the concepts of conduct problems, externalization, and antisocial behavior, a cluster of hyperactivity, distractibility, low perseverance, and low concentration can be differentiated from antisocial aggression. A two-dimensional analysis of ratings that had factor loadings on a global dimension of adjustment-maladjustment revealed two independent factors: 1) distractibility, hyperactivity, work fluctuation, inappropriate talkativeness, low calmness, and low conscientiousness which was labeled low task-oriented behavior and 2) cruelty, resentfulness, irritability, covert hostility, and suspiciousness which was labeled hostility. Subsequent analyses of teachers' ratings of classroom behavior confirmed the factor of hostility and defined the positive pole of the independent factor of task-oriented behavior with scales of perseverance, conscientiousness, attentiveness, concentration, methodicalness, academic seriousness, and achievement orientation (Schaefer, 1971).

Many earlier studies did not identify a factor of task-oriented behavior because those behaviors were not sampled. Studies identifying what appeared to be task-oriented behaviors have assigned many different labels to them. For example, Smith (1967) isolated a factor which he labeled strength of character, which included major loadings for ratings of perseverance, responsibility, conscientiousness, self-reliance, and orderliness. The label autonomous achievement striving has been given to a similar set of behaviors by Beller (1959) and Digman (1972) has also identified a factor of industriousness which was highly correlated with high school grade point average. In addition, Douglas (1964) reports high correlations between ratings by teachers of perseverance and hard work in school and Miller (1972) has identified a dimension of need achievement versus task avoidance from ratings of classroom behavior.

The dimension of task-oriented behavior has been isolated from ratings of classroom behavior by several different investigators. Perhaps the differentiation of hyperactive, distractible behavior from hostile behavior has been made more clearly from classroom data than from clinical data. Evidence that task orientation is correlated with academic achievement would justify including that dimension as a major component of social competence. Intelligence is also a major component of social competence that has been emphasized far more than task orientation in research on academic achievement and on social competence. The major dimensions of adjustment and competence discussed here are integrated into a hierarchical model for adaptation in Figure 1. The research reviewed suggests that each of these major dimensions of adjustment and competence should be included in comprehensive studies of socialization.

Negative extremes of the specific dimensions of the model for social adaptation might be associated with specific diagnoses, e.g., low intelligence with mental retardation, distractibility with minimal brain dysfunction, hostility with delinquency, and introversion and withdrawal with neurosis. Yet, the degree of statistical independence of the dimensions suggests that the negative extremes of the dimensions may coexist in the same person, i.e., that a mentally retarded person might also be distractible, hostile, and withdrawn. Perhaps a fruitful direction for research on socialization and on mental

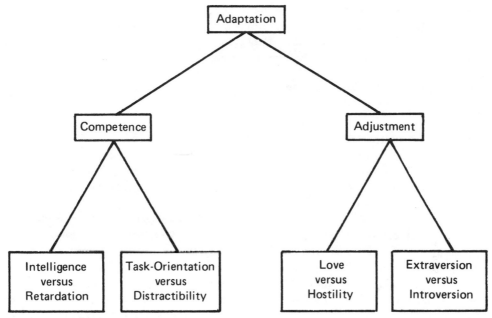

Figure 1. A hierarchical model for adaptation.

retardation would be to investigate the antecedents and correlates of these major dimensions of adaptation.

Stability of Major Dimensions of Adaptation through Time

The importance of the early socialization of major dimensions of adaptation can be partially evaluated by the stability of the child's behavior through time. If the child's behavior shows great change through time, the social significance of early socialization would be reduced. The contrary conclusion, illustrated by Bloom's (1964, p. 88) statement that "about 50 percent of intellectual development takes place between conception and age 4 and about 80 percent by age 8" has provided much of the motivation for research on early intellectual development. Examination of the evidence concerning early stabilization of child behavior and alternative interpretations of those data will contribute to planning for both research and service programs.

Bloom's summary of the evidence that intelligence stabilizes during the early years of life was derived from longitudinal studies of children reared in their own families. Therefore those studies were not able to differentiate genetic influences from environmental influences or to differentiate the early environment from the continuing environment of the family. Studies of children who leave an initially depriving environment for a more stimulating environment suggest that major changes in environment can result in substantial increases in intellectual functioning, even in late adolescence or early maturity. Clarke and Clarke (1959) report mean IQ increases of 16 points from mentally retarded subjects during the 6 years after they left their severely depriving environments. Feuerstein (1970, p. 357) summarized the effects of a 4- to 6-year educational and training program in an Israeli kibbutzim for immigrant youth with retarded development and concluded:

> The achievements marked by the Youth Aliya wards in terms of quantity and quality can be considered as massive evidence that reversibility of severely retarded performance is an attainable goal, even at such a late stage as adolescence.

The extent to which intelligence tends to be stable in the absence of major changes in environment is suggested by correlations between 18-year and 40-year IQ's for Berkeley Guidance Study males of 0.74 and for females of 0.75 (Honzig, 1972). These correlations are substantially smaller than the stability of IQ scores for short time periods, suggesting that changes in functioning occur even during maturity.

Determination of the stability of a dimension of task-oriented behavior is minimal due to the lack of concensus in conceptualization and measurement, the typical lack of differentiation of hyperactivity and distractibility from antisocial aggression, and the resultant lack of longitudinal studies. However, Digman's (1972) report for a sample from a university school that a factor of industriousness rated during the first and second grade predicted high school grade point average with a correlation of 0.51 suggests that these behaviors may stabilize early. Similarly, Wender's (1971) discussion of the minimal brain damage (MBD) syndrome, which prominently includes distractibility, indicates that early symptoms of this syndrome suggest a poor prognosis at maturity. He further indicates that Robins' (1966) follow-up of acting out psychiatric clinic patients may be relevant to the prognosis of MBD since, "many children having symptoms which overlap those seen in the MBD syndrome developed a variety of serious psychiatric disorders, while children with symptoms unlike those seen in MBD did not develop such disorders."

Studies by Robins (1966) and Roff (1971), as well as Robins' (1972) review of follow-up studies of behavior disorders of children, show that antisocial, aggressive children have a relatively poor prognosis for recovery from illness and for adult outcome. Roff's studies have shown that both rejections and discharges from military services for psychiatric or behavior problems can be predicted by delinquent behavior found in case histories from child guidance clinics of 8- to 12-year old children. In addition, Robins (1966) found that cases of antisocial behavior from child guidance clinics showed a variety of maladaptive behaviors as adults.

In contrast to the poor outcome of antisocial behavior, a number of follow-ups of clinic patients with neurotic disturbances show relatively high rates of recovery (Cunningham, Westerman, and Fischhoff, 1956; Masterson, 1958; Warren, 1965; Robins, 1966). Summarizing her work, Robins (1972, p. 437) states

> . . . poor outcomes were largely confined to *antisocial* children. . . . Indeed, children seen for neurotic disturbances had almost as good adult adjustment as had normal school children selected for freedom from school problems. . . .

Robins (1972) also states that, "*no* childhood variables, neither the child's behavior problems nor his family type, predicted adult neurosis."

This cursory examination of the stability of major dimensions of adaptation suggests that three dimensions, low intelligence, low task-oriented behavior, and hostility or antisocial aggression, tend to be predictive of the child's future adaptation, while the dimension of introverted, inhibited, neurotic behavior has a more favorable prognosis. Since much of the existing research has been on psychiatric clinic populations, longitudinal studies of more representative samples are needed to determine the significance of lesser degrees of maladaptation during childhood.

CONCEPTUALIZATION OF
FAMILY VARIABLES THAT INFLUENCE SOCIALIZATION

An analysis of major characteristics of the parent's interaction with the child may justify the focus of this paper as to family influence upon socialization. As contrasted to other institutions, the family's *priority* in influencing the child's early socialization is complemented by the *duration* and by the *continuity* of that influence, and by the total *amount* of interaction and care. These characteristics of family care are related to the *extensity* of sharing in many different situations, the *intensity* of involvement and affect, and the *pervasiveness* of the parent's influence upon the child's total experience with society. The degree of parental influence is also related to the *consistency* of the patterns of parent-child interaction, the great *variability* in parental care, and the *responsibility* for child care that is assigned to the family by society (Schaefer, 1972). The early, continuing, and cumulative influence of parental care, as contrasted to care provided by professionals, is shown by these characteristics.

A model of early parent-child interaction and of the parent's influence upon the child's interaction with other persons, objects and activities is reproduced in Figure 2 (Schaefer, 1970). The first stage of the socialization process, which is often omitted in psychological analyses, is the parent's development of a positive attachment to the child. Thus, an analysis of factors that block parental attachment to the child would contribute to an analysis of factors impeding the socialization process. In the second stage, the child develops a positive attachment to the parent. More emphasis in recent research upon the child's response to the parent is a needed complement to research emphasizing the parent's response to the child (Bell, 1968; 1971). In the third stage, the parent and child together engage in an activity, with an object or with another person. Through these shared activities the child may develop new relationships, interests, skills, and task-oriented behaviors. Thus, the model outlines the development of mediated learning experiences which Feuerstein (1970) suggests are the most significant impetus to intellectual development.

The degree of importance attached to parent behavior as an antecedent of child development has led to numerous attempts to develop detailed conceptualizations of such behavior. The diversity of conceptual schemes and of methods has led to attempts to develop major concepts or dimensions that would include many different parent behaviors. Symonds (1939) was among the first to attempt integration of empirical studies of

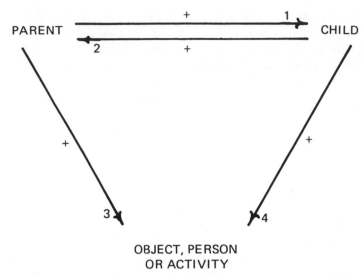

Figure 2. A model for early parent-child interaction, socialization, and mediated learning.

parent-child relationships into a two-dimensional conceptual model of acceptance-rejection and dominance-submission. A second order factor analysis of the Fels Parent Behavior Rating Scales by Lorr and Jenkins (1953) anticipated later three-dimensional models by the isolation of three major factors of democracy in child training, dependency-encouraging, and organization and effectiveness of control. From her clinical insights, Roe (1957) developed a hierarchical circular model for parent behavior that included a major dimension of loving versus rejecting and a second dimension that emphasized high or low emotional concentration upon the child. She also suggested concepts for combinations of the two major dimensions, e.g., the concept "overprotective" was shown as a combination of loving with high emotional concentration as contrasted to "neglecting" which was shown as a combination of rejecting with low emotional concentration.

From a factor analysis of a set of maternal behavior ratings, Schaefer (1959) developed a two-dimensional circumplex model for maternal behavior. The model included major dimensions of love versus hostility and autonomy versus control. Becker (1964), from parent behavior ratings that included some of the Fels scales, developed a three-dimensional model of warmth versus hostility, anxious emotional involvement versus calm detachment, and restrictiveness versus permissiveness. A factor analysis of the Child Report of Parent Behavior Inventory (Schaefer, 1965a) generated a very similar three-dimensional model with dimensions of acceptance versus rejection, psychological control, and lax control versus firm control. Roe and Siegelman (1963) also reported three dimensions of loving-rejection, overt attention, and casual-demanding. In addition, Siegelman's factor analysis (1965) of another method of collecting children's perceptions of parent behavior resulted in three factors of loving, demanding, and punishment.

The repeated replication of a three-dimensional factor structure for the Child Report of Parent Behavior Inventory for different national samples and age groups (Schaefer, 1965b; Renson, Schaefer, and Levy, 1968; Kojima, 1967; Burger and Armentrout, 1972; Schluderman and Schluderman, 1970) suggests that differences among the various conceptual schemes are probably due to differences in conceptualization and measurement. Despite these differences, all two- and three-dimensional analyses of parent behavior have identified a major dimension of acceptance, democracy, love, and warmth as contrasted to hostility and rejection. The two-dimensional analyses have identified dimensions of dominance-submission, emotional concentration, and autonomy-control. The three-dimensional organizations differentiate a dimension of control that has been labeled organization and effectiveness of control, restrictiveness versus permissiveness, and lax control versus firm control from a dimension of involvement that has been labeled dependency-encouraging, anxious emotional involvement versus calm detachment, psychological control, and demanding. The degree of convergence in these concepts suggests that three major dimensions of acceptance, control, and involvement can be identified in comprehensive samples of parent behavior. Perhaps these dimensions might also be isolated in comprehensive studies of other dyadic relationships.

Despite the convergence in empirical psychological studies of parent behavior, those studies have had little influence in another research tradition that stems from Bowlby's (1951) work on maternal deprivation. Much of the early research that contributed to analyses of maternal deprivation was summarized by Ainsworth (1962), who differentiated three aspects of maternal deprivation: separation from the mother, insufficiency of maternal care, and distortions of maternal care. Insufficiency of maternal care might be related to the dimensions of low involvement and low acceptance reviewed above, as well as to the social welfare concept of neglect. Distortions of maternal care might be related to high involvement combined with hostility and rejection, as well as the social welfare concept of abuse (Helfer and Kempe, 1968; Kempe and Helfer, 1972).

Rutter's (1971) analysis of data on family relationships suggested that brief separations from the family, if not accompanied by persistent family tension and/or negative relationships, may have minimal long term effect upon the child's socialization. His analysis of family relationships also significantly broadened the focus of research on deprivation by finding that the husband-wife relationship, as well as the father-child and mother-child relationship, is significantly related to the social adjustment of sons. By combining data on husband-wife, father-son, and mother-son relationships, Rutter found relatively high correlations with sons' antisocial, delinquent behavior. Inclusion of several family relationships in prediction of the adaptation of the child would significantly broaden the focus of current psychological research on socialization. This research has previously had a primary focus on mother-child relationships, a minor secondary focus on the father-child relationship, and an almost total neglect of husband-wife relationships (Mussen, 1970).

Recent family research suggests the need to study the entire network of family relationships among father, mother, child, and sibling shown in Figure 3. Integrated studies of the entire network of relationships would investigate Burgess' (1926) concept

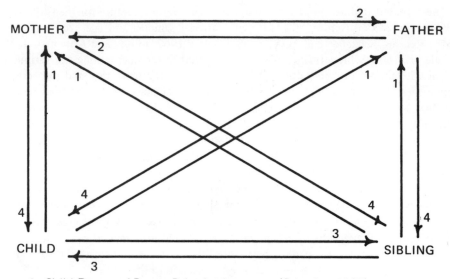

1. Child Report of Parent Behavior Inventory (Schaefer, 1965)

2. Communication in Marriage Inventory (Schaefer and Phillips, Unpublished)

3. Sibling Behavior Inventory (Aaronson and Schaefer, Unpublished)

4. Child Behavior toward the Parent Inventory (Schaefer and Finkelstein, Unpublished)

Figure 3. A network of family relationships: inventories of perceptions by family members. 1. Child report of parent behavior inventory (Schaefer, 1965). 2. Communication in marriage inventory (Schaefer and Phillips, unpublished). 3. Sibling behavior inventory (Aaronson and Schaefer, unpublished). 4. Child behavior toward the parent inventory (Schaefer and Finkelstein, unpublished).

of the "family as a unity of interacting personalities" and would contribute to the "psychological study of whole families" advocated by Handel (1965). Although earlier research has focused upon maternal behavior with the child, more studies are analyzing the effects of paternal behavior upon the child (Biller, 1970; Radin, 1972; 1973). Indicating that child behavior also influences parent behavior, Bell's (1968; 1971) reviews have integrated earlier research and have stimulated additional study. The controversy about the direction of influence from parent to child or vice-versa suggests that more detailed analyses of the circular interactions of parent and child will contribute to an understanding of family relationships. Research on relationships among siblings (Sutton-Smith and Rosenberg, 1970; Bowerman and Dobash, 1974) is also needed to understand family relationships. Although research on the triadic interaction of mother, father, and child may be most fruitful in investigating the socialization of the individual child, studies of differences in the family relationships of siblings will contribute to the understanding of the antecedents of different parental behavior with different children.

Although the entire network of family relationships of Figure 3, apart from clinical case studies, has not been studied simultaneously, a set of inventories has been developed for the multivariate measurement of each of these relationships.

The validity of children's perceptions of parent behavior, shown by correlations with other data on parent behavior (Schaefer and Bayley, 1967), and the reliable measurements and clear factor structures that have been found for each of the vectors of Figure 3 open up a broad field of research on family relationships and socialization.

RELATIONSHIP OF FAMILY VARIABLES
TO MAJOR DIMENSIONS OF CHILD BEHAVIOR

Theories of Socialization: Processes and Mechanisms

Several theoretical explanations of the socialization process have been developed, with many of them focusing upon explanations of parental influence upon child development. An analysis of how different theories of socialization might explain the influence upon child behavior of the most pervasive dimension of parent behavior, parental love, warmth, and acceptance versus hostility and rejection, will indicate that the different theories do not contradict, but rather complement one another. This analysis will support the conclusion derived from empirical research that major dimensions of parent behavior have a significant effect upon major dimensions of child behavior.

Developmental identification or anaclitic identification suggests that the child is socialized because of his attachment to a rewarding and nurturant parent (Mowrer, 1950; Mussen, 1967). Thus, parental warmth, love, and acceptance would increase the effectiveness of this process in socializing the child. Evidence for this theory includes Mussen and Distler's (1960) and Mussen and Rutherford's (1963) findings that affectionate, warm fathers and mothers had more appropriately sex-typed boys and girls.

Bandura (1962; 1970) has shown that many of the phenomena included under the concept of identification can be explained by *modeling,* imitation, or incidental learning. Ample experimental evidence has been provided that modeling can influence both aggression (Bandura, 1970) and pro-social behavior (Bandura, 1969; Rosenhan, 1972). Thus, it is reasonable to assume that consistent loving or hostile parent behavior will lead to similar behavior patterns in the child.

Reinforcement of specific behaviors also has a major effect upon child behavior. Research on the effects of training parents to modify the behavior of their children has influenced many clinical programs directed at both parents and teachers (Brown, 1971; Johnson and Katz, 1973). Parents who are more warm, accepting, and loving apparently perceive and reinforce more positive behaviors of their children than hostile and rejecting parents. Patterns of positive reinforcement may partially explain the success of parental acceptance in socializing the child.

Mediated learning (Feuerstein, 1970) may contribute both to cognitive learning and to other socialized behavior through shared experiences of parent and child. If the parent has a positive relationship with the child and with another person, the parent can mediate the child's development of a relationship with the other person. The positive affect, the enriched experience, and the skills developed through shared experiences with a warm, accepting parent may be related to the other processes of identification, modeling, and reinforcement.

The concept of identification with the aggressor suggests that fear may also lead to the child's identification with the hostile, aggressive parent. Such an identification might lead to hostility directed toward other weaker persons. Mussen (1967) has interpreted his own research as providing some evidence for this process, but as providing more evidence for developmental identification with the nurturant parent.

The frustration-aggression hypothesis (Dollard et al., 1939) that has influenced much of the research on aggression has been reviewed in depth by Zigler and Child (1969) and Feshback (1970). Clearly, a hostile, rejecting parent would frustrate many of the social and emotional needs of the child. From their review of the evidence Feshbach and Feshbach (1972) state:

> It would appear . . . that the frustration-aggression hypothesis best applies to particular types of children as well as to particular types of frustrating experiences, and that one cannot assume that frustration necessarily increases aggressive tendencies in all children at all times.

Levy's (1937) concept of primary affect hunger arising from early deprivation is most clearly supported by studies of children reared in institutions (Goldfarb, 1945; Pringle and Bossio, 1958). However, it may also apply to the acting-out behavior of neglected and rejected children reared in families.

This brief discussion suggests that the effects of warm, loving, accepting parent behavior upon the socialization of children might be explained by a combination of the processes of *developmental identification, modeling, reinforcement,* and *mediated learning,* while the effects of hostile, rejecting parent behavior might be explained by the mechanisms of *identification with the aggressor, frustration-aggression,* and *primary affect hunger.* Perhaps the relevance of these processes to the child's hostile, aggressive behavior is most apparent. However, the effects of modeling, reinforcement, and mediated learning might also influence the child's intellectual development and task-oriented behavior. The effects of parental involvement and control upon child behavior might also be interpreted through these processes of socialization. However, the changing needs of the child from birth to maturity, from a need for high involvement during infancy to a need for autonomy at maturity, as well as the varying appropriateness of parental control at different ages, do not allow a brief discussion of those issues. The apparent stability of the parent's love and acceptance versus hostility and rejection from infancy to adolescence (Schaefer and Bayley, 1960) and the pervasive effects of this dimension upon the processes of socialization may explain the correlations of parental acceptance versus rejection with major dimensions of child behavior.

Evidence of Family Influence on Major Dimensions of Child Adaptation

Although many different researchers support the conclusion that family functioning influences the intellectual development of the child (Hess, 1969; Schaefer, 1972), only a few studies will be noted here. Douglas' (1964) analysis of a national sample of British children showed that the parent's interest in the child's education was correlated with mental test scores even after controlling for social class. Similarly, Moore (1968) showed that ratings of verbal stimulation and toys, books, and experiences provided at 30 months predicted the child's reading scores at 7 years and mental test scores at 8 years even after controlling for parent education. Werner, Bierman, and French (1971, p. 134) concluded from a longitudinal study from the prenatal period to age 10 years:

> Ratings of the families' socioeconomic status, educational stimulation, and emotional support showed significant associations with achievement, intellectual development and emotional problems at age 10. *Ten times more children had problems attributed to the effects of a poor environment than to the effects of serious perinatal stress.*

Radin (1972; 1973) demonstrated that observations of paternal behavior with 4-year-old sons during an interview are significantly correlated with the sons' IQ both at that time and with the sons' IQ test scores a year later. Paternal nurturance, including reinforcement, sensitivity, and consultation with the child, showed significant correlations with sons' IQ for both middle class and lower class subjects. Sons' IQ was also significantly correlated with an interview measure of educationally supportive activities. Both paternal nurturance and educationally supportive activities were also significantly related to social class.

Parent behaviors have been shown to correlate with reading skills as well as IQ. Rupp (1969) studied a group of lower socioeconomic status children with high and low reading skills. After matching for a number of family structure and socioeconomic variables, differences between high and low reading groups were found in the amount of intellectual stimulation in the home and the parents' involvement in the child's schooling.

Briggs and Elkind (1973) compared a sample of children who were early readers with a group of matched controls and found that the fathers of the early readers had read to them more often. In addition, the early readers had other children reading to them more often and had been exposed to reading instruction on television. Significant differences between the two groups on the Matching Familiar Figures Test, a measure of reflection-impulsivity that has also been related to reading skills by Kagan (1965), suggests that early, mediated learning experiences in reading may influence both reading skills and task-oriented behavior. Douglas' (1964) finding that parents' interest in the child's education was related both to mental test scores and to teacher ratings of the child's perseverance and hard work in school would support that conclusion.

Digman's (1972) finding of a high multiple correlation of ratings of industriousness and of academic achievement test scores with the child's grade point average in high school also suggests that school competence is highly related to both task-oriented behavior and intelligence. Both reading skills and referral for special education are significantly related to task-oriented behavior, and reading skills have been related to parental behavior (Douglas, 1964; Rupp, 1969; Briggs and Elkind, 1973). The higher correlation of family process variables with academic achievement (Dave, 1963) than with intelligence (Wolfe, 1964) in parallel studies can be explained by the cumulative effects of family process variables upon both intelligence and task-oriented behavior that together predict academic achievement.

Schaefer and Bayley's (1963) finding that a dimension of maternal love versus hostility, identified during infancy, predicts sons' task-oriented behavior in the mental test situation would also support a relationship between parent variables and task-oriented behavior. Findings by Goldfarb (1945) that children reared in institutions have little impulse control, frustration tolerance, or goal directedness have been confirmed by Pringle and Bossio (1958). Despite these indications that early rearing may have a powerful effect upon task-oriented behavior, clinical studies of hyperactive, distractible children (Keogh, 1971; Fish, 1972; Weiss et al., 1972) show a number of other possible antecedents. From a study of twins, Willerman (1973) presents evidence that hyper-activity may be inherited, and Wender (1971) stresses biological rather than social-psychological antecedents of minimal brain dysfunction. Further study of the dimension of task-oriented behavior is necessary to clarify the importance of different factors. However, behavior modification studies in classrooms suggest that reinforcement can change these behaviors. Perhaps parental modeling, the child's identification with the task-oriented parent, mediated learning experiences, and parental reinforcement are important environmental influences even though brain damage and genetic differences also influence the child's hyperactivity and distractibility.

The literature on antisocial aggression and delinquency is clear in finding a related family background of both maternal and paternal rejection and hostility, particularly for sons (Hewitt and Jenkins, 1946; Lewis, 1954; Glueck and Glueck, 1950; Andry, 1960; Rutter, 1971). Achenbach (1966) found that parents of externalizers show a history of divorce, psychiatric problems, criminality, alcoholism, unemployment, desertion, having illegitimate children, and charges of child neglect. This is paralleled by Robins and Lewis' (1966) and Roff's (1971) findings that antisocial behavior of parents is related to antisocial behavior of sons. Robins and Lewis (1966) found this relationship in both white-collar and blue-collar families and also reported that the greater the number of antisocial relatives, the greater the effect upon the boy. The several different socialization processes of modeling, identification, reinforcement, identification with the aggressor, and frustration-aggression might be used to interpret these findings.

Rutter's (1971) report that marital tension and conflict are related to antisocial behavior of sons is paralleled by Kimmel and van der Veen's (1974) finding that reports by husband and wife of low compatibility in marriage are related to the child's aggressive behavior. Reviews of research on aggression (Feshbach, 1970; Feshbach and Feshbach, 1972) would also support a conclusion that parental hostility and rejection are related to the child's aggression and delinquency. Rutter's (1971) report on family relationship antecedents of delinquency refers almost entirely to data for boys. Perhaps the high boy to girl ratio for delinquency (Jenkins et al., 1966) is caused by a greater tendency for sons to respond to family hostility and rejection with antisocial aggression.

Achenbach (1966) reports that parents of internalizers show greater involvement with the child than parents of externalizers, but does not compare his groups with normal children. Levy (1943) reported more submissiveness, passivity, timidity, and poor peer relationships for children of dominating overprotecting mothers, and Hewitt and Jenkins (1946) found more overinhibited behavior in children associated with parental repression.

Jenkins et al. (1966) also concluded that neurotic, overanxious children have close ties to overanxious, neurotic mothers. Corresponding to Jenkins' findings, Hagman (1932) reports correlations between the mother's and the child's fears as reported by the mother. Through processes of identification, modeling, and reinforcement, parents may influence the fearful, anxious, neurotic behavior of their children. However, the conflicting findings, as contrasted to the clear correlations of family functioning with hostility and delinquency, suggest that more subtle and detailed studies are needed to correlate family functioning with neurosis.

Regarding the antecedents of introversion-extroversion, twin studies indicate that this dimension may be highly heritable (Vandenberg, 1967). Relatively high consistency of active, extroverted behaviors through time (Kagan and Moss, 1962; Schaefer and Bayley, 1963; Tuddenham, 1959) and low and inconsistent correlations between ratings of introversion versus extraversion and ratings of parent behavior (Schaefer and Bayley, 1963; Becker and Krug, 1964) also suggest that introversion-extraversion may be influenced more by genetic than environmental factors.

This discussion has emphasized family influence upon major dimensions of child adaptation. However, intelligence is influenced by heredity and neurological impairment as well as environmental variables. On this issue, Werner, Bierman, and French (1971) state that family environmental factors show far more correlation with IQ scores than perinatal stress factors. Scarr-Salapatek (1971) reports that heritability estimates for intelligence may be different for low socioeconomic groups than for high socioeconomic groups. This suggests that proportions of variance related to genetic and environmental factors may be different depending on the population. Similarly for the dimension of task-oriented behavior, heredity and neurological impairment as well as environmental variables appear to be important antecedent variables. Perhaps the clearest evidence of family influence upon socialization is shown for hostile, delinquent behavior and the least evidence for a dimension of introversion-extraversion. However, the importance of the family in the socialization process justifies an examination of the factors that may influence the family's ability to socialize the child despite the evidence that neurological impairment and/or genetic differences may be related to individual differences in intelligence, task-oriented behavior, and introversion-extroversion.

IDENTIFICATION OF VARIABLES THAT INFLUENCE FAMILY FUNCTIONING

Social Stresses and Social Supports

An analysis of the stresses and supports that influence family functioning may contribute to prevention of problems in socialization. Leadership in such an analysis has come from clinical investigators, perhaps because of their responsibility for coping with the problems of child and family. For example, Helfer and Kempe (1968) initially analyzed factors that contributed to battering and then reported methods for helping the battered child and his family (Kempe and Helfer, 1972). Although an exhaustive analysis of the social stresses and supports that influence family functioning would be desirable, only a few studies will be reviewed that illustrate the importance of these factors.

Gordon and Gordon's (1959) review of the social factors that predict emotional disturbance of the mother during the first 4 months after delivery found many predisposing factors in the family of origin, including family history of emotional disorders, divorce or separation, and homes broken by death of a parent. Characteristics of the woman that have been found predictive include greater tendency to serious physical illness, previous personal emotional disorders, more physical complications of pregnancy, unplanned pregnancies, and 33 years or older at the time of emotional upset. Lack of social supports contributing to emotional disturbance included husband's frequent unavailability and less other help in the first weeks after return home from the hospital. Gordon and Gordon's study (1959) supported a conclusion that:

> A definite trend appears for parents with few environmental strains to respond without undue emotional upset, while those with many environmental difficulties tend to react with considerable emotional upset.

The potential effectiveness of family variables in predicting serious illness and, presumably, maternal care is shown by a study of low birth weight infants by Glass, Kolko, and Evans (1971). Initially an index was developed to predict rehospitalization or death of premature infants. This index included failure to attend to prenatal care, absence of father, receipt of public assistance, and one or more siblings at home. These variables were related to utilization of the follow-up clinic and also predicted rehospitalization or death of the child. Utilization of the prognostic index on a second sample yielded a rehospitalization rate of 11.4% for women with low scores, but 41.7% for women with high scores. This was essentially the same differentiation that was found for the initial sample. The predictive index is being used by the authors "to identify low birth weight infants at highest risk of serious illness and rehospitalization . . ." in order to provide more thorough medical supervision for those infants.

Elmer's (1967) study of abusive and nonabusive mothers found that marital difficulties, household disorganization, and lack of associations outside the home differentiated the two groups significantly. Elmer also reported a set of childbearing and family structure variables significantly more characteristic of mothers of abused children. These include: three or more children at the time of admission of the abused child, mother less than 21 years of age, the abused child conceived out of wedlock, less than 1 year intervening between the births of the children in the family, the mother pregnant at the time of admission, and the birth of a sibling less than 1 year before the time of admission. Perhaps the stresses of childbearing and childrearing reduce both the amount and quality of maternal care. This hypothesis is supported by Douglas' (1964) study, which found a number of indices of family care and education of the child negatively related to family size, even after controlling for social class.

Giovannoni and Billingsley (1970) have confirmed some of the characteristics of less adequate families in a study of low income white, black, and Spanish-speaking mothers. The subjects were adequate and potentially neglectful mothers nominated by public health nurses and neglectful mothers known to Protective Services. Among the findings were that adequate mothers had fewer children than the potentially neglectful or neglectful in all social groups. Neglectful families more frequently had only one parent, while the adequate families more frequently had two parents. A higher incidence of extreme poverty was found in the neglectful group as well as fewer material resources such as adequate housing, telephones, and automobiles. For the black and white women, daily contact with relatives was more characteristic of the adequate mothers, and the adequate mothers were more often engaged in church activities. Giovannoni and Billingsley (1970, p. 332) conclude:

> In sum, the low-income neglectful parent is under greater environmental and situational stress and has fewer resources and supports in coping with these stresses than does the adequate mother. It is the current situational strains that predominate among neglectful parents, not those of their past life.

Schaefer (1959) reported correlations between marital conflict, financial distress, and poor physical health of mothers and ratings of maternal hostility and rejection within a more representative community sample. Studies done by Bayley and Schaefer (1960) and Milner (1951) also report correlations between socioeconomic status and maternal behavior, and Hess (1970) has reviewed the correlations of socioeconomic status and ethnic group with child care. Perhaps many of the differences in parental care between social groups are related to differences in social stresses and social supports, which tend to be correlated with socioeconomic status and minority group status. However, just as family process variables seem to be better predictors of child development than socioeconomic status, family stress and support variables may be better predictors of parental care than ratings of socioeconomic status.

Evidence has been cited that the number of children in the family may be a stress that reduces the adequacy of parental care (Douglas, 1964) or increases the probability of neglect and abuse (Elmer, 1967; Giovannoni and Billingsley, 1970). From clinical studies it also seems probable that characteristics of the children, by the stresses they place on family resources, may also influence the adequacy of family care (Glass et al., 1970; Elmer, 1967; Klaus and Kennell, 1970). In an interview study of mothers of mentally retarded children, Schonell and Watts (1956) found that the child's condition affected family plans, caused difficulties in obtaining schooling or training for the child, curtailed family social activities, and seemed related to emotional disturbances in family members. Stresses upon the family caused by the presence of the mentally retarded child have also been recognized by Kershner (1970) and by Stone (1967).

Professional Support for Family Functioning

In the presence of many stresses and few social supports, to what extent can parents obtain consultation, support, and assistance from the professions and institutions that relate to children and families? Schonell and Watts (1956) found that 32 of 50 mothers of mentally retarded children reported they had received no outside help in the care of their child, although 37 reported they had the support and encouragement of the rest of their family. Thirty-three reported they would like more information on the cause, treatment, future prospects, and other aspects of the child's condition. In contrast, Fowle (1968) studied families whose children were enrolled in centers for the mentally retarded and from her study of marital integration speculated "that the availability and utilization of community centers for the retarded may be contributing to a substantial extent to the harmony and integration of the marriages of the parents of the children served." Stone (1967) also found that: "Active participation in parents' organizations was associated with both accurate knowledge about mongolism and willingness to care for the retarded child in the home." Studies of random samples, rather than self-selected samples, of parents receiving services are needed to demonstrate the effectiveness of these supports.

Not only parents of retarded children but also unselected samples of middle class parents may receive little help from professionals. Chamberlin (1974) interviewed 190 mothers of 4-year-olds who were receiving pediatric care for their children. Of the mothers who identified a conflict with the child and/or a concern about the child, approximately 81 to 84% had not talked to a professional about the problem, and a maximum of 15% had talked with the pediatrician. Fifty-one percent of the mothers who identified their children as having a definite behavioral or emotional problem had not talked to a professional about the problem. Thirty-three percent had talked with the pediatrician, and the remainder had talked with either a teacher, a social worker, or psychiatrist. Of the mothers who had talked with the pediatrician, 60% saw the interactions as very helpful, and only 20% found the interactions of little or no value. These results suggest that middle class parents are receiving little assistance from professionals, but that the assistance received is often helpful.

In investigating professional support for parents, Stine (1962) found very little discussion of child behavior and development in 673 well child visits with 42 physicians. Similarly, Starfield and Barkowf (1969) reported that mother's questions about child behavior in well baby visits were often unacknowledged and unanswered. Further analyses of the barriers that reduce the support for family care would help in understanding findings such as these.

Thus far the discussion of factors that influence family functioning has suggested that many different stresses, including the stresses of frequent, closely spaced children and those associated with rearing a handicapped child, may predict problems in childrearing. Similarly, the lack of social supports, from one's spouse and extended family and community, apparently contributes to inadequate child care. Some evidence that middle class parents receive little assistance from the professions and abundant evidence that lower class parents receive even less indicate that current professions and institutions offer little support for family functioning. Examination of parent-centered early intervention programs designed to provide training and support for parental care suggests that a change in policies and practices by health, education, and child care professions could significantly influence family care and education and could have more positive effects upon child development.

Intervention Research on Professional Support for Family Functioning

Evidence from intervention research indicates that positive maternal attachment to the infant may develop and stabilize in the first days or weeks of life. In animal studies, it has been found that separation of a mother goat from her kid during the first day of life often results in inadequate maternal care (Hersher, Moore and Richmond, 1958). Converging evidence also suggests that separation of mother and infants in intensive care may be related to failure-to-thrive and child abuse (Fananoff, Kennell, and Klaus, 1972). The possibility that current amounts of mother-infant contact at the time of birth, even for normal infants, may be reducing the amount of positive maternal attachment to the child motivated a study by Klaus et al., (1972). In this study the amount of mother-infant contact was increased to 1 hour during the first 3 hours after birth and to at least 5 hours each day during the first 3 days while a control group received the usual low level of contact. A follow-up with an interview and observations of the physical examination and of feeding the infant at 1 month of age showed highly significant differences between groups, with the increased contact group showing much greater positive involvement than the usual hospital routine control group. The study suggests that changing hospital policies and practices might have significant effects on maternal behavior. The question might be asked whether separation of the father from the mother and infant during this period might also significantly influence mother-father-child interaction. In addition, the study raises the important question of whether the professions, in supplementing parental care through direct care of the child, might not also be implicitly supplanting family care of the child. On the other hand, the health professions' potential for contributing to family functioning is suggested by the positive results of a program conducted by a pediatrician and public health nurse that was designed to strengthen and support family care and education of the child (Gutelius et al., 1972).

The positive effects of parent-centered early education programs have been reviewed by Lazar and Chapman (1972), who conclude:

> Consideration of the results of all four of the studies in which the effects of schooling for the child, home visits, and parent meetings were compared, either singly or in combination, reveals the following: in each of the four studies parent involvement, with or without a preschool component, resulted in more beneficial effects on children's language or intellectual development or academic achievement and on parents' IQ, feelings, attitudes, or life style than the school component only.

Lazar and Chapman (1972) report that the parent-centered approach appears to be more effective even during first grade:

> In the project sponsored by Mobilization for Youth, the first grade children whose parents were trained one hour per week to read to their children scored higher on nine different reading tests than did matched children who received special schooling—two hours of remediation per week from professionals—or a control group receiving no intervention.

Other studies show that parent-centered early education programs (Levenstein, 1970; Karnes et al., 1970; Gray, 1971) have greater long term effects upon the target child, influence the development of younger children in the family, and are less expensive than child-centered early intervention programs (Schaefer, 1972; Schaefer and Aaronson, 1972).

The success of the programs that strengthen rather than supplement family care and education suggests the need to examine the current policies and practices of the professions and institutions that relate to families and children. Apart from the activities of parent-centered early intervention programs, both health and education professionals working in hospitals, clinics, and schools appear to devote most of their attention to direct involvement with the child. Much less attention to professional-parent interaction and to the roles of professionals in supporting and strengthening parent involvement with the child is given in traditional training programs, policies, and practices than to the direct care and education of the child. The model for parent-professional interaction and involvement seen in Figure 4 suggests that characteristics of parents, teachers, and health professionals influence both their direct involvement with the child and their interaction with one another. Vectors between involvement and interaction indicate that the parent may influence the professional's involvement, and the professional may influence the parent's involvement with the child. The needs of parents for training and support, the deficiencies in current professional support for parents, and the promising results of intervention programs providing training and support for parents point to the need for more research on parent-professional interaction and for the application of that research to renewal of our professions and institutions.

SUMMARY AND CONCLUSIONS

This analysis of factors impeding the process of socialization has attempted to integrate clinical psychiatric and personality research identifying major dimensions of child adjustment and competence. Four major dimensions of child behavior were identified. These dimensions have been repeatedly isolated from multivariate statistical studies and have been demonstrated to be major components of the child's social adaptation: intelligence versus retardation, task orientation versus distractibility, love versus hostility, and extraversion versus introversion. Complementing the traditional mental test measures with data on the other three dimensions of adaptation may significantly increase understanding of the social adaptation of the mentally retarded as well as other populations.

After a discussion of characteristics of family care that result in the major impact of the family on the child's socialization, a model for early parent-child interaction was developed which emphasized the contribution of that interaction to socialization and to mediated learning of the child. A review of psychological research on parent behavior suggested convergence on major parent behavior dimensions of acceptance, control, and involvement. Those dimensions were related to the maternal deprivation concepts of insufficiency and distortions of maternal care and to the social welfare concepts of neglect and abuse. Recent research suggests that the entire network of relationships among mother, father, child, and sibling may predict the child's socialization. The development of family therapy would support the potential fruitfulness of a focus upon the network of family relationships.

A brief discussion of processes and mechanisms of socialization including developmental identification, modeling, reinforcement, mediated learning, identification with the aggressor, frustration-aggression, and primary affect hunger preceded an interpretation of the probable effects of a major dimension of parental warmth, love and acceptance,

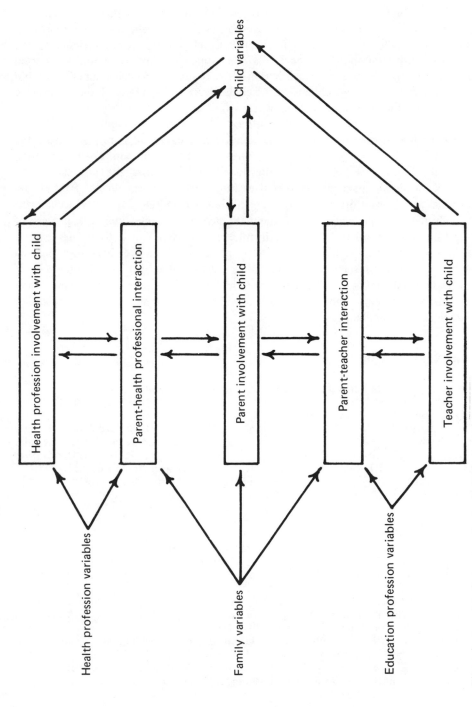

Figure 4. A model of parent-professional-child interaction.

versus hostility and rejection. Research was reviewed that suggests that family environment has a major impact on the child's hostile, aggressive, delinquent behavior; contributes substantially to the child's intellectual development; may contribute to the
child's task-orientation; but may have less effect upon extraverted versus introverted
behaviors. Although the varying contributions of heredity, neurological impairment and
family environment to major dimensions of child adaptation were noted, the importance
of the family for the child's socialization was emphasized.

The social stresses and supports that influence family functioning were then briefly
reviewed. In the absence of support from nuclear and extended family and from the
community, the family may turn to the professions for support and assistance. Often
families receive minimal help from professionals and at times the professions and
institutions may even be counterproductive. In an effort to supplement family care,
professional policies and practices may supplant family care, reduce parental attachment
and involvement in the child's care, and have negative effects upon the process of
socialization. On the other hand, experimental programs designed to strengthen and
support family care of the child appear to be more cost effective than child-centered
programs. Finally, the results of those programs suggest the need to examine the roles of
the professions and institutions dealing with children and with families, to study their
interaction with parents, and the extent to which they supplement and supplant or
strengthen and support family care of the child.

REFERENCES

Aaronson, M. and E. S. Schaefer. 1970. Sibling Behavior Inventory. Unpublished.
Achenbach, T. M. 1966. The classification of children's psychiatric symptoms: A factor
    analytic study. Psych. Monogr. 80, No. 6.
Ackerson, F. 1942. Children's Behavior Problems. University of Chicago Press, Chicago.
Ainsworth, M. D. 1962. The effects of maternal deprivation. A review of findings and
    controversy in the context of research strategy. In Public Health Papers 14, Deprivation
    of Maternal Care: A Reassessment of Its Effects. World Health Organization, Geneva.
Andry, R. G. 1960. Delinquency and parental pathology. Methusen, London.
Anthony, E. J. 1970. The behavior disorders of childhood. In P. H. Mussen (ed.),
    Carmichael's Manual of Child Psychology, Vol. 2, pp. 667–764. John Wiley & Sons,
    Inc., New York.
Bandura, A. 1962. Social learning through imitation. In M. R. Jones (ed.), Nebraska
    Symposium on Motivation, pp. 211–269. University of Nebraska Press, Lincoln.
Bandura, A. 1969. Social-learning theory of identificatory processes. In D. A. Goslin
    (ed.), Handbook of Socialization Theory and Research, pp. 213–262. Rand McNally,
    Chicago.
Bandura, A. 1970. The role of modeling processes in personality development. In W. W.
    Hartup (ed.), The Young Child. Reviews of Research, pp. 42–58. National Association
    for the Education of Young Children, Washington, D.C.
Baumrind, D. and A. E. Black. 1967. Socialization patterns associated with dimensions of
    competence in preschool boys and girls. Child Develop. 38: 291–327.
Bayley, N. and E. S. Schaefer. 1960. Relationships between socioeconomic variables and
    the behavior of mothers toward young children. J. Genetic Psychol. 95: 83–104.

Becker, W. C. 1964. Consequences of different kinds of parental discipline. *In* M. L. Hoffman and L. W. Hoffman (eds.), Review of Child Development Research, pp. 169–208. Russel Sage Foundation, New York.

Becker, W. C. and R. S. Krug. 1964. A circumplex model for social behavior in children. Child Develop. 35: 371–396.

Bell, R. Q. 1968. A reinterpretation of the direction of effects in studies of socialization. Psychol. Rev. 85: 81–95.

Bell, R. Q. 1971. Stimulus control of parent or caretaker behavior by offspring. Devel. Psychol. 75: 81–85.

Beller, E. K. 1959. Exploratory studies of dependency. Trans. N.Y. Acad. Sci. Ser II 21: 414–426.

Biller, H. B. 1970. Father-absence and the personality development of the male child. Devel. Psychol. 2: 181–201.

Bloom, B. S. 1964. Stability and Change in Human Characteristics. Wiley, New York.

Bowerman, C. E. and R. M. Dobash. 1974. Structural variations in inter-sibling affect. J. Marr. Family 36: 408–456.

Bowlby, J. 1951. Maternal Care and Infant Health. Monograph Series No. 2. New York, World Health Organization.

Briggs, C. and D. Elkind. 1973. Cognitive development in early readers. Devel. Psychol. 9: 279–280.

Brown, D. G. 1971. Behavior Modification in Child and School Mental Health. A Bibliography on Applications with Parents and Teachers. U.S. DHEW Pub. No. (HSM) 71-9043. Government Printing Office, Washington, D.C.

Burger, G. K. and J. A. Armetrout. 1972. A factor analysis of fifth and sixth graders' reports of parental child-rearing behavior. Devel. Psychol. 4: 483.

Burgess, E. A. 1926. The family as a unity of interacting personalities. The Family 7: 3–9.

Chamberlin, R. W. 1974. Management of preschool behavior problems. Pediatr. Clin. North Am. 21: 33–47.

Child, I. L. 1954. Socialization. *In* G. Lindzey (ed.), Handbook of Social Psychology, pp. 655–692. Addison-Wesley, Cambridge, Mass.

Clarke, A. D. B. and A. M. Clarke. 1959. Recovery from the effects of deprivation. Acta Psychol. 16: 137–144.

Collins, L. F., A. E. Maxwell, and K. Cameron. 1962. A factor analysis of some child psychiatric clinic data. J. Ment. Sci. 108: 274–285.

Cunningham, J. M., H. H. Westerman, and J. Fischhoff. 1956. A follow-up study of patients seen in a psychiatric clinic for children. Am. J. Orthopsychiatr. 26: 606–612.

Dave, R. T. 1963. The Identification and Measurement of Environmental Process Variables that are Related to Educational Achievement. Unpublished doctoral dissertation, University of Chicago, Chicago, Ill.

Digman, J. M. 1972. High school academic achievement as seen in the content of a longitudinal study of personality. *In* Proceedings, 80th Annual Convention of the American Psychological Association, pp. 19–20. APA, Washington, D.C.

Dollard, J., L. W. Doob, N. E. Miller, D. H. Mowrer, and R. R. Sears. 1939. Frustration and Aggression. Yale University Press, New Haven, Conn.

Douglas, J. W. 1964. The Home and The School: A Study of Ability and Attainment in the Primary School. MacGibbon and Kee, London.

Elmer, E. 1967. Children in Jeopardy: A Study of Abused Minors and Their Families. University of Pennsylvania Press, Pittsburgh.

Erikson, E. 1959. Identity and the life cycle. Psychol. Issues 1: 1–171.

Eysenck, H. J. 1953. The Structure of Human Personality. Methusen, London.

Faranoff, A. A., J. H. Kennell, and M. H. Klaus. 1972. Follow-up of low birth weight infants—the predictive value of maternal visiting patterns. Pediatrics 49: 287—290.

Feshbach, S. 1970. Aggression. *In* P. H. Mussen (ed.), Carmichael's Manual of Child Psychology, Vol. 2. John Wiley & Sons, Inc., New York.

Feshbach, N. and S. Feshbach. 1972. Children's aggression. *In* W. H. Hartup (ed.), The Young Child. Reviews of Research, Vol. 2, pp. 284—302. National Association for Education of Young Children, Washington, D.C.

Feuerstein, R. A. 1970. A dynamic approach to the causation, prevention, and alleviation of retarded performance. *In* H. C. Haywood (ed.), Socio-cultural Aspects of Mental Retardation, pp. 341—377. Appleton-Century-Crofts, New York.

Fish, B. 1972. The "one child, one drug" myth of stimulants in hyperkinesis: The importance of diagnostic categories in evaluating treatment. *In* S. Chess and A. Thomas (eds.), Annual Progress in Child Psychiatry and Child Development, 1972. Brunner/Mazel, New York.

Fowle, C. 1968. Effect of the severely retarded child on his family. Am. J. Ment. Defic. 73: 468—473.

Fromm, E. 1947. Man For Himself. Rinehart, New York.

Giovannoni, J. M. and A. Billingsley. 1970. Child neglect among the poor: A study of parental adequacy in three ethnic groups. Child Welfare 49: 196—204.

Glass, L., N. Kolko, and H. Evans. 1971. Factors influencing disposition to serious illness in low birth weight infants. Pediatrics 48: 368—371.

Glueck, S. and E. T. Glueck. 1950. Unraveling Juvenile Delinquency. Harvard University Press, Cambridge, Mass.

Goldfarb, W. 1945. Psychological privation in infancy and subsequent adjustment. Am. J. Orthopsychiatr. 15: 247.

Gordon, R. S. and K. Gordon. 1959. Social factors in the prediction and treatment of emotional disorders of pregnancy. Am. J. Obstet. Gynecol. 77: 1074—1083.

Gray, S. W. 1971. Home visiting programs for parents of young children. Peabody J. Educ. 48: 106—111.

Gutelius, M. F., A. D. Kirsch, S. MacDonald, M. R. Brooks, T. McErlean, and C. Newcomb. 1972. Promising results from a cognitive stimulation program in infancy. A preliminary report. Clin. Pediatr. 11: 585—593.

Guttman, L. 1954. A new approach to factor analysis: The radex. *In* P. F. Lazarsfeld (ed.), Mathematical Thinking in the Social Sciences. The Free Press, Glencoe, Ill.

Hagman, E. R. 1932. A study of fears of children of preschool age. J. Exp. Educ. 1: 110—130.

Handel, G. 1965. Psychological study of whole families. Psychol. Bull. 63: 19—41.

Helfer, R. E. and C. H. Kempe. 1968. (eds.) The Battered Child. University of Chicago Press, Chicago, Ill.

Hersher, L., A. U. Moore, and J. B. Richmond. 1958. Effect of postpartum separation of mother and kid on maternal care in the domestic goat. Science 128: 1343—1348.

Hess, R. D. 1969. Parental behavior and children's school achievement: Implications for Head Start. *In* E. Grotberg (ed.), Critical Issues in Research Related to Disadvantaged Children. Educational Testing Service, Princeton.

Hess, R. D. 1970. Social class and ethnic influences on socialization. *In* P. H. Mussen (ed.), Carmichael's Manual of Child Psychology. 3rd Ed., Vol. 2, pp. 457—557. John Wiley & Sons, Inc., New York.

Hewitt, L. E. and R. L. Jenkins. 1946. Fundamental Patterns of Maladjustment: The Dynamics of Their Origin. State of Illinois, Chicago.

Honzig, M. P. 1972. Intellectual abilities at age 40 years in relation to the early family environment. *In* F. D. Monks, W. W. Hartup and J. de Witt (eds.), Determinants of Behavioral Development, pp. 653—656. Academic Press, New York.

Horney, L. 1945. Our Inner Conflicts. W. W. Norton & Co., New York.

Jenkins, R. L., E. Nur Eddin, and I. Shapiro. 1966. Children's behavior syndromes and parental responses. Genet. Psychol. Monogr. 74: 261–329.

Johnson, C. A. and R. C. Katz. 1973. Using parents as change agents for their children: A review. J. Child Psychol. Psychiatr. 14: 181–200.

Kagan, J. 1965. Reflection–impulsivity and reading ability in primary grade children. Child Devel. 36: 609–628.

Karnes, M. B., J. A. Teska, A. S. Hodgins, and E. D. Badger. 1970. Educational intervention at home by mothers of disadvantaged infants. Child Devel. 41: 925–935.

Kassenbuam, G. G., A. J. Couch, and P. E. Slater. 1959. The factorial dimensions of the MMPI. J. Consult. Psychol. 23: 226–236.

Kempe, C. H. and R. E. Helfer. 1972. (eds.) Helping the Battered Child and His Family. J. B. Lippincott Co., Philadelphia.

Keogh, B. 1971. Hyperactivity and learning disorders: Review and speculation. Except. Child. 38: 101–110.

Kershner, J. R. 1970. Intellectual and social development in relation to family functioning: A longitudinal comparison of home vs. institutional effects. Am. J. Ment. Defic. 75: 276–283.

Kimmel, D. and F. van der Veen. 1974. Factors of marital adjustment in Locke's Marital Adjustment Test. J. Marr. Family 36: 57–63.

Klaus, M. H. and J. H. Kennell. 1970. Mothers separated from their newborn infants. Pediat. Clin. N. Am. 17: 1015–1037.

Klaus, M. H., R. Jerauld, N. C. Kreger, W. McAlphine, M. Steffa, and J. H. Kennell. 1972. Maternal attachment: Importance of the first postpartum days. New Engl. J. Med. 286: 460–463.

Kohn, M. and B. L. Rosman. 1972. A social competence scale and symptom checklist for the preschool child: Factor dimensions, their cross-instrument generality and longitudinal persistence. Devel. Psychol. 6: 430–444.

Kojima, J. 1967. Children's reports of parental behavior and attitudes: Semantic differential questionnaire and personality factors. Bulletin of the Faculty of Education, Kanazawa University of Japan. Humanities and Social Educational Sciences. 16: 47–61.

Lazar, J. B. and I. Chapman. 1972. A review of the present status and future needs of programs to develop parenting skills. Prepared for the Interagency Panel on Early Childhood Research and Development. Social Research Group. (April). The George Washington University, Washington, D.C.

Levenstein, P. 1970. Cognitive growth in preschoolers through verbal interaction with mothers. Am. J. Orthopsychiatr. 40: 426–432.

Levy, D. M. 1937. Primary affect hunger. Am. J. Psychiatr. 2: 212–227.

Levy, D. M. 1943. Maternal Overprotection. Columbia University Press, New York.

Lewis, H. 1954. Deprived Children. Oxford University Press, London.

Lorr, M. and R. L. Jenkins. 1953. Three factors in parent behavior. J. Consult. Psychol. 17: 306–308.

Masterson, J. F., Jr. 1958. Prognosis in adolescent disorders. Am. J. Psychiatr. 114: 1097–1103.

Miller, L. C. 1972. School behavior checklist: An inventory of deviant behavior for elementary school children. J. Consult. Clin. Psychol. 38: 134–144.

Milner, E. A. 1951. A study of the relationship between reading readiness in grade one school children and patterns of parent-child interaction. Child Devel. 22: 95–112.

Moore, T. 1968. Language and intelligence: A longitudinal study of the first eight years. Part II: Environmental correlates of mental growth. Human Devel. 11: 1–24.

Moss, H. A. and J. Kagan. 1961. Stability of achievement and recognition seeking behaviors from early childhood through adulthood. J. Abnorm. Soc. Psychol. 63: 629–635.

Mowrer, O. H. 1950. Learning Theory and Personality Dynamics. Ronald Press Co., New York.

Mussen, P. 1967. Early socialization: Learning and identification. New Directions in Psychology III. Holt, Rinehart and Winston, New York.

Mussen, P. H. 1970. Carmichael's Manual of Child Psychology. 3rd Ed., Vol. 2. John Wiley & Sons, Inc., New York.

Mussen, P. H. and L. Distler. 1960. Child rearing antecedents of masculine identification in kindergarten boys. Child. Devel. 31: 89–100.

Mussen, P. H. and E. Rutherford. 1963. Parent-child relations and parental personality in relation to young children's sex-role preferences. Child Devel. 34: 589–607.

Peterson, D. R. 1960. The age generality of personality factors derived from ratings. Educ. Psychol. Meas. 20: 461–474.

Peterson, D. R. 1961. Behavior problems of middle childhood. J. Consult. Psychol. 25: 205–209.

Pringle, M. L. and K. V. Bossieo. 1958. Intellectual, emotional and social development of deprived children. Vita Humana 1: 66–92.

Quay, H. C. 1972. Patterns of aggression, withdrawal and immaturity. In H. C. Quay and J. S. Werry (eds.), Psychopathological Disorders of Childhood, pp. 1–29. John Wiley & Sons, Inc., New York.

Radin, V. 1972. Father-child interaction and the intellectual development of four-year-old boys. Devel. Psychol. 6: 363–371.

Radin, V. 1973. Observed paternal behavior as antecedents of intellectual functioning in young boys. Devel. Psychol. 8: 369–376.

Renson, G. J., E. S. Schaefer, and B. I. Levy. 1968. Cross-national validity of a spherical conceptual model for parent behavior. Child Devel. 39: 1229–1235.

Robins, L. N. 1966. Deviant Children Grown Up. Williams & Wilkins, Baltimore.

Robins, L. N. 1972. Follow-up studies of behavior disorders in children. In H. C. Quay and J. S. Werry (eds.), Psychopathological Disorders of Childhood. John Wiley & Sons, Inc., New York.

Robins, L. N. and R. C. Lewis. 1966. The role of the antisocial family in school completion and delinquency: A three-generation study. Sociol. Quart. 7: 500–514.

Roe, A. 1957. Early determinants of vocational choice. J. Counsel. Psychol. 4: 212–217.

Roe, A. and M. Siegelman. 1963. A parent-child relations questionnaire. Child Devel. 34: 355–369.

Roff, M. 1971. Childhood antecedents in the mental health development of three groups of adult males: Neurotics, severe bad conduct and controls. Project Report. National Institute of Mental Health, Bethesda, Md.

Rosenhan, D. L. 1972, Prosocial behavior of children. In W. W. Hartup (ed.), The Young Child. Reviews of Research, Vol. 2, pp. 340–360. National Association for the Education of Young Children, Washington, D.C.

Rosenzweig, S. 1945. An outline of frustration theory. In J. McV. Hunt (ed.), Personality and the Behavior Disorders, Vol. 1. Ronald Press, New York.

Rupp, J. C. C. 1969. Helping the Child to Cope with the School: A Study of the Importance of Parent-Child Relationships with Regard to Elementary School Success. Walters-Noordhoof, Gronigen.

Rutter, M. 1967. A child's behavior questionnaire for completion by teachers. Preliminary findings. J. Child Psychol. Psychiatr. 8: 1–11.

Rutter, M. 1971. Parent-child separation: Psychological effects on the children. J. Child Psychol. Psychiatr. 12: 233–260.

Scarr-Salapatek, S. 1971. Race, social class, and I.Q. Science 174: 1285–1295.

Schaefer, E. S. 1959. A circumplex model for maternal behavior. J. Abn. Soc. Psychol. 59: 222–234.

Schaefer, E. S. 1961. Converging conceptual models for maternal behavior and for child behavior. In J. C. Glidewell (ed.), Parental Attitudes and Child Behavior, pp. 124–146. Charles C Thomas, Springfield, Ill.

Schaefer, E. S. 1965a. Children's reports of parental behavior. An inventory. Child Devel. 36: 413–424 (a).

Schaefer, E. S. 1965b. A configurational analysis of children's reports of parental behavior. J. Consult. Psychol. 29: 552–557 (b).

Schaefer, E. S. 1970. Need for early and continuing education. In V. M. Dennenberg (ed.), Education of the Infant and Young Child. Academic Press, New York.

Schaefer, E. S. 1971. Development of hierarchial configurational models for parent behavior and child behavior. In J. E. Hill (ed.), Minnesota Symposia on Child Psychology, Vol. 5, pp. 1301–1316. University of Minnesota Press, Minneapolis.

Schaefer, E. S. 1972. Parents as educators: Evidence from cross-sectional, longitudinal research. Young Children 27: 227–239.

Schaefer, E. S. and M. Aaronson. 1972. Infant education research project: Implementation and implications of a home tutoring program. In R. K. Parker (ed.), The Preschool in Action: Exploring Early Childhood Programs, pp. 410–434. Allyn and Bacon, Boston, Mass.

Schaefer, E. S. and N. Bayley. 1960. Consistency of maternal behavior from infancy to preadolescence. J. Abn. Soc. Psychol. 61: 106.

Schaefer, E. S. and N. Bayley. 1963. Maternal behavior, child behavior and their intercorrelations from infancy through adolescence. Monogr. Soc. Res. Child Devel. 28: (3) (87).

Schaefer, E. S. and N. Bayley. 1967. Validity and consistency of mother-infant observations, adolescent maternal interviews, and adult retrospective reports of maternal behavior. In Proceedings, 75th Annual Convention of the American Psychological Association, 2: 147–148. APA, Washington, D.C.

Schaefer, E. S. and N. Finkelstein. 1973. Child behavior toward the parent inventory. Unpublished.

Schaefer, E. S. and J. Phillips. 1970. Communication in marriage inventory. Unpublished.

Schaefer, E. S. and R. Plutchik. 1966. Interrelationships of emotions, traits, and diagnostic constructs. Psychol. Reports 18: 399–410.

Schuldermann, E. and S. Schuldermann. 1970. Replicability of factors in children's report of parent behavior (CR-PBI). J. Psychol. 76: 239–249.

Schonell, F. I. and Rorke, M. 1960. A second survey of the effects of a subnormal child on the family unit. Am. J. Ment. Defic. 64: 862–868.

Schonell, F. I. and B. H. Watts. 1956. A first survey of the effects of a subnormal child on the family unit. Am. J. Ment. Defic. 61: 210–219.

Siegelman, M. 1965. Evaluation of Bronfenbrenner's questionnaire for children concerning parent behavior. Child Devel. 36: 163–174.

Smith, G. M. 1967. Usefulness of peer ratings of personality in educational research. Educ. Psychol. Meas. 27: 967–984.

Starfield, B. and S. Barkowf. 1969. Physician's recognition of complaints made by parents about their children's health. Pediatrics 43: 168–172.

Stine, O. 1962. Content and method of health supervision by physicians in child health conferences in Baltimore. Am. J. Public Health 52: 1858–1865.

Stone, N. D. 1967. Family factors in willingness to place the mongoloid child. Am. J. Ment. Defic. 72: 16–20.

Sutton-Smith, B. and B. G. Rosenberg. 1970. The Sibling. Holt, Rinehart, and Winston, Inc., New York.

Symonds, P. M. 1939. The Psychology of Parent-Child Relationships. Appleton-Century-Crofts, New York.

Tuddenham, R. D. 1959. The constancy of personality ratings over two decades. Genetic Psychol. Monog. 60: 3–29.

Vandenberg, S. G. 1967. Heredity factors in normal personality traits (as measured by inventories). Rec. Adv. Biol. Psychiatr. 9: 65–103.

Warren, W. 1965. A study of adolescent psychiatric in-patients and the outcome six or more years later. II. The follow-up study. J. Child Psychol. Psychiatr. 6: 141–160.

Wender, P. H. 1971. Minimal Brain Dysfunction in Children. Wiley–Interscience, New York.

Weiss, G., K. Minde, J. Werry, V. Douglas, and E. Nemeth. 1972. Studies on the hyperactive child: Five-year follow-up. In S. Chess and A. Thomas (eds.), Annual Progress in Child Psychiatry and Child Development, 1972. Brunner/Mazel, New York.

Werner, E. E., J. M. Bierman, and F. F. French. 1971. The Children of Kauai: A Longitudinal Study from the Prenatal Period to Age Ten. University of Hawaii Press, Honolulu.

Willerman, L. 1973. Activity level and hyperactivity in twins. Child Devel. 44: 288–293.

Wolfe, R. M. 1964. The identification and measurement of environmental process variables related to intelligence. Unpublished doctoral dissertation. University of Chicago, Chicago, Ill.

Zigler, E. and I. L. Child. 1969. Socialization. In G. Lindzey and E. Aronson (eds.), The Handbook of Social Psychology, 2nd Ed., Vol. 3, pp. 450–589. Addison-Wesley, Cambridge, Mass.

Zigler, E. and L. Phillips. 1960. Social effectiveness of symptomatic behaviors. J. Abn. Soc. Psychol. 61: 231–238.

Oral and Non-Oral Representations of Communicative and Social Competence

Aaron V. Cicourel

THE PROBLEM

Mentally retarded children present scientists with a broad range of problems because the spectrum of biological, medical, psychological, and socio-cultural issues that must be addressed challenges the foundations of these disciplines. Children with identifiable organic damage (Lesch-Nyhan, de Lange, Prader-Willi, Down's, and other chromosomal anomalies) exhibit behavioral displays that may be specific for each syndrome. These behavioral displays, however, often lead to different psychological and socio-cultural interpretations. Moderately retarded and mildly retarded children, those children that constitute the largest population of the mentally retarded, pose more subtle psychological and socio-cultural problems because their study is complicated by a lack of clear criteria for understanding the relationships between normal language acquisition, the measurement of intelligence, and socio-cultural definitions of acceptable social behavior.

In this paper I will confine myself to a few issues in the study of oral and non-oral representations of communicative and social competence as they can relate to the kind of base lines that researchers presuppose or assume exist with normal children and adults. The central point of my discussion will be to argue that our understanding of the mentally retarded is guided by a narrow view of oral communication and non-oral representations of information processing. Hence we must use our studies of the mentally retarded to challenge existing views of normal communicative and social competence based on abstract auditory-oral representational systems.

The complexity of normal human language acquisition and social competence is often a barrier to our understanding of the social world of the mentally retarded because the

229

basis for evaluating the latter group is usually dependent on many unstated conditions making up some ambiguous notion of normal social competence. We lack a clear model of what we mean by normal children and adults. The problem is exacerbated when we realize that the idea of mental retardation is itself ambiguous, because it does not subsume a clear class of behavioral events but is rather a broad range of phenotypes that are often evaluated by conceptions derived from severely retarded cases.

In our dealings with the mentally retarded we immediately assume and incorporate implicit ideas about normal ways of handling daily social interaction and bureaucratic practices. The assumed normal forms of social organization and practices make it difficult to conceptualize the everyday experiences of the mentally retarded because we do not know how their different social worlds are being filtered or attenuated by distinctive cognitive and linguistic systems.

We can begin to approximate a more realistic model of mental retardation by studies of the deaf or the blind. These groups provide examples of different socialization experiences *vis-à-vis* implicit notions of normal communicative competence. I shall initially mean by normal communicative competence the ability to employ a native system of signals that can represent appropriate past, present, and future temporal conditions of personal and group life that can be normatively identified and represented in ideal-typical terms.

What I am proposing, therefore, is that we can approximate a model of communicative competence for the mentally retarded by examining what happens when a key modality like hearing or vision is absent from otherwise normal children. This is a delaying tactic but one calculated to avoid the reification that occurs when normal adult researchers study mentally retarded children and adults with an implicit model of normal communicative and social competence.

Another strategy (not pursued here) would examine research on subhuman primates subjected to different experimental conditions of social isolation and brain damage. The research would follow several sub-strategies. One would catalogue how primates have been taught "language" by some form of manual sign system in order to discern the exemplars of communicative competence the researcher attributes to these subjects based on performance criteria. Another sub-strategy requires devising experiments that can specify the organization of memory that primates can exhibit, where the tasks are carried out under conditions of non-verbal communication that could be similar to those that would prevail with severely retarded children.

In this paper, however, I will focus on the communicative competence of children born deaf and discuss the consequences of such impairment for the study of the mentally retarded. The study of the communicative competence of the deaf provides a springboard for examining basic issues like the relationship between internal imagery and normative systems we call "language," and how we are to conceive of the relationship between cultural experiences that are not auditory-oral and their representation in signaling systems that are normatively sanctioned. The thesis of this paper can be stated in more general terms as follows: communicative competence need not have started or be linked to a vocal or acoustical signaling system, but must be compatible with the complexity and form of life that could generate cognitive abilities associated with observable and experimentally defined information processing tasks. Contrasting models of information processing systems would provide criteria for attributing cognitive abilities associated with specifiable levels of communicative and social competence.

THE TESTING FRAMEWORK

The child's acquisition of language and his development of cognitive processes is central to acquiring interpretive abilities for gradually comprehending and producing adult forms of behavior. These developmental activities enable the child to create a cultural and normative sense in on-going settings and to make judgments about the significance of information, thus helping the child to decide what is "normal," "bizarre," "threatening," "humorous," etc.

The child's ability to deal with everyday social organization as a system of norms or rules presupposes a language system, and language in turn presupposes cognitive processes that are integral to the development of interpretive abilities that can articulate immediate experiences with rule systems that imply past and future experiences and knowledge about the world. It is difficult, however, to reveal how language acquisition, the development of cognitive processes, and interpretive abilities are indexed by the psychological tests used to measure intelligence and communicative and social competence. Most tests for measuring intelligence and general knowledge were developed before recent advances in developmental psycholinguistics and cognitive psychology. But the tests have many advantages because they facilitate categorizing individuals into bureaucratically convenient groups that enable decisions to be made about education and institutionalization.

The general format of psychological testing is to provide subjects with a few instructions that are standard introductions to the task that lies ahead. The test is then presented in the form of standardized and presumably objective questions like "point to the thing that can walk in this picture," that can be answered by an open (oral remark or pointing gesture) or a closed response like "circle the thing that is most like what is in the box on the left." The assumed connection between the stimulus questions and the expected responses is based on prior work with some pretest group that enabled the researcher to claim that his test has been normalized with respect to some sample of a larger population. The normalizing process is designed to eliminate problems in the test and to ensure that "appropriate" items are included: items that subjects or respondents seem to find answerable and that, when collected, will give some kind of numerical distribution to their aggregated responses. But this testing paradigm tends to ignore the role of language acquisition and the stages at which different instructions and responses can be expected of children whose cognitive, emotional, and language development is contingent on the cultural setting of the family.

In a recent study of two classrooms in two schools (Cicourel et al., 1974), an analysis of testing situations created a contrast between the official version of the meaning of test materials and the child's interpretation of these materials. Standardized reading, intelligence, and language development tests were given to the first grade children in two schools. A small group of children were asked to explain their answers and to provide the reasons for their answers. The children's accounts were then compared to the official versions provided by the testing protocol. Many children seemed to attend to the testing material in different ways. The differential perception often led to a wrong answer and a low test score. MacKay (1974), Mehan (1971; 1974), and Roth (1974) challenged the conclusion usually drawn from incorrect responses, that the children being examined lacked particular abilities. Instead they suggest that it is necessary to examine the structure of the child's accounting practices and reasoning processes in order to draw valid inferences about his competence.

Observations of the performances of teacher, tester, and children in testing situations suggest that children do not always share the tester's idea of what the test is about. Different substantive conclusions are drawn from the same materials. Problems of selective attention, memory, dialect differences, incorrect guesses, and general misunderstandings routinely emerge in educational interaction, but are not addressed as central ingredients of learning and evaluation that take place in the classroom (Cicourel, 1974a). Errors and misunderstandings are natural aspects of educational encounters and the problem of what is right and wrong cannot be resolved by some absolute notion of a correct answer.

Mehan (1971; 1974) has shown how the teacher and child can arrive at different interpretations of a classroom lesson because of the complexity of the interactional situation. The child's conception of location was seen to have a variable quality that the simple designation of a correct or incorrect response did not capture. The features of the interaction scene contributed to judgments of "correct" and "incorrect" answers in the lesson.

Roth (1974) demonstrated that the reasoning abilities of the child who received a low score on the Peabody Picture Vocabulary Test could be seen as similar to the child who obtained a high test score. But an anlysis of the responses to the test items did not permit careful judgments about the child's reasoning ability. An analysis of the audio and visual materials revealed that all of the children could produce elaborate cross-referenced interactions, regardless of test scores. All of the children had abstract understandings of the items far in excess of those indicated by their actual test score. An understanding of the child's competence requires that we at least recognize the complexity of the interactional setting which produces test results.

Further documentation of the observations of Mehan and Roth are found in MacKay's (1974) work in which a study was made of a group-administered reading test employed by school districts throughout the state of California. MacKay demonstrated that the test fails on its own terms. The group test is even more likely to mask the child's reasoning ability than the individualized test or classroom lesson. The materials that MacKay discussed with the children revealed the contingent character of the test for the child. The test did not reflect the child's classroom learning experiences. The child's reasoning strategies for decoding the meaning and intent of the task he was asked to do were hidden from review by the teacher's and tester's procedures.

Of especial importance for comprehending the role of interactional competence in classroom and testing situations is the child's and adult's cross-modal integration of information within a socially emergent setting. The child and teacher must reflexively recognize and use multiple sources of information including body movement and non-verbal acoustical materials, as they interact with their language abilities in these socially organized settings. Our studies stress that changes in the evaluation of classroom and testing situations cannot come about unless we are willing to recognize the poverty of existing theories of education and the bureaucratic expediency of classroom and testing procedures. We need to make better use of recent work on language acquisition, cognitive processes, and interactional competence.

The developmental psycholinguist employs a model of child language acquisition that revolves around the notion of a bounded sentence defined as a string of lexical items or their presumed equivalents that conform to a subject-verb-object (SVO) construction. This SVO construction is presumed to be self-contained: rules that can operate on the notion of an auditorially perceived sentence presumably can ignore information that is visual, kinesthetic, or tactile. Blind adults, for example, seem to use oral language with the same facility as a seeing adult, but their ability to reference objects and events by their speech is not always clear because of the visual information presumed in all talk (Ima, 1972). Linguistic theory claims that the acoustical signals are mediated by a formal system of rules said to underlie the acoustical information. But the work of cognitive psychologists forces us to recognize that sound patterns are organized by immediate and underlying selective processes in their reception. These cognitive judgments occur in social contexts that are subject to alterations by reflexive thought. Hence the perception of acoustical or auditory signals is more than a simple pattern recognition problem.

The linguist views language as bounded utterances whose internal structure can be described by clearly identifiable rules. He refers to syntactic and phonological rules, and to the idea of a lexicon. In the lexicon each item or entry possesses a phonological matrix as well as inherent and contextual features that can specify the item as animate or abstract, and, for example, whether it follows a definite or indefinite article. This model provides the linguist with carefully constructed ideals that can be studied and described independently of actual language use in social settings.

The linguist's syntax-based theory of language provides the ideal structures needed to construct standardized tests. The linguist's normative theory of language describes prescriptive and proscriptive rules or practices. Such practices are like recipes for deciding what is socially acceptable and unacceptable behavior. The language of the psychological test achieves its limited objectivity by relying on idealized language structures. The linguist's idealized grammatical and phonological rules, and standardized dictionary, however, are not helpful in explaining how children understand instructions and test items, or in the study of actual language use in settings where it is not clear how the mentally retarded child employs specific utterances.

What is missing from the educational psychologist's model of intelligence is the psycholinguist's conception of the child's linguistic competence and how this competence is presumed in the assessment of intelligence. But both the educational psychologist and psycholinguist need a model of how attention and memory are integral to an interpretive ability necessary for learning and carrying out the tasks that comprise tests of intelligence and experiments in language.

COMMUNICATION AND INFORMATION PROCESSING

If we are to understand the communicative and social competence of the mentally retarded child, we cannot rely on the static conditions assumed by the psychological test, and we must modify the linguist's model. Research on information processing suggests that the human organism processes information using both a "filter model" and something like analysis-by-synthesis (Broadbent, 1958; Neisser, 1967; Norman, 1969). The filter model seeks to explain the limitations of our ability to perceive competing messages by reference to perceptual factors. The brain is seen as capable of filter operations that are oriented to accepting some message while rejecting others considered "undesirable" or perhaps not receivable.

The differential reception of some signals through the filtering operations that result in further processing is not clearly understood. Presumably information from a channel to which the organism is "tuned," despite the exposure to other channels, is processed further, remembered and used as a basis for a response. Challenges to this notion (Moray, 1959; Triesman, 1960; Gray and Wedderburn, 1960) have noted that there are psychological features associated with attention as well as physical characteristics, and that the content of a rejected message does leave an impression on the subject depending on the content of the rejected message and how it is presented to the subject. Material submitted to the 'wrong' ear produced a response from the subject. The information received by both ears will reach the same perceptual and discriminatory mechanisms involved (Deutsch and Deutsch, 1963). Sensory cues alone were found to be inadequate to explain the kind of selection going on when subjects receive information from several channels.

Modern linguistic theory does not address language competence and performance by reference to the above information processing activities. Hence whatever is called the comprehension of utterances requires extending the linguistic model to include explicit cognitive processes. Complex information processing goes on in selecting different channels and every incoming signal receives some kind of selective attention *vis-à-vis* its meaning by reference to memory storage and the sensory features of the incoming signals. Therefore, we must specify some of the complexities of attending to information while recognizing that we are capable of simultaneously generating several types of informational particulars.

Linguistic theory recognizes but does not address the fact that we make tacit use of information from visual and other sources when speaking, including thinking processes that enable us to expand utterance fragments into meaningful items because of culturally organized memory. This is not a matter of simple pattern recognition whereby the linguist could claim that sound patterns are organized by immediate and underlying rules in the act of reception. The shortcomings of any simple pattern match theory of reception can be shown by examining the effects of context on the interpretation of letters, sentences, and visual appearances, where the same physical signals are interpreted quite differently when different surrounding contexts are introduced. Kolers and Pomerantz (1971) note that adult subjects create moving visual illusions from stationary stimuli that cannot be explained by gestalt principles or feature analysis extraction. Thus the contour of the stimuli is not primary, nor is any set of features said to index the stimuli presented. The interpretation of visual stimulus conditions seems to begin with a response to movement and is followed by the creation of recognizable patterns. The visual system is said to supplement inputs to it through cognitive organization and reorganization.

The processing of information seems to occur at several levels simultaneously despite the fact that our representation of what we are thinking, feeling, or perceiving is being channeled into a verbal coding that is oral and/or written, and thus linear. This coding does not adequately represent the information we experience, but what we experience at different levels is important for what we say because our talk relies on this experience.

The psychological model is not clear about how such cognitive processes are articulated with culture meanings that are negotiated in the setting. The processing presupposes that a pair of speaker-hearers are responding in a "normal" way to informational particulars that can be seen as "familiar" or "normal" forms of everyday representations. But speaker-hearers must negotiate the discrepancy between what they may have stored in memory about substantive qualities of the everyday world and the variety of informational particulars selectively available to their senses during social exchanges.

Multiple sources of information processed by different modalities limit what we learn in simple description or from an interview. The limitations of cross-modal information processing are especially difficult when we must rely on non-verbal communication. We have no precise way of discussing non-oral communication (Cicourel, 1974b). What is at issue is the organism's ability to execute many disconnected conceptual processes simultaneously. Several points should be noted: 1) the difficulty of the tasks involved, 2) the number of events the subject can attend to and follow, 3) the respondent's ability to retain and retrieve variable amounts and types of information, 4) the subject's ability to organize and store experiences as socially meaningful chunks of information that can be retrieved by reference to the original conditions of the experiences.

The description of social competence among normal children and adults is useful for indicating the kind of adult-oriented conception that we tend to rely on as researchers of the mentally retarded. It is important to keep emphasizing that our studies of the mentally retarded depend often on unclear conceptions of what is normal. If our research on normal cognitive, linguistic, and social development is not clear, we can ill afford to describe the mentally retarded as if the contrast with normal subjects is understood.

One way of approximating an understanding of language development with the mentally retarded is to examine children with normal intelligence but whose language facility is ambiguous because they are born deaf. I am not implying that the deaf approximate the mentally retarded but that the language acquisition problems of the deaf can help us to understand the general issue of communicative and social competence since the latter notion is often dependent on verbal measures of competence.

GESTURAL SIGN LANGUAGE AND VISUAL INFORMATION

A broad spectrum of researchers interested in language origins, language acquistion and use, and semantic information processing have found common ground through studies of oral and non-oral communication (Cicourel, 1974b).

A recent paper by Hewes (1973) refers to work on teaching some form of gestural or pictorial sign language to chimpanzees to trace the possible gestural origin of language. Hewes refers to papers by Hockett (1960) and Hockett and Asher (1964) to indicate how conditions basic to the development of language like productivity, displacement, the designation of semantic qualities, and the like can be found in a gestural system. Hence language need not have started as a vocal or acoustical system. Hewes, like others before him, argues that a gestural language was probably more appropriate to the form of life of early hominids. He notes how the complexity and form of life would give rise to cognitive abilities associated with a particular form of language development. Hence during man's early use of oral language, forms like embedded nouns and passives were probably not developed. Recent studies of present-day hunting and gathering groups reveal, of course, complex oral language forms. Therefore, we cannot extrapolate too readily from present conditions to those that might have existed for early hominids. The central point is that language development is said to have evolved according to the complexity of man's cognitive and social life. Complex social institutions, therefore, presuppose important cognitive and linguistic foundations.

Hewes notes that despite the fact that we cannot 'go back' and capture the nature of early language development in hominids, we can seek evidence based on neurophysiological development, brain capacity, tool-making and use, and the like, to piece together how language developed.

A number of researchers (cf. Hewes) has suggested that vocalization was probably not the basis for propositional language, but rather primarily for emotional displays. In primate studies it has been claimed that vocalizations have been used for territorial markings or spacing to set off local troops, but there is no implication that a propositional format was involved. They appear to be situational and triggered by internal and external stimuli that do not come under the animal's explicit control.

The studies of teaching some form of gestural or arbitrary pictorial sign language to chimpanzees (Gardner and Gardner, 1969; Premack, 1971) are cited as possible evidence for the gestural origin of language, Hewes (1973) notes that in these studies the chimps do not originate signs, nor do we know if they could teach such signs to other chimps. The generative aspect of language, not in Chomsky's sense, but in a broader sense that would include interaction settings and specific cognitive structures, is what is at stake here. Present-day gestural language as used among the deaf does not require any use of the vocal-auditory channel of communication, and this system of manual signs can be communicated to deaf children or hearing children with ease in the same "natural" sense as when we talk of the hearing-seeing child who acquires oral language.

A recent paper by Stokoe (1972) answers Hewes' (1973) suggestion that gestural sign language does not contain the complexity that oral language possesses. Stokoe notes that unlike oral signs, gestural signs have more information attached to them than the vocal sign and also act as indicators of more details. Gestural sign language includes many connotations that become marked in the context of using manual signs.

The general thesis explored by Hewes is that gestural language is prior in evolution to or independent of oral language. Studies of deaf communities reveal that man has always been capable of developing a gestural system of language regardless of which system, gestural or acoustical, comes first. The study of gestural sign language sheds new light on information processing systems by stressing the role of several modalities and different levels of analysis.

A general point is that if auditory language began to displace some form of gestural system (if this thesis is to be believed), then the gestural significance of language would become less organized as a codified system of gestures used propositionally, and therefore more and more residual as an index of the informational particulars available in everyday social interaction. The representational context would become radically altered. The considerable information we can experience through several modalities as modified by our thinking, and the interaction that occurs with our memory, become compressed into sequential auditory-oral expressions whose limitations are seldom examined. Thus we find non-oral communication is always present in everyday interaction but inadequately indexed by acoustical forms. Our accounts of our experiences, therefore, must always be represented by unexamined limiting factors associated with speech. The context of interaction becomes crucial for understanding the role of non-oral communication. This is not simply a question of how context-free expressions presuppose ethnographic details, as articulated in particular settings, but how the idea of social structure requires a model that is not limited by the oral accounts of members, despite our reliance on such accounts to claim findings. The general problem is how to represent a broader conception of everyday life by recognizing and formalizing non-oral activities in interaction, while also examining the limitations of oral accounts for understanding everyday communication. Additional constraints are introduced because of having to speak sequentially while experiencing information from several modalities simultaneously. Finally, the study of gestural signs forces us to reexamine whether morphemes or morpheme-like units, much less sentential structures, provide necessary and sufficient conditions for the analysis of everyday human and primate communication.

We need to study how the emergence of social organization is related to the development of cognitive and communicational skills regardless of the specific form of language that is used. The problem of teaching "language" to mentally retarded children who do not speak requires clarification of the relationship between internal and external representations of knowledge, and the complexity of the mentally retarded child's everyday existence, before we use a language derived from more complex group life where oral forms have become quite elaborate in displacing various types of information over time and space.

LANGUAGE SOCIALIZATION AND THE DEAF

In my study of British gestural sign language and verbal communication among the deaf (Cicourel, 1974b), I have stressed my attempts to create a context for the analysis or description of materials. This creation of a context is necessary to suggest what the meaning of the materials might signify. Hence what particular gestural signs mean in some dictionary sense is of less interest to me than how I come to appreciate their production by observing their manual generation and their oral description by others and myself. The gestural sign language produced, therefore, becomes oriented to an oral conception of social reality. This oral language orientation forced upon the deaf by the hearing world is not to be equated with a deaf person's interpretation of some event explained to him by another deaf person using gestural sign language.

The way in which hearing-seeing children learn to represent their thought and remembered experiences through an oral modality remains unclear, despite the fact that they initially rely on the perception and processing of information from other modalities to satisfy their everyday activities. The activities I want to outline are as follows:

The child's acquisition of communicational devices is assumed to begin at birth, although we cannot pinpoint the time at which these devices can be used competently in an adult sense. The use of different modalities is integral to the child's receiving information about social orientation, nourishment, physical security, emotional security, etc. A vast array of potential information can impinge upon the child. Depending on his culture, the child must convert experiences from several modalities into oral representations and also interpret oral signals as signifying various types of details available from other modalities.

What is the relationship between sound and the representation of everyday experiences? The sound system presumably characterizes the experiences and thought processes, including non-oral forms, through an arbitrary set of acoustical signals. If our experiences and thought processes can also be represented and indexed by iconic, pictographic, or organized gestural forms, then we can have two competing or complementary types of representational abilities. This view presumes the dominance of an acoustical interpretational system for mediating our experiences and thought processes in everyday exchanges, as well as relying on the oral modality for representing non-oral activities.

Humans are obviously capable of creating communicational systems that do not depend on an acoustical representational system. Exploratory research on hearing children born to deaf parents whose first language was gestural sign (Cicourel and Boese,

1972) supports the idea that having normal hearing does not lead to an automatic acquisition of oral language. Both languages can be learned fluently.

There is another problem here. We can easily acknowledge that a hearing-seeing child often cannot represent his intentions or understanding by verbal means. But it is difficult to obtain clear measures of this problem because any description of the child's difficulties entails references to a setting whose features require adult description (and condensed descriptions at best). But descriptive statements of the child's activities are available and are not unusual. What is difficult to assess is what the child seems "to know" despite not being able to represent himself or herself through some kind of oral expression. Acting out the meaning of sentences provides some basis for revealing comprehension, but the problem persists in classroom settings where the teacher must make a judgment he or she cannot objectify for others and where the demands of the educational bureaucracy require that the child demonstrate his or her comprehension through oral activities or verbal activities that are written. The child's written expressions can provide indirect evidence of his thought processes and their relationship to some of his verbal skills.

In the case of the deaf child the problem is more complicated and perhaps more interesting because the deaf child can seldom express himself verbally with the same proficiency as the hearing child. Hence the deaf child's written expressions can be important for understanding concepts that have been presented in an oral form through lip reading, and then in written form. A child who has learned gestural sign language at home as a first language and from peers in school may use this gestural system to mediate the verbal information he or she receives. This implies differences in how information is received, organized, stored, and retrieved. There are several issues here. Some researchers are interested in the organization of manual sign language and how it can be seen to possess a structure that is similar to or different from oral language structure. The hearing researcher's conception of language is based on his own and others' conception of oral language syntactic structure and the role of phonology and semantics. Hence the prior significance of the oral model is paramount.

Another problem is the extent to which all gestural sign language users today are educated in orally dominated contexts, and how much of their use of gestural sign is a reflection of oral language syntax and semantic interpretations. Gestural signs are described and compared to oral language structures in a context of communicating results and an understanding of what is produced for consumption by a hearing audience. The oral dominance is unavoidable despite the hearing researcher's strong interest in the elements of "natural" gestural sign as used by persons born deaf whose first language is manual sign.

In a study of deaf children in one American and two English schools (Cicourel, in press) an attempt was made to replicate a study of hearing children (Cromer, 1970) with the use of crazy adjective sentences (*The wolf is tasty to bite, The duck is horrible to bite*) to observe how deaf children would perform with lip-read versus gestural sign versions of the sentences. The basic design of the study was to have the child's teacher read each of 16 sentences to the child. The child was to lip-read the teacher's spoken sentences and act out what was said by using two brightly colored foam rubber puppets of a wolf and a duck. A second trial used the same sentences but this time they were presented by gestural sign translations.

The children's performances on the crazy adjective sentences proved ambiguous and very difficult to score. Not having a base line of the children's prior language socialization made it difficult to interpret their relative success with the lip-read and gestural sign versions of the sentences. The crazy adjective exercise could perhaps best be understood within the context of learning a foreign language, but where it is not clear that an equivalent "native language" has been acquired by all of the children regardless of age. Nor can we employ an unambiguous conception of mental age when the tests used to measure this concept usually presuppose unspecified competence with oral language structures. The various fragments of linguistic codes used in the crazy adjective exercise by different children and teachers complicate our study of sign language use because we cannot assume that native competence in oral language exists, nor can we clearly identify beforehand a native sign system base line with which to study the variations that can be observed. Base lines have not been identified for subjects, teachers, or experimenters. Hence the deaf situation is not easy to compare with conditions that exist for hearing subjects. We are faced with the intrusion of implicit oral language models of performance at every step. Hence we are forced to pretend that some base line exists, and this assumption immediately prejudices our analysis. Our subjects too are put into very constrained settings because what is "natural" for them as "language" consists of unspecified mixtures of fragments of different linguistic codes often used as or derived from an oral language mode.

The study of deaf children using criteria of communicative competence based on work with hearing children points to a parallel I have been making between the mentally retarded and normal children. We cannot specify what would be a "native" language for many persons considered "retarded." We do not have clear base lines with normal children and adults for making comparisons between persons presumed to have severe, moderate, or mild conditions of "mental retardation" and persons from a comparable cultural background we would call "normal." We do not have unambiguous conceptions of mental age that enable us to compare test behavior with daily life situations in which the persons labeled mentally retarded can be judged according to how they exhibit communicative and social competence under conditions where others do not have knowledge of the deficiency attributed to them. The different *cultural* contexts in which attributions of mental deficiency are made are not part of our understanding of mental retardation. These attributions of mental deficiency are not linked to test performance and actual social interaction between persons considered to be mentally retarded and "normals" who do not know that this attribution has been made to the other participants.

CONCLUDING REMARKS

When we describe language origins and the structure of oral and non-oral systems of communication we often do so by ignoring the historical evolution of representational systems. It is difficult to compare the nature and complexity of everyday living under relentless historical conditions of harsh survival with the organization of oral and non-oral communication in industrialized and technologically complex societies. The existence of researcher-oriented elegant rule systems for describing speech codes or levels of auditory abstraction (phonetic, phonological, syntactic, semantic, conversational) can mask the ways in which speaker-hearers receive and process auditory inputs during actual exchanges. If the complexity and form of human cognitive and social life are associated with the form and organization of oral and non-oral communication (Hewes, 1973), how do we suspend or refrain from imposing idealized rule systems on communication that has not achieved the same rule structures (Cicourel, 1974b)? The study of the gestural sign language of the deaf poses such a problem because the vocal-auditory channel is not needed for communication of complex ideas in a productive or generative manner. Hence, it is not clear how we should impose levels of abstraction or phonetic, phonological, or morpheme-like units onto our study of native gestural sign language. The convenience, power, and normative sanctioning of formal speech and notation or writing systems tend to obscure the role of cognition, visual appearances, movement, and culturally organized conceptions of knowledge in achieving comprehension and communication in everyday social interaction.

The study of gestural sign language use among the deaf born to deaf parents is central to a theory of language origins and the role of cognitive processes because no formal prescriptive syntax or orthographic system exists. Hence gestural sign usage among uneducated native signers should not be expected to represent the activities and logical constructions experienced by oral language users. It is therefore possible to study the complexity of some native signers' everyday existence before their communicational strategies became more elaborate because of the influence of oral language rules and constructions.

The problem of internal and external representations of our experiences poses many questions about the basis of everyday communication among and between subhuman and human subjects. We are faced with a complex phenomenon whereby members of a group experience far more than they can describe, more than they can or want to react to, and their descriptions of their experiences require that they and others attribute unstated elements to their remarks to render them comprehensible. Oral and non-oral descriptions or accounts provide the speaker and hearer or deaf member with information for recovering or imagining the experiences or settings that went into the creation of the account. Hence the member's general knowledge is a basic resource for assigning meaning to experiences and descriptive accounts or visual or kinesthetic information.

The existence of at least two generative or self-contained representational systems, oral-symbolic and gestural-symbolic, for communicating our thoughts and emotions, raises the question of what do we mean by the term "language"? How do languages correspond to thought or cognitive processes? Can we understand cognitive processes by a careful study of oral or gestural sign representational systems? How much faith are we to put into the discovery of phonetic, phonological, syntactic, semantic, conversational, or narrative rules for understanding memory and reasoning processes? If the representational systems are culturally evolved forms of communication, how do we credit the ingenuity of the cognitive processes that produced the elegant rule systems developed by native speakers and signers in cultures where written forms do not exist? Our general practice is to focus on the structure of the socially organized and sanctioned rules or constraints. We tend to focus on the notion of phonological and syntactic universals of representational systems rather than on the social conditions of education and use that seem to motivate the rule structures of the researcher's attention. But since the rule structures or elements of representational systems are the product of memory and reasoning processes, we need to worry about the relationship between the internal processes of reception, storage, retrieval, and reorganization of information and the external representational systems that are often the focus of attention.

Present-day theories of communication are tied to the rule systems said to index previous and possible future settings and the settings in which the accounts are expressed. These theories are informed by the careful study of representations that are presumed to be standardized indicators of the unobserved settings. Day-to-day experiences that are tied to a past or a possible future condition of the lived present presuppose a memory system and normative conceptions of normal events and thoughts. It is difficult to speculate about the nature of internal representations experienced despite the lack of a generative, normatively sanctioned external signaling system. But this is the problem faced by severely retarded children and children born both deaf and blind. Since we always begin our description and analysis of communication with the observation that some sort of "system" exists externally, it is difficult for us to speculate about the organization of internal processes that are not informed by prescriptive and proscriptive external representations.

In summary, therefore, I have urged a view of "language" that suggests the possibility that we have placed too much emphasis on several identifiable rule systems said to form the structure of auditory-verbal displays. We rely on these rule systems when we seek to infer a native speaker-hearer's or signer's intuition or cognitive processes. The communicational systems we call "language" can be viewed sociologically as normatively sanctioned representations that impose arbitrary idealizations on auditory-oral or visual-kinesthetic activities. When we designate some persons as "retarded" we often rely on these normative communication systems for documenting our evaluations. Our reliance on these rule systems tends to obscure how persons designated as "retarded" can be capable of comprehending and implementing activities that are not revealed by their facility with an oral representational system or its written form.

Cognitive processes are tied to daily social exchanges where the settings themselves inform the participants about what is happening in addition to the use of auditory-oral and visual-kinesthetic displays to index experiences and activities. We still lack an adequate conceptual and empirical basis for understanding the role of the setting and the participants' methods of reflecting on the import of their selectively attended experiences of the setting, themselves, and others. Instead we tend to focus on the representational displays, relying on the formal aspects of culturally created and sanctioned rule systems to describe and claim an analysis of native intuition and comprehension in our study of communicative and social competence. The study of deaf sign language from a sociolinguistic perspective suggests that we should spend more time observing the social and cognitive processes that organize communication and representational systems rather than allow our analysis to reflect primarily the elegant rule-governed displays we call "language." "Language" then becomes an important, but not necessarily the only dominant, aspect of the recognition, comprehension, and production of socially organized displays of communicative and social competence.

REFERENCES

Broadbent, D. E. 1958. Perception and Communication. Permagon Press, London.

Cicourel, A. V. In press. Sociolinguistic aspects of the use of sign language. *In* I. M. Schlesinger and L. Namir (eds.), Current Trends in The Study of Sign Languages of the Deaf. Mouton, The Hague.

Cicourel, A. V. 1974a. Some basic theoretical issues in the assessment of the child's performance in testing and classroom settings. *In* Cicourel et al., Language Use and School Performance. Academic Press, New York.

Cicourel, A. V. 1974b. Gestural sign language and the study of non-verbal communication. Sign Language Studies 4: 35–76.

Cicourel, A. V. and R. J. Boese. 1972. The acquisition of manual sign language and generative semantics. Semiotica 5: 225–256.

Cicourel, A. V., K. Jennings, S. Jennings, K. Leiter, R. MacKay, H. Mehan, and D. Roth. 1974. Language Use and School Performance. Academic Press, New York.

Cromer, R. F. 1970. 'Children Are Nice to Understand': Surface structure clues for the recovery of a deep structure. Br. J. Psychol. 61: 397–408.

Deutsch, J. A. and D. Deutsch. 1963. Attention: Some theoretical considerations. Psychol. Rev. 70: 80–90.

Gardner, R. A. and B. T. Gardner. 1969. Teaching sign-language to a chimpanzee. Science 165: 664–672.

Gray, J. A. and A. A. Wedderburn. 1960. Grouping strategies with simultaneous stimuli. Q. J. Exp. Psychol. 12: 180–184.

Hewes, G. W. 1973. Primate communication and the gestural origin of language. Curr. Anthropol. 14: 5–24.

Hockett, C. T. 1960. The origin of speech. Sci. Am. 203: 88–96.

Hockett, C. T. and R. Asher. 1964. The human revolution. Curr. Anthropol. 5: 135–168.

Ima, K. 1972. Unpublished manuscript.

Kolers, P. and J. R. Pomerantz. 1971. Figural change in apparent motion. J. Exper. Psychol. 87: 99–108.

MacKay, R. 1974. Standardized tests: Objective/objectified measures of "competence." *In* Cicourel et al. Language Use and School Performance. Academic Press, New York.

Mehan, H. B., Jr. 1971. Accomplishing Understanding in Educational Settings. Dissertation, University of California, Santa Barbara.

Mehan, H. B., Jr. 1974. Accomplishing classroom lessons. *In* Cicourel et al. Language Use and School Performance. Academic Press, New York.

Moray, N. 1959. Attention in dichotic listening: Affective cues and the influence of instructions. Q. J. Exp. Psychol. 11: 56–60.

Neisser, U. 1967. Cognitive Psychology. Appleton-Century-Crofts, New York.

Norman, D. A. 1969. Memory and Attention. Wiley, New York.

Premack, D. 1971. Language in chimpanzee? Science 172: 808–822.

244   Aaron V. Cicourel

Roth, D. 1974. Intelligence testing as a social activity. *In* Cicourel et al. Language Use and School Performance. Academic Press, New York.

Stokoe, W. C. 1972. Motor Signs as the First Form of Language. American Anthropology Association annual meeting, Toronto.

Triesman, A. M. 1960. Contextual cues in selective listening. Q. J. Exp. Psychol. 12: 242–248.

FORMS OF
FAMILY ADAPTATION
AND INTERVENTION

Family Adaptions to Severely Mentally Retarded Children

Bernard Farber

Generally, social scientists regard families with severely retarded children as curiosities. Focusing upon the mental retardation label, they try to ferret out ways in which families cope specifically with their stigmatized child and with the courtesy stigma which the parents themselves earn (Goffman, 1963). They view their task as that of identifying the peculiar modes of behavior, the unique strategems employed by these families in reacting to stigma. But regarding families with severe retardates as curiosities ignores the fact that in most respects these families resemble others in the society. Most of their roles and values are drawn from and are sustained in a flow of events similar to that experienced by other families. Rather, the plight of the parents of retarded children stems from the necessity of handling various kinds of offensive situations associated with their offspring.

By focusing instead on the mobilization of the family to handle the continuing *offensive* situations and *offensive* behavior, we can then study the dynamics of family interaction in trying to live with unpleasantness. Yet, not all families or family members find living with a severely retarded child equally offensive. There are variations in the sense of stigma, in the amount of time and energy demanded, in the extent of family resources, in prior loyalties and commitments, and so on. These variations require more extreme adaptations on the part of some families (and some family members) than others. The presence of such differences in adapting to a retarded child evokes the question: how do families decide on how much they must change their mode of existence in order to permit their lives to be bearable?

As a means of suggesting directions of further research on families with retarded children, this paper deals with this question of the extent of adaptation which families are prepared to undergo. The first section is concerned with assumptions about the adaptational process, the second section with a putative description of this process, and the third with the effect of the social context on the process of adaptation. The term adaptation, incidentally, is not to be confused with "adjustment" or "acceptance." It is used rather in the traditional sense in which social scientist have applied the term, that of creating means for dealing with functional problems, as a basis for cultural change.

ASSUMPTIONS REGARDING THE ADAPTATIONAL PROCESS

This section will suggest some basic assumptions underlying the process of adaptation to problematic family situations. It will first present the principle of minimal adaptation as a basis for ordering changes in family relationships. Then following the lead of theories on social exchange (Goode, 1960), it will relate the principle of minimal adaptation to questions pertaining to role renegotiation. Afterward, it will outline a tentative progression of successive minimal adaptations.

The Principle of Minimal Adaptation

In the analysis of change in family interaction, one can make various alternative assumptions about the choice of adaptations by family members. One possible assumption is that adaptations are capricious and depend mainly upon the power structure of the family. This, in one sense, is the assumption made in the stimulus-response approach. This assumption implies a basic family disorder in problem situations and a reliance for solutions, in the final analysis, upon the psychological make-up and resources of the family members. On the basis of this assumption, families in crisis have been variously characterized in terms of coping behavior, adaptability, flexibility, need-response pattern, and patterns of behavioral influence. In the past, the stimulus-response approach has not yielded significant hypotheses regarding generic processes of family adaptations to crisis (Hill and Hansen, 1964; Geismar, 1961; Parad and Caplan, 1960).

A second alternative assumption is to regard the adaptational process as a "rational" means for attaining ends in family life. One then observes how the most and least rational families differ in their choice of action. This is an approach I used in applying a strategic games analogy to the study of families with severely retarded children. I was concerned with the conditions under which strategies of institutionalization versus home residence were effective in maintaining a high marital integration of the parents. This procedure assumed that high marital integration was the major end (the payoff) for all families. Although the rationality assumption is useful when 1) there is a limited number of strategies to be examined and 2) there is a general consensus about the importance of the characteristic regarded as the payoff, its utility is diminished when these conditions do not hold.

A third assumption, which will be explored in this paper, is that of minimal adaptation. This assumption implies that, *ceteris paribus*, families will make as minimal an adaptation as possible to solve problems involving family relationships (or at least to create a situation making it possible to live with these problems). A family problem is regarded here as any event or chronic situation which the family members collectively perceive as interfering with the successful attainment of their goals in family life. Ideally, before the onset of the offensive situation, family relationships had been sufficiently gratifying so that family members are reluctant to change their mode of living. I consider an adaptation to be any sustained change in roles, norms, or family interaction which family members make (individually or collectively) with the intention of effectively handling (either solving or living with) the offensive situation. The minimal adaptation assumption implies a *temporal* progression of adaptations from the simple to the complex, from the least disruptive to the potentially fully disruptive of family relationships. Since these adaptations represent means for counteracting a threat to the integrity of the family, members are not likely to resort to more extreme measures until those less risky have been tried. Especially as adaptations become more extreme, variations in the opinions of family members as to the appropriateness of adaptations may themselves generate additional family problems.

The idea of change as a series of successive minimal adaptations to a critical event, with each adaptation more profound in its influence than the preceding one, appears in various guises in sociological analysis. It is found in Nisbet's (1969, p. 270) "priority of fixity," by which he means "apart from all interferences and external impacts, social behavior tends to remain fixed and unchanging." It is implied in models of stable equilibrium (Smelser, 1968, pp. 262–268), which involve eventual recovery to a steady state of functioning by a social system. Applied to a concrete event, the principle of progressive minimal adaptations has been invoked to explain the slow but extensive escalation of U.S. involvement in the Vietnamese conflict of the 1960's. Briefly, it is the position that as a general rule major changes do not occur precipitously, without a long buildup of preliminary adaptations which do not themselves produce the desired ends. Thus, in response to a critical event, changes in family interaction may inch along, intruding upon different domains of interaction (possible imperceptibly), until a profound revision eventually occurs in the organization of interaction.

ROLE, RENEGOTIATION, AND ADAPTATION

The principle of successive minimal adaptations involves a series of renegotiations of family relationships. If we assume that at any given time partners in a social relationship have negotiated a set of understandings, then any potential new allocation of time, funds, or hierarchy of loyalties must be pitted against old ones in revising commitments. The mechanism of renegotiation assumes an inelastic amount of time, economic resources, and hierarchy of loyalties. If these were elastic, they would not have to be renegotiated every time a new potential allocation presented itself. Since an acceptable arrangement of time and resources allocation and loyalty hierarchy would have been negotiated to begin with, people would be reluctant to give up the existing pattern of allocations without trading off. This reluctance to renegotiate an existing pattern of allocations of time, resource, and personal loyalty commitments inhibits the speed and amount of negotiation that occurs.

Ordinarily, problematic situations either hit at one person's area of responsibility harder than at another's or strike at different roles in different ways. A consequence of this differential effect on roles is that the cost of a crisis is greater for one family member than another. This person must then "purchase" a far larger reallocation of time, loyalty, or resource than is required by another family member as a result of this crisis. In this asymmetrical situation, the other family member may 1) demand an exchange of commitments equal to those given, which results in a "profit," or 2) reallocate time, resources, or loyalty as a "loan" to be repaid at some future time, or 3) give only that much commitment as is appropriate to his own requirements in the crisis, sustaining an allocation deficit for the more affected person, or 4) provide the required allocation as a "gift" and expect nothing in return, treating the other as an object of one's unilateral action rather than as an interacting participant, or 5) negotiate an exchange which neither had anticipated earlier. I suggest that in an asymmetrical situation such as that just described, those persons less affected by the problem would tend to choose alternative 3, which maintains an allocation deficit for the more affected persons.

This choice of a minimal adaptation by the lesser affected persons sets the stage for later negotiation to balance allocation deficits in the family. As roles are renegotiated to eliminate these deficits for the more affected persons, those who are less affected may demand considerable compensation for their cooperation. For example, since the maternal role is most affected by the presence of a retarded child, the husband may be unwilling to reallocate his efforts without an increase in the wife's submissiveness or attentiveness. The process thus hinges upon the willingness of the lesser affected persons to renegotiate roles. The lesser affected persons are thereby in a strong position to define the major value orientations of the family.

At each phase of the adaptation process, the parents and siblings probably "test" their role arrangements on each other and on outsiders. Apparently, as long as the parents feel that they can manage the child's disability, they can regard themselves as competent to handle offensive situations. It is only as they come to regard themselves as powerless that their role bargaining ability would deteriorate (Voysey, 1972).

If interaction were uniformly intensive among all family members, one might anticipate that the family would progress as a unit through successive adaptations. However, because of variations in intensity of interaction, these phases refer more to family dyads: husband-wife, parent-and-normal child, parent-and-retarded child, and sibling-sibling. The necessity of living with a retarded sibling or child may stimulate a variety of offenses in these relationships. As secondary issues arise within these dyads, subordinate progressions of successive adaptations are apparently generated. Whereas the initial series of adaptations may refer to the retarded child as a problem, in later phases the focus may be on difficulties between parents or on a disturbed sibling. Eventually, the issue of divorce as a possible adaptation may overshadow that of institutionalization of the retarded child. The secondary offenses created in renegotiating roles influence the direction of later adaptations. As in the case of kidney donors, persons may drift into adaptations. Having negotiated or stalemated on one offense they are ready for a next step on that issue without considerable deliberation (Simmons, Klein, and Thornton, 1973).

The Progression of Successive Minimal Adaptations

The previous paragraphs indicated that hypothetically, other things being equal, families start out with the most minimal adaptations to their problems and proceed to successively more extensive and drastic ones only when the simpler adaptations are not effective. This characterization of family adaptation to crisis suggests the need to identify adaptations along a continuum from the most minimal to the most extensive and then to determine the extent to which families do indeed follow this sequence in reacting to critical events. One would anticipate, as a general principle, that the families would stabilize a mode of adaptation when the solutions developed are, at least in their view, inoffensive. Otherwise, the adaptational process would continue until the family units dissolved. What follows below is, of course, an ideal progression of adaptations to crisis and cannot apply to all empirical situations. The manner by which various conditions may affect this process will be discussed later.

Assuming the principle of successive minimal adaptations, one can postulate a process in terms of the phases outlined below. At any stage, if the kind of adaptation is effective, the family would cease seeking further adaptations to this problem, stabilize in its organization, and the crisis-meetingprocess would cease.

The progression of minimal adaptations in families with a severely mentally retarded child illustrates the effect which the presence of this child may have on family relationships. The successive adaptations include the following:

1. *Labeling phase*, in which the bases for the existing role arrangements are removed, and there is a realization that major understandings underpinning family relationships may have to be renegotiated.

2. *Normalization phase*, in which the family makes a pretense of maintaining its normal set of roles, all the while being considerate of each other for role lapses in an attempt to keep family life as normal as possible. The family presents a face of normality to the outside and seeks to maintain liaisons with the world of normal families.

3. *Mobilization phase*, in which the family members intensify the time and effort given to family demands, without, however, giving up their claim to normality as a family.

4. *Revisionist phase*, in which the family, in isolating itself from community involvements, can no longer maintain an identity of normality, and it revises age and sex standards in its organization of family roles. This revision represents an attempt to maintain cohesiveness in an uncaring and misunderstanding world.

5. *Polarization phase*, in which the family, finding itself unable to maintain its coherence in a complacent or perhaps hostile world, turns its attention inward to seek the sources of this complacency or hostility within the family.

6. *Elimination phase*, in which the polarization eventuates in arrangements to preclude contact with the offending person himself. In this phase, the family seeks to renegotiate (with whatever resources remain) to regain those roles regarded as normal.

PHASES IN THE ADAPTATIONAL PROCESS

The previous section outlined a series of putative phases in the adaptational process. It is difficult to determine from that outline the special features of each phase and the ways which these phases are related to recent research on families with deviant children. This section presents a more detailed discussion of these phases.

The continued presence of a severely retarded child in the home represents a dynamic set of problems rather than a static problem which the term "stigma" might imply. Even in so-called normal families, relationships are under continual pressure to change. This inherent instability derives from the fact that age-sex roles vary with movement in the family life cycle. As both children and their parents age, role expectations are modified.

The presence of a severely handicapped child in the family can be regarded as a factor in the arrest of the family cycle (Farber, 1959). This assumption is made on the following basis:

1. In interaction with their children, parents tend to assign a status to each child commensurate with the capabilities they impute to him.

a. The roles embodied in the status are classified on the basis of age grading. By definition, normally, mental age is approximately equal to chronological age.

b. Age grading in a culture is regarded more as a psychological and social activity than as a chronological variable, e.g., the chronologicaly middle aged severely retarded individual is generally regarded as a "boy" or "girl" by those with whom he interacts. According to Eaton and Weil (1955) the Hutterite religious group excludes the mentally retarded from adult responsibility by cancelling baptism requirements, thereby giving them the moral status of children.

2. As the child proceeds in his life career, the parents normally tend to revise their self-concepts and roles. With respect to their normal children, ideally, parents continually redefine their roles, obligations, and values to adjust to the changing role of the child. With respect to their retarded children, the parental role is fairly constant. Regardless of his birth order in the family, the severely handicapped child eventually becomes the youngest child socially. A very severely handicapped child at home would not engage in dating and courtship, belong to organizations, seek part-time employment, or take part in other activities characteristic of adolescents. In his progressive movement to the youngest-child status, the severely retarded child would not merely slow down movement in the family cycle but also prevent the development of the later stages in the cycle. Birenbaum (1970) ascribes an increasing severity of family problems as the retarded child reaches adolescence.

The relative ages of a retarded child and his siblings seem to affect the extent to which there will be a revision in their birth order socially. Shere (1955) investigated 30 pairs of twins. Within each pair, one child was cerebral palsied. The behavior of the parents toward the twins differed in certain respects: 1) the parents generally expected the non-cerebral palsied child to assume more responsibilities and to act older than his age or capabilities would warrant, 2) the parents tended to be more responsive to the problems of the cerebral palsied child and oblivious to those of his twin, 3) the parents overprotected the cerebral palsied twin, permitting him little discretion in his activities. The non-cerebral palsied twin was more curious and adventurous, less patient, more excitable, less cheerful, more resistant to authority, and more prone to emotional outbursts than the cerebral-palsied twin.

The Farber (1960a) study of 240 Chicago area families with severely retarded children investigated characteristics of those normal siblings who were closest in age to the retarded child. Farber found that the retarded child's siblings were affected by his high degree of dependency, which adversely affected the siblings' relationships with their mother. When the children were young, interaction between the normal and the retarded brothers and sisters tended to be on an egalitarian basis. As they grew older, the normal siblings frequently assumed a superordinate position in the relationship. However, siblings who did not interact frequently with their retarded brother or sister generally were affected less than those who interacted frequently.

Factors related to the family life cycle provide an impetus for revising adaptations. What may be merely an impropriety at one phase of the family life cycle becomes offensive in another. The minimal amount of adaptation at one stage of the family life cycle is insufficient to handle offensive behavior that may emerge at a later stage.

Labeling Phase: Improprieties and Offensive Behavior

When a child fails to develop according to a normal developmental time table, ordinarily we try to fit a number of labels to explain this failure, usually choosing the less offensive labels first and dreading the most stigmatizing ones (Davis, 1961, 1963). The father who regards his young son with Down's syndrome as having a slight speech impediment, correctable through speech therapy, does not yet require significant strategies of adaptation. As yet, this behavior is an impropriety, but not offensive. To the outsider who had to point out the behavior, however, this failure must have somehow been offensive.

What makes behavior offensive? Evidently, the consequences of the behavior are important. For example, suppose a child does not walk when he normally might be expected to or does not start using language at the appropriate developmental time. The parents might not consider this proper, nor would it, however, be offensive. They could merely regard the child as a late walker or a late talker. They might regard the same behavior as extremely offensive, though, if they believed it to be symptomatic of mental retardation. Having a personal diagnosis validated by a physician or psychologist would reinforce the parents' view of the behavior as offensive.

The redefinition of a retarded child's behavior from merely "improper" to "grossly offensive" undoubtedly produces a shock to the parents. Parents almost without exception report this realization as constituting a major tragedy in their life. Sometimes, the parents may take this occasion to turn against their spouse, regarding him (or her) in turn as offensive for having some sort of role in this event. Occasionally, it is the physician who is regarded as offensive. To regard another as offensive is not to discredit him (or her) personally as one might do in denying the validity of a diagnosis, but instead one blames the other for offending him. Unlike stigmatization, which in effect implies that the "spoiled" individual does not have a right to continue interaction, offensiveness constitutes a transgression, which does not damage an individual's right to interaction, but does make continued interaction disagreeable. Having reached the point of defining the child's failure to develop normally as offensive to them, the parents must now decide how to handle this offensiveness.

Normalization Phase

Having defined the child's inappropriate behavior as offensive, the parents must either eliminate this offensiveness or learn to live with it. Parents, when asked to participate in a study of families with severely retarded children, have responded, "But we don't have any special problems; we are a normal family, everything about us is normal. The fact that one of our children has a special problem makes us no different. In most families some children have problems of one kind or another." The minimal family adaptation, following the communication of the deviance label, is to try to handle the offending child within the existing arrangements of family roles and norms (see, for example, Graliker et al., 1962). The maintenance of deviance within the normal scheme of things, despite the family consensus that something is amiss, can occur in several ways: 1) some family members may suppress their perceptions about the existence of a problem, 2) some family members may convince others to change their perceptions (i.e., their labels), or 3) as in "pseudo mutuality," the family members may all pretend that all is well (Wynne, 1969). Although pseudo mutuality has been discussed mainly in connection with mental illness, the fiction of normality in family relationships occurs in numerous offensive situations: deviance disavowal in interaction with physically disabled persons (Davis, 1961), the pretense of uncertainty of prognosis in polio and leukemia (Davis, 1963; Murstein, 1960), shopping around for a favorable diagnosis for severely mentally retarded children, the family's denial of a parent's compulsion to drink or to take drugs (Jackson, 1956), or the denial of bizarre behavior of a psychotic parent (Clausen et al., 1955). As long as the deviant person and his family can carry off the fiction of normality, there is no need for further adaptations in family roles or norms. It is only when the fiction of normality cannot be sustained (or itself interferes with the attainment of family goals) that more complex adaptations must be sought.

In his discussion of courtesy stigma (i.e., someone who has a spoiled identity because he is affiliated with a stigmatized person (Goffman, 1963)), Birenbaum (1970, p. 198) writes that "to the extent that mothers of retardates are able to perform roles similar to those performed by mothers of normal children, the consequences of the courtesy stigma they bear are manageable." These are manageable when 1) under conditions of role nonconformity, others are "considerate" in accepting "the plight of the family with a disabled child," or 2) situations can be avoided in which the risk of exposing the nonconformity is high. As long as others with whom one interacts "forgive" failures in role performance, there is no need to renegotiate the basis for continuing the relationship. The failures are seen as improper but not offensive.

When do people stop forgiving failures in role performance? Presumably, when 1) these failures are no longer seen as unavoidable lapses, 2) the failure itself (regardless of basis) produces bitter disappointment and interferes with important goals and is viewed as a permanent state, 3) the demands on one's resources exceed his or her ability to fill in for these failures, and/or 4) the costs of carrying a courtesy stigma outweigh the gains from maintaining the relationship. There is then a time when an existing role arrangement may flounder, and, finding the situation offensive, the person calls for renegotiation of the allocation of family roles, either directly or through an intermediary (such as a professional or a relative).

Mobilization Phase

When the family cannot resolve the offensiveness within existing arrangements, it must make minor adaptations to fill lacunae or exert greater efforts in existing roles. This extension of responsibilities requires a change in expectations of all the family members in a systematic reapportionment of duties. The family members then retain many of their previous privileges and obligations, but are faced with a change (probably minor) in the authority structure and division of labor. Thus, the wife may encroach upon the husband's household domain, or the husband on the wife's, or perhaps the child on the mother's. Yet, the original person retains primary responsibility for that domain.

In "normal" family life, participation in organizations with friends outside the family ordinarily supports the norms and values associated with everyday life. For the family in crisis, these ordinary community relationships do not support norms and values pertinent to handling "the problem." On the other hand, other extrafamily coalitions do assist family members in handling the crisis. Women with husbands in the military service shift reliance to grandparents and relatives; the wife of the mental patient withdraws from family and friends and forms coalitions with the mental hospital staff; parenthood ordinarily involves a curtailment of social activities (especially activities with friends who have no children); attempts are made to decrease the social visibility of drinking and eventually coalitions are formed with doctors, social workers, psychologists, and the like, and with nondrinking alcoholics; the family of the unemployed tends to withdraw from friends at the old social level and to find new friends at the lower socioeconomic level.

There is widespread evidence that parents of severely retarded children tend to isolate themselves socially (Schonell et al., 1959; Kramm, 1963; Tizard and Grad, 1961; Birenbaum, 1968). Birenbaum (1970) suggests further that while reciprocal visiting may decrease significantly, parents "found it more comfortable to receive guests in their home than to visit other people's houses"; there was apparently less awkwardness and embarrassment. This isolation does not seem to extend so much to relatives. Either relationships with kinsmen do not change or they may even be intensified as the relatives show "consideration" for lapses in role performance.

Yet, defense against outside intrusion does not by itself imply conformity to normal parental roles in families with retarded children. McAllister, Butler, and Lei (1973) report a lesser amount of reading stories to children or talking with children in families with retarded than with all normal children. The parents may thereby cut down on socializing behavior at the same time they also diminish their visits with relatives, neighbors, friends, and co-workers. The avoidance of failure-validating situations seems to mark the early adaptations made.

The principle of minimal adaptation suggests an uneven kind of transformation of the family in handling the offensive behavior. The less important conveniences and more threatening actions are given up in role trade-offs, and the more significant aspects of existence are clung to. In an earlier study (Farber, 1960a), it was feasible to identify families as home oriented, parent oriented, or child oriented in decision making and to classify other families as relying upon residual strategies. These residual category families had apparently not been able to retain or to agree on these more significant elements in their family life, and the parents were evidencing some difficulty in their marital relationship. Bermann's (1973) more recent analysis of family interaction patterns also indicates strongly that, in the process of eventual polarization, the preferences of the individual members become highlighted above common concerns.

There is a danger in the mobilization phase that resentments may arise over extensions of roles which have been negotiated or enforced. Family members may believe that 1) the social debt owed them may never be paid off or 2) the social interest accruing in this debt is not sufficient to compensate them for their sacrifices. Yet, the mere resentment of a possibly unfair division of labor is not enough to force a change. Children may resent additional attention that parents give the retarded child without the parents even becoming aware of this resentment. For example, in one family the brothers and sisters of a retarded boy felt sorry for their parents, and although they felt "hurt" by their own relative neglect, they kept this resentment from the parents even after achieving adulthood. This hidden sense of oppression may, however, not be restricted to children. Husbands as well may resent additional household duties which might interfere with social mobility or leisure activities. As long as this resentment is seen merely as a necessary imposition, it can be maintained and justified. However, when the impropriety seems unjust, the family members feel offended, and they seek further role renegotiation.

Revisionist Phase

At some point, family members begin to regard themselves as having "special problems." The minor revision in family roles may not handle the offensiveness in family relationships effectively. In fact, there may be a diffusion of offensive behavior throughout the family. When everyone is offended by what is required (in contrast to the large investment of time, energy, and/or personal trauma), there is a general demand for changing the basic role structure of the family. The continuation of family life in a crisis situation may be sustained eventually through a rearrangement of age, sex, and generation roles in the family. The duty and power structure of the family is rearranged. In the case of the chronic alcoholic, the drinking husband is demoted in generation to the role of a recalcitrant child, and the mother assumes her husband's responsibilities, while sharing some of her own with the children. Similarly, the unreliable behavior of the mentally ill husband causes a comparable demotion. The unemployed husband withdraws from planning and management; children assume adultlike roles, contribute financially, and demand a change in power structure in the family. In these instances, the family members have departed from conventional age, sex, and generation roles. The family organization itself becomes deviant.

One of the organizational problems that occurs with extensive revision of family roles is how to maintain a coherent set of social relationships in the face of high tension. Since there is a general conception that retarded children do generate family problems, the parents can feel free to blame the state of the family upon the presence of the retarded child. The child is in a powerless position. He cannot effectively counteract the parents' efforts to regard him as a scapegoat, and he obviously represents a symbol of failure to them (Vogel and Bell, 1960). Moreover, the retarded child can carry out the role of a problem child without any special effort: he has seriously violated social norms, but he is rewarded for his offensiveness by being exempt from any responsibilities and obligations. Thus, the child has earned his role by drawing off aggression and thereby permitting the family to maintain its solidarity.

In the extensive revision of family roles, the mother, faced with a daily life she finds impossible to endure, may become sick. This situation tends to occur more often in lower socioeconomic level families (Farber, 1960b). However, like any other role, a "sick role" in the family must be negotiated with other family members. The absence of a parent, for example, would eliminate the possibility of negotiating such a role. The obvious need for personnel and resources in order to negotiate a sick role is indicated by Koss' (1954, p. 30) quotation: "I wish I really knew what you mean about being sick. Sometimes I felt so bad I could curl up and die, but had to go on because the kids had to be taken care of, and besides we didn't have the money to spend for the doctor—How could I be sick?" Consistent with this speculation concerning the inability of some families to renegotiate sick roles in crisis, Roghmann, Hecht, and Haggerty (1973, p. 58) find that persons in incomplete families tend to report more chronic conditions and more difficulty in coping with illness and other family problems than is the case of people in complete families.

The extensive revision of role bargains in the family may be negotiated at a high cost in extrafamilial relationships. Farber (1959) and others have noted how daughters (when the retarded child lives at home) are called upon to provide much household and childcare assistance. They have also noted the tension which exists between the retarded child's mother and sister in this situation. This tension extends beyond the household. Gath (1973) has found that sisters of mongoloid children show a high amount of antisocial behavior in school. At the same time, however, Farber and Jenne (1963) have also found that the siblings who interact a good deal with their retarded brothers and sisters tend to be more serious in outlook on life and less concerned with acceptance by peers. This alienation seems to pervade interaction with outsiders.

Polarization Phase: Identities in Danger

At a minimum, family members would regard extensive revision of family roles to meet the exigencies of the situation as departing from the ordinary norms of propriety. One would expect such families to manage carefully information about themselves to the outside world (Goffman, 1963). As family members encounter situations within the home (as well as outside) which they see becoming offensive to themselves and to each other, their careful information management extends into the household itself.

Eventually, family members may participate in pseudo-negotiation with each other whereby superficially "offers" of services are made and accepted, but actually the contracted roles are never played out. Nor is there overt redress over failure to comply with contracted roles. In describing interaction process analysis in a troubled family, Bermann (1973) writes that as the crisis continues, the family members "pointedly behave in ways that seem calculated to abort extensive interaction, that appear designed to attenuate continuing exchange between family members." Whereas in the earlier phases of the crisis family members had been placed in a position where they were encouraged to sustain interaction, in later stages:

> There is a polarization of behaviors in crisis—initiations [of interaction] are either inconsequentially noncontroversial or [are] threatening antagonism; reactions are either those of ready acquiescence or of withdrawal. . . . Person A can act on Person B, so as to have no impact on him, or so as to terrorize him. One or the other. Nothing between. Person B, for his part, is merely intent on getting out of A's way. He, as much as A, wants to be left alone. To this end he acquiesces or withdraws. The facade of social exchange is maintained. . . . In the end people do not want to be disturbed. It is not that they don't care. It is because they care more than they can admit (Bermann, 1973, p. 86).

Although family members may remain under the same roof, they establish a tacit agreement to interact as briefly as possible in order to permit them to coexist with as little sense of abuse as possible. In this manner, some shred of belongingness as a family can be maintained.

Wynne et al. (1958, p. 638) emphasize the large role that secrecy and privacy play in families which are pseudo-mutual in their interaction. "Each family member may be expected to conceal large areas of his experience and not open to communication with the others." The norm for the family is based on a perhaps "exaggerated" right of privacy, with the amount of sharing intimate, personal things the prerogative of each family member. In an effort to maintain a visage of cohesion, there may be sweeping approval of any kind of behavior, with departures from acceptable standards explained away by some rationalization. In this manner, all semblance of the family as an interacting group which socializes its members and guides their conduct is lost. One finds that in families with a severely retarded child, normal brothers may be given free reign as long as they do not get in the way at home. Similarly, in those families in which the parents' marriage shows signs of low integration, there is a tendency (where there is a retarded child in the home) for the parents to seek escape outside the home.

In the end, however, the accumulation of problems generated by the failure of successive adaptations may be so great that the entire complex of family relationships loses its viability. Both parents may, for various reasons, have become incapable of filling family roles, and the children may have to be parceled out. Fortunately, few families reach this stage. One extreme case might be mentioned in which the father had been idle because of a bad heart for at least a decade, the mother was in the home with cancer at its terminal stages, the adolescent daughter was having incestuous relations with her severely retarded brother and doing poorly in school, while the normal brother understandably was failing all of his subjects. (These pieces of information were garnered from various sources.) Yet, the father earnestly believed that his wife's "wasting away" would miraculously stop, a spine adjustment by a chiropractor would halt further deterioration of his retarded son, his daughter would be a nurse, and his normal son a doctor. With the children away from the house most of the time and the mother too weak and too much in pain to be active, there was little family interaction. What interaction there was tended to be highly guarded. No one was interested in ridding the father of his delusions, least of all the mother.

Elimination Phase: The Formation of New Identities

Ordinarily, when we think about eliminating the offending person in families with severely mentally retarded children, we have in mind institutionalization of the retardate. Indeed, in most families when the offense of the retarded child is sufficiently grave (e.g., interfering with the parents' and/or siblings' mental health or social mobility), institutionalization seems an appropriate solution (Culver, 1967; Downey, 1965; Farber, Jenne, and Toigo, 1960).

Yet, in some families the progression of adaptations may have generated so much offensive behavior in the family, that "transgressions" of a spouse or normal child may be considered as more serious than the retarded child's. As a consequence, the parents may divorce or a sibling sent to live with a relative. Thus, for example, one parent who had completely identified herself with the "cause" of the mentally retarded gave up her marriage to a man who resented her almost total involvement with her parent group, her disdain of those who were not sympathetic to her cause, and her delusion that her group's continued existence depended solely upon her leadership. Or, in another family, even after the retarded child had been institutionalized, the parents threw themselves into volunteer work related to the mentally retarded and later were considering hospitalizing their child of normal intelligence for a "nervous breakdown."

One might review conceptions of institutionalization to determine how families with retarded children handle the elimination phase. Some parents, particularly those of middle class background, prefer to regard the institutionalized child as dead or depersoned. Their contact with him or her is minimal. Those of lower socioeconomic background, however, more often regard institutionalization as living-away-from-home, and their contact and readiness to reincorporate the child may be strong (Downey, 1963; Mercer, 1965). Perhaps lower class families are less inclined to avoid crises, regarding them as part of family life.

THE CONTEXT OF ADAPTATION

The progression of successive minimal adaptations described in the previous paragraphs requires the qualification that all other things are equal. Empirically, however, numerous factors impinge upon family interaction and affect the course of events, and given different conditions, the succession of adaptations may be modified. Families may skip some phases of the process, or complex adaptations may precede simpler ones. It thus seems advisable to suggest conditions under which modifications of the adaptation process occur. Some of these conditions are sketched briefly below.

Prior Role of the Offending Deviant

If the offensive person has been regarded by the other family members as essential to fulfilling dreams and goals, then the family would be more reluctant to make changes which might reduce the status and participation of this person. For example, in an earlier study, I found it useful to distinguish among families with a strong parent orientation, child orientation, general home orientation, and mixed or vague orientations (Farber, 1960a). These families differed by age of parents, social-mobility orientation, handling of their retarded and normal children, and in adaptations to family problems. Especially among parent-oriented, upwardly mobile families, there was a tendency to institutionalize the retarded child as soon as possible (Culver, 1967; Farber, 1960a). Many of them skipped any attempt to live with the retarded child and immediately eliminated him from their lives (Downey, 1965). Not so with the child-oriented families wherein jobs, social life, and home life were all organized around the children. In any case, an offending member, whose presence otherwise promotes familial goals about which there is consensus, would be more likely to generate successive minimal adaptations than one whose presence contributes less to the overall family goals.

Prior Family Loyalty

In some families, for a variety of reasons, marital or filial ties may have been fragile even prior to the retardate's presence. Here again we would not anticipate a continual development of a series of successive minimal adaptations which goes on until a satisfactory arrangement has been attained. Instead, members whose family bonds are fragile might extend their activities outside the family or might dissolve family relationships altogether. For example, among families with severely retarded children, parents whose own ties to their family orientation outweighed their loyalties to spouse and children sometimes escaped into many activities outside the home. These marriages seemed tenuous to begin with and could not readily withstand the problems generated by the presence of the retarded child. Hence, in contrast to these examples, the development of a process of successive minimal adaptations seems to require that the family bonds be fairly strong to begin with.

Reliance on Experiential Guides

The family may not build up a succession of minimal adaptations itself but may rely instead upon previous experiences of others (or its own prior adaptations to crisis). Influences here may include 1) professional therapy or advice, 2) the experiences of relatives or friends facing similar crises, 3) the family's previous experiences with problem situations, 4) mental experiments which anticipate probable consequences of different adaptations, or 5) cultural prescriptions. In any of these situations, the family members may discard lesser adaptations as unworkable and go on to ostensibly more complicated, more drastic ones. However, knowledge that these adaptations do work precludes the necessity of having to renegotiate roles from scratch.

Changes in Family Composition

The development of a series of successive adaptations requires that the composition of the family remain unchanged from that in existence prior to the crisis. Otherwise (as in death, imprisonment, or involuntary military separations) where families lose members or (as in homecomings from prison or military service) where they gain members, families do not have options regarding simple minimal adaptations, the required changes in role tend to be drastic. Yet, we do not know how extensive the adaptations must be. Thus, even where simpler adaptations are impossible, it may be instructive to view the progressive development of more complex, more drastic ways of meeting critical situations.

Community Relationships of Family and Offending Members

The description of successive family adaptations to a critical event starts with labeling by family members. Adams (1971, pp. 32–322), however, indicates that the critical event may be of such a nature that the family problem is labeled first in the community and only afterwards within the family, and he suggests that revisions of family relationships with outsiders may occur even while the family denies the existence of a problem (e.g., avoidance or ostracism). While Adams is accurate in his remarks, his criticism does not preclude another later revision in community relationships in the order of adaptations described in the previous section. His comments provoke a question with regard to the initiation of labeling: does it make a difference in the progression of phases of adaptation if the initial labeling is done outside the home (e.g., a school problem or a neighborhood nuisance)?

DISCUSSION

Although there have been numerous investigations of families in crisis, little progress has been made regarding the understanding of the adaptations of families to these critical events. The major findings have been tautological: flexible families more readily make changes in meeting problems. Few studies have suggested any mechanisms as to how these changes are accomplished. Bakke's (1940) investigation of unemployment during the 1930's Depression, Jackson's (1956) study of the father's alcoholism, or Farber's (1964, pp. 406–438) analysis of families with a severely mentally retarded child all do *describe* some sort of progression of stages. Yet, they omit mention of a basis for this progression. Without positing a mechanism for justifying the stages they have described, they have been unable to counter criticisms regarding the sufficiency or necessity of the stages they describe in explaining family reactions to crisis. (See, for example, Adams, 1971, pp. 321–322).

This paper has presented a set of assumptions which appear to justify the formulation of a progression of phases in the adaptation of families to crisis. Briefly, the argument is that, *ceteris paribus,* families try to make as few changes as possible in roles, norms, and values to the problems they perceive. Only as the simplest adaptations fail to produce an acceptable accommodation to the offending problem do they go on to a more complex solution. As a more complex solution fails, they go on to a still more complex solution, and so on. This principle of minimal adaptation to crisis seems to account for a predictable progression of phases of adaptation. This theoretical progression is present in Figure 1.

The qualification about other-things-being-equal may facilitate the formulation of a theoretical statement, but it also evokes questions regarding the kind of conditions which can affect the progression of phases of family adaptation. The paper has listed several of these conditions: 1) roles of the problem members of the family prior to the deviance (or potential roles imputed to them), 2) priorities of family orientations and loyalties of the so-called non-deviant members who are called upon to develop adaptations to the problem, 3) the changes in family composition which provoke the crisis, 4) the presence of experiental guides, and 5) the possible emergence of the family problem first as a community problem. These conditions (and probably others) may influence families to depart from the principle of successive minimal adaptations and to skip or change the sequence of phases in the adaptational process.

Three other matters should be dealt with in relation to questions about conditions which may affect in the adaptational process. These include 1) voluntarism as a factor, 2) the duration of adaptations, and 3) the content of adaptations. These constitute additional problems for empirical investigation.

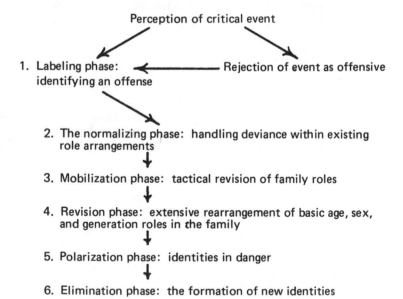

Figure 1. Phases in the theoretical progression of successive minimal adaptations of families in crisis. Note: Each phase in the progression is capable of being (1) a transitional state to the next phase if the adaptation is not satisfactory (or at least an acceptable) accommodation for the family or (2) an end state, which arrests the progression, if the adaptation is acceptable.

Voluntarism in Crisis and Adaptations

Adams (1971) suggests that crises wrought by voluntary actions (e.g., divorce or illegitimacy) are different in effects on family relationships than those brought about by involuntary action (e.g., unemployment or death). He points out that they differ, for instance, in the extent of guilt attached to the critical event. But what sets in motion a series of adaptations generally is not the intended action, but the unintended elements. Voluntarism may become an aspect of a critical event only when family members intentionally create disruption (e.g., cruel treatment of others). Still familial adaptations to this offense may follow the same sequence of progressively more profound adaptations that might take place if the stressful behavior were involuntary. (There is, to be sure, usually a blending of what is intentional and what is compulsive and unconscious in offending behavior.)

With respect to voluntarism of adaptations, similar questions may be posed: Does it make a difference if everyone willingly makes certain kinds of adaptations? In one sense, the principle of minimal adaptations presupposes an unwillingness to depart from the original order of roles, norms, and values. Does it make a difference in the adaptational process if the family members themselves are aware of the changes they have undertaken? They may be aware of only some of these modifications in family organization; other adaptations may be dimly at the edge of consciousness. While the question of voluntarism may be important for psychological analysis, it may not be particularly significant for the study of adaptations in role, norms, or values of the family unit.

Duration of Adaptations

A second dimension not handled in this paper is that of the duration of adaptations in relation to that of the problem situation. Presumably, as the need for the adaptation disappears, the shift in roles, norms, or values tends to dissolve. Still, in some instances the offensive situation which generated the crisis may disappear (e.g., illness or unemployment), but the adaptive measures may endure. It may be useful to regard the elimination of the critical event as still another problem situation (e.g., the returned military veteran (Hill, 1949)). One would then anticipate, other things being equal, that the family would handle the reversion to its "normal" situation with the same kind of progression of successive adaptations as those provoked by the initial crisis. This perspective suggests, for example, that the sick role (Parsons, 1951), which verges on a revision of age-sex-generation roles, be considered as undesirable not only by the patient, but perhaps even more so by other family members (as placing undue burdens upon them). Otherwise, as it happens in some families, the adaptations made initially to the illness might become permanent.

Another possible problem that may emerge with respect to duration of adaptations is that adaptations may fade before the problem has been solved and before another adaptation has been attempted. The study of the abandonment of adaptations has received little attention in family research. Yet, in order to understand conditions under which families reorganize themselves, it is necessary to investigate this topic: how do families become disillusioned with the efficacy of their adaptive measures?

Content of Adaptations

Whereas this paper has been concerned with the form of the adaptation process, it has given little attention to the content of these adaptations. Yet, the application of the theoretical scheme outlined in the paper depends for its efficacy upon the appropriateness of adaptations for arresting the process and in that sense solving the family problem. I mentioned earlier 1) the part played by family values in determining the appropriateness of the particular adaptation and 2) the use of "games of strategy" as a research model for determining the "rationality" of any given adaptation. It is thus necessary to examine empirically the kinds of conditions under which these adaptations "work" in creating an acceptable solution or accommodation to the family problem. In doing so, it may be advisable to establish the costs and utilities of specific adaptations in order to determine a continuum of complexity or profoundness of changes in role organization, norms, and values in different phases of the process. This procedure would permit an empirical test of the theoretical scheme and might provide guidelines for therapy.

While the empirical test of the principle of minimal adaptations (and the progression of successive changes derived from it) would undoubtedly reveal shortcomings of the scheme, it should also suggest directions for revision of sociological analysis of family crisis (for example, the development of crisis fugues, in which stresses are multiplied). Such an analysis might suggest, for example, how adaptations to an offensive situation may be eufunctional up to a certain point in terms of continuity of general values or mental health, yet as the family continues to introduce further adaptations in an effort to handle the offense, these later efforts are destructive of the basic conditions for the family's integrity.

REFERENCES

Adams, B. N. 1971. The American Family, A Sociological Interpretation. Markham Publishing Co., Chicago.
Bakke, E. W. 1940. Citizens Without Work. Yale University Press, New Haven.
Bermann, E. 1973. Regrouping for survival: Approaching dread and three phases of family interaction. J. Comp. Family Stud. 4: 63–87.
Birenbaum, A. 1968. Non-institutionalized roles and role formation: A study of mothers of mentally retarded children. Columbia University, New York. (Unpublished Ph.D. dissertation)
Birenbaum, A. 1970. On managing a courtesy stigma. J. Health Soc. Behav. 11: 196–206.
Clausen, J. A., M. R. Yarrow, L. C. Deasy, and C. G. Schwartz. 1955. Impact of mental illness of the family. J. Soc. Issues 11(4): 6–11.
Culver, M. 1967. Intergenerational social mobility among families with a severely mentally retarded child. University of Illinois, Urbana. (Unpublished Ph.D. dissertation)

Davis, F. 1961. Deviance disavowal: The management of strained interaction by the visibly handicapped. Soc. Problems 9: 120–132.

Davis, F. 1963. Passage Through Crisis: Polio Victims and Their Families. Bobbs-Merrill, New York.

Downey, K. J. 1963. Parental interest in the institutionalized severely mentally retarded child. Soc. Problems 11: 185–193.

Downey, K. J. 1965. Parents' reasons for institutionalizing severely mentally retarded children. J. Health Hum. Behav. 6: 163–169.

Eaton, J. W. and R. J. Weil. 1955. Culture and Mental Disorders. Free Press, New York.

Farber, B. 1959. Effects of a severely mentally retarded child on family integration. Monogr. Soc. Res. Child Develop. No. 71.

Farber, B. 1960a. Family organization and crisis: Maintenance of integration in families with a severely mentally retarded child. Monogr. Soc. Res. Child Develop. No. 75.

Farber, B. 1960b. Perceptions of crisis and related variables in the impact of a retarded child on the mother. J. Health Hum. Behav. 1: 108–118.

Farber, B. 1964. Family: Organization and Interaction. Chandler Publishing Co, San Francisco.

Farber, B. and W. C. Jenne. 1963. Interaction with retarded siblings and life goals of children. Marr. Family Living 25: 96–98.

Farber, B., W. C. Jenne, and T. Toigo. 1960. Family crisis and the decision to institutionalize the retarded child. Council Except. Child., NEA, Res. Monogr. Series, No. A-1.

Gath, A. 1972. The mental health of siblings of a congenitally abnormal child. J. Child Psychol. Psychiatr. 13: 211–218.

Geismar, L. L. 1961. Three levels of treatment for the multiproblem family. Soc. Casework 42: 124–127.

Goffman, E. 1963. Stigma: Notes on the Management of Spoiled Identity. Prentice-Hall, Englewood Cliffs, N.J.

Goode, W. J. 1960. A theory of role strain. Am. Sociolog. Rev. 25: 483–496.

Graliker, B. V., K. Fishler, and R. Koch. 1962. Teenage reaction to a mentally retarded sibling. Am. J. Ment. Defic. 66: 838–843.

Hill, R. 1949. Families Under Stress. Harper, New York.

Hill, R. and D. A. Hansen. 1964. Families under stress. In H. T. Christensen (ed.), Handbook of Marriage and the Family, pp. 782–819. Rand McNally and Co., Chicago.

Jackson, J. K. 1956. The adjustment of the family to alcoholism. J. Marr. Family 18: 361–369.

Koos, E. L. 1954. The Health of Regionville: What People Thought and Did About It. Hafner, New York.

Kramm, E. 1963. Families of Mongoloid Children. Children's Bureau No. 401. U.S. Government Printing Office, Washington, D.D.

McAllister, R. J., E. W. Butler, and T. J. Lei. 1973. Patterns of social interaction among families of behaviorally retarded children. (Unpublished)

Mercer, J. R. 1965. Social system perspective and clinical perspective: Frames of reference for understanding career patterns of persons labeled as mentally retarded. Soc. Problems 13: 18–34.

Murstein, B. I. 1960. The effect of long-term illness on children on the emotional adjustment of parents. Child Devel. 31: 157–171.

Nisbet, R. A. 1969. Social Change and History. Oxford University Press, New York.

Parad, H. J. and G. A. Caplan. 1960. A framework for studying families in crisis. Soc. Work 3–15.

Parsons, T. 1951. The Social System. Free Press, New York.

Roghmann, K. J., P. K. Hecht, and R. J. Haggerty. 1973. Family coping with everyday illness: Self reports from a household survey. J. Comp. Family Stud. 4: 49–62.

Schonell, F. J., I. G. Middleton, B. H. Watts, and M. W. Rorke. 1959. First and second surveys of the effects of a subnormal child of the family unit. University of Queensland Papers, Brisbane, Australia.

Simmons, R. G., S. D. Klein, and K. Thompson. 1973. The family member's decision to be a kidney transplant donor. J. Comp. Family Stud. 4: 116–130.

Smelser, N. J. 1968. Essays in Sociological Explanation. Prentice-Hall, Englewood Cliffs, N.J.

Tizard, J. and J. Grad. 1961. The Mentally Handicapped and Their Families. Oxford University Press, New York.

Vogel, E. F. and N. W. Bell. 1960. The emotionally disturbed child as the family scapegoat. In N. W. Bell and E. F. Vogel (eds.), A Modern Introduction to the Family, pp. 382–397. Free Press, New York.

Voysey, M. 1972. Impression management by parents with disabled children. J. Health Soc. Behav. 13: 80–89.

Wynne, L. C., I. M. Ryckoff, J. Day, and S. I. Hirsch. 1958. Pseudo-mutuality in the family relations of schizophrenics. Psychiatry 21: 205–220.

Foster Family Care For the Intellectually Disadvantaged Child: The Current State Of Practice and Some Research Perspectives

Margaret Adams

The social institution of foster family care is founded on a paradox, which may help to explain why this service to dependent children is a highly promoted tool of child welfare even while it is recognized to contain many potential problems that require constant surveillance and reassessment. This paradox stems from the *nature of the service demanded,* the care of children deprived of parental protection and nurture; the *social purpose it serves,* safeguarding the successful survival of the next generation; and the *resources required* to meet these ends, stable family households in which the adult members are motivated by the fundamental, even primitive, emotions necessary to the nurturing parent role. Beyond these rudimentary basics modern foster care must also encompass a clear understanding of the social and psychological dynamics that provide its motivation and rationale. A formal foster care service is of itself evidence that the cohesive, emotionally based social network which formerly could absorb the vulnerable members of society has broken down, transforming an earlier implicit social process of reciprocal obligations within the extended kinship group or close-knit, face-to-face society into a complex and explicit organization.

This more impersonal professional system depends on strangers for caretaking tasks, monetary recompense rather than reciprocal service, and checks and balances to ensure that it works efficiently and to the child's maximum advantage. Foster care practice, as we know it today, is the end-product of this evolutionary metamorphosis, and its different ingredients reveal an attempt to balance intimate gut-motivated nurturing with more self-conscious professional insights and techniques about how to provide this in its optimal form.

Research undertaken in this field over the past 15 to 20 years illustrates the need to reconcile these two complementary but often conflicting aspects and the theoretical application of foster care to the specifically handicapped population which is our concern today, namely the intellectually disadvantaged child, presents a particularly telling paradigm for this paradox. The word "theoretical" is used advisedly because despite valiant sporadic efforts to provide this alternative to institutionalization for children identified as retarded (Burgess and Morrissey, 1964, 1966; Morrissey, 1966), foster family care for this group has not been developed as a consistently available service under the general child welfare rubric.

Very little research is reported on this subject and I suspect not much more being carried out. In consequence, exhaustive and rigorous raking has failed to assemble much straw for the bricks of this paper. So, I am offering a summary of the significant areas of research that have been burgeoning in the foster care field in the past two decades, prefacing it with a thumbnail history of foster family care in America and England. From these beginnings I hope to extract the generic elements of foster care that have clear relevance for our specialized field and will point the directions in which a research thrust of the future could be made. I shall garnish this basic diet with brief accounts of the rare research ventures and findings that have been undertaken in regard to handicapped children, in which are included those with our specialized disability.

I shall start by outlining the reasons why, in my opinion, foster care is today an important social issue for mental retardation. In analyzing this subject we need, as always, to bear in mind the complex and varied character of the constituency under discussion, and to realize that its social implications are likely to be different for children with different types and grade of handicap. Mild retardation, with its inseparable social concomitants, presents another set of problems from those associated with the more conspicuous socio-clinical condition due to severe neurological damage.

However it is equally important not to lose sight of the fact that these two disparate groups have problems in common when it comes to needing substitute parental care. I shall therefore begin by looking at those components of foster care that apply across the board to all retarded children and then branch into those aspects that relate more specifically to the different categories.

Foster family care is important to all retarded children because it represents one segment of the coordinated spectrum of services that may be required to counter some of the social needs and hazards that arise from their social and intellectual handicap. Its particular social significance lies in the fact that it offers a type of substitute parental care that most closely resembles the normal situation of family living. The normalcy of this situation is more likely to maximize the social and emotional development of a retarded child than the more familiar alternative of large-scale institutional care (Birch and Belmont, 1961; Stedman and Eichorn, 1964).

At this point it may be useful to examine the concept of residential care for the mentally retarded, and particularly why it continues to be an integral feature of any comprehensive service provision. The reasons are complex and tend to be different for the two categories of the mildly retarded and their more severely handicapped peers. For the latter, residential care must be potentially available because of the long-standing tradition that has allowed, even encouraged, parents to institutionalize (sometimes from birth) children with conspicuous developmental and intellectual deficit that carries a prognosis of permanent social and intellectual disability.

We may promote the philosophical concept that a handicapped child has a right to his own home and family and is likely to flourish better in that normal setting than elsewhere (Stedman and Eichorn, 1964) and even support this pious hope with an efficient and comprehensive battery of supportive services within the community. But until all families and professionals abandon the residual belief that it is acceptable to abrogate responsibility for a retarded child's upbringing and delegate his care to society's organized welfare system, we must include appropriate, nurturing, and stimulating surrogate care within our service continuum. There will always be some children with neurological impairment and severe behavior deficits whose management is too taxing for a normal family. Likewise the impoverished psychological and material resources of some families prevent them from accommodating even minor deviance without detriment to their own viability. For these situations foster family care may be the happiest solution (Adams, 1970). The project of the Retarded Infants' Services in New York City was initiated to meet these sorts of need (Arnold, 1971).

For the mildly retarded, foster family care is an even more serious issue that implicates both rehabilitation and prevention, because a proportion of all children with defined mild retardation faces the prospect of having to be placed in substitute care, due to the precarious and often deleterious character of their own homes and the social disorganization which characterizes them. In Massachusetts 18% of all the children in foster care on November 18, 1971 were deemed to have some intellectual disability, and an analysis of home backgrounds showed that around one-third of this sample came from families of low socioeconomic status. Their parents had not completed high school, were unemployed or in unskilled work, and maintained their families on incomes of less than $3000 per annum (Gruber, 1973).

These findings speak to the now familiar fact (to this audience it is documented coals to several Newcastles) that the mildly retarded are heavily distributed in the lowest socioeconomic strata of society both in America and Great Britain (Stein and Susser, 1969). An impressive body of research into this epidemiological phenomenon has enabled us to identify some of the specific components of the environment of poverty and low socioeconomic status that appear to be closely associated with retardation. These are overcrowded homes, run down neighborhoods densely populated by less competent households, low income, large family size, parents of low intelligence, education and occupational skill (Birch et al., 1970; Heber et al., 1972), plus various manifestations of social aberrance such as delinquency and child neglect (Stein and Susser, 1960).

Looking at some of the research findings in foster family care, we see that the same characteristics of poverty and social pathology prevail to an overweighted degree among the families of children placed and are often the predominant reason for placement. Child neglect was one of the characteristics identified by Stein and Susser (1960) in the dysmorphic families of the mildly retarded sample they studied, and this problem appears in one guise or another as one of the leading causes of placement in at least three foster care studies. Deviant parental behavior (neglect, abuse, abandonment, and exploitation) accounted for 21% of the placement requests in the Child Welfare League Study of foster care placement in seven cities (Shyne, 1969); neglect, abuse and family dysfunctioning appeared as a placement reason in 25% of the cases in the Columbia University Child Welfare Research program studies (Jenkins and Norman, 1972, 1969), and in 14.4% of the cases in the study of foster care done in Massachusetts (Gruber, 1973). Characteristics of the children's families in all three studies indicate that a considerable proportion of parents had incomes less than $3000 per annum, did not graduate from high school, and were in unskilled work, unemployed, or supported by Welfare.

To sum up, foster family care is an invaluable resource for children who are markedly retarded with residual chronic impairment, for children with functional retardation due to improper upbringing and children who are at risk of becoming retarded because of their social circumstances, if appropriate intervention is not provided. Its practical possibilities are preventing placement in a large-scale institutional setting and assisting the resettlement of children into the community from such a setting, if they have been previously placed there. It can also provide an especially tailored therapeutic milieu which will include the special insights and expert knowledge of social and psychological factors required to meet the unusual needs created by retardation. At the same time it will offer a living situation with all the components of normalcy built into it, which will prevent the alienating and stigmatized prescription that results from segregated institutional placement (Goffman, 1961; Vail, 1966). Foster care is therefore an important social instrument of the normalizing principle which informs the conceptual thinking and practical policy behind care in the mental retardation field (Nirje, 1969; Wolfensberger, 1973).

If theoretically foster family care seems appropriate, even desirable, for our constituency of intellectually disadvantaged children, we need to look at why it has not been hitherto utilized. Are these reasons valid? If not, how can we reverse them? What social science insights can transform this rather impoverished wilderness into a flourishing kindergarten in that word's original sense? A brief backward look at history of both child welfare and services for the retarded is necessary to this understanding. When neighborliness no longer sufficed to take care of children who had no family of their own, the English Poor Law discharged this responsibility by apprenticing them to families for work. Foster care proper came into being when the charitable foundation of Christ's Hospital boarded out those under age for apprenticeship with nurses in the suburbs of London (George, 1970). America followed this model by indenturing (Encylopedia of Social Work, 1965) and town governments boarded out homeless families for a fee (Modell and Hareven, 1973). Thus the initial blueprint for foster care was laid down in both countries.

Two centuries later the social upheavals of industrialization forced both countries to develop more complex and sophisticated social services, and philanthropically disposed individuals with a sense of the social dialectics of cause, effect, and long term outcome began to experiment with better services for destitute or at-risk children. In England a clergyman made an arrangement with the local Poor Law authority to finance the maintenance of children from workhouses in private foster homes which he undertook to find and supervise himself (George, 1970). In the identical year a reverend gentleman, Charles Loring Brace, had the same idea in New York City and founded the Children's Aid Society (Encyclopedia of Social Work, 1965). This venture included an extensive foster home placement system in rural New York, the purpose of which was to provide a better environment for children to grow up than was offered by their own overburdened and impoverished homes or the alternative of a city orphan asylum. The English cleric's goal was to offer training as well as a setting that would be beneficial to emotional and social development.

Almost at the same time, Howe was harassing the legislature of the Commonwealth of Massachusetts to provide funds for a special school for the "idiotic children" it had in its care, mainly in the County Poor Houses, with the express intention of giving them a milieu and training that was suited to their limited capacities but would also stimulate them appropriately so that they would "be more of a man and less of a beast" (Howe, 1851): the 19th century concept of humanization and normalization. This excellently intended effort started the system of specialized residential care, so that while the *normal* children under County Care were salvaged by assimilation into the foster home model the retarded were marshalled into their specialized educational establishments.

The separation of these two paths started here and became more sharply pronounced as different bureaucratic structures took different services under their aegis. Thus when nearly a century later progressive minded institutions wanted to resettle their residents out into community situations, this service had to be developed as an offshoot of the institutional model as Family Care, financed by funds from the mental health rather than child welfare bureaucracy. In this way the expertise and experience of fostering retarded children remained the province of social workers located in the institutions (Bishop, 1959; Crutcher, 1940; Doll, 1940; Kuenzell, 1938; Vaux, 1935), and did not generally infiltrate into, and so modify, child welfare philosophy, policy, and practice. When the First White House Conference on Children (1909) emphasized foster family care as a vital resource of child welfare, it did not include retarded children in its plans for promoting this service. The Conference on Research in the Children's Field meeting in Chicago in 1956 similarly overlooked this group of deprived children.

This landmark conference, however, has relevance to our theme because it highlighted the paucity of research findings by which practitioners could evaluate foster care, modify shortcomings, and plan for more effective programs in the future. In an important paper entitled "Unanswered Questions about Foster Care," Meisels and Loeb (1956) refer to the dearth of formal research about foster home care, observing that:

> In spite of concern with the results of the programs and recognition of problems . . .
> the methods which are suggested or tried are based not so much on systematic

exploration of the facts in the situation as on the acceptance of axioms, speculations and inferences, and . . . there is practically no formulation of hypotheses growing out of the newly found knowledge and there is no research to test them.

After this rather castigatory start the paper proceeds to outline areas for which research data would be valuable. These are 1) an objective and scientifically based assessment of what constitutes a home sufficiently inadequate or detrimental to warrant the child's removal, 2) criteria for assessing foster homes, particularly their capacity for meeting the psychosocial needs of the child who has been separated from his natural family setting, 3) social work strategies for dealing with parents, foster parents, and community and maintaining a carefully balanced stance between the rights of each constituent, 4) the economic basis for foster home care and its costs relative to other forms of substitute care, 5) devising of a model for ideal psychosocial development to be striven towards for the children in care.

Either by dialectical process or happy coincidence a series of significant research projects were initiated in the next few years, resulting in a veritable renaissance of publications. These were concerned with reassessing current practice and suggesting new directions for the future that would meet emerging needs and the innovative practices these demanded. Maas and Engler (1959) published "Children in Need of Parents," which combined some telling insights about community differences in child care with a cogent picture of the status of children in foster care. "Selecting foster parents. The ideal and the reality" (Wolins, 1963) dealt with the process involved in foster parent selection and the role ascribed to this task. This important aspect of foster care was pursued in greater detail by Fanschel (1961a, 1961b, 1966) who was able to identify personal and social attributes in foster parents that tuned in favorably with certain characteristics of foster children.

In England Parker (1966) analyzed the variables that seemed crucially related to success or failure in placement (judged by whether it lasted for 5 years or more), with a view to offering a predictive instrument for child care workers. At the same time the Child Welfare League of America was involved in a nationwide study of the decision-making factors involved in the placement process of children into substitute care of any form (Shyne, 1969). Since 1966 Columbia University has been engaged in a comprehensive study of child placement based on New York City. This project has focused on the implications of placement for the biological family, for the agency taking charge of the child, and for the child, with emphasis on his chances for being successfully assimilated into his natural home (Fanschel, 1971; Jenkins, 1969; Jenkins and Norman, 1972; Shapiro, 1972, 1973). More recently the Governor's Commission on Adoption and Foster Care in Massachusetts published a report on foster home care in the Commonwealth (Gruber, 1973). Its purpose was to identify the characteristics and problems of children currently in foster care in that state.

These research projects cited do not claim to be an exhaustive survey of work carried out in this field. Rather they have been selected because their scope and content have most visible relevance, direct or indirect, to our specialized topic of foster family care for the mentally retarded child. Since this particular area of child care has been so little explored we must look to services for normal children and extrapolate those features that fit our group and can serve as a model for both program development and research. Many of the points made by the investigators just quoted relate closely to handicapped children and by implication refute the traditional conviction that foster family care is not appropriate for them.

Before looking at these relevant "normal" features it may be enlightening to glance briefly at the theoretical arguments and practical obstacles that have hampered the development of this service. The bureaucratic barriers of categorical funding and assigned responsibility have already been mentioned. Others may be hypothesized as follows:

1. The management of a child with intellectual handicap requires special skills and expert knowledge that are unlikely to be found in ordinary run-of-the-mill foster families.

2. The supposedly static nature of this disability makes the task of raising a retarded child unrewarding at the best and exceedingly frustrating at worst.

3. The behavior problems and lack of social skills that may be manifested by retarded children, who cannot be managed in their own homes or have been institutionalized, would militate against their successful assimilation into the nuclear unit of the foster family and the broader network of the community and school system, which supports the family.

4. Given the limited supply of foster homes available and the inverse ratio of supply and demand it is not politic to waste them on children whose placement success is in doubt and whose long term future social adjustment and productivity do not warrant the utilization of this scarce resource. This argument is an offshoot of the thinking that locates the retarded in permanent institutional placement and does not actively envisage their either remaining in the community-at-large or being rehabilitated into it. Therefore the normalizing experience of foster home care is less necessary as a preparation for adult life than it is for children of normal social and intellectual potential whose future role is theoretically not in doubt.

5. Families of the more conspicuously handicapped children have many misconceptions about foster care, associate it with social pathology and a negative social image, and are often resistant to accepting this form of care, much preferring the traditional socially affirmed option of institutional placement.

Several of the research studies on generic (as opposed to specialized) foster care speak cogently to these various points and if we examine their findings and those from research in mental retardation, we get an idea of how erroneous these assumptions are. Let us take first the point that retarded children are unlikely to appeal to prospective foster parents because of the developmental limitations inherent in their condition of residual neurological deficit and the anticipated lack of progress and resultant frustration for the child-caring persons. To begin with, only the most profound degree of basic neurological deficit results in a *totally static* condition. Studies on behavior have indicated that given appropriate care, which involves emotional nurturance, stimulation, and structure, children with considerable deficit can sometimes show dramatic improvement (Hollis, Gorton, and Chester, 1967; Mackay and Sidman, 1968).

Further, in his study of the foster care role Fanschel was able to identify clusters of characteristics and attitudes (styled "factors") in foster parents which suggested different capacities for raising children with different developmental and behavioral characteristics. One distinction was between foster parents who preferred infants to older children, and another between those who showed an aptitude for aggressive, acting-out children as against those who did better with children showing exceptional dependency needs. The latter category comprised children with physical or mental handicap or emotional problems manifested in bizarre and dependent behavior, and colicky infants. These data suggest that if we could identify potential foster parents with these personality characteristics they might respond enthusiastically to the challenge of a retarded child. Another point in Fanschel's study relevant to our theme is that mothers fostering infants tended to find role satisfaction in the close personal interaction with the children in their care. Fathers on the other hand were much less involved in the fostering situation with infants. With older children they perceived their role in terms of "desiring to serve a worthy cause" and to provide a masculine model for the foster child to round out the family paradigm.

The study of foster placement success carried out in England by Gray and Parr (1957) showed that the highest rate of failure was in children with identified mental disability, i.e., who were in the educable and trainable ranges of retardation, severely maladjusted, or mentally ill. This group of children was the smallest subcategory within the studied sample (11%). Of these, only 15% were boarded out in foster families, the other 85% being distributed in larger scale homes, nearly half of which were a specialized residential facility. These results are disappointing from our point of view because children with other types of handicap were successful in 62% of the cases. Building up a viable foster care service for the retarded depends very much on being able to recruit parents with the sort of attitude and motivations that will neutralize potential failure. Fanschel's work offers a useful tool for identifying this invaluable resource. To balance it, it would be useful to have a parallel study which identifies those behavioral problems associated with retardation that are least tolerable to foster parents. Kushlick's (1970) criteria for children requiring placement could serve as a baseline, reinforced by other studies of reasons for placement (State of Illinois Department of Public Health, 1965), and the family stress factors reported by Tizard and Grad (1961).

This point leads into a discussion of another barrier to foster care for the retarded, namely the uncertainty of success and the potential waste of valuable foster home resources on a child who cannot utilize them, and may also undermine the good will of the foster parent constituency because of the failure they symbolize. If we can establish some reliable predictability criteria about the sort of child likely to succeed, given his specific characteristics and their fit with the dominant characteristics of foster parents, this argument will be greatly diminished. Parker's study (1966) offers other useful predictive pointers. One consistently crucial variable was the presence of other children in the foster family setting and their relationship in age to the foster child. Where there is a birth child of the foster parents of under 5 or within 5 years of the foster child there is a strong likelihood of the placement failing. This is significant for our population because of the discrepancy between chronological and mental or social age and the prolonged dependency on foster parents, and it needs to be carefully balanced with the Fanschel findings that some foster mothers do well with children who have greater dependency needs.

The other and more cogent rebuttal of the implication that scarce foster homes should not be squandered on retarded children has already been briefly suggested by my earlier observations on the relationship between mild retardation, adverse socioeconomic living conditions, and admission to foster care. With the well documented evidence we now have that mild retardation of non-organic origin is susceptible to being either reversed (Heber et al., 1972) or substantially mitigated (Kugel and Parsons, 1967) through exposure to more stimulating, nurturing, and stable living conditions, it is hard to accept that foster care placement would be a waste when it has such rehabilitative potential. Children from socially depriving backgrounds who have experienced the culminating trauma of being removed from their homes are in equal, if not greater, need of a restitutive environment to counteract the stultifying influences they have been subjected to. This may well be provided best in a foster home rather than in a large scale institutional setting. By the very nature of its structure this type of facility has its own built-in deprivative features which only serve to compound the initial insult produced by a deleterious home and summary removal therefrom (Braginsky and Braginsky, 1974).

Although the actual environment of foster family care is less alienating and tends to a normalizing model, it does not necessarily meet the quite stringent rehabilitative needs of this category of mildly retarded children. A specific effort must, therefore, be made to reinforce these natural therapeutic influences by providing some professional expertise for the foster parents and special remedial services for the retarded child. In Massachusetts, Gruber (1973, 1974) found that around 40% of the children in foster care had some form of disability and that of this number nearly a quarter had not had their handicap evaluated. For those that were evaluated, recommended treatment had not been implemented in 26% of the cases. Seventeen percent of these "untreated" children had intellectual deficits but other disabilities frequently associated with retardation received similar non-attention. For example, behavior problems which many retarded children in care demonstrate were neither assessed nor treated in around one-third of the children manifesting this handicap. The role of foster parents in regard to this problem is illuminating. Seventy-five percent indicated that they were not aware of the existence nor extent of the child's disability prior to placement, and 13.8% who were fostering children with *identified* handicap denied any problem.

This suggests that many children with borderline or mildly retarded intellectual function are being absorbed into the main stream of child welfare without having due attention paid to their specific deficits until these manifest themselves in deviant functioning. This often results in disruption of the placement with a strong likelihood of transfer to a specialized facility for the retarded and consequent abrogation of the normalizing goals. In these situations, which I suspect are not uncommon, we have to develop a precise understanding of the range and nature of services an intellectually disabled child needs, devise reliable mechanisms for identifying children at such risk and build in a system for ensuring that these support services are a routine component of the overall therapeutic goal of the foster placement. This is an area that lends itself to research.

In contrast to this bleak picture, we do have both information and structured data about specialized care for the more seriously handicapped in foster homes. This care is mediated through the provision of a comprehensive back-up service to foster parents and their involvement in specialized training. The latter includes didactic knowledge about normal and deviant child development, the range of handicap and its behavioral manifestations liable to be encountered, and specific techniques for managing the latter. This support may also take the form of structuring specific programs to be carried out in the foster homes with direct professional assistance or consultation. An unpublished report from the Metropolitan Children's Aid Society of Toronto (Green, 1973) describes both its training schedule and the progress made by the children since its inception. Several other projects are reported in the literature (Justice, Bradley, and O'Connor, 1971; Mamula, 1970, 1971; Tomkiewicz, Biny, and Zucman, 1971). This component of foster care is also being vigorously pursued in many innovative programs being developed in the Macomb-Oakland Centre in Michigan (Rosen, 1974), the Residential Services Program of the Developmental Disabilities Council of Ohio (McAvoy, 1974), at the Levinson Center, Bangor, Maine (Valentine, 1974) and at Fernald (Peters, 1974).

Closely allied to this trend toward expertise are two other movements in the foster care field. One deals with the question of appropriate additional reimbursement for foster parenting. The other relates to the change in the foster parent role *vis-à-vis* the child welfare agency and its staff, and the much more sharply delineated roles that this so-called lay segment of the child welfare armamentum is defining, projecting, and consolidating for itself (Anderson, 1971; Hunzeker, 1971; Rosendorf, 1972). Recognition of the skilled expertise that goes into fostering has permeated the literature for a good decade, resulting in a redefinition of both tasks and roles. This new perception of function raises some conflicts around the quasi-supervisor-client relationship that has prevailed in the foster care situation.

Reimbursement is part of this new movement which defines motivation in more sophisticated terms than the simple desire to mother, and recognizes skills in the task that should be paid for like any other form of labor, over and above the subsistence allowance paid for the child's upkeep (Garrett, 1968; Pratt, 1966). This crystallizes the paradox I mentioned in my opening paragraphs in that new skills involving fresh remunerative obligations from the responsible welfare institution are being grafted on, or rather seen to emerge from, the older pattern of what is considered simple substitute parenting, and the hitherto implicit amateur status is being transformed to one with at least some dimensions of professionalism.

The question of how to determine what is suitable reimbursement for this new professionally slanted occupation has been systematically studied by the Children's Aid Society of Vancouver, B.C. This agency has devised a scale for measuring the degree of additional or unusual care required by children with different handicapping conditions, and has worked out a system for additional reimbursement commensurate with extra demands for time and more highly developed skills involved in their care (Shah, 1971; Shah and Poulos, 1974). The repertoire of handicaps includes emotional, intellectual, and physical deficits and so has clear relevance to our topic.

These extra inevitable demands on foster parents' time and energy are being recognized in other practical ways. The Community Evaluation Rehabilitation Center of the Walter E. Fernald State School is developing a foster care program for children with multiple handicaps from community families, in lieu of institutionalization. This project includes a relief worker in the planning to give the foster parents officially sanctioned and reliably predictable time off (Peters, 1974). The Home Training Program (a form of foster home care for children already placed in the institution) of the Elizabeth Levinson Center in Bangor, Maine provides respite care on a regular monthly basis as well as on demand for emergencies (Valentine, 1974). Arrangements of this kind not only give foster parents much needed relief but also underscore the fact that they are doing the equivalent of a normal paid job and are subject to employment conditions generally prevailing in our society.

The new uses to which foster care may be put makes it especially important to accentuate its professional aspects. In addition to serving the more familiar type of dependent, neglected, or abandoned child who has been removed from parental care, it may now cover the very different contingency of another sort of child whose specific disabilities create management problems that are beyond the capacity of his natural family, no matter how well intended or devoted they may be (Lobenstein, 1973). Because of the unusual and specialized nature of the fostering task involved in such situations it is essential to implicate the foster parents as equal colleagues with other agency staff in making plans for a child's placement (Reistroffer, 1972). It also means that the natural parents must be equally involved in arrangements, from their moment of inception until they are concluded, in order to forestall the psychological and social amputation of child from family, and to make subsequent reassimilation, *if feasible,* easier and part of a dynamic continuum. This new development will inevitably trigger off conflicts about the respective roles of biological and foster parents which the latter will have to be prepared to deal with appropriately, and this task will be easier to handle if their own expectations are to be professional caretakers rather than surrogate parents. George (1971) has tried to sharpen up this role distinction by designating foster parents as "foster care workers."

From another angle it is important that foster care for the more obviously retarded child has a strong visible professional image, to allay the reluctance natural parents may have about delegating their child's care to individuals rather than to an impersonal institution. Placement in the latter has been traditionally seen as an acceptable measure within the medical treatment model but foster care is not vested with equivalent professional status. Instead it carries implications of failure in the parental role which have serious practical concequences, in that many parents seeking residential placement for their child are adamantly resistant to foster care even though it is clearly most suitable for his needs.

Associated with this is the understandable fear concerning the long term security of foster home placement. Families who decide to place a severely handicapped child on a permanent basis are often unable to envisage foster care as a long term arrangement equally reliable as an institution, but are inclined to see it as an informal arrangement liable to land the child back in their laps. The other side of the coin is that ordinary households who have an interest and aptitude for fostering a handicapped child may be hesitant to do so, in case the placement is not successful and there is no guaranteed way of their being relieved of the child, since specialized foster care is in short supply and institutional waiting lists extremely long.

Both of these points have relevance to another recurring theme in the foster care field, namely the length of stay within a specific placement, duration of time in care, and the limbo-like character of foster care, which is the concern of several of the studies on foster care for normal children. Maas' followup study (1969) of his earlier work (Maas and Engler, 1959) indicated that over half the children were in foster care for over 6 years. This finding was supported by the Massachusetts survey (Gruber, 1973) where the average length of stay was over 5 years. Both reports showed that for a substantial number of children ongoing contact with their families of origin was extremely tenuous and their chances of being reassimilated during their growing up period very slight indeed. Maas (1969) found that this risk was higher for children of low intelligence from families of low socioeconomic status.

The philosophy on this aspect of care provides an interesting contrast to that of the studies done in England on foster home recruitment (Gray et al., 1957) and placement prediction (Parker, 1966), which both used a minimum stay of 5 years in one foster home as their criteria of success. Although professional opinion in the United States has not generally favored long term foster care, we should start to reassess its potential value for our specialized population. The sustained long range rehabilitative programming needed by the more incapacitated child, and the abrogation of parental responsibility that often accompanies placement, suggest that it could be a very valuable resource. The same consideration often applies to the midly retarded in care who can be predicted, from research evidence, to come from socially disorganized homes which, even with help, cannot be guaranteed to reassimilate them. The crucial factor in both instances is that placement is done on a planned rather than haphazard crisis-precipitated basis (Andrews, 1970; Madison and Shapiro, 1970). Efforts must also be made to keep the foster parents consistently motivated to manage this type of child, and a carefully structured program of professional guidance and support to help them in the difficult task is essential.

However, this policy may not be without its conflicting elements that will need to be considered and resolved. Fanschel (1961), for instance, noted that foster mothers who enjoyed taking care of children with higher dependency needs had difficulty separating from them when the placement terminated, and were also inclined to an overprotective reinforcement of their dependency. While this latter tendency can be detrimental to a handicapped child if overdone, it could be exploited to advantage provided it is explicitly geared to the exceptional needs of a disabled child; these must be specifically identified by professional rehabilitative criteria. Another interesting facet to this problem of length of stay and foster parent roles comes from England. Fletcher (1974) found that short term foster mothers were more easily able to assume the professional role because of the decreased motivation to be substitute parents that is inherent to their situation.

My final point has sociological rather than psychosocial significance. Studies done in America, England, and France (Gray and Parr, 1957; Gruber, 1973; Maas and Engler, 1959; Tomkiewicz, Biny, and Zucman, 1971) have generally revealed that the majority of foster parents come from the middle to lower socioeconomic strata of society, have modest standards of living and limited education. For many of them fostering is an intuitive task, the skills which have either accumulated as a residual by-product of raising their own children or by osmosis. If the residual pool of foster parents continues to be recruited mainly from sections of society manifesting these sociocultural characteristics we shall face the delicate task of trying to graft professional insights and specialized child-rearing skills and techniques onto this essentially untutored constituency, as well as redefining its role along much more consciously professional lines. Fanschel (1966) suggests that:

in a rapidly moving society such as our own there is an increasing tendency for middle class orientations to take hold, even among unskilled blue collar workers.

This trend may significantly reduce the numbers of old style foster parents, compelling the child welfare field to look to other better educated social categories for recruitment of homes. It is unlikely, however, that this new resource group can be mobilized in sufficient strength right away and in the interim our attention must be directed to developing specialized skills in the existing body of personnel (Dorgan, 1974).

This should not present great difficulties because it is in line with modern social welfare policy that favors utilizing the particular skills of community residents irrespective of their level of formal education. The past decade has seen an impressive reservoir of untapped human resources that are susceptible to training in a variety of educational, professional, and social parameters (Ayres, 1973; Birnbaum and Jones, 1967; Brager, 1965; Epstein and Shainline, 1974; Pearl and Riessman, 1965; Specht, Hawkins, and McGee, 1968). In our particular field there has been a number of innovative projects utilizing personnel of this kind. The Retarded Infants Service of New York initiated a pilot program for training low income, unskilled personnel to work with retarded children and their families under the surveillance of professional staff in an outpatient clinic (Budner, Arnold, and Goodman, 1971). The more recent home stimulation program reported elsewhere by Levenstein (1974) utilized workers from the same backgrounds as the families they were helping, and the Child Development Program of Mississippi was organized and run entirely by local women working with professional consultation (Levin, 1967).

Along the same lines a report in Child Welfare (Garber, 1970) describes a program for recruiting foster homes from low income families in the Spanish Harlem section of New York City, emphasizing the precise and carefully planned system for recruitment and three successive stages of screening and training. Since a high proportion of dependent neglected children coming into care are from ethnic minority groups, the question of mobilizing homes that can provide a continuation of the child's native cultural milieu is crucial. In the studies done by Columbia University and the Commonwealth of Massachusetts the percentages of children of minority group origin were respectively: black c. 40 and 14.8; Spanish speaking 31 and 1.8. Approximately 20% of the children in the Child Welfare League study were from non-white families. Some mildly retarded children are likely to be included in these figures, as they are in every child welfare caseload.

Equally important, however, is to ensure that such homes are capable of understanding the special needs of an intellectually or emotionally disabled child and able to develop the skills necessary for his rehabilitation. Two different research projects speak to this point. Fanschel (1966) noted that Negro foster mothers were more apt to have originated from rural backgrounds and made the comment that "on the basis of PARI scores foster mothers from rural backgrounds had a distinctive tendency to avoid communication with the children." This characteristic represents a rather serious deficit in relation to foster children with retarded development because consistent verbal stimulation from articulate adults is an important factor in their mental and social development.

In the Milwaukee Study, Heber and his associates (1972) reported that the children in their control group were significantly behind their experimental peers in language and the social and cognitive functioning associated with this basic skill. They attributed this lag to the fact that the main source of interpersonal communication for the control group was their siblings or intellectually disadvantaged and not very articulate mothers.

Before closing I will briefly summarize the principal points on which this paper's main thesis rests. The first is that foster home care for intellectually handicapped children is an invaluable social resource that has been hitherto largely ignored. Its suitability for this type of deprived child is suggested by the following points:

1. Its close resemblance to ordinary family living exerts a normalizing influence on the social development of a retarded child and assists in promoting his integration into the normal fabric of society. This is in contrast to the institutional experience which is alienating and reinforces deviance.

2. A substantial proportion of all children in foster care come from environments which have socioeconomic characteristics similar to those associated with a high incidence of mild mental retardation: overcrowding, poorly educated parents, low and unreliable income, and pathological patterns of parenting.

3. To compensate for their earlier depriving experience these socially deprived and intellectually stunted children require an exceptionally understanding and stimulating form of substitute care if they are to develop normal emotional, cognitive, and social functioning.

4. Foster family care lends itself to this sort of therapeutic regime provided the undermentioned conditions are met:

   (a) a systematic attempt must be made to select foster parents whose personality and perception of the fostering role indicate a special aptitude for managing handicapped children with the behavioral characteristics associated with organic impairment or social deprivation or both combined.

(b) foster parents must be given substantial and consistent support in this challenging and unfamiliar task, through professional guidance in how to handle a retarded child and ongoing consultation to reinforce their efforts.

(c) the basic caretaking task of fostering must be supplemented by a battery of services, generic or specialized according to need, that will promote the physical, psychological, educational, and social development of the child.

(d) wherever feasible the child's natural parents should be kept in touch with the child and his foster home and the foster parents should be encouraged to support the formers' interest in their child's progress.

5. The professional character that is now being ascribed to the function and role of foster parenting has a special relevance for mentally handicapped children due to the specialized skills and knowledge implicit in their care, and increased demands on time. Both points demand a reassessment of rates of reimbursement.

6. This inevitable trend may encounter problems because traditionally foster parents have been recruited from lower socioeconomic segments of society, with modest living standards and limited education.

7. Until a more intellectually sophisticated constituency of foster parents can be recruited from other social classes, a concerted effort is needed to educate the current reserve of foster parents about the special needs of intellectually handicapped children, including more subtle ones such as stimulation of speech and language.

8. The example of involving endogenous personnel in community social welfare programs has demonstrated that lack of formal education need not be an insuperable barrier to efficient practice if appropriate training and guidance are available.

9. Research on foster home care for organically impaired children has indicated that specialized training within this setting can substantially improve their developmental progress.

10. Research on intact children remaining in their own socially deprived homes has highlighted the sort of intervention that is effective in neutralizing retarded cognitive and social development.

11. This intervention relates to stimulating interpersonal relationships and interchange and was carried out in an informal numerically small setting. The inference to be drawn is that a well planned, carefully structured foster care program which combines these insights and techniques with regular child-rearing practices could have a similar preventive or rehabilitative impact.

The ideas, practical facts, and research perspectives that I have projected reinforce my frequently reiterated contention that foster family care is both feasible and desirable for the intellectually disadvantaged child. Although proven research from our field is slim, we can claim enough accumulated general evidence to carry our point and to indicate ways in which this emerging service can be extended, improved upon, and even garnished with innovative experiments that may benefit foster care as a whole.

REFERENCES

Adams, M. 1970. Foster care for mentally retarded children. How does child welfare meet this challenge? Child Welfare 49(5): 260–269.

Anderson, S. 1971. Foster parent organizations: How a provincewide federation was formed in British Columbia. Child Welfare 50(7): 408–412.

Andrews, R. G. 1968. Permanent placement of Negro children through quasiadoption. Child Welfare 47(10): 583–586.

Arnold, I. L. 1971. Report on a project to establish a central facility for recruitment of foster care homes for mentally retarded children. Presented at the 9th Convention of the American Association for Mental Deficiency, Houston, Texas.

Ayres, A. Q. 1973. Neighborhood services: People caring for people. Social Casework. 54(4): 195–215.

Birch, H. G. and L. Belmont. 1961. The problem of comparing home rearing versus foster-home rearing in defective children. Pediatrics 128:(6) 956–961.

Birch, H. G., S. A. Richardson, D. Baird, G. Horobin, and R. Illsley. 1970. Mental Subnormality in the Community: A Clinical and Epidemiological Study. Williams & Wilkins Company, Baltimore.

Birnbaum, M. L. and C. H. Jones. 1967. Activities of the social work aides. Social Casework 48(10): 626–632.

Bishop, E. B. 1959. Family Care boarding homes. Am. J. Ment. Defic. 63: 703–706.

Brager, G. 1965. The indigenous worker: A new approach to the social work technician. Social Work 10(2): 33–40.

Braginsky, B. M. and D. D. Braginsky. 1974. Stimulus response: The mentally retarded. Society's Hansels and Gretels. Psychol. Today 7(10): 18–30.

Budner, S. A., I. Arnold, and L. Goodman. 1971. The plan and the reality: Training and utilization of paraprofessionals for services to the retarded. Am. J. Public Health 61(2): 297–307.

Burgess, M. and J. Morrissey. 1964. Family care and adoption of retarded children. Annotated bibliography. Ment. Retard. Abs. 1: 332–333.

Burgess, M. and J. Morrissey. 1966. Family Care. An Annotated Bibliography, pp. 17–21. Fresno State College, Fresno, Calif.

Crutcher, H. 1940. Family care of mental defectives. Am. J. Ment. Defic. 45: 127–138.

Doll, E. 1940. Foster care for mental defectives. Training School Bulletin 36: 193–205.

Dorgan, M. 1974. Initiating a program of foster parent education. Child Welfare 53(9): 588–593.

Encyclopedia of Social Work. 1965. 15th Issue. National Association of Social Workers, New York.

Epstein, N. and A. Shainline. 1974. Paraprofessional parent-aides and disadvantaged families. Social Casework. 55(4): 230–236.

Fanshel, D. 1961a. Specializations within the foster care role: Part I. Child Welfare 40(4) II: 19–23.

Fanshel, D. 1961b. Specializations within the foster care role: A Research Report. Part II. Foster parents caring for the "acting out" and the handicapped child. Child Welfare 40(4): 19–23.

Fanshel, D. 1966. Foster Parenthood: A Role Analysis. University of Minnesota Press, Minneapolis.

Fanshel, D. 1971. The exit of children from foster care: An Interim Research Report. Child Welfare 50(2): 65–81.

Fletcher, M. 1974. Short-stay foster parents. Soc. Work Today 4(22): 698.

Galaway, G. 1972. Clarifying the role of foster parents. Children Today 1(4): 32–33.

Garber, M., Sister Mary Patrick, and L. Casal. 1970. The ghetto as a source of foster homes. Child Welfare 49(5): 246–251.

Garrett, B. L. 1968. Foster care for children. Children 15(1): 32–34.

George, V. 1970. Foster care, theory and practice. Routledge and Kegan Paul, London.

George, V. 1971. Foster care workers. Soc. Work Today 2(17).

Goffman, E. 1961. Asylums: Essays on the Social Situation of Mental Patients and other Inmates. Anchor Books, Doubleday, New York.

Gray, P. A. and E. A. Parr. 1957. Children in Care and the Recruitment of Foster Parents. Social Survey SS. 249, London.

Green, M. L. 1973. A Comprehensive Evaluation of the Home Care Program. Children's Aid Society of Metropolitan Toronto.

Gruber, A. 1973. Foster Home Care in Massachusetts. A Study of Foster Children—Their Biological and Foster Parents. Commonwealth of Massachusetts Governor's Commission on Adoption and Foster Care.

Gruber, A. 1974. The Developmentally Disabled Child in Foster Home Care. Commonwealth of Massachusetts Governor's Commission on Adoption and Foster Care and Boston Children's Services Association.

Heber, R., H. Garber, S. Harrington, C. Hoffman, and C. Falender. 1972. Rehabilitation of Families at Risk for Mental Retardation Progress Report. Rehabilitation Research and Training Center in Mental Retardation, University of Wisconsin, Madison.

Hollis, J. H., E. Gorton, and E. Chester. 1967. Training severely and profoundly developmentally retarded children. Ment. Retard. 5:(4) 20–24.

Howe, S. G. 1851. On the training of idiots. Am. J. Insanity 8(2): 97–116.

Hunzeker, J. 1971. Organization and implementation of foster parent associations. Child Welfare. 50:(8) 468–476.

Jenkins, S. 1969. Separation experiences of parents whose children are in foster care. Child Welfare 43(6): 334–340. Commentary, 340–354.

Jenkins, S. and E. Norman. 1969. Families of children in foster care. Children 16(4): 155–159.

Jenkins, S. and E. Norman. 1972. Filial Deprivation and Foster Care. Columbia University Press, New York.

Justice, R. S., J. Bradley, and G. O'Connor. 1971. Foster family care for the retarded. Management concerns for the caretaker. Ment. Retard. 9(4): 12–15.

Kuenzell, M. 1938. Training of the mentally deficient in foster families. Proc. Amer. Assoc. Ment. Defic. 43(2): 135–139.

Kugel, R. B. and M. H. Parsons. 1967. Children of Deprivation: Changing the Course of Familial Retardation. U.S. DHEW Social and Rehabilitation Service. Children's Bureau, Washington, D.C.

Kushlick, A. 1970. Residential care for the mentally subnormal. R. Soc. Health J. 5: 225–261.

Leven, T. 1967. The child development group of Mississippi: A hot sector of the quiet front in the war on poverty. Am. J. Orthopsychiatr. 38(1): 139–145.

Levenstein, P. 1974. A message from home: Findings from a program for non-retarded, low income preschoolers. This volume.

Lobenstein, J. H. 1973. Guidelines to Community Living Systems for the Developmentally Disabled. Wisconsin Department of Health and Social Services, Division of Mental Hygiene, Bureau of Mental Retardation.

Maas, H. S. 1969. Children in long-term foster care. Child Welfare 18(6): 321–333.

Maas, H. S. and R. Engler. 1959. Children in need of parents. Columbia University Press, New York.

Mackay, H. A. and M. Sidman. 1968. Instructing the mentally retarded in an institutional environment. *In* G. Jervis (ed.), Expanding Concepts in Mental Retardation. Charles C Thomas, Springfield, Ill.

Madison, B. and M. Schapiro. 1970. Permanent and long-term foster family care as a planned service. Child Welfare 49(3): 131–136.

Mamula, R. A. 1970. Developing a training program for family caretakers. Ment. Retard. 8(2): 30–35.

Mamula, R. A. 1971. The use of developmental plans for mentally retarded children in foster family care. Children 18(2): 65–68.

McAvoy, J. 1974. Personal communication.

Meisels, J. and M. Loeb. 1956. Unanswered questions about foster care. Soc. Serv. Rev. 30: 239–246.

Modell, J. and T. K. Hareven. 1973. Urbanization and the malleable household: An examination of boarding and lodging in American families. J. Marr. Fam. 35: 447–479.

Morrissey, J. R. 1966. Status of family-care programs. Ment. Retard. 4(5): 8–11.

Nirje, B. 1969. The normalization principle and its human management implications. *In* R. B. Kugel and W. Wolfensberger (Eds.), Changing Patterns in Residential Services for the Mentally Retarded. President's Committee on Mental Retardation, Washington, D.C.

Parker, R. A. 1966. Decision in Child Care. A Study of Prediction in Fostering. George Allen and Unwin, London.

Pearl, A. and F. Riessman. 1965. New Careers for the Poor. Free Press, New York.

Peters, K. 1974. Integrated foster home care (Eunice Kennedy Shriver Center; Gaebler School–Children's Unit; Family and Youth Resource Center). Personal communication.

Pratt, C. 1966. Foster parents as agency employees. Children 13(1): 14–22.

Reistroffer, M. E. 1972. Participation of foster parents in decision-making: The concept of collegiality. Child Welfare 51(1): 25–28.

Roberts, P. 1974. Boarding-out allowances and fostering practices. Soc. Work Today 5(8): 238–242.

Rosen, D. 1974. Inservice Training Objectives for Family Care Training Home Parents. Macomb-Oakland Regional Centre, Michigan.

Rosendorf, S. 1972. Joining together to help foster children. Children Today 1(4): 2–6.

Shah, C. P. 1971. Assessing needs and board rates for handicapped children in foster family care. Child Welfare 50:(10) 588–592.

Shah, C. P. and S. Poulos. 1974. Assessing needs and board rates for handicapped children in foster family care: Progress Report. Child Welfare 53:(1): 31–38.

Shapiro, D. 1972. Agency investment in foster care: A study. Social Work 17(4): 20–28.

Shapiro, D. 1973. Agency investment in foster care: A followup. Social Work: 18(6).

Shyne, A. W. 1969. The need for foster care. Child Welfare League of America.

Specht, H., A. Hawkins and F. McGee. 1968. Case Conference on: The Neighborhood Subprofessional Worker. Children: 15(1).

State of Illinois Department of Public Health. 1965. The Waiting List: A Study of the Mentally Retarded.

Stedman, D. J. and D. H. Eichorn. 1964. A comparison of the growth and development of institutionalized and home-reared mongoloids during infancy and early childhood. Am. J. Ment. Defic.: 69: 391–401.

Stein, A. and M. Susser. 1960. Families of dull children. J. Ment. Sci. 106: 1296–1319.

Stein, Z. A. and M. Susser. 1969. Mild mental subnormality: Social and epidemiological studies. Res. Publ. Assoc. Res. Nerv. Ment. Dis. 47: 62–85.

Tizard, J. and J. Grad. 1961. The Mentally Handicapped and Their Families. Oxford University Press, Oxford.

Tomkiewicz, S., Y. Biny, and E. Zucman. 1971. Le placement familiale specialisé pour enfants arriérés profond. Rev. Neuropsychiatr. Infant. 19(3–4): 165–175.

Vail, D. J. 1966. Dehumanization and the Institutional Career. Charles C Thomas, Springfield, Ill.

Valentine, S. 1974. Elizabeth Levinson Center Home Training Program. (Personal communication).

Vaux, C. 1935. Family care of mental defectives. Psychiatr. Q. 9: 349–367.

Wolfensberger, W. 1973. Normalization: The principle of normalization in human services. National Institute of Mental Retardation, Ontario, Canada.

Wolins, M. 1963. Selecting foster parents. The ideal and reality. Columbia University Press, New York.

Intervention in Infancy:
A Developmental Approach

Howard L. Garber

For any number of reasons we as a nation have increasingly committed ourselves to a concern for human welfare. There does not need to be any justification for such a concern because what is there of greater value to a nation than its people and their welfare? However, as the scientific educators responsible for successive generations, we are required to obtain justification, empirical justification, in order to guide our nation's hands in implementing its programs. To a considerable extent we have been distracted from our charge by reacting emotionally and radically to issues. In particular, I speak about the issue of cultural-familial mental retardation, a mild form of mental retardation, the etiology of which has generated both some of the most intense controversy and some of the poorest research.

Our most recent efforts originate from our social concerns of the 1960's for the disadvantaged. In good conscience, we could not allow poverty and inequality to exist in our nation.

When we began with our latest efforts at early intervention or early enrichment, we had a large number of reasons to justify them. Those with a strong social conscience said that an enriched environment through compensatory education would wipe out the effects of disadvantagement and the deprived environment. No one asked if all poor people are mildly retarded, which, by far, they are not. Others of us offered the critical periods hypothesis, based mainly on research in animals, as evidence that early stimulation was necessary, otherwise there would be irreversible damage. No one questioned that although we were in some ways similar to animals, how many ways were we different, nor did they compare the degree or quality of deprivation in the animal studies which was far more extreme and not usually in the cognitive domain. Further, we have continued to confuse epidemiology and etiology, i.e., even though there are certain epidemiological characteristics in common to individuals, some of whom show low IQ scores, this does not mean all should have the same IQ.

In our work at Wisconsin we committed ourselves to the examination of the epidemiological characteristics of the mildly retarded. By and large, the intensity of the controversy regarding the origins of this form of retardation results as much from the inadequacy of the research as it does from the emotion of human social problems.

Central to the controversy is the source of the excess prevalence of low IQ's in low socioeconomic status (SES) populations. We undertook to examine the problem by first surveying a part of the inner city of Milwaukee which showed the highest number of educable mentally retarded (EMR) school children, in order to develop information regarding the epidemiological characteristics of one such low SES population.

We found a differential course of intellectual development for children born to mothers with above 80 IQ and those born to mothers with below 80 IQ. After the infancy period, the children whose mothers had IQ's greater than 80 maintain a steady intellectual level, while the children whose mothers had IQ's less than 80 show a marked progressive decline.

This trend toward a decline in measured intelligence for children in disadvantaged environments is widely accepted as a general characteristic of a "slum" environment population, yet these data indicate that the trend of declining intelligence with increasing age is restricted to offspring of low IQ mothers. In fact, we found the variable of maternal intelligence was the best single predictor of low intelligence in the offspring. The data indicated that the lower the maternal IQ, the greater the probability of the children scoring low on intelligence tests, particularly for the offspring of mothers with IQ's below 80.

These observations from our survey data suggested our strategy to approach the prevention of sociocultural mental retardation by attempting to rehabilitate the family rather than simply the individual retarded adult. The ability to select families "at risk" for mental retardation on the basis of maternal intelligence made it possible to initiate a program to study "high risk" children before they became identified as mentally retarded.

The project has differed from previous enrichment or intervention efforts in at least two ways. First, the subjects were selected on the basis of epidemiological studies which indicated that children born to parents who are poverty stricken as well as of low intelligence are at high risk of being identified as mentally retarded. Secondly, the program began in very early infancy and continued intensive intervention until the children enter first grade. The intention of the program was the prevention of mental retardation, in contrast to attempts at remediation (See Heber, Dever, and Conry, 1968).

PROJECT DESIGN

As babies were born in our study area, trained surveyors employed by the University of Wisconsin Survey Research Center contacted the family within a few weeks of birth and completed a family history questionnaire which included a vocabulary screening test administered to the mother. Those mothers falling below a cutoff score on the vocabulary test were administered a full scale WAIS (Wechsler Adult Intelligence Scale) by a trained psychometrist. A maternal IQ on the WAIS of less than 75 was the selection criterion in accumulating a sample of 40 families. These 40 families were assigned to either the Experimental or Control condition.

The design of the Milwaukee Project study for the Experimental group called for a comprehensive family intervention effort beginning in the home. The Experimental program (e.g., see Garber and Heber, 1973; Heber, Garber, Hoffman, Harrington, and Falender, 1972) was composed of two components: 1) the infant, early childhood stimulation program and 2) a maternal rehabilitation program. Intervention into the experiential environment of the Experimental infants began as soon as was feasible after birth (within 6 months) and has continued to the age of regular school entry, approximately 6 years. Its objective was to provide experiences potentially lacking in the natural environment of the "high risk" infant which could facilitate the development of cognitive skills.

Obviously, I can discuss only a portion of the data. Let me begin with some of the findings of our evaluation of the maternal rehabilitation program.

Essentially, the occupational rehabilitation component of the maternal program appears to have been quite successful to date. Some problems remain for the mothers with respect to their adequacy in homemaking skills and some problems remain in the care and treatment of their children. After an initial training phase was finished, resulting in a number of the mothers becoming employed, the maternal program shifted to an increased emphasis on training in general care of family and home, budgeting, nutrition, and food preparation.

In one part of our effort to evaluate the effectiveness of the intervention effort on the mother, i.e., the maternal rehabilitation program, we used a series of measures to provide information about differences in the home life, attitudes, self-concept, etc., between the Experimental and Control mothers, as well as a study of how these mothers interacted with their children.

Interestingly, we found no differences between the Experimental or Control families on any section or scale of the Home Inventory. There were no between-group differences in father absence, size of family, mobility, nature of the extended family, books and materials in the home, or any other variable. This finding is particularly interesting in view of the between-group differences found on our measure of maternal attitudes. The Experimental group mothers showed attitudes which encouraged reciprocal communication between themselves and their infants. The result of this attitude is manifested in the mother's engaging in verbally informative behavior as compared to non-risk-oriented physical behavior. In contrast, the attitudes of the Control mothers showed no relationship to the behavior observed when in interaction with their child.

These findings are comparable to Gordon's (1969) results, which revealed similar attitudinal and behavioral changes as a result of participation in a stimulation group, but revealed no changes in the home environment. Further evidence for changes having occurred in the mother's behavior because of her involvement in the maternal rehabilitation program appears in our measure of "locus of control." Locus of control gives an indication of how the mother views her ability to control her life. We found the Experimental mothers showed a greater tendency to an internal locus of control, indicating she felt more in control of environmental consequences. Such feelings of control are transmitted to the child, whose self-confidence is thereby enhanced.

Such changes in the mother's attitude are significant because they signal not only an increased sensitivity both to their needs and the needs of their families, but indicate an increased receptivity to the suggestions of respected and responsible outsiders. There can now be, therefore, more hope for these parents to make use of community resources.

Thus, it seems that as a result of the long term family rehabilitation effort of families with a retarded mother, there has been a change in the motivation of these families to seek out, participate in, and profit from the rehabilitation resources in the community. It appears that the organized maternal rehabilitation program, together with continued guidance by the parent coordinator, has effected the changes observed in the mothers, including job and homemaking skills. The mothers have shown significant changes in self-concept; they are more positive and more self-confident, and they have shown an increased sensitivity to the needs of their children in terms of nutritional and health care.

ASSESSMENT OF BEHAVIOR

The assessment of the children's development consisted of a comprehensive array of standardized and non-standardized measures of behavioral development. The schedule of measurement included 1) developmental schedules of infant adaptive behavior, 2) experimental learning tasks, 3) measures of language development, 4) measures of social development, and 5) standardized tests of general intellectual functioning.

The Experimental and Control infants were on an identical measurement schedule, with assessment sessions every 3 weeks. The particular measures administered at a given session depended upon the predetermined schedule of measures for that age level. A particular test or task was administered to both Experimental and Control infants by the same person. The testers were not involved in any component of the infant stimulation or maternal program.

The Gesell Developmental Schedules were administered to both the Experimental and Control infants, beginning at age 6 months. Through the 14-month testing, the groups responded comparably on the four schedules: Motor, Adaptive, Language, and Personal-Social.

At 18 months the Control group began to fall 3 to 4 months below the Experimental group, although still performing close to Gesell norms. At 22 months the Experimental group scores were from 4½ to 6 months in advance of the Control group on all four schedules, while the Control group had fallen below the Gesell norms on the Adaptive and Language schedules.

Beginning at 24 months, increased emphasis was given to experimental, direct measures of learning and performance, as well as to the standardized tests of general intelligence.

We were concerned with delineating some of the characteristics of early learning behavior that either facilitate or interfere with performance. We wanted information on the response patterns or behavior styles, and how a child's simple response choice may reveal his general response tendencies and his ability to select and order incoming stimulation. Furthermore, the role of this part of the assessment program was to provide more comprehensive information about cognitive growth than we were deriving from the IQ tests and various language measures.

We employed a series of tasks including color form and probability matching. Our concern was with the child's strategy of responding, i.e., did he adopt a developmentally sophisticated strategy of consistent responding, either to color or form, or did he respond randomly, or perseverate to position? These learning measures have been administered every year since the children were 2½ years of age.

These data revealed more developmentally sophisticated patterns of responding by the Experimental group. Generally, the Experimental children have utilized a response strategy which demonstrates that they tend to alter successive responses according to the outcome of their previous responses. The Controls showed a tendency to perseverate on a response, e.g., to choose one position or to alternate from left to right, indicating that the children are insensitive to previous feedback and make no attempt to adopt a strategy. Moreover, they are more passive and less enthusiastic in their response behavior, which is partly responsible for their low level of attention to the details of the stimulus display.

Thus, a response behavior which is important for future performance, the strategy or style of responding, appears to develop in the early years. The Control children's strategies may interfere with their later learning while the style of the Experimental children should facilitate problem-solving performance.

The ability to differentiate various aspects of a stimulus display is not limited to these kinds of experimental learning tasks. We have also administered several other kinds of tasks requiring analytical sorting ability and a demonstration of developmentally sophisticated perceptual learning skills. With such tasks as the Matching Familiar Figures Test (MFFT), the Kansas Reflection-Impulsivity Scale (KRISP), the Sigel Sorting Task (SST), and the Embedded Figures Test (EFT), we could observe whether the apparently developmentally sophisticated performance by the Experimental children on our learning tasks was reliable. Indeed, the Experimental children tended to analyze the stimulus array in a more thorough manner before responding than did the Controls, which resulted in a significant performance difference superior to the Controls. Consistently, on all the measures employed, the Experimentals exhibit developmentally more sophisticated behavior, typically associated with older, middle SES children. The Experimental children demonstrate the use of strategy behavior in how they approach a stimulus display. For example, they are more field independent: they are able to ignore misleading cues and analyze the stimulus display more efficiently. This is the same behavior basic to performance on the SST. The Experimental children use sortings based upon categorization and description, while in contrast, the Controls not only tend to use strictly relational sorting, which requires a minimal analysis of the display, but also find difficulty in verbalizing the type of sorting they have done.

Our second major area of concern was the children's development of language and the measurement of this development.

The first statistically significant difference in language development appeared at 18 months on the language scale of the Gesell Developmental Schedules. By 22 months the Experimental children were over 4 months ahead of the norms and 6 months ahead of the Controls. This trend of differential language development has continued in an even more dramatic way. In fact, some of the most striking differences in the performance of the Experimental and Control children are reflected in the research measures of language performance.

The analysis of free speech language samples indicated that the Experimental children between the ages of 1½ and 3 years say more in conversation. Using this measurement technique, we find that it is not until 3 years of age that the Control group produces a vocabulary comparable to that of the Experimental children.

At the age of 3 years we began to test imitation with a sentence repetition test. This is an easily administered instrument which requires the child to repeat 34 sentences of varying length and grammatical complexity. The children's replies are analyzed for omission, substitutions, and additions. By the age of 4 years the Experimental group made significantly more exact repetitions than the Control group, whose performance is comparable to the Experimental group's performance at 3 years. This same performance differential continues through age 6 years.

Also beginning at age 3 years, we tested grammatical comprehension with a modified version of a test developed by Bellugi-Klima (Fraser et al., 1963). This measure is a game in which the child manipulates objects in order to demonstrate his ability to understand 16 grammatical constructions. (The tester gives instructions for the child to fulfill a command, i.e., "Put the ball *under* the cup.") The results show that the Experimental group's performance is significantly superior at all age levels tested (3, 4, 5, and 6 years). Their grammatical comprehension is 1 year or more in advance of the Control group.

Our standardized language instrument has been the Illinois Test of Psycholinguistic Abilities (ITPA), which has been administered to all children at 4½ and 6½ years of age. The results have supported the differential performance of the Experimental and Control groups on our other measures. At 6½ years the difference between groups found at 4½ has been maintained: the Experimentals performed 6 months above their mean chronological age (CA) while the Controls were 11 months below their mean CA. Mean Psycholinguistic Quotient (PLQ) for the Experimentals was 108.3 versus 86.3 for the Controls, a difference of 22 points.

In describing the language behavior of the Experimental children, one would find them expressive, verbally fluent, and, according to the ITPA, linguistically sophisticated. They speak their own dialect and they are proud of their own speech and yet their performance is developmentally advanced on sophisticated tests of the English language.

The next area we have given attention is mother-child interaction. In the mother-child interaction most sophisticated behavior such as the initiation of problem-solving behavior by verbal clues and verbal prods, or the organization of tasks with respect to goals in problem-solving situations, etc. is done by the mother. However, where the mother has a low IQ, the interaction is more physical, less organized, and less direction is given to the child. Indeed, while this was the case in the Control group mother-child dyads, it was quite different in the Experimental dyads.

We found that the Experimental dyads transmitted more information than the Control dyads, and this was a function of the quality of the Experimental child's verbal behavior. The Experimental children supplied more information verbally and initiated more verbal communication than the Control dyads. The children in the Experimental dyad took responsibility for guiding the flow in information, providing most of the verbal information and direction. The mothers of both dyads showed little differences in their teaching ability during the testing session. However, in the Experimental dyads, the children structured the interaction session either by their questioning or by teaching the mother. Also, the Experimental mothers appeared to be modelling some of the behaviors of their children. Consequently, they used more verbal positive reinforcement and more verbal responses.

As a result, a developmentally more sophisticated interaction pattern has developed between the Experimental children and their mothers, which contributed to faster and more successful problem completion.

It became apparent from these data that the intervention effort has effectively changed the expected pattern of development for the Experimental dyads. Moreover, the result of what might be termed a reciprocal feedback system initiated by the child has been to create a more sophisticated and satisfying interaction pattern in the Experimental dyad. In fact, as previously noted, the Experimental mothers seem to have undergone changes in attitude and self-confidence. The Experimental mothers appear to be adopting more of an "internal locus of control," an attitude that "things happen" because of their decisions and actions and not purely by chance or fate.

The mother who feels more in control of environmental consequences is more likely to regulate her behavior towards her child in a way that is compatible with her attitudes, whereas the "external locus of control mother" sees herself as being "put-upon" by her children. Thus, the intensive stimulation program, in which the Experimental children participated, has benefited both the children and their mothers by broadening their verbal and expressive repertoire.

INTELLIGENCE TEST SCORES

A clearer picture of the differences between groups is given by the results from standardized measures of intelligence.

We have presented the summary data from intelligence testing in Figure 1. For Figure 1, the data from 12 to 21 months is derived from the Gesell developmental Schedules, standardized intelligence scores from Cattrell and Binet tests beginning at 24 months until 66 months, Wechsler Preschool and Primary Scale of Intelligence (WPPSI) scores at 72 months, and Wechsler Intelligence Scale for Children (WISC) at 84 months.

As can be seen in Figure 1, the mean IQ of the Experimental group is consistently more than 20 points above that of the Control group. For example, at 60 months the

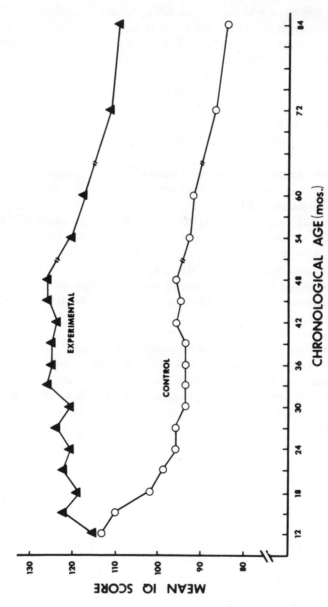

Figure 1. Summary data from intelligence testing.

mean IQ of the Experimental group was 118, in comparison to the Control mean IQ of 92, a difference of 26 points. We have calculated the mean IQ at the 72- and 84-month points: WPPSI scores at 72 months are complete; WISC scores at 84 months represent less than the complete samples.

These latter points are particularly important, for they are some of the first evaluative data obtained since the children have been out of the intense educational program and on their own. There was a drop in the scores of both groups: those of the Experimental children to 111 (SD = 8.7) at 72 months and 106 (SD = 8.2) at 84 months, and those of the Control children to 87 (SD = 11.4) at 72 months and 85 (SD = 8.9) at 84 months. It is particularly significant that even with the decline in test scores, a large difference in mean IQ has remained: at 84 months there is still a 20+ point difference between the groups.

The remarkably high mean IQ attained by the Experimental group has diverted attention from the more fundamental concerns of the Intervention program. The accelerated IQ performance, albeit to a rather remarkable level, is a *by-product* of the intensive educational program *and was expected to occur but not to be maintained.* The hypothesis of our study predicted normal intelligence levels if intervention was effective in mitigating intellectually depressing environmental events which are presumed to occur during early development.

We remain encouraged, therefore, by these preliminary results, for thus far the Experimental children have shown no indication that their intellectual functioning will decline to the retarded mean IQ level of their siblings and mothers. This decline is already in evidence for the Control group, whereas it seems likely that the Experimental group will level off at a mean IQ of about 100.

The tendency for declining IQ in this population is further illustrated by the comparison data in Figure 2. The bottom dotted curve is the original survey group. The longer solid line curve is the mean IQ of siblings from both the Experimental and Control families. In general, these older siblings of our actual subjects show the same trend toward declining IQ's with increasing age, as do the actual Control children, whose mean IQ data are represented in the shorter solid line curve. Thus, it appears that we have prevented in the Experimental group the relative decline in intellectual development that we now see in the Control group, and that we have found in the siblings of both groups and in the original survey groups.

We tested nearly all of the siblings of the subjects in both the Experimental and Control groups. This represents the third testing of these children over a 6-year period. Although the testing has not been completed, the performance data available so far appear to substantiate evidence for declining performance found for this sample in the two previous testings. At the 84- and 96-month mark, for example, the mean IQ's for the siblings are 85 and 83 respectively, levels entirely comparable to those of the Control group children.

These data answer two pivotal questions about the study at this time. The first question concerns the basis for predicting that these children are at risk for retardation. Can we be sure that the downward trend in IQ for this population is reliable? The data we

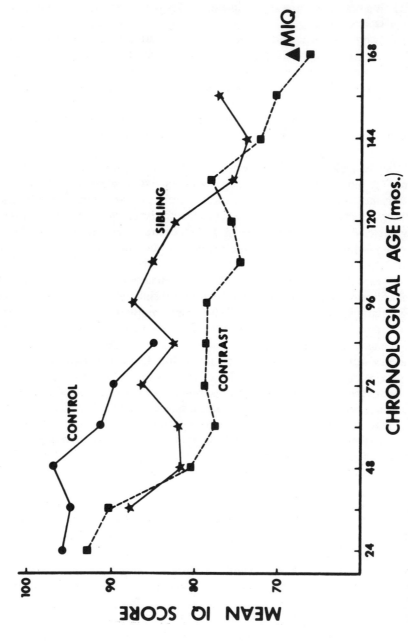

Figure 2. Comparison data.

have just reported indicate that it is: successive samplings from three generations of offspring have shown the same tendency for IQ's to decline. The second major question at this time is whether the present differential performance favoring the Experimental children is merely an artifact of training. The strength of the present differential performance is borne out not only by standardized test scores and performance levels on the various experimental tasks, but also by the differential behavior patterns displayed by the two groups. The behavior pattern of the Experimental children demonstrates a sincere and concerted effort to work at the task, while the Control children have tended to be apathetic and to perseverate in their responses.

Still it remains for time to tell us what will be the eventual course of development of our Experimental and Control children. What we know at this time is that we have prevented from occurring in the Experimentals, thus far, a level of retarded functioning that we see in the Controls and all of the siblings. There is, therefore, far more hope for these children to have normal intellectual development than there would have been without intervention.

It is difficult to draw conclusions at this time, especially with regard to the more general question about the effectiveness of early education programs. All of the children in our program are not through even 1 year of school. Moreover, our study needs to be replicated by others, with considerable attention to delineating additional variables. In the light of the results from so many other studies in one way or another similar to the Milwaukee study, it is obviously necessary to be cautious in our interpretation of data. Furthermore, it would seem that in spite of this large number of studies, there remains a confounding of the major questions regarding the efficacy of early education programs. I think it would be valuable at this time both to reevaluate the basis for the concept of compensatory education and to reorientate our thinking with regard to the long term social and educational implications of the current emphasis on early education.

The concept of intervention, as it has been practiced, is partly derived from the social deprivation hypothesis, which is the assumption that the problem of development for some children is that their early environment is not "normal." Intervention, then, requires that a normal environment be conceptualized and implemented to correct the environment and make it normal, and in turn make the child become normal. However, time after time, intervention efforts, in one form or another, have seen performance gains dissipate. Why do these IQ gains dissipate? The major contention by early education opponents is the obvious genetic inferiority of the experimental population. Well, there are *at least* five or six other reasons besides genetic failure that can be offered for the loss in performance scores, and in addition, they contain some important concerns about the success of early intervention efforts.

1. To begin with, there is a problem with our detection techniques. The reaction to the genetic or nature argument has been quite radical, even to the point where some will tell you the genes have nothing to do with development. Obviously genetics is a major influence, perhaps even the major influence in development, but we do not really know how it works yet. It is not only considerably easier to study development from the

environmental side, but there is a tremendous amount of research that remains to be done about the environmental influences on development.

However, we must not ignore the fact that the detection technique for our population of concern, the high risk child, probably ends up including many kinds of children, including a number of children who can not be helped because of their genetic inheritance. Let me consider for the moment the genetic factor as a threshold factor such that it predisposes some individuals to the ills of the environment, but not all to the same extent. Take the threshold concept together with what we do know about the distribution of the gene pool. Then we can assume that some proportion of the high risk population indeed have "genetic failure" and will not be able to achieve normal levels of intellectual development, and some others at the threshold will succumb to the ills of their environment, sooner or later, even if they get some help. Therefore a number of cultural-familial mentally retarded (CFMR) or high risk children will fail in spite of intervention or compensatory education. We must improve our detection techniques if we are to determine which children will benefit by intervention. Some children may be better served by a different form of education. The key to the threshold factor may be partly in the IQ level of the mother, from which we can determine a probability risk factor, e.g., based on IQ and regression to the mean.

One way that this genetic threshold factor works to help dissipate performance scores is that many, or maybe even all, the children in a program develop in the normal range. Later, however, a proportion will fail because they cannot and could not sustain normal intellect, except as a performance artifact during intense training and because of the unreliability of testing, while another few at the threshold cannot sustain normal levels because of the environmental disadvantagement (both physical and psychological) and succumb later. Then the remainder who maintain normal performance are those individuals who do not need help and of course, those who once helped can maintain normal development. These latter individuals, at least, should be very carefully examined. With additional research we should be able to diagnose the high risk factor more thoroughly and better provide for each kind of child's development. We need to examine much more closely those who succeed and those who do not, and not accept simply the mean group performance as the criterion for program success.

Moreover, the use of a statistical definition for mental retardation, even though the individual may be diagnosed as being only "at risk" for retardation is a very serious concern. Labeling a child "at risk" for retardation can jeopardize his future as much as if he were actually labeled retarded. Thus, even in the name of prevention, we must be careful that we do not statistically transcend the rights to privacy and freedom of the individual. In fact, some responsible Black leaders have already cautioned against any suggestions for a national compulsory preschool program if selection is based on something even as impartial as a statistical criterion of probability. Intervention for the sake of normalization must not become an obsession even if it is in good conscience. We do not really know what normal is anyhow, or whether it would really be any good.

Therefore poor detection not only results in diluting the measured effectiveness of early programs, but as Kirp (1974) points out, "adverse school classification may result in two kinds of injury; educational ineffectiveness and stigmatization of the children."

2. A second factor in performance loss I mentioned briefly before has to do with the methodology of IQ tests: the problems with which all of us are all too familiar. This factor can explain some performance loss for example, because scores usually reach spuriously high levels.

There is a host of problems with both the validity and the reliability of tests, especially those for younger children. In programs of early stimulation, intensive training and repeated testing lead to inflated scores because the instruments are sensitive to the training, because of test sophistication, because in longitudinal assessment cognitive and language skills change and are measured differently, because the initial levels of the children vary, often considerably, and for that matter are not typically controlled, and because of the influences of cultural factors. We need both better tests and more comprehensive assessment programs in order better to understand development on an individual basis. At the same time, however, there is good reason to believe that the tests are valid and the poor performance is in part the result of the individual's deprived or inadequate early life experience. Also, interim learning, between childhood and adolescence, can significantly change performance which is reflected in low retest correlations. The implications of this factor for human development are being ignored, and are remarked upon only in terms of test-retest reliability. I shall mention this again below.

3. A third problem area is the nature of the preschool curriculum, i.e., what is learned in preschool is not the same as what is learned, or has to be learned, in school. The research in this area is minimal and poor. There is need for some coordination and organization between preschool and regular public school.

We have been so concerned with early education and the manipulation of the immediate ability structure that we have tended to ignore the consequences of the other aspects of an individual's life, most of which is yet to come. In most cases, there is a marked difference for the child between his preschool and school experience (e.g., in terms of teacher-child ratio, available equipment, flexibility of curriculum). This difference can have a traumatic effect when no provision is made for the transition into a markedly different experience.

4. The fourth problem is with the poor schools, with the poor teachers and the poor curriculum, and the prejudice, and so on. This is something we can correct now. I think we need to reorganize our total school system and our concept of education, particularly where we find high problem areas.

With respect to teachers and teaching, I would like to make some suggestions:

a. I think all teachers need training in special education during their school training, and through their professional teacher careers.

b. I think that even with better training as we now know it, we need to examine the differences between teachers, successful and unsuccessful, and to put this information to work to make better teachers.

c. I think we need to put more emphasis on improving teaching in the early years. As a result I think we will keep more children in school longer and minimize many of the problems occurring at the higher levels.

d. I think teachers are going to have to go back to walking the beat to learn about the neighborhood and the families. Of course, we will need smaller classes and more teachers.

Most often good teachers are good only so long as the children are good. When there is a deviation from the text book pupil, the majority of teachers is lost. Teacher training programs are not facing up to their responsibility, and where they are, it will be several years before even the basic needs are met. Furthermore, it may well be that some special kind of tutoring is needed more or less continuously for certain children, and this should be carefully coordinated with the home.

5. A fifth factor is the continued oppressive environment. After the preschool program is over, the mother (and father) are still retarded and are inadequate in helping. There is a growing negative influence of the peers, increasing negative self-concept with increasing awareness of the world, a decrease in whatever appreciation exists in the relevance of school, and continued health and nutrition problems.

This factor requires, in part, the realization that some families will continuously and actively need some kind of support to help them through crises as well as through daily living, which in itself is a continuous crisis.

6. My sixth factor is the behavior system that develops in the high risk child because of the nature of his development. This behavior system is actually antagonistic to the system of behavior skills and response patterns appropriate and required if there is to be successful performance in school and life in general. It includes what is referred to in the literature as a failure syndrome. We find it in the cognitive or behavior style, developing already in the preschool years. It is the passive-compliant behavior referred to by Hess and Shipman (1967). It is the rigid, perseverative response style of problem-solving referred to by Bresnahan and Shapiro (1972) and Kofsky and Osler (1967), and so on. Moreover, it develops before the child enters school and in school it is reinforced.

In one way, however, if such a behavior system exists, there is the possibility that it can be undone. Previously, we have talked about early education as a necessity because disadvantagement and deprivation cause irreversibly poor development, but such a notion as an *antagonistic behavior system* could provide hope for recovering many individuals.

7. The ultimate effectiveness of any intervention effort must rest on the fundamental principles of learning, i.e., if there is to be more than a transitory effect the psychological experience must demonstrate true learning, which can be defined as a modification of behavior possessing some measurable extension in time (See Clarke, 1968).

As Clarke (1968) points out, the effectiveness of such an early learning experience will and should vary according to the length and potency of the experience, the age of the learner, etc., and what is more, it should vary according to the amount, intensity, and duration of subsequent reinforcement. Why should we assume, considering all of our research into learning psychology, that there will be no extinction or learned interference of the behavior we worked so hard to develop but somewhat foolishly think will sustain itself in a non-supportive environment? The potential for learning may remain while the dissipation of the IQ scores and performance scores we see are actually reflecting several things: e.g., reinforced "bad" behavior, non-reinforced appropriate behavior, the dissipation of motivational components of learning, etc.

We have assumed that the influences on early development are critical, because the effects are essentially irreversible. Yet, as Clarke (1968) for example, has pointed out, there is room, if you will, in the correlations for a lot of learning to go on between the early years and adulthood. In other words, we may be victims of our reaction to both our research and that of others regarding the prepotence of early stimulation. We are too quick perhaps to accept the developmental failure in some children as due either to the failure of intervention or to the failure of heredity. There is a lot more room between the two. Clarke has carefully pointed out a number of instances in the data where there is inconsistency between early development and later development, particularly when in the intervening years there has been a generally positive environment. For example, Clarke and Clarke (1975) point to Skeels and Skodak's follow-up of that now classic study in which one member of the contrast group has performed quite well in adult life. After the early years in the barren institution he was transferred to a school for the deaf. There he received some special care from a matron of his cottage. His life is remarkably different from all of the other contrast group members. Clarke scores this as one for the effect of a positive environment after the early years, and also points out that in the Skeel's experimental group there was a positive environment maintained all through the adolescent years as well.

It would seem, therefore, that in the long run a single early intervention effort must be inadequate since it ignores the effects of later training, poor schools, the continuance of a non-supporting environment and so on.

When we consider the effectiveness of early intervention in preventing mental retardation, we can mean that we have helped to avoid in some individuals a low IQ score early in life, but we can not say yet if we have helped an individual to be self-sufficient, independent and to have a normal life. In the first instance, it appears that we can prevent mental retardation, but in regard to the latter situation, we shall either have to wait until adulthood to see if intervention has been effective for high risk individuals in preventing retardation, or reevaluate the evidence upon which we have based our hope that early intervention is sufficient to prevent mental retardation. If we do, then we may well see that we need to consider the possibility for modifying behavior in the middle years.

I have tried to identify some areas needing attention, all of which are relevant to the overall problem. They can become tools for sorting out the kinds of individuals who are at risk for retardation. If we do not consider our data in this way we will continue to be shocked every time we add up all the time and effort seemingly wasted when accelerated performance is not maintained and IQ scores are dissipated by the first years in school.

For example, even if you accept the threshold factor as an additional variable, it is still just that. Its value is methodological, in the immediate sense, and only if we recognize its value for our research can we hope for any value in the ultimate sense:

educationally and socially. In other words, to accept the hypothesis that a portion of the children who participate in some kind of early education or early stimulation project will fail in spite of their training should not for one moment excuse our responsibility as educators to improve the lot of all children. No matter how much money we have spent on early education in the hope that it would make all children normal, it is still nowhere near too much, even if only a portion of them benefit.

For the most part, we have been lax in sorting out the kinds of children in early education programs: which children succeed and which fail, how do they compare to non-early education program participants, how does success vary with the schools they enter, etc. Therefore the condemnation in summary fashion, by some, of the early intervention efforts must be partly blamed on ourselves as researchers. In research the hardest data to defend against criticism is your own, and we have not as a field of research done a particularly good job with ours. Early intervention efforts should not be distracted by theory building, particularly since we are and will continue to be pursued by others in and out of our field to derive the theoretical implications of early intervention in regard to heredity. Obviously heredity is important, but the problem now is to strengthen the arguments regarding the influence of other variables: psychological, environmental, social, etc., such that the opponents of early education will have to develop their own data, rather than use ours against us. Although some excellent research is now being done, the preponderance of research has been poor.

It is not education's job to relegate individuals to a level of development, but to help each individual realize his potential, to help him make a contribution to society, and to provide him with the tools that will make him independent and help him to lead as normal a life as he wants to.

REFERENCES

Bresnahan, J. and M. M. Shapiro. 1972. Learning strategies in children from different socioeconomic levels. *In* Advances in Child Development and Behavior, H. W. Reese (ed.), 7: 32–77. Academic Press, New York.

Clarke, A. D. B. 1968. Learning and human development. Br. J. Psychiatr. 114: 1061–1077.

Clarke, A. M. and A. D. B. Clarke. 1975. Genetic-environmental interactions in cognitive development. To be published in the third edition of Mental Deficiency: The Changing Outlook, A. M. Clarke and A. D. B. Clarke, (eds.). Methuen, London. In press.

Fraser, C., U. Bellugi, and R. Brown. 1963. Control of grammar in imitation, comprehension, and production. J. Verbal Learning Verbal Behav. 44: 7–52.

Garber, H. and R. Heber. 1973. The Milwaukee Project: early intervention as a technique to prevent mental retardation. The University of Connecticut Technical Papers. The University of Connecticut, Storrs, Conn.

Gordon, I. J. 1969. Early child stimulation through parent education. Final report of the Children's Bureau for Development of Human Resources. College of Education, University of Florida, Gainesville, Florida.

Heber, R., R. Dever, and J. Conry. 1968. The influence of environmental and genetic variables on intellectual development. *In* Behavioral Research in Mental Retardation, H.

J. Prehm, L. A. Hamerlynck, and J. E. Crosson (eds.), University of Oregon, Eugene, Oregon.

Heber, R., H. Garber, S. Harrington, C. Hoffman, and C. Falender. 1972. Rehabilitation of families at risk for mental retardation. Annual report. University of Wisconsin, Madison, Wisc.

Hess, R. and J. Shipman. 1967. Cognitive elements in maternal behavior. *In* Minnesota Symposia on Child Psychology. J. P. Hill (ed.), Vol. I, pp. 58–81. University of Minnesota Press, Minnesota.

Kirp, D. L. 1974. Student classification, public policy and the courts. Harvard Ed. Rev. 44: 7–52.

Kofsky, E. and S. F. Osler. 1967. Free classification in children. Child Devel. 38: 927–937.

Message from Home: Findings from a Program For Non-Retarded, Low Income Preschoolers[1]

Phyllis Levenstein

All children in western society require enough education to prepare for the vocational complexities of a technologically based civilization. Yet children from low income families frequently have trouble with academic tasks when they enter elementary school. This is a cross-cultural phenomenon hardly confined to this country (Davie, Butler, Goldstein, 1972; Thorndike, 1973). Several years ago the mounting, and indeed hierarchical, nature of this educational handicap as the low-income child proceeds through higher and higher school grades was identified as a "cumulative academic disadvantage" (Deutsch, 1965) whose roots are already established by the time the child has entered school, compounding whatever inadequacies the school has in dealing with the problem.

Children at the high end of the mental retardation continuum, the mildly retarded, enter school at a lower level of academic functioning than those from the low income population. Thus, they may demonstrate the cumulative academic disadvantage earlier in their school careers. However, the educational problems of the low income and the mildly retarded populations appear very similar, with considerable demographic overlap between the two populations (Stein and Susser, 1970) suggesting that a preventive program found effective thus far for the low income population may have similar hopeful implications for the mildly retarded.

---

[1] Supported by U.S. Department of Health, Education, and Welfare: Children's Bureau, National Institute of Mental Health, and Office of Education; and by the Carnegie Corporation of New York, the Foundation for Child Development, The Grant Foundation of New York, and the Rockefeller Brothers Fund.

FAMILY AS COGNITIVE RESOURCE

The prevention or amelioration of mild retardation may ultimately rest where society has its beginnings, the home. This chapter is, most literally, a message from home, both in its abstract sense and in some of its concrete manifestations. In this study, the data come from the homes of 93 low income mothers who have been actively engaged in the Verbal Interaction Project's Mother-Child Home Program in their own homes to prevent educational disadvantage in their 2- to 4-year-olds. By age 2 years, before the program began, the mean group IQ of their children, reported in many studies to be normal in infancy for all populations in this country (e.g., Bayley, 1965), had apparently already started on the downward slide to a point above the edge of retardation but one predictive of educational disability. That trend was reversed when the mothers became more directly involved in the education of their youngsters than had been hitherto allowed by poverty and insufficient awareness by the parents of the importance of incorporating simple verbal interaction techniques into their play with the children.

The family, embodied in the dyadic mother-child relationship within the home, appears to provide a potent system to foster the child's cognitive development. To release the power of that system, certain crucial conditions appear necessary in an intervention program. These conditions seem to be met in the Mother-Child Home Program. That they are not all present in other systematically researched programs with a home visit component (Gordon, 1969; Gray and Klaus, 1965; Karnes et al., 1970; Payne et al., 1973; Schaefer, 1969; Weikart and Lambie, 1968) is no more surprising than that school-based programs also differ greatly from each other. But the differences among such programs in long term effectiveness has been recently noted (Bronfenbrenner, 1974).

THEORETICAL FOUNDATIONS OF THE MOTHER-CHILD HOME PROGRAM

The theoretical base of all parent-involving programs includes a belief in the profound importance of parents as primary change agents or teachers of their own children. The Mother-Child Home Program (MCHP) added to this the idea that the "teaching" should occur at home through concept-building verbal interaction, in play around permanently assigned, perceptually rich and ordered stimuli, and should be embedded in the affective matrix of the child's most enduring relationships, especially that with his mother. Further, the intervention to assist this process must be through means which provide maximum motivation for mother and child (and home intervener-visitor). It should cause minimum disturbance to their relationship, especially since the optimum time in the child's life for the intervention is between ages 2 to 4 years, partly because of the peaking then of that relationship.

These propositions were developed from an interdisciplinary, far flung network of theory and investigations concerning the disparate, yet often intertwining, roles in the child's intellectual development of language, of early family relationships and motivations, of sensory-motor development, of play, and of optimum age periods for intervention.

Most fundamental was a belief in the critical role of language in cognitive development and in the assumption that man's most distinctive attribute is his capacity both for abstract conceptualization and for symbolization of abstract thought through language. Sapir (1962) was among the first to pronounce language a perfect symbol system, the vocal actualization of the human tendency to see reality symbolically. He posited that language may originate through vocalization of the "abstract attitude," summarizing numerous concrete perceptual-conceptual encounters. This theme was expanded philosophically by Cassirer (1944) but with so many references to empirically based evidence (from the language of a central Brazil Indian tribe to the early learning of Helen Keller) as to make his discussion almost as much a far ranging review of actual observation as theoretical reflection. Werner's seminal theories of symbol formation (e.g., 1967), closely related to Cassirer's, were also supported by the work of investigators such as Vygotsky (1962) and Rapaport (1945), who cited experimental evidence for the development and greater efficiency of language as a verbal symbol system for abstracting and summarizing common traits among unlike experiences, as compared to the compilation of many concrete instances to convey a general concept. Bruner et al. (1966) provided a useful, stage-referenced framework for viewing the development of symbolization in children by dividing the attainment of symbolic representation of reality into three steps: the enactive (to about the end of the 1st year of life), the iconic (imaginal predominance which may persist in very primitive societies as a dominant mode of presentation into adult life), and finally, the symbolic, which begins when the child, who formerly employed words only as labels for immediate experience, uses words to generalize the common attributes of many such experiences and so uses words as verbal concepts.

Brunner had noted in an earlier article (1964) that the process of internalizing language as the child grows older probably depends on his interaction with others in what was called by Brown the Original Word Game (1958). Bruner commented that this may end up by being the Human Thinking Game, a phrase which neatly encapsules what may well be the most important underlying function of language, superseding its communication aspects. A similarly economical summarization is furnished by Sigel's (1971) "distancing hypothesis," which elaborated Werner's observations on the function of language as an aid to abstract conceptualization. Sigel took the theory a step further by proposing that children need practice in using language to represent increasingly distant referents for their intellectual development, those most out of sight, for example, requiring the most abstract use of language.

The emphasis on the importance of language interaction with others leads inevitably to considering the relationship of language-induced conceptual growth within the family, and the contrasting cognitive development of middle and low income children. Bernstein (e.g., 1961) was perhaps the most influential of those who suggested that patterns of limited abstract language (and syntax) exchanges in British families of working class children might account for parallel limitations in the children's intellectual development. When Hess and Shipman tested this idea with the families of Black American middle class and poor children, they found enough support in their data to conclude: "The structure of the social system, and the structure of the family, shape communication and language; and language shapes thought and cognitive styles of problem solving" (1965).

Whatever the constrictions on concept-building verbal interaction in low income families, the studies detected no significant differences in the amount of warmth and affection present in middle income and low income families. Observers like Bernstein, and Hess and Shipman, had noted a tendency in low income families toward "status" orientation rather than "person" orientation, but this was a difference in social, interpersonal style, not in feeling. It was obvious that healthy mother-infant attachment was developing through the interaction of mother and child, regarded as essential to this basic attachment by many investigators of family relationships, notably Bowlby (1952) and Ainsworth (1967; 1973). Increased parent-child interaction was also functional for monkeys (Harlow, Harlow, and Suomi, 1971; Ruppenthal, Harlow, Eisele, Harlow, and Suomi, 1974). Indeed, the quality of that interaction may well influence the child's development of competence (Ainsworth and Bell, ERIC reports). This appears to be especially true in relation to language development (Eveloff, 1971). It is noteworthy that an early home-centered intervention program (Irwin, 1960) demonstrated its effect on language through the mother's reading stories to her child, thus utilizing the enhancement of mother-child interaction in its conative as well as cognitive aspects. Many mothers, particularly those of the college-educated, middle income group, carry on such "intervention" spontaneously, as part of a now well known "hidden curriculum" of the family. Increased cognitive development results for the child. Schaefer, indeed, suggested that early, basic informal home education be given a name, "Ur-Education," and be recognized as a legitimate supplement to conventional academic education (1970). Implicit in the concept is the inseparability of the mother-child emotional interchange from the cognitive interaction, and intermingling of cognitive stimulation and deepening of the attachment between the mother and child. The futility of trying to separate the two factors conceptually in their deprivation consequences seemed amply demonstrated by Bronfenbrenner in his meticulously documented review of the effects of early deprivation on humans and animals (1968).

One of the most remarkable and valuable features of "Ur-Education" is that the Teacher (mother) and Student (child) involved in it need little incentive beyond the interaction itself and the activities attached to it, so strong is the motivation provided by what Bronfenbrenner once noted as "that irrational affect called love." But certainly the interaction, and especially the verbal interaction, will be very much reinforced by stabilizing a "situation" (Cazden, 1970) rich in potentialities for encouraging conversation and it concomitants. Such interaction also effects the development of sensory-motor skills in the child through "reafference" (sensory feedback accompanying self-initiated movement, described by Held, 1965), as well as the utilization and encouragement of the child's intrinsic motivation to master the environment through play (Hunt, 1961, 1969;

White, 1963). The child's intrinsically motivated play, self-motivated and self-rewarding (Ellis, 1973; Millar, 1968), is probably also self-teaching. The youngster's problem solving, using materials with many motor, perceptual, and conceptual properties matched to his maturational stage, can, in itself, benefit cognitive development (Bruner, 1972; Hunt, 1969). It seems obvious that the "situation" should be playful, and centered about durable, attractive toys and picture books owned by the child so that they can be used again and again, with constant reinforcement of the intermingling of the conative and the cognitive (especially the verbal).

The interaction between mother and child, embedded in the attachment relation between them is a major component of the cognitive stimulation of the child. This stimulation probably begins almost at the infant's birth. If verbal interaction is a central feature of the cognitive stimulation, the full effects of the cognitive stimulation begin to have their impact as the child is emerging from the stage of sensory-motor learning into the period of what Cassirer called "reflective intelligence," a stage signaled and reinforced by beginning language development. This occurs at about age 2 years. This age also coincides with heightened attachment to mother (Maccoby and Feldman, 1972), greatly increased curiosity about the environment, and developing sophistication in the use of limbs for walking and manipulation, in short, with a near explosion of rapidly developing skills and feelings. By about 4 years the child has incorporated the main effects of this revolution and begins to be impatient to turn to experiences outside of the mother-child relationship (Bronfenbrenner, 1968). If the cognitive possibilities of this age period have for some reason not been fully exploited, perhaps because of the constrictions put on parents by poverty, then the child's intellectual development may already have taken the downward turn which is so handicapping to academic achievement (e.g., Bloom, 1964). Logic and the evidence seem overwhelmingly to indicate that intervention to prevent that cognitive dip should occur between the ages of 2 and 4 years, as the optimal, and possibly critical, period for preparation for school learning.

RESPONSE FROM THE PROFESSIONAL FIELD

A little more than a decade ago, tremendous impetus was given to the whole field of early childhood intervention research by the appearance of Hunt's review of the role of environment in the growth of individual intelligence (1961). It promised new hope for the prevention of the personal tragedy and social problems generally posed by the educational disadvantage of the poor. Attempts were made to provide, in carefully structured preschool learning centers, duplications of what one major investigator aptly called the "optimal learning environment": the child in his own home within the context of a warm and nurturant emotional relationship with his mother or a reasonable facsimile thereof, under conditions of varied sensory and cognitive input (Caldwell, 1967).

The long term effectiveness of such centers, as well as of the home-based programs mentioned earlier, was often found to be social rather than cognitive when follow-up results, sometimes made equivocal by research termination (e.g., Karnes et al., 1970; Palmer, 1969), were available. As the need to intervene directly with parents became more evident, the formation of parent education groups rose to prominence as an intervention method, but their impact on the low income population was disappointing (Chilman, 1973).

Curiously, an intervention program which appeared to have great impact and was impressively documented as having lasting effects into the adult years, originated in the 1930's in an institution for the retarded. The "parents" in this program (retarded, adult females) were given little training or direction, yet provided for the children ample conative, verbal, and cognitive stimulation (Skeels, 1966). This seemed a broad hint to the Verbal Interaction Project not only to operationalize through the Mother-Child Home Program the theoretical propositions elaborated above, but to introduce the program into the family with the least disruption possible to child and family. A careful attempt was made to work out a delicate balance in the program between building sufficient structure to turn theory into concrete program reality, while preserving to a maximum degree the autonomy of the mother and the intactness of the family's interpersonal relationships. The general aim of the ur-education to be fostered by the program could be summarized by a paragraph from Bronfenbrenner's recent review of early childhood education research:

> In the early years of life, the psychological development of the child is enhanced through his involvement in progressively more complex, enduring patterns of reciprocal, contingent interaction with persons with whom he has established a mutual and enduring attachment (Bronfenbrenner, 1974).

THE PROGRAM

The Mother-Child Home Program (MCHP) was created and researched by the Verbal Interaction Project (VIP), starting with a pilot study in 1965, (Levenstein and Sunley, 1968). The program had developed by 1968 into its current form after its first full year of operation in 1967 to 1968 (Levenstein, 1970). Its goals are cognitive and affective. They are aimed at supporting the mother (and through her, the family) in fostering the intellectual and socioemotional development of her child. The following general conditions were met by the program as a means of actualizing its theoretical base. It:

1. was conducted in the home,
2. addressed the mother-child dyad as an interacting, mutually supportive social system,
3. began when the child was 2 years of age and continued to age 4 years,
4. actively involved the mother without teaching, counseling, or subtly coercing her,
5. assigned permanent toys and books as self-motivating, stable curriculum materials as the focus of verbal interaction techniques,
6. employed these toys and books to demonstrate to the mother a simple, structured, yet flexible curriculum of verbal interaction techniques,

7. provided non-didactic home interveners to model the curriculum techniques and use of the curriculum materials.

Extrapolating the social implications of the theory, the VIP anticipated feasibility for implementation outside of the research project by keeping the program simple and eliminating requirements of formal education, previous special skill, or particular charisma for the home visitors.

The method has been described in detail (Levenstein, in press; Levenstein and Levenstein, 1971; Levenstein, 1973; and in a repetitive, cumulative curriculum called "The Toy Demonstrator's VISIT Handbook," Levenstein, 1970–1974). Briefly, the MCHP consisted of 92 semi-weekly, half-hour Home Sessions spread over 2 years, by interveners called "Toy Demonstrators." The latter were trained in non-didactic techniques to show a mother, by participating in play sessions with her and her child together, how to interact verbally to enhance the child's conceptual and socioemotional development. Commercially available toys and books were used as the curriculum materials permanently assigned to the child. The Toy Demonstrator, after involving the mother early in the Home Session, gradually faded into the background and the mother was free to adopt the modeled behavior, or not, as she wished.

The 46 Home Sessions during each year roughly followed the local school calendar for a total of about 7 months from October to May. Altogether the program required about 23 clock hours of the dyad's time with a Toy Demonstrator each year, aside from the time mothers might spend outside of sessions playing and reading with their children each day (suggested but not stressed to the mothers). The cost of thus giving low income mothers the materials and access to the techniques of the "hidden cognitive curriculum" of some middle income families, was estimated at about $400 a year for each child. The cost could be kept relatively low because it included the free manpower of the mothers acting as their children's main teachers and the free working space contributed by the participating families.

The Toy Demonstrators were paid former mother-participants of high-school education and unpaid woman volunteers, usually college educated. They were trained together in an initial training workshop and in weekly group supervisory conferences throughout the program year. Twelve books and eleven toys, selected on 26 explicit criteria by VIP staff, were given to the mother for the child each year in a planned weekly sequence of increasingly complex curriculum materials. The Toy Demonstrator modeled verbal interaction techniques and interpersonal behavior functional to learning, utilizing the toys and books (called Verbal Interaction Stimulus Materials, or "VISM") as the structured cognitive curriculum with a different guide sheet for each VISM. The "curriculum" actually consisted of a list of concepts and behaviors which remained the same on every guide sheet but were illustrated and elaborated differently by each toy or book which formed the content of each new guide sheet. The chief lesson conveyed to the Toy Demonstrator in supervision was that the program was aimed more at the mother than at the child. The main and enduring responsibility for the child's education at this age must be the mother's, not the Toy Demonstrator's. Therefore, ability to eliminate herself early as an active participant from Home Sessions was her best sign of success.

RESEARCH DATA: THE MESSAGE FROM HOME

Since 1968, each September a new group of children was pretested by the Verbal Interaction Project (Cattell, Binet, Peabody Picture Vocabulary Test) and enrolled in the full, 2-year MCHP, to be post-tested 2 years later after completion of the program. By June of 1973 the 93 mothers and children mentioned earlier had participated in the MCHP in four successive yearly cohorts (1968, 1969, 1970, 1971). All were of low income with the usual cluster of demographic attributes characteristic of this socio-economic status and with the cohorts ranging in ethnic composition from 70% to 100% Black.

The research of the program's cognitive and socioemotional effects included the goals indispensable to intervention evaluations: tests of internal validity ("Does it work in the research project?") and of external validity or generalization ("Will it work in other settings?").

The measures used to answer these questions were standardized and project-developed tests of the cognitive and affective development of treated and untreated children.

The research went beyond these goals, however. It was concerned with the *feasibility* (including quality control) of the program in other settings and with other low income populations than those of the project. It was concerned, too, with the *desirability* of the program, not only in terms of its attractiveness to the target low income population, but in relation to the values of a democratic society. Since the issues of feasibility and desirability are of pivotal importance to the social usefulness of an intervention program no matter what the significance of the basic research findings, the VIP attempted to carry a triple burden from the beginning. The program had to be developed for acceptability to the target population and to society, for the possibility of broad and perhaps national implementation, and the research data had to warrant dissemination.

The results for the four cohorts of children entering the 2-year Mother-Child Home Program from 1968 to 1971 indicate that the program did indeed seem to work. The children showed significant IQ gains and above norm IQ's by the end of the 2 years (Table 1).

These short term results remained stable for the two cohorts (1968 and 1969) which had entered kindergarten and first grade at the time of the fourth annual follow-up study conducted from November 1972 to March 1973. The mean IQ was 105.4 for the group in which the majority had reached first grade, and at 113.3 for the group in which most were in kindergarten. On the other hand, a group of first grade children (Group C_5), recruited in 1972 for participation as an "after only" untreated group with no previous contact with the VIP but matched to the 1968 treated cohort (Group T_1) on the same low income criteria met by the treated groups, demonstrated a much lower IQ mean of

Table 1. Comparisons of treated and control groups, by IQ 1968–1973

Entry year	Group and program	Pretest	Number of months after pretest					Control group
			8	20	28	40	52	
1968	T_1	IQ 90.4	101.8^a	109.0^a	108.3^a	107.3^a	105.4^a	
	$N = 21$	SD 9.1	9.0	8.5	11.1	11.6	13.0	
1969	T_6	IQ 88.8	105.6^a	108.2^a		113.3^a		
	$N = 23$	SD 13.8	16.5	15.6		15.9		
1970	T_8	IQ 90.0	106.4^a	106.9^a				
	$N = 23$	SD 9.6	15.1	13.1				
1971	T_9	IQ 91.6	105.8^a	108.1^a				
	$N = 26$	SD 13.0	9.8	9.4				
1972	C_5	IQ						91.0
	$N = 30$	SD						11.5

[a]p is less than 0.01.

91. (The low income criteria were eligibility for low income housing, residence in rented housing, parents not above the 12th grade education or semi-skilled occupation.)

Moreover, when the two matched groups were compared with each other, the treated T_1 group was found to be significantly superior to the untreated C_5 group, not only in general IQ but also in other cognitive areas: verbal IQ, reading achievement, and arithmetic achievement (Table 2).

The two groups also differed significantly in socioemotional coping skills (on an instrument developed by the Verbal Interaction Project), as rated by their classroom teachers, who were unaware of the treated or untreated status of the children. The instrument was the "Child's Behavior Traits," a 20-item, criterion-based, Likert-type scale yielding a summative score ranging from 20 to 100, with a score of 60 indicating generally "moderate" presence of coping skills. The treated T_1 group scored significantly higher than the untreated C_5 group on the CBT. (The split-half reliability coefficient for the CBT was 0.97, indicating the very high internal consistency of the instrument. It is currently being tested for inter-rater reliability and for validity.)

These findings must be viewed with some reserve, since they were based on a quasi-experimental research design (Campbell and Stanley, 1963), with subjects not randomly selected, but recruited from the populations of two low income housing projects and from referrals by local social agencies (e.g., social workers of Headstart programs and public health nurses). All families had to meet low income criteria and the acceptance rate of eligible families was high, at least 80% each year. The fact remains that without random assignment of individuals to treated and untreated groups, the conditions

Table 2. Comparison of matched two-year treated (T_1) and untreated (C_5) groups on cognitive and socioemotional measures at follow-up 1972–1973

Measures	T_1 Group 1968 2-year treated			C_5 Group 1972 tested "after only"			Difference of means t		
	N	Mean	SD	N	Mean	SD	Score	value	p <
Stanford-Binet and WISC: general IQ	21	105.4	13.0	30	91.0	11.5	14.4	4.18	0.01
Peabody picture vocabulary test: verbal IQ	21	97.6	13.6	30	89.7	11.6	7.9	2.22	0.05
Reading standard score,[a] wide range achievement test	15[b]	103.9	7.7	30	95.0	12.9	8.9	2.45	0.02
Arithmetic standard score,[a] wide range achievement test	15[b]	106.0	13.3	30	95.0	13.9	11.0	2.55	0.02
Child's behavior traits, raw score: socioemotional coping skills	21	77.2	16.7	30	66.1	15.9	11.1	2.41	0.02

[a]As calculated in Schaie and Roberts, 1970.
[b]Six Ss were too young for the age-based standard scores.

of a true experiment were missing and thus it cannot be said with a high degree of confidence that the differences between groups were due only to treatment effects. In view of the possible import of the findings, this caveat must be taken seriously and not as a standard academic disclaimer. The basic requirement of random assignment of subjects to different conditions is now being met for 50 children (25 treated and 25 untreated) in the 1973 to 1974 cohort, and it remains to be seen whether similar outcome differences within and between treated and untreated groups will be found.

REPLICATION OUTSIDE OF THE VERBAL INTERACTION PROJECT

To study the generalizability of the method's effectiveness, the Mother-Child Home Program is now being tested outside of the research project in ten states of the country, from Alaska to Maine. The research project's Demonstration Center has been guiding its replication at 30 locations in a variety of organizational settings, such as schools, family service agencies, churches, mental health clinics, and American Indian reservations. The replications provide feedback of demographic data on their samples and of before-after IQ's to measure the replications' effectiveness and thus answer the question of the external validity of the model program's effectiveness. At the same time, the replications provide a practical test for the feasibility of applying the program in settings with fewer resources than the research project. For example, a replication is not likely to be staffed by personnel with the specialized skills and long program experience of the research project's team.

IQ data have been analyzed from the first eight replicators (1970 to 1972). Their combined pre-post IQ differences after 1 and 2 years were similar to those of the model program's sample, using the same measures (Cattell and Stanford-Binet): about 15 IQ points for combined replication results after 2 years, and about 17 points for children in the model program during the same year. Again a word of caution is in order. The range of IQ differences among the replications was wide, immediately suggesting that the program had varying effects on different target populations among the poor. But important factors obscured the reliability of these test results. The N's in most of the replications were very small, and the comparability, in terms of skill and experience of the psychologists who examined the children came into question when actual protocols were scrutinized with some attention. It became clear that it was difficult to know which of three replication variables was influencing the results: small N's, uneven tester performance, or actual differences in program effectiveness. To remedy the first two factors, replications have enrolled larger numbers of subjects this year and the testing procedures for seven of the replications are being closely monitored for reliability by an outside testing agency, the Educational Testing Service of Princeton, New Jersey. By July, 1976, the replication results would lend themselves to clearer interpretation.

However, the labor of the project's Demonstration Center in this pilot dissemination experience has already yielded a great deal of valuable information about the feasibility and the desirability of the program's broad implementation. There are advantages and disadvantages. One of the disadvantages is that organizations are often prevented by lack of money from adopting the program for large enough numbers of children to demonstrate program effects reliably. Even when they do, the maintenance of model program standards, though effective in almost all replications, requires hard work.

Clear advantages lie in the areas of desirability and feasibility. In terms of desirability, the program appears to be as attractive to dyads reached by replications as it is to the project sample. It is received enthusiastically both by the dyads and by the sponsoring organizations. Also, the individualized dissemination techniques developed by the Demonstration Center (Levenstein, Kochman and Roth, 1973) appear to preserve the low key, low pressure nature of the intervention as well in replication as in the model MCHP, so as to interfere minimally with family privacy, style, and autonomy. This approach is not only necessary for effectiveness, but is also congruent with a democratic society's respect for human values and human beings. Milgram's (1974) sobering studies at Yale on obedience to authority underscore the social risks of gaining mothers' cooperation too easily with a program which can destroy the privacy of their homes. They also vividly illustrate the covert sabotage which can occur when mothers give surface obedience to accepting a program they do not really like. Against these dangers, the Mother-Child Home Program has incorporated explicit safeguards which seem to work in replication as well as in the model program.

The program is also feasible. Although difficult, it does seem possible, at a financial cost similar to the model program's, to maintain program quality control through firm guidelines and personal training and monitoring of replication coordinators. The program's techniques, curriculum, and materials appear to be transmittable and they are used effectively by a wide variety of personnel throughout the country trained as Toy Demonstrators, under the direction of coordinators trained at the VIP Demonstration Center. A large number of well established organizations, with demonstrated capacity to provide program stability, are enthusiastic about the program and are willing to support it. Many more have indicated they would do so if they had minimal financial supplementation from government or other sources. In short, the dissemination of this family enhancing program appears to be socially feasible.

Some questions remain to be answered. Will future out-of-project replications return more reliable demonstrations of program effectiveness? Will the 1968 to 1971 graduates continue to show long range effects? Will the outcome data repeat the findings for these four cohorts when collected from new groups within a true experimental design? Yet, the data even at this time may warrant consideration of the program's applicability to other populations vulnerable to educational disadvantage, such as the mildly retarded.

A re-phrasing of the "message from home" appears to be that a surprisingly small amount of intervention geared specifically to tapping the mighty resources of the mother-child interactional system within the family has had relatively strong and long-lasting effects for children with normal capabilities. Perhaps the same can be true for many mentally retared children as well.

REFERENCES

Ainsworth, M. D. 1973. The development of infant-mother attachment. *In* B. M. Caldwell and H. N. Ricciuti (eds.), Review of Child Development Research, Vol. 3, pp. 1–94. Child Development and Social Policy, University of Chicago Press, Chicago.

Ainsworth, M. D. 1967. Patterns of infantile attachment to mother. *In* Y. Brackhill and G. Thompson (eds.), Behavior in Infancy and Early Childhood, pp. 607–615. The Free Press, New York.

Ainsworth, M. D. and S. M. Bell. Mother-infant interaction and the development of competence. *ERIC Reports:* N.Y. Office of Child Development. Ed 065 180 - PS 005 704.

Bayley, N. 1965. Comparisons of mental and motor test scores for ages 1–15 months by sex, birth order, race, geographic location, and education of parents. Child Devel. 36: 379–411.

Bernstein, B. 1961. Social class and linguistic development: a theory of social learning. *In* A. H. Halsey, J. Floud, and C. A. Anderson (eds.), Education, Economy and Society, pp. 288–314. The Free Press, Glencoe, Ill.

Bloom, B. S. 1964. Stability and change in human characteristics. John Wiley and Sons, New York.

Bowlby, J. 1952. Maternal care and mental health. World Health Organization, Geneva.

Bronfenbrenner, U. 1968. Early deprivation: a cross-species analysis. *In* G. Newton and S. Levine (eds.), Early Experience and Behavior, pp. 627–764. Charles C Thomas, Springfield, Ill.

Bronfenbrenner, U. 1974. Is early intervention effective? Vol. II of A Report on Longitudinal Evaluation of Preschool Programs. D/HEW Publication No. (OHD) 74-25.

Brown, R. 1958. Words and things. The Free Press, Glencoe, Ill.

Bruner, J. S. 1964. The course of cognitive growth. Am. Psychol. 19: 1–15.

Bruner, J. S. 1972. Nature and uses of immaturity. Am. Psychol. 27: 687–708.

Bruner, J. S. et al. 1966. Studies in cognitive growth. John Wiley & Sons, New York.

Caldwell, B. M. 1967. What is the optimal learning environment for the young child? Am. J. Orthopsychiatr. 37: 8–21.

Campbell, D. T. and J. C. Stanley. 1969. Experimental and quasi-experimental designs for research. Rand McNally & Co., Chicago.

Cassirer, E. 1944. An essay on man. Yale University Press, New Haven.

Cazden, C. B. 1970. The situation: a neglected source of social class differences in language use. J. Soc. Iss. 26: 35–60.

Chilman, C. S. 1973. Programs for disadvantaged parents: some major trends and related research. In M. Caldwell and H. N. Ricciuti (eds.), Review of Child Development Research, Vol. 3, pp. 403–465. Child Development and Social Policy. University of Chicago Press, Chicago.

Davie, R., N. Butler, and H. Goldstein. 1972. From Birth to Seven: A report of the national child development study. Longman Group Ltd., London.

Deutsch, M. 1965. The role of social class in language development and cognition. Am. J. Orthopsychiatr. 35: 78–88.

Ellis, M. J. 1973. Why people play. Prentice-Hall, Inc., Englewood Cliffs, N.J.

Eveloff, H. H. 1971. Some cognitive and affective aspects of early language development. Child Devel. 42: 1895–1908.

Gordon, I. J. 1969. Stimulation via parent education. Children 16: 57–59.

Gray, S. W. and R. A. Klaus. 1965. An experimental preschool program for culturally deprived children. Child Devel. 36: 887–898.

Harlow, H. F., M. K. Harlow, and S. J. Suomi. 1971. From thought to therapy: lessons from a primate laboratory. Am. Scientist 59: 538–549.

Held, R. 1965. Plasticity in sensory-motor systems. Sci. Am. 213: 84–94.

Hess, R. D. and V. C. Shipman. 1965. Early experience and the socialization of cognitive modes in children. Child Devel. 36: 869–886.

Hunt, J. McV. 1961. Intelligence and experience. Ronald Press, New York.

Hunt, J. McV. 1969. The challenge of incompetence and poverty. University of Illinois Press, Urbana.

Irwin, O. C. 1960. Infant speech: effect of systematic reading of stories. J. Speech Hearing Res. 3: 187–190.

Karnes, M. B., J. A. Teska, A. S. Hodgins, and E. D. Badger. 1970. Educational intervention at home by mothers of disadvantaged infants. Child. Devel. 41: 925–935.

Levenstein, P. 1970. Cognitive growth in preschoolers through verbal interaction with mothers. Am. J. Orthopsychiat. 40: 426–432.

Levenstein, P. 1973. Manual for replication of the mother-child home program. 2nd Ed. Verbal Interaction Project, Freeport, N.Y.

Levenstein, P. Mother-child home program. In R. K. Parker (ed.), The Preschool in Action. Allyn and Bacon, Boston. In press.

Levenstein, P. 1974. Toy demonstrator's VISIT handbook. 5th Ed. Verbal Interaction Project, Freeport, N. Y. Mimeographed.

Levenstein, P., A. Kochman, and H. A. Roth. 1973. From laboratory to real world: service delivery of the Mother-Child Home Program. Am. J. Orthopsychiatr. 43: 72–78.

Levenstein, P. and S. Levenstein. 1971. Fostering learning potential in preschoolers. Social Casework 52: 74–78.

Levenstein, P. and R. Sunley. Stimulation of verbal interaction between disadvantaged mothers and children. Am. J. Orthopsychiatr. 38: 116–121.

Maccoby, E. E. and S. S. Feldman. 1972. Mother-attachment and stranger-reactions in the third year of life. Monogr. Soc. Res. Child Devel. 27: Serial No. 146.

Milgram, S. 1974. Obedience to authority. Harper & Row, Inc., New York.

Millar, S. 1968. The psychology of play. Penguin Books, Baltimore.

Palmer, F. H. 1969. Learning at two. Children 16: 55–57.

Payne, J. S., C. D. Mercer, R. A. Payne, and R. G. Davison. 1973. Headstart: A tragicomedy with epilogue, pp. 40–48. Behavioral Publications, New York.

Rapaport, D., M. M. Gill, and R. Schafer. 1945. Diagnostic psychological testing. Vols. 1 and 2, The Year Books Publishers, Inc., Chicago.

Ruppenthal, G. C., M. K. Harlow, C. D. Eisele, H. F. Harlow, and S. J. Suomi. 1974. Development of peer interactions of monkeys reared in a nuclear-family environment. Child Devel. 45: 670–682.

Sapir, E. 1962. Culture, language and personality. Berkeley: University of California Press, Berkeley. (First published 1921).

Schaefer, E. S. 1969. A home tutoring program. Children 16: 59–61.

Schaefer, E. S. 1970. Need for early and continuing education. In V. M. Denenberg (eds.), Education of the Infant and Young Child, pp. 61–82. Academic Press, New York.

Schaie, K. W. and J. Roberts. 1970. School achievement of children 6–11 years as measured by the reading and arithmetic subtests of the Wide Range Achievement Test. Series 11, number 103, National Health Survey, National Center for Health Statistics, Public Health Service, DHEW.

Sigel, I. E. 1971. Language of the disadvantaged: the distancing hypothesis. In C. S. Lavatelli, (ed.), Language Training in Early Childhood Education, pp. 60–76. Univeristy of Illinois Press, Urbana.

Skeels, H. M. 1966. Adult status of children with contrasting early life experiences. Monogr. Soc. Res. Child Devel. 31: Serial No. 105.

Stein, Z. and M. Susser. 1970. Mutability of intelligence and epidemiology of mild mental retardation. Rev. Educ. Res. 40: 29–67.

Thorndike, R. L. 1973. Reading comprehension education in fifteen countries. John Wiley & Sons (Halstead Press), New York.

Vygotsky, L. S. 1962. Thought and language. Massachusetts Institute of Technology Press, Boston.

Weikart, D. P. and D. A. Mambie. 1968. Preschool intervention through a home teaching program. In J. Hellmuth, (ed.), The Disadvantaged Child, Special Child Publications, Seattle.

Werner, H. and B. Kaplan. 1967. Symbol formation. John Wiley & Sons, New York.

White, R. W. 1963. Ego and reality in psychoanalytic theory. Psychol. Issues 3: Monogr. 11.

Discussion:
Forms of Family Adaptation
And Intervention

Discussion following the Adams paper on foster parent care for the intellectually dis-advantaged child centered on program evaluation. Although the country is serious about foster family care (FFC) as an alternative to institutional care, the adequacy of FFC as a treatment and educational service has not been closely examined, including pro-blems revolving around the placement procedure and the nature of the placement process. The FFC services should be compared in terms of program effectiveness with other possible community-based approaches such as keeping the child with his natural parents, subsidized adoption, and residential home programs. Initial discussion focused on the problems confronted by foster family care programs. Children who are quite retarded, physically different, older, or who have behavioral problems are particularly difficult to place. The child's characteristics, however, might be less important than the value system of social workers who place retarded children. More specifically, it was stated that social workers: 1) try to find "idealized" foster parents and as a consequence place fewer children, 2) typically expend much of their energy trying to place the more "normal" child and do not explore as vigorously new avenues for placement of the "stigmatized" child, and 3) underestimate the desirability to certain parents of the "stigmatized" child. New mechanisms of recruitment, particularly the use of television and other mass media presentations, should be explored. The way a child is described to the public might be a critical factor determining placement. Moreover it was pointed out that although the "stereotyped" foster parent of the past might have been that of a low income minority individual, the possibilities of placing children in middle class white families appear at present to be definitely more favorable.

In discussions with potential foster parents, social workers should fully inform such candidates as to what having a foster retarded child in their home means and what types of problems they will face. The prognosis for a successful family placement would be more favorable if the foster parents were initially aware of and could be prepared for the problems that commonly occur with foster parent responsibility. The need for backup support, e.g., respite care for the foster care parent was emphasized. It was also pointed out that the federal government's policy not to subsidize the services as well as the care provided by foster parents in contrast to the practice in some progressive states, was perhaps unfortunate.

The question of whether and under what circumstances natural parents should be allowed to divest themselves of their child was explored, although it was clearly recognized that some parents could not psychologically accept a retarded child and that in such cases, home care could be harmful. If supportive community programs such as respite care and financial aid were available to the parents as they are sometimes to foster parents, keeping the child in his natural home might prove therapeutic, educational, and economic. A subsidized adoption program or an FFC program leading to subsidized adoption might also provide greater benefits to the child. The critical questions pervading the discussion of FFC were: for which retarded child was it really beneficial, under what circumstances and provisions is it effective, and is it more desirable than programs which assist the natural parents or which lead to the child's legal adoption?

The advantages of a home-based versus a preschool-based program as presented by Garber were examined at length. Several discussants agreed with the author that early intervention programs based in a nursery or preschool setting should not preclude, but rather involve, the parents to as great an extent as is possible. Home-based parent programs, such as Levenstein's, would be more intensive and extensive in their influence on the child given the amount of daily and potentially reinforcing contact the child has with his parents. With parents who are retarded or otherwise inadequate, however, home-based programs might be less successful, because there would be a more difficult educational problem in training such parents how to teach or optimally stimulate their child. Ideally, it was agreed intervention programs for the retarded should be home and preschool-based.

The question of what the content focus of intervention programs should be for the "culturally disadvantaged" and minority groups was explored. "White Anglo" curricula may not be acceptable to these groups. Recent litigation in California decreed that educational programs should be culturally relevant. The desirability of bi-cultural programs in contrast to an exclusive unicultural centered curriculum, whatever its emphasis, was pointed out by several participants. From a broad cultural standpoint the format of presentation of curriculum needs to be adjusted to the specific ethnic group and might be more important than the content of curriculum. The skills necessary for cultural preparation (e.g., concept training and arithmetic) should be a constant across curricula. In addition it was stressed that the question of what the content and mode of presentation of early intervention programs should be is secondary to the ultimate goals of educational programs. That is, the nature of the society the child is being prepared for educationally should dictate ultimately the nature and structure of educational delivery systems.

Interest in the IQ trends of children since the termination of the Milwaukee intervention program was expressed. Comparisons in this regard with the Coleman and Gray studies were made. The importance of follow-up as a critical validation device for evaluating the goodness of early intervention programs was generally acknowledged.

Discussion of the Levenstein presentation focused initially on methodological and procedural issues surrounding her project and later on the results of the study and their implication for the area of early childhood education.

The mothers who participated in this study came from familes 1) which were frequently on welfare (30%), 2) in which the father was often absent (40%), 3) in which the father and/or mother were employed in semiskilled jobs, and 4) in which the average educational level of the father and mother was about eleventh grade. In contrast, the mothers who refused to participate in the project were characterized as being from families with upward social mobility. These mothers usually worked and thus could not participate in intervention programs.

The percentage of mothers approached willing to participate in the program (80%) was surprising. Levenstein indicated that this figure was comparable to that found in the numerous replications of her study currently being conducted in various parts of the country under her supervision. Given the results that the home intervention procedures were successful, the question was raised but not discussed as to how mothers not willing to engage in the program could be motivated to participate.

Mothers in the project were taught the skill of toy demonstration immediately at the onset of the program and maintained their skill throughout the program. It was suggested that videotape procedures along with various coding procedures could be quite helpful in differentiating the interaction style of mothers and children in the experimental and control groups.

Levenstein's intervention projects' results were contrasted with other programs where children were provided early stimulation. In contrast to earlier studies, the IQ gains found by her were relatively long term. Critical differences in the Levenstein procedures were that it was home based, involved the mother as teacher, and provided a structure for stimulation of the child throughout the day. The change in mother-child interaction patterns tended to avoid the observed contrast between home and preschool day care environments in other child-focused only intervention programs.

Suggestions for future research in this area were made by several participants. These included examining whether there is a "critical" period during which intervention should take place and whether still earlier intervention is better than the traditional 2- to 4-year onset of intervention efforts. It was also suggested that the "optimal" length of time over which the intervention procedure should be applied needs to be examined. Levenstein stated that her data indicated that a "prolonged" period of 2 years was needed, but it was noted that most advocates of intervention consider this a short time span. Concern was expressed that the influence of the father on their children's development has been greatly ignored in the intervention literature and should in future research be closely examined. Throughout discussion the need for this study to be replicated with intellectually limited parents of retarded children was stressed to determine the general applicability of this method.

EMERGENT PATTERNS OF SERVICE FOR YOUNG PEOPLE AND ADULTS

Epidemiology and Evaluation Of Services for the Mentally Handicapped[1]

Albert Kushlick

As part of the British National Health Service, the Wessex Regional Hospital Board was created in 1958 to provide and administer hospital services for a geographic region in the south of England with a population of about two million. The responsibilities of the Board included provision of hospital care for the mentally handicapped, when considered appropriate, by the agency personnel from health and social services. It is, of course, in general the most severely mentally handicapped who live in continuous hospital care. Of those mentally handicapped persons who do not, many live in private households, some in privately run institutions, and (at the present, although not in 1958) an increasing number in hostels provided by the county authorities.

The Board was faced with the problems of overcrowding in their institutions for the mentally handicapped and a growing waiting list for institutional placement. Professor Jack Tizard, when approached for advice on the number and type of places needed, advised the Board to undertake a prevalence survey of mental handicap in the Region as the data available were insufficient for the purpose of planning further provisions. The author joined the Wessex Hospital Board in 1963 in order to undertake the survey.

Data for the survey are supplied by hospitals within and outside the Region, as well as by local authority social service, health, and education departments in the Region. These authorities, in addition to authorizing the special collection of data for the team, also allow the team members access to facilities for the collection of additional data based on direct observation.

[1] I would like to thank my team colleagues: Geraldine Cansick, for undertaking a major editing revision of several drafts of this paper; John Palmer, John Smith, and Ron Whatmore respectively for contributions and editorial arrangement on epidemiology, changes in children's scores, and quality of care results presented in the paper; and Sally Scott for typing and re-typing drafts of the paper. In addition, I am indebted to Stephen Richardson for detailed editorial contributions.

The following questions guided the kinds of data collected in the Wessex survey and the kinds of analyses undertaken.

1. What is the size of the target population for which services are being made available? For example, how many people at any time, and in a population of given size and demographic characteristics, have the "problem," for example, mental handicap?

2. What is the nature of the "problem"?

(a) What are the types or ranges of disability (incapacity to do things normally expected) among the people identified? For example, inability to walk at all even with help, inability to walk alone but able with help, inability to feed oneself at all, inability to talk in sentences.

(b) What are the types and ranges of inappropriate behaviors (difficult, disruptive, or potentially dangerous behaviors) among the people identified? For example, over-activity, physically aggressive behavior, behavior destructive of furniture, fittings, clothing, etc., attention seeking, self-injuring behavior (Kushlick, Blunden and Cox, 1973).

(c) What are the associated clinical conditions found among people identified? For example, epilepsy, spasticity, congenital abnormality (mongolism, hydrocephalus, heart, or other abnormalities). Estimates are made of the proportions of identified people with different degrees of handicap, inappropriate behavior or associated clinical conditions. (Kushlick and Cox, 1973).

3. How are the people identified being cared for? What are the characteristics of people to whom the services are being delivered? How do these people differ from those not receiving services?

(a) How many are living with their own families, and how many are in hospitals, in local authority homes, or private homes, etc?

(b) How many are receiving defined specialist services believed to be appropriate? For example, education, occupational therapy, or physiotherapy?

The data from the survey for answering some of the questions are contained in Tables 1 and 2. They show the number of children and adults who were recognized as mentally handicapped by health and social service agencies in the Wessex Region on July 1, 1963 (Kushlick, 1973) and are the crude rates in a total standard population of 100,000. The low rates of "mildly handicapped" children are accounted for by the fact that most of such children are dealt with by the Education Authorities and are not included in the survey data.

Of the 48 children known to health and social services and who are severely subnormal, two-thirds are living at home. Of the 130 adults, only about one-third are living at home (Table 1).

It can be seen that the majority of children who are non-ambulant with severe behavior problems or severely incontinent, and all severely subnormal adults with these handicaps, are in institutional care. However, it can also be seen that there is almost one child with these severe disabilities living at home for every one in a hospital. In addition, the proportion of those handicapped who are continent, ambulant, and without severe

Table 1. Wessex survey: Grade, social or physical incapacity, place of care and education of mentally handicapped persons known to health or social services (rates per 100,000 total population)

Age group	Grade	Place of care	Incapacity category				
			NA	All SB	SI	CAN	Total[a]
Children	SSN[b]	Home	4[c]	4	2	20	30
under 16	(IQ < 50)	Institution	5	5	3	4	18
	MSN	Home	1	1	1	7	9
	(IQ > 50)	Institution	0	1	0	1	2
Adults	SSN	Home	2	2	1	45	50
16 and	(IQ < 50)	Institution	6	14	6	53	80
over	MSN	Home	1	0	0	69	75
	(IQ > 50)	Institution	2	4	1	45	53

[a]Where figures do not add exactly to the row totals this is due 1) to rounding to the nearest whole number and, 2) to inclusion of a few persons for whom incapacity ratings could not be obtained.
[b]SSN, severely subnormal (IQ < 50); MSN, mildly subnormal (IQ > 50); NA, non-ambulant (unable to walk); All SB, all severely behavior disordered (able to walk but presenting seriously disruptive behavior); SI, severely incontinent (not in the NA or All SB categories but severely incontinent); CAN, continent, ambulant, and with no severe behavior disorders.
[c]The figures shown here are the known or 'administrative' prevalence. The 'true' prevalence, especially of mild subnormality, is much greater, but the majority of mildly subnormal persons make no contact with health or social services.

behavior disorders in institutions is considerable, and this is particularly marked among the adults.

A standard total population of 100,000 had only 20 mentally handicapped children in institutions, 18 severely subnormal and 2 mildly subnormal. Of the 20 children in institutions, 14 or 70% were incontinent, non-ambulant, or had severe behavior problems. Of the 30 severely subnormal children at home, 10 had similar problems. For the same overall population there are 133 mentally handicapped adults in institutions. Of these, 33 or 25% were incontinent, non-ambulant, or had severe behavior problems. Clearly there is a higher proportion of adults than children in institutional care with "problems" other than being unable to walk, behavior disturbance, and severe incontinence. Further, there is a higher proportion of adults than children in institutional care who are mildly subnormal (40% compared to 10%).

Table 2 shows level of functioning by clinical diagnosis of Wessex adolescents between 15 and 19 years, the age group at which our ascertainment is known to be most complete (Kushlick and Cox, 1973). There appears to be little or no relationship between level of functioning and medical diagnosis.

The only significant associations are a higher proportion of non-ambulant (NA) people among those with conditions nearly always associated with mental handicap (MD)

Table 2. Severely subnormal persons aged 15–19 years, Wessex including all Wiltshire, 1963; social and physical incapacities in persons of different diagnostic groups

Diagnostic group[a]	Number of cases	Cases with incapacity rating (= 100%)	Incapacity category (%)			
			NA[b]	All SB	SI	CAN
Down's Syndrome	167	163	2.5	6.1	0.6	90.8
Conditions almost always associated with mental handicap[c]	32	32	28.1	9.4	9.4	53.1
Cerebral Palsy	61	61	37.7	6.6	9.8	45.9
Major congenital abnormalities	37	37	8.1	16.2	8.1	67.6
Epilepsy	74	73	2.7	32.9	15.1	49.3
No clinical evidence of brain damage	220	213	2.3	14.6	5.2	77.9
Not known	17	17	5.9	11.8	0	82.3
All diagnoses	608	596	7.9	13.4	5.9	72.8

[a]The clinical conditions are mutually exclusive and have been derived in serial order from above down. E.g., the people categorized "Epilepsy" have *not* associated major congenital abnormalities or cerebral palsy, etc. Similarly, people categorized 'Cerebral Palsy' may have associated major congenital abnormalities or epilepsy.
[b]NA, non-ambulant (unable to walk); ALL SB, all severely behavior disordered (able to walk but presenting seriously disruptive behaviors); SI, severely incontinent; CAN, continent, ambulant, and with no severe behavior disorders.
[c]Examples: phenylketonuria, lipoidoses, microcephaly, hydrocephaly, craniostenosis.

or with cerebral palsy (CP) and of severe behavior disorders (all SB) among the ambulant people with epilepsy.

An earlier study of Tizard (1960) had demonstrated that a small residential unit for moderately retarded children who were ambulant and had no severe behavior disorders, that was organized separately from the traditional hospital, on principles of "nursery education," provided an alternative pattern of care from the more traditional mental retardation hospital. At the end of the study children in the small residence had made significantly higher increments of verbal IQ scores than a control group of children who had remained in the mental retardation hospital. No differences were observed in the performance IQ scores of the two groups. Both sets of children had originally been in the mental retardation hospital and the study determined, on a random basis, those who remained in the hospital or moved to the small residence. Further studies of different forms of residential care were conducted by King, Raynes, and Tizard (1971). These studies developed objective criteria for measuring certain staff practices within residential settings. The measures discriminated between units which were recognized intuitively as "good" or "bad." The results of these studies, together with the Wessex Survey, were used to make a series of recommendations to the Wessex Hospital Board Administrators for the planning of new residential facilities for the mentally handicapped.

Evidence from the research suggested that there would be major advantages if people in hospitals or residential care were grouped in relation to the area in which their families lived rather than by their incapacity level or by the clinical condition from which they were suffering. The advantages of geographical grouping, both in small residential units and within existing hospitals, appear to be:

1. The spreading out of the most dependent and disruptive residents among those more able who could also contribute to their care.

2. Bridging the traditional gap at operational level between home and institutional care. Parents from any area would know which unit serves their particular area and the living unit staff might get to know the families with the clients still at home in their areas.

3. Bridging the gap between hospital and local authority and general practitioner services. General practitioners, pediatricians, social workers, teachers, home nurses, and health visitors from an area might know the unit and the staff serving that particular area.

4. Representatives of local government and parents' societies might also be able to identify with one or two residential units or hospital wards, and take a special interest in achieving, maintaining, and improving standards on that unit. Thus, not only would there be more effective demands for higher standards of care in the residential settings, but it would be easier to deliver those resources that were available to the residential settings and to coordinate them.

The team suggested using geographic catchment areas for planning, and that new facilities for all mentally handicapped children requiring residential care be set up in each catchment area. From the prevalence study it was estimated that the residential needs for the mentally handicapped children in each catchment area of 100,000 would be met by 25 places, including 4 to 5 for short term care and an additional 130 places for mentally handicapped adults.

It was recommended that the new residential units be domestic in character. The term "domestic" is used here to emphasize a move away from what are commonly regarded as "institutional" characteristics in existing hospitals, towards those in "ordinary" households. The features of "domestic" or "institutional-type" units include their size (number of residents), physical design, furnishings and fittings, as well as the way in which they are organized and in which staff and residents relate with one another. While the new units are still considerably larger than "ordinary" family houses (20 to 25) residents with, at any time, about 5 members of caring staff) they should be smaller than many existing hospital wards which contain about 40 children and 8 staff. The residents should sleep in bedrooms for 1 to 5 people as opposed to dormitories for around 20. They should have a separate dining room, lounge, and playrooms, as opposed to a large single, "day room" which doubles as a dining room. The units should prepare their own food in their kitchen rather than receiving food, prepared in a central kitchen, in trolleys. They should have ordinary bathrooms which contain a single bath, washbasin, and toilet, rather than an "ablution-block" with up to 20 toilet bowls and basins in a row. The furnishings and fittings should be those found in homes: wooden beds, cupboards, carpets, instead of iron bedsteads, lockers, and linoleum-covered floors. The staff should not wear uniforms, they should sit down with the residents at meal times and eat with them, and some staff should live within the units, albeit in separate flats or bed-sitters. The staff of "domestic-type" units should be recruited for that unit only; that is, they cannot be transferred as in existing hospitals from one ward to another when needs arise in other wards. The new units should be locally based; that is, they are sited in residential areas within the locality from which they receive their residents.

To meet the immediate problems of overcrowded institutions and waiting lists for institutional placements, it was recommended that two small residential units be established with 25 children in each unit. Each unit was to be placed in, and to serve, an area of approximately 100,000 population. A similar area of the same size, served by the traditional mental retardation hospitals would serve as a control in an experiment to evaluate and compare the two patterns of care.

The recommendations were accepted and the author was involved in the establishment of the two small residential units and in their evaluation. Since the recommendations were made and based on initial experience with the two small residential units for children, three additional residential units for children and one for adults have been established. It is already clear that locally based residential units serving catchment areas of 100,000 total population can effectively care for the most severely mentally handicapped children and adults within the catchment area.

The following are some of our findings since these small locally based residential units have been established:

1. It has (in spite of earlier doubts) proved possible to find sites for both childrens' and adults' units with little difficulty or neighborhood opposition.

2. The new units have recruited staff for all positions, although existing traditional units are still unable to fill all positions.

3. (a) The numbers and behavioral characteristics of children and adults in each locality who were identified from the system and admitted to the new units are very close to those predicted from the prevalence data. (b) Very few parents with a child in existing units declined the offer of a place for their child in the new local units. (c) Only one geographically eligible child in an existing unit was not transferred to the appropriate new unit. Her behavioral characteristics were very much more capable than most of the children admitted, but it was considered unwise to admit her to a unit with no qualified nursing staff because she has bouts of status epilepticus. (d) Since the admission of children and adults to the new units, only one individual from each unit has been removed from the unit and transferred to the existing large hospitals. These residents have been regarded as too aggressive or disruptive for the local unit. Their disruptive behaviors

continue in the existing units. (e) The demand for residential care in the areas serving the new units has not increased, despite the fact that no additional services have been provided in the intervening period to serve families in these areas with a handicapped person at home. Such clients are given day care at the new units when transport is available.

4. The general medical care of the residents of the small units has been managed by the local General Practitioner. When specialized acute medical or surgical care has been needed, this has been obtained from the local District General Hospital specialists.

5. The local pediatrician, social workers, and special educators all form part of the multidisciplinary team following the progress of clients in the units. (The consultant in charge of one children's unit is a pediatrician. In the other units, the consultant in charge is the psychiatrist specialized in mental handicap from the existing hospital for the mentally handicapped.)

6. Those children and adults who live at home and who are acceptable to the local day schools or training centers for children or adults attend these daily. This affects just over half of the residents. Those not accepted by the local education and training facilities are very physically handicapped or are regarded as too disruptive. Most are incontinent more than once a week, during the day.

Home teachers visit the children's units daily to undertake teaching programs and a physiotherapist visits for 2 to 3 sessions weekly.

7. The costs of these units have been described in detail elsewhere (1). Briefly: (a) these units use up less land per resident than traditional units. (b) The running costs are related to the staffing ratios. Thus, when traditional hospital costs are adjusted to allow for the fact that their staffing ratios are lower, there are no differences in running costs per week between new units and traditional units in our region. (c) The running costs of these new units are lower than average running costs for existing units in the Oxford Region of England, where a new large traditional hospital has recently been built.

The approach to evaluation consisted of attempting to measure the different degrees of "effectiveness" of different methods of care.

In order to measure effectiveness, it has been necessary to define the aims of care in a way that makes it possible to measure (that is, to quantify) whether and to what extent they are being met.

Any measures of effectiveness must be reliable (replicable), valid (measure what they claim to measure), and agreed upon and seen to be relevant by the people planning, administering, or running the service at all levels.

The criteria of effectiveness used by the research team were incorporated in operational policy documents and statements of administrative aims with respect to all hospital services for the mentally handicapped in the Wessex Region.

Work continues on refining these measures of effectiveness which have been divided into two main areas:

1. (a) Measures of change, over time, in the behavior (appropriate and inappropriate) of the handicapped person. (b) Measures of change, over time, in the "problems" and

experiences which the family of the handicapped person encounter while caring for the handicapped person, and especially in relation to contacts with the residential services for the mentally handicapped.

The assumptions are that the "better" the service, the greater will be the "progress" made by the handicapped people, and the lower will be the level of difficulties experienced by their families.

2. Measures of the "quality of care" received by the handicapped person and the families. The "quality of care" has been operationally defined to include the following: the daily routine of the residential units for the handicapped. The sequencing of staff and patient activities for the whole of the waking day (including weekdays and weekends) is observed and systematically recorded. This allows the collection of standardized data including: (a) Number of staff assigned to a living unit as well as those on duty at any time. (b) The time spent by the residents in groups of different sizes throughout the day. (c) The time spent by the residents in different activities in which they might acquire or lose important social skills (for example, in getting out of bed, toiletting, dressing, eating, formal training, and recreation). (d) The proportions of residents with personalized possessions and living space. (e) The extent to which the staff sequencing of activities is influenced by the individual differences among the residents at any time, or whether these routines affecting all residents are modified at different times of the week (weekends) or at different seasons of the year.

RESULTS

Quality of Care

Preliminary findings are discussed elsewhere (Kushlick, 1973; Durward and Whatmore, 1975; Whatmore, Durward, and Kushlick, 1975).

The original aims of the new units were to avoid the undesirable features and practices described by King, Raynes and Tizard, (1961), namely, "depersonalization," "social distance," "rigidity," and "block treatment." These aims have been achieved in the units by providing adequate staff-resident ratios, and facilities for acquiring, storing, maintaining, laundering, and distributing personal clothes and effects, and by providing high quality catering standards. (Costs per head of food are the same as for existing hospitals, costs per head on clothes are *lower* than in existing units.) Clothes are now often provided by parents who can be reasonably sure that clothes will not be lost or destroyed in existing hospital laundries. In the units in the hospitals for the mentally handicapped the same aims have so far not been achieved.

Further measures of quality of care have been developed by the team (Durward and Whatmore, 1975); Whatmore, Durward, and Kushlick, 1975). Another most interesting measure has been developed by Professor Todd Risley's Living Environments Group of the Department of Human Development, University of Kansas (Risley, 1974). In these measures we study, by a time-sampling procedure, the behavior of the children, classifying it into Appropriate, Neutral, Inappropriate and Disruptive, and also the behavior of the staff, noting when they contact children and the child behavior with which this contact is associated. Initial results using this procedure show that children in the local experimental units display a higher proportion of "appropriate" behavior at nearly all times of day than their counterparts in the traditional hospitals. The results also show that staff contact the children more in the experimental units, and particularly that "appropriate" child behavior is more likely to be followed by staff contact in the experimental units than in the control units. The main exception noted was that a small group of children (the partly mobile) seemed to be better cared for in a traditional unit, but this was only noted for certain times of day, recreation periods and mealtimes.

A comparison of the "progress" of children living in the first small, locally based unit and equivalent children living in hospital was made by means of a Child Development Interview Schedule administered at baseline (T1) and again after 4 years (T3). The interview schedule has 13 sections, each dealing with a particular type of behavior (for example, mobility, washing, etc.). The questions in two of the sections enable a subdivision of General Behavior and Emotional Response into "appropriate" and "inappropriate" sections. The questions in the interview were devised after 24-hour observations had been made on groups of severely mentally handicapped children and an analysis of behavior scales already successfully used, such as Vineland (Doll, 1953), and that of Griffiths (1954).

Table 3(a) lists the 13 behavioral areas of the CD schedule, together with the mean raw scores at T1 and T3 of the two groups of children. Results (Smith et al., 1973) show that, as measured by the changes in mean raw scores, the group of children receiving residential care in the locally based unit made more "progress" than those in the hospital unit in 9 out of the 13 behavioral areas. In 3 of these, eating (a), dressing and appropriate general behavior, the differences in the change in scores of the two groups between T1 and T3 reached statistical significance.

In the section eating (a), all the 18 children in the locally based unit gained in score over the 4-year period, whereas of the children in hospital, 11 showed a gain in score, 8 showed a loss, and 1 child remained at exactly the same score.

In the section on dressing, 17 of the children in the locally based unit showed a gain in score and 1 scored the same at T1 and T3. Of the children in hospital, 11 showed a gain, 8 showed a drop in score, and 1 remained at the same score.

In the section on appropriate general behavior, 11 of the children in the locally based unit showed a gain in score, 5 showed a drop in score, and 2 remained at the same score. Of the children in hospital, 7 showed a gain in score, 10 showed a deficit, and 3 scored the same at T1 and T3.

In the section eating (a) the scores are derived from questions about how the child eats his food, what type of food he eats, and whether he makes a mess. (Eating (b) includes questions on the child's table manners.)

In the section on dressing, scores are derived from questions on the child's dressing and undressing skills, whether he fastens buttons, puts on socks, ties laces, etc.

Table 3(a). A comparison of the changes in raw scores over 4 years on the CD schedule of two groups of SSN children receiving different types of residential care

Section of CD schedule (and maximum possible score)		Mean raw score		
		TI	T3	Difference
Mobility	E[a]	7.06	7.20	0.25
(11)	C	7.45	7.20	−0.25
Speech	E	9.89	11.89	2.00
(24)	C	11.00	10.55	−0.45
Eating (a)	E	11.61	16.22	4.61 p<0.01
(22)	C	13.15	14.00	0.85
Eating (b)	E	14.44	16.33	1.89
(21)	C	15.30	16.95	1.65
Washing	E	3.44	5.38	1.94
(17)	C	3.00	4.10	1.10
Dressing	E	9.28	14.34	5.06 p<0.02
(27)	C	10.90	12.20	1.30
Toilet	E	8.16	12.22	4.06
(20)	C	6.90	9.90	3.00
Habits	E	18.94	19.16	0.22
(24)	C	20.40	20.70	0.30
Sleep	E	10.56	10.89	0.33
(14)	C	10.20	11.20	1.00
Appropriate general	E	8.17	10.11	1.94 p<0.02
Behavior (25)	C	11.80	10.00	−1.80
Inappropriate general	E	11.50	11.50	0
Behavior (16)	C	10.25	12.00	1.75
Appropriate emotional	E	15.50	16.22	0.72
Response (24)	C	15.85	16.25	0.40
Inappropriate emotional	E	13.94	14.83	0.89
Response (19)	C	13.70	15.30	1.60

[a]E, children in locally based residential units (N = 18); C, children in large mental handicap hospitals. (N = 20).

The section on appropriate general behavior includes questions on the child's level of activity, whether he does small jobs, goes on errands, plays with toys, looks at picture books, etc.

Table 3(b) compares the two groups on whether the change in score for each child in each section was positive or negative. This tabulation of changes reveals that overall the children living in the locally based unit made 154 gains (66%) out of a possible 234 (18 children X 13 sections) against an overall improvement for the children living in hospital of 133 (51%) out of a possible 260 (20 children X 13 sections). The differences between the gains and losses of the two groups reached statistical significance.

Among children in the locally based unit those who showed most gains in behavior over their counterparts in hospital were those with the most severe handicaps, that is, children who remained non-ambulant throughout the 4 years of the study.

These data relate only to the first locally based unit and its control group, hence the numbers are small. More data will be added when the other locally based units have been open 4 years.

At present, no special educational programs or goal setting activities are being undertaken in the new units, although the environment would facilitate their implementation should the staff working there and their supervisors decide that these are desirable.

Despite the fact that they are the only ways of comparing changes in groups of people over long periods of time, measures derived from averaging scores accorded answers to questions on a wide range of specific aspects of the child's behavior have severe

Table 3(b). Sections of CP in which there was a statistically significant difference between the "progress" of experimental and control groups; a comparison of the two groups on overall gains and losses in scores on the interview schedule[a]

	Gains[b]	Losses[c]	Same[d]	Total
E ($N = 18$)	154	62	18	234[e]
C ($N = 20$)	133	94	33	260
Total	287	156	51	494

[a]$\chi^2 = 11.07$ with 2 off; $P < 1\%$ (9.21).
[b]Gains = number of cases in which a child showed a gain in score between T_1 and T_3 on a section of the interview schedule.
[c]Losses = number of cases in which a child showed a drop in score between T_1 and T_3 on a section of the interview schedule.
[d]Same = number of cases in which a child scored the same at T_1 and T_3.
[e]Thus the total for E represents the number of children in the group (18) multiplied by the number of sections on the interview schedule (13) = 234.

limitations as criteria of effectiveness of different forms of care. The measures of child behavior in different situations and activities throughout the day are very much more sensitive to subtle changes in behavior which are relevant to other people living with and caring for them. They are also more sensitive to the physical and social environments in which the children live, appear very useful proxies for the "quality of care," and can be used by the direct care staff to monitor the effect of changes in routine. These measures are therefore being developed within the team and will be undertaken in all of the experimental and traditional units.

Other measures of comparative effectiveness include the extent to which family members are able to maintain contact with the handicapped person in residential care and their feelings about the care expressed in positive or negative comments on the care received. The preliminary results show that parents of children in the locally based units maintained contact (visited and took the children home) more frequently than those with children in traditional units. They also expressed positive comments more frequently and negative comments less frequently (Horner et al., 1973).

FUTURE PLANS FOR SERVICES FOR THE MENTALLY HANDICAPPED

Based on the experience gained from the research in Wessex and from elsewhere, a plan has been drawn up for the structure of service facilities for the mentally handicapped in England and Wales (Department of Health and Social Security, 1971).

The unit for planning is a population of one million people. The present and future structures of services is shown on Figures 1 and 2. Figure 3 gives the key to the symbols used in the diagrams.

In Figures 1 and 2, the total population covered by the whole page is one million. The population covered by one of the four columns is a quarter of a million (250,000). Each column is divided into five rows or five areas each of total population 50,000.

The squares within, which extend over two areas of 50,000, represent the team of multi-disciplinary professionals shown in Figure 3. These are key professionals from different disciplines, already available outside the hospitals for the mentally handicapped, whose efforts might, if there were the will to do so, be collectively directed towards the needs of the mentally handicapped and their families.

The smaller squares represent residential facilities. The diamonds represent schools or training facilities. Those with double lines are for children (age under 16 years). Those with single lines are for adults. Symbols which are "shaded" represent facilities administered by local authorities; symbols without "shading" represent those administered by the hospital service.

The main features of the present service can be seen in Figure 1.

This shows a total population of one million served by two hospitals for the mentally handicapped. In other words, each hospital serves a total population of half a million people (two columns).

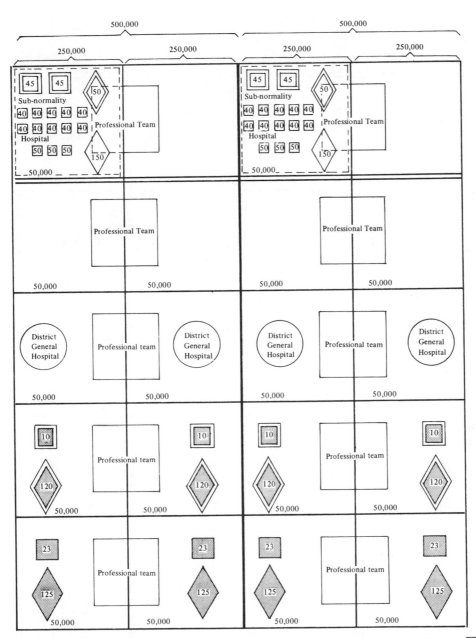

Figure 1. Existing services for mentally handicapped in a total population of 1,000,000. Key: ▣ , residential facility for children; ☐ , residential facility for adults; ◈ , training facility for children; ◇ , training facility for adults. Non-shaded areas represent hospital facilities, and shaded areas represent local authority services.

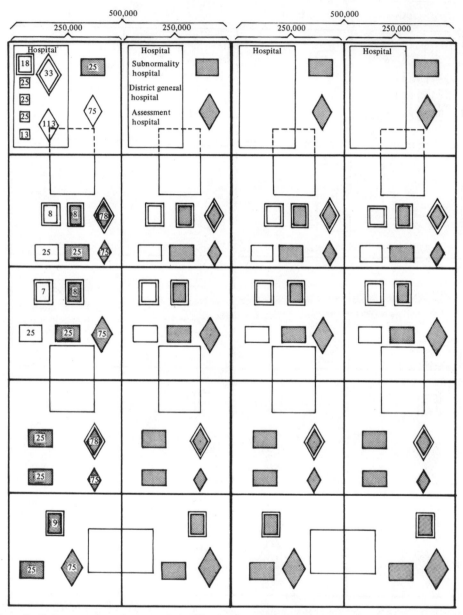

Figure 2. Future services (command 4,683) for mentally handicapped in a total population of 1,000,000. For key, see Figure 1.

G.P.'s	40
Local health authority medical officers	5
Pediatricians or child psychiatrists	1
Physicians	1.8
Psychiatrists	1.5
Educational psychologists	1
Social workers	12+
Home helps	63+
Health visitors	12+
Home nurses	18+
Teachers	5+

Figure 3. Personnel available to population of 10,000.

Each hospital has about 90 children (50 of whom attend school) in two wards, and about 550 adults in about 13 wards, 10 wards of 40 places each for SSN adults, and 3 of 50 places each for MSN adults. Of the adults, about 150 attend training centers either on or off hospital premises. (There are hospitals which serve total populations of one million or more. These would have at least double the numbers of children and adults on double the number of wards or villas.)

The mental handicap hospital is separately sited from the district general hospital where most sophisticated early diagnosis and assessment takes place.

The "shaded" symbols show the existing local authority residential and training facilities available in each area of 250,000 population.

The professional team (in the internal square) is responsible for the care, among other responsibilities, of *all* mentally handicapped people living at home or in local authority facilities. If they wish to follow up their clients in hospital facilities for the mentally handicapped, they must go to the site of the hospital. In this hospital, the clients may be on any of the 15 wards. Indeed, it is more usual that the mentally handicapped from an area of 100,000 population will *not* be in *one* hospital serving 500,000. They are more likely to be scattered around in three or four such hospitals and they will accordingly be dispersed through between 15 and 45 wards.

The same problem of geographical dispersal faces parents from the population of 500,000 who wish to visit and maintain contact with their children in hospital, and hospital staff, particularly nurses, who wish to maintain contact with the families of their clients.

Similarly, distances involved make it impossible for the hospital facilities to be used on a day basis for people from the area of 500,000. They also make it difficult or impossible for hospital residents to attend local authority schools or training centers.

Most of the areas on the page have neither residential nor training facilities for the subnormal.

If the policies outlined in Command Paper 4683 are implemented, half of all mentally handicapped people in traditional hospitals will be cared for in small domestic-type residential units, based near their own homes, staffed and managed by the social service departments of the Local Authority. Many of the people remaining in hospital will be cared for in units of the same type, similarly located but staffed and managed by the health authority. The education and training facilities like the residential facilities will be sited in the local areas, close to the professional team providing a wide range of services to people living at home.

The main features of the future service are shown in Figure 2:

1. Where there were two mental handicap hospitals there will be four, each serving a total population of 250,000. These hospitals will be either on, or closely associated with, the local District General Hospital.

2. Where each hospital had about 15 wards of about 50 people each, there will be about 5 wards ("domestic" in character) each holding around 25 people. The remainder of those in residential care will be in local authority accommodation.

3. Some of the hospital facilities will be developed in the middle of the residential areas where the families live. (The diagram shows two such children's units and two adults units in each area of 250,000.)

4. Because of the geographical siting of the mental handicap hospitals, half of the people attending the hospital school and training center will come daily from their own homes. Similarly, nearly half of the hospital residents will attend local authority school and training center facilities outside the hospital on a day basis.

5. The hospital will be "aligned" (for example, take only clients from its 250,000 population) and wards will be "sectorized" (for example, take only clients from a subarea, say; 5,000 of the whole area). (Paragraphs 266, 267). This arrangement will enable the professionals from outside the hospital to maintain easy continuing contact with their clients who are in a ward of one hospital. Moreover, the doctors, teachers, and particularly the nurses staffing a "sectorized" ward of the hospital will be able to take an increasing interest in the care of the mentally handicapped living at home. The area with which they need to become familiar will be small and they should easily be able to liaise with the non-hospital professionals from the area.

6. There will be a very large expansion of local authority residential and training facilities in areas previously completely without such services.

Provided that these are also "sectorized," the clients will be easily accessible to their families and to the professional teams undertaking their continuous assessment.

FUTURE DEVELOPMENTS IN THE RESEARCH TEAM

In our work for the mentally handicapped we have found ourselves following a cycle of action and research, like this:

Stage I: Survey of existing demands, resources and problems, (The 1973 survey of mental handicap in Wessex).

Stage II: Recommendation of a solution and experimental implementation (setting up the locally based hostels, with traditional services as a control).

Stage III: Evaluation of the experimental solution (studies of quality of care and family experience).

Stage IV: Reassessing the demands, resources, and problems and recommending further solutions and modifications to earlier solutions. These will in turn be evaluated.

We are currently approaching the end of Stage III in our mental handicap work. However, many features of this work appear also to be relevant to other fields. The team is in the early stages of a similar project on services for the elderly. In this project we are still at Stage I and moving into Stage II. Some aspects of the relative sizes of the two target populations, the old with behavioral deficits and the mentally handicapped, can be seen from Table 4, which compares, in crude rates per 100,000, the number of people involved (Kushlick, 1972).

It has been necessary to develop a conceptual framework which allows the team members to research the two target populations collectively. The early stages of these developments and the research objectives are described in our latest report to our Scientific Advisory Committee (Health Care Evaluation Research Team, 1973).

Table 4. Social incapacities in a total population of 100,000 among (A) elderly, (B) mentally handicapped of all ages

(A) Elderly (aged 65+)		(B) Mentally handicapped (all ages)		
Bedfast	350 (220)[a]	21 (8)	Non-ambulant
Confined to home	1410 (1300)	31 (7)	Severe behavior problems
Mobile outside with difficulty	1020 (910)	14 (4)	Severely incontinent
None of above	9240 (9100)	247 (142)	None of above

[a]Parentheses show those living at home.

Effort will be directed towards setting up a locally based, comprehensive, service for both elderly people and mentally handicapped people. In this a key ingredient will be that the locally based personnel servicing clients both at home and residential care jointly set, attain, and monitor specified goals with respect to their clients. This will include goals with respect to identification and manipulation of organic variables affecting the clients' behavior (the medical or biological aspect), the clients' behavior itself, and the environment in which it takes place (social, educational or rehabilitation aspect) (Kushlick, 1974).

REFERENCES

Callingham, M. 1973. Some problems involved in studying the costs of alternative services for the mentally handicapped. Appendix 18 to Report to Scientific Advisory Committee, Health Care Evaluation Research Team, December 1973.

Department of Health and Social Security. 1971. Better Services for the Mentally Handicapped. Cmnd. 4683. HMSO, London.

Doll, E. A. 1953. The measurement of social competence: A Manual for the Vineland Social Maturity Scale. Educational Test Bureau: Education.

Durward, L. and R. Whatmore. 1975. Testing measures of the quality of care: A pilot study. Behavior Research and Therapy. In press.

Griffiths, R. 1954. The Abilities of Babies. University of London Press, London.

Health Care Evaluation Research Team. 1973. Report to the Scientific Advisory Committee (with Appendices 1–24).

Horner, D., J. Smith, J. Hall, P. Williams, S. Nicholson, and A. Kushlick. 1973. Differences in pre-admission or pre-transfer experience, admission or transfer experiences, and present knowledge of residential care practices between parents whose child is currently receiving residential care in a hostel and parents whose child is currently receiving residential care in an institution. Appendix 14 to Report to the Scientific Advisory Committee, Health Care Evaluation Research Team.

King, R. D., N. V. Raynes, and J. Tizard. 1961. Patterns of Residential Care. Routledge & Kegan Paul, London.

Kushlick, A. 1972. Research into care for the elderly. The Elderly Mind. Suppl. to Hospital International, pp. 27–30.

Kushlick, A. 1973. The need for residential care. Presented to Conference "Action for the Retarded," Dublin, March 1971. National Society for Mentally Handicapped Children, London.

Kushlick, A. 1974. The rehabilitation or habilitation of severely or profoundly retarded people. Presented in a panel "Strategies for Prevention: Mental Illness and Mental Retardation" at 1974 Annual Health Conference of New York Academy of Medicine "Prevention and Health Maintenance Revisited," New York, April 1974. Bull. N.Y. Acad. Med. 51(1): 143–161.

Kushlick, A. and G. R. Cox. 1973. The epidemiology of mental handicap. Develop. Med. and Child Neurol. 15: 748–759.

Kushlick, A., R. Blunden, and G. R. Cox. 1973. A method of rating behavior characteristics for use in large scale surveys of mental handicap. Psychol. Med. 3: 466–478.

Smith, J., S. Nicholson, P. Williams, A. Tamplin, and A. Kushlick. 1973. A comparison of the changes which took place among two groups of severely subnormal children who were receiving different forms of residential care. Appendix 11 to Report to the Scientific Advisory Committee, Health Care Evaluation Research Team.

Risley, T. R. 1974. Designing Living Environments. Workshop held at the International Practicum Behavior Modification Workshop, Cardiff, August 1974.

Tizard, J. 1960. Residential care of mentally handicapped children. Br. Med. J. 1: 1041–1046.

Whatmore, R., L. Durward, and A. Kushlick. 1975. Measuring the quality of residential care. Behav. Res. Ther. In press.

The Changing Lives
Of Mentally Retarded Adults[1]

Arnold Birenbaum

The human services revolution in Scandinavia, England, and other welfare state countries has called into question prior models of care for those who cannot take care of themselves in the United States. A movement has developed at the state level to decentralize services in localities and to close down the large and isolated institutions which provided shelter for psychiatric patients and mentally retarded people. It has yet to be demonstrated that mentally retarded adults who have spent many years in state schools are capable of returning to society after living in these large and isolated maximum care facilities. Only in the last few years has it been possible for patients from state schools in the United States to leave voluntarily these institutions and legally return to community living. This is a report of a study of the changing lives of 51 former patients from state schools and their first year returning to the community where they once lived with their families.

At the same time that new concepts for the management of the retarded have been developed, the large and isolated institution for the mentally retarded has become the subject of investigative reporting (Rivera, 1972) and class action suits on behalf of residents at these facilities (Goodman, 1974). Lacking social stimulation and privacy as well, persons in these environments become apathetic and acquire an "institutional" demeanor while the overcrowded conditions have produced serious neglect of basic care (Blatt, 1970). Furthermore, few efforts were undertaken to prepare residents to return to the community. Consequently, Federal district courts have ruled that some institutions could not provide a safe and wholesome environment for so many people and state agencies in charge of these facilities were ordered by the courts to alleviate the conditions of overcrowding and neglect.

[1] This research was supported by NIH Grant HD-01799. Valuable criticism of this paper was provided by Stephen A. Richardson. Sara Goldsmith, Wendy Walker, and Samuel Seiffer were invaluable coworkers in data collection and analysis stages of the research. The Rose F. Kennedy Center provided appropriate facilities and encouraged the development of this study.

According to surveys performed by state mental hygiene officials in New York, as many as one-third of the mentally retarded persons living in these institutions could have remained in the community if alternative local services had been available (Rosenberg, 1969). Large and isolated custodial institutions for the mentally retarded were created to remove them from the complexities of the modern, urbanized and industrialized environment (Wolfensberger, 1969, pp. 94–100). The idea of creating asylums for those who could not compete led to the development of these protective residences, emphasing "benevolent shelter" (Wolfensberger, 1968, p. 97). Ironically, the courts have ruled that these facilities provide little protection and may be hazardous to the well-being of their inmates. Under court orders, the responsible state agencies are required to develop a plan for improving living conditions at the large and isolated institutions.

State and private agencies have attempted to create some alternate living arrangements to large and isolated institutions. Rather than build additional residential units and hire more staff at these large institutions, some mental health and developmental services have attempted to return state school patients to the community, either through independent living arrangements, foster care, or community residential facilities of various types. Today, increasingly large numbers of mentally retarded persons, some with little in the way of adaptive skills to commend them for independent community living, are being resettled.

There have so far been few studies of the functioning of community-based services for the retarded because the efforts to create effective halfway houses, hostels, and group homes on a large scale are very recent. Current efforts in California to return mentally retarded adults to community living have involved extensive use of board-and-care facilities, containing 30, 40, or even more residents. Lacking supportive services and individualized goals to increase the independence of the residents, the board-and-care facilities are in the community but do not utilize it for programs in vocational rehabilitation or recreation. Furthermore, caretakers operate to make a profit and do so maximally when facilities are filled to their capacity. Consequently there is great reluctance to permit a resident to strike out on his own unless a replacement is made available (Edgerton, 1974).

Other investigators in California have provided a different set of facts on board-and-care facilities. Bjannes and Butler (1974) compared the activities of residents at board-and-care facilities and family care and observed that the former encouraged more independent behavior. Furthermore, board-and-care facilities seem more closely to realize the goals of developing social skills and providing a varied round of life than other types of residential facilities in the community. Extensive exposure to the community was found to be an important aspect of reintegrating former state school patients.

This study examines the life experience of 33 men and 18 women who voluntarily left three large and isolated state schools for the mentally retarded and went to live at a community residence we shall call Gatewood. While an original total of 63 persons were resettled, 51 residents who stayed at Gatewood were interviewed twice: first, during their initial week of living at Gatewood to obtain a picture of past activities at state schools and second, 7 to 10 months later to determine the extent to which their lives had changed. Out of the additional 12 who were in the first interview, three residents had gone to live with their parents and one had voluntarily returned to a state school. Seven were transferred back to the original state school because of occasional outbursts. One person was struck by a car and killed.

Through participant observation and standardized open ended interviews at two different times, during the resident's first week at Gatewood and some 7 to 10 months later, data were collected on the experiences of the persons resettled. Comprising some 65 hours, participant observation began during the screening of potential residents at the state schools and continued at Gatewood. In addition, important anecdotal information about the behavior of residents and the problems faced in making policy at Gatewood has been volunteered by staff informants, frequently through conversations. The interviews with residents were conducted by the author and a research assistant. Men were interviewed by a male interviewer and women by a female interviewer. The interviews were concerned with self-image, interpersonal relationships, work experience, use of leisure time, personal decision making, and social competency. One person refused to complete an initial interview and was not reinterviewed. Comparisons are made between answers received during the first and second interviews to assess whether change has taken place and in what direction. A third and final interview focusing on the participation of Gatewood residents in community activities took place 7 to 10 months after the second interview but the data have not been analyzed.

The residents of Gatewood were from that area of the city in which Gatewood is located. Their selection took place at the state schools and persons were removed from further consideration when they had a history of violent behavior, required medical care beyond oral medication, or were regarded as not capable of either competitive employment, achieving sheltered workshop status, or attending a day center program in the community. Each candidate was then brought to Gatewood and asked whether he or she would like to transfer. In a few cases even when guardians refused to approve the move, residents were resettled at Gatewood.

The three state institutions from which residents were selected were among the largest in the United States. Overcrowding prevailed at all three state schools, with one facility providing 47.5 square feet of sleeping space for each patient when state law mandated 80 square feet. In the most publicized state school, there were 5000 residents in facilities designed for 3000. Dormitories generally held up to 70 people and had available one toilet for every ten and one showerhead for every 40. All of these institutions were located in areas far from the families of the patients, with poor public transportation and few opportunities for competitive or sheltered work in the community.

The people who went to live at Gatewood were mainly young adults, with a mean age of 33 years. Many had lived in state schools for most of their adolescent and adult lives. The mean age at time of admission was 16 years and the mean number of years lived in state schools was 18. Before placement in state schools, half of the population were in classes for educable children. When last tested during the past 2 or 3 years, the mean IQ was 51. All persons selected for Gatewood were able to walk, bathe, toilet, dress, and feed themselves. One-third of the population had some medical condition and 16% were subject to seizures and were receiving antiseizure medication when transferred to the community residence. People of different ethnic backgrounds came to live at Gatewood. By virtue of the ethnic composition of the region at the time the population was admitted to the state schools, the predominant groups were 27% Jewish, 23% Puerto Rican, and 20% Black (Table 1).

Gatewood residents were selected for resettlement in 1972 and there has been a substantial change in the characteristics of the populations at state schools since that time. Many of the more able people have been relocated in small and more centrally located residential facilities, leaving behind many people who require maximum care because they can do little for themselves. Even when the local branch of the state developmental service was screening candidates for Gatewood, about 30 able men and women from one state school were already living in a community residence which had been initiated a few years earlier by the developmental service in another catchment area.

While data were not available about the characteristics of the populations of the three state schools that provided residents for Gatewood, one state school with which the local developmental service was working closely provided some interesting comparisons. The Gatewood residents were among the least intellectually and functionally impaired of the residents of that school who came from the geographic area where Gatewood is located.

Table 1. Background characteristics of Gatewood residents

Characteristic	% (N = 51)
Sex	
Male	67
Female	33
Ethnicity	
European	28
Jewish	27
Hispanic	25
Black	20
Age (years)	
Less than 21	14
22–26	18
27–31	22
32–41	20
42 or older	27
IQ	
0–39	16
40–54	49
55–69	23
70–84	12
Recorded associated handicaps	
No recorded medical problems	76
Epilepsy	17
Motor disabilities	7

While 87% of that population is considered severely and profoundly retarded, only 16% of Gatewood residents are in this category. Gatewood residents were older than the state school population, with only 14% being under 21 years compared to 59% in the state schools.

LIVING AT STATE SCHOOLS

The Gatewood residents were interviewed about their activities at the state schools in order to obtain a picture of their daily round of life. While referred to as patients at state schools, they were used to serve others more than they were provided with services, falling somewhere between the totally disabled patient who needed maximum care and supervision and the attendants who provided that care and supervision. Half of the respondents said they worked while at the state schools, being involved mainly in the care and feeding of less able persons, cleaning the ward where they lived, or doing odd jobs such as helping to pick up papers on the ground or the loading or unloading of service trucks. Five residents had steady work in one of the many service shops which provide supplies, repair buildings or clothing, or do other forms of maintenance. One person helped the shoemaker and another had a hand in delivery of supplies from the store room to the ward buildings. Two women worked in the sewing room repairing torn clothing and these were the only people at Gatewood who received minimum wages for work they did at state schools. A large portion of the women's pay went to the state school in partial compensation for their support. Income or pay for residents usually meant a tip for work done for attendants in the form of money or food, with food being used quite often in lieu of cash.

Three residents worked off the grounds doing day labor at local restaurants, garages, bowling alleys, or in domestic service. One man earned the nickname of "the nightbird" from the staff because of his late hour of return from work as a dishwasher in restaurants in the towns near the state school. In no cases were any state school residents involved in vocational rehabilitation either at the state school or in nearby communities.

The lack of available public transportation made working in the community difficult. Isolation in the countryside or low density residential areas made travel in and out of a state school a very time-consuming task. Public transportation in these areas was limited to movement to the large metropolitan area and travel from town to town was dependent on the use of automobiles, taxis, or buses operated by the state schools. The "nightbird" recounted how he often had to walk long distances back from his place of employment because he did not have enough money for a taxi.

Programmed activities at the state school were geared toward adult education or occupational therapy, comprising no more than 10 hours per week or 2 hours per day. A quarter of the Gatewood residents listed these programs as the major daily activity. Adult education and occupational therapy were regarded as not very satisfying and were discussed with little enthusiasm or interest. Attendance at these programs was not compulsory and two residents told interviewers that they skipped these programs regularly and were punished by being locked up during hours when they were not scheduled for a program. In addition, those who cut classes were escorted by attendants to programs and back to their dormitories.

Twenty percent of the respondents said that they did nothing during the day at state schools or sat around the day room, generally watching television. No one seemed enthusiastic about this inactivity but they also did not mention any self-initiated activities such as playing ball with other residents or having conversations.

For many of the Gatewood residents who had worked regularly with an employee of the state school, "the job" was an important way of organizing their lives. Contact between the "boss" and the state school resident could be warm and affectionate as well as a way of "keeping busy" or "staying out of trouble." Residents appeared to welcome any work experience. Some people who did not have steady work often mentioned that they once helped to move beds, or went to pick up some equipment with employees in a trailer truck, indicating that these moments were important in their lives.

Independent entrepreneurial work was also possible as a way of making money. A few respondents reported that they washed and waxed cars or shined shoes on the days when employees received their bi-weekly pay checks. In addition, earnings could be made by receiving tips from attendants for going to the institution's community store for refreshments. Residents were very proud of earning money at the state schools and complained about others who stole money from them. The lack of cash was a universal problem for all residents and they were enthusiastic about opportunities to perform a service for an employee or an attendant.

Spending as a daily activity was possible but did not take place very often on the grounds of the state schools. Residents received an allowance for clothing and incidentals from the Social Security Administration's Aide to the Disabled, which was credited directly to the resident's account at the state school. These funds paid for such items as special toilet articles and refreshment at the community store, but residents did not pay in cash or have control over deductions from these funds. Choice of items was generally limited to a few standard commodities and a few residents said that these stores did not stock the things they wanted to acquire, such as watches, radios, or fashionable clothing.

Gatewood residents reported that recreation, entertainment, and opportunities for sociability were generally organized at state schools as mass activities such as movies, dances, and parties related to holidays. One resident viewed these programs as not providing satisfying social contact, with the summer recreation program being better for him than during other seasons because of the presence of volunteers from neighboring communities. Occasions at which informal sociability could take place were few, particularly cross-sex social contact. Men and women ate their meals in large, sex-segregated dining halls, noted for their noise. At any meal, one might sit at a large rectangular table and 500 residents might be served at one sitting. Places for quiet conversation or to be alone were few and far between at the state schools and residents had a difficult time finding privacy.

Some cross-sex social contact did take place between residents outside of the sponsored activities provided by the staff. A fleeting smile exchanged between residents was often suggested by respondents as the basis for regarding the other as a sweetheart. Residents often said they were too shy to tell others of their fondness for them or often did it indirectly through teasing. Respondents admitted that their sweethears did not always feel the same way towards them. Having a boyfriend or girlfriend was regarded as a desired relationship, even when the love went unrequited.

Sexual activity did take place at the state schools between residents. What psychiatric hospital patients humorously refer to as "bush therapy" seemed to be a common unsponsored activity at state schools as well. Illegitimate births among the women at state schools did take place and new policies did permit the performance of therapeutic abortions on patients. State school policy did not permit birth control information or the means of birth control to be dispensed.

For most Gatewood residents, contact with the wider community outside of the state school was limited to either visits by parents or visits to their parents' homes. Parents were more likely to visit residents than residents were to go to their parents' homes. Only one person said he was able to travel to his parents' homes by himself. Only 25% of the residents claimed to have celebrated their birthday with their family and 25% of the residents had no contact with family at all.

The development of interpersonal relations between residents and attendants was made difficult by the conditions of work for the staff. By virtue of the low rate of pay, difficult working conditions, and shift work, there was a turnover rate of 50 attendants per month at one state school, with few replacements available due to economies in the state budget. Attendants also seemed to know little about the lives of the people in their wards, with a day attendant not able to say whether a patient received medication if the medication was not given during the evening hours.

Relations of Gatewood residents with attendants can be characterized as one of strong dependency. Attendants were not only the source of additional income and some important daily activities but were also the major allocators of other resources as well, such as clothing, beds, soap, etc. Any change in daily routine required the permission of the attendants. Self-reliant behavior could not be encouraged where resources were limited and use of facilities had to be tightly scheduled. Attendants were regarded as the major source of punishment at state schools. Disobedience or the failure to move quickly enough by residents could lead to physical coercion by attendants. There was an isolation room available for locking up more serious offenders or those who could not be controlled. Other punishments were of a more humiliating kind, such as having their clothing removed or being put on a ward for profoundly retarded people, known as a "locked ward." Residents were most sensitive to being subject to unjust punishments, particularly when others who committed violations of the rules did not get caught.

LIVING AT GATEWOOD

Gatewood compared very favorably to the state schools both in physical appearance and the availability of useable space. Each resident shares a bedroom with one other person.

Every two bedrooms are connected through a bathroom. All rooms are carpeted and well furnished and there is a large lounge area and dining area with small tables. Gatewood is operated as a business venture by a proprietor who is licensed and regulated by various state agencies.

Gatewood residents were told that they would leave the state schools to come and live in these pleasant surrounds and learn how to work at a sheltered workshop. The goals of vocational rehabilitation would be to train residents either to become employable in competitive work or to remain permanently as sheltered workshop employees. Placement in vocational rehabilitation training programs at sheltered workshops did not take place until 6 months after the transfer to Gatewood. Moving from a state school to Gatewood ended work routines which had been socially rewarding to residents when they were at state schools. Some of the residents had acquired a great deal of prestige from success-fully performing as helpers in various service shops at the large institutions. These people who had supervised jobs were most severely tried by the long period of inactivity at Gatewood before receiving vocational training.

Life at the state school had prepared residents to keep busy when few activities were available. During the first 6 months at Gatewood, the slow rate of evaluation of candidates for vocational training left many persons at a loss for what to do. The women, who were at first concerned about not working, later became less concerned, and expressed the view that they were content staying home while the men went out to work. Men were more likely to go outside for recreation and entertainment, while women were more likely to remain inside Gatewood.

Spending provided a form of activity during the months of inactivity. The acquisition and use of toilet articles was of great interest. Residents often used up the entire contents of the vials, jars, and cans of bath powder and creams in one day. In addition, at the beginning of each month, a fad of movie-going developed, particularly among the male residents, and singly and in two and threes, they would go off to neighborhood theaters. Once these funds were exhausted, however, there were few ways of earning money.

At the time of the second interview, some 7 to 10 months after having left the state schools, 80% of the residents of Gatewood had been placed in vocational rehabilitation programs at sheltered workshops in the community, permitting residents to follow a daily round of life which included at least 4 hours a day or 20 hours a week of training for work and actual piece work for which they were paid between 5 and 10 dollars per week. All residents in training programs used public transportation (buses and subways) to get to and from the various sheltered workshops and training centers, with some of the more able travelers serving as guides for those who could not travel alone or who had not as yet learned the route from domicile to workplace.

The training received at the sheltered workshops was predominately in assembly work or packing, to be completed while seated at benches and tables. A few residents were putting tickets on garments for a department store, while others were trained for porter-maintenance work or for messenger work. It is important to note that age proved to be no limitation to training and some of the men and women in their fifties would go off to work with other people who were 30 years younger.

The work experience provided an opportunity to meet other people as well as earn some additional spending money. A few residents mentioned that they had found boyfriends and girlfriends among the other trainees at their workshops. In addition, the workshop experience became something to talk about with other residents who attended different workshops.

Money was much more easily available at Gatewood than at the state school. Residents were given cash by staff upon request, up to the amount in their monthly allowances. These funds were intended for clothing and incidentals and the staff tried to get residents to put away part of each allowance for future purchases of clothing. The money could not be spent at Gatewood since no community store existed. Residents learned to use shops and services in their neighborhoods to take care of their needs.

While weekly free entertainment in the form of documentary films from such sources as the telephone company were available at the facility, many residents preferred current adventure movies at local theaters (e.g., James Bond), trips to downtown areas of the city, and amusement parks. A few residents who were able to travel around the city on their own went to these places alone or with one or two other residents. Group trips were also organized for residents for entertainment and recreation.

Most of the attempts to find entertainment began to shift to weekends since residents spend a good part of the daytime hours in travel to vocational rehabilitation training programs or at the workshops. An arts and crafts program at Gatewood provided some activity in the evening but most residents preferred to talk to others or watch television. A few said they were extremely tired from their jobs and went to bed around eight o'clock at night.

Travel to parents' homes was facilitated for residents by relocation in the city because of their total reliance on mass transportation. Initially, parents were curious about Gatewood and came to visit to see how their children were adjusting to the new residential setting. Later, at the time of the second interview, most residents visited their families at their parents' homes rather than having their families visit them at Gatewood. These visits also took place on weekends, with 60% of those who visited their parents able to travel to them on their own.

Living at Gatewood contributed to greater contact between residents, particularly around questions concerning care of the bedrooms. Residents were now responsible for the care of their rooms, which they shared with one other person. Rooms also received many personal touches, both inside and on the outside of the door. Few residents had pictures of their families to display in their rooms. Some disputes ensued between roommates about living arrangements, particularly related to cleaning and to playing radios loudly at night. Some disputes lead to changes of room assignments where people were found to be incompatible.

Opportunity for informal cross-sex social contact occurred frequently at Gatewood. These contacts took place in the public rooms of the facility, and in all probability, in private rooms as well. These opportunities may also have increased the direct conflict between men and women because there were some people who found it hard to avoid teasing and taunting residents of the opposite sex. Residents were often seen embracing in the public rooms and were rarely reprimanded by staff for this behavior. Birth control devices and information were made available to women living at Gatewood.

Small groups tended to form at Gatewood, generally among people who had known each other at the previous state school. These groups would provide a protective social environment within the larger environment of Gatewood. These people would take their meals together, go for walks together or to stores. Sometimes they could be found sitting in the same location, night after night, in the lounge area.

Contact between staff and residents at Gatewood was not characterized by the strong dependency found at the state schools but was oriented more toward counseling the mentally retarded adult about neglected aspects of personal hygiene and how to get along in the community. In addition, certain personal services such as letter writing were performed by the staff for residents, but residents were able to buy many things for themselves for which they previously had to ask the staff at state schools or do without. Staff also helped to arrange for services available only outside of Gatewood such as vocational rehabilitation, health service, and recreation at local community centers. Punishment by the staff was limited to reprimands and threats to send people back to the state schools. As noted earlier, seven residents were transferred back to state schools after violent episodes.

Location in the urban community makes available the opportunity to try new things. Ten percent of the respondents focused on such self-initiated activities as travel to zoos and museums when asked about their activities. While residents are not encouraged to go out at night by staff or each other, many do go places on weekends. They are oriented toward the community as a place where they will find activities and do expect to use the community.

The experiences described here require a more precise focus on the work and travel experience. The new opportunities of being able to work, travel, and have purchasing power are central to the story of what has happened in the lives of Gatewood residents. While initially the pressures quickly to take patients from state schools and return them to the community led to a lengthy period of inactivity, the work experience at the vocational rehabilitation programs in sheltered workshops has provided opportunities for residents not only to develop a life independent of the residential facility, but also to take pride in their accomplishments at the work place.

WORKING IN THE COMMUNITY

The workplace functioned both to maintain existing relationships and to establish new relationships. The social separation of home from workplace for these mentally retarded men and women is not as extreme as it is for other people in the community who work. As many as ten people from Gatewood may be in training at a single workshop. Most residents said that they ate their lunch at the workshop with other people from Gatewood. Still, the workshop was a place where eight respondents say they have found new boyfriends and girlfriends.

Pride of accomplishment in work was evident in responses to questions concerning how jobs were acquired, whether they felt they were doing a good job, and whether the trainee enjoyed his work. Opportunity for steady work provided benchmarks or ways for respondents to recognize and measure their personal progress as well as ability, as illustrated in the following interviews. Here, three workshop trainees show different levels of achievement in their training experience.

Interviewer: How did you get the job?

Respondent No. 1: The first job I got was in a workshop. You do a test first. After the test you go to a metal job. I worked there for 3 weeks, then I got out of there.

Interviewer: How come you got out of there?

Respondent No. 1: Well, they think I was good.

Interviewer: Do you do a good job?

Respondent No. 2: I'm doing good. I know it. I know it. I know I'm doing 3 pounds of metal. I know I'm doing good.

Interviewer: What do you do?

Respondent No. 3: I bend metal.

Interviewer: Do you like it?

Respondent No. 3: Yeah.

The experience of attending a workshop also provides some of the residents with something to talk about when they return in the evening. Residents were observed conversing about some of the features of their respective workshops, with particular interest paid to the different refreshment vending machines. Other people at Gatewood discussed the different kinds of jobs they have done at workshops or complained about not getting the job they wanted. Even getting lost in the transit system while traveling to and from their jobs has become a topic of conversation on occasion. Working, then, may be considered to be a new experience which is conducive to expanding the number of social contacts of the respondents as well as expanding the experiences which can be related to others at Gatewood.

The work experience has also become a source of great pride for people who were seldom regularly paid for work at state schools or who were provided with tips, often in the form of food or cigarettes. Residents returning to Gatewood with checks in the modest amounts of $5 to $10 per week took great pleasure in being able to earn money. Money is now far more important in their lives when there is a variety of places to spend and when purchases are not restricted to what is available in the PX or community store. In fact, when asked "What would you do if you had $300?" respondents were far more likely to say they wanted light consumer items which they could now afford, such as radios and tape recorders, during the second interview than the first. Residents could now save up for those purchases whereas before such desires were not as realizable. During the first interview there was greater emphasis on consumables such as candy or cigarettes, but these differences were not statistically significant.

The intrinsic nature of the work experience is quite different from what was previously experienced at state schools. Assembly work at benches and tables is far more disciplined in the sheltered workshop than at state schools. The programs focus on increasing the attention span and capacity to follow instructions of trainees as well as providing specific skills in assembly and packing tasks. Significantly, far more respondents said they could not talk to each other at work when at sheltered workshops than at state schools. In order to prevent wandering, workshop trainees were often not permitted to get up from their work and were not encouraged to find materials and tools for themselves.

Finally, the work experience creates expectations about whether the task was done well or not. Sheltered workshop supervisors are far more concerned with day to day evaluation and long run predictive trends in performance than state school staff. Given the workshop supervisors' goal of work as a source or rehabilitation, it is no surprise that they are concerned with these questions of productivity and quality of performance. The workshop experience provides the Gatewood resident with a sense that the activities he is expected to perform are serious. They are paid on a piece-rate basis and if output is unsatisfactory they receive less pay or no pay. Given the important place money now occupies in the lives of these retarded people, the evaluation received from workshop counselors and supervisors can be of central concern.

Vocational rehabilitation programs were organized to transmit the habits of work as well as skills. Work was structured to stimulate the environment of competitive employment, where the standards of performance would have to be met if persons in training would be able to keep their jobs. While the tasks performed in sheltered workshops were geared to the abilities of the trainees, a serious atmosphere prevails in order to encourage dedication. Everyone, including those persons who are not expected to keep up productivity so as to qualify for competitive employment, are trained in following the rules of the workplace and are expected to meet the role re-quirements of a trainee. Staying at an assigned place was one habit imparted to Gatewood residents.

> Interviewer: Do you work?
> Respondent No. 4: Yes.
> Interviewer: What do you do?
> Respondent No. 4: I stay at the table at which the man put me.
> Interviewer: What kind of work is it?
> Respondent No. 4: You know, these needles with the cards in them? We put the needles through the cards and thread.

Training in a vocational rehabilitation setting approximated the atmosphere of the world of work, including all of the details of arrival, departure, and starting the day's work. Most importantly, learning how to work with others in a cooperative manner was stressed in the program along with the acquisition of specific skills. Working with others sometimes was shown to involve interdependency as well as the companionship, as depicted in the following description.

> Well, we wait out there on the fifth floor. They open the doors. Then each one punches the time clock. Then you get a sheet of paper, either white, blue, or yellow. That tells you what you are going to work on. You work on needles. Someone else puts them in, we take them out.

Work may be considered then to constitute a central interest of mentally retarded adults once they are located at a community residence and placed in a vocational rehabilitation sheltered workshop. Work also becomes a way of creating responsibility among residents for increased control of their own lives. Personal decision making is encouraged by the new responsibilities demanded by attending the sheltered workshop programs.

Work provides a new orientation to the consequences of their own actions, providing a more self-reliant way to live. Respondents frequently reported that attendants hit patients at state schools. For example, in answer to the question, "What happens if you want to stay in bed late in the morning at a state school?" over half the respondents said they they would be hit, have water thrown on them, or be tossed out of bed. In contrast, no respondent mentioned physical punishment if such a situation emerged at Gatewood. Over half of the respondents said they would be late for work if they stayed in bed in the morning. A similar result was obtained when respondents are asked "What would happen if you want to stay up late?" At the second interview, 23% reported that they would be late for work the next morning, while no such answers were presented when living at state schools was discussed.

CHANGING SELF-EXPECTATIONS

The residents' sense of what others expected from them and what they expected from others changed during the transition period of living in the community. Although the workshop experience provided residents at Gatewood with a central purpose around which they could organize their lives, a long wait of 6 months took place before vocational rehabilitation was made available, a period in which residents had to learn a new way of living. During this period of transition, residents did establish attitudes which recognized the advantages of community living made possible by their new situation. These changes occurred even though programs were not created to orient former state school patients to new expectations for cooperative living at Gatewood or for appropriate behavior in public places. Despite this additional gap in programming, residents acquired a recognition that self-reliance and self-initiated activities were advantageous to them.

Plans for resettlement rarely take into account the subjective reactions of the people being relocated. The meaning of the transfer from the state school to Gatewood is important to report, not only because it provides a way of evaluating consumer response to public services but because it is a way of knowing when further demands can be placed on residents for increased self-reliance. In addition, it reflects a high degree of motivation to learn new skills which can help residents integrate themselves still further into the community.

When residents were presented with the opportunity to move to Gatewood and learn how to work in a sheltered workshop program, initial reactions to this prospect were wide ranging, from the view that "I thought that the only way I would ever get out of here is in a pine box" to an interpretation that this was a response to good behavior. In general, when the screening team from the mental retardation service in charge of resettlement appeared at state schools, residents seemed resigned rather than being overjoyed at the prospect of leaving. One attendant at a state school commented that the women she cared for were used to being told to move from one place to the next.

While visiting Gatewood, prospective residents began to ask questions about the extent to which currently achieved privileges could be maintained. Men were very concerned about whether they would be allowed to travel on their own. Women rarely asked such questions about outside activities, having rarely been granted the right to go off the grounds of the state schools without escort. Prospective residents admired the newness of Gatewood and its appointments but were most astonished by its non-institutional look. One resident noted that the windows were free of the protective metal screening characteristically found on state school buildings. Sometimes the difference in size and appearance confused visitors from state schools, with one person asking about the location of the dining hall while standing in the far smaller dining area at Gatewood.

By all available measures, residents liked Gatewood and preferred living there to living at state schools. A distinct change in the quality of life was recognized by residents to have taken place as well as the evident improvement in physical surroundings. During the first and second interview, respondents were asked about the things they liked about state schools and Gatewood. The freedom and independence available at Gatewood was recognized as its most desirable feature. These qualities were not mentioned at all when asked about state schools. As one person remarked:

> There are two to a room here. I can take a bath whenever I want to. I can go to the store whenever I want to.

To what extent were unfavorable aspects of the two facilities mentioned? Fighting with other residents, poor treatment by staff, and inadequate facilities were suggested by almost all respondents when asked about state schools while fighting among residents was the only complaint about Gatewood. A major source of disappointment, although not expressed directly as a complaint against Gatewood, was the failure to fulfill the promise that they would soon learn how to work, once in the community.

Despite large gaps in programming, residents found the freedom available at Gatewood to be a desired feature.

> Interviewer: Is it different here than at state school?
> Respondent No. 1: They lock the doors and this and that at state school.
> Respondent No. 2: Here it is better. There they always say where are you going and you got to get back on time. If you fight and fool around they put you on the locked ward. Here they don't.

Some respondents found the state school to be full of conflict.

> Respondent No. 3: There was too much trouble and everything. So many fights and everything like that.
> Respondent No. 4: I like it here. I don't have the aggravation I had with the attendants.

A few respondents conceived of the differences in terms of having a stimulating life in the city and leading a round of life like others in the community.

Respondent No. 5: State school is so dead, you know. You don't go out working like most people. . . .

Sometimes the protective environs of institutional living were appreciated in comparison with the dangers of city life. Although this view was exceptional, a few residents were anxious about traffic or the complications of travel on the mass transit system. Residents often told me stories of their commuting difficulties and their preferences for buses over trains. These travel problems became less evident as residents became accustomed to the route they used to get to work and return.

The aspirations of residents also shifted in accommodation to the lack of work and/or increased travel skills. Respondents showed an increased interest in engaging in self-initiated activities with their peers or alone, such as traveling to ball games, going to local stores, parks, and other places. When asked about what they would like to do while living at Gatewood, 41% mentioned these activities the second time as compared with 20% the first time.

The trend toward self-initiated activity was also found in comparing answers to the question, "What are some of the things you can do?" A 15% increase in self-initiated activities was found in answers to this question concerning definition of self as well as a 15% decrease among those who mentioned work as their prime skill or ability. In addition, fewer respondents said during the second interview that they could do nothing or mentioned passive behaviors such as sitting or watching television as a defining activity, indicating a trend away from apathy if not the apathetic behavior characteristically found among institutionalized people.

This change in subjective definition of what they could do may result from the change in situation for Gatewood residents. Most respondents simply did not expect to be inactive. Answers to a question concerning things they did not wish to do or wished to avoid doing confirmed this impression. Respondents desired to avoid inactivity, with the frequency of this answer increasing over time so that 80% of the respondents answered in this way the second time compared with over half during the first interview. Paradoxically, even though fewer activities might have been available at Gatewood than at the larger state schools, idleness seemed to be less socially accepted at Gatewood.

Many of these relocated mentally retarded adults recognized that they had been kept away from society and now wished to become part of it again. Travel represents participation, not just in the sense of something to do, but also something which gives each person a unique history and something to talk about.

Interviewer: What are some of the things you want to do here?

Respondent No. 2: I like to go out and visit different people and see things that I never saw before.

Along the same lines, the more able residents saw living at Gatewood as a step toward further independence. While no resident wished to live on his or her own during the first interview, about 10% at the second interview wished to get "out on my own for good." Others were more specific, seeking "to be out on my own ... to live in a real good apartment."

RESEARCH ISSUES IN THE ESTABLISHMENT OF SMALL RESIDENCES

The experiences of living in large and isolated state schools, while uniform in requiring the acquisition of skills for living at a maximum care residential facility, did vary to the extent that some people were able to find and keep a steady albeit unpaid job. These residents were most out of place at the state school and were also the most vocal in their complaints about not receiving the training at vocational rehabilitation settings during the first 6 months at Gatewood. At this time it is not known to what extent prior work experience facilitates adaptation to community living. As far as adaptation to sheltered workshops is concerned, because the rhythms and discipline of benchwork are quite routine and standardized, they appear to be quite different from the more episodic tasks performed at the state schools.

What we have learned about the transition period suggests that resocialization and even desocialization programs are needed for residents, starting before the return to the community. These programs should include how to get along with roommates, a new social relationship rarely found in state schools; learning how to present themselves in public places in an unobtrusive manner; or alternatively, learning how to ask for help when they need it rather than merely standing around and waiting until it arrives; learning how to deal with interpersonal conflict without involving staff or using physical force; unlearning the obsequious behavior which they brought with them from state schools. Further study is needed of the skills required for living at a community residence and how to teach these skills.

The movement from the state school to the community residence also raises questions about the consequences of different methods of transferring people.

Residents who were moved with others from state schools seem to depend on each other for social support and constitute a peer group while those who are relocated alone have a much sharper break with past associations and are forced often to either form new peer groups or to break into existing closed groups.

The rate of movement also may have an impact upon staff training. When a facility is filled slowly, residents are regarded by a staff as not requiring a program to orient them to the facility and the community. In turn, staff skills may be regarded as unimportant because of the high ratio of staff to residents, making the need for a training program less visible to planners.

A number of other research issues are raised by this case study on the relocation of mentally retarded adults, which are related to the background characteristics and potential for adaptation to community living, particularly for medium or minimum care residential facilities. The trend toward diversification in providing services for the mentally retarded in the community raises many questions about the appropriateness of certain kinds of residential units for homogeneous as compared with heterogeneous populations. These questions were rarely raised when Gatewood residents were originally selected for relocation from state schools because of the pressure to comply with court orders to reduce the populations at these large and isolated institutions. While it would not have been necessary for most of the Gatewood residents to live at state schools if adequate community services were available at the time of placement, not every community residential facility is appropriate for every mentally retarded adult.

There seems to be no direct relationship between IQ and success in return to community living, at least insofar as it can be defined by managing to stay out of trouble in the community or at the residential facility. Mildly retarded persons are often found to have difficulties in getting along with staff members at community residential facilities and often act "bossy" with less able residents. Furthermore, they are more physically mobile in the community outside of the residence and may get into trouble with neighbors and the police much more frequently than moderately retarded persons. Such persons may be in need of supportive services in the form of individual or group counseling, while more severely retarded persons may not require or benefit from such efforts.

Mildly retarded persons may not wish to be in a facility with other mentally retarded people and may thrive in a smaller residential setting, such as family care, which does not call attention to their disabilities or where they would not be in close contact with the profoundly mentally retarded. In the larger state school, mildly retarded persons often were used in service shops as helpers or were informally employed in the "back wards" to take care of what are called by these persons as "low grades" or "vegetables." A community residence provides fewer opportunities for mildly retarded persons to demonstrate their competency and differentiate themselves from those who are less able. Some residents have taken to not mentioning the fact that they were once in state schools and will refer euphemistically to their former location as "upstate."

The length of time spent at a state school may have an important impact on the extent to which resettlement in the community is possible. The person who has spent many years at a state school may initially find it difficult in an open-ended situation where his limitations are not known to others and where he cannot always explain himself. The staff of the community residence were concerned about residents who stood in front of the building, looking not only idle, but unengaged and purposeless. Because Gatewood is on a busy street, the staff seem very conscious of inappropriate behavior and dress, and are constantly correcting residents. In contrast, such behavior at state schools seems to be ignored by the staff, and may be regarded as an attribute of mental retardation rather than as alterable behavior. Similarly, residents had to learn how to walk quietly through the corridors of a public building and other forms of appropriate behavior in public places.

While persons who spent long periods of time in state schools had some difficulty in learning to give off the appropriate cues while in public places, they also had to learn how to get along with each other when there was a greater responsibility for personal decision making in their hands than before. Residents now in control of their direct allowance of

$17 per month for personal expenses had to decide how to spend their money. At the state school, they had an account at the store on the grounds. Since residents had to share a room with one other person, they now had to decide who would do what to maintain the room rather than being told by attendants, as at the state schools, to do different tasks in the wards. Sharing was something that was not encouraged when these persons lived in dormitories with 70 other people. The kinds of social relationships between residents which are possible under differing social and ecological conditions may influence the extent to which self-reliant behavior in the community and at the residence is encouraged or discouraged. Similarly, the relationship established between the resident and members of the staff may take on a different character under differing conditions. If staff spend less of their time directing and supervising residents in basic tasks of daily living (e.g., cleaning rooms), then they may become more available to residents to counsel them in more complicated aspects of living in an urban community. The counseling role may be maximized when authoritative or punitive roles are downplayed or are differentiated.

A residential facility may be conceived of as a microsocial environment within a larger social environment. Many times the points of contact with the larger social environment encourage the development of appropriate behavior on the part of residents and self-reliance. When a facility is in close proximity to neighbors, staff become genuinely concerned about the appearance and mannerisms of residents. When a resident attends a vocational rehabilitation program in the community, he may become more self-regulating, knowing that if he does not get up at seven in the morning he will be late for work.

The resettlement of mentally retarded adults at one community residence can only provide a way of raising research questions about the extent to which mentally retarded adults can be reintegrated in the community. It is important to initiate and complete comparative sociological research on the subject of resettlement, organized around the following questions:

1. What kinds of social skills are needed to live in different residential settings?
2. What socially learned and utilized skills acquired at state schools are appropriate and inappropriate for community living? It is important to develop a typology of social environments, based on different residential facilities, and the different combinations of social skills needed to live in those environments.

A number of organizational characteristics of residential programs can be suggested as constituting some of the dimensions of the social environment in which mentally retarded adults, with differing combinations of characteristics might be fitted. These programs vary by 1) size, 2) availability of supportive human service networks, 3) availability of future placements in more independent settings, 4) availability of candidates for open places in their program, 5) the extent to which the facility is integrated in the community, 6) the extent of coordination with vocational and recreational services, 7) the homogeneity of the population of the facility, 8) the degree of specialization of the facility, 9) the extent to which residents have contact with family, friends, neighbors in the community, 10) staff training and staff-residents ratios, and 11) administrative goals and means of implementation.

The issues examined in the present study arose because of the existence of large and isolated institutions for the mentally retarded and because it has become public policy that residential facilities should be near the families and homes of those who are retarded, with close coordination with community services. This issue is presently the focus of great concern and interest both for professionals and the general public. The current problem of the resettlement of mentally retarded people from state schools has deflected attention from the related social policy issue of providing supporting services, including residential care where needed for the mentally retarded living with their families. The often pressing unmet needs of these families require careful study because the adaptation process of mentally retarded who have been living with their families in moving to residential care are probably different in many respects from the mentally retarded moving away from long term stays in large and isolated institutions. Finally, it can be anticipated that public policy and planning will lead to an increased flow of mentally retarded adults from the community into facilities like Gatewood, perhaps by the end of the decade, reversing current trends to fill community-based residential facilities mainly with former state school patients.

In conclusion, there is a need to develop a model of the network of services that are required by the returning state school patients (and other mentally retarded adults), while carefully avoiding the dangers of overprogramming which can lead to a situation in which mentally retarded adults never learn to act in a self-reliant way or ask for and acquire the services they need. Such a network of services would have to include a variety of models of clients and their behavior, fitting into different residential situations. Future research on resettlement could identify the characteristics of mentally retarded persons who are resettled from state schools and be able to make precise determinations of the relationship between these characteristics and their success in community living.

REFERENCES

Bjaanes, A. T. and E. W. Butler. 1974. Environmental Variation in Community Care Facilities for Mentally Retarded Persons. Am. J. Ment. Defic. 78: 429–439.

Blatt, B. 1970. Exit from Pandemonium. Allyn and Bacon, Boston.

Edgerton, R. 1974. Issues Relating to the Quality of Life Among Mentally Retarded Persons. This volume.

Goodman, W. 1974. The Constitution vs. the Snakepit: How Lawyers are Proving That Mental Inmates Have A Right to Treatment. New York Times Magazine, March 17, pp. 21–37.

Rivera, G. 1972. Willowbrook. Random House, New York.

Rosenberg, A. D. 1969. Appropriateness of the Continued Institutionalization of the State School Population of New York State. Department of Mental Hygiene, Buffalo, N.Y.

Wolfensberger, W. 1969. The Origin and Nature of Our Institutional Models. In R. B. Kugel and W. Wolfensberger (eds.), Changing Patterns of Residential Services for the Mentally Retarded, pp. 59–172. Department of Health, Education and Welfare, Washington, D.C.

Vocational Adjustment
Of the Mentally Retarded

Andrew S. Halpern, Philip L. Browning, and Esther R. Brummer

Questions have been raised since the beginning of this century about the potential of mentally retarded adults for survival outside of an institutional environment. Not surprisingly, vocational adjustment has been an important component of this concern. Early follow-up studies of retarded adults released from state institutions frequently found a relatively high level of vocational adjustment, even though vocational training for these people was either extremely inadequate or non-existent. In spite of these research results, a public attitude favoring separation and segregation of retarded people remained predominant during the first half of this century.

During the past 15 years a great change has occurred in the public stance of our country toward mentally retarded citizens, culminating in a widespread interest in the concept of normalization as developed and applied in the Scandinavian countries. One significant component of this change in attitude has been a renewed and intensified interest in the vocational adjustment of retarded adults.

Thorough reviews of the literature on vocational adjustment of mentally retarded people have been well accomplished elsewhere (Browning, 1974a; Cobb, 1972; Gold, 1973; Goldstein, 1964; Gunzberg, 1965; Wolfensberger, 1967). Rather than repeating such efforts, this chapter focuses on five major neglected areas which still persist in the field: 1) general theoretical inadequacy, 2) the importance of vocational interests, 3) the relevance of social and prevocational skills, 4) vocational training for severely retarded people, and 5) career development.

ONE THEORETICAL APPROACH

Considering the rapid growth and development which the field has continuously experienced since the beginning of the 1960's, it is surprising to note that the topic of theory has received practically no attention throughout this span of time. This is especially puzzling since a conceptual framework concerning the vocational development and adjustment of mentally retarded adults would undoubtedly serve to suggest a limited number of major and interrelated parameters and thus systematically reduce a complex phenomenon to more manageable proportions. The following theory represents one important effort in this area, even though its development has occurred primarily within the context of a non-retarded population.

The U. S. Department of Health, Education, and Welfare for the past 15 years has financially supported a research program entitled, "The Minnesota Studies in Vocational Rehabilitation-Work Adjustment Project." The project focus has been the general area of adjustment to work, with particular attention directed to problems relevant to the vocational rehabilitation of disabled people.

The major achievement of the Work Adjustment Project has been the Theory of Work Adjustment, which provides a conceptual and operational framework for vocational practice and research. The first formulation of the theory was published in 1964 (Dawis, 1964), followed by a revision in 1968 (Lofquist and Dawis, 1969). The final project phase has been devoted to the development of a set of instruments designed to measure the major concepts of the theory.

The Theory of Work Adjustment is presented in Figure 1. A basic premise underlying the theory is that each individual seeks to achieve and maintain a *dual* correspondence with his work environment. This correspondence is viewed as the individual meeting the ability requirements of the job, and the job or work environment fulfilling the need requirements of the individual. The presence of this dual correspondence is manifested when the individual is both satisfactory and satisfied within his work environment. A high degree of satisfactoriness (employer index) and satisfaction (employee index) frequently results in job tenure.

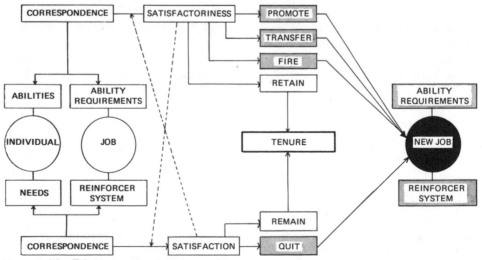

Figure 1. The theory of work adjustment.

The two essential components of an individual's work personality are abilities and needs or preferences. Abilities are basic verbal and motoric response capabilities which a person can utilize, whereas needs are basic preferences for responding to reinforcement stimulus conditions in the environment.

The two basic components of the work environment are analogous to the two components of work personality. Accordingly, a job is described both in terms of its ability requirements and the reinforcement system it offers. To an extent, one can predict satisfactoriness from the ability/ability requirement correspondence and satisfaction from the needs/reinforcement system correspondence.

The Theory of Work Adjustment is an expansion and refinement upon the occupational matching model first articulated by Parsons in 1909. Parsons' approach focused only upon the correspondence between job skills and work requirements, whereas the Minnesota Theory suggests that an individual's occupational preferences and the reinforcement system in the work setting are equally crucial factors in accounting for a person's vocational adjustment. In addition, the authors of the Minnesota Theory have developed a set of instruments which can be used to measure individual differences with respect to each of the major constructs in the theory.

Since the Theory of Work Adjustment is based upon a correspondence paradigm, it gives primary emphasis to the individuality of persons and jobs. This emphasis on individual differences is especially significant in the area of mental retardation, where stereotyping of abilities, needs or preferences, and work placements has been all too prevalent. In commenting upon the applicability of this theory to mentally retarded persons, the authors state that "The individual differences in the abilities and needs [preferences] of mentally retarded persons should have a significance for work adjustment. The mentally retarded individual, just as the normal individual, has a unique work personality, and his own work adjustment possibilities" (Lofquist et al., 1964, p. 10).

Since specific implications of this theory to the vocational world of retarded people have been discussed elsewhere (Browning, 1972; 1974b), they will be mentioned only briefly in this chapter. First, the theory has practical implications in respect to 1) definition of disability and work adjustment, 2) evaluation and training, 3) counseling, and 4) placement. Second, the theory has research implications with respect to 1) framework for empirical findings, 2) systematic basis for selection of variables to be investigated, 3) instrumentation, and 4) generation of hypotheses. A major utility of the theory is that it provides a systematic frame of reference for both practice and research considerations, and they relate to each of the above areas.

In spite of the utility of the Theory of Work Adjustment for understanding vocational adjustment of the mentally retarded, there are certain shortcomings in this theory which need to be remedied through further inquiry. The Theory of Work Adjustment is basically a placement model and, as such, a static model of vocational adjustment. Evaluation is viewed primarily as a tool for placement and only secondarily as a tool for training. Because of this bias, the developmental aspects of vocational adjustment are largely neglected, including the impact of vocational training.

Many studies and demonstrations, however, suggest that training and experience can have a profound impact upon both vocational abilities and needs of retarded people, implying that the development and maintenance of vocational adjustment is a lifelong task, subject to possible frequent change. Further theoretical exploration of the vocational *development* of mentally retarded workers should help our understanding of their vocational adjustment. Perhaps some of the theoretical approaches from vocational psychology will be useful in this regard.

VOCATIONAL NEEDS AND INTERESTS

The Theory of Work Adjustment focuses attention not only upon abilities which are specific to the job situation, but also upon the individual's preferences for a unique set of work-related reinforcers. Unfortunately, the work interests of retarded people have received only scant research attention.

In referring to this aspect of the work personality, the most commonly used terms have been vocational interests and vocational needs or preferences. Vocational interests have been defined as the degree to which an individual is favorably inclined toward performing activities involved in a specific occupational category (Parnicky, Kahn, and Burdette, 1965). By contrast, vocational needs have been defined as preferences for the reinforcement values of general stimulus conditions in a work setting (Lofquist and Dawis, 1969). Both constructs are motivational variables applying to the attitudes, feelings, or drives an individual implements in the world of work.

There are very few instruments that have been developed to measure the needs or interests of mentally retarded people, and most of what does exist has utilized a pictorial approach. Nonverbal instruments devised to elicit choices among occupations include: The Picture Inventory of Semi-skilled Jobs (Urich, 1960), The Reading-Free Vocational Interest Inventory (Becker, ND), and the Vocational Interest and Sophistication Assessment (Parnicky, Kahn, and Burdette, 1968). Burg and Barrett (1965) used a bisensory approach by presenting both visual and verbal cues, showing pictures from the Geist Picture Inventory (Geist, 1959), and simultaneously presenting a question and an oral description of the picture. In the area of vocational needs, the Minnesota Importance Questionnaire-Form S has been developed for use with mentally retarded people (Lofquist and Dawis, 1970).

Studies conducted with these instruments, however, have not clarified the relationship between experience and interest, a question of vocational development. Wolfensberger (1967, p. 248) makes the following statement while discussing studies of retarded persons' vocational interests:

> . . . preliminary findings suggest that the relevant interests of retardates (sic) are easily affected by experience. If that should be the case, training should probably aim at shaping interest rather than be based upon it.

A study conducted by one of the present authors (Brummer, 1973) examined the impact of one potential influence on the vocational needs and interests of mildly retarded young adults, a paid work experience. One of the hypotheses investigated was whether or not a paid work experience would broaden and clarify the vocational needs and interests of mildly retarded adolescents.

Experimental subjects were 31 educable mentally retarded young persons chosen by their vocational rehabilitation counselors in Lane County, Oregon to participate in a summer employment program. Criteria for selection were: 1) age 16 to 22 years, 2) ability, according to counselor judgment, to benefit from a paid summer work experience, 3) no previous work experience, and 4) current enrollment in or recent termination from a work/study program in one of Oregon's high schools.

Comparison subjects were 35 mentally retarded young persons in the Portland area. Portland Vocational Rehabilitation Division counselors were asked to select clients from their work/study caseloads, according to the same criteria as the Lane County counselors, *as if* these persons were to be participating in a summer work experience.

Over an 8-week period, program participants worked 32 hours per week for $1.60 an hour at job sites selected to provide meaningful work, individual supervision, and training in relevant work skills and habits. Weekly counseling sessions were held with each participant. All efforts were made to insure that the work experience provided was as realistic as possible while still attempting to meet the needs of beginning retarded workers.

Two instruments were used to measure vocational interests and needs. The VISA (Vocational Interest and Sophistication Assessment) is a pictorial interest inventory developed for and standardized on mentally retarded adolescents and adults (Parnicky and Kahn, 1963; Parnicky, Kahn and Burdette, 1968). The male form of the VISA has 75 pictures covering seven job areas: farm/grounds, food service, garage, industry, laundry, maintenance, and materials handling. The female form consists of 53 pictures covering four job areas: business/clerical, food service, housekeeping, and laundry/sewing. Degrees of preference for each picture are elicited. Raw scores are plotted on profiles which are based on standardization norms (Parnicky, Kahn, and Burdette, 1971).

The MIQ-Form S (Lofquist and Dawis, 1970) is a revision of the Minnesota Importance Questionnaire (Gay et al., 1971) modified for use with mentally retarded persons. The MIQ-Form S is a paired-comparison questionnaire which yields scores on twenty vocational need scales. Examples of vocational needs tapped by this instrument are: 1) ability utilization, 2) creativity, and 3) job security.

The major finding of this study was that the range of responses on the MIQ-S increased significantly for the experimental group from pretest to post-test while the comparison group range did not. This suggests that the paid work experience did indeed have an impact upon work personality, causing some needs to emerge as highly important and other needs to emerge as relatively unimportant.

Although this study represents some initial effort in a highly neglected area, there is obviously much additional work that needs to be done. In order for this area to be more researchable, a first priority must be the development of improved instrumentation, especially in the area of vocational interests. Once improved instruments are available, we may begin to explore an indefinite number of research questions which pertain to how well the work setting is meeting the retarded person's requirements in terms of his vocational interests or needs. The following are but a few questions which might be investigated:

1. To what extent do differing prevocational experiences affect the vocational interest and need patterns of mentally retarded workers?

2. What is the relationship between the retarded person's actual vocational choice and expressed vocational interests?

3. What is the relationship between differing levels of subaverage intelligence and vocational interest patterns?

4. Does ability level have a greater moderating effect on occupational interests of mentally retarded workers than on non-retarded workers?

SOCIAL AND PREVOCATIONAL SKILLS

Several reviewers of relevant research have suggested that social and prevocational skills may be as important as or more important than specific vocational skills in facilitating the ultimate vocational adjustment of mentally retarded workers, especially those whose level of retardation is mild (Goldstein, 1964; Wolfensberger, 1967). Although this has been a very popular hypothesis for a number of years, little research evidence is available to provide empirical support. A major reason for the lack of appropriate research has been the unavailability of instrumentation for measuring social and prevocational skills.

A current project of one of the present authors has resulted in the development of a battery of instruments designed to measure knowledge of social and prevocational competencies among mildly retarded respondents. The package of instruments, developed over a 3-year period, is known as the Social and Prevocational Information Battery (SPIB). This battery consists of a series of nine tests that relate to five broad clusters of social and prevocational competencies: employability, economic self-sufficiency, family living, personal habits, and communication (Halpern et al., in press). The SPIB can now be purchased from the California Test Bureau/McGraw-Hill.

There are, of course, many component skills that are included in these five broad clusters. Although the nine tests in the SPIB represent only a portion of these component skills, they were selected because of their importance in school and rehabilitation programs for mildly retarded adolescents. The title of each test refers to a component skill, and the relationship between component skills and skill clusters is shown in Table 1.

Each test in the SPIB consists of approximately 30 items, either true/false or picture selection in format. The tests are administered orally, thus eliminating the effect of differential reading ability. Each test requires 15 to 25 minutes of testing time, and group administration is possible. A thorough account of the test development procedures has been published elsewhere (Halpern et al., in press).

Nearly 2000 pupils from EMR classrooms in Oregon have been tested on various developmental forms of the SPIB. The difficulty levels range from a mean of 61% correct

Table 1. Relationship between skill clusters and SPIB tests

Skill cluster	SPIB tests
Employability	Job search skills
	Job-related behaviors
Economic self-sufficiency	Banking
	Budgeting
	Purchasing
Family living	Home management
	Physical health care
Personal habits	Hygiene and grooming
Communication	Functional signs

for the hardest test (banking) to a mean of 79% correct for the easiest test (functional signs). Internal consistency reliabilities (Coefficient Alpha) range from 0.65 to 0.82 for the individual tests, and the value for the total battery is around 0.93. Test-retest reliabilities are nearly identical with the measures of internal consistency.

One of the samples that has been tested on the SPIB is the population of seniors who graduated from work/study programs in Oregon during June, 1973 ($N = 220$). Approximately 130 of these pupils were assigned to a vocational rehabilitation counselor as part of the work experience program in Oregon. Since the vocational rehabilitation counselors had known these students during some portion of their high school years and had continued contact with some of them after graduation, it was possible to request an assessment of post-school adjustment from these counselors. To facilitate this assessment, a rating instrument was designed in collaboration with the counselors that would provide five scores reflecting general adaptation in the areas of community integration, economic self-sufficiency, communication, family living, and personal habits. Clients were then rated on these scales, approximately 1 year after graduating from high school.

A first order cannonical correlation of 0.58 was found between the nine tests of the SPIB and the five criterion subscales, indicating a moderate predictive relationship between the two sets of variables. This correlation was probably attenuated to some degree since 50% of the 105 follow-up clients received some type of post-school training or education during the 1 year interval since graduation.

The correlations between the SPIB and employment status, however, were not significant, which raises some questions about the presumed relationship between social and prevocational skills and *vocational* adjustment. There are a number of alternative hypotheses that would be more consistent with the current findings:

1. Social and prevocational skills other than those measured by the SPIB are good predictors of vocational adjustment.
2. Performance rather than knowledge of social and prevocational skills is a good predictor of vocational adjustment.
3. Vocational adjustment is independent of social and prevocational skills.

Additional research is clearly needed in order to explore these and other competing hypotheses.

VOCATIONAL TRAINING FOR SEVERELY RETARDED PEOPLE

Several research reports have shown that moderately and severely retarded adults can learn surprisingly complex vocational tasks. Clark and Hermelin (1955) taught six such adults a number of work tasks, including manufacture of a television plug by soldering color-coded wires to correct terminals, and assembly of a bicycle pump which required nine manual operations with small parts. More recently, moderately retarded workers have been taught to assemble electrical relay panels (Tate and Barhoff, 1967), television rectifier units (Huddle, 1967), and 14-piece and 24-piece bicycle brakes (Gold, 1972), to use a drill press in the manufacture of pencil holders (Crosson, 1969), and to insert circuit board components (Gold, 1973). In a demonstration workshop presently operating at the University of Oregon, moderately and severely retarded individuals have been taught to complete a 52-piece cam switch assembly which requires the use of five different hand tools, a 24-piece and 26-piece printhead assembly for a labeling gun such as the kind used in most grocery stores, a four-piece electrical cord assembly involving the use of three different hand tools, and a six-piece battery pack assembly which requires soldering.

A careful examination of these various studies and demonstrations shows one common factor to run throughout: in each instance, the vocational task, although potentially complex, was broken down into a series of sequential subtasks. Each resulting subtask was relatively simple, requiring neither complex discriminations, complex responses, nor complex judgments connecting appropriate discriminations with appropriate responses. Retarded subjects were then taught these subtasks, using procedures based on the findings of laboratory research on operant learning, imitation, and discrimination learning.

Results such as these raise new questions about how we should define and measure vocational abilities, since they appear to be a function not only of personal characteristics, but also of task complexity and method of training. One possible and practical approach would be to define level of vocational ability as the *amount of time* required for training within the context of the type of training employed and complexity of the vocational task. Such a definition would focus attention on the possibility that vocational performance is constantly amenable to change, and can be manipulated effectively through training, even with moderately and severely retarded persons. The question for evaluation would then become one of predicting training time for a task of given complexity with prescribed training methods, using readily available client characteristics as the predictors.

In defining *level* of vocational ability as the training time required to accomplish a task of given complexity using prescribed training methods, the focus of evaluation clearly is shifted from placement to training. Different *abilities* are defined in terms of *environmental* variables, i.e., varying levels of task complexity and alternate methods of training. The evaluation problem becomes the identification, if possible, of client characteristics that will predict training time of individuals within the context of different abilities.

Such an approach to vocational evaluation of severely retarded people would appear to be warranted from the impressive results that are currently being reported about vocational training for this population. There is no good reason to assume *a priori* that most vocational tasks are too complex for severely retarded people to accomplish. Given the correct approach to training and a sufficient amount of time, severely retarded people are clearly capable of much greater accomplishments than their performance on the back wards of institutions would lead one to believe.

CAREER DEVELOPMENT

Since vocational needs and abilities develop over time and are subject to change as a consequence of new experience, it is important to conceptualize and then investigate the important events and processes that contribute to a person's career development. The tremendous surge of interest in career education during the 1970's would suggest that career development has been greatly neglected by our traditional educational system. This has certainly been true with respect to educational programs for mentally retarded pupils, in spite of the widespread proliferation of work-study programs during the past 15 years. These programs do focus on vocational adjustment, but the process is late in starting and frequently builds on a weak foundation.

In order to maximize an individual's potential for career development, career education should begin at a very early age, perhaps even during the primary school years. The first level of instruction should focus on career awareness, somehow exposing the pupil to information and experience that has vocational ramifications. The next level of instruction involves career exploration, where the information and experiences become more focused on specific vocational opportunities, and the intensity of involvement is increased as its importance continues to grow. The final level of instruction involves vocational evaluation and training. The purpose at this level is to prepare the pupil for entry into his or her first job. If vocational evaluation and training have been built upon a strong foundation, the pupil's abilities and needs should have been well recognized and developed, enhancing the likelihood that his or her first job will be a satisfying and satisfactory first step in the implementation of a career.

Career development, in its broadest sense, involves more than the development of a repertoire of vocational behaviors. Such a repertoire is certainly important, and can be described generally in terms of two categories: work habits and work productivity. Work habits refer to those behaviors that are critical to survival on a job but which are not denoted in the specific requirements of the job. Typical examples include punctuality, reliability, motivation, willingness to accept supervision and ability to get along with fellow employees. Work productivity refers to how well the employee meets standards (both his own and his employer's) for the production of goods or services.

There are other skills, however, which can also be stressed in a curriculum for mentally retarded pupils which may have an equally important impact upon their career development. Some of these skills are primarily personal in nature while others are primarily social. The personal domain includes motor, affective, and cognitive skills. Traditional educational objectives, of course, have always focused heavily on the development of cognitive skills. The social domain includes self-help skills, communication skills, interpersonal skills, and independent living skills. Some of these skills have been addressed in traditional educational programs, but not nearly to the extent that is possible and desirable, especially with mentally retarded pupils. As a result, the hypothesized relationships among personal, social, and vocational behaviors have had little opportunity for either empirical verification or theoretical elaboration.

One noteworthy alternative to traditional educational programs for mentally retarded pupils is the Social Learning Curriculum being developed by Goldstein (1972) and his associates at Yeshiva University. This curriculum incorporates many of the personal, social, and vocational objectives mentioned above into a developmental framework that begins with knowledge about one's self and expands to include the broader environments of family, neighborhood and community. Using an inductive problem-solving approach as the primary method of instruction, this curriculum is concerned mainly with preparing its pupils for ultimate community adjustment. At this time the curriculum has been largely developed at the primary and intermediate levels, and work is just underway at the junior and senior high levels. When this curriculum is completed and implemented, it should provide one good opportunity for exploring the personal, social, and vocational dimensions of career development.

SUMMARY AND CONCLUSIONS

The five topics discussed in this chapter are important current concerns which relate to the vocational adjustment of mentally retarded people. Theoretical development is sorely needed in order to provide guidance to both research and practice in the field. Attention must be paid to vocational interests and needs, as well as vocational abilities. In addition, social and prevocational skills need to be explored further in order to ascertain their significance as a predictor and/or component of vocational adjustment.

The extraordinary success of recent vocational training efforts for the severely retarded brings into question the traditional view that vocational abilities are extremely limited in this population. A new perspective was suggested which would define vocational abilities in terms of *environmental* variables (task complexity and training methods), and ability level in terms of the amount of time required to learn a task of given complexity with prescribed training techniques.

Vocational adjustment was then placed in the broader context of career development, implying a central role for public education in this field. As efforts in this area proliferate, it should become possible to explore more carefully the relationships between personal, social, and prevocational skills and vocational adjustment.

REFERENCES

Browning, P. L. 1972. Research: A consideration for theory. *In* M. Cohen (ed.), International research seminar on vocational rehabilitation of the mentally retarded. American Association on Mental Deficiency, Special Publication Series, Washington, D.C. No. 1, pp. 269–275.

Browning, P. L. (ed.) 1974a. Mental retardation: Rehabilitation and counseling. Charles C Thomas, Springfield, Illinois.

Browning, P. L. 1974b. The work adjustment of the mentally retarded: A frame of reference for practice and research. *In* P. L. Browning (ed.), Mental retardation: Rchabilitation and counseling, pp. 177–197. Charles C Thomas, Springfield, Illinois.

Brummer, E. R. 1973. The effects of a paid work experience upon the measured vocational needs and interests of mentally retarded adolescents. Unpublished doctoral dissertation, State University of New York at Buffalo.

Burg, B. W. and A. M. Barrett. 1965. Interest testing with the mentally retarded: A bi-sensory approach. Am. J. Ment. Defic. 69: 542–552.

Clarke, A. and F. Hermelin. 1955. Adult imbeciles: Their abilities and trainability. Lancet 2: 337–339.

Cobb, H. V. 1972. The forecast of fulfillment: A review of research on predictive assessment of the adult retarded for social and vocational adjustment. Teachers College Press, Teachers College, Columbia University, New York.

Crosson, J. 1969. A technique for programming sheltered workshop environments for training severely retarded workers. Am. J. Ment. Defic. 73: 814–818.

Dawis, R. V., G. W. England, and L. H. Lofquist. 1964. A theory of work adjustment. Minnesota studies in vocational rehabilitation. Monograph No. XV.

Gay, E. G., D. J. Weiss, D. D. Hendel, R. V. Dawis, and L. H. Lofquist. 1971. Manual for the Minnesota Importance Questionnaire. Minnesota Studies in Vocational Rehabilitation, Monograph No. XXVIII.

Geist, H. 1959. The Geist Picture Interest Inventory: General Form. Psychological Test Specialists, Missoula, Montana. Monograph Supplement No. 3.

Gold, M. 1972. Stimulus factors in skill training of the retarded on a complex assembly task: Acquisition, transfer, and retention. Am. J. Ment. Defic. 76: 517–526.

Gold, M. 1973. Research on the vocational habilitation of the retarded: The present, the future. *In* N. Ellis (ed.), International review of research in mental retardation, Vol. 6. Academic Press, New York.

Gold, M. 1973. Printed circuit board assembly for the moderately and severely retarded. Paper presented at the American Association on Mental Deficiency, Annual Convention, Atlanta, Georgia.

Goldstein, H. 1964. Social and occupational adjustment. *In* H. A. Stevens and R. F. Heber (eds.), Mental retardation: A review of research, pp. 214–258. University of Chicago Press, Chicago.

Goldstein, H. 1972. Construction of a social learning curriculum. *In* E. Meyer, G. Vergason, and R. Whelen (eds.), Strategies for teaching exceptional children. Love Publishing Co., Denver.

Gunzberg, H. C. 1965. Vocational and social rehabilitation of the subnormal. *In* A. M. Clarke and A. B. Clarke (eds.), Mental deficiency: The changing outlook, pp. 385–416. The Free Press. New York.

Halpern, A., P. Raffeld, L. Irvin, and R. Link. Measuring social and prevocational awareness in mildly retarded adolescents. Am. J. Ment. Defic. In press.

Huddle, D. 1967. Work performance of trainable adults as influenced by competition, cooperation, and monetary reward. Am. J. Ment. Defic. 72: 198–211.

Lofquist, L. H., T. F. Siess, R. V. Dawis, G. W. England, and D. J. Weiss. 1964. Disability and work. Minnesota Studies in Vocational Rehabilitation, Monograph No. XVII.

Lofquist, L. H. and R. V. Dawis. 1969. Adjustment to work: A psychological view of man's problems in a work-oriented society. Appleton-Century-Crofts, New York.

Lofquist, L. H., and R. V. Dawis. 1970. Assessing the work personalities of mentally retarded adults. Department of Psychology, University of Minnesota, Final Report, Minneapolis.

Parnicky, J. J. and H. Kahn. (eds.) 1963. Evaluating and developing vocational potential of institutionalized retarded adolescents. Edward R. Johnstone Training and Research Center, Bordentown, New Jersey.

Parnicky, J. J., H. Kahn, and A. B. Burdette. 1965. Preliminary efforts at determining the significance of retardates' vocational interests. Am. J. Ment. Defic. 70: 393–398.

Parnicky, J. J., H. Kahn, and A. B. Burdette. 1968. Standardization of the vocational interest and sophistication assessment (VISA): A reading free test for retardates. Edward R. Johnstone Training and Research Center, Bordentown, New Jersey.

Parnicky, J. J., H. Kahn, and A. B. Burdette. 1968. Manual for the vocational interest and sophistication assessment. Edward R. Johnstone Training and Research Center, Bordentown, New Jersey.

Parnicky, J. J., H. Kahn, and A. B. Burdette. 1971. Standardization of the VISA (vocational interest and sophistication assessment) technique. Am. J. Ment. Defic. 75: 442–448.

Tate, B., and G. Barhoff. 1967. Training the mentally retarded in the production of a complex product: A demonstration of work potential. Exceptional Children 33: 405–408.

Urich, D. A. 1960. Picture inventory of semi-skilled jobs (male and female forms). Brandon Training School, Brandon, Vermont.

Wolfensberger, W. 1967. Vocational preparation and occupation. *In* A. Baumeister (ed.), Mental retardation: Appraisal, education and rehabilitation, pp. 232–273. Aldine Publishing Co., Chicago.

Advocacy for The Mentally Retarded: The Development Of a New Social Role

Richard A. Kurtz

While any specific date is more symbolic than real, for convenience we may use October 1950, i.e., the date of the founding convention of the parent-sponsored National Association for Retarded Children (NARC), as the starting point for current ideas about advocacy for the mentally retarded. There had been attempts to start such organizations before this date, but none succeeded until the NARC stimulated local and state organizations to bring parents together to discuss mutual problems and to plan strategies for bringing about social change. Consequently, local branches of the NARC used their knowledge of and familiarity with decision makers in such organizations as school boards and state legislatures to point to a lack of programs for the retarded and to call for community recognition of a responsibility to invest social resources in the search for alleviation and amelioration. Parents learned that pressures can lead to action, and this in turn contributed to the emergence of community-based service programs for the retarded and their families.

This progress of the 1950's was followed by a dramatic new emphasis on mental retardation in the 1960's, primarily because of President Kennedy's publicly expressed interest in the condition. Frequently neglected by both professionals and legislators until this time, the identification of mental retardation as a problem in need of attention led to an about-face in interest, changing from a situation of benign neglect to one of an enormous social investment in problems of the condition. Politically sophisticated about procedures which would bring conditions before the public eye and conscience, President Kennedy appointed a panel of mental retardation experts with a charge to prepare a plan to combat the problem. One year later, the President's Panel on Mental Retardation Report (1962) was published under the title "A Proposed Program for National Action to Combat Mental Retardation." Four months later President Kennedy sent a Special

Message on Mental Illness and Mental Retardation to Congress, using the President's Panel Report as the guide for a national mental retardation program. There is no doubt that President Kennedy served as the catalyst in "elevating" mental retardation to social problem status in the American society, which is a status that it has retained ever since.

NORMALIZATION OF THE RETARDED: A NEW SYSTEM OF VALUES

The 1960's were important to the retarded for another reason. Toward the end of the decade a new system of values spread rapidly among workers in the field, as the principles of normalization captured the imagination of both parents and professionals. Quite suddenly, these principles came to dominate much of the field, as they served to identify areas of neglect for the retarded. Few problems have experienced so rapid a transformation in social perceptions as did mental retardation when the new value system was introduced. Almost overnight, normalization became the guiding light and the battle cry of laymen, parents, and professionals.

The first major spokesman for normalization was Bengt Nirje, a Scandinavian visitor to the United States who detailed the implications of the principle through a chapter in a monograph published under the auspices of the President's Committee on Mental Retardation (Nirje, 1969). Declaring that normalization applies to all of the retarded, irrespective of their degree of retardation and their residential patterns, Nirje (1969) declares that " ... the normalization principle means making available to the mentally retarded patterns and conditions of everyday life which are as close as possible to the norms and patterns of the mainstream of society" (p. 181). At root, the message of the normalization principle is that the human needs of the retarded must be recognized and must be taken under consideration in the community. In each of eight major points Nirje suggests that the retarded are human beings who have needs which are similar to the needs of the non-retarded. By implication, if the retarded are being denied an opportunity for normal experiences because of their retardation, the society must be restructured to make certain that opportunities for normal behavior, given the presence of limitations, are possible.

Nirje's presentation is a compelling one which states the principles in theoretical terms and then quickly removes the message from a purely idealistic level with the disarming statement that "it may be sobering to many Americans that in Sweden, programs based on normalization principles are not dreams but actual realities ... " (p. 188). In an enthusiastic statement he suggests that the normalization principle cannot be dismissed as some idealistic, unrealistic, unachievable, theoretical statement of desire on the part of a few strongly committed individuals. Rather, it is uncritically described as a workable public policy which is based on recognition of the human character of the mentally retarded. Nirje thus became the spokesman for a system of values which set an idealistic context within which the human rights of the retarded could be advocated.

RIGHTS OF THE RETARDED: A NEW SYSTEM OF NORMS

In many ways the American Association on Mental Deficiency (AAMD) official statement on the Rights of Mentally Retarded Persons (AAMD, 1973) calls for a reformulation of programs and services to meet the human needs which are identified in the normalization principle. Thus, while normalization spells out the normal needs of the retarded individual, in many respects the AAMD statement reinterprets normalization as a series of rights which emphasize that "mentally retarded citizens are entitled to enjoy and to exercise the same rights as are available to nonretarded citizens, to the limits of their ability to do so" (AAMD, 1973, p. 56). In this context the AAMD statement on the Rights of Mentally Retarded Persons presents a specific charge to professionals to commit themselves to the securing of these rights for retarded individuals. Thus, in an almost emotional call to action, the AAMD aggressively declares that:

> Professionals in the field, individually and in concert, should assert leadership in the protection of these rights, in assuring their exercise and enjoyment by retarded citizens, and in the implementation of these rights to provide for more satisfying circumstances of life for retarded persons.... *When a professional sees that retarded individuals are being dealt with in a manner inconsistent with the principles expressed in this document, then that professional person should act in a conscientious manner to remedy the situation immediately,* through individual or group action, and by formal or informal process. This may be accomplished through job action, through administrative action, through legislative action, through judicial action, or *through whatever public or private means are available, moral, ethical, and legal.* The Association pledges to support such efforts.... When an individual retarded citizen is unable to enjoy or exercise his or her rights, *it is the obligation of the society to intervene so as to safeguard these rights,* and to act humanely and conscientiously on that person's behalf (AAMD, 1973, p. 56; emphasis added).

There is clearly a significant difference in tone between the principles of normalization and the statement of rights for the mentally retarded. Whereas the Nirje (1969) statement is written as an enthusiastic series of principles affecting the normal life of the retarded individual, the AAMD (1973) statement may be seen as an action-oriented listing of demands. Interpreting these events historically, it may be concluded that the normalization principle has provided the value base and the direction for the development of an aggressive series of specific demands upon society.

ADVOCACY FOR THE RETARDED: A NEW SYSTEM OF ROLES

The final right of the retarded which is listed in the official AAMD statement is of particular interest to this discussion. It reads as follows:

> The right, for a retarded individual who may not be able to act effectively in his or her own behalf, to have a responsible impartial guardian or advocate appointed by the society to protect and effect the exercise and enjoyment of these foregoing rights, insofar as this guardian, in accord with responsible professional opinion, determines

that the retarded citizen is able to enjoy and exercise these rights (AAMD, 1973, p. 58; original underlined).

Utilizing a historical perspective once again, the right to a guardian or advocate may be interpreted as the culmination of a series of ideas which start with the normalization principle, reach a mid-position with a charge to workers in the field to commit themselves to securing human rights for the retarded, and end with a suggestion of means for reaching goals. In other terms, the normalization principle has legitimized a new value definition of the mentally retarded, the statement on rights has legitimized a new social norm definition for professionals *vis-à-vis* the retarded, and advocacy represents a statement of the need for a new role for those who wish to protect the retarded in their associations with the community.

To a large degree, the idea of an advocacy role for the mentally retarded is a specific outcome of a general revival of interest in advocacy among social workers, who have recently been engaged in journal discussions of new dimensions concerning the relationship between the profession and its clients (McCormick, 1970). In its most general sense advocacy denotes ". . . the actions and role that social workers are committed to when the human, moral, civil, and legal rights of their clients are transgressed by individuals, groups, or social institutions" (Adams, 1973, p. 840). In this context, a National Association of Social Workers (NASW) Ad Hoc Committee on Advocacy has stated that in playing the role the social worker is a "champion of social victims," further declaring that the role comes directly from this organization's Code of Ethics and that " . . . the professional social worker is ethically bound to take on the advocacy role if he is to fulfill his professional responsibilities" (NASW Ad Hoc Committee on Advocacy, 1969, p. 16). While "the nature of such a role and the responsibilities attached to it were recognized half a century ago by the leaders of what was then an emerging profession" (McCormick, 1970, p. 4), social worker interest in advocacy has been revived during the past few years.

Most of the literature about advocacy in these publications cite the social worker's advocacy obligations toward large groupings of individuals who are in deprived social circumstances. In this context the beneficiaries of social worker advocacy are social categories which lack spokesmen and the ability to bring about needed changes, e.g., children, the poor, the handicapped, members of minority groups, etc. (Grosser, 1965; Brager, 1968; NASW Ad Hoc Committee on Advocacy, 1969; McCormick, 1970; Paull, 1971; Mahaffey, 1972). While the retarded may be added to this listing, the development of an advocacy role for the mentally handicapped has taken a different turn. Thus, while social workers refer to "social advocacy" for large groupings, those who have written about the role for the mentally retarded refer to "citizen advocacy," which emphasizes a relationship between the advocate and only one individual.

Citizen Advocacy

In tracing the development of the advocacy role as it has been operationalized for the mentally retarded, it is appropriate to initiate the discussion with Edgerton's (1967) study of the community adjustments of former residents of an institution for the retarded. In this study it was suggested that "benefactors" in the community, normal persons who help the retarded with their practical everyday affairs, are extremely important in helping former residents of the institution to maintain themselves in the community by providing " . . . welcome assistance with the practical difficulties of coping with everyday problems, with the multifold problems of passing, and even with the delicate need for denial" (p. 172). This description of the benefactor role is not precisely consistent with the AAMD and social worker charges to advocates to intervene when the rights of the individual are transgressed since the latter two statements suggest a reactive role for the advocate, while Edgerton is describing a more general everyday activity role. The citizen advocate role is described in both cases, although the emphases differ.

Given the fact that the advocacy role is a new one for the retarded, there has been a flurry of recent discussion among professionals who are attempting to understand the emerging associations between the advocate and the retarded person, and between the advocate and the community. Standing in a central position between the retardate and the social system, questions of legitimate rights and obligations arise for the incumbents of the advocate status. It is to such discussions of the advocacy role that attention will now be turned.

A leading contributor to this discussion has been Wolfensberger (1972), whose monograph on citizen advocacy was published by the President's Committee on Mental Retardation. Defining the advocate as "a mature, competent citizen volunteer representing, as if they were his own, the interests of another citizen who is impaired in his instrumental competency, or who has major expressive needs which are unmet and which are likely to remain unmet without special intervention" (p. 12; for a discussion of instrumental and expressive needs see Parsons and Bales, 1955), Wolfensberger suggests that the citizen advocate should attempt to make certain that the practical and emotional necessities of the retarded person are fulfilled. The one-to-one nature of the Wolfensberger delineation of expectations is clear: "representing, *as if they were his own,* the interests of another." This means that the incumbent of the advocacy status is expected to put himself in the place of the other, to monitor the meeting of instrumental and expressive needs. If such needs are not being met, there is a clear expectation of advocate intervention in an attempt to turn the situation around so the interests of the retardate are not denied.

If the citizen advocate represents the interests of the retarded individual as if they are his own, there is no dividing line between the rights of the advocate and the rights of the retarded person, which would surely be a most difficult role for most people. However, differentiation is maintained through implications that the advocate is expected to act much like a parent who oversees the daily behavior of a child. Therefore, irrespective of the chronological age of the retarded person, the advocate is expected to play a parental-type role while the retarded person plays a child-type role. This is a basic problem since such a dependency relationship is not viewed as desirable by many professionals who have written of the social life of the retarded (e.g., Edgerton, this volume). In fact, the image of the retarded adult as a child is inconsistent with the principles of normalization, the philosophy of the AAMD listing of rights, and the value viewpoint of the National Association of Retarded Children, which recently changed its name to the National Association of Retarded *Citizens.*

Why is Wolfensberger (1972) so adamant about the one-citizen-to-one-citizen nature of advocacy? Why does he state that " ... the advocacy concept demands that advocacy for an impaired person is to be exercised *not* by agencies, and *not* by professionals acting in professional roles, but by competent and suitable citizens" (p. 12), while also indicating that " ... the heart of the proposed advocacy scheme is individual advocacy, in which one citizen is the advocate for one other citizen" (p. 13)? At least part of his answer to this question rests on a position that to this point protective service laws and practices for the retarded have suffered from a number of major shortcomings (Wolfensberger, 1972, pp. 7–11). From this perspective, if the systems had been more successful in protecting the human rights of the retarded, there would have been no need for the emergence of the citizen advocate role. Parenthetically, it should be noted that while the arguments for one-to-one citizen advocacy are very appealing, a data-based objective evaluation of public guardianship programs, in which one person is an advocate for several people, has not yet been presented by social scientists.

From a different perspective, the issue of social system versus individual advocacy actually revolves around another, more general, issue which was discussed by Szasz (1961) in his critique of psychiatric practice. In a discussion of the therapist-patient relationship Szasz suggests that if the therapist is the agent of the patient, his rewards come from the patient, while if the therapist is the agent of a larger social system (such as an agency or the state), rewards are received from the larger system. In situations of conflict of interest between the individual and the system, under the first arrangement the therapist may be primarily concerned about the rights of the individual, while under the second he may be more concerned with the rights of the larger social system. Consequently, if the therapist is employed by the system he may be tempted toward decisions which reflect the more generous rewards which can be dispensed by large-scale organizations, in comparison to the relatively meager rewards which can usually be given by the individual. Recognizing the seriousness of such conflict, the NASW Ad Hoc Committee on Advocacy (1969) takes the position that " ... the obligation to the client takes primacy over the obligation to the employer when the two interests compete with one another" (p. 18).

In this context, a system of citizen or individual advocacy is designed to act as a safeguard of the rights of the individual while avoiding the potential temptations of self-interest which are seen as inherent in agency advocacy. If the citizen advocate puts himself in the place of the other and represents the interests of the retarded person *as if they were his own,* there would be little reason to doubt his motivations. At the very least, citizen advocacy thus avoids a potential conflict of interest in playing the advocacy role. It also helps to define clearly the interests of the individual retardate as lying at the very heart of the advocacy role.

Objections to agency or professional advocacy are shared by Adams (1973), who has expressed concern about some of the dilemmas faced by social workers who find themselves called upon to function as advocates. In a penetrating discussion of issues concerning research and social priorities, medical exigencies and human rights, informed consent and intellectual handicap, and genetic knowledge and family integrity, she raises the same issue which was discussed by Szasz by asking the following question: "Are social workers advocates for individuals or for society, of whom an individual is one fraction? Where should the profession's protective efforts be directed?" (Adams, 1973, p. 842). Actually, Adams hedges an answer to this question with a statement that "I have no answer . . . " (p. 842) but she seems to take this position because she is discussing some dilemmas of advocacy for the social worker. Thus, in elaborating on implications of the question, Adams (1973) asks: "What line should the social worker adopt when research workers desperately need to perform some technological procedure on a living child, or a postmortem on a dead one, either of which will cause serious distress to a family who have probably been tested to the utmost of their emotional limits?" (p. 841). Continuing, she also asks: "If a retarded child or adult indicates a clear dislike of being part of a research project, even after every human precaution has been taken to minimize danger and anxiety, do social workers have an obligation to interfere on his behalf to prevent this involvement?" (p. 841). What if the retarded child decides against cooperation while the parents feel that cooperation is desirable? Who has the right to decide consent—the scientist, the parent, the social worker, the superintendent of an institution in which the retarded person is a resident, or the retarded individual himself? And, does the answer change if the experiment has the potential of providing new and significant knowledge about prevention or "cure" of a damaging disease which affects large numbers of others? These are, indeed, dilemmas for those who play the advocacy role.

Wolfensberger's (1972) specification of the role helps to frame an answer to Adams' general question: citizen advocates are to function by directing protective efforts toward the individual, rather than the social system. Such role specification, however, seems clearer on a theoretical level than in an empirical situation. For example, does citizen advocacy also function for unborn "citizens"? The broadness of the Wolfensberger proposition suggests a positive answer, which means that the fetus (i.e., the individual) must be protected from decisions which may lead to distress, injury, or death. However, the very simplicity of the statement is deceiving. For example, the advocate may find himself in a position in which he must choose from among more than one person, e.g., what is beneficial for the mother may be detrimental for the fetus, and vice versa.

To further complicate matters, Adams (1973) raises a significant value problem with the statement that "a great deal of rhetoric is uttered in anti-abortion arguments about the rights of the fetus, but I would like to voice an appeal on behalf of the damaged fetus not to be born to a life-long sentence of subnormal functioning and potential misery" (p. 841). Wolfensberger's position that advocacy consists of one citizen protecting the rights of one other citizen is too simplistic to help in arriving at a solution to the value problem which is posed by Adams. Since many of the decisions which an advocate must make on behalf of the other individual are of a value nature, such problems may be constant and real. Thus, although some of the expectations of the role may be spelled out, this may not help in reaching appropriate value decisions in specific cases.

There is, however, one dominating value which is held to be central to the advocacy role by those who suggest that citizen advocacy must focus on the human rights of the individual: whoever plays the advocacy role is broadly expected to protect the humanness of the individual whenever human rights are found to be denied. Standing between the individual and the social systems with which the retardate comes into contact, the advocate is expected to intercede whenever it seems that the system is functioning unfairly toward the retarded person because of his handicap. It is not that the system is looked upon as particularly evil but, rather, that systems are viewed as impersonal institutions which can lose contact with human needs, human rights, and human behavior in general. For example, in discussing "stumbling blocks to change" in institutions for the retarded, Elkin (1972) suggests the establishment of an Advocacy Agency to represent the individual who faces institutional retaliation, a bureaucratic emphasis on empire building and self-interest, unrealistic civil service regulations, and community misconceptions about the mentally retarded. Elkin further suggests that the Advocacy Agency should stand alone, independent of the social institutions which are involved with the delivery of services.

This raises another serious question for the advocate: in referring to social workers, Payne (1970) speculates on " . . . how far a social worker can go in effecting an advocacy role without transgressing his commitment to professional behavior" (p. 16). The range of professional behavior may be from helping the retarded person to fill out agency forms in order to receive some benefit, to an outrightly militant action, such as a sit-in demonstration that forces the closing of a welfare office (Payne, 1970, p. 15). Grosser (1965) presents the extreme view in a discussion of advocacy for the urban poor when he states that the advocate mut be "a partisan in a social conflict" (p. 18).

However, precisely in this area the social worker faces serious problems of role definition. Thus, by tradition at least, the members of the profession are expected to be neutral in their relationships with clients. Since the advocacy role is clearly not a neutral one, can the social worker legitimately claim both professionalism and the advocate role at the same time? Judging from the intensity of the discussion which has been generated in social work journals, this question is very important to the social worker's self-image. Thus, Brager (1968) indicates that "the dynamism of the times has resulted in dissatisfaction with such concepts as worker neutrality . . . " (p. 5), the NASW Ad Hoc Committee on Advocacy (1969) states that " . . . the professional social worker is ethically bound to take on the advocacy role if he is to fulfill his professional responsibilities" (p. 16), McCormick (1970) refers to " . . . the potential conflict that exists between political-social action and professional action" (p. 7), Knitzer (1971) writes of " . . . the limits and hypocrisies of the traditional 'neutral' professional role . . . " (p. 800), and Paull (1971) suggests that "social work is giving less attention to soul-searching about whether social action is proper professional behavior" (p. 31). Apparently, the growing significance of advocacy in social work has led practitioners to modify their traditional roles, but this has not taken place without serious discussion about the proper function of social work in the larger society. From the social worker's perspective, the discussion may be described as one of soul-searching, while from the sociologist's perspective, it may be described as one of role-searching.

It is significant to note that, as viewed by Wolfensberger (1972), " . . . the mission of the advocate is to use culturally appropriate means to fulfill the instrumental *and expressive needs* of such a person, consistent with cultural norms and with the person's impairments and potentials" (p. 12, emphasis added). The expressive or affective dimension is emphasized here because this considerably broadens the expectations of advocacy role players. In fact, this addition extends role expectations to a point where it is difficult to differentiate between the role of advocate and the role of parent.

It should also be noted that the emphasis on expressive functions actually extends the advocacy concept well beyond the normalization concept. In the Nirje (1969) statement, there is emphasis on " . . . making available to the mentally retarded patterns and conditions of everyday life which are as close as possible to the norms and patterns of the mainstream of society" (p. 181). Therefore, emphasis is on such principles as a normal rhythm of day, a normal routine of life, a normal rhythm of the year, and the opportunity to undergo normal developmental experiences of the life cycle. Such principles emphasize instrumental rather than expressive needs. Even sexual contact is listed in non-expressive terms by Nirje (1969): "normalization also means living in a bisexual world" (p. 184) seems a curious attempt to avoid specifically implications of expressive associations. In contrast, the AAMD (1973) listing extends to such statements as "the right to be part of a family" whenever the developmental needs of the retarded individual can be met satisfactorily in this manner and "the right to marry and have a family of his or her own" (p. 57) if the individual can be effectively self-supporting and can reasonably be expected to meet effectively the obligations of marriage and parenthood, which clearly suggests that the retarded person has a right to both instrumental and expressive life experiences.

The tone and language used by both the AAMD (1973) and Adams (1973) suggest that the advocate should function in a watchdog capacity, responding (perhaps aggressively) when it seems that the human rights of the person are being denied by the social system. Illustrative is the AAMD (1973) directive to "remedy the situation immediately" through certain "actions," utilizing "whatever . . . means are available" since "it is the obligation of the society to intervene to safeguard these rights" (both instrumental and expressive; all quotes from p. 56). Similarly, Adams (1973) states that advocacy denotes " . . . the actions and the role that social workers are committed to when the . . . rights of their clients are transgressed. . ." (p. 840). Wolfensberger (1972) is less aggressive in tone and language, implying a supervisory or monitoring function for the advocate, which brings the role somewhat closer to a parent-child type of association. In practice, the responsive feature of the AAMD-Adams statement and the monitoring nature of the Wolfensberger statement of function may be the same, but the difference in tone may attract different personality types to the advocacy role.

This is only speculative, however, since information about characteristics of advocacy role players is not currently available. In fact, this is an interesting empirical question, which some social scientist will, it is hoped, approach when the number of incumbents increases and their efforts are felt throughout society. Presently, empirical information about the motivation of advocacy role players is limited to such passing observations as Edgerton's (1967) statement that the benefactors in his study indicated that they were functioning in the role for altruistic reasons, and that the motivations of spouse-benefactors are not always altruistic (p. 203). Even today, the pursuit of information about advocacy role players may form the basis for an interesting doctoral dissertation in sociology, psychology, or social psychology. A sociologically-oriented doctoral dissertation would capture the role at a fairly early stage of development, which can therefore broaden an understanding of those who choose to play the role, and can add significant knowledge about how roles are specified and modified over time.

Lack of information about characteristics of advocates is probably related to the recent development of the advocacy role, which is associated with a lack of precise definitions of rights and obligations for status incumbents. Presently, outside of some broad agreed-upon principles, there is a lack of role standardization. In fact, the present broadness and undefined nature of the role may be part of its appeal to present incumbents, since this allows advocates to be recruited on the basis of idealism, rather than on the basis of demonstrated abilities or accomplishments.

Given this background, an examination of the literature was undertaken, to ascertain the nature of characteristics deemed desirable for filling the advocate status and playing the role. This examination revealed that the advocate must be mature, competent, unpaid, committed, motivated, inspired, stable, must have continuity in the community, be willing to undergo orientation, understand his specific advocacy mission, have good moral character, have desirable characteristics, share common interests with the retardate, have time free to carry on the relationship, and have sincere humanitarian reasons for wanting to enter into the relationship (Wolfensberger, 1972; Novak, 1973). He or she would be expected to know something about mental retardation and have some knowledge of the law and of the structure and function of bureaucratic organization.

One cannot help wondering about the availability of individuals who fit the criteria. Even if it is assumed that there are enough altruistically oriented people available who meet the criteria, who in society would have the enormous amount of time available to invest in monitoring the daily needs of another person? Such an investment may be expected of some particular roles in society, such as parents and, in limited ways, clergymen and social workers, but it seems naive to expect a large number of people to step forward as volunteers to reorganize their daily lives around the human rights of another person. This would especially be the case if the volunteer understands the lifetime commitment which seems inherent in the advocacy for the retarded role.

A key to differences in how the role is being played lies in whether emphasis of the advocate is given to expressive or instrumental features. While the point needs further elaboration, it would seem that sole commitment to instrumental functions comes closer to representation of the agency or the social system than the individual, while sole commitment to expressive functions suggests that the needs of the individual whose rights are being advocated receives primacy over the system. Perhaps this is a continuum which can be utilized as a methodological tool to understand advocacy role playing.

There does seem to be at least one very important consistency in the role, which reflects the conditions which led to its development. In the final analysis the necessity for the role may be interpreted as a response to observations that the social system has not been even-handed toward all its citizens, especially the mentally handicapped. In response, a major function of the advocate is to correct the imbalance which has short-changed the retarded person and to monitor relationships to make certain that deprivations do not occur because of the handicapping condition (cf. the NASW Ad Hoc Committee on Advocacy, 1969, image of the advocate as a "champion of social victims"). Consequently, the successful advocacy role player will often find himself in a position in which it is necessary to challenge and attack a discriminating social system. In this respect role conflict is a necessary feature of the very structure of the advocacy role. Some examples of such conflict will now be presented and discussed.

It would be folly to believe that all of those who are significant to the life experiences of the retarded individual will always agree with the advocate's decisions. The advocate may find that others who feel they are also responsible for the welfare of the retarded person, such as parents, siblings, or friends, have different ideas about correct decisions. This may put the advocate into a confrontation position in which the best interests of the retarded person are up for debate. Thus, the advocate may find himself at the center of conflict with a variety of individuals who also have the interests of the retarded person at heart.

A probably infrequent rendition of this type of conflict may place the advocate in a conflict situation with the retarded person himself, since the advocate and the individual may reach different decisions about any given situation. Under these conditions the individual whose rights are being monitored and protected may make demands which are unacceptable to the advocate. For example, the retarded person may want a driver's license or may want to enroll in a correspondence course being advertised on television. As presently structured, neither the citizen advocate nor the retarded individual are provided with a means of solving the disagreement. Just how are compromises to be reached between an advocate and a retarded person? What workable options have been developed by advocates and the retarded? These are interesting questions which can only be answered through empirical research.

In discussing the social worker as advocate, the NASW Ad Hoc Committee on Advocacy (1969) has pointed to some particular and unique problems for members of the profession. Thus, in discussing the social worker advocate the Committee states that " . . . in promoting his clients' interest the social worker may be injuring other aggrieved persons with an equally just claim" (p. 19). Thus, while promulgating the claims of the individual being represented, the social worker may find himself in a position whereby he is denying the same rights to others, who are not represented by advocates. Consequently, the discriminations of the social system may simply be transferred to a new level of available services, suggesting that problems of the welfare delivery system would only be intensified, although the language which describes the problem may make it more palatable. In an interesting aside, such a situation also raises the possibility of advocate-advocate conflict.

A most interesting case of role conflict would occur if the social worker finds that his own agency is not meeting the needs of the individual whose rights he is supervising. Under these conditions the advocate may find it necessary to challenge the agency which pays his salary, in an attempt to stop transgressing the rights of the person whose cause he is championing. Consequently, the social worker may have to instigate change in his own agency of employment (Brager, 1968, p. 7), and may find himself in the unenviable position of challenging the structure and function of the agency which pays his salary (NASW Ad Hoc Committee on Advocacy, 1969, p. 29).

Given the wide ranging nature of the discussion of the citizen advocate role, a summary is in order. However, rather than simply reviewing what has already been stated, many of the points previously presented will be cast into a different series of concepts, in an attempt to provide a heuristic review. In presenting the review, some elements of the "pattern variable" schema of Parsons (1951) will be utilized since this provides a framework for further insight into some of the specific features of the citizen advocate role. In this context, four of the pattern variables can be utilized to construct a model which describes orientations of incumbents of the status.

1. Affectivity-affective neutrality. In the Parsonian framework this pattern variable indicates that some role relationships are expected to be expressively based, while others are rooted in an objectivity which helps to prevent subjective relationships. Clearly, the citizen advocate role is expected to be an affective one. The advocate is expected to exhibit an emotional commitment to the interests of the retarded person and to take action on behalf of the individual when these interests are not being fulfilled.

2. Specificity-diffuseness. This variable refers to the scope or inclusiveness of the relationship between two roles. From the sociological perspective specificity-diffuseness may be seen as the degree of involvement of one's social position with another, or other, social positions. The advocate-retardate relationship is clearly a diffuse one since the basic right of the retarded person which is being monitored by the advocate is perhaps the most general of mankind: the right to the human experience. Based upon normalization, the citizen advocate is expected to deal with society on behalf of the retarded individual to make certain that this right is not denied.

3. Universalism-particularism. This refers to whether an individual is treated as a member of a universally defined class of objects or as a particular individual in a social relationship. In this context, the citizen advocate is expected to be in a particularistic relationship with the mentally handicapped person since he is expected to relate to the retarded individual as a particular person with needs and as one whose handicap may be preventing fulfillment.

4. Collectivity orientation—self-orientation. This refers to whether an individual is participating in the association for self-benefit or for the benefit of others. It is clear that the citizen advocate role is a collectivity oriented one in which the advocate is expected to carry out the rights and obligations of the role for the benefit of the retarded individual, rather than for personal gain.

Legal Advocacy

Despite declarations that citizen advocacy is "an idea whose time has come" (Helsel, 1973, p. 131) and despite reports which show that the citizen advocacy idea has been spreading rapidly throughout the United States and Canada (Zauha and Korn, 1973), without some means of backing up citizen advocate demands, the movement would not have become significant. Some parallel means had to be developed which would threaten social systems which were nonresponsive or slow to respond to advocate-sponsored demands. Without some clout the cry for human needs would undoubtedly still be left in the hands of idealists who lacked knowledge of how to bring about social change. It is fortuitious for the retarded that a practical methodology to bring change about has become readily available to the proponents of the human needs of the mentally retarded.

To understand the development of the means which have served an instrumental function in the creation of a methodology for the proponents of human needs, focus will be shifted to the "student revolt" which affected many college campuses throughout the United States in the late 1960's. Seemingly, this nationwide protest was concerned with the war in Vietnam, but there was an additional point to the student protests. Students during the latter part of the 1960's were demanding something new from college administrators and professors. They demanded that these members of the establishment must vacate their ivory towers and enter into the thick of the action to bring about elimination or amelioration of many societal problems.

As this paper is being written from the perspective of the mid-1970's, it may be conjectured that these student demands have not made a lasting impact on most academic disciplines, and that among those fields affected, some have moved more strongly toward social action than others. Judging the past from the perspective of the present, it may be concluded that law as an academic enterprise has responded to student demands by making one of the more quantitative and qualitative moves toward social action. In retrospect it is also important to recognize that it was not only the administrators and professors who were radicalized during the student protests. In disciplines such as law it was the students themselves who were most saliently and lastingly affected by their own protests.

Crucial to the history which is being presented here is the observation that these "radical" students in the late 1960's are the young practicing attorneys of today. As students they learned how to protest, and win, against a system considered discriminatory and repressive. As attorneys they have at their command the knowledge which can be used to force systemic change through legal means. Many of these attorneys believe that if the established system denies human rights to an individual, retarded or non-retarded, the system must be challenged and changed.

A combination of commitment to the principles of normalization, emerging notions of citizen advocacy, concern for the rights of every individual in the American society, and knowledge of how to change the social system has led to a powerful new influence on public policy planning. This new approach is known as legal advocacy for the mentally retarded. In this approach if the rights of the retarded are being denied by the state, the state must be sued; if the rights of the retarded are being denied by private enterprise, private enterprise must be sued; if the rights of the retarded are being denied by an individual, the individual must be sued. Consequently, members of the community power structure must recognize that their actions are under scrutiny by a cadre of young attorneys who are monitoring the rights of the mentally handicapped. What parents and professionals found it almost impossible to achieve, because of much idealism and little technique, is almost taken for granted by this new group of independent professionals who only a few years ago were sitting in the hallways of the administration building of some formerly quiet college campus.

Setting the tone for this association between normalization, advocacy, and the legal approach has been the President's Committee on Mental Retardation (1973), which has declared that "retarded people have rights, too" (p. 22), and which has coupled this declaration with the observation that "cases are being brought to court, on behalf of the mentally retarded, asserting the *right* to education (including protection against assignment based on unfair labeling), the *right* to treatment, and the *right* to be free from involuntary servitude" (p. 22). Furthermore, "a deluge of such cases is flooding the courts. They may mark the beginning of a new national attitude toward people who are mentally retarded" (p. 22).

In summary, the significant coalition which has emerged consists of the proponents of normalization, citizen advocates, and legal advocates for the rights of the retarded. Emerging from this new association is a growing feeling that citizen advocacy and the legal approach supplement one another, with the advocate pointing to the problems and the attorney utilizing professional skills to make certain that the proper authorities become aware of societal oversights and discriminations. While the mentally retarded have not themselves become a militant social category which is demanding equal rights, and while they have not banded together in Nader-like consumer groups which have never before known how to approach the established institutions, the retarded have become the beneficiaries of a new set of principles and the development of new roles. Furthermore, it is likely that the surface has only been scratched, especially as cases are won and legal precedents are established. From this perspective it is possible that policy planners will have no choice but to recognize the rights of the mentally retarded when economic, educational, and political issues are under discussion.

There are some obvious differences between citizen advocacy and legal advocacy, which become especially clear when it is recognized that the legal advocacy approach is a strictly instrumental one within the confines of a professional relationship. Thus, while the citizen advocate may be described as affective and particularistic, the legal advocate must be affectively neutral and universalistic. The scope of the relationship is broad in both instances and the humanitarian collectivity orientation emphasis is present in both cases. Thus, while citizen advocacy consists of one citizen protecting the human rights of another, legal advocacy consists of a professional relationship in which the rights of one individual may be used as precedent-setting for all of the retarded. In the legal advocacy approach, in fact, all of the retarded may be grouped into one category for the purposes of a class-action suit.

SOME SIGNIFICANT ISSUES

Because the advocacy role for the mentally retarded is a recent social development, there has been little time for reactions by individuals other than proponents who are attempting to legitimize its place in society. Recency also accounts for a lack of empirical information about individual and community experiences with advocates. Not yet available are such basic data as the number of individuals who are in advocacy positions, the characteristics of incumbents of the role, the physical and social location of advocates, and the specific characteristics of recipients. Therefore, this paper cannot close with a summary of the experiences of advocates, the community, and the mentally retarded. Instead, closure will concentrate on the identification of issues which suggest some of the important questions concerning advocacy for the mentally retarded. Eventually, the answers to some of these questions will help toward the development of a social science literature which will help us to understand advocacy for the mentally retarded as a significant social phenomenon.

1. Potential conflict between incumbents of the advocacy role and incumbents of other roles. To what extent does the extreme partisanship and aggressiveness of the advocacy role lead to conflict between the advocate and others who are in contact with the retarded? Some of the significant others for the retarded who may be in conflict roles relative to the advocate are parents, teachers, policemen, clergymen, physicians, social workers, and the executive directors of health and welfare agencies. The extent and nature of conflict are questions which can only be answered by research contact with individuals who are playing advocacy and related roles. An associated research question concerns the nature of the social patterns which have been developed in response to conflict.

This issue becomes significant in another context when a question is raised about the extent to which and conditions under which role conflict occurs between the advocate and the retarded person. And, given the presence of such conflict, how are disagreements resolved? Furthermore, the diffuseness of the advocacy role suggests a question of whether disagreement in one area of the relationship between the advocate and the retardate influences the total interaction pattern. As in the case of conflict between the advocate and incumbents of related roles, this area is a ripe one for empirical research. In designing the research in this particular case, the investigator would find it important to plan interviews with the retarded, as well as with advocates.

2. Potential conflict between the rights of the retarded and the rights of others. A significant question may be raised about whether advocacy for the rights of the retarded may result in deprivations in the rights of others. For example, if scarce health, educational, and welfare resources are made available to a retarded person to meet the demands of the advocate, will it be necessary to neglect some individuals who are otherwise handicapped from receiving similar benefits? It is also significant to note that if others are also represented by advocates, this also suggests the possibility of advocate-advocate conflict.

3. Lack of information about characteristics of advocacy role players. Related to the first two issues, it is important to ask: what are the demographic, social, and psychological characteristics of individuals who volunteer to play the advocacy role? And, if characteristics can be identified, there should be interest in how such characteristics are associated with successful and unsuccessful role playing (if success is actually subject to objective definition and measurement). Of course, it would be incorrect simply to assume that

there is an abundance of competent people who are standing ready to volunteer to play the advocacy role. Comparisons between individuals who do and do not volunteer for the role, and between successful and unsuccessful advocates, seem critical to future directions of the advocacy movement.

4. Possible importance of social class factors. Is it fair to interpret the emerging advocacy system as still another example of a middle class incursion into the lower class subculture? Since most advocacy role players are probably middle class individuals, and since most of the retarded who need an advocate are probably of the lower class (both generalizations await empirical backing) such a pattern is possible. The temptation may be great for a massive ethnocentrism in which the mentally retarded are considered "empty vessels" who must be filled with "proper" values so their behavior patterns are considered "acceptable" by community gatekeepers (e.g., social workers).

5. Possible undesirable latent consequences of the advocacy role. Are there undesirable latent consequences of the advocacy role and, if the answer to this question is yes, what are some of these? For example, Edgerton states in his chapter in this volume that "our experiences with independently-living retarded persons showed again and again that these people did not look upon us as potential advocates of their rights, but as resources for the maintenance or augmentation of their everyday dependencies: for small loans, transportation, advice about bureaucratic matters, help in health and medical or dental appointments, shopping, handling money, reading, and the like" (p. 132). Are such dependency patterns desirable for the community adjustments of the retarded? And, if such dependency is allowed to develop, what will be the outcome if the advocate finds it impossible to continue in the role or finds new interests which lead to a breaking of the relationship? Is incumbency in the advocacy role a lifelong commitment?

6. Societal reactions to the demand for change. Finally, and perhaps most importantly, is the American public ready to accept some of the modifications in life styles which may become necessary if the advocate-sponsored principle of full human rights for the retarded became a reality? While most people would probably be willing to accept ideological principles and would give verbal support to a listing of rights, it is questionable whether they would be willing to make the practical everyday adjustments which the fulfillment of principles and rights for the retarded would necessitate. For example, while the public may accept the principle that every retarded individual, within his capabilities, is entitled to a publicly supported and administered program of training and education (AAMD, 1973, p. 57), a question here is whether people would be willing to contribute to the sizable tax increase which such a program would necessitate, at least initially.

Furthermore, a comprehensive system of citizen advocacy could also be extremely threatening to some of this country's most powerful social institutions. Thus, if the economic, educational, and political institutions found it necessary to recognize the rights of the mentally retarded, many unquestioned institutional policies would have to undergo major changes. This could necessitate important modifications in industrial hiring practices and compensation rates, a significant extension of educational programs to include presently ignored and excluded children, and governmental guarantees that services will be provided and that rights will be protected. To the degree that institutions are concerned with maintaining the status quo, the citizen advocate may find himself challenging some of the most significant vested interest groupings in American society. This suggests that the advocacy role will not be successful unless it can go further than moral persuasion, perhaps by being provided with community-supported means of forcing resistant vested interests to respond positively to demands. The coalition of citizen and legal advocacy is, perhaps, the key to convincing American business, unions, government, professional groupings, and boards of trustees that social change is necessary.

In the final analysis, the viability of the social experiment of advocacy may rest on the willingness of the American public and American institutions to allow challenges to the present system. The question of whether the advocate is a prime mover in social change, or an impractical idealist, will be better answered by the next generation of social scientists.

REFERENCES

Adams, M. 1973. Science, technology, and some dilemmas of advocacy. Science 180: 840–842.

American Association on Mental Deficiency (AAMD). 1973. Rights of mentally retarded persons: An official statement of the American Association on Mental Deficiency. Ment. Retard. 11: 56–58.

Brager, G. A. 1968. Advocacy and political behavior. Soc. Work 13: 5–15.

Edgerton, R. B. 1967. The Cloak of Competence: Stigma in the Lives of the Mentally Retarded. University of California Press, Berkeley.

Edgerton, R. B. Issues relating to the quality of life among mentally retarded persons. This volume.

Elkin, E. 1972. Editorial. Mental Retardation News. 21: 4, National Association for Retarded Citizens.

Grosser, C. F. 1965. Community development programs serving the urban poor. Soc. Work 10: 15–21.

Helsel, E. 1973. History and present status of protective services. In W. Wolfensberger and H. Zauha (eds.), Citizen Advocacy, pp. 131–146. National Institute on Mental Retardation, Toronto.

Knitzer, J. 1971. Advocacy and the children's crisis. Am. J. Orthopsychiatr. 41: 799–806.

Mahaffey, M. 1972. Lobbying and social work. Soc. Work 17: 3–11.

McCormick, M. J. 1970. Social advocacy: A new dimension in social work. Soc. Casework 51: 3–11.

National Association of Social Workers (NASW) Ad Hoc Committee on Advocacy. 1969. The social worker as advocate: Champion of social victims. Soc. Work 14: 16–22.

Nirje, B. 1969. The normalization principle and its human management implications. In R. B. Kugel and W. Wolfensberger (eds.), Changing Patterns In Services For The Mentally Retarded, pp. 179–195. President's Committee on Mental Retardation, Washington, D.C.

Novak, L. 1973. Operation of the citizen advocate program in Lincoln, Nebraska. In W. Wolfensberger and H. Zauha (eds.), Citizen Advocacy, pp. 45–78. National Institute on Mental Retardation, Toronto.

Parsons, T. 1951. The Social System. The Free Press, New York.

Parsons, T. and R. F. Bales. 1955. Family, Socialization and Interaction Process. The Free Press, Glencoe, Ill.

Paull, J. E. 1971. Social action for a different decade. Soc. Serv. Rev. 45: 30–36.

Payne, J. E. 1970. Ombudsman and advocate: New roles for social workers. Unpublished paper.

President's Committee on Mental Retardation. 1973. MR 72: Islands of Excellence. DHEW Publication No. (OS) 73–7. U.S. Government Printing Office, Washington, D.C.

President's Panel on Mental Retardation. 1962. A Proposed Program for National Action to Combat Mental Retardation. U.S. Government Printing Office, Washington, D.C.

Szasz, T. S. 1961. The Myth of Mental Illness. Harper and Row, Publishers, Inc., New York.

Wolfensberger, W. 1972. Citizen advocacy for the handicapped, impaired, and disadvantaged: An overview. President's Committee on Mental Retardation, DHEW Publication No. (OS) 72–42. U.S. Government Printing Office, Washington, D.C.

Zauha, H. and M. Korn. 1973. Implementation of citizen advocacy to date. *In* W. Wolfensberger and H. Zauha (eds.), Citizen Advocacy, pp. 81–89. National Institute on Mental Retardation, Toronto.

Discussion:
Emergent Patterns of Service
For Young People and Adults

Initial discussion of Kushlick's presentation centered around the interplay between his residential units for the severely and profoundly retarded and visitation by parents and others. The frequency of parental visitations had not increased, although each unit maintained an open visitation policy. However, no active effort had been made to encourage visitations. He commented further that little or no community resistance was encountered in setting up the homes which are financed by the National Health Service. The presence of the first group of homes provided a fine example to the community regarding the nature of the facilities and the patients served. Through such demonstrations, the ease of establishing new homes was enhanced.

Regarding the behavioral effectiveness of the residential units, the author reported that all children had made progress on self-help skills and language acquisition whereas similar children in institutions typically regress. The greatest of such changes was noted in nonambulant children. Several questions centered on the possible factors responsible for these gains. The following factors were considered important: 1) a staffing ratio of one attendant for every five children (constant throughout the day), 2) the environmental setting evoked a whole range of educational-oriented behaviors from the staff, e.g., an increase in toilet training activities because of the limited bathroom facilities, 3) the location of homes in the midst of residential communities providing more respectable occupational status for the staff and forcing more responsibility on adminstrators in that their mistakes are more visible.

With respect to medical care, local pediatricians were reported to handle most of the problems and seem to be providing better care than occurs in most institutions. Specialists are, of course, called in for the "hard cases." Psychiatrists are involved to a much lesser extent than in institutions. Apparently, a "special kind of medicine" does not need to be practiced in treating the mentally retarded. The key seems to be in securing the cooperation of pediatricians before setting up the residential units and then encouraging the staff to act as medical advocates.

The assumption that the mentally retarded are the first to be laid off during periods of high unemployment does not appear, in fact, to be borne out, according to Halpern. There are data suggesting that job placement for the retarded is not at all correlated with the extent of unemployment. Advocacy, both by professionals and by citizens, appears as an important factor in effective placement, especially during periods of general unemployment. The interests of the retarded individual are best protected when his abilities and needs are carefully matched with the available jobs.

A common pattern in job placement was seen to emerge: seemingly successful placement, followed by a year or two of "settling in," then dissatisfaction because peers are advancing, then termination. Clearly more research on initial placement, career development and advancement, and follow-up procedures for maintaining job satisfaction are needed.

In the long run, how will retarded individuals be effected by the new, technological society? One possibility is the establishment of industries created especially for the retarded, such as has been done in Illinois. Such a strategy might be financially sound as well as healthy in terms of developing pride and dignity. However, advocates of integration would likely criticize "industries for the retarded" because they would tend to insulate and cut off retarded employees from the society at large. In any case, a more technological society will probably not work to the detriment of the mentally retarded if jobs can be broken down into component skills, which can, in turn, be taught in step-wise fashion. Also, unskilled labor is likely to be required by society for the foreseeable future.

The discussion turned to whether the retarded person fails in job placement for lack of appropriate social skills. In general, it was felt that the development of social and personal skills was important in successful placement and job maintenance. The final comment dealt with the changing values of retarded individuals. In some areas of the country, for instance Los Angeles, the retarded individual who is living in the community may not necessarily want to work, preferring a girl friend and a welfare check to tedious, often boring, employment. Certainly many of the values of our society will influence the job satisfaction attitudes of the retarded in a manner similar to those found in normal individuals. This trend will be increasingly true as the deinstitutionalization movement expands.

In the presentation of the community residence program at Gatewood, the lack of information on sexual adjustment merited special attention. Although sexual activity was not examined directly, it was observed that birth control and gynecological information were provided. Sexual activity in this facility seemed to take a more personal, social form although the frequency of sexual intercourse had not markedly increased. It was agreed that this area of behavior was critical and that more data on the sexual adjustment of retarded individuals in community settings need to be gathered, both for mildly and moderately retarded adolescents and adults.

What is the professional's responsibility before an individual is transferred from an institution to a residential setting? A graded series of experiences facilitating the transition seems most desirable. For instance, it is possible to set aside units in the institution that might serve as a preplacement training unit before moving individuals into the community. Then a graded series of structured and unstructured residential units might be provided. Research is needed on how one can make adjustment to community living less traumatic.

Is Gatewood any less socially isolated than an institution? In many respects, the answer is no. Apparently, retarded individuals in Gatewood and in similar homes are not really integrated into the community. In other words small size and good location per se do not lead to improved living and training conditions, nor are they necessarily more normalizing.

One member of the group felt that residential homes, such as Gatewood, are really academic experiments rather than viable social programs. The reasoning here is that the high staff ratios are too costly for widespread use. Why should such efforts be instituted at the expense of other worthwhile societal needs (e.g., education and housing in urban ghetto areas)? Some of the points of disagreement included: 1) money is actually saved by establishing residential centers (it should be noted that there were many divergent opinions on this matter, with several discussants arguing that homes were more costly than institutions), 2) small homes are administratively manageable and programming is likely to be more effective, 3) early intervention, e.g., toilet training, saves money in the long run and can best be carried out in residential centers, 4) operating costs are high at the outset as people move from institutions but costs will go down as institutions are closed and job placement becomes more efficient, 5) replacement into the homes of biological or adoptive parents is desirable where possible.

The issue of how society will choose to allocate its resources for mental retardation versus other uses remained unsolved and is deeply rooted in its value system and assigned priorities. Yet it was seen as a key issue requiring further research in implementing programs of deinstitutionalization and alternative systems of community care.

SOCIAL CHANGE: PROBLEMS AND STRATEGIES

Obstacles to Developing Community Services For the Mentally Retarded

Herbert J. Cohen

The purpose of this paper is to present a case study of the kinds of obstacles encountered in establishing and maintaining community services for the mentally retarded. To do this, it is necessary to draw on some of the experiences of the author during the past 4 years in his professional roles and to describe the services he directs.

The development of community services for the mentally retarded has generally proceeded slowly in the United States. As Director of a multidisciplinary diagnostic evaluation and rehabilitation clinic in the Bronx, one of the five boroughs (counties) of New York City, I became keenly aware of the lack of satisfactory treatment services for the mentally retarded in our borough. As a result of this experience, 4 years ago I accepted an invitation from the Department of Mental Hygiene of New York State to direct the development of new community services for the mentally retarded in the Bronx.

My position, as originally envisioned by the State Department of Mental Hygiene, was to direct a "Bronx State School," a residential facility with 750 beds which was in the planning stage and not yet built. During negotiations before taking the post, and as the result of planning and circumstances after assuming the position, architectural changes were made to alter the original character and purposes of the building. It will have apartment-style living quarters and will provide intensive habilitation for both children and adults, day programs, workshops, in-patient physical rehabilitation services, crisis and respite care, plus innovative educational programs. The residential facilities have been reduced to a maximum of 384 occupants. A substantial amount of space will be allocated to our six Community Service Teams to permit each Bronx region to develop programs responsive to its needs. The building is now named the "Bronx Developmental Center" and will be the headquarters of the parent organization that we have named Bronx Developmental Services (BDS).

Five weeks after the project started, New York State instituted a job freeze for 1 year. During this period, some program activities were carried out using existing physical facilities in the Bronx. Recruitment of staff was planned and, as a result of discussions with officials of New York State, the Director's role was broadened to include responsibility for program planning for all of the developmentally disabled in the assigned borough.

The job freeze was lifted in the Spring of 1972, partially as the result of the adverse publicity about Willowbrook and other New York State Schools for the retarded where already unsatisfactory conditions had been markedly exacerbated by the budget freeze. In the past 2½ years since the freeze was removed, BDS has expanded its staff to over 130 with 11 operating units or programs. A plan was implemented for resettlement of former institutional residents and for the development of a broad range of community services for the mentally retarded in the Bronx. Particular attention was given to creation of alternatives to institutional care.

To assist in developing services of high quality with associated training and research, from the outset Bronx Developmental Services was formally affiliated with Albert Einstein College of Medicine of Yeshiva University and with the Rose F. Kennedy Center for Research in Mental Retardation and Human Development, and the University Affiliated Facility for Training in Mental Retardation.

A DESCRIPTION OF BRONX DEVELOPMENTAL SERVICES (BDS)

The core of BDS's services and operation are its Community Services Teams, whose offices are geographically distributed in the various parts of the Bronx. Four Community Services Teams currently exist, one each in the northeast, southeast, west, and south Bronx. BDS eventually intends to have a Community Services Team serving each of the six comprehensive health planning districts of the Bronx. Each district has a population of approximately 250,000. The Teams function in a relatively autonomous fashion, but are supervised by a Chief of Community Services. Each Team is developing its own consumer and community advisory board. The Teams consist of social workers, nurses, a psychologist, special educators, or ohter professionals and paraprofessions (Table 1) who know the resources in the borough and have established contact with other organizations and individuals working with the developmentally disabled. Each team acts as a resource and referral service, provides crisis intervention, helps to arrange for homemakers, family care, and residential care, and for pre-school, school, workshop, recreation, and hostel programs. In addition, each team is either operating or planning a direct service program out of its community office. The initial philosophy of the teams was to utilize existing services for the disabled whenever possible, while providing consultation, support, and advocacy services. They now also provide direct services when the skills needed to operate a new program are otherwise unavailable in the community or no one else can be found to provide the needed services. An example is in the rehabilitation of physically handicapped mentally retarded children and adults where few agencies have the expertise or

Table 1. Staff of community services team

Team leader
Psychologist
Social workers
Community mental retardation nurse
Special educators—child and adult
Nursing home consultant
Community workers and paraprofessionals
Part-time:
  Occupational therapist
  Physical therapist
  Vocational counselor
Secretaries

Consultants:
  Medical specialists
  including
  psychiatrist and physiatrist
  Other chiefs of services
  (psychology, social work, etc.)
  Speech therapist

---

interest in providing direct services, so that BDS, with its medical school affiliation, has directly developed new programs in this important area. In situations in which existing agency assumes primary responsibility for a client's care, BDS continues to maintain a liaison with most clients and their families, since our expertise and consultative skills are often necessary to assist in sustaining the client and to act as an advocate in the community. All clients resettled from institutions continue to be followed by BDS staff.

The full scope of the activities of the community services teams are illustrated in Figure 1.

An important function of the Community Service Teams is to help community agencies develop habilitation, educational, and residential programs. The teams provide advice and staff training for existing health care and social agencies while assisting them in whatever way possible in their work. Another obligation of the Community Service Teams has been the resettlement into the community of those residents of Willowbrook and other New York State Schools who originally resided in the Bronx. Team members have participated in the screening of current residents in the State Schools and, where they exist and can be located, established contact with the families of these clients. In the past 30 months, the teams have arranged for resettlement of about 182 people from State Schools, including 157 from Willowbrook, and the teams now monitor the care and services that resettled clients are receiving.

BDS, in addition to the teams, has staff situated at seven other locations in the Bronx where space is borrowed or shared with community or State agencies. Special treatment programs directly operated by BDS, or in conjunction with a community agency, include a 12-bed in-patient Short Term Intervention Treatment Unit for behavior modification of

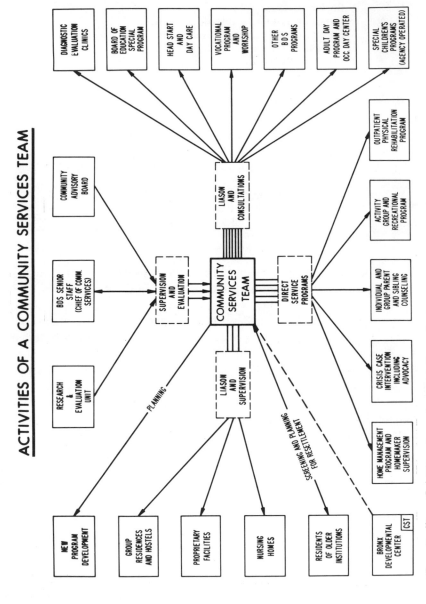

Figure 1. The role and functions of community service teams.

severely retarded children, a Home Management Unit, a Family Care Program, an Adolescent Treatment Service, Parent-Child Education Day Programs, an Adult Multidisciplinary Diagnostic Clinic, and a day program for severely retarded adults.

The opportunity to develop and provide these decentralized community services and direct treatment programs was enhanced by the specific local situation. If BDS had been located in a community in which there was an existing large residential institution for the retarded or other easily available centralized space, both political and fiscal pressures would have inhibited the implementation of a plan for decentralized services. Furthermore, a completed building would have evoked pressures to provide classical institutional type of care rather than community oriented programming of the type that has been described.

DIFFICULTIES ENCOUNTERED IN DEVELOPING COMMUNITY SERVICES

Fiscal Difficulties

A critical factor affecting the ability to plan and deliver effective services is the amount of funds allocated for that purpose. Unfortunately, until recently, budgeting for mental retardation services at a State governmental level has been primarily based on allocations of funds to residential institutions. This has been almost entirely tied to a formula for the costs per patient served in a bed. In New York State, institutional services have been funded on a 100% basis. On the other hand, limited State aid funds for local or outpatient programming are available via a formula requiring that State aid is matched by local support on a dollar for dollar basis.

Conversion to a system of services, based on the concept of providing a diversity of services to the developmentally disabled within their community, has been a painfully slow process. Part of the problem is related to the apparent conservatism of State control agencies. Budgetary staff are familiar with and used to allocating funds and dealing with costs of traditional institutional care, including staffing ratios and indirect (other than personnel services) costs, since these are both components of the standard hospital-medical model. Auditors can control costs in a known model and can clearly identify discrepancies. In this situation, Civil Servants can apply existing patterns of staffing and enforce adherence to prior, usually inflexible, standards. On the other hand, community services currently appear too open ended to control agencies. The costs are uncertain, the staffing requirements vary, prior experience of fiscal control based on a hospital model is of little use, the charting of staff utilization and activities is more complicated, and the patient statistics are confusing. For example, When promoting the concept, the staffing and the role of the Community Services Teams, we have had difficulty with State fiscal control agencies on issues such as: 1) the size of the catchment area that a staff team should cover, 2) the number of staff needed to serve a population base, 3) the type of staff requested for a community services operation, 4) the need for flexibility in hiring to enable recruitment of indigenous staff, to expand the use of paraprofessionals and to develop new career opportunities, 5) utilization of staff in new roles, as advocates, consultants and advisors rather than primary care deliverers, 6) the problem of record keeping and statistics on a decentralized basis. It is particularly difficult to account for time spent on indirect services, team meetings, meetings with agencies, telephone calls, assisting clients at social security offices, etc., 7) in trying to staff an intensive behavior modification program for severely retarded children, it has been difficult to convince the control agency that a higher staff to client ratio is needed to develop an effective program, than for caretaker or custodial services, 8) it is difficult to convince the authorities that an isolated program location justifies authorization of a senior clerical and secretarial position, when these positions have previously always been allocated by civil service on the basis of whom the person works for rather than on the basis of functions performed, 9) in addition to these staffing or personnel problems, the difficulties in obtaining space, providing transportation, and supplying equipment are a logistical nightmare, since the separate actions of all of the State control agencies usually result in staff recruitment, space allocation, or rental and equipment purchasing being thrown completely out of synchrony, 10) another serious obstacle is the complex bureaucratic procedure which impedes arrangements to rent space in the community. This is despite the Joint Commission on Accreditation of Hospitals (JCAH) Standards for Community Mental Retardation Programs (1973), which recommends that space be located in the midst of the community that the program is intended to serve. Central Office budget and program administrators do not yet seem to be aware of the need to decentralize programming to serve local needs. This is an additional example of the undesirable effects of arbitrary decisions made at points far distant from the program provider.

The lack of understanding of community services by State Fiscal authorities, as well as misplaced priorities, has caused grave problems with community oriented programs. For example, expansion plans for BDS were eliminated from the Governor's final budget proposal in each of the past 3 years. The reason, as verified by official letter, was that we had no new beds to operate and, therefore, presumably did not need new funds. Our eventual staff expansion came through reallocations within the Department of Mental Hygiene with staff being reassigned to BDS based on our plans to resettle a specific number of former institutional residents. Thus, even the latter arrangements still excluded any consideration by senior officials of the needs of the mentally retarded clients now in the community who are not now receiving needed services.

Competition for limited resources by competing special interest groups within the mental retardation field presents major obstacles. Allocations based on revenue sharing rarely seem to find their way directly into categorical programs for the developmentally disabled. Tax levy funds for new programs are becoming scarcer as are voluntary, privately raised dollars. Then, there is the bane of program developer's existence: matching formulae requiring local dollars, which are in diminishing supply, to provide a dollar for dollar match for State or federal governmental allocations.

One of the ways we have tried to deal with the budgetary problem has been to lobby actively via calls, mail, and by contacting people until we get what we ask for. Another method has been to mobilize consumer groups, public opinion, and local legislators. Unfortunately, it has been disappointing to observe how powerless the latter have been to alter the stance of the executive branch of State government.

Attempts to educate the control agencies in the executive branch have, thus far, been of limited benefit. This seems to be due to a conscious attempt on their part to remain aloof in order to be objective. An example of this is the fact that the budget staff assigned to Mental Hygiene in the executive branch of government are rotated every 3 years, with the apparent intent of discouraging budget analysts from becoming too identified with a Departmental program and, thereby, being in danger of showing favoritism. Of course, if the cost effectiveness of new programs could be clearly demonstrated, then this would be an effective means of educating control agency staff. However, demonstrating cost effectiveness in a human services operation is a most difficult task and may not even be a reasonable or appropriate one.

In order to make certain that the developmentally disabled get their share of needed governmental funds, it is clear that the best insurance is the earmarking of funds for that purpose with matching formulae eliminated.

Finally, when all else fails, as it often has, we have been forced to: Assign staff to activities and in locations for which they were not originally allocated, juggle staffing patterns, make informal shared services arrangements, both internally and with outside agencies, and, generally, do whatever appears best for client services and care that seems prudent.

Bureaucratic Difficulties

One of the major problems BDS has enountered is the impression that many state officials appear more concerned about "the system" than the clients that the system is intended to serve. The Civil Service system, while useful as a merit system, often appears as an instrument to prevent change. In the program area, new proposals seem to face irrational and "penny wise and pound foolish" decisions by bureaucrats who claim to be "protecting the tax payer's dollar." Plans for custodial care seem to encounter few delays, while plans for preventive services face interminable delays in being initiated.

Decisions in the bureaucracy are often made by decision makers who are far from the point of delivery. A case in point is that despite our carefully formulated budget and staffing proposals, we were never consulted, spoken to, or visited when specific cuts were made or when priorities were altered, based on political or other unspecified considerations. Then, when programs were finally at the point of implementation in the community, the process of approval of staffing, equipment, locations, or agreements on sharing responsibility with agencies are delayed weeks and months by state paperwork procedures.

One practical recommendation for overcoming these bureaucratic obstacles would be to provide remote bureaucrats with firing line experience, both before their central office assignments and on a rotating basis while they are in their jobs, in order to broaden their perspectives and range of experience. Ideally, decision making should be decentralized as much as possible without creating additional layers of bureaucracy, while maintaining carefully controlled, but not stifling, procedures assuring accountability. There should be an expeditor whose sole responsibility is to identify the obstacles and to follow up on or push program plans forward. The system should be kept flexible so that new ideas and proposals can be introduced and, perhaps, be given a clinical trial. Such trials should be accompanied by evaluations involving techniques to assess client acceptability, cost effectiveness, and staff productivity and morale.

Problems with Consumer Participation

It is natural and desirable in a community program to actively encourage consumer participation in service development and decision making. Consumers and the community have a right to participate in making decisions and formulating policies which affect themselves and their families. This view has led community-oriented programs such as BDS to plan for the gradual development of a community advisory board and for consumer participation on policy making committees. In our case, the consumer advisory board was intended to be representative of all program components of BDS, all sub-regions of the Bronx, and all ethnic groups.

Unfortunately, this objective has encountered serious difficulties. Foremost is the basic ambivalence of both consumers and professionals. Both feel that those in authority possess skill and expertise that the public is not equipped to evaluate or regulate. This "medical model" views the consumer as a patient to whom help is given and who cannot "prescribe" for himself. This reasoning is often applied to both service and administrative judgments. The professional is often threatened by parents projected into decision-making positions on policy-making boards, while the parent or client often prefers to be placed in a passive role of being given treatment. Here are some examples of how the ambivalence on both sides has caused considerable problems. When the consumer advisory board of BDS was being planned, considerable difficulty was encountered recruiting parents representative of all sections and ethnic groups in the Bronx. It was predominantly middle class parents who came to the meetings. Old timers discouraged newcomers with tales of past failures and lack of progress when they lobbied to help the developmentally disabled. The consumers who showed up at all community meetings to express their own views were often not representative and tended to dominate the meetings. Language barriers inhibited Spanish-speaking clients from participating.

When the consumer advisory board started developing its bylaws, they stated a desire for final decision-making power over policy, hiring, and firing. The Director then indicated that he was legally responsible for program decisions and, therefore, must have final authority. In doing so, he stressed the advisory role of consumers and how a consensus should be obtained about important decisions. The Director also pointed out the Civil Service regulations which control hiring and firing and which must be adhered to by BDS. Then, apparently as the result of frustrations that the parents seemed to feel when confronted by the regulatory procedures, the parents expressed feelings of distrust towards the professionals who were planning services for their children. This occurred at the same time that the parents were asking the professionals for new types of services which the parents had difficulty defining.

As the process of forming the consumer advisory board continued, senior professional staff began to show anxiety about its creation and possible powers. One particularly difficult problem was the anger expressed by certain parents aimed at individual professionals who provided specific programs. Examples of such conflicts were: 1) when short term residential or intensive treatment was offered by staff, but long term residential programming was the primary goal of the specific parent or family, 2) when the staff felt that a child was no longer appropriate for a program and the parents were approached about a referral to another program, the child's parents vocalized their hostility, 3) some parents disliked parent group counseling, while other parents lobbied for more group counseling, 4) parental overprotectiveness obstructed program participation for certain retarded children, keeping these children from attending more advanced programs for which they were clearly qualified.

Although all parents who attended meetings were encouraged to participate and make their views known, most preferred to remain quiet. It appeared that a few more aggressive or angry parents, were the dominant participants at meetings. Few parents were able to generalize from their own specific problem to the larger problem of the whole community.

There is a serious problem in enlisting community support for programs for the developmentally disabled, since many people have other major priorities, including unemployment, poor housing, and overwhelming poverty. It is hard, under the circumstances, for consumers or professionals to raise the visibility of mental retardation as an important issue at community meetings.

Conflict arises when staff assume an advocacy role for the disabled client and believe that the parental preference for institutional placement is not in the client's best interest. When staff decide it is preferable to maintain a particular client in the community rather than arrange placement in an older overcrowded institution, the staff's position may be in direct opposition to the parent's wishes. The legal rights of the disabled person, the related guardianship issue, and the State's role in this regard are still not very clear, although as a guding principal, the courts have stated in Wyatt *vs.* Stickney (Civil Action No. 72 2634 M.D. Ala. 1972) that "the mentally retarded person is entitled to the least restrictive setting necessary for rehabilitation."

To work out some of these difficulties, we are attempting to form an alliance and collaborative relationship with concerned interested consumer and community groups, and are evolving a policy for joint decision making through consumer participation in BDS policy and planning committees. Furthermore, program evaluation will be jointly performed by consumers and professionals. We are establishing a mechanism to assist parents and consumer groups in providing legal assistance for clients and their families when needed. Finally, since it is hoped that better informed consumers and public officials will be more effective collaborators with involved professionals, we have embarked on a serious effort in consumer and community education via radio and T.V. programs, posters, speaking engagements, and workshops, including special presentations to public officials, court personnel, and clergy.

Despite the effort to encourage consumer participation in planning and program development and the efforts BDS has made in community education, there are basic unresolved questions which cause concern and reservations among community service planners. The concerns include whether consumer participation, or even control, is as helpful in creating better programs as it appears to be in lobbying for needed services. Is joint decision making too cumbersome? Too time consuming? How much will conflicts of interest interfere with consumers' participation in deciding global issues? How productive are community education efforts? Since there are few data to answer any of these questions, creative thinking and extensive research will be needed to attempt to resolve these issues.

PHILOSOPHICAL AND ATTITUDINAL OBSTACLES

An obstacle impeding service development and delivery is the stereotypes some hold about the mentally retarded. The general belief of many is that "nothing can really be done" to help the retarded. Fear and ignorance are prevalent.

Health Professionals

Attitudes held by different medical specialists vary. For example, pediatricians are trained primarily to care for the acutely ill. Although they commiserate with the plight of the handicappped, as Cooke (1966) and Burg and Wright (1972) have reported, pediatricians often feel that they have a low level of competence to handle the problems of the chronically ill and would rather not treat these patients. In addition, their experience and training as counsellors are rather limited. Among obstetricians, a common reaction encountered is to advise the family immediately to instituionalize the child, regardless of whether this is wise, appropriate, or even feasible. Many psychiatrists appear to avoid becoming involved in therapeutic relationships with physically handicapped, brain damaged, or retarded patients and this is reflected by the very limited literature concerning psychiatric treatment of such patients. Yet psychiatrists in many states still exercise political and fiscal control over mental retardation, as a branch or a subsidiary of mental health.

Nurses usually have little exposure to mental retardation in their training and curriculum. However, in our experience, nurses can play a major role in delivery of services to the retarded. While mental health nursing has long been considered a recognized subspecialty, it is only in recent years that mental retardation nursing is gaining any recognition either inside or outside of institutions.

In general, medical centers appear to have "ivory tower" attitudes in that they are willing to do research or study the retarded, but will usually not assume service responsibilities or initiate outreach service programs for these patients. As Rosen and Callan (1972) have reported, only a small number of institutional programs for the retarded have formal university affiliations that affect programs or training, while community programs have an even lower frequency of university ties. These observations contrast with biological researchers' past proclivity for using institutionalized retarded subjects in research studies.

Many health professionals have had rigid attitudes which tended to reinforce the concept that successfully to serve the handicapped, job qualifications and professional degrees are more valuable than life experiences. In addition, the problem of finding staff who have had previous experience in the mental retardation field has made staff recruitment difficult. This is, in part, the consequence of the failure of many training programs for health professionals to spell out their objectives. When they have, those objectives are usually too general. For example, we may train social workers to be case workers or psychologists to be psychometricians, but we do not adequately prepare these professionals for roles in community mental retardation programs, residential settings, and specific program areas where more goal-directed training would assist them in their later functioning. The lack of such training has forced new programs such as ours to provide extensive on-the-job and in-service training for most new professional employees. To deal with the problems of the insensitivity, callousness, or ignorance of many service providers, including health professionals, it is clear that more and better training is needed to develop the kinds of interviewing, counseling, and related skills and knowledge that are required to work more satisfactorily with and help the developmentally handicapped. With regard to rigidity in job classifications, the use of multi-disciplinary team approaches, although not always commodious or efficient, tends to break down some of the rigidities of the more traditionally trained professionals. In addition, use of more paraprofessionals and lay personnel should be encouraged.

Teachers

Teachers have little or no training in special education as part of their regular curriculum. It is, therefore, not unexpected that they are fearful of integrating mentally handicapped children into their programs. Furthermore, special educators emphasize training programs to accommodate the needs of the more mildly learning-disabled and educable retarded children and often neglect the problems and needs of the severely retarded and multiply handicapped. The latter groups were for a long time regarded as primarily having medical problems and their care regarded as a medical responsibility.

As developmentally disabled children of all types are increasingly being integrated into community schools, it is essential that educators familiarize themselves with the problems of handicapped children. Furthermore, the thrust of training for new special educators must be on expanding their range of skills to enable them better to deal with more severely disabled children. This involves learning methods such as behavior modification and working with parents to encourage carry over of school experiences into the home. It also means developing early educational intervention techniques with preschool handicapped children. Greater attention must also be given to vocational training programs.

A progressive approach to the educational needs of the retarded is to emphasize the value of investing in services now and intervening with treatment as early as possible in order to translate the early intervention into long range benefits. Early and more intensive treatment may reduce unnecessary dependency, social difficulties and, in some cases, avert permanent residential placement. As Conley (1973) has reported, investments in vocational training have certainly demonstrated long range cost savings in terms of the productivity of the individuals who have received the necessary training and support services.

The approach of BDS to educators has been to offer workshops and training sessions for both special educators and teachers with limited special education backgrounds. The Community Service Teams and special program staff have, when feasible, established close relationships with preschool programs such as head start and day care centers to assist relatively untrained staff to include handicapped children in their programs. BDS has provided back-up services both inside and outside of the schools. In some cases, programs are jointly sponsored by the N.Y. City Board of Education and BDS, and in other cases, one or the other agency with appropriate liaison between the staffs. Training for teachers is an essential component of all such programs.

Legislators

A number of issues related to mental retardation cause difficulties for legislators. In a situation where responsibility for mental retardation services is subsumed under the label "mental health," legislators naturally tend to lump the two groups together in their thinking. Thus, institutions for the mentally ill are assumed to be programmatically similar to those for the mentally retarded. Problems of aftercare and community placement are assumed to be similar and community reactions to and fear of the mentally ill are assumed by politically sensitive legislators to apply equally to those of the mentally retarded. This encourages a "lock them up and keep them off the streets" attitude. It is clear that legislators have not received accurate information about mental retardation and, particularly, about the current movement toward community mental retardation services.

In attempting to educate legislators on these issues, public and voluntary agencies have sponsored legislative forums. Public agencies such as BDS are limited in their ability to lobby for their objectives and views. However, a militant and informed consumer advisory board, led by parents who seek services for their children, can be an effective voice at public hearings that legislators attend.

Parent's Groups

Over the years, the parents and relatives of the retarded have developed into an important lobby for better services for the retarded. In states such as New York, leading parent-

sponsored organizations have aggressively advocated direct consumer control and operation of services. Even when a recent series of court rulings ordered local Boards of
Education to pay for all of the educational costs for children now being served by
parent-sponsored agencies, the reaction of parent's groups was ambivalent, since they
were concerned about diminishing their role as direct providers. The issue of control of
educational activities or fear of job loss by some agency workers appeared for some to be
more important than the opportunity to divert "hard to raise" dollars, now used for
primary education services (which the government should and now agrees to pay for),
into the development of needed supplementary recreational programs, social activities,
parent counseling groups, etc.

In dealing with these difficult problems it is essential to build trust between consumers and professionals. Opportunities for joint planning for common objectives seem to
foster collaboration and trust. Openness on the part of professionals is also useful. A
community-oriented program such as BDS sees no contradiction in consumers operating
their own programs provided the programs are effective, well run, and do not duplicate
existing services. Another reasonable way of promoting better professional and consumer
understanding is through the mechanism of establishing procedures for the joint evaluation of the effectiveness of services and "normalization" experiences for the handicapped.
The results of these studies would enable us to plan more realistically and collaboratively
in the future.

Minority and Other Community Groups

The development and maintenance of services for the mentally retarded is not a priority
for most community groups. Some ethnic and racial minority groups in relatively poor communities appear to prefer not having their children classified as being mentally retarded
unless the retardation is severe. Most community leaders appear to be unaware of the
extent of the broader problem of developmental disability in their own geographic area.

Another problem is the skepticism of the minority groups members because of what
they view as the unfulfilled promises that have been made to them by governmental and
voluntary agencies as well as community mental health groups who encouraged community participation and then reacted defensively when control become the central issue.
Their anger at governmental institutions, in general, inhibits attempts at cooperative and
collaborative arrangements.

The pragmatic way we are trying to deal with these feelings is by establishing a visible
presence in the community including those areas dominated by minority groups. The
Community Service Teams operating in these areas are staffed largely by indigenous
professionals and paraprofessionals who come from similar minority backgrounds. Some
belong to local families who have retarded children. These staff assist local agencies in
developing their own programs. Staff attempt to educate the local community by
whatever forums exist, and then assist the local groups to provide needed services.
Whenever possible, local people are selected for jobs and trained to work in mental
retardation programs.

The Media

Few radio and television programs accurately portray the plight of the mentally handi-capped, particularly of the more severely disabled. The media appear primarily to describe the extremes, namely the mildly retarded who have an optimistic prognosis or the profoundly retarded who are abandoned in abhorrent circumstances. The latter group make cogent and profitable journalistic material for exposé purposes. This approach may be effective in lobbying for improved programs, but it can also engender attitudes of hopelessness and the image of incurability for all of the retarded. On the other hand, a preoccupation with happy endings and more palatable commercial fare can lead to distortion and misinterpretation on the public's part. It is obvious that the issue of mental subnormality and, particularly, severe mental subnormality must be given more promi-nence. We need more research, however, to tell us what the most fruitful mechanism for this may be.

OVERLAPPING JURISDICTIONS

Planning Responsibilities

An issue of considerable importance in developing new services in the community is defining the responsibilities and interrelationships of the various agencies who serve the mentally etarded as a result of a legal mandate or a voluntary effort.

The role of BDS, a new state agency to serve the mentally retarded, has been the subject of considerable debate. No guidelines for community-oriented state programs existed in the past. The leaders and staff of BDS constructed their role to be not only as an agent to channel State funds into new programs, but also as coordinators and advocates to mobilize all available resources in the county to help develop services for mentally retarded and developmentally disabled Bronx citizens. As a result of these efforts, BDS has been involved with other agencies, both public and voluntary, in a process of clarifying whose role it is to provide specific types of services. This issue has significant political ramifications, since it tends to aggravate existing controversies and fiscal entan-glements between City, State, and voluntary agencies. Examples of these types of difficulties that are frequently encountered involve responsibilities for social welfare, education, health services, and transportation.

Social Services

Local social service agencies are required by law to provide payments for medical care and for the maintenance of all eligible handicapped citizens, including the mentally retarded, in nursing homes and intermediate care facilities via Medicaid. Local communities are reimbursed by the Federal Government for 75% of these costs. Local social services officials resist certifying retarded people as being eligible for these facilities while claiming that the responsibility for the cost of care for the retarded rests solely with the State

Department of Mental Hygiene, which pays for 100% of the costs of the retarded in State Institutions. Community services staff, functioning as advocates, often must resort to legal pressure to make local Department of Social Services officials approve payments for the care of the retarded. Another example involves the Bureau of Child Welfare, a branch of the Department of Social Services (or Human Resources Agency as it is called in New York). Although this agency is required by law to accept guardianship responsibilities and assist or directly arrange for emergency placement for homeless or abandoned children, the agency often refuses to accept responsibility for guardianship and placement of retarded children who, due to a family crisis, need emergency alternative living arrangements. As a consequence, out of necessity, mental hygiene agencies, such as ourselves, have been forced to set up their own family care or foster care programs for the retarded. At the same time, we have offered ourselves as consultants to the social welfare agency so that we can eventually assist a government agency to assume fully their legally mandated responsibilities in this area of child care. The guardianship issue is an excellent example of how, under appropriate circumstances, responsibilities can be delineated. When and if the social service agency assumes its responsibility as guardian of the retarded child, it is appropriate for that agency to act as an advocate and a monitor to assure that a state agency, such as BDS, responsible for developing programs for the retarded child, appropriately carries out its mandate. In fact, in N.Y. Family Court proceedings, BDS recently convinced a Judge to assign guardianship responsibility for a mongoloid child to the Bureau of Child Welfare (BCW), after BDS guaranteed that it would directly provide or arrange the appropriate treatment and educational programs. Despite the Judge's acceptance of this plan, which placed the authority of the court squarely behind BCW in any effort they might have to make to assure that BDS would keep its part of the bargain, BCW officials refused to accept this plan. BCW is currently appealing this ruling to a higher court. BDS has been assured by the N.Y. State Attorney General's office that BDS is legally correct in its assertions that the separation of responsibility for treatment from guardianship is a correct one and that the Mental Hygiene and the Social services or Welfare agencies respectively have distinct responsibilities in such cases.

Another important example of a problem with social service agencies is related to the new legislation for Supplemental Security Income. The new guidelines and payment procedures have created chaos for the mentally retarded, since the definition of who is eligible, in terms of degree of retardation, is unclear. The mechanisms for implementation of this new program are also unclear and the resultant delays have slowed down the process of deinstitutionalization, since these payments were counted on to support part of the retarded clients expenses in the community. This has, again, caused conflict between community services staff, playing an advocacy role, and those administering the local Supplementary Security Income program.

Education

Recent court rulings clearly indicate that the legal responsibility for educating the retarded unquestionably rests with the local education authority. Board of Education programs have not, however, previously included many severely handicapped children and, therefore, their teachers are usually not prepared to deal with these youngsters, despite the legal mandate. This has also been the case with Head Start and Day Care programs, which have been ordered by federal authorities to integrate handicapped youngsters with normal children so that a minimum of 10% of their total program population will be developmentally disabled youngsters. Implementation of this has caused tension between the advocates for the handicapped and the program providers. However, as a result of discussions between BDS with local education officials we have agreed to train teachers funded by the Board of Education who will then teach handicapped clients that we serve, while we also provide necessary back-up and support services. Once these roles and responsibilities, including the Board of Education's fiscal and programmatic commitments were clarified, we were then able to operate successful collaborative education and habilitation programs.

Health Services

In the area of health services, there has been a general lack of availability of medical services for the handicapped. This has been fostered by exclusionary policies. Families of retarded children and adults who come to medical or psychiatric emergency rooms frequently report that the retarded are mistreated and excluded from services that others receive. One of the often heard complaints among advocates and service providers for the mentally retarded is their inability to obtain psychiatric services, despite the fact that the control of mental retardation funding is in the hands of the Department of Mental Hygiene. BDS has engaged in delicate and sometimes frustrating negotiations with medical and psychiatric departments of local municipal hospitals, attempting to arrange needed care for retarded clients. In doing so, BDS stresses its role in liaison and providing follow-up, but not primary or acute health and psychiatric care for the retarded.

Transportation

One of the greatest barriers to effective programming for the mentally retarded and physically handicapped has been inadequate transportation. Although most urban communities have reasonably adequate public transportation, it does not meet the needs of those who are severely handicapped. The development of special transportation for the handicapped has been inhibited by lack of funds and by difficulty in defining whether it is the responsibility of the Department of Mental Hygiene or the Department of Transportation and whether this should be a state, local, or agency-operated program. The development of transportation for the handicapped has also been inhibited by attitudes, both on the parts of parents and professionals, toward increased travel for the handicapped. Some parents express fear of permitting their handicapped offspring to travel alone, citing the dangers of travel on urban public transport even for normal people. Compounding this fear is the tendency of some parents to overprotect their handicapped child. In many cases, this has never been effectively dealt with by the professional staff working with the family.

Among the solutions to the problems of transportation for the handicapped is early training in the use of public transport. This should be an essential component of all public education programs for the retarded. Although it does not appear to be feasible to modify current public transportation to accommodate the needs of all retarded and physically handicapped people, it is still important to remove as many physical barriers as possible to enable the handicapped to utilize this mode of transport as often as possible. However, recognizing the limitations that would still exist, a single special transportation system would still be necessary for those who would otherwise be home bound. This could be developed as a public program whereby anyone with a severe disability could call a central number and a special vehicle suited to accommodate physically handicapped people would be dispatched to transport the person to his or her destination. This is the essence of some experimental "dial-a-ride" systems. Another possibility is that all agencies serving retarded and physically handicapped people pool their resources and form a consortium to develop an efficient centralized system within the community. Public mental retardation agencies, such as BDS, must be willing to volunteer to coordinate such an effort.

DETERMINING PRIORITIES

The problem of setting priorities in a relatively underserved area such as the Bronx would ordinarily be a serious one. However, since the Bronx has always had strong diagnostic services for children, there was no need to set up a mechanism for additional case finding and assessment of developmentally disabled children. What was evident, as a result of the clinics' experiences, was the necessity for rapid development of day treatment programs for severely retarded children, especially in poverty areas. In addition, there was an immediate desperate need for community residential services. These priorities and others became even clearer as a result of BDS's efforts to serve local community needs via visible community service teams and through an effort to coordinate its activities with other agencies. Formal coordination with other agencies has taken place through a Bronx Mental Retardation Regional Council. All provider agencies and consumer groups are invited to participate on the Council. With 30 or more members, the Council is too large a body to be effective in determining priorities. However, through subcommittees that deal with specific problems, such as residential care, adult programs, children's day program, etc., the Council voices its approval or disapproval of new proposals. But the subcommittees have not usually rated priorities within their specific area of interest, nor has the Council itself recorded its priorities among the various competing types of proposals.

Because of the Mental Retardation Council's and the participating agencies' failure to effectively set priorities and do joint planning, BDS pushed for the development of what we call an Implementation Committee. Difficult cases are brought to this committee on which all important provider agencies are represented. This committee formulates a "treatment" plan or plan for needed services. By applying pressure from peers and colleagues, responsibility for implementation is assured. Although this type of collective decision making is cumbersome, it is useful in obtaining some consensus on the location of services gaps and who should try to fill them.

With information obtained from sources such as the implementation committee and from the types of problems confronted as a result of their own field experiences and agency referrals, BDS staff realized that their first priority had to be crisis intervention for the handicapped individuals or their families who present serious social emergencies. BDS' second priority has been planning and arranging for the removal of former Bronx residents from large State institutions for the retarded and providing or developing programs and more normal living accommodations for the people back in their community of origin. This process has commonly been called deinstitutionalization. This has been a very high priority for BDS because of the wretched state of the large public institutions and the pressures to diminish rapidly their size. Thirdly, as a result of our own and the referring agencies' assessment of the current needs in the Bronx, we have attempted to plug huge gaps in terms of available programs. This led to the creation of our short term treatment unit, a 24-hour intensive treatment program for severely retarded children. The crisis intervention activities also clearly pointed to a need for a multi-disciplinary diagnostic clinic for adults, since the existing clinics only served children. Other units that BDS has developed include a day program for severely retarded adults, a home management program for both children and adults, and an adolescent treatment service. While the development of these programs has represented short term solutions to deal with the immediate problems, a final important priority has involved a serious attempt to plan, coordinate, advise, and advocate for the development of a network of new services to meet intermediate and long range projected needs.

Priorities can obviously be altered by fiscal and political pressures. In the case of BDS, developing programs for people currently in need of services in the community would have remained our primary commitment had it not been for the political situation and the fiscal incentive tied to removing former Bronx residents from large distant institutions and returning them to the community.

Since the large institutions were considered a "State" problem because a State agency ran them, City and voluntary agencies felt little obligation, until pressured, to change their priorities to include aiding in the removal of the retarded from institutions. Furthermore, the return of former institutionalized residents to the community provoked concern among the more vocal constituency within the community who saw the possibility of deinstitutionalized people competing with their agency clients or retarded relatives for the limited services currently available within the Bronx. These concerns, coupled with fear of "dumping" the institutionalized retarded into the community and the difficulties in developing smaller community residences in an urban setting, have all impeded the process of deinstitutionalization. Added to this, at the institutional level, has been the active and passive resistance of the employees of the large State facilities, the fear of individual job loss and economic loss to the institution's local community, plus resentment toward the BDS staff "outsiders" who appear to institutional employees to be trying to change the status quo. All of these combine to delay deinstitutionalization efforts.

In planning services and seeking priorities within the community, numerous conflicts have also existed between agencies that give service to children and adults with different types of handicaps. Agencies serving the cerebral palsied, the mentally retarded, the autistic, the birth defects population, and the learning disabled, with the objective of aiding their specific clients, compete for control and funds. In doing so, they try to influence decisions about funding for new programs, whether the funds emanate from Federal, State, or City sources. With all of these governmental agencies also often indicating different priorities and conflicts in their respective planning functions, this complex situation obviously creates obstacles that inhibit rational planning and fail to satisfy competing special interest groups.

There is almost universal agreement that large State institutions are undesirable places for the retarded to live. Most professionals and consumers favor providing as normal or home-like an environment for the retarded, plus as normal participation in community activities as is possible. This is what is commonly called "normalization."

However, though everyone usually appears sympathetic to the goal of "normalization," some parents as well as professionals differ as to whether the first priority should be the immediate development of basic, although segregated services, even when "normalization" does not appear to be feasible. Some professional program planners and parents also question whether normalization in terms of near normal community living is a realistic goal for any but the mild to moderately retarded. Those with more pragmatic attitudes appear to want development of as many basic services as possible (e.g., residential, education, habilitation, vocational, etc.) where none currently exist, and do not concern themselves with how well integrated the handicapped are into the rest of society. The pragmatists point out that it is unrealistic to expect society to change with sufficient alacrity to adapt to the needs of the handicapped as fast as parents or professional planners desire.

There are conflicting views on the methods of eliminating the large dehumanizing State institutions. There are those who desire to close large institutions immediately versus those who prefer gradually to phase out these large institutions and avoid "dumping" clients back into communities that are unprepared to provide adequate services. The preferred alternative goal of almost everyone is the development of smaller residential facilities. However, practical considerations, such as locating appropriate space, rebuilding older suitable housing to meet the needs of the handicapped, complying with local building codes, and overcoming community opposition and zoning laws, make the development of smaller residential centers a difficult and exasperating task. It is unfortunate that a recent Supreme Court ruling permitting communities to exclude groupings of unrelated people in residential areas may further inhibit progress in developing local community residences.

A key priority for BDS, as a community-oriented program, has been a strong advocacy role for all the retarded and developmentally disabled, irrespective of current location and degree of disability. Few agencies, public or voluntary, appear anxious to serve the severely retarded. In addition to the advocacy role, when dealing with community agencies, the most effective means of demonstrating our interest, concern, and value has been when staff acted as coordinators and collaborators in helping the agency and community obtain new resources and programs. This is carried out while making it clear that we do not have a desire to control other agencies programs. This approach has been most successful when coupled with our efforts in providing education and training to agency and community staff.

BDS has chosen the development of geographically distributed community-based programs as the primary means of meeting the goals of dealing with crisis cases, deinstitutionalization, and developing a network of needed services in the Bronx. It has become quite clear, however, in managing a community services operations, that we are far more exposed and open to criticism than if we hid behind the walls of an institutional program. Bringing the handicapped into the community and next door to people makes them more familiar with the problem. There is a serious question as to whether familiarity breeds contempt, acceptance, fear, or children. The latter may seem facetious, but fears of overt sexual activity and pregnancies among retarded adolescents and adults cause widespread concern. In a community service operation, our successes and failures are more obvious than they would otherwise be. While program staff usually try to maintain a relatively low profile, they are often accused of trying to change society when they act in an advocacy role. Furthermore, it has not been uncommon for the media to report inaccurately community program activities.

Finally, since there is no proof of the effectiveness of community services of the type we are attempting to develop, it remains an important priority for BDS to develop a system to evaluate the results of its programs. This will require a systematic program and cost evaluation effort, plus an automated information-gathering system which has concomitant safeguards to maintain confidentiality. A system of this type could be used for both planning and evaluation purposes. This system could correlate the demographic data, the program activities, the status pre- and post-program, particularly the pre- and post-institutionalization functional levels and behavior of the deinstitutionalized, plus the relative costs of the various treatment alternatives. Due to fiscal restraints and the pressures to develop rapidly new service programs, BDS has not yet been able to make a sustained effort to develop this type of evaluation system. However, it remains an important priority for the future.

SUMMARY

This paper has discussed the practical problems that have confronted a new ambitious program aimed at developing community mental retardation services in an urban setting. Many of the problems reported are generalizable to other communities and service situations. In examining the obstacles inhibiting the development of new services and innovative approaches, we have described the new model of community services which we are utilizing. We have also discussed some of the pragmatic methods of dealing with the problems and the reactionary and bureaucratic forces that have accentuated our difficulties and slowed us down, but, fortunately, not stopped us.

REFERENCES

Burg, F. and F. H. Wright. 1972. Evaluation of Pediatric Residents and their training programs. Pediatrics 80: 183—189.

Conley, R. W. 1973. The Economics of Mental Retardation. Johns Hopkins Press, Baltimore.

Cooke, R. E. 1966. Residency Training—A summary of findings of the PREP Committee. Pediatrics 38: Part II, 720—725.

Joint Commission on Accreditation of Hospitals (JCAH). 1973. Standards for Community Agencies Serving Persons with Mental Retardation and other Developmental Disabilities. Chicago.

Rosen, D. and L. B. Callan. 1972. TRENDS: Residential Services for the Mentally Retarded. Report by the National Association of Superintendents of Public Residential Facilities.

Reforming Programs
For Youth in Trouble

Lloyd E. Ohlin

In the last decade public policy governing the treatment of children with problems has shifted to a greater reliance on treatment in community-based programs as opposed to large isolated institutions. This trend has been especially striking in programs of mental health, mental retardation, and juvenile corrections (Joint Commission on Mental Illness and Health, 1961; President's Commission on Law Enforcement and Administration of Justice, 1967). The cost of operating large, congregate institutions has become prohibitive and the services provided are seldom able to respond adequately to each client's needs (Dean and Reppucci, 1974). Institutional services tend to drift down to the lowest common denominator of need in the client population and to hover at the minimum daily requirement of effort on the part of staff. Consequently, they tend primarily to serve the ends of physical sustenance and custodial security for the confined population. But these ends are gained at the expense of severe exacerbation of client problems, alienation of clients from constructive social roles, and stigmatization as the result of commitment to these institutions.

Although this dramatic change in public policy away from large institutions has pervaded the whole area of children services, there has been little exchange of experience of the problems of transition and the relative effectiveness of the newer modalities of treatment. It is, of course, often an accident of personal circumstance whether a child with problems comes to official attention as a person who is mentally ill, retarded, delinquent, or simply in need of special welfare, education, or other social services (Polier, 1974). Nevertheless, each type of service has developed its own institutional resources, professional commitments, treatment ideology and communication network. Although they all draw on the insights and knowledge of the social, psychological, and medical sciences, the structure and organization of their professional activities tend to confine interaction and communication to their own fields of specialization. It is on the assumption that these fields of specialization do in fact have common problems and much to learn from one another that I shall try in the following account to outline major trends in the treatment of delinquents and strategic problems that arise in the movement from institutional to community-based services.

JUVENILE CORRECTIONS IN TRANSITION

The basic philosophy and effectiveness of juvenile justice policies are being critically reexamined throughout the country. The high saliency of the crime problem and federal grants to the states to deal with it have been partly responsible. However, other sources of dissatisfaction with the present system have added even more significantly to the current climate of criticism and search for new solutions.

In nearly all states the large, traditional training school continues to be the most common resource for the confinement of adjudicated delinquent boys and girls in a residential setting. A recent census as of June 30, 1971, found that 84% of the 42,642 children confined in correctional facilities (other than those used for detention or temporary care) resided in these training schools (U.S. Department of Justice, 1974). Recidivism rates of the graduates run as high as 90% depending upon the age of the youth, length of follow-up, and the criterion of recidivism employed (Ohlin et al., 1975). The costs of such confinement also are increasing due to inflation and attempts to introduce more intensive treatment experiences of a therapeutic character. Cost estimates vary from $2,500 to $20,000 a year per child depending on the amount of professional services provided, the inclusion or exclusion of capital amortization costs, and regional variations in cost of living factors (Dean and Reppucci, 1974). There have been repeated public exposés of the repressive, brutal, and punishment-oriented practices that constantly reoccur in these schools despite periodic reform efforts. Such an exposé laid the ground in Massachusetts in 1969 for the resignation of the former Director of the Division of Youth Services, the passage of new legislation, and the appointment of a reform-mandated Commissioner (Ohlin et al, 1974). More recently, a federal district court judge in Texas ordered the closing down of two of the most repressive training schools and major changes to protect the rights of children and their access to treatment opportunities (Morales v. Turman, 1974). These trends have all contributed to an increasing repudiation of large institutions as a treatment resource for delinquent children.

A second major source of dissatisfaction has been the discouraging results from studies of new treatment programs and demonstration projects. Martinson (1974) has recently reported his analysis of 231 studies completed between 1945 and 1967 that utilized a control or comparison group and a clear measure of outcome of treatment. He concluded that, "With few and isolated exceptions, the rehabilitative efforts that have been reported so far have had no appreciable effect on recidivism." An NIMH survey of community-based correctional programs reported essentially the same results in 1971. Lerman (1968)[1] comes to similar conclusions after reviewing some of the most progressive and innovative residential treatment programs. A recent report (Bondeson, 1968) on youth facilities for delinquent boys and girls in Sweden used sensitive argot measures of socialization. The results showed a failure rate of 70% and strong criminalization effects resulting from socialization processes within the institutions.

---

[1] For a more detailed analysis of the highly regarded probation subsidy and community treatment programs in California see Lerman, 1975. Community Treatment and Social Control: An Analysis of Juvenile Correctional Policy, University of Chicago Press, Chicago.

These evaluative studies thus far suggest that the newer treatment programs do not significantly increase the success rates of those exposed to them, at least as measured by subsequent recidivism, although admittedly this is a somewhat complex and insensitive criterion of actual behavior. A recent notable exception to this generalization has been the report on the experiment in Provo, Utah (Empey and Erickson, 1972). This program offered nonresidential guided group interaction for the experimental group combined with attempts to open up conventional opportunities in the community. Although the initial differences were small, the experimental group was doing much better at the end of a 4-year follow-up period. The experimental group showed a success rate of 60 to 70% compared to 25% for the incarcerated control group. Furthermore, the experimental group's average 7-month stay in the program cost $609 as compared to $2,015 for an average stay of 9½ months for the incarcerated boys. In general, this study concludes that youth diverted from traditional training schools show lower recidivism rates and tend to spend less time in treatment at lower cost.

Another major source of dissatisfaction with the existing juvenile justice system arises from a strong upsurge of concern for protecting the civil rights of minors. Since the historic Gault decision in 1967, there has been a series of cases which have challenged the unconstrained discretion and procedural informality of the juvenile court process (Fox, 1972). These U. S. Supreme Court decisions have imposed upon the juvenile court certain constitutional requirements of due process such as the right to appropriate notice, to counsel, to confrontation and cross examination, and the privilege against self-incrimination. They also require that the standard of proof should be beyond a reasonable doubt. The Court, however, stopped short of imposing a constitutional requirement of access to trial by jury as part of the juvenile court's adjudicative procedures. The Court is still not ready to reject the underlying philosophy that has motivated the juvenile court movement. The appeals courts have however been impressed by the studies, opinions and arguments of experts that challenge the ability of juvenile courts to act in the "best interest of the child" as a substitute parent. The overloaded process of the court and its limited treatment resources severely limit its capability to fulfill this role properly (Polier, 1974).

Accordingly, recent decisions have moved in the direction of providing the protections for the juvenile which are regularly provided for the adult in a criminal court procedure. This change in policy recognizes that the informal, nonadversary, civil process of the juvenile court has not been able to remove the stigma attaching to delinquency proceedings and further recognizes that the deprivations of confinement and separation from home imposed on the juvenile may be more severe than the sanctions meted out to adults in criminal court for similar conduct. More recently legal advocates for children have argued that there is a right to treatment for young offenders confined in residential training schools (Morales v. Turman, 1974). Others have asserted that young offenders should also have the right to choose to accept either treatment or whatever punitive penalty is imposed (Fox, 1972). This concern for the child's rights during the correctional process has undoubtedly been reinforced by recent successful efforts to induce the court to intervene to protect the civil rights of adult prisoners during confinement. The scope and depth of court intervention on matters relating to the rights of prisoners in confinement has greatly increased (Orlando, 1973). It is argued that children should not be denied rights available to adult prisoners. Part of this concern for civil rights of children also arises from the apparent discriminatory impact of the juvenile court in the correctional process. Deeper penetration into the juvenile justice system to the point of confinement in training schools appears to be disproportionately the fate of poor minority group youth unable to obtain access to private alternative services (Polier, 1974).

TRENDS IN JUVENILE JUSTICE

These criticisms of the juvenile court and correctional process have generated pressures toward reform of the existing system. This reform movement is halting and uneven, varying considerably in both pace and direction in different states. For example, the National Assessment of Juvenile Corrections Project recently reported that half of the states has been increasing the institutionalization of delinquents while the other half has been reducing this type of confinement (Grichting, 1973). In the following account I shall be concerned primarily with those trends generally regarded by authorities in juvenile justice as "progressive" or "liberal."

There are three dominant models for the residential treatment of juvenile offenders presently competing for control of resources. As noted in Table 1, I have designated these models protective custody, clinical treatment, and therapeutic community. Table 1 highlights contrasting differences in various organizational features of these models (Ohlin, 1974). Each is grounded in more or less explicit assumptions about the sources of delinquent behavior. The organizational characteristics of each model tend to be congruent with these perspectives on delinquency and lead to notable differences in such features as the type of correctional remedy, the allocation of decision-making authority, the control techniques employed, the subcultural pattern of inmate response, the level of staff education, training, preferred abilities, and competence, the relation of the institutions to the central office, institutional and aftercare services.

As noted earlier, the protective custody model reflected in traditional training school practices is still the dominant model for youth correctional treatment in many states. Since World War II, however, the clinical treatment model has made substantial inroads. It exists in its purest form in privately operated residential schools to which young offenders may be sent as an alternative to the public institutions. More commonly, however, certain features of the clinical treatment model have been added to the protective custody model in a subordinate capacity to carry out diagnoses for classification and release decisions or to deal with youth who exhibit loss of emotional control. The therapeutic community model is a more recent importation to the field of juvenile corrections. It is most likely to be found in newly established small group homes modeled with many variations after the Highfields program in New Jersey (McCorkle et al., 1958). It provides in most states an alternative to the protective custody or clinical treatment model for some seriously delinquent youth deemed likely to respond to peer group pressures. From an historical standpoint the trend has been from protective custody

Table 1. Juvenile correctional models

Organizational characteristics	Protective custody	Clinical treatment	Therapeutic community
Theory of delinquency	Deficient character training and loss of respect for authority	Emotional deprivation and psychological conflicts, blockage of insight to emotional problems	Loss of respect for self and others, failure of interpersonal socialization, or moral development
Correctional remedy and procedure	Teach respect for authority and good character through obedience to adults and proper conduct in cottage, school and work	Encourage insight into sources of emotional disturbance through individual counseling with professional clinicians	Teach respect for self and others through understanding one's own feeling and those of others in group therapy and discussion sessions with inmates and staff
Decision-making authority	Centralized in cottage life staff	Centralized in clinical staff	Decentralized to therapy group (subject to staff approval in most situations)
Control techniques	Regimentation, segregation, loss of privileges, physical force, broad discretion to discipline, informal sharing of authority with inmate leaders, use of special privileges, transfer, withholding of parole or home visits	Additional clinical sessions, special privileges or loss of privileges, segregation or transfer, control of release and home visit decisions by clinical staff, low visibility of criteria of decisions	Group discussion of rule violations or disruptive conduct, group advice on disciplinary measures subject to staff veto, group advice on release, furloughs and other special rewards of achievement, high visibility of criteria of decision

continued

Table 1. *continued*

Organizational characteristics	Protective custody	Clinical treatment	Therapeutic community
Inmate subcultural roles and norms	Domination by inmate clique of leaders sharing power with staff for special prerogatives despite ideology of equal treatment, stress doing one's own time, no ratting, minimal contact with staff, ritual conformity to rules, subculture closed to staff and resists character training approach	Inmate role model is "right" guy defending self integrity against staff intervention, stress conformity to group norms against ratting or discussing behavior of others with staff and not threatening group privileges by conduct, subculture closed to staff and resists treatment approach	Subculture open to staff through group discussion with some taboo topics that put others on spot, role model is active participant in group discussion, decisions visible to group more acceptable, norm is to participate but not at expense of others
Staff training and desired abilities	No professional training needed except for school teachers. Cottage life model is an authoritative but protective parent. Reliance on previous experience as parent, tradesman or teacher. Appointment by political patronage is likely	Stress specialized professional training for clinicians, teachers, recreational directors, vocational instructors and special competence as cottage parents to create receptive and understanding climate. Clinicians try to match inmates with appropriate cottage parents. Professional recruitment	Preference for professional training in group therapy or discussion methods for group leaders. All staff including maintenance staff capable of warm and empathic responses to children and especially capable of handling aggressive, hostile verbal assaults. Professional recruitment

Relations to central office	Largely autonomous, rely on central office for administrative support and crisis management	Central office furnishes administrative support, general policy, technical assistance, crisis intervention	Central office exercises strong planning and development function, back-up services, expert supervision and training
Relation to aftercare services	Little contact, no regular institutional visiting. High parole case-loads, nominal supervision, patronage appointment, no professional training required	Professional training required, low case-loads, some institutional pre-release visiting, regular client visiting and counseling expected	Close integration of institutional and aftercare program. Use of group discussion approach continued in aftercare. Part-time voluntary participation in institutional program by client group of parolees. Professionally trained aftercare workers

through clinical treatment to therapeutic community facilities, although in most states all three of these approaches currently coexist in varying proportions in the total network of public and private residential services for juvenile offenders.

Current trends reveal the emergence of a new model of treatment utilizing more non-residential services oriented toward reintegration and community advocacy of client needs (Coates, 1974). The basic premise of this approach is that changes in attitude and behaviour achieved in isolated residential settings will not result in a less deviant community adjustment unless strong supportive reinforcement for these changes exists in the communities to which offenders return. In addition, there is a clear preference for services which intervene as unobtrusively as possible in the everyday life of offenders in their local communities while providing support with problems of adjustment they usually encounter. The emphasis, therefore, is on creating a better integration of the youthful offender into the basic institutions of the community through supportive services of a residential or non-residential character involving such services as counseling, tutoring, vocational training and placement, etc., or through strategically relevant forms of advocacy on the behalf of the client with relevant groups or agencies. In this approach the assumption is that problems of individual adjustment or institutional inadequacy and unresponsiveness to client needs must be confronted and worked through in the community where the problem arises, if at all possible. This community-oriented perspective is apparent in three basic strategies of treatment which are gaining increasing acceptance in the field: radical nonintervention, diversion and advocacy, and deinstitutionalization.

Radical Nonintervention

In the felicitous phrase "radical nonintervention," Shur reflects a greater sensitivity among youth workers to the harmful effects of official intervention which may often produce seriously disruptive and stigmatizing effects on youthful career development (Schur, 1973). In essence, this approach suggests that we normalize as much as possible the recurrent troubles and problems in the adjustment of youth to their everyday life circumstances. It assumes that the successful prevention of serious future misconduct may require considerable tolerance and judicious handling of minor infractions that do not pose serious threats to the person or property of others. The problem is perceived to be one of tiding youth over the inevitable adjustment problems and identity crises experienced during adolescence until they are prepared to enter the job market, military service, marriage, or other adult roles which furnish a reputational stake and set of obligations conducive to law-abiding activities. These policy implications of the labeling perspective are countered, on the other hand, by increasing public concern about the rising rates of serious youth crime at younger ages and a pervasive public preference for stronger law and order control measures in response (Morgan, 1975).

Diversion and Advocacy

The increasing reliance on policies of diversion and advocacy for youthful offenders rests on several observations and beliefs about the current state of services for such offenders.

Disenchantment with the ability of juvenile courts or training schools to rehabilitate delinquent youth or reduce the high rates of recidivism is reinforced by the stigmatizing effects on delinquent adjudication and training school commitment which make it even more difficult for these young people to solve successfully problems they may have with their families, school authorities, employers, the police, or other neighborhood residents (Coates et al., 1974). Also, many of the public and private agencies responsible for providing services tend to reject delinquent youth as unsuited to the type of treatment they can provide.

The policy of diversion, therefore, urges that the juvenile court should be used only as a last resort for youth who have commited frequent and serious offenses (Vorenberg and Vorenberg, 1973). Instead, youth are diverted to non-juvenile justice alternatives. This diversion is coupled with some form of advocacy on behalf of individual youth to encourage school services, mental health, social welfare, and vocational training and placement programs to work seriously and intensively on the problems of adjustment these youth present. A trend in this direction is evident in new statutes limiting delinquency proceedings in a juvenile court to only those offenses by youth which are also crimes for adults (Fox, 1972). This means that child status offenses such as truancy, running away, being ungovernable, incorrigible, or stubborn can no longer constitute grounds for a delinquency petition. Instead, most of the states pursuing this policy have created a new category of problem youth variously designated as persons in need of service (pins), children in need of service (chins), and minors in need of service (mins). These statutes ordinarily also require that youth with these problems of conflict with authority must not be referred to the correctional services but must be dealt with by mental health, child welfare, or other private or public services of a similar nature. There is still a considerable amount of confusion in making appropriate dispositions since these agencies are already overburdened with excessive caseloads.

It is still not clear how successful the new child status offender statutes will be in keeping youthful rebels against adult authority out of the youth correctional services. In the past, juvenile court judges often adjudicated youth as child status offenders when they had actually committed criminal acts for which adults could be punished as well. This device protected the child from acquring a juvenile court record for a more serious offense, while still exposing him to comparable treatment measures. It is likely that under the new law judges may employ this device less often, especially when young offenders appear to the court to require a period of intensive and secure treatment. This possibility is reenforced by the views of many knowledgeable observers that there is ordinarily very little difference between the child who is brought to court as a child status offender and one who appears on a delinquency petition. They are perceived as children with very similar types of treatment needs involving both delinquency and acts of rebellion against adult authority (Office of Children's Service, 1973).

There is also concern that the transfer of jurisdiction of child status offenders from youth correctional authorities to welfare and mental health agencies will cause the court to cast a wider net, bringing into treatment children whose cases otherwise would be dismissed or settled out of court (Empey, 1973). A related concern is that child status offenders will not receive adequate care because of the lack of resources for dealing with these often difficult cases in welfare and mental health agencies. It is too soon to tell in most jurisdictions whether any or all of these fears will be realized, but the expressions of concern demonstrate a more sophisticated recognition that major new innovations undertaken by "child savers" with benign motives may have unexpected and possibly harmful consequences (Platt, 1969).

Deinstitutionalization

Perhaps the most radical policy change emerging in the field of youth corrections is the abandonment of traditional training schools and reliance on treatment in community-based residential and non-residential services. Movement toward this objective has varied considerably among the different states. As has been noted, training schools, next to probation, are the primary treatment resource for juvenile correctional services and, furthermore, as many states are increasing as decreasing the use of such institutions. Some states have tried to make the training schools work more successfully by introducing intensive group or individual therapy and also behavior modification programs.

In those few states where deinstitutionalization has emerged as the preferred public policy, the traditional training schools are being replaced by a new network of public and private small group homes, more use of foster home placement, independent living arrangements for youth, and non-residential therapeutic, counseling, remedial education, and vocational training services (Bakal, 1973). In these new service arrangements greater reliance is being placed on the purchase of service from private agencies. The resulting network seeks to draw on the greater organizational flexibility and capacity for innovation in the private sector as well as the legally mandated accountability of public agencies. Such a mixture of public and private services is not in itself a new phenomena, especially in the eastern states where the development of institutional services for children by private charities and agencies has a long history. What is new is the rejection of treatment in large institutions for delinquent youth under either private or public auspices as the major treatment resource or even as a last resort.

Here again, however, proponents of the new policies of community-based services are conscious of potential pitfalls. Even small detention shelters or community residential treatment centers for delinquent youth can assume the character of jails or prisons depending upon the correctional philosophy which guides their organization and operation. In the past, private agencies have tended to skim off the cases more amenable to treatment, leaving the more difficult and disturbed youth to the public agencies. Thus the twin problems of accountability and quality of service are not automatically solved with the rejection of large institutions as a treatment resource (Ohlin, Coates, and Miller, 1974). Instead it places even greater demand on the system to create a truly effective system of accounting and monitoring of the quality and integrity of the services provided.

The Process of Change

More than anything else, the new trends in juvenile justice and especially the new policies of deinstitutionalization have underscored the enormous difficulty of effecting even limited changes in traditional practices. One of the greatest obstacles to improving the effectiveness of human services resides in the lack of systematic understanding of the means for effecting major changes in policies and organizational arrangements. The processes of social change as they naturally affect public policy and agency operations in every day life have not been studied sufficiently. Strategies for mobilizing the political and organizational processes of change in the policies of public bureaucracies are still regarded as dependent on the intuitive artfulness of politicians and successful administrators. Yet widespread improvement in the delivery of human services cannot be achieved unless such knowledge and skill are analyzed and made communicable. This means gaining greater understanding about the roots of the conservatism of established agencies and policies, the nature of other barriers to change, the strategies and processes which can create a climate for change, and procedures for creating supportive coalitions of interest groups (Ohlin, 1974).

In the current movement toward deinstitutionalization in corrections and other human services, we are provided with an excellent opportunity to develop this type of knowledge. The shift in policy is radical enough to require a massive dislocation in the organization and operation of existing services. The change requires a public mandate sufficiently strong to overcome the stake of vested interests in the existing system. Comparative studies of both the successes and failures of deinstitutionalization will begin to provide better understanding of how to achieve major social change in public agencies.

In youth corrections the most radical and pervasive pursuit of a policy of deinstitutionalization has occurred in the last few years in the State of Massachusetts. At the Center for Criminal Justice at the Harvard Law School we have been studying reforms in the youth correctional services in Massachusetts for the past five years. Although our studies are not yet complete, the Department of Youth Services has been successful in closing its traditional training schools and creating a diversified network of community-based services throughout the seven mental health regions of the state. In the following account, I would like to describe in summary fashion the reforms which took place, the strategies employed, the problems encountered, and the current state of the system of services.

YOUTH CORRECTIONAL REFORM IN MASSACHUSETTS[2]

The progress of recent reforms in the Massachusetts Department of Youth Services (DYS) can be separated into four relatively distinct phases. In the first phase, from 1965 to 1968, the DYS was the object of six investigations. These investigations were precipitated by severe public criticism of outmoded and punitive practices in the institutional treatment of youthful offenders. Departmental policies were criticized for favoring

---

[2] The most complete account of the Massachusetts program as yet published by the Center is contained in Ohlin, L. E., R. B. Coates, and A. D. Miller. 1974. Radical correctional reform: A case study of The Massachusetts Youth Correctional System. Harv. Ed. Rev. 44: 74–111. An independent report on the reforms is also provided by Rutherford, A. 1974. The Dissolution of the Training Schools in Massachusetts. Academy for Contemporary Problems, Columbus Ohio.

custodial confinement over treatment and failing to provide sufficient professional supervision and care of committed youth. This series of studies served to mobilize a liberal coalition determined to introduce more progressive practices and professional competence into the DYS.

A new set of public charges concerning the punitive treatment of youth at the Institution of Juvenile Guidance at Bridgewater in 1968 lent impetus to the reform movement and finally precipitated a major crisis that resulted in the resignation of the Director in March 1969. The Governor promptly selected a blue-ribbon committee to conduct a nation-wide search for a new Commissioner, and, in the interim, appointed an acting director of the DYS. The crisis in the Department won new support for reform legislation, which was signed into law in September 1969. On the recommendation of the search committee, the Governor appointed Dr. Jerome Miller as Commissioner of the Department in October 1969.

The chief thrust of the reform legislation was to strengthen the authority of the central office by creating the positions of Deputy Commissioner and four Assistant Commissioners in charge of the newly established central bureaus of Institutional Care, Education, Clinical Services, and Aftercare. The new legislation also specified the required levels of competence and experience of the Commissioner and his new aides and established salary levels making these positions competitive with comparable posts in other States. Although the direction of reform in the policies of the Department was not specified in the legislation, it was generally assumed by the liberal coalition, led by the Massachusetts Committee on Children and Youth, that the new Commissioner and his assistants would professionalize the work of the Department along the lines suggested by the earlier investigations. Thus, in this first phase, there emerged a mandate for reform which could lead to more humane and professional treatment of children committed to the care of the Department.

The second phase of reform, covering the first 2 years under the new Commissioner, was characterized by strenuous efforts to introduce more humane and therapeutic treatment of youth. When Miller assumed office, the Department operated four detention and reception centers, a forestry camp, a newly acquired former novitiate and also five institutions where most of the 800 boys and girls committed to the Department were confined. These five facilities included an institution for rebellious or emotionally disturbed boys at Bridgewater, a school for preadolescent boys at Oakdale, a school for adolescent boys at Lyman, the industrial school for older boys at Shirley, and an industrial school for girls at Lancaster. These institutions were organized after the pattern of a traditional training school which relied primarily on the threat of punishment and deprivation to maintain order, custodial control, and obedience to authority.

The lack of new funds during the 1st year severely limited the Commissioner's ability to hire new staff or introduce new programs. He, therefore, began by issuing a series of directives to change some of the more offensive practices. He ordered that youth in the institution should be allowed to wear their hair as they chose and, henceforth, haircuts were not to be used as a form of punishment. Youth were to be allowed to wear their own streetclothes rather than garments provided by the institution. The practice of marching youth in silent formation from one activity to another was to be discontinued. Youth eligible to smoke should be allowed to carry their own cigarettes, and the staff practice of doling out cigarettes or denying access to them was no longer to be permitted as a control measure. Staff members were forbidden to strike or physically abuse youth. Enforced idleness and silence in the punishment units, the use of strip cells, and other severe deprivations were not to be tolerated.

These measures to humanize practices in the institutions served to articulate some of the new goals of the Department, but they also attacked some of the basic supports of the traditional system. Many of the staff long accustomed to take for granted the use of punishment, personal degradation or deprivation as essential to the maintenance of authority bitterly resented the new "permissiveness." They perceived the new directives as undermining their authority and capacity to exact obedience from the committed youth. They fought back by relaxing controls, exaggerating stories about the chaos in the institution to legislators and the press, and attending public meetings to denounce the permissiveness of the new regime. The reform administration countered by vigorously defending the new policies in the mass media, in legislative hearings, and in innumerable public meetings around the state. Miller succeeded in capturing for the new administration a public image as youth advocates and casting disaffected staff in the role of self-serving bureaucrats unconcerned with the welfare of children (Miller and Ohlin, 1975).

In addition to these administrative measures to humanize child care practices in the institutions, the Commissioner and his aides tried to create therapeutic communities in the cottages at several of the institutions, following the model developed by Jones in England (Jones et al., 1953). The idea was to decentralize all treatment programs to the individual cottages, creating therein a therapeutic climate where staff and youth would share responsibilities for decisions not only relating to cottage affairs and privileges but also to home visits and ultimately to release on parole. Programs for girls and boys in the same institution and even in the same cottage were also tried out.

Despite the hostile staff climate in the institutions, several of the cottages utilizing the group therapy approach proved remarkably successful (Ohlin, Coates, and Miller, 1974). However, most of the cottages continued to be run in traditional fashion. The staff members did not understand the new concept of a therapeutic community and felt threatened by the demand that they make radical changes in their attitudes toward delinquent youth and their expectations of staff and youth roles. As a consequence, the first 2 years of the administration were characterized by a progressive polarization of youth and staff, periodic crises, confrontation, and confusion. Attempts to retrain staff met with little success but demonstrated that at best the re-education of staff would be a long and difficult process. Most of the DYS appropriation was still tied to the operation of the institutions with little flexibility for bringing in new staff or programs. However, with federal funds, the Commissioner was able to recruit top staff committed to his philosophy and capable of implementing some of the treatment concepts. By the spring of 1971, the new planning unit together with key departmental administrators worked out a seven point plan for further reform. It called for 1) regionalization, 2) community based treatment centers, 3) expansion of the forestry program, 4) relocation of detention, 5) increased placement alternatives, 6) grants in aid to cities and towns, and 7) a small intensive care security unit. As the Department shifted toward the implementation of these goals the stage was set for the third phase of the reform effort.

The strong resistance of staff in the institutions and in the parole services, the rigidity of civil service protections, the absence of funds to hire staff members committed to running the programs, and a general impatience with the slow pace of change led Miller and his aides to conclude that new and more radical strategies had to be adopted. They reasoned that if the therapeutic communities could be organized successfully in a few cottages in the institutions, they could perhaps more easily be organized as small community-based group homes. Instead of making child care the responsibility of institution administrators, responsibility for treatment could be lodged with the new regional directors. Purchase of service funds would permit the Department to obtain from the private sector or from other public agencies a diversity of treatment options that could not be generated within the existing institutions. Thus the challenge of the third phase of reform became the closing of the institutions and the creation of a new structure of services integrated into community life. In the summer of 1970, Miller had already succeeded in paroling or transferring youth from the crisis-ridden Institute of Juvenile Guidance at Bridgewater and closing the institution as a facility for DYS youth. Now, more than a year later, the staff moved swiftly to depopulate the other institutions and succeeded in closing the two largest institutions for boys, Shirley and Lyman, in the winter of 1971–1972. The girl's institution at Lancaster was gradually converted to privately-run programs on the institutional grounds later in 1972, and Oakdale also was finally closed late in 1972.

The closing of the institutions was accompanied by considerable fanfare and yet evoked little public reaction. The Commissioner succeeded in further consolidating his public image as an advocate of new opportunities for youth and his opponents as advocates of the older forms of punishment and repression which he had exposed. A dramatic illustration of the strategies employed to close the institution was provided by the University of Massachusetts Conference, (Coates, Miller, and Ohlin, 1973). For a month in January and February 1972, 99 boys and girls were taken from Lyman, Lancaster, and two detention centers accompanied by news reporters in a caravan of cars to the University of Massachusetts campus at Amherst. The Conference had been worked out between DYS staff, University authorities, and a University student organization. The youth lived with their volunteer student advocates in the University residences while the advocates worked to arrange placements for the youth in cooperation with DYS staff. The Governor appeared at the Conference to lend his support and the whole program received favorable press attention.

Such radical changes in the organization and character of human services are not achieved in a short time without a considerable amount of confusion, frustrated hopes, and charges and countercharges of bad faith, administrative ineptitude, and fiscal irre-sponsibility. In the rapid transition to the emerging community-based network of ser-vices, such charges were frequently voiced (Miller and Ohlin, 1975). Several legislative investigations were initiated based on the complaints of embittered employees or disappointed contractors for private services. Fiscal reform lagged far behind program reforms and payment for services far behind their delivery. A complicated procedure for payment authorizations and for rate setting in the case of contracted services created administrative confusion, bureaucratic delays, and in some cases, the termination of services. A number of juvenile court judges and probation staff members expressed special concern about the inability or unwillingness of the Department to provide intensive and secure care for those youth the courts judged to be in need of such care. Staff members in the old institutions who could not be absorbed into the new services looked toward early retirement while others simply awaited transfer to some other state service along with the expected transfer of the institutions to other Departments.

On the positive side, these rapid changes in the organization of services also released a considerable amount of suppressed creativity and capacity for implementing the new treatment philosophy on the part of a number of the older staff members. They also brought forth a wide range of professional and volunteer talents not previously regarded as capable of being interested or effectively involved in youth corrections. The regional offices responded to the need for new services by securing the assistance of a variety of private agencies and individuals. New court liaison units were created to work out voluntary referrals from the courts to the Department and to develop appropriate services in difficult cases. New shelter care units were set up in several regions to provide better care for youth awaiting court disposition and the use of foster homes was greatly expanded for both detained and committed or referred youth.[3]

Phase three of the reform movement came to a close with the resignation of Commissioner Miller to accept a new post as Director of the Department of Family and Children Services in Illinois, in January 1973. He received some criticism for leaving the state before the old institutions had been converted to new functions and the new system of services had become more fully developed. In response he expressed his belief that his successor, Joseph Leavey, a DYS staff member committed to the new reforms and raised to the position of Deputy Commissioner under Miller, would have an easier time consolidating the new system of services. He argued that the tenure of reform commissioners inevitably must be brief since the hostility aroused during the change process creates so much personalized animosity that it becomes a serious impediment to further progress.

Since Miller's departure, the reform movement has entered a fourth phase of consolidation involving the refinement and further development of the service network and administrative reorganization and tightening. By December 1974, most of the problems of transition have been resolved. The former institutional budgets have been converted to a purchase of service budget and the training schools transferred to other Departments. The Department continues to operate a forestry camp and three of the former detention centers, now used partly for committed youth needing secure treatment and partly as

---

[3] The distribution of youth among the various placements is reported in unpublished quarterly and annual reports by the Center projects.

detention-reception centers. Most of the services required for detained, committed, and referred youth are purchased from private agencies or other public agencies. Responsibility for the placement of youth, initiation of many of the new services, and the working out of cooperative arrangements with the courts and probation services are decentralized to the regional offices. A new unit in the central office screens and secures appropriate placement for those youth requiring intensive or secure care. A new quality control unit evaluates purchased services on a regular basis to ensure that contracts are fulfilled and appropriate standards of service are maintained. The fiscal reforms have helped to eliminate the lag in the payment of services to vendors and procedures for contracting and paying services have been regularized.

There are, of course, continuing problems. Cutbacks in service funds can be expected with the new, recession-created demands for austerity in state government. The quality control monitoring units have still not fully developed to ensure the operation of effective programs for youth. Services for girls appear less adequate and more difficult to procure than services for boys. The problem of providing appropriate programs for youthful offenders regarded as dangerous or deeply disturbed is still a bone of contention between certain courts in the state and the Department. A small number of former employees are still carried by the Department without appropriate assignments, although virtually all of the former institutional employees have been absorbed into the new system of services, have resigned, or have been transferred to other Departments.

The transformation of the Department of Youth Services from a program based on traditional training schools to a new network of diversified community-based residential and non-residential services is now virtually completed. This pioneering correctional reform has demonstrated that radical changes in treatment policies and programs for delinquent youth can be achieved over a relatively short period of time. Both youth and staff perceive the new system as much more helpful and responsive to youth needs. The diversity of services provides a more flexible range of options for reintegrating youth into their home communities. Preliminary data on recidivism currently available indicate that the new treatment services are achieving a better record, although insufficient time has yet elapsed for a firm conclusion to be reached (Ohlin, Coates, and Miller, 1975).

Critics of the reform process have questioned whether the institutions should have been closed so abruptly before the new system of services was in place. They have argued that the changes could have been affected with less administrative and fiscal confusion, less hardship for older employees, and more adequate provision of services for youth during the transition period if the new policies had been implemented more slowly (Miller and Ohlin, 1975). The counterconsideration is whether they would have been implemented at all under such circumstances. A slower transition would have allowed the consolidation of interest groups opposed to the reforms taking place. The Massachusetts process of reform suggests that efforts to implement new human service policies, programs, and goals must proceed simultaneously with actions designed to affect the internal distribution of responsibility, power, and reward in the interest groups and organizations involved and in their relationships with each other. The change effort mobilizes greater power to be effective if actions of both types are taken at the same time.[4] Further analysis of the Massachusetts reforms is expected to yield a more precise formulation of the strategies, actions, and relationships that proved pivotal in the ability of the reform movement to overcome change and reform of services. Such an analysis together with the principles of social action derived from them should prove of general utility to the field of corrections, mental retardation, and other human services confronted with similar change problems.

REFERENCES

Bakal, Y. 1973. Closing correctional institutions: New Strategies for Youth Services. D. C. Heath & Co., Lexington, Mass.

Bondeson, V. 1968. Argot knowledge as an indication of criminal socialization. A study of a training school for girls. Scand. Stud. Criminol. 2: 73–107.

Coates, R. B. 1974. A working paper on community based corrections: Concept, historical development, impact and potential. Unpublished paper presented in Massachusetts Conference on Standards and Goals, November 1974, Center for Criminal Justice, Harvard Law School.

Coates, R. B., A. D. Miller, and L. E. Ohlin. 1974. The labeling perspective and innovations in juvenile correctional systems. In N. Hobbs (ed.), Issues in Classification of Children: A Source Book on Categories, Labels, and Their Consequences, Vol. II, pp. 123–149. Josey Bass, San Francisco.

Coates, R. B., A. D. Miller, and L. E. Ohlin. 1973. A strategic innovation in the process of deinstituionalization: The University of Massachusetts Conference. In Y. Bakal (ed.), Closing Correctional Institutions: New Strategies for Youth Services, pp. 127–145. D. C. Heath & Co., Lexington Mass.

Dean, C. W. and N. D. Reppucci. 1974. Juvenile correctional institutions. In D. Glaser (ed.), Handbook of Criminology, pp. 865–894. Rand McNally, Chicago.

Empey, L. T. 1973. Juvenile justice reform: Diversion, due process, and deinstitutionalization. In L. E. Ohlin (ed.), Prisoners in America, pp. 13–48. Prentice-Hall Inc., Englewood Cliffs, N.J.

Empey, L. T. and M. L. Erickson. 1972. The Provo Experiment Evaluating Community Control of Delinquency. D. C. Heath and Co., Lexington, Mass.

Fox, S. J. 1972. Modern Juvenile Justice: Cases and Materials, pp. 1–133. West Publishing Co., St. Paul, Minn.

Grichting, W. I. 1973. Sampling Plans and Results, The University of Michigan National Assessment of Juvenile Corrections Project. University of Michigan, Institute of Continuing Legal Education, School of Social Work, Ann Arbor.

Joint Commission on Mental Illness and Health. 1961. Action for Mental Health. Wiley, New York.

Jones, M. et al. 1953. The Therapeutic Community. Basic Books, New York.

Lerman, P. 1968. Evaluative Studies of institutions for Delinquents. Reprinted from Social Work 13. In P. Lerman (ed.), Delinquency and Social Policy, pp. 317–328. Praeeser Publishers, New York, 1970.

---

[4] An extensive theoretical analysis of the process of change in the DYS reforms has been sketched in an unpublished paper by Miller, A.D., L. E. Ohlin, and R. B. Coates. 1975. Logical analysis of the process of change in human services: A simulation of youth correctional reforms in Massachusetts. Center for Criminal Justice, Harvard Law School.

Martinson, R. 1974. What works? Questions and answers about prison reform. Public Interest 35: 22–54.

McCorkle, L., A. Elias, and F. Bixby. 1958. The Highfields Story: A Unique Experiment in the Treatment of Juvenile Delinquency. Henry Holt, New York.

Miller, J. and L. E. Ohlin. 1975. The new corrections: The case of Massachusetts. In M. K. Rosenheim (ed.), Pursuing Justice for the Child. University of Chicago Press, Chicago. In press.

Morales v. Turman. 383 F. Supp. 53, 1974.

Morgan, T. 1975. They think, "I can kill because I'm 14," The New York Times Magazine, January 19, p. 9.

National Institute of Mental Health, Center for Studies of Crime and Delinquency. 1971. Community Based Correctional Programs. U.S. Government Printing Office, Washington, D.C.

Office of Children's Services. 1973. PINS, A Puthora of Problems. Judicial Conference of the State of New York.

Ohlin, L. E. 1974. Organizational reform in correctional agencies. In D. Glaser (ed.), Handbook of Criminology, pp. 1000–1007. Rand McNally, Chicago.

Ohlin, L. E., R. B. Coates, and A. D. Miller. 1974. Radical correctional reform: A case study of the Massachusetts youth correctional system. Harv. Ed. Rev. 44: 74–111.

Ohlin, L. E., R. B. Coates, and A. D. Miller. 1975. Evaluating the reform of youth corrections in Massachusetts. J. Res. Crime Delinq. 12: 3–16.

Orlando, L. 1973. Justice, Punishment, Treatment: The Correctional Process, pp. 125–397. The Free Press, New York.

Platt, A. 1969. The Child-Savers: The invention of delinquency. University of Chicago Press, Chicago.

Polier, J. W. 1974. Myths and realities in the search for juvenile justice. Harv. Ed. Rev. 44: 112–124.

Prensident's Commission on Law Enforcement and Administration of Justice. 1967. Task Force Report: Corrections. U.S. Government Printing Office, Washington, D.C.

Schur, E. M. 1973. Radical Non-intervention, Rethinking the Delinquency Problem. Prentice Hall, New York.

U.S. Department of Justice, Law Enforcement Assistance Administration, National Criminal Information and Statistics Service, 1974. Children in Custody: A Report on the Juvenile Detention and Correctional Facility Census of 1971, pp. 1–2. U.S. Government Printing Office, Washington, D.C.

Vorenberg, E. and J. Vorenberg. 1973. Early diversion from the criminal justice system: Practice in search of a theory. In L. E. Ohlin (ed.), Prisoners in America, pp. 151–183. Prentice-Hall, Englewood Cliffs, N.J.

Legal, Legislative, and Bureaucratic Factors Affecting Planned and Unplanned Change In the Delivery of Services To the Mentally Retarded

Elizabeth M. Boggs

Every man is in some respects -
like all other men
like some other men
like no other man. . . .

It will be the purpose of this paper to explore some of the implications of that statement for the manner in which the judicial, legislative, and executive branches of the federal government address the social problems of which mental retardation is a manifestation. Within a general framework illustrative case studies will be presented.

It is not necessary to quote Shakespeare, Aristotle, or modern theories of taxonomy in order to educe from the opening quotation certain corollaries. One respect in which all persons are like all other persons is that each is unique; every mentally retarded person is in some respects like all other mentally retarded persons, and in some respects like some other retarded persons, but each mentally retarded person is also in some (but not necessarily the same) respects like some persons not called mentally retarded.

The terms "like" and "non-like" are easy to conceptualize, but are more difficult to apply in social systems than in mathematics. An integer is either even or odd, prime or not prime, but it is not quite so clear that a person is either male or female, white or non-white, disabled or not disabled, competent or incompetent, retarded or not retarded. Yet laws can do, and, indeed, for some purposes must, deal with such distinctions. Human beings, human needs, human behavior are infinitely variable. Human dimensions are potentially infinite in number and each is a continuum, but human institutions are finite and discrete.

This is the dilemma underlying all our social structures, and particularly our governmental institutions: our courts, our legislative bodies, and our administrative agencies. All are bureaucracies which divide their missions into defined tasks, along ostensibly rational lines, and assign each task to an organization unit.

Bureaucracies exist and division of labor is made necessary not merely because there are jobs to be done, but because human capacities are limited. Each of us has a life defined in time and space. Missions are divided into tasks of manageable size, i.e., human dimensions. Yet no person, and no institution for that matter, can be all things to all people, or indeed, even to one other person. Human institutions, social, political, industrial, or other, are therefore devised to provide defined structures in which a limited number of human beings can exercise their respectively limited capacities in a mutually complementary manner so as to produce desired but limited outcomes which no member could produce by himself.

Insofar as the task relates to the needs of human beings, it is usually defined in terms of a certain class or classes of persons and of certain defined services, privileges, rights, or prerogatives which may be dispensed or adjudicated, or authorized. The issue then becomes one of the closeness-of-fit of these classifications, definitions, task assignments, and structural relationships, discrete and circumscribed as they are, to the range, variety, and continuity of the changing human conditions they address. If the fit offends our sense of continuity, we complain that services are fragmented; if it appears to be more than one-to-one, we complain of duplication.

Organizations are systems which usually have subsystems and are also simultaneously parts of hierarchies of supersystems. These relationships may be stable or unstable over time. The ultimate supersystem is the human race, and the ultimate unit of the subsystem (socially although not biologically) is the individual. The human race is not currently organized effectively, and the individual cannot long survive without the social supports of a variety of subsystems.

These unities, the universal and the unique, are, like the global poles, conceptually attractive but practically uninhabitable. In the Arctic Eden, all men are created equal; in Antarctica, each is in a class by himself. In the habitable regions of human services, most legislation is, in fact, class legislation. A given law identifies a "respect" in which "some men" are "like" some others, and share some common privilege or deprivation.

The law applies its principles of classification not only to individuals, but to agencies and organizations (e.g., profit versus nonprofit) and, very importantly in our context, to services themselves. Whether a service is defined in or out of th term "health care" creates for the provider a continental divide with respect to funding under any proposed version of national health insurance.

LEGAL, LEGISLATIVE, AND ADMINISTRATIVE PROBLEMS IN CLASSIFICATION

There is a tendency in the law to binary classifications. A consumer or provider or agency or service is either eligible or ineligible. The notion of being more or less eligible has been hard for the law to accommodate. This mismatch between the yes/no dichotomy and the graduated character of human needs leads to what is known in the welfare field as the "notch problem," equivalent to a golfer's "sudden death" or a tennis player's match point, except that the contestants are not playing games and are not in the arena by choice. The notch problem occurs when eligibility for a free health or social service or for public housing is based on a specified income level. If the level is exceeded by 1 dollar, the otherwise eligible individual loses potential benefits worth many times the income increment. The situation has many analogues. For example, in most states guardianship laws are still structured on the assumption that individuals are either totally competent or totally incompetent (Boggs, 1966).

Another problem related to the foregoing is the overburdening of a given classification, attaching to it implications beyond that for which it was devised. A mentally retarded person returning to the community from an institution is presumed to present a social hazard, for example. It is assumed that a retarded woman will not be able to care adequately for her child, and so on. These are the dangers of "labeling," dealt with elsewhere in this volume, and by Hobbs (1974).

Obviously there are some classifications which are incompatible with a classification of mental retardation: candidacy for graduate school, for instance. However, a designation as "retarded" usually does not preclude participation in other classes and should not automatically disqualify one from enjoying the rights specific to age or residence or employment, for example. Yet such denials are not infrequent. For instance, in the mid-sixties there were still a few states which denied crippled children's benefits to physically handicapped children who were also of "unsound mind." Experience with such denials on a worldwide basis led to a Declaration on the Rights of Mentally Retarded Persons (United Nations, 1971).

The widespread use of class legislation for purposes of enfranchising or disenfranchising the members of some defined group reflects an understanding that "equal protection of the laws" may require recognition of inherent inequalities (Smith, 1955). It follows, however, that the criteria for specifying the class must be relevant to the purposes of the legislation and equitable in that light. Capricious or vague criteria may be struck down as unconstitutional by the courts. In some instances criteria are specified which are usually applicable without much expertise: age, employment status, and marital status are examples. In other cases, expert judgment may be required, in which case a procedure is usually specified. It is necessary in these cases to assure that anyone denied a benefit by virtue of exclusion from the favored class must have "due process protections."

The most pertinent example of expert classification in the federal domain lies in the field of Social Security benefits payable on account of "disability." *Disability* for purposes of Social Security and similar income maintenance programs, and *handicap* for purposes of the Rehabilitation Act, are both defined in relation to the ability, present or potential, of an applicant to engage in substantial gainful employment. The presence or absence of a particular clinical condition is not, in and of itself, conclusive evidence that such a disability exists. However, the laws require medical determination that a physical or mental impairment is present which is causally related to the inability to work.

Administering bureaucracies are chronically beset with the mismatch between classification systems designed and used by clinicians for clinical purposes and the classification criteria designed to meet the purpose of legislation which is social rather than clinical. An example of bureaucratic confusion in dealing with such a mismatch (in another context) is provided in one of the case studies to follow.

Finally, it must be pointed out that in respect to classification, as in other aspects of implementing federal legislation, the "intent of Congress" plays an important role. Changing approaches to that concept deserve special treatment and are addressed as such later in this paper.

Case Studies in Classification of Individuals and Services

1. Immigration of Mentally Retarded Aliens   Before 1965 there was, under Section 212(a) of the Immigration and Nationality Act, an absolute prohibition against the immigration into the United States of any alien who was 1) "feebleminded," 2) insane, 3) formerly insane, or 4) "afflicted with psychopathic personality or mental defect." The effect was not merely to prevent immigration of individuals in these categories but to prevent entire families from immigrating or even visiting the United States if a "feebleminded" member were included. The only way around the difficulty was to secure a "private bill," i.e., an Act of Congress specifically "for the relief of" a named individual. Obviously to obtain such relief, an alien family had to have "contacts" in the Congress.

An omnibus bill to amend the Immigration Act, introduced during the Kennedy administration, would have authorized administrative procedures for the granting of individual waivers of this prohibition under certain circumstances. Basically, such aliens could accompany or join their spouses or parents if the relatives would guarantee their support and if there was an undertaking for 5 years of medical surveillance following arrival. The proposal followed closely (perhaps too closely, considering that contagion was not an issue) the precedent set earlier in permitting immigration of persons with a history of tuberculosis.

The bill did not pass in 1963 and was reintroduced with certain modifications in 1965. One of these modifications was to change "feebleminded" to "mentally retarded." The implications of this change were discussed in the hearings before the House Committee on the Judiciary by Dr. Andrew Sackett, speaking for the Public Health Service:

The change of the term "feebleminded" to "mentally retarded" is in itself simply a change of nomenclature. But its implications are significant. It connotes the change in attitude toward the mentally retarded and in the philosophy of programs for their care that prompted the new laws enacted by Congress in 1963. . . .

The change in nomenclature from "feebleminded" to "mentally retarded" in the immigration law will connote something of this change of attitude and philosophy. It will fit into the proposed substantive changes which would permit the family with a mentally retarded child to remain together, or to be reunited, with assurances that the services necessary for the retarded child will be provided without his becoming a public charge. . . .

A typical situation in the exclusion for feeblemindedness is that of a child, most or all of whose family members have been granted immigrant visas to proceed to the

United States. The child is often borderline in its retardation and either trainable or educable. The family must elect to remain abroad, refusing to be separated from the child, or leave the child behind with relatives or strangers. The medical notification of feeblemindedness allows the consul no alternative but to refuse a visa. . . .
(House Committee on the Judiciary, 1965, pp. 138–9).

At the time of the hearing, the bill under discussion authorized waivers for persons in any of the four classes, hence distinctions among them seemed unimportant. In the light of subsequent events, however, the following interchange between Congressman Michael Feighan, the Chairman of Subcommittee No. 1, and Dr. Sackett assumes significance:

Mr. Feighan: Well, just what is the difference between mental retardation and mental defect?

Dr. Sackett: Sir, the term "mental retardation" implies a lack of intellectual capacity, something below normal. It also implies that this condition has been present throughout the individual's life. It is detected early in childhood.

On the other hand, mental defect implies a behavioral or intellectual deficiency that results from some physical cause, maybe a degenerative cause. The person may have been normal at one time and has suffered an injury or some progressive or acute disease that has reduced his intellectual capacity or has caused a behavioral problem.

So this category we call defect (House Committee on the Judiciary, 1965, p. 141).

"Legislative history" recorded in hearings or floor debate is intended to guide the executive branch in its subsequent administration.

There was some subsequent informal discussion of the proposed waiver authority with Congressman Feighan, who felt that perhaps the application of the waiver should be limited only to those retarded persons who had a prospect of becoming self-supporting. It was pointed out to him that the very seriously retarded person whose family is prepared to care for him may present less of a genetic or economic threat than a more able person, and that such a distinction was likely to be arbitrary as well as inhumane. Mr. Feighan expressed some concern that such persons would preempt space in public institutions needed by native Americans.

It came as a surprise to those concerned, therefore, that the bill, as reported in the House, contained no provision for any waivers of 212(a) (1–4); no mention of this deletion was contained in the Committee report (House Report No. 1101, 89th Congress, First Session). The National Association for Retarded Children sought to remedy this defect by securing the addition of amending language which would be less comprehensive than that originally proposed and hence less objectionable to the Committee. The Committee had added "sexual deviation" as a cause for exclusion in Section 212(a)(4), and it was understood that they wanted no waivers of that provision. With drafting help from the Department of Justice, Congressman John Fogarty successfully proposed from the floor an amendment which restored, but only in part, the waiver as it would apply to classes (1) and (3), i.e., the mentally retarded and the recovered mentally ill person. The Senate, led by Senator Edward Kennedy, accepted the original Administration proposal for these two categories, and this broader language prevailed in the House-Senate Conference Committee.

The legislative history and debate on this topic made it clear that the members of Congress who voted for this amendment considered that it applied to the "mentally retarded" as that term is generally accepted in the United States by the professional community[1] and informed lay public. Specific mention was made of mongolism as a form of mental retardation. However, the U.S. Public Health Service (PHS), which writes and implements the regulations covering the health aspects of Section 212, was using a terminology in which the distinction made between "mental retardation" (equated to feeblemindedness or mental deficiency) and "mental defect" placed in the former category only those with nonspecific or nonorganic forms of mental retardation, "with functional reaction alone manifest." All clinical forms were classed as "defect."

The PHS *Manual on the Medical Examination of Aliens* (1963) is based on a system of classification as to mental diseases and defects adopted in 1952, and very much outdated. While the immigration bill was being debated in the Congress in 1965, the International Conference for the Eighth Revision of the International Classification of Diseases was in progress in Geneva. This conference adopted a classification system for mental deficiency similar to that promulgated by the American Association on Mental Deficiency in 1959 (Heber, 1959, see also International Classification of Diseases (ICD) 1965), in Appendix III to the U.S. Delegation to the International Conference, 1966).

As a result of continued adherence to the outdated manual, the hopes raised by the 1965 legislation were not realized in a number of specific cases in which organic defect was apparent. These included cases where there was a combination of mental retardation with cerebral palsy, as well as cases of "mongolism." Private bills to assist individuals adversely classified continued to be introduced in Congress. Several Congressmen introduced public bills to clarify the general intent. One of them, Congressman Hanley of New York, entered an excellent review in the Congressional Record (Hanley, 1966) covering the extended history of provisions for exclusion under the Act.

The exclusion of persons with mongolism represented a particularly interesting example of bureaucratic involution inasmuch as the PHS Manual classified "Chronic Brain Syndrome associated with Mongolism" as "code C - Certify as feeblemindedness" on page 6-12, but on page 6-2 used mongolism as an example of "mental defect." A NARC spokesman who attempted to point this out in May 1966 to Dr. Louis Jacobs, then Chief of the Division of Foreign Quarantine, was told that persons with mongolism were absolutely excluded and that this would continue to be the policy. This contradiction of congressional intent was brought to the attention of Congressman Fogarty, who spoke personally to The Surgeon General, Dr. William Stewart, pointing out the language of the Congressional debate. In July, 1966, the regulations were modified so that aliens with mongolism, who met the other stringent requirements, would be classed 212(a)(1). This change resolved a patent inconsistency in the Department's own regulations, but did not address itself to the arbitrary nature (from a social point of view) of the distinction still

---

[1] It is only proper to point out that there was and continues to be a broad spectrum of opinion in the psychiatric and nonpsychiatric community on many of the problems of classification in mental retardation (Begab et al., 1972).

being made in the PHS Manual (and PHS practice) between those classified as "retarded" and those classified as "mental defective."

The matter was not brought to resolution until 2 years later, after a reorganization and change in personnel. In March of 1968, holders of the Manual were advised that all aliens who "demonstrate reduced intellectual functioning which originates during the developmental period and is associated with impairment of adaptive behavior" regardless of degree or etiology were to be classed under 212(a)(1) and permitted to apply for a waiver of excludability.

By 1972, all operations of the Foreign Quarantine Program had been assembled at the Center for Disease Control in Atlanta. In that year, FQP did a 5-year retrospective survey of their experience. They found that about 250 "mental waivers" are being granted annually, of which the majority (about 85%) are for mental retardation, as contrasted with "previous attacks of insanity." The following retrospective observations are particularly relevant to the "intent of Congress":

> . . . review of the background papers and discussion in 1964 and 1965 reveals that institutionalization was expected for virtually all persons granted mental waivers, if not for the full 5 years at least for some period of time. Again the facts are that of the 184 persons arriving in 1966 who were considered mentally retarded, only 4 were institutionalized—2 of these in private institutions. Of the 24 considered to have a "previous attack of insanity" one was institutionalized, 4 years after arrival (U.S. PHS, Foreign Quarantine Program, internal memorandum, 1972).

2. Housing   In the previous case study, we have an example of inappropriate classification to the extent that the distinction made between forms of mental retardation with an apparent organic component and those in which no such "defect" was manifest was not highly relevant to the purposes of the Immigration Act, although it was apparently based (in the minds of some) on the assumption that organic etiology carried with it a necessity for institutional care. Most informed persons would agree, however, that the social purposes of most legislation benefiting or penalizing the retarded are not highly correlated with such etiological criteria and that indeed it is still uncertain whether some "unspecified" forms of retardation do or do not have an organic base. The following example raises the same issue from the opposite perspective. Here an even less rational presumed "physical" basis was used as an opening wedge in broadening the housing options for mentally retarded persons.

The Housing and Community Development Act, signed by President Ford in August 1974 (P.L. 93-383), represents a comprehensive revision of the mass of housing and urban development legislation that has accrued since 1949. One of its objects is to make available suitable housing for low income families. Early in the history of the legislation, it was recognized that elderly people (individuals or couples) not only are at risk of being "low income" but may need housing designed to accommodate their physical infirmities and their special social needs. The Housing Act of 1964 extended to the "handicapped" the loan, mortgage insurance, low rent, and demonstration provisions previously enacted to benefit the elderly (House Committee on Banking and Currency , 1971, p. 316). Section 202(d)(4) of the Housing Act of 1959, as amended in 1964, reads:

A person shall be considered handicapped if such a person is determined, pursuant to regulations issued by the Secretary, to have a physical impairment which (A) is expected to be of long-continued and indefinite duration, (B) substantially impedes his ability to live independently, and (C) is of such a nature that such ability could be improved by more suitable housing conditions (p. 218).

There is little doubt that the original authors of this definition were thinking of architectural design features which affect the orthopedically handicapped, the infirm, the chronically ill, the blind. Yet the functional portion of the definition well describes a group of mentally retarded adults for whom "community living arrangements" were, and are, being increasingly sought, beginning in the late sixties.

In its efforts to follow President Nixon's "deinstitutionalization" mandate of 1971 (Nixon, 1971), the President's Committee on Mental Retardation (PCMR) pressed the Department of Housing and Urban Development for a more affirmative stance and a broader interpretation. The results are described as follows:

Using the programs for the physically handicapped, the HUD General Counsel then undertook a close examination of this legislation to determine whether or under what conditions mental retardation could be considered to be an eligibility factor for housing for the handicapped. The initial conclusion related to mortgage insurance under Section 221(d)(3) and 236, for the subsidies available under these programs. The opinion stated that "Although this Department's earlier position was that the statutory definition of handicap, which was based on "physical impairment" did not include the mentally retarded, the Department's position is now that if the mental retardation of an individual can be determined to be the result of a physical impairment, such as brain damage problem, or chemical or neurological physical impediment to normal growth, then that individual legally could be considered 'handicapped' for purposes of determining eligibility as a tenant in Section 221(d)(3) or 236 housing.

As a result of this decision, on April 28, 1972, HUD approved two plans under State-Federal financing in the 236 program for four group homes and one two-story apartment building to provide housing for mentally retarded adults capable of an independent life style in their communities (PCMR, 1972, pp. 106–7).

The initial programs were both in Michigan and are now operational.

Obviously this was a breakthrough, yet one which was based on a tenuous distinction. State and local housing authorities could continue to maintain a conservative posture in interpreting the federal statute by citing its language. Major housing legislation, pending in mid-1972, presented an opportunity to drive home the advantage. However, a political impasse within the House Committee on Banking and Currency prevented passage during that session of Congress. More time was available for the development of legislative strategies. Over the next two years, The President's Committee on Mental Retardation (PCMR), National Association for Retarded Citizens (NARC), United Cerebral Palsy Association (UCPA) and others, formed a coalition and maintained an active interaction with the Congress as it struggled with new legislation. The result in 1974 was a triple button down: 1) the definition of handicapped, cited above, was retained but without the word "physical, 2) specific reference was made to the Developmental Disabilities legislation (P.L. 91-517, Section 102(b)(b)) to incorporate by reference persons meeting that definition, and 3) persons meeting the Social Security definition of disability were also incorporated by reference. It is estimated that at least a quarter of a million mentally retarded adults meet both the income and disability tests thus defined.

3. Vocational Rehabilitation   The state-federal vocational rehabilitation program began in 1920 as an effort to restore the physically disabled to competitive employment. Although the mentally disabled became eligible during World War II (P.L. 113 of 1943), the language used throughout the Act continued to refer to the "physically handicapped." One had to look at the list of definitions to find that "a physically handicapped individual is one who is under a physical or mental disability." The editorial change to delete "physical" was made by P.L. 89-333 in 1965 at the instigation of the late Senator Robert F. Kennedy.

The number of mentally retarded persons reported rehabilitated rose from 106 in 1945, to 531 in 1955, to 10,248 in 1965 (DHEW-SRS, 1970). It is estimated that 45,400 will be reached in 1975. However, a reduction in these reported figures may be anticipated in the future as a result of two unrelated developments.

During the early seventies, Congress began receiving increasingly vocal messages from organizations representing the handicapped, complaining that the State rehabilitation agencies were "creaming," i.e., giving priority to the least handicapped for whom the minimum investment of rehabilitation resources would produce the maximum number of successful case closures into employment. The complaints alleged that the employment potential, not to mention the capacity for improved self-care, of the "severely handicapped" was being ignored. Rehabilitation professionals did not attempt to deny that there was some basis for these allegations. The bureaucratic response had two thrusts:

1. The administering agency took a number of steps internally to place greater priority on work with the severely disabled. These included working on protocols for "weighted case closures" through which more difficult (and costly) cases would be given more "credit" in statistics, and advising the monitoring agencies to expect a reduction in the number of annual rehabilitations per million dollars expended.

2. The administration successfully held out against a Congressional push to make eligible (for rehabilitation services) persons so severely handicapped as to have dubious prospects for becoming employable through rehabilitation.

The Rehabilitation Act of 1973 (P.L. 93-112) reflects the administration's success in keeping the "vocational" thrust in the program, if not in the title of the Act. The net effect may be to reduce the apparent number of retarded served since emphasis will be placed on persons whose rehabilitation is costly, but eventually dollar productive, such as persons with spinal cord injuries.

A completely unrelated development may also contribute to the same outcome, i.e., reduction in the number of mentally retarded persons reported as served by vocational rehabilitation programs. As a result of professional responses to the social pressures against "labeling" of mildly retarded persons, the background for which is described elsewhere by Mercer and others, the American Association on Mental Deficiency in the 1973 revision of its *Manual on Terminology* (Grossman et al., 1973) decided to exclude "borderline" (IQ above 70 or less than two standard deviations below normal) from the range of measured intelligence to be characteristicly included in the definition of mental retardation, even if accompanied by "impairment of adaptive behavior" originating in the developmental period. In August 1974, the Rehabilitation Services Administration, Department of Health, Education, and Welfare wrote its Regional offices, calling attention to this change and noting that "the current deletion of the borderline IQ ranges in the AAMD manual definition, if adopted by the VR program, would have considerable impact in serving those with scores within one standard deviation below the norm. Such persons might be considered as learning disabled, a category not presently considered as a disability per se under the rehabilitation program" (RSA internal memorandum).

4. What Is an Institution? A Case Study in Classifying Services When the public assistance provisions of the Social Security Act were first enacted in 1935, the primary beneficiaries were impoverished elderly people and "dependent" children, i.e., those who were orphaned, neglected, or deprived of parental support. (Aid to the disabled was not authorized until 1950.) Persons in public institutions and all mental institutions were excluded. There appears to have been a dual motive for the exclusion: 1) the federal government did not want to take on a fiscal responsibility which had been assumed by the states and local governments, and 2) no one wanted to open the Pandora's box of county almshouses, jails, and mental institutions.

Although exceptions were later made for public "medical institutions," both public and private institutions for mental diseases remained proscribed until 1965. In that year, it became legal for a state to claim federal financial participation (under Title XIX) in the cost of care of indigent persons over 65 who were patients in "institutions for mental diseases." As long as such institutions had been out of bounds, it had been assumed that the term covered all kinds of mental institutions, including those for the retarded. As soon as the possibility of paying for care was opened up, however, a narrower definition was immediately devised, one which, in effect, limits the term to those psychiatric hospitals accredited as such by the Joint Commission on Accreditation of Hospitals. At that time, approximately one-third of the state mental hospital population was over 65, so the new option was attractive to the states. The fact that the narrowed definition of "institution for mental disease" did not include institutions for the retarded was of little practical consequence since there were relatively few people over 65 in such institutions.

There was, however, an incidental benefit to the retarded, whose significance has grown in recent years. Because private residential facilities for the retarded are not usually psychiatric hospitals, they no longer come within the definition of "institutions for mental diseases"; therefore, otherwise eligible retarded persons of any age need not lose their eligibility for public assistance upon entering such a private facility. On this basis, it became possible to promote a wide variety of old and new residential arrangements for the retarded, particularly adults, many of whom qualified for disability assistance.

These alternatives were timely since, while it may be true that one-third of the residents of public institutions for the retarded in 1971 could have lived in "less restrictive" settings (Nixon, 1971), unsupervised independent living is not a realistic prospect for many. A statewide survey in Ohio in 1973 to 1974 found twenty thousand retarded persons not currently receiving residential care who would require some form of sheltered living arrangement in the foreseeable future (Turner and Butler, 1974). This figure is additional to the ten thousand currently enrolled with the Ohio state agency. The combined total represents just under 0.3 percent of the population.

But how are these new living arrangements to be rationalized? Are they institutions? What is an institution? Congress, in defining an intermediate care facility ("ICF") referred to persons who "require care and services above the level of room and board which can be made available to them only through institutional facilities" (Social Security Act, Section 1905(c)). What mental images did the members of Congress, or more pertinently the staff of the Ways and Means and Senate Finance Committees, intend to project? Was it as broad as the HEW definition which refers to any "establishment which furnishes . . . food and shelter to four or more persons unrelated to the proprietor, and in addition, provides some treatment or services which meet some need beyond basic provision of food and shelter" (CFR, 1973)? Does this definition meet the popular conception? Or does the public expect an "institution" to accept a responsibility beyond "some services"? A group of lay and professional leaders in mental retardation met in November 1973 to consider this question. Their definition: "an institution is a residential facility which is responsible for providing (directly or by purchase) professional and supportive services to meet most of the health, rehabilitative and social needs of most of its residents." Such a definition leaves room for a range of non-institutional living arrangements which can be separately delineated (NARC, unpublished, 1973).

The definition just cited also recognizes that an underlying but usually unstated issue in defining *institution* is the degree of authority, the degree of responsibility, and the degree of control (over the individual) exercised by the administration of the facility. By contrast, many newly emerging models of "community based special living arrangements" emphasize the function of *residence* apart from service or custody, a place to live similar to a family home, from which the residents sally forth to utilize community facilities which are not part of the residential "establishment" (Wolfensberger, 1973,b). Thus, residents may engage in learning, working, leisure time pursuits, or other activities in a manner analogous to, if not indistinguishable from, the "normal" population. Such facilities are not perceived by the residents and their families as "institutions," although many administrators so define them. If, however, the residential facility has a legal or contractual obligation to provide, or to arrange, or to pay for the off-campus services, and is responsible for the well-being of the residents while they are at large in the community as well as while they are on the residential premises, there will be more general agreement that it is legitimate to consider the facility as an "institution."

These concepts are compatible with HEW's definition of ICF/MR:

"Institution for the mentally retarded or persons with related conditions" means an institution (or distinct part thereof) primarily for the diagnosis, treatment, or rehabilitation of the mentally retarded or persons with related conditions, which provides in a protected residential setting, individualized ongoing evaluation, planning, 24 hour supervision, coordination and integration of health or rehabilitative services to help each individual reach his maximum of functioning capabilities (DHEW/SRS, 1974, Section 248.60(b)(10)).

Certainly in 1974 the stereotypic "institution" was in disrepute. The promulgation of distinct regulations and standards for "intermediate care facilities for the mentally retarded" (ICF/MR) represented a giant step forward for the cause of quality in their institutional care.

One of the standards which the ICF must meet is periodic review of each resident's need for its services. Where does he go who is found not to need that level defined above? Most "community alternatives" are also "instituions" by HEW's general criterion of "food and shelter . . . and some other service . . . for four or more."

Under "Medicaid," an all-in vendor payment is available to pay board and care costs for eligible persons who are admitted to a licensed ICF, public or private. But what is the best way to finance the group home, or supervised living arrangement, or any of the variety of near "normal" residences which provide "something more" than board and lodging but which no one wants to see forced into an "institutional" mold? Can we not replace the "table d'hôte" of the institutional care package with a menu à la carte, in which the handicapped adult uses his "income maintenance" (earned or provided as assistance) to pay for his board and lodging, while receiving an assortment of community services, financed as "rehabilitation" or "adult education" or "social services" as appropriate. If *some* of these services, such as social supervision, are more properly provided in-home, should there be a prohibition against using the same funding mechanisms because the facility is publicly owned, or because the value of the service will somehow be charged off against the client's disability assistance, or because the policy makers in Washington cannot deal conceptually with a facility which is neither a "medical institution" nor a foster home?

During 1974, reconceptualization of these issues was strongly influenced by considerations of funding. Specifically, with the displacement of state-administered disability assistance by the new federal supplemental security income program inaugurated on January 1, 1974 (Callison, 1974) and the separation of income maintenance activities from social services, for both of which federal funding had previously flowed under the welfare titles (Title IV A, I, X, XIV, and XVI) of the Social Security Act, major readjustments were set in motion involving realignment of money streams classified under the headings of *income maintenance, medical assistance,* and *social services.*

In theory, these three components (with some infusion from vocational rehabilitation) should be delineated to form smoothly interlocking sectors of a continuum of human services. In practice, each of these components is the province of one or more different organizational units at the federal level alone.

States were initially advised by the district or regional offices of the Social Security Administration that subsidies paid by state agencies on behalf of mentally retarded children and adults in private residential facilities not qualifying as ICF's would be regarded as unearned income to the residents, and hence would reduce their entitlements to supplemental security income (SSI). A resolution was eventually worked out by which the states would differentiate their payments as to purpose: board and lodging versus services. If the state payments were restricted in use to "social services," the residents' SSI payments could be maintained for board and lodging.

This solution was being worked out within the Social Security Administration during the summer of 1974 at the same time that the staff of the Assistant Secretary for Planning and Evaluation in Washington was invoking different criteria, while collaterally negotiating a major legislative revision of those provisions of the Social Security Act dealing with federal support of state-administered social service programs (Mondale et al., 1974). One of the most intractable issues revolved around federal financial participation in the cost of social services provided to eligible persons "in institutions." The HEW posture, liberal on many new provisions of the proposed legislation, was resistive to opening up state options in this area. Stereotypical judgments on the distinctions between "good" and "appropriate" institutional care versus "bad" or "custodial" care, together with a determination not to open the door to paying foster parents anything for their "services" and a fear that costs of services previously borne entirely out of state funds would be refinanced by the states out of federal funds made available under the bill at the favorable 75% matching ratio, all were set against notions of state autonomy and of portability of entitlements for the client who would be eligible if he were not in one of the proscribed facilities. To the different ways of viewing the problems of children and the elderly, drug addicts and alcoholics, the retarded and the blind, were added the provider interests: the nonprofit child-caring institutions and homes for the aged, the employees of state and local government, who resent the assumed superiority of private facilities, and the frank entrepreneurs.

Once again, the underlying legislative and bureaucratic problem lay in finding the match between complex dynamic human needs and the finite bounds which agencies and legislators find it necessary to set. Yet to say that either the legislators or the bureaucrats imposed barriers to change would be to deny that change was what they sought and what they would ultimately produce in good measure. On January 4, 1975, President Ford signed P.L. 93-647, adding a new Title XX to the Social Security Act, an event with major implications for community services to the retarded.

ORGANIZATIONAL DILEMMAS IN MENTAL RETARDATION

The ideology of "normalization" for the retarded, which was widely acclaimed in the early seventies (Wolfensberger, 1973a), has important implications for the structure of governmental agencies responsible for delivering human services. Normalization implies maximum feasible participation of the retarded in the generic service systems. Such participation calls for outposting or diffusion of units of expertise and advocacy throughout the systems, rather than aggregation of responsibility in one larger and more visible entity. Again the match of real structures against the philosophical model is an issue.

Mental retardation is a peculiarly pervasive disability, affecting the individual throughout his life span, and usually requiring special as well as generic interventions in respect to education, health, social adjustment, work, and living arrangements. Klein (1968) has discussed the delivery of services to clients with many needs:

The simple reality as it emerges is that the same client may and often does have several needs at the same time, calling for different kinds of services, and these in different combinations. How shall these services be given? How can they be given—by the same agency, same personnel, or some elaborate design, flexible and adequate? How, in fact, are they given if given at all? The simple answer is that there is no effective and dependable system now in existence to assure requisite services for the multiproblem client in this country at this time. The principal methods utilized for clients with many needs have been referral, diversification, and coordination (Klein, 1968, p. 127).

By *diversification,* Klein means the process by which a single agency acquires the competence within itself to meet the multiple needs of the client. This has been the rationale for the residential institution in the past. Currently, referral and coordination, despite their known hazards, are being promoted with some new twists. At the point of delivery to the client, he is seen as needing continuity of personal advocacy. More emphasis is being placed on on-going individual program planning, client-oriented advocacy, and continuing case management, independent of any one major provider (Accreditation Council, 1973). This emphasis seeks to meet the criticism voiced by Klein that the concept of coordination of agencies is naively believed by many to be the "same as coordination for the explicit needs of the client" (Klein, 1968, p. 129). Such beliefs are not widespread among those who work for or with the retarded these days.

Unlike health services, mental health services, vocational rehabilitation, and special education, "mental retardation services" do not draw on a well-defined disciplinary base. Indeed, the American Association on Mental Deficiency is atypical as professional organizations go because of the diversity of professional backgrounds from which its membership is drawn. Failure to recognize that services to the mentally retarded are defined primarily by the client group rather than the provider group is behind some of the confusion attending their place in the organizational scheme of things. Etzioni's (1964) analysis of the principles of organization in the classical sense sheds some light on this issue.

He points out that although it is agreed that the distribution of tasks among organizational units should reflect some rationale and some sort of search for the most effective or most efficient structure, there is often disagreement as to the best basis for dividing the labor (p. 23). Some seek assignment according to *purpose,* grouping together workers with similar goals or subgoals. Others advocate using *process* as the informing principle. Specialization according to the type of *clientele* or according to *geographical area* also has its proponents. Etzioni goes on to note:

> In reality, organizations are made up of a combination of various layers that differ in their degree of specialization. The tendency is often for the lower layers to be organized according to area and/or clientele principles, and the higher ones by purpose and/or process. But even this statement should be viewed only as a probability statement which says that effective organizations are *likely* to be this way, rather than saying that they always or even usually are. . . . In actuality organizations often combine work units and divisions whose organizational principles are only partially compatible. We will see that it is not only possible to find contradictory

principles operating simultaneously in the same organization, but that such a "mix" provides the most effective organization (p. 24).

These observations can be applied to explain in part the multiplicity of foci of responsibility for programs for the retarded within the Department of Health, Education, and Welfare. The department as a whole (like other departments) is assigned a purpose: its major operating divisions are concerned with health, education, social, and rehabilitation services. These can be considered as processes mediated by disciplinary clusters. The general scheme is indicated in Figure 1, based on the recommendations of the Ash Council for reorganization of the Executive Branch. Except for "manpower," which has gone to Labor, the present Department of Health, Education, and Welfare follows closely the model for Human Resources. Figure 2 indicates the current disposition of principal "operating agencies" concerned with services to the disabled within HEW.

As for geographical groupings, HEW casts its shadow into its ten regional offices, where most major central offices have their counterparts, each ranked one echelon below the Washington original.

Specialization according to type of clientele is a principle which can be found at work in the lower layers of HEW. Education for the handicapped and health services for crippled children still maintain an organizational locus in the next echelon despite recent efforts to "decategorize." These operational agencies are not to be confused with those offices whose primary purpose is cross-agency advocacy for a special population. These offices are clustered in the Office of Human Development (OHD).

In a statement before the Senate Subcommittee on the Handicapped of the Labor and Public Welfare Committee, HEW Under Secretary Frank C. Carlucci, (1974) described the mission of OHD thus:

> To bring together a series of relatively small programs which were then scattered with no particular logic throughout the Department and administered by the larger operational agencies and the Office of the Secretary. For example, the Office of Child Development, administering the Head Start program and the Children's Bureau, was floating free in the Office of the Secretary, nominally reporting to the Assistant Secretary for Administration and Management. The Administration on Aging and the Youth Development Administration could appropriately serve as focal points for all the Department's agencies serving the elderly and youth, respectively. The President's Committee on Mental Retardation reported to the Assistant Secretary for Community and Field Services and the various functions relating to Native Americans were located throughout the Department with no single coordinating office. What all these agencies now in the Office of Human Development have in common is that they act as advocates on behalf of specific target populations. The Office of Human Development was designed to bring these advocacy agencies together to ensure that these special populations—the elderly, children and youth, Native Americans and the handicapped—are adequately served by the larger operational agencies of the Department.

The totality of funds flowing to and through OHD in 1974 was $700 million.

Carlucci was here describing a conscious departmental effort to reduce the number of operational units organized according to the principle of clientele, while recognizing that

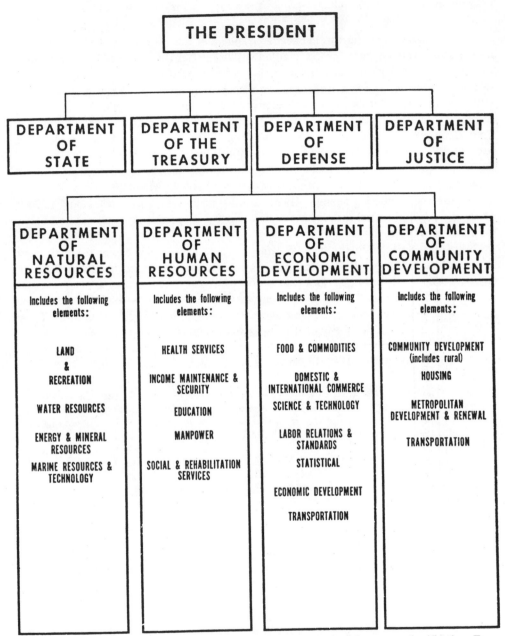

Figure 1. A rationale for organizing the federal government by broad purpose classification. From *The Case for Executive Reorganization:* The Domestic Council, Executive Office of the President, Washington, 1971, p. 16.

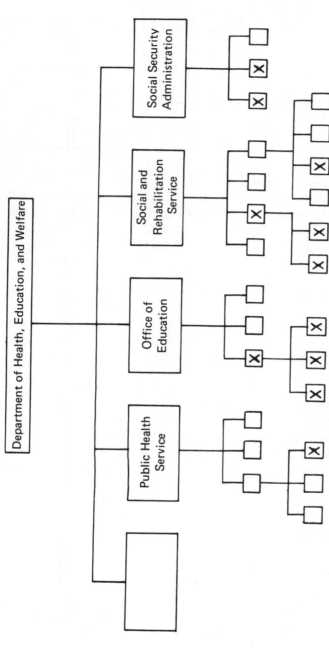

Figure 2. Schematic representation of relationships between major "operating" agencies (within the Department of Health, Education, and Welfare) having responsibilities for funding direct services or income maintenance programs, as of December, 1974. X indicates the principal sub agencies with major responsibilities for services to the handicapped, including the mentally retarded. The operating agencies are defined primarily by "process" (discipline); within the sub agencies "client characteristics" begin to show up as an organizing principal.

certain populations with special needs require special advocacy within the overall system. He also knows that if the members of these populations see no manifestation of attention to their needs they will demand a visible focal point. Such demands, if expressed through the political process, and especially through Congress, may result in distortion of administrative patterns. The establishment of OHD, therefore, served a political purpose, but it also served a valid organizational function. It generated a kind of staff input into the line activities, giving a legitimate client oriented cross cut to a structure in which "process" is the dominant organizing principle.

It is worth noting that the need for identified advocacy for certain special populations has been recognized even in HEW, which is an "umbrella agency" of broader scope than any at the state level. This need persists even when state health and welfare departments are regrouped into "human services" agencies. Gettings (1973) notes that 19 states now administer ten or more human service programs in consolidated departments. These agencies usually include health, mental health, social services, public assistance, corrections, and frequently vocational rehabilitation, but never education. (Partly because of the sheer size of the state effort, partly because of its wide political base, and partly because in many states the chief state school officer is elected, education continues as a separate department in all states.) Such consolidations have in many instances made generic funding sources, such as social services and child health, more accessible to the retarded, but they accentuate rather than eliminate the need for expert collective and individual advocacy on behalf of individuals with special needs.

The primary original purpose of the Developmental Disabilities Act (as stated in Section 130 of P.L. 91-517) is to "assist the several States in developing and implementing a comprehensive and continuing plan for meeting the present and future needs for services to persons affected by developmental disabilities." There is a fundamental similarity between this Act and the Older Americans Act, (P.L. 89-73 as amended) administered by the Administration on Aging in OHD, in that its thrust is to assist states in cross cutting the generic systems on behalf of a vulnerable clientele, at the state and intrastate regional levels, and ultimately at the point of delivery to the client.

In line with this similarity, there were many people in and out of HEW who believed that by 1974 the time had come to transfer the Division of Developmental Disabilities into OHD from its relatively obscure position in the bowels of a major operating agency, the Rehabilitation Services Administration. The Division's budget of some $50 million is dwarfed by RSA's which is nearing $1 billion. DDD's location was a vestige of a reorganization which took place in 1967 at which time the Division of Mental Retardation was a small operating agency dispensing project grants for construction and services (Boggs, 1972). Its present mission is much more clearly directed toward planning, resource development, and collective advocacy on behalf of children and adults with long term substantial disabilities originating in childhood. In view of this shift Carlucci's statement quoted above could scarcely have set forth more clearly the arguments for moving DDD into this context.[2]

---

[2] In fact, DDD was transferred to OHD as part of RSA in February, 1975; in July, it was rechristened Developmental Disabilities Office, at which time it was separated from RSA and put in a position to report directly to the Assistant Secretary for Human Development.

As Stedman (1974) has pointed out, developmental disability is not a new syndrome, but an administrative concept. It is designed to address problems common to persons who are and have been severely handicapped since very early in life. Such people are doubly vulnerable in a system that is organized by process rather than clientele. First they are clients with many needs, secondly the nature of their handicap puts them at a personal disadvantage in seeking to mobilize their own solutions.

Approximately one-third of all recipients of disability assistance in 1970 were disabled before age 18 years, and of these 80% were disabled from birth. More than half have mental retardation as a primary or secondary disability (National Center for Social Statistics, 1972). Comparable findings characterize those adults who receive social security benefits as adults disabled in childhool (Social Security Administration, Office of Research and Statistics, 1973).

It is known that those disabled in childhood have a different life experience than those disabled later in life (Richardson, 1963; Battle, 1974), and that their social and demographic characteristics also differ. Early onset of disability militates against marriage and increases the probability that the disabled person will live in dependent family situations, e.g., with parents. Likelihood of entering the labor market is also decreased, with attendant loss of benefits associated with a work history. Those disabled in childhood are twice as likely to be without public income benefits, although this may be changing with the advent of Supplemental Security Income (Haber, 1969).

Not apparent in any demographic data is a more subtle but significant difference between those who become disabled after growing up normal and those who have never known normalcy. It is clearer to the former what they have lost, not only in personal capacities but in prerogatives, rights, and status. Demands, whether polite or clamorous, for compensatory privileges are more likely to be effectively directed and pursued by those first disabled in maturity. In seeking their own advantage, legitimately, through the political process, these handicapped citizens may well elbow aside the less vocal developmentally disabled.

Among adults disabled in childhood who receive social security benefits, mental retardation, cerebral palsy, epilepsy, and childhood schizophrenia are the most common diagnoses, accounting for more than 80% of recently qualifying applicants (Social Security Administration Office of Research and Statistics, 1973). The explicit naming of the first three in the Developmental Disabilities Act (1970) was more illustrative than functional. Omission of autism and related syndromes was not so much a programmatic as a political distinction. Officially the childhood mental illnesses "belong to" the National Institute of Mental Health. The National Society for Autistic Children however, quite correctly, sees autism as a chronic disabling condition originating in childhood and leading to the same social and economic constraints as other developmental disabilities. The explicit mention of some disabilities and omission of others in the legislation, however, gave rise in the early seventies to some of the same difficulties and mismatches described in the case studies on classification. An enormous amount of bureaucratic and, later, legislative energy was addressed to the issue of who is "in" and who is "out," based on diagnostic distinctions rather than social need. An analysis of many of the activities spawned by the Act would show, however, that the benefits of planning, casefinding, comprehensive diagnostic programs, information and referral, advocacy, infant stimulation projects, and the like simply cannot be confined by diagnosis. The name of the grantee agency is not necessarily a good guide to the range of its clientele. Indeed the whole program is directed less to a defined set of eligible individuals than to the ambiance surrounding a target population.

Four years after enactment, disparities among the perceptions of the consumer representatives, the providers, the state and federal bureaucracies, and the Congressional staff members concerned continued to produce barriers, not to change, but to progress. The mismatches were less a matter of ends than of means. Although there had developed by 1974 an increasing consensus that the Act should stimulate cross-agency planning and a stance toward resource development that included accessing generic resources as needed by developmentally disabled persons along the stages of their life span, there was an increasing predisposition on the part of the Congress, more particularly the Senate Subcommittee on the Handicapped, to dictate in detail the procedures, structures, and time frames to which the states (as well as HEW) should conform in striving toward this goal.

Gettings and Ziegler (1974) have summarized graphically the diversity among the states in their organization of public health, education, and welfare activities. The Developmental Disabilities Act as conceived in 1969 addressed these realities by permitting great fluidity in the use of the relatively small amount of money flowing to states through the Act. The Act requires no "single state agency" to control the funds, for example. The thrust was "interstitial," to fill gaps between the larger health, education, rehabilitation, and social service structures as they impact on this population with many special needs. As Richardson said (1972), the resources must not only be brought together but fitted together. It seems apparent that such melding must be engineered to a large extent at the state level. Federal funding should enable rather than direct. Initial fumbling was to be expected. Stedman (1974), as director of a nationwide project of technical assistance to the state councils generated under the Act, was in a unique position to overview the national scene. He noted:

> The mechanism was new and unique. It was widely misunderstood. The length of the leash provided by the simply written legislation was not fully appreciated. Consequently the initial activities of the state developmental disabilities councils were to emulate those bureaucratic structures they knew and to use federal formula grant funds for direct service program development.

As mistakes were made, there arose some clamor to write into law restrictions which might have prevented such mistakes. That such laws also prevent creative new solutions is less well recognized. Stedman's further observation is relevant.

> This national program is now at a critical point in its transition from its earlier, competitive form to an initiating-advocacy posture. Whether this can be fully implemented remains to be seen, for it will depend on the creativity, flexibility and adaptive capacity of both bureaucratic and informal non-governmental structures. My own hope and expectation is that it will succeed if given a fair opportunity to be fully explored over the next three to five years.

In recommending continuation of the legislation without major structural changes, the Department of Health, Education, and Welfare put itself on the side of providing this "fair opportunity." The Department thus clearly distinguished between the purposes of this program and those of the community mental health centers program, which it applauded but wanted to set loose from federal support. CMHC is part of the same original legislation (P.L. 88-164, 1963) and the two programs had initially been seen as parallel.

However, the predisposition of the Senate staff in 1974 was to elaborate on the 1970 text of the Developmental Disabilities Act and to limit the opportunities for "creativity, flexibility and adaptive capacity" at the state level. It was foreseen by some observers that many of the staff proposals, if enacted, would conflict with state law and practice, and even with civil rights thrusts. For example, there was a proposed specification that the staff of the state council should be "solely responsible to the council," and another that mandated individual client tracking for evaluation purposes (U.S. Senate, Subcommittee on the Handicapped, 1974).

The Senate bill also called for the creation of an "Office of Developmental Disabilities" within the Office of Human Development. As indicated earlier, there exists a strong rationale for such a move. However, the attempt to legislate this change represented one more in a series of unilateral moves on the part of the legislative branch to impose its own organizational patterns on the executive branch.

THE ROLE OF THE CONGRESS

The Congress, as the body which writes the laws, clearly has a prime responsibility for the definitions which lead to the legal and administrative classification systems which, in turn, determine individual entitlements under a wide variety of human services legislation. This is not to say that Congress is not advised by the executive branch. However, it is likely to be more responsive to organized constituencies. The effects of constituency structure may be illustrated by the following example.

Part of the Ford strategy for combatting inflation is to reduce federal spending. Within the first month of his tenure he proposed (on two separate occasions) two steps, each of which would reduce federal payroll. First, he would permit reduction of the payroll by attrition, a freeze on replacement hiring; secondly, he asked Congress to delay a proposed 5% federal pay hike for three months. The latter suggestion would spread the effect of "belt tightening" over a large number of people who would remain employed. The former suggestion would, in effect, add to unemployment by significantly reducing the number of career-related job openings throughout the country. (This suggestion was made simultaneously with a proposal for increasing temporary "public service" employment.) Congress responded with immediate opposition to the proposal to hold the line on pay across the board. Federal civil servants are well organized. The people who are unemployed because of the job freeze are faceless and unorganized, and no Congressional opposition to this proposal surfaced, although from several points of view it could be seen as the more destructive. Few people realize, for example, the reduction in efficiency which results from an unplanned reduction in force. Such a reduction leaves gaps in an agency's competencies, whether the posts lost be clerical or professional. The constituent who complains to his Congressman about the poor service he gets from the Social Security District Office, or the IRS, seldom connects this dissatisfaction with the reduction in the federal bureaucracy which he applauded. Nor does his Congressman.

Constitutencies tend to organize themselves along lines which divide consumers from providers. The provider group is further fractured along lines of organized (agency) providers (nursing homes, community mental health centers, etc.) versus professionals as individuals (AMA, NASW, AAMD). Among organized providers there are further splits along the lines of public, proprietary, and non-profit. Consumers, on the other hand, tend to be split along lines which reflect their own perceptions of common interests (National Council of Senior Citizens, National Federation of the Blind, National Welfare Rights Organization, United Cerebral Palsy, National Association for Retarded Citizens).

In the past there have been some rather significant matches between such constituencies and the programmatic units within HEW. When the providers are state agencies, this kind of linkage is fostered by the usual statutory specification that to take advantage of a federal program of grants-in-aid to states, a state must "designate a single state agency" to administer the funds in the state. Such linkages exist in respect to maternal and child health funds, child welfare funds, vocational rehabilitation funds and many others. A federal attempt in 1974 to relax this "single state agency" mandate with respect to social services funds for low income persons as authorized under the Social Security Act was strongly resisted by the American Public Welfare Association, whose most influential members are the heads of the presently designated "single state agencies" for social services.

Consumers of human services organize themselves into what are perceived by HEW and the Congress as "special interest" or "categorical" groups. The Nixon administration sought to reduce the extent to which the organization of HEW was molded by these categorical interests, as a reflection of "categorical" legislation which the department was and is called on to administer.

Members of Congress, on the other hand, tend to identify particular constituencies (as well as official agencies) with particular pieces of legislation. In fact organizations such as the National Association for Retarded Citizens have had difficulty in making clear to the appropriations committees why they, the organizations, want to speak to more than one agency budget. The idea that the National Association for Mental Health has interests beyond NIMH is puzzling to them. Committees having jurisdiction over substantive legislation also look for clearly identified supportive constituencies with articulate spokesmen.

Congress As a Bureaucracy

Like other organizations, Congress is structured to divide the labor. In its case, the organizational units are its committees. Those that deal with the drafting and recommending of legislation are assigned tasks according to the purpose of the legislation. Some committees have developed a body of law which is contained in a single large Act, such as the Social Security Act, or the Public Health Act. Any bills which take the form of an amendment to such an act, even if only tangentially related, will be assigned to the committee having jurisdiction. Jurisdictional power struggles are not infrequent, but are not usually publicized.

The President and his cabinet members are not bound to assign the administration of all portions of any one act to the same agency, however. Thus the one-to-one relationship between Congressional committees and administering agencies is by no means complete. Moreover, the two houses of Congress do not see the division of labor in the same way. Rehabilitation is handled in the House by Education and Labor, but, until recently, was handled in the Subcommittee on Health within Labor and Public Welfare in the Senate. The Developmental Disabilities Act, on the other hand, was seen initially as health legislation in both houses. Thus it lines up along side rehabilitation in the Senate, but in the House is assigned to the Interstate and Foreign Commerce Committee. These mismatches mean that different personnel are involved and that natural parallels and opportunities for inter-program consistencies may be overlooked. For example, the Rehabilitation Act and the Developmental Disabilities Act are administered by the same agency within HEW but they use different definitions of construction. The DD definition is consistent with that used by the Hill-Burton Hospital and Medical Facilities Construction Act, with which it is associated historically in the minds of the House Subcommittee on Public Health and the Environment (Boggs, 1972, p. 177).

In 1972, the Senate Committee on Labor and Public Welfare (which does not handle welfare legislation) created a new Subcommittee on the Handicapped and assigned both rehabilitation and developmental disabilities to it. They remain in separate full committees in the House.

Although a committee chairman in either house has considerable latitude in defining and redefining subcommittees, the restructuring of the overall committee assignments proceeds, if at all, with much greater difficulty. This is because the principle of unity of control of the organizational structure is grossly violated (Etzioni, 1964, p. 23). Restructuring committee assignments can proceed in either house only with the consent of the majority of the members. A major planful effort to "modernize" the House committee structure in 1973 to 1974 (House Report #93-916, 1974) was largely annulled by the resistance of the members themselves (Malbin, 1974). In this, Committees which were resisting change were reinforced by their identifiable organizational constituencies. For example, the AFL-CIO successfully opposed splitting up the Education and Labor Committee, and eliminating the Merchant Marine Committee (AFL-CIO, 1974).

Congress As an External Constraint on HEW Management

By contrast, the executive branch, and especially HEW, has been undergoing major reorganizations for the past 8 years, partly as a reflection of general concerns for better management but even more as a reflection of the changing rationale of the leaders and their view of their mission. Etzioni (1964, p. 30) suggests that the search will be stopped when performance appears "reasonably good." It may be that HEW's search will continue to be incessant. In any case, while decision making authority on organizational structure in HEW is centralized, it is subject to certain restraints including a strong tendency on the part of Congress to interfere, to mandate certain changes, and to prohibit others. Frequently Congressional intervention reflects the interests of particular constituencies. For example, HEW's general thrust toward decentralization to its regional offices has been thwarted in the case of the Office of Education by the education interests (Carlucci and Essex, 1973). Similar resistance to the growth of the regional offices (geographical principle) at the expense of the categorical agencies in the central office (clientele principle) is expressed in the Rehabilitation Act of 1973 (P.L. 93-112) and in 1974 amendments which were passed over President Ford's veto (P.L. 93-516). Congress sought therein to prevent delegation of the RSA Commissioner's functions and to force transfer of the Rehabilitation program to the Office of Human Development. This transfer was, of course, opposed by HEW (Carlucci, 1974) as well as OMB.

Congressional Intent As a Program Determinant

The drafting of laws requires a highly skilled combination of art and technology. To avoid overly elaborate verbiage in the statutes themselves, with the opportunities which this affords for post facto reconstruction by the courts, it is customary to leave much of the detail to "rule making" by the administrating agency. In the past most major bills were originally drafted by the agency, and the testimony of administration witnesses (heard first during any hearing) was designed not only to justify the provisions but to clarify how the agency intended to interpret and carry them out. Changes made by the two congressional committees before reporting a bill were similarly explained in their reports. Any remaining questions were subsequently dealt with during the debate on the floor. Occasionally a planned colloquy is staged to clarify the intent. Question: "Do I understand that it is the Committee's intention to include the mentally handicapped within the term 'handicapped' for the purposes of Section 100?" Answer: "The distinguished Senator is quite right."

In recent years the entente between Congress and the administration has deteriorated. This is not merely a reflection of a greater discrepancy in goals and objectives as expressed in legislation, but of poorer communication. Restraints have been placed on informal exchanges between middle level program managers in HEW and the staffs of the Congressional committees, partly because their loyalties to program or constituency were seen as conflicting with the administration goals. The credibility of those administration spokesmen who are permitted to communicate has declined. Congress complains that its intent as expressed in its report language is not respected. This has led to more elaboration of provisions in the enacted text. Such provisions are, in turn, found to be unworkable in execution. What makes the administration's dilemma even more acute is the frequent lack of underlying agreement between the two houses of Congress.

The role of Congressional staff members in molding the ever increasing proliferation of legislation is also increasing (U.S. News and World Report, 1974). Not only are their numbers increasing, but their competence in program fields is often (although not always) impressive. For instance, it is little known that there have been at least two and sometimes three physicians on the staff of the Senate Health Subcommittee since 1972. With increasing numbers, the delegation of decision making from the Senator or Representative tends to increase. Staff members tend to take on the cloak of power with which the electorate have clothed their principals. It is not uncommon for a staff member to aver quite earnestly, "I know that was the intent of Congress because that is what I had in mind during the executive mark-up session." Clearly this kind of "intent" attached to the same language emanating from two separate mark-up sessions may lead to ambiguities, not to say contradictions, at the point of application.

Congressional intent is obviously shaped to some extent by the kind of information it receives. Policy decisions need hard factual as well as broad philosophical justification (National Academy of Science, 1969). In the human services area such facts are not always obtainable. The demand for measurable objectives and "accountability" against them has led to the increased use of a social science tool, the social indicator (National Academy of Science, 1969; U.S. Office of Management and Budget, 1973; Henriot, 1972). Here, too, a mismatch may occur. For example, we have had to use reduction in perinatal mortality as an indicator of the success of the comprehensive maternity and infant care programs which were originally presented to Congress as for the purpose of preventing mental retardation. But some approximation is needed, and this is better than none. Occasionally, however, the indicator is substituted for the real goal, as, for example, when President Nixon announced as a goal "to enable one third of the more than 200,000 retarded persons in public institutions to return to useful lives in the community" (Nixon, 1971). It is sometimes necessary (and difficult) to divert Congressional attention from "the numbers game" to the less tractable problems of people, from *how many persons were served,* to *how well they were served.*

Nobody denies that responsible lobbyists serve an important information purveying function. Congressional committees are largely dependent on their recognized constituencies and on the executive branch for much of their information. Commenting on this point in relation to proposals to establish an Office of Technology Assessment for Congress, Congressman Charles Mosher (1972) said:

> We need much more adequate and accurate evidence and expert advice concerning both the immediate impact of any proposal and its probable secondary and tertiary consequences, whether economic, social, or environmental.
>
> Many of the decisions we must make concern proposals from the federal executive agencies. The Congress is today seriously outmanned and outgunned by the expertise in the executive branch. That is an added reason for our need for a professional source of informational and advisory help that shall be solely responsible to the Congress.

Since then the OTA has in fact been established, but to date its emphases have been on technologies relating to engineering and the environment rather than social impacts. Congress still lacks adequate machinery for assessing the social and economic variables which underly decision making on behalf of the mentally retarded. A study such as Conley's (1973) takes years to complete, and must be updated to be useful in on-going policy development. Moreover, the meaning of the information is obscure if not set in a still larger context.

The Judicial Branch

Although this paper has not dealt in depth with the courts, their interventions in recent years are well publicized. The judicial system is also a bureaucracy. The problems of perception and classification are as present there as in the other branches of government. To some attorneys, the admission of a mentally retarded person to a residential facility is viewed as incarceration, and the action of a parent in applying for care is viewed as "divesting." To the professionals the admission may be seen as improving the environment of the child or adult, and to the parent it may mean offering him opportunities for enriched services. Thus the question asked earlier: "What is an institution?" takes on a different set of dimensions in a judicial context. Some court decisions have, in fact, been adverse to the current values of normalization. Courts also enlarge on or interpret Congressional intent, as in Souder v. Brennan (1974), which required institutions to pay patients for useful work performed, in accordance with the Fair Labor Standards Act.

CONCLUSION

The interaction between the three traditional branches of government and the citizenry, professional and lay, takes place at various levels within a complex multi-organizational framework in which we can see at work many of the principles of social science as applied to organizations in general and bureaucracies in particular. The application of these principles to public policy making which affects the mentally retarded is an especially interesting study because of the pervasiveness of the subject, and the many cross linkages between conventional systems which it invokes. There is a critical need at this time for studies of organizational models on the one hand, and of basic public policy decision-making on the other, as they impact on the often unidentified or invisible component of our population, who, for some purpose or other, are called mentally retarded.

REFERENCES

Accreditation Council on Facilities for the Mentally Retarded. 1973. Standards for Community Agencies. The Joint Commission on the Accreditation of Hospitals, Chicago. 154 pp.

American Federation of Labor-Council of Industrial Organizations. 1974. Statements Adopted by AFL-CIO Executive Council, Washington. 21 pp.

Battle, C. U. 1974. Disruptions in the Socialization of a Young Severely Handicapped Child. Rehab. Lit. 35: 131–140.

Begab, M. et al. 1972. Classification in Mental Retardation. Am. J. Psychiatr. 128 (Suppl. 11): 1–45.

Boggs, E. M. 1966. Legal Aspects of Mental Retardation. In I. Philips (ed.), Prevention and Treatment of Mental Retardation, pp. 407–428. Basic Books, New York.

Boggs, E. M. 1972. Federal Legislation 1966–71. In J. Wortis (ed.), Mental Retardation, An Annual Review, IV, pp. 165–206. Grune and Stratton, Inc., New York.

Callison, J. C. 1974. Early Experience Under the Supplemental Security Income Program. Social Security Bull. 37:6: 3–11.

Carlucci, F. 1974. Statement before the Subcommittee on the Handicapped, U.S. Senate Committee on Labor and Public Welfare.

Carlucci, F. and M. W. Essex. 1974. Should HEW Decentralize? Compact-Bimonthly Magazine of the Education Commission of the States, VIII: 3: 20–22.

CFR (Code of Federal Regulations) 1973: 45 CFR 233.60(b), 45 CFR 248.70(b).

Conley, R. W. 1973. The Economics of Mental Retardation. The Johns Hopkins University Press, Baltimore, 377 pp.

Department of Health, Education, and Welfare, Social and Rehabilitation Service. 1970. Statistical History: Federal State Program of Vocational Rehabilitation 1920–1969. U.S. Government Printing Office, Washington, D.C. 72 pp.

Department of Health, Education, and Welfare. 1974. Regulations, Intermediate Care Facilities. Federal Register 39:12:2220-2235, 248.60(b)(10).

Etzioni, A. 1964. Modern Organizations. Prentice-Hall, Englewood Cliffs, N.J. 120 pp.

Gettings, R. M. 1973. Impact of Politics in the Next Decade. In Manpower Projections for Developmental Disabilities in the 80's. pp. 18–27. Temple University, Philadelphia.

Gehings, R. M. and W. A. Ziegler, 1973. Organization of State Services for the Mentally Retarded: A Source Book. National Association of Coordinators of State Programs for the Mentally Retarded, Inc., Washington, D.C. 242 pp.

Grossman, H. J. et al. 1973. Manual on Terminology and Classification. In Mental Retardation 1973 Revision. American Association on Mental Deficiency, Washington, D.C.

Haber, L. D. 1969. The Disabled Beneficiary—A Comparison of Factors Related to Benefit Entitlement: Report # 7 from the Social Security Survey of the Disabled, 1966. Social Security Administration, Office of Research and Statistics. Washington, D.C. 33 pp.

Hanley, E. 1966. Amending the Immigration and Nationality Act. Remarks. Congressional Record (daily edition) April 18, pp. 7806–7807.

Henriot, P. J. 1972. Political Aspects of Social Indicators: Implications for Research. # 4 in series Social Science Frontiers. Russell Sage Foundation, New York. 34 pp.

Heber, R. 1959. Manual on Terminology and Classification in Mental Retardation, 1959 revision. American Association on Mental Deficiency.

Hobbs, N. 1974. The Futures of Children. Josey-Bass, San Francisco. 309 pp.

Klein, P. 1968. From Philanthropy to Social Welfare. Josey-Bass, San Francisco. 307 pp.

Malbin, M. J. 1974. Congress Report. Democratic Caucus Panel Works to Revise Bolling Plan. National Journal Reports. 6: 1059.

Mondale, W. et al. 1974. S. 4082, A Bill to amend the Social Security Act to establish a consolidated program of Federal financial assistance to encourage provision of services by the States. U.S. Senate.

Mosher, C. A. 1972. Needs and Trends in Congressional Decision Making. Science 178: 134–139.

National Academy of Sciences-Social Science Research Council. 1969. The Behavioral and Social Sciences—Outlook and Needs, pp. 88–100. Prentice-Hall, Englewood Cliffs, N.J.

National Center for Social Statistics (DHEW). 1972. Findings of the 1970 APTD Study, Part I, Demographic and Program Characteristics. DHEW Publication No. (SRS) 73-3853, Washington, D.C.

Nixon, R. N. (President). 1971. Statement on Mental Retardation, November 16, 1971. Presidential Documents, Washington, D.C.

President's Committee on Mental Retardation. 1972. Federal Programs for the Retarded— A Review and Evaluation, U.S. Government Printing Office, Washington, D.C. 271 pp.

Richardson, E. L. 1972. Responsibility and Responsiveness. Publication No.(OS) 72-19, Washington, D.C.

Richardson, S. A. 1963. Some Psychological Consequences of Handicapping. Pediatrics 30:7: 291—297.

Smith, A. D. 1955. The Right to Life, pp. 105—106. The University of North Carolina Press, Chapel Hill, N.C.

Social Security Administration (DHEW) Office of Research and Statistics. 1973. Social Security Applicant Statistics, 1971. Washington, D.C.

Souder et al. v. Brennan et al., Civil Action No. 482-73, (United States District Court, District of Columbia).

Stedman, D. J. 1974. Developmental Disabilities: State of the Nation. 1974. Paper delivered at the annual conference of the American Association on Mental Deficiency.

Turner, S. and Butler, H. (eds.). 1974. Community Living for Ohio's Developmentally Disabled Citizens, Ohio Developmental Disabilities, Inc., Columbus, Ohio. 98 pp.

United Nations. 1971. Declaration on the Rights of Mentally Retarded Persons, The Assembly, New York.

U.S. Delegation to the International Conference for the Eighth Revision of the International Classification of Diseases. 1966. Report. Public Health Service (DHEW), Washington, D.C.

U.S. House of Representatives, Committee on Banking and Currency. 1971. Basic Laws and Authorities on Housing and Urban Development. Revised through January 31, 1971. U.S. Government Printing Office, Washington, D.C. 1132 pp.

U.S. House of Representatives, Committee on the Judiciary. 1965. Hearings before Subcommittee, # 1 on H.R. 2580 to Amend the Immigration and Nationality Act, Serial # 7. U.S. Government Printing Office, Washington, D.C. pp. 138—9.

U.S. News and World Report. 1974. Those Staffs on Capitol Hill: Power Behind the Scenes, pp. 26—28.

U.S. Office of Management and Budget. 1973. Social Indicators, 1973. U.S. Government Printing Office, Washington, D.C. 258 pp.

U.S. Office of Management and Budget, Public Health Service. 1963. Manual for the Medical Examination of Aliens. U.S. Government Printing Office, Washington, D.C.

U.S. Senate, Committee on Labor and Public Welfare. 1974. Report No. 93-1169: Developmental Disabilities Assistance and Bill of Rights Act, Washington, D.C.

Wolfensberger, W. 1973a. The Principle of Normalization in Human Services. National Institute on Mental Retardation. Toronto, Canada, 258 pp.

Wolfensberger, W. 1973b. The Future of Residential Services for the Retarded. J. Clin. Child Psych. II:1: 19—20.

Guided Societal Change
And Mental Retardation

Amitai Etzioni and Stephen A. Richardson

The purpose of this chapter is to take some of the concepts in Etzioni's theory of guided social change and illustrate their application to mental retardation. Particular attention will be paid to the role of the social scientist. The study of social change is based on the premise that the greater the ability of individuals and collectivities to guide social change, the freer they are of their history. Where the ability is not present or exercised, the more they are bound by policies and conditions they had no hand in shaping. The theory of societal guidance focuses on specifying the conditions under which societal units can become more active in guidance.[1]

Societal guidance consists of "downward" factors which include the collection, processing, analysis, and evaluation of information as well as the use of knowledge in making and implementing decisions. It also includes the use of power to bring about compliance to implement decisions. There are also "upward" factors which change the "downward" factors of societal control into societal guidance. These upward factors are necessary to take into account human preferences and to develop concensus. This is achieved through the understanding and modification of public opinion and the mobilization of various individual and group purposes through organizations which endeavor to exert influence over the course of public policy. The chief locus of capacities for societal guidance is government.

The guidance of society in actions related to mental retardation must be related to the goals toward which the society is directed. And yet it is clear that such goals are neither explicit nor generally agreed upon at any one time. The goals are heavily influenced by societal attitudes toward mental retardation.

Even this brief introduction to theoretical constructs related to societal guidance raises numerous questions about mental retardation, e.g., what are the desired goals of meeting the human needs of those who are mentally retarded? What are the ways in

---

[1] The basic elements of the theory of societal guidance are presented in Etzioni (1968), Ch. 5. In addition, for a brief overview of the theory, see Etzioni (1967).

469

which the proportion of guided to unguided planning for the mentally retarded can be increased? In the process of guidance, who is involved in downward control, upward consensus building, and power mobilization?

The goals of mental retardation services are heavily influenced by societal attitudes toward the mentally retarded. Several of the authors of this book have traced the historical development of services for the retarded showing the influence of the genetic concepts of mental retardation, the eugenics movement, and the creation of asylums where the mentally retarded could be sheltered and cared for separate from the society. More recently, it is becoming recognized that the system of care in isolated residential institutions often provides little to meet the social, emotional, and developmental needs of the retarded with emphasis being more on the bodily needs of feeding, clothing, and cleanliness. Increasingly, emphasis has been placed on the goal of providing a variety of services to meet the human needs of the retarded and their families within existing communities where possible, using existing services rather than services especially for the mentally retarded. The change in emphasis has not only come from the evidence that many isolated institutions provided subhuman standards, a barren existence and made continued contacts between the residents and their families difficult. The change also comes as the values of minorities have become more recognized and individual rights to treatment, humane care, and education are now more articulated and supported. The expression and spread of these newer values are accompanied by the development of terms which have developed some of the attributes of slogans: "normalization," "decentralization," "integration," "habilitation," "mainstreaming." The translation of these very general goals into specific objectives, policies, and programs is a difficult exercise in societal guidance.

At any time, various and in part contradictory values will be held. An illustration of this is when parents are asked to take their child back into the home after years of placement in an institution and little or no contact. The more the parents have accepted the earlier institutional placement and its presumed underlying values, the more difficult it becomes, suddenly to change to the values of decentralization and normalization. Conceivably, they might have welcomed these latter values at the time they were considering institutionalizing their child.

Explicating the goals of planning for mental retardation is made difficult by the variety and range of needs of people with different sub-types of mental retardation. Further, while they have some needs which may sometimes be unique to certain forms of retardation, many of their needs are shared with persons who are not mentally retarded. This is the dilemma of human classification discussed in the chapter by Boggs (this volume).

The implementation of goals to meet the human needs of the mentally retarded becomes a far more complex human and political process working within and utilizing existing community facilities than does the operation of an isolated total institution.

Many institutions for the mentally retarded have not fully implemented the therapeutic, educational, and rehabilitative goals of service for which they were originally created and have directed their efforts instead to custodial care, asylum, and segregation from society. Without clear goals for societal guidance of the institutions, guidance was left largely in the hands of those responsible for running or financially supporting the institutions—a fact that resulted in strong "downward" social control. The "upward" mechanisms that transform control into guidance were weak or nonexistent either in terms of channels for taking into account the preferences of the institutionalized mentally retarded or through external societal monitoring of what went on in the institutions. The mentally handicapped have been largely passive and almost never consulted to determine their wishes, needs, and reactions to their experiences with programs and services on their absence. They have contributed to reconsideration of goals through being the recipients of neglect, ill treatment, and abuse in programs intended to provide beneficial services. Their sufferings, when identified and made known, have resulted in public outcry and demands for reform. Unfortunately such public concern has rarely led to a basic reexamination of goals and services. The ignoring of the needs of the consumer of mental retardation services has been based on the assumption that the mentally retarded would challenge these assumptions for a large proportion of those who are classified as mentally retarded. With time, patience, and experience, all but the most severely retarded have the capability to communicate to some degree their feelings, needs, and wishes. This has recently received some recognition in the advocacy program discussed in the chapter by Kurtz (this volume).

In the gradual shift now occurring toward decentralized multiple services in the community using a wide variety of community resources, the problems of societal guidance have become enormously more complex because of the major increase in the "upward" factors of concensus building and power mobilization. State and local departments of mental hygiene are staffed largely by officials whose background and experience was with a central authority structure which exercised tight downward social control and where little change occurred in the forms and patterns of service. The present rapidly changing services in the community are far more open to public scrutiny and multiple and diverse collectives which mobilize power to challenge social control. Societal guidance of resources for the mentally retarded is presenting difficult new problems for government agencies whose officials are unprepared for dealing with these new circumstances and conditions. The chapter by Cohen (this volume) provides a case history to illustrate some of the changes occurring in societal guidance of services for the mentally retarded.

Any consideration of societal guidance and mental retardation requires the identification of various types of individuals and collectivities and the roles they play. Those who are retarded and government officials have already been given brief attention. Here it is possible only to illustrate and leave to others a systematic analysis of this component of societal guidance.

Perhaps the greatest experience about the needs of the mentally retarded is the collective knowledge and experience of the parents of those who are mentally handicapped. While this may appear obvious, parents were largely ignored in the development of goals and programs for the retarded. It was not until parents formed organizations first at the local level and then at the state and national levels that they obtained a voice which was heeded by officials in mental retardation, in politics, and in government.

Early parent organizations were predominately concerned with service for and the prevention of severe mental retardation. This was not accidental. The parents who organized had to have time, funds, and contact, and some influence with persons in power. Such parents largely came from professional or upper income families and their concerns arose from their experiences related to their own retarded children. From epidemiological studies it is known that severe mental retardation is randomly distributed across all socio-economic groupings, but that mild mental retardation is heavily overrepresented in low socio-economic groups and is rare among families of high socio-economic status (Abramowicz and Richardson, 1975; Birch et al., 1970). The personal experience of upper income families is then almost exclusively with severe mental retardation. Further, the degree of severity of the mental retardation and associated handicaps which are more common among the severely retarded made it difficult for their parents to conceal from themselves and others the existence of their child's impairments, and the parents' needs for help with their children which were multiple and serious. The set of factors just described suggests why parents of mildly retarded children were less frequently in the leadership roles in the parent organizations. The development of societal guidance for developing goals, policies, and programs for the mildly mentally subnormal comes largely from collectives in the society other than parents.

The number and kinds of professionals who have become permanently involved in planning and providing services for the mentally retarded and their families have grown steadily. In addition there are many who have some connection with mental retardation in some secondary role. Professionals have been influential in the ways in which mental retardation policies and services have developed. The organizations of services which they have evolved have been heavily influenced by the professional backgrounds from which they came. For example, the large scale institutions for residential care have been modeled in large part on hospital organization and conduct. Frequently mental retardation services are organized within state or city departments of mental hygiene. Psychiatry is a medical speciality which has been particularly influential in guiding, planning, and directing services. Services have frequently become parts of large bureaucratic structures. Residential facilities have taken on the characteristics of large isolated total institutions where pressures to maintain the status quo and maintain a growing body of vested interests develop. The roles of the professionals became increasingly prescribed by institutional restraints and the options and alternatives for services were delimited. A conflict of interest can easily develop among the professionals' concern and obligations to those they serve, self interests of professional security, and advancement and expectations of loyalty to the institution and to the particular profession of the individual.

The decentralization of services with the accompanying emphasis on maintaining the mentally retarded outside of institutional residential care where possible has led to increased participation by parents and other community members and collectives. This has broadened the base for articulating the needs, goals, and plans for services. Innovation of new services has also led to the recognition of service skills which are not necessarily possessed by those who filled the more traditional staff positions in mental retardation services. The newer forms of services include establishing adults who are moderately retarded in apartments where they are given help and support in daily activities related to apartment living and to functioning in the community. Services also include help in use of transportation, legal assistance, and foster care of children. Effective societal guidance for such activities requires forms of knowledge about the lives of the retarded and how they live in the community. There is a need to expand these forms of knowledge.

Knowledge tied to transformation is concerned with exploring potential challenges to the basic assumptions of established social policy. Production of "stable" knowledge elaborates and respecifies, even revises secondary assumptions within the basic framework of the ongoing programs; that the basic character of the program will remain the same is taken for granted. Decision-making elites, we suggest, tend to prefer the production of "stable" to transforming knowledge and seek closure on basic knowledge assumptions. One reason for this preference is that basic assumptions cannot be selected and reviewed on wholly empirical grounds. Hence, once consensus has been reached on the basic assumptions of a world view, a self view, a strategic doctrine, it is expensive politically, economically, and psychologically for the elite, to allow these assumptions to be questioned, which is necessary if they are to be transformed. They therefore tend to become tabooed assumptions, and the elite attempt to guide knowledge production toward elaboration, additions, and revisions within their limits.

Structurally, then, research and development units within administrative hierarchies are often subject to intense pressure from policy makers toward selective perception in knowledge collecting and even distortion, especially when it comes to communicating what they learned to their superiors.

Outside researchers are comparatively free of political pressure to produce only stable knowledge. But their effectiveness may be hampered by other kinds of structural constraints. Outside researchers are generally academically based and as such think in terms of analytic disciplines such as psychology, sociology, economics, etc. which slice the world quite differently from the way a policy maker has to confront a problem, i.e., perhaps only one problem, such as mental retardation, but in terms of its economic, social and psychological dimensions simultaneously. Analytic scientists tend to work under the assumption that all other variables besides the one they are interested in remain constant. Of course they know that in reality this is not the case, but for their work this does not matter. The policy maker, however, cannot work with these assumptions and cannot directly use research findings based on this notion. Theoretically, the problem can be handled by piecing together the inputs of various analytic disciplines into a synthesized recommendation. In practice, however, such a task can rarely be accomplished by either policy makers or researchers.

An alternative approach is for policy research to be based on a less formalized, less analytic discipline that falls between the analytic sciences and policy recommendations, the way medicine comes between physiology and pharmacy. Perhaps the most significant difference between policy science and the more analytic disciplines would be that the former would focus its attention to a much higher degree on differences in malleability of variables. That is, it must concentrate on those variables which are inherently more changeable (e.g., income vs. sex) and on the conditions under which less moveable variables can become more open to modification.

Finally, for the knowledge obtained to have an actual impact on policy making, policy researchers, unlike basic researchers, must be willing to invest a significant amount of time and energy in communicating. This is obviously especially true if the findings suggest a major change in policy. The policy researcher can in many instances fulfill his contractual obligations merely by turning in a written report, but this is likely to have little impact on decision making. To make his or her findings of use to policy making the policy researcher must learn how the world looks to the policy makers, how best the policy makers will absorb new ideas, which means of documentation and presentation will be most successful. Unlike the basic researcher who is often a "loner," the policy researcher needs to be able to interact effectively with politicians, bureaucrats, citizen representatives, organization leaders, etc.

In sum, transforming knowledge is best produced and channeled into the policy-making structures from a position which is sufficiently autonomous to be free of political pressure to distort knowledge yet sufficiently close to the decision makers to be able to respond realistically to the constraints imposed upon them by the differential malleability of variables and to be able to communicate effectively.[2]

An initial area that requires exploration is what forms of knowledge are known to legislators and policy makers when dealing with mental retardation. Clearly their approach to and conception of mental retardation will vary widely depending on the type and content of their knowledge and attitudes. The knowledge of some people is deeply affected by personal experiences they have had with a family member, relative, or friend, who has a particular form of retardation and this particular experience may be generalized and applied to all mental retardation without recognition of the great variety of manifestations of mental retardation. Knowledge will also be influenced by attitudes and stereotypes the individual possesses toward mental retardation. This factor is discussed in the chapters by Richardson, Gottlieb, and Edgerton. The motivation of policy makers to learn from the knowledge available about mental retardation may well be weak if the legislators believe that the mentally retarded have little political strength and influence.

For those who guide social change, there are changes in societal attitudes of which they must be aware and sensitive: for example, the increase in the willingness of parents to bring out in the open for discussion and review the needs and problems of mental retardation, the increased recognition that the mentally retarded must be considered in the broad context of the family and the community rather than as "patients," the growing insistence and recent court decisions on rights to treatment, rights to receive education and health care, and to be protected from abuse and harm and to be treated in a humane manner.

A factor influencing research workers who are a part of existing services and have service as well as research responsibilities is that they are likely to assume rather than question the organizational constraints of their roles. This together with the questions that are asked in the context of their work will lead to the pursuit and production of stable knowledge.

The production of transformational knowledge in mental retardation does appear to come largely from investigators who were outside of and independent of the service

---

[2] For a fuller discussion of the distinctive characteristics of policy, as opposed to pure or applied research methodology, see Etzioni (1971).

system. Another factor which seems to have given a major impetus to transformational knowledge was the entry of new scientific disciplines into the study of mental retardation. Representatives of these new disciplines, through having different perspectives, conceptualizations, and methods, looked at issues which were previously largely neglected. This occurred when social scientists who were members of universities and other research institutions not connected with mental retardation services began studying residential care of the retarded at a time when the policy and administration of the institutions was largely in the hands of those with training in the biological sciences, medicine, and traditional psychiatry. Some physicians and psychiatrists readily accepted and themselves contributed to the production of transforming knowledge.

An illustration of these points about transformational knowledge comes from the work of a social psychologist, Jack Tizard and some of his colleagues, who, after the Second World War, joined newly formed research units established by the British Medical Research Council. These units were placed in university settings. Tizard's first task was to inquire into problems of occupational adaptation of the mentally sub-normal, and he set to work with Neil O'Connor in a large mental deficiency institution (Tizard, 1967). They found to their surprise that those classified as feebleminded in one institution had an average IQ of 70, and that this finding was typical of similar London institutions. Many appeared quite capable of open employment in the society. Tizard and O'Connor restructured the work environment of the institution so that occupational therapy and ward work were changed to occupational training. The work was economically useful and socially meaningful to the trainees. Many were quickly placed in work outside the institution and most later left the hospital to live in the community. Other institutions followed suit by beginning similar programs. Tizard and his colleagues came to think that principles of education and social work which have been developed to deal with ordinary children and young people in trouble could be applied with little modification to the subnormal.

Together with O'Connor, the Clarkes, and Hermalin, Tizard worked with the retarded with IQ's below 50 in studies of learning and motivation. They were able to demonstrate that the work environment could be re-structured to provide a socially meaningful and challenging experience. These demonstrations had effects on the attitudes of the staff of the institutions toward the seriously subnormal. Staff came to see them as handicapped persons rather than "vegetables" or "creatures."

In the United States, Caudill (1958), Goffman (1961), Stanton and Schwartz (1954), and in Britain, Rapoport (1961), and Brown et al. (1966) conducted studies of psychiatric hospitals in the 1950's which challenged the stable knowledge that focused attention of the doctor- or psychiatrist-patient relationship, and showed the importance of the overall social and physical institutional environment in influencing the behavior of the residents. These studies led to new progress in community psychiatry which attempted to use the overall environment for therapeutic processes. They also led to more attention being given to the overall environment of the mental retardation institution. Tizard (1964) published an influential study in which the effects of care in a mental retardation institution, administered in a traditional hospital fashion, were compared to

Brooklands, a small residential care facility organized along " . . . principles of child care that today are regarded as meeting the needs of normal children deprived of normal home life," (p.85). The study showed the beneficial effect of Brooklands for the physical health of the children and their motor, social, and emotional development compared with the children at the traditional institution. Tizard followed up this work with studies of residential facilities with King and Raynes (1971). He was also instrumental in starting the work reported in the chapter by Kushlick (this volume).

In addition to studies of institutions, a second important body of transformational knowledge encompasses research dealing with the socialization of children and the experiences necessary at different ages, to fully develop a child's overall functional development. Early work of Spitz and Wolf (1946) and Bowlby (1951) pointed to the potentially harmful consequences of maternal deprivation. While some of Bowlby's findings were questioned, the work stimulated wider research into the consequences for socialization of various forms of human and social deprivation. (U.S. DHEW 1968). In the late 1950's and early 1960's major interest developed in the learning problems of children from poor families, in which poor school performance and mild mental retardation occurred with far greater frequency than in middle and upper income families. For some, "the culturally disadvantaged" became almost synonymous with "the poor." In animal research the effects of various forms of stimulation were studied. Levine (1960) and Harlow (1959) showed that for monkeys various forms of deprivation had harmful consequences for emotional development. This overall body of research stimulated interest in mild mental retardation and environmental factors which may contribute to its cause. A part of this work has been intervention studies to change the socialization experiences of children to provide them with experiences believed to enable the child more fully to develop his intellectual and social capacities. Some of this work is described in the chapters by Levenstein and Garber. The research has shown the importance of the experiences gained in living within a family structure and a community, and the need for a diversity of role models. The results have given impetus to the decentralization of services, to keeping retarded children in close contact with their families wherever possible and to working with families and the social conditions that make adequate parenting difficult if not impossible.

While the role of research in developing transformational knowledge is important, it should not be overstated. The choice of research is heavily influenced by values and attitudes to which the researcher is exposed. Transformational knowledge antedates research by many centuries and research results may be ignored if they are too disparate from prevailing attitudes.

At the end of the 19th century there were many studies supporting the stabilizing knowledge that mental retardation was caused by genetic factors and that the retarded had criminal tendencies. Fernald made a follow-up study of inmates of Waverly State School who had been discharged and were living in the community. Many of them had married, obtained jobs, were living at home, and had not gotten into any trouble with the law. Davies (1930) reported, "Dr. Fernald told the writer that he had hesitated for two years to publish the results of this study because they seemed so much at variance with the then accepted theories dealing with mental deficiency" (p. 196). After the publication of the reports a number of other similar studies were undertaken and published over the years which generally support Fernald's results (Goldstein, 1964). The implications of this work for changing mental retardation services was not fully seen or acted on for many years.

When behavioral research results in transformational knowledge it adds to our understanding of existing services and suggests valuable concepts and provides evidence for planning changes which may lead to more effective service. There are dangers that the research findings may not be generalizable because they were based on a particular set of circumstances and conditions which held only for the particular sample of the population studied. There is also danger that in planning and executing social change there may be unintended consequences that may be harmful to those for whom the plans are designed. It is for these reasons that it is so important to evaluate the introduction of new programs.

When an institution functions for long periods using primarily stablizing knowledge it may become so inflexible that the staff and organization are unable to adapt to new requirements that transformational knowledge demands, and it becomes necessary to close the institution and start new ones. An example of this situation is given in the chapter by Ohlin. One of the difficulties in applying transformational knowledge to services is that although in the long run the new services may result in fiscal savings, during the transition, increased costs may result because the old and new forms of services will both have to be maintained for some time. For example, during the period of transition from large isolated mental retardation institutions to smaller residential facilities, the large institutions continue to function with many continuing expenses at the same time that funds are needed to develop the new services. This dual expense during the transition should be recognized as a necessary cost worthwhile in terms of the long term benefits which accrue from the changes.

Public policy toward the retarded, as with any other social program oriented toward dealing with a difficult social problem, is subject to the influence of changes in intellectual outlook, often stemming from the development of new social sciences. Under certain circumstances, specifically, when a new theoretical approach emerges at the same time that broader societal values are undergoing change and there is strong disenchantment with ongoing attempts to cope with a problem, policy makers and professionals may yield to the temptation to look on a promising new outlook as a panacea. The upshot is that under the spell of some charismatic but untested and perhaps latently utopian ideas (among which "maximum feasible participation" of ghetto dwellers in federal anti-poverty programs has probably gained the greatest notoriety), programs effecting the well-being of millions of people and the allocation of billions of tax dollars are sweepingly recast. With little if any prior experimentation whole agencies are disbanded, dismembered, or submerged; new bureaucracies, centers, and services created; laws and regulations re-written. Only then does it become apparent that the new policy's merits were from the start poorly documented and now turn out to be illusory in many cases. When, in addition, the unforeseen negative side effects appear, the overall effect on the agency and its constituency can be highly deleterious.

The impact of deinstitutionalization of large numbers of psychiatric patients in the absence of a serious effort to set up services in the community to meet their needs is a case in point. In many instances, released psychiatric patients were later found to the roaming the streets or living in welfare hotels or for-profit nursing homes where they were less well cared for and more frequently neglected or abused than they had been in the huge state psychiatric hospitals.

To prevent new, untested theoretical approaches from being turned overnight into administrative cure-alls, with the havoc this threatens to wreak on social programs, a procedure which may be valuable is a "data court" in which proponents and opponents could argue the basis of evidence for a radical program overhaul before it is undertaken. This court may need to be held in stages. The first stage would be a peer review where those fully conversant with the theory, methods, and scientific knowledge related to the research would consider the validity and generalizability of the findings and whether there was counter evidence. If this review is satisfactory a second stage would be a discourse between research workers and those who would bear responsibility for putting into effect the changes suggested by the investigators. At this stage the desirability and design of small scale field trials could be considered to test the utility of the changes recommended.

Some of the elements of the data court that have been suggested were used by the President's Panel on Mental Retardation which was established by President Kennedy in 1961 with the mandate to prepare "a national plan to combat mental retardation." The panel held public hearings, reviewed research, visited existing services, and developed recommendations concerning research and manpower, treatment and care, education and preparation for employment, legal protection and development of Federal, state, and local programs. In Britain, Royal Commissions are appointed to review social issues and several have considered issues related to mental retardation.[3]

In the implementing of social change in the community setting, the people in the community may well question and demand participation in the planning and implementation of the changes. Opposition to proposed changes is likely to be encountered in varying degrees and may even prevent change. Research workers often have difficulty communicating with administrators and government officials. The data court is one means of improving communications. Research workers often have even more difficulty in communicating with members of the community, especially when those in the community are antagonistic to the proposed changes or to data gathering that may be related to the changes. Generally the task of working and dealing with the community is one researchers leave to others while they remain politically naive. Increasingly, research workers will need to become involved in social policy and social change and enter into the

---

[3] For a related suggestion concerning a national advisory commission or "council of wise elders" to oversee research and its impact on public policy in the area of genetic engineering (a field that clearly has many implications for mental retardation) see Etzioni (1973) Ch. 7-8 and App. 6.

political process at the community level. Researchers will have to become spokesmen for an increased emphasis on transformational knowledge if they are to help guide societal change.

ACKNOWLEDGMENT

The authors are indebted to Pamela Doty and Helene Koller for research and editorial assistance through several drafts of this paper.

REFERENCES

Abramowicz, H.K. and Richardson, S.A. 1975. Epidemiology of severe mental subnormality in children: Community studies. Am. J. Ment. Defic. In Press
Birch, H.G., Richardson, S.A., Baird, D., Horobin, G., and Illsley, R. 1970. Mental Subnormality in the Community. The Williams & Wilkins Co. Baltimore.
Bowlby, J. 1951. Maternal Care and Mental Health. World Health Organization. Geneva.
Brown, G.W., Bone, M., Dalison, B., and Wing, J.K. 1966. Schizophrenia and Social Care. Oxford University Press. London.
Caudill, W. 1958. The Psychiatric Hospital as a Small Society. Harvard University Press. Cambridge, Mass.
Davies, S.P. 1930. Social Control of the Mentally Deficient. Crowell. New York.
Etzioni, A. 1967. Toward a theory of societal guidance. Am. J. Sociol. 00:15-50.
Etzioni, A. 1968. The Active Society. Free Press. New York.
Etzioni, A. 1971. Policy research. Am. Sociol. (Suppl.) 6:000.
Etzioni, A. 1973. Genetic Fix. MacMillan. New York.
Goffman, E. 1961. Asylums: Essays on the Social Situation of Mental Patients and Other Inmates. Aldine. Chicago.
Goldstein, H. 1964. Social and occupational adjustment. In H. A. Stevens and R. Heber (eds.), Mental Retardation. University of Chicago Press. Chicago.
Harlow, H.F. 1959. Basic social capacities of primates. Hum. Biol. 31: 40-53.
King, R.D., Raynes, N.V., and Tizard, J. 1971. Patterns of Residential Care. Routledge & Kegan Paul. London.
Levine, S. 1960. Stimulation in infancy. Sci. Am. 202. 80-86.
Rapoport, R.N. 1961. Community as Doctor. Charles C Thomas, Springfield, Ill.
Spitz, R.A. and Wolf, K.M. 1946. Anaclitic depression: an inquiry into the genesis of psychiatric conditions in early childhood. (II). Psychoan. Stud. Child. 2: 313-342.
Stanton, A.H. and Schwartz, M.S. 1954. The Mental Hospital: A Study of Institutional Participation in Psychiatric Illness and Treatment. Basic Books. New York.
U.S. Department of Health, Education, and Welfare. 1968. Perspectives on Human Deprivation: Biological, Psychological and Sociological. Public Health Service, National Institutes of Health. Government Printing Office. Washington, D.C.
Tizard, J. 1964. Community Services for the Mentally Handicapped. Oxford University Press. London.
Tizard, J. 1967. Survey and Experiment in Special Education. George G. Harrap & Co., Ltd. London.

Discussion:
Social Change:
Problems and Strategies

The discussion of Cohen's paper centered around three major topics: 1) conceptual issues which may significantly modify program development, 2) priorities and value judgments which influence programs, and 3) critical external events that impinge on program development. Individual comments are summarized in this framework.

According to one discussant, the author, at some time, must have decided to organize his paper by focusing first on the service program itself and by describing the impact of the programs upon the clientele thereafter. This sequence may have influenced only the paper as presented, but if used also in the development of the program, it could have substantially influenced the nature of the services themselves.

As examples, the discussant proposed two alternative approaches and suggested that had either of these been used in conceptualization, the outcome may have been different, either as far as the paper or the characteristics of the program were concerned. One possibility would have been to utilize a model which starts with an enumeration of the typology and frequency of specific problems encountered among the retarded and their families. The services would have then derived from the epidemiological, more specifically, the prevalence data. Another model could have used as a starting point, characteristics of the community including the presence or absence of specified services with a subsequent planning of the program in accordance with identified gaps. From the viewpoint of sociology, these models are preferable because through their use programs result from needs rather than needs being identified to fit the specific available programs.

The opinion was then expressed that a service program which is rapidly overwhelmed by demands cannot spend too much time on epidemiology, conceptualization, and planning because families with problems of a critical nature immediately appear at the door in large numbers. However, it was also pointed out that the moment a "crisis service" is established, the number of problems identified as crises increases accordingly.

Ensuing comments focused further on priorities and social values. The first issue pertained to the decision-making process that assigns a higher priority to service or planning in relationship to one another. This, then, led to a discussion of the high priority which was given to "deinstitutionalization." It was thought that prevention of institutionalization and the proper placement of individuals currently in the community could have and probably should have been given a higher priority. Deinstitutionalization focuses only on the "residual" problem. In fact, the high weight assigned to deinstitutionalization may have been related to emotional or political overtones. On the other hand, such elements and the strong emphasis on deinstitutionalization may have been key factors which contributed to the rapid development of multifaceted service systems.

The discussion moved from priorities within mental retardation programs to broader scopes. It next focused on inevitable conflicts which arise within leadership personnel of community programs. Questions concerned the locus of primary loyalty of such individuals: should it be the agency for which they work, the community which they serve, or the clients who happen to be on their roster? No solution was offered except for the observation that the resolution of the conflict usually represents a compromise highly specific to the person involved.

Along another dimension pertaining to priorities, the discussion focused on a recurrent theme. That is, even if priorities are resolved within the realm of mental retardation, how are they to be fitted into the broader network of general social priorities? How much of the resources of a community should be spent on the retarded as contrasted with other disadvantaged or, for that matter, not disadvantaged subgroups, or on society as a whole? Are the retarded receiving preferential treatment in comparison to other needy groups? A consensus evolved that in general the retarded have not fared well in the marketplace in the past and that therefore those individuals who are charged with responsibilities for their care are justified in advocating their needs forcefully.

It was pointed out that some issues are of greater theoretical relevance than of practical significance. In daily life unanticipated events often exert as much if not more influence on programs than do systematic planning or advance conceptualization. Publicity related to unacceptable conditions in one service component is apt to influence developments in another component of the same system rather rapidly. In public programs such issues often become entangled with political forces which magnify their impact manifold. Politically motivated forces may be viewed as undesirable from a professional viewpoint, but they often serve as springboards for significant advances.

Final comments emphasized the need for balanced and stable progress which can reconcile highly divergent viewpoints like those held by clinicians, on the one hand, or biomedical and behavioral scientists, on the other.

In response to Ohlin's paper, the group observed that there were very close parallels between reform in the juvenile justice area as experienced in Massachusetts and mental retardation reforms. There were expressions of agreement with the Massachusetts project in philosophy but concern that emptying institutions without preparation and the failure to provide services or protection for children who were removed from institutions was "incredible." The group wondered what reports were available on the "fate" of youngsters who were deinstitutionalized in addition to the general recidivism figures quoted by Ohlin.

It is clear that the Massachusetts experiment data is not all in. The length of the stay in institutions had reduced from approximately 8 months to approximately 3 months immediately before the closing of the institution. There was, however, no aftercare available for children. Funding for the changes in Massachusetts lagged far behind commitments and this caused uncertainty and difficulties after the change. Ohlin believes that funding was the major problem since universities and others responded warmly and extensively to the needs of children removed from institutional settings.

It was observed that the length of stay which Ohlin was describing was very different from those experienced in the mental retardation field. In addition, the community perception of juvenile delinquency is quite different from that of mental retardation.

Ohlin took issue with this latter statement and indicated that he believed the stigma were not all that different. He went on to illustrate this by saying that efforts to establish group homes in certain areas had failed because those backing the effort were unaware of earlier opposition to the attempts of other groups to do the same thing. The stigma was sufficient to carry over against the juvenile delinquent and could not be combatted. In other instances which he cited, the opposition in the community were not that well mobilized. He suggested that euphemisms for "delinquent" or "juvenile" behavior helped to change some public attitudes and that acronyms should be avoided. He further observed that the use of existing community leadership could often make a major difference in dealing with the stigma which was found.

Some believe that the juvenile delinquency problems were substantially different than the mentally retarded because the former are part of the "prison problem." The issue of evaluation of results in both adult and juvenile corrections were causes of severe problems. Five functions of corrections were cited, including: 1) treatment, 2) general deterrence, 3) specific deterrence, 4) punishment, and 5) removal from or protection of society. The evaluation of these components in a mass context is very difficult. Issues around general deterrence are typically only subjective rhetoric with little hard data.

The group observed that in social reform, it is sometimes possible to make a fundamental change by the use of sheer power rather than basing change upon objective evidence that the change should indeed be instituted. It was observed that political action can "undermine anything."

Ohlin indicated that there are intensive efforts to keep track of delinquency rates but this really does not help deal with the question of general deterrence in the society. He reiterated that institutions were viewed as punitive symbols and that their removal may effect the public view of delinquency itself.

The observation was made that the Massachusetts effort was effective only when society is focusing on the "client interest" model. Society "sanctions" as well as "treats" when antisocial behavior occurs. Failure to sanction affects moral judgments and such effect cannot be accurately measured. It is very difficult to know the impact on moral judgments when such changes are made. Society has as one of its purposes to sustain the moral sentiments of the community and, therefore, moral sanctions should not be ignored. Ohlin responded that the adult system is more appropriate for dealing with moral sanction. The adult system can provide "cover" to give the juvenile system time to digest reforms and "settle down." Ohlin also wondered whether the "retribution" approach may well be unworkable for current groups, particularly minority black groups, even though such a model may have worked a hundred years ago for the "Irish" and others.

Some expressed an interest in a more careful view of the impact of ending institutionalization in juvenile delinquency since our normative system would benefit.

One member observed that New England has a long tradition of private sanctions that do not exist elsewhere. This is especially true when comparing New England to the West. Massachusetts was observed to be a very particular climate and some questioned whether such a reform would work in other places.

Ohlin indicated that private organizations do exist which parallel the judicial juvenile delinquency system in the East. These were religious as well as non-sectarian private groups. On the other hand, Ohlin observed that the private sector has creamed off the top of the most easy to treat for years. Now money is helping private organizations to get to the most difficult and baffling of the delinquency problems.

The discussion of Boggs' presentation generally focused on issues related to "advocacy," with specific comments on the typology of the mentally retarded, from the viewpoint of their needs for advocacy, on the typology of advocates and advocacy systems, and on possible conflicts of interest between advocate and provider roles, particularly when these two functions are performed either by the same person or the same agency.

The number of mentally retarded individuals who are in need of a personal advocate on a continuous and intensive basis is quite limited. They are persons who are profoundly, severely, or at least moderately handicapped and they often suffer from additional chronic disabilities. Their needs are multifaceted and complex, and they are unable to represent their own interests. Parents, parent surrogates, and/or advocates are essential on a continuous and intensive basis if these children and adults are to receive the benefits of services.

Most of the mildly retarded, on the other hand, require advocates only for limited periods and with lesser frequency and intensity. Particularly during their adult years, they require advocates only under rather unusual circumstances and only for a limited time. Their general needs can be met through representation as groups rather than as individuals. It was repeatedly emphasized, however, that the IQ is not a good measure of social competency, so that the above dichotomy based on the IQ is useful only as a general guide-line and is not necessarily valid in individual instances.

A host of different types of advocates and advocacy systems was described. They ranged from persons whose roles most closely resemble those of "friends" to persons who have assigned legal authorities and responsibilities, *vis-à-vis* their clients. The concerns of other advocates involve not individuals but groups. The latter types included functions described as administrative advocacy and agency advocacy at various levels from the community to the federal government.

Curiously, the issue of conflict of interest did not enter the discussion when personal advocates or personal advocacies were discussed. It gained center stage *vis-à-vis* administrative advocacy by agencies, particularly at the federal level. Two somewhat opposing viewpoints were presented although it was acknowledged that ideally the advocacy role should be maximally separated from responsibility for the delivery of services. One view maintained that at the federal level, quite often, the two functions have been inter-mingled, usually with undesirable outcomes. The other view maintained that in the complex federal system meaningful advocacy is difficult to carry out by any agency unless that agency has some "power or clout" customarily expressed in available program-matic dollars. That is to say, the most effective federal governmental tool for the initiation of a needed service is the support of demonstration projects or the funding of new programs at least during their start-up phase. If a federal agency is not in a position to back its advocacy role with such resources, it is unlikely to succeed. Although the conflict is clear, the benefits, this view held, outweigh the disadvantages. Some of the specific examples pertained to the Office of Human Development, which has a clear advocacy role but at the same time is also responsible for a number of federal programs. The list might include the program for the developmentally disabled in the future.

In this latter connection it was emphasized that the program for the developmentally disabled was originally conceptualized at a time when only a relatively small proportion of the federal dollars allocated for mental retardation was used for the payment of services. It was hoped that this new financing system would fill the gaps that usually develop as federally funded service programs expanded. History has proven this predic-tion correct. In spite of a host of funding opportunities now available, gaps still exist. Yet as long as those responsible for programs at the state and local levels know how to access the various funding channels, the retarded can greatly benefit through several more generic resources.

Local mental retardation service programs have a particular problem around the issue of conflict of interest, as was pointed out. Many of them see themselves as "control" agencies and would prefer to utilize the generic services available in the community. In this fashion, they could function primarily as advocacy agencies. On the other hand, the clients see them as mental retardation service agencies and expect direct service from them rather than referrals to other community units. Practical resolution of this conflict requires substantial skill, insight, and most importantly, a sizable endowment of human-ism and social conscience.

Index

Evaluation of services for mentally retarded, 325–343

Family
adaptations to severely mentally retarded children, 247–266
changes in composition, 261
changing role of, with mentally retarded child, 21–26
as cognitive resource, 306
community relationships, 261
forms of adaptation and intervention,
245–321
foster, 267–285
identity, in adaptation process,
257–259
influence on child adaptation, 212–215
prior loyalty, in family adaptation, 260
professional support for functioning of,
217–220
reliance on experiential guides, 260
variables affecting child behavior,
211–215
variables influencing functioning of,
215–220
variables influencing socialization,
207–211
Family supports, administrative classification of mental subnormality in absence of, 83–84
Forced compliance paradigm, attitude
change, 168–169
Foster family care, 267–285

Gatewood, living at, 351–354
Gestural sign language, visual information, 236–238

History
educational institutions and mental subnormality, 33–52
mental retardation, 1–73
Housing, 447–449

Identification of mentally retarded,
85–95

Identity, family
formation of new, in adaptation process, 259
in danger, in adaptation process,
257–259
Immigration of mentally retarded,
444–447
Improprieties in adaptation process, 253
Incidence
of mental retardation, 54
uses of measures of, 55–60
Incompetence, sociocultural contexts,
136–139
Infancy, intervention in, 287–303
Information processing, communication,
234–236
Institutions, future role, 17–21
Intelligence test scores, 293–302
Intergroup attitudes and behavior, procedures for altering, 165–170
Intergroup relations, negative, cognitive-
affective syndromes, 163–165
Intervention
family, 245–321
in infancy, 287–303

Judicial branch of government, 466
Jurisdictions, overlapping, as obstacles to
developing community services for
mentally retarded, 414–417
Juvenile corrections in transition,
424–426
Juvenile justice, trends, 426–433

Labeling
educational, sociocultural factors,
141–157
impact of, 26–29
of mentally retarded, 134–136
phase in adaptation process, 253
Legislators as obstacles to developing
community services for mentally retarded, 412

Massachusetts, youth correctional reform,
433–439